MICHAEL D. O'BRIEN

THE
ISLAND OF
THE WORLD

A Novel

IGNATIUS PRESS   SAN FRANCISCO

Cover art: *Transcendence*, painting by Michael D. O'Brien

Cover design by Riz Boncan Marsella

© 2007 Ignatius Press, San Francisco
All rights reserved
ISBN 978-1-58617-216-9
Library of Congress Control Number 2007927189
Printed in the United States of America ⊚

For those who, dying young,
now sleep in the earth
with their unspoken poems,
waiting for the Last Day.

Contents

Prologue

I am old. Time has revealed itself and shed its pretense of eternity, though it is of course contained within eternity. I clean the hallways, take out the garbage, try not to be irritated by the roar of ten million automobiles, and by the jackhammers that are breaking up the street outside the front door, only to lay down another stratum of tar for future generations to dig up. This is a big city, and though I have lived within it for close to forty years, I still do not understand how it survives.

Its people display an astonishing variety of colors, languages, temperaments, and ratios of good and evil (as is everywhere), but they do not seem unhappy. Neither do they contemplate the body of the world. Its foundations are below them, they believe, in the concrete and tar, the pipes and wires. During my time among them I have noticed this delusion particularly. Seldom have I encountered the few who are awake, who cast their gaze to the real foundations, which, as human beings should know, are above.

Soon I will leave this place and return to my first home. Perhaps I will find myself waiting for me there. Is this a candid admission that I have failed to know myself? Yes, of course it is. What else is there to learn save that we know almost nothing? I am not referring to biographical data, but to something more important, the character of presence that appears to be displacement, as a stone or tree displaces air as it fills space. That I am a displaced person is true enough. Yet this is true of all men, each in his way. What is to be learned of me now rests in memory, the interior, a country that contains ranges of mountains and their shadowed vales, the beds of alpine glens, the crevasse and its fall from which there is no return, and the summit from which one does not wish to return.

Why do we in memory seek ourselves, when it is ourselves who shape the memories? The truth is, we shape and are shaped. In the beginning we unwittingly find our forms, as the first steps of a child. Later we take our longer strides, with secret timorousness, preferring a crowd of companions. Then, in time, we go farther out into the world with blind and knowing willfulness, with good intent and ill, alone inside ourselves. For in solitude the blur of safe indistinction becomes sharp and dangerous identity. Then, when identity has sealed its form, we seek union with the other islands, within the island of the world.

Of my life I can only resort to pictures. It began, as most lives do, with warmth and milk and love.

The village was hidden from the world. At least it thought itself so, for it was ringed by peaks, and its people assumed that a valley suspended so high above all others was exempt from tribulation. We the young believed this. Our elders encouraged the illusion. They did not want to rob us of our joy and perhaps desired to share in it a little. And so the mountains were the meridians of all creation. The brook that came to us from the upper crags ran unfailing, clear and swift between the houses. The little fields and flocks fed us well. From other places men of wisdom came from time to time and taught us of the world beyond, which was a place of fear and confusion. For us, the children of Rajska Polja, which is the fields of heaven, their accounts seemed more remote than the tales of Anthony and Francis, who could talk to fish and birds.

In this place where we first appeared, we did not doubt that love is the path of ascent. We did not think of it, as we did not think of the air we breathed. In time our flesh received instruction as we grew, and our hearts and our souls. We came to know that love is the soul of the world, though its body bleeds, and we must learn to bleed with it. Love is also the seed and milk and the fruit of the world, though we can partake of it in greed or reverence.

We are born, we eat, and learn, and die. We leave a tracery of messages in the lives of others, a little shifting of the soil, a stone moved from here to there, a word uttered, a song, a poem left behind. I was here, each of these declare. I was here.

THE MOUNTAINS

I

That summer, three gifts come to him.

Because the entire year has been full of interesting events, it is not clear at first that they are gifts. The first is the journey he makes with his father to the sea, leaving the mountains behind, though they cannot be left behind really, because they reach as far as the waters of the coast, and tower always in the composition of his mind. The sea itself is the second gift, for it is not an aspect of the world that he has seen before. The third is the miracle of the swallow. This last gift, it seems to him, is the least of the three.

"Josip, tomorrow you will see a great thing", says his father as they rise by candlelight before dawn, putting on their clothes beside the stove while mother makes a fire. "You will see the waters of the Adriatic."

"Is it like a lake?" Josip asks. He has seen photographs of the ocean in one of his father's books, but it is hard to tell its size from them.

"Much bigger than a lake."

"How big is it, really, Tata?" he presses with earnest curiosity, for he believes that his father has an answer for everything.

"It is beyond measuring, Josip."

"Is it as big as the sky?"

"That is a difficult question. When you go there you will see that the sky above it is greater than the sky above our mountains."

Josip furrows his brow in concentration.

"This I do not understand!"

"You must see it with your own eyes and then you will understand."

The boy closes his eyelids and touches them with his finger-tips.

"The sea will show you many things, Josip."

"Fish?"

"Yes, fish", says his father, smiling, as he lights the oil lamp above the kitchen table. "But more than fish."

"Squid?" He has seen a picture of squid and read a little about them.

"Perhaps we will see a squid."

"With a spear I will catch one, and we will cook rice in its ink."

"First you will have to catch one."

"Will we play in the sea?"

"We will play in it."

"Miro," interjects his mother, "do not let him be too . . ."

"Too?"

"Too like himself. If you see him about to throw himself into deep water, stop him."

"I will stop him", laughs his father.

"He cannot swim. He is nine years old, and he cannot swim."

"Marija, if we do not play in the dangerous surf, we will drown in puddles."

She scowls and crosses her arms—her usual response whenever her husband is too witty.

"No one swims in Rajska Polja," Josip pipes, "except in the rain."

"You and your friends *pretend* to swim," says his mother, kissing him on the forehead, "but if it was anything more than rain, you would drown, you would die, and how would you like that!"

"I wouldn't drown", says Josip, cramming bread into one side of his mouth and tilting a crock of warm milk toward the other. He chokes on it, coughing and sputtering.

"Already you're drowning!" cries his mother.

As they eat the remainder of their meal on the little wooden table beside the window, the roosters begin crowing. A slice of red flame slips over the crest of the mountain, drawing in its train a veil of pink. His father's eyes wander toward it.

"Rose-fingered dawn", he murmurs.

"Will we bring *The Iliad* or *The Odyssey* with us?" Josip asks. "Will you read aloud to me when we sleep at the sisters' convent?"

"Finish chewing before you speak", says his mother. "Miro, please, enough of war."

"It is an old, old war, Mamica", Josip pleads. "The rage of Achilles is *very* interesting."

"We will bring no books", the father answers. "Instead we will see with our own eyes what Odysseus saw. We will see the waters he sailed upon in *Argo*."

"Will we see monsters?"

"That is always possible."

The sun is just rolling over the ridge of Zamak mountain by the time Josip and his father are ready to go. In the yard the night-chill lingers, and the smell of sheep droppings is pleasant to the nose. While his father leads Svez the donkey from the shed behind the house and harnesses him to the cart, Josip gazes down the lane, which is the only street in Rajska Polja. Two dozen houses are scattered haphazardly along its muddy ruts. Most of them are made of field stone, a few of wood, many with their back walls under the slopes of the hills. On both sides of the village, pastures rise to the east and the west. Beyond the grass there is forest, and above the trees high bare ridges merge with sharper peaks.

Svez is harnessed and snorting little bursts of frosty breath.

Onto the cart his father loads the carry-box with a food bag and sheepskin water flasks. When those tasks are completed, he opens his arms wide and drops to his knees. He and the mother and Josip kneel with their arms around each other and pray that God will give a safe journey and for a blessing on everything that will occur between the going and the coming. They all make the sign of the cross and stand, brushing dirt from their knees. Then father bows to the stone church at the end of the street, kisses his wife, and lifts Josip onto the plank where they will sit.

"Bye-bye, Mamica", Josip waves. "I will miss you very much, but I must go and see the world."

"Of course you must go and see the world, my Josip. And you must come home again too. I will make a beautiful supper."

"I will explain to him, Marija, that *The Odyssey* is all about a man trying to get home again."

She folds her arms and smiles into her husband's eyes, but man and boy can see that she does not like them to go away, even if only for a few days.

"Pray for a door to open", father says.

"I will pray. In Split, there are many good people. Stay away from soldiers. And beware of gypsies."

"There are good gypsies."

"I know, just as there are good beggars and bad beggars. But we cannot afford to give our few coins to frauds. A school-teacher's income . . ."

"In the city there may be jobs, new schools. It would be better for him . . ."

Him, Josip knows, is the singular object of their affection, their only child—himself.

Father flicks the reins, and Svez reluctantly hobbles forward, pulling the creaking cart slowly along the lane and out into the eastern pasture toward the mountain pass. All around them the peaks are white, the morning birds swim in the liquid air, and the purples, reds and yellows of meadow flowers sway in the wind. The air is scented by the pine trees above the schoolhouse and combed by the oak forest on the mountain slopes, and the bell in the church begins to ring with laughter.

Theirs is a small valley, higher than most in the region, containing little more than a hundred souls. It is not long before they leave it behind and enter the folds in the range that lead downward to the coast.

By noon they arrive at the nearest village. From there they go by another route, no longer a path but a track of rutted dirt. There is a lot of up and down, though they are slowly, slowly winding their way lower in the mountains. When the sun sets, father pulls off into a grove of trees sprouting new leaves. They are hidden from view; no one passing by would know they are here; there are no houses to be seen in any direction. A fox barks, and night birds call to each other. The stars are very bright. The chill settles in quickly. It is the first time in many years Josip sleeps with his father, curled inside his arms, wrapped in a blanket. It feels warm and safe.

Before dawn they resume their journey, passing into the lower foothills of a narrow gorge flanked by brutally sharp ranges. Now the rutted dirt is firmer underfoot and becomes a road with a noisy creek babbling beside it. The sun is high in the sky by the time the gorge opens up and enters a wider valley. Here the creek flows into a river. Father directs Svez across a clattering wooden bridge and then turns right onto a gravel road that runs beside the river.

"The Neretva", says father.

"It is very big", says Josip, with wide eyes.

"At this point it is not so big. It grows as it nears the coast."

They proceed along the road for many hours, and occasionally they must plug their ears against the roar of trucks that father says are going north to Sarajevo, and of others going south to Mostar. The valley through which the river passes is like a canyon, its lower slopes covered with low brush and small trees, growing barer as the cut in the earth soars toward the great white peaks.

At one point his father pulls the cart to the side of the road, and they walk down to the riverbank. How dark the water is, more silent than the mountain creeks, more powerful too. They kneel on a patch of sand to fill the water-skins. When Josip's is full and the cork firmly in place, he stands and notices a boat floating a few meters downstream, tethered to a bush by a rope. This is the first real boat he has ever seen. It is nothing like the pictures of such vessels that he has looked at in books. It is shaped like a knife blade, two man-lengths long, and painted blue. This blue is unlike the other blues that he loves, such as the sky or the flashes on a *lastavica*. This blue is like the robe of a king.

"Oh", he breathes, opening his mouth and spreading his arms.

His father is standing beside Josip, looking down at him with a small smile of amusement.

"So, you want to go fishing?"

Josip shakes his head.

"You are really staring at that boat. Would you like to have such a boat?"

Yes—rather, *no*! To possess it is not what he is thinking. He is merely loving its shape, its color, and the way it floats as if weightless upon the swift green water.

"Tata?"

"Yes?"

"Are we like this?"

"Like what?"

"Are *we* boats?"

His father laughs, then shakes his son's shoulder. "No time for daydreams, Josip. We'd better get moving if we want to reach Mostar by nightfall."

So, Svez ambles steadily along the road, and the motion of the cart induces drowsiness. An hour or two pass while Josip dozes with his head leaning on his father's shoulder. When he opens his eyes, he sits bolt upright and points.

"Look, Tata, castles!"

On promontories above their heads, enormous towers of stone jut toward the sky, the solitary fortresses of giants who guard the river.

His father smiles. "They are natural formations, Josip, made by God, not by man."

By evening they arrive at a city—Mostar. It is enormous. Dozens of streets, like a hundred villages all pushed together. Josip stares in wonder. Everything about it is a beauty and a shock. The many people, the market, the colorful buildings, and the needles of Muslim prayer-towers on one side of the river, the church spires on the other. Soldiers in different uniforms patrol the streets, guarding the post office and bank. On these buildings the Italian flag is flying. The soldiers' faces are not quite the same as the faces of the people of Yugoslavia.

As their cart crosses a square, a gunshot echoes against the buildings. Seconds later, a man runs past, into the shadow of an alleyway. He is carrying a hunting rifle tipped by a bayonet.

"Ustasha?" his father whispers.

"Why do you whisper to me like that, Tata?"

"In cities there are many ears, Josip."

"Is that man with the gun a bad person?"

"He may be one of the Ustashe."

"What is Ustashe?"

"A group of Croats who fight our enemies. But they are wrong in some of their thoughts and their actions."

"Why are they wrong in some of their thoughts and their actions?"

"They are very brutal."

"Maybe he is not a Ustasha. Maybe he is a shepherd who is guarding his flock."

Father scowls.

"Do wolves come into big cities like this?" Josip asks, gazing longingly after the place where the shadow disappeared. "Maybe he has seen a wolf."

"Yes, I think he has seen a wolf."

"And will he kill it, if it attacks the sheep?"

"He will."

"Then he is not wrong in his thoughts and his actions."

Father says nothing, just shakes his head.

"What kind of wolf is it? A big one?"

"Yes, very big and growing."

"A black wolf or a grey one?"

"Maybe a Chetnik wolf", his father mutters distractedly, as if to himself.

"What is a Chetnik?"

Josip has, on occasion, overheard the men of the village using this word. They do not like the young to listen when it appears in their conversation.

"My son," says his father rubbing his eyes, "it is one thing to defend. It is another thing to attack and degrade . . ."

"What do you mean, Tata?"

"I cannot explain it to you now. Later I will tell you, after we have seen the sea."

There is no more time for questions because they have arrived at a stable where people can leave their donkeys and carts. Father pays a few coins to the man who looks after the animals. He will feed Svez while they are gone. They joke with each other, trading a few details about their lives. He is a Croat, and it turns out that he grew up in a village near Rajska Polja. Now he lives in the city and hates it. Then they talk about the gunshot. Who was firing upon whom?

"I don't think he was after Italian blood", says the stableman in a quiet voice. "Though he'd like some of that too. If he shot an Italian you can be sure their soldiers would be stampeding through the city like pigs at slaughter time. Still, they're not Germans. If he had killed a German you can be sure they'd be rounding up hundreds of people right now to shoot them in reprisal."

Father purses his lips. "The Italians have imprisoned thousands in camps", he says in a voice just above a whisper. "They have been shooting hostages too. At Primošten they shot and stabbed eighty people in retaliation for the death of fourteen sailors."

Suddenly father catches himself and glances over at Josip, who is studiously observing the other animals in the shed. He is listening, though he pretends not to be.

The stableman lowers his voice: "Maybe he was Ustasha. Maybe Chetnik. Maybe Partisan. With everyone carrying guns, who can tell! I hear the Ustashe are after a Chetnik chief who crept into town last night. Maybe it was Baćović."

"Who is Baćović?"

"He's one of Mihailović's gang of murderers. On their way to Makarska they burned several Croat villages and killed all the men and boys fifteen and older. They tortured and killed three Catholic priests too."

Father frowns and puts a finger to his lips. The man nods. He gives Josip a dry fig, a great treat. The boy chews it ravenously, eyes shining with euphoric pleasure. The man gives him another, which Josip packs into his mouth even as he chews the first, eyeing his benefactor's pockets in hopes of more.

"The children must eat", the man says to father. "They are our future, they are our hope."

There is more discussion about travel to Split, which Josip ignores because a goat has nibbled the donkey's ear and a quarrel has broken out between the animals. It is very funny.

That night they sleep in a room for travelers—a big room

attached to the stables. Josip is a little frightened of the strangers who are lying so close on the other cots, but his father reassures him and holds him snugly until he is asleep. In the morning they walk about the city. Father agrees to risk a little time, although the autobus that will take them to the coast departs within the hour. They walk back and forth on an arching stone bridge connecting two ancient towers on either side of the river. It soars in the middle, but to Josip it seems no higher than a hillock on the pastures of home.

"Castles?" he asks pausing in the center of the span to gape at the towers.

"Yes, like castles. Guard towers on the river."

"It is very, very wide", he says peering down into the water.

"It is narrow."

Josip does not respond, for in his mind he is now standing on the topmost battlement, brandishing a sword, or shooting arrows down into the ships of invaders.

Then a race to catch the autobus. Josip has never seen one before. It is a tremendous thing, like a beast that eats people, then spews them out alive. There are a lot of people inside it. His father pays some coins to the driver, who is standing by the door with an anxious look and the palm of his hand open. They find an empty seat for two persons halfway to the rear. When the beast roars, coughs black exhaust, and begins to move, Josip's eyes widen as the seat bounces him up and down.

"Oh!" he cries, half in amazement and a little fear, half in delight.

His father smiles and puts an arm around his shoulders to keep him from banging against the glass window. The bus plunges along at a terrifying speed and lurches as it rounds corners of the mountain road, which is very narrow.

"How far is it to the sea, Tata?"

"As the crow flies, Josip, it is only eighty kilometers. We are too late to catch the bus that would have taken us directly to the coast at Ploče. Now we will take a different route, northwest through the mountains. It is longer and slower, but we are in no rush. Are you in a rush?"

Josip grins. "I am not in a rush, Tata."

"Good. This way, also, we will pass through Široki Brijeg, where Fra Anto became a priest. It is a school for boys and a seminary. It is also a great shrine in honor of the Assumption of Our Lady into Heaven. Many Franciscans live there."

"Will we meet them?"

"No, the autobus will pass through the town, but we can see the church and the school up on a hilltop. It is a blessed place."

The bus rumbles along, up and down on the winding and unwinding roads, which are better than the roads leading to Rajska Polja, but still rough. Now and then the bus stops and must back up, sometimes a kilometer, to allow oncoming army trucks to pass. It bounces all the way, backward or forward, squealing and rattling. It is a great thrill. There are animals on the bus. Chickens in a crate. A few goats tethered to the legs of the seats. A piglet in a burlap sack elicits Josip's sympathy, for though the weave of the cloth is rough, permitting air, the top is tied with twine, and the piglet is thrashing and squealing.

The road plunges down into a valley full of trees, and there on the heights of a promontory is a big church made of fine yellow bricks, with several large buildings about it. Beyond are fields and groves of fruit trees. The bus stops below to drop off a few passengers and pick up others. Then it roars and continues on its way.

So, that is where Fra Anto was a boy, thinks Josip. Yes, he must have been a boy at one time, long ago. Then a seminarian, and then a priest. This is a good place.

"There are more than a hundred thousand books in its library", says father. "Great scholars teach there, friars who studied in Paris and Budapest. Someday, Josip, perhaps you will study here." He makes a sign of the cross as he looks back to the church, just as the bus climbs out of the valley and leaves everything behind.

Hours pass. Old men begin arguing in subdued voices that grow louder as the journey stretches on.

The word *Chetnici* again. *Ustashe* too is repeated. Also *HSS* and *NDH* and *Domobrani*. None of these or other subjects seem to be happy ones. The old men are worried. A king is mentioned—Petar. The old men approve of the Croatian Peasants' Party, but think it has been destroyed. They do not approve of the king who has run away, but their dislike of Ustashe and Chetnici is greater.

"Do we have a king?" Josip asks his father. "I did not know we had a king."

"He is in exile", his father whispers. Again he whispers. This is strange. Tata never whispers. None of the men of Rajska Polja whisper. Only women whisper, and then it is usually with smiles for happy secrets, new babies sprouting in their mothers' bodies, or youths and maidens engaged to be married.

The autobus driver honks his horn, and a roadside donkey barely escapes from its path. Across the aisle, two old women pray the Rosary. Smaller children watch every passing detail of the scenery, their heads held high and mouths wide open. The youngest are nursed at their mothers' breasts. Some of the women, the poorest, do not cover themselves with shawls. Josip disapproves of this exposure, though he is fascinated.

The bus stops at a narrow ravine that cuts the road. Its stone bridge has collapsed, and only two wooden beams have replaced it. The driver gets out, scratching his head. His passengers spill out while he is trying to decide if he should risk a crossing. The ravine is no more than three meters wide, and it is not very deep, but to fall into it would precipitate a longer plunge down the mountain side. The passengers scatter into the roadside bushes, startling flocks of small golden birds. Joseph observes their flight, pondering the patterns they make in the air.

The driver widens the distance between the two planks, measures with his eyes, sighs, and shouts for everyone to get back on board. Father suggests to him that this is not a good idea, because, if the tires slip off the beams, a lot of people will die.

"You think it's better for me to die alone?" asks the driver with an offended tone.

Father looks back at him with an expression that is usually readable only by his wife and child: the one he uses when he does not wish to speak his mind. It says, "So far beyond rational thought is your attitude, that nothing I can say will change it. A lifetime of reasoning with you would not alter your amazing inability to comprehend reality."

So, everyone but his father and Josip gets back on board. Except for the murmur of prayers, silence reigns as the autobus rolls slowly across the ravine. It arrives safely on the other side, and everyone within it bursts into applause. Josip and his father walk across while the bus waits for them. The driver graciously, without comment, opens the door for them to climb in. The journey resumes.

An hour later, a barricade brings the bus to a stop. There are about a dozen Italian soldiers waiting there with their rifles cocked. Three of them get on board and go up and down the aisle inspecting every face. Silence reigns. They question a young man, and unsatisfied by his answers, drag him out of his seat and push him through the door into the arms of the waiting soldiers. The Italians get out, then wave the bus onward. The silence continues for a time, and then a chorus of muttering begins. An old woman bursts into wails, though it is uncertain if she is related to the young man. Other old women go to her and comfort her.

"Why did they take that man?" Josip whispers into his father's ear. He is learning to whisper.

Father flashes a warning look at him: the look says, *Be silent!*

Not long after, the road makes a wide curve, then descends more steeply. Another curve, and father says, "There it is. The sea."

Josip presses his face to the window, his eyes straining, mouth open like a baby, head stretched high on his thin neck. Beyond the folds of the foothills the sea is the shape of a feather held sideways at arm's length. The sun is glinting on it, but he notes how blue it is, a shade of blue he has never seen before.

"What do you think?" his father asks.

He cannot think. He can only see it, only drown in its presence, for it grows and grows. It is bigger than the world, this sea.

Now the bus rushes down the last incline and screeches to a halt where the mountain road meets another road, one that runs along the coastline. Josip and his father gather their belongings, stumble through the chickens and children and goats, reach the open door, and hop down into the dust. The engine roars, the bus turns right and begins to chug into the north toward Split.

"Why do we stop here?" Josip asks.

"Because I am going to show you the sea. In Split we will see it too, but it is a harbor with many wharves of stone and cement, and it is not so nice. Here the sea is as it was when Odysseus sailed upon it."

The road is hundreds of meters above the shore. They shoulder their baggage and leave the road, making their way down a steep incline through a grove of olive trees. The hill is rough underfoot but less stony than the pastures of the mountains. Trees and wild plants grow taller here. There are many flowers, some of them new to Josip. The air is hotter and drier. The sun beats down. They stop beneath a tree and in its shade drink from their water-skins. But neither of them wants to rest. They press on, picking their way through outcroppings of white stone, clumps of thorn, and low bushes bursting with red flowers.

At last they arrive at a cliff and stop to survey the terrain in search of a way down. On its crest is a tree that Josip does not recognize. Round golden fruit litter the grass beneath it. Josip throws himself onto his knees and picks one up. Oh, such a color!

"It's an orange", his father says.

"Can I eat it?"

"You can try. But it's a winter orange, very sour."

Josip carefully bites into the skin, spews it out with a look of disgust. But the smell makes him dizzy with desire. He peels the rest with his fingers and sinks his teeth into its flesh. It is very wet inside. Oh! It is sweet!

His father picks up one of the windfalls, peels it, and splits the insides into pieces shaped like a quarter moon. He nibbles one, then spits it out.

"These are really sour", he says.

Josip divides his into moons and gives one to his father. "This one is sweet", he says.

Father bites into it, spits it out, and makes a face. "Even more sour!"

Convinced that his father is joking, Josip eats the remainder of his own, then opens another and eats it. He has eaten six by the time he is full.

"Sour?" asks his father.

"Sweet", Josip replies.

Now they are ready to undertake the final stage. Going with caution among the jumbled rocks of the cliff, they traverse it at an angle and, within minutes, are standing on a beach of smooth white stones, millions upon millions of them, the largest as big as a dove's egg, the smallest like peas. There is no wind, and the ocean is calm, yet it heaves continually. It is breathing. It casts gentle sighs upon the shore where a lip of water rises and falls back, leaving a line of wetness.

Josip runs forward to touch it, his heart beating wildly. He is totally in love for the first time in his life. He loves it all—the water, the new sounds, the little stones, the vastness of the space above the sea, the sense of infinity that opens up before him. He has never seen so much sky gathered in a single place.

He kicks off his shoes, strips off his clothes down to his undershorts, and wades in. He grins in surprise, shouts inarticulately, a half laugh, half cry. Jumping up and down, splashing, feeling with his toes the underwater bed of round white stones, the spray on his bare limbs, the heat of the sun, he is so happy. He knows now that he can penetrate the infinite. It would be worth drowning in it just to have this moment of play. He takes a few more steps, pressing against the sea's power, and now it swells above his knees.

"Josip, that's enough. Come out, it is very cold."

Oh, it is so warm!

"Please, Tata!"

"A minute only. I don't want you to catch a chill."

All sounds, especially the voice of caution, fade away because of the impelling command of the sea and the force of his youth. He thinks of nothing, only feels it. There is ecstasy in his face and exultation in his heart. He flings his arms high above his head and runs forward. Laughing, he plunges in.

Underwater, it is not necessary to think about breathing, because it is full of light: blue light and white light and golden light. He opens his eyes, the salt in the water stings them, but this is fine, this is part of it. He can see lacy weeds moving backward and forward, and a school of little yellow fish darting about, a crab walking away on its tiptoes, a purple star crawling.

Then his body is seized, the arms of a giant squid wrap around him and heave him up into the air. He gasps for breath, struggles to escape, for he has read about giant squids.

But it is his giant father, standing in water up to his neck, dragging-swimming back to shore with Josip in his arms.

The man drops his son onto the white stones, and the boy

lies on his back with arms stretched above his head, eyes closed, grinning like a madman. His father sits down beside him, his shoes and clothing soaked. He removes them and spreads them around to dry in the sun. He does not look pleased. He says nothing, just watches the distant horizon, where a ship with red sails is passing from south to north.

After a while, father lies down on his stomach, head on his forearms, and dozes. Josip sits up and watches the sea. He can see *Argo* far out, can hear the shouts of the Argonauts. Monsters are trying to seize the ship and pull it down forever.

Bird songs mix with the sound of surf. Not songs, really, but chirping and cheeping. It is familiar to him because there are swallows in the mountains too. He glances around trying to find them. Farther along the shore stands an embankment of sand, part of the cliff face, about ten meters high. The swallows are there, darting in their unique way, soaring sometimes, and plunging. They have wings and tails like no other bird. Josip jumps to his feet and heads toward the cliff.

Standing at its base, he sees that the swallows have made homes in the wall of hard sand, hundreds of holes. Now and then little heads pop out for an instant, take a look around, and then go back in. Birds on the wing swoop down and enter this or that hole, others leave. There are probably chicks inside. It's a very busy place.

Josip has been entranced by them since his earliest years. Their qualities are sufficient cause for this, but there is, as well, the name they share. The *lastavice* are family. He has learned that this is of no interest to them. The admiration is not mutual. They are as elusive as other birds, but swifter and smarter. He has tried to capture them at various times, with no good results. They have dive-bombed him at nesting time. They have sat on the roof of Svez's shed, observing his activities out of the corners of their eyes, scolding him or discussing him (he is never sure which), as he gazes out of the bedroom window. If he climbs to the roof of the shed, they fly across to the roof of the house. If he climbs to the roof of the house, they fly to the shed. They devour enormous amounts of insects, a habit for which all human residents of Rajska Polja respect them. They hunt at nightfall. They are small but amazingly courageous. They fear nothing, not even the alpine eagles, or the crows, or the vultures. They regard the earthbound domestic hens with pity or perhaps with lofty disdain. It is possible that their estimation of people is the same. They are never, never, interested in contact.

Josip imitates their calls, which draws their attention. The patterns of their flight, their arrivals and departures, change for a minute before returning to normal. Then, remembering that the sea is near, he leaves the swallows, goes back to the shore, and sits down by the edge of the surf. A wind has risen over the water. The sea is now making waves, and the stones are chattering. Whenever a wave comes in, it strains to reach his feet, but he has cleverly placed himself so that it can only touch his toes for an instant before retreating.

His knees are under his chin, arms wrapped around his legs, as he gazes out at the horizon, without a thought in his head. He is drowsy and feeling very peaceful. For a time he closes his eyes and listens to the surf. As he is resting in this way, a swallow makes its high chipping sound nearby. He opens his eyes.

It is suspended in the air a meter in front of him, facing him, its wings tilting this way and that as it floats on a draft. Josip opens both his hands, offering a perch, though he knows it is futile.

The swallow flits forward and alights on his fingertips. Josip ceases to breathe.

It flutters a little, settles. He has never seen one this close. It weighs next to nothing, it is warm, and through the trembling of its tiny feet he can feel its heartbeat. He knows that he cannot, must not, seize it. The swallow has come of its own accord and will depart in the same way. He must not hasten this moment, which he feels is the most important of his life.

The swallow grows completely still, perching tentatively, with extreme delicacy. It is regarding him with a fathomless attention, just as he is regarding it.

"Who are you?" he breathes at last.

Still the swallow does not depart.

"Where have you come from?"

For a few seconds only—seconds that might stretch into the eternal—the boy and bird look into each other's eyes, reaching across the gaps between the ranks of creatures. Then, without warning, the swallow flashes and is gone before the eye can follow.

"Where are you going?" Josip whispers.

2

Josip and his father sleep under the orange tree. His father has made him unload his pockets, which are crammed with the white stones he has collected from the beach. He will take them home to remember the sea. They are stacked in a little pile not far from his hand.

Wrapped in their blankets, listening to the surf, they watch the stars over the Adriatic. They pray together, and in a sleepy voice father recites some lines from Homer, about the sea. Josip blinks, and it is morning.

Cheese and bread, and more oranges for breakfast.

"Sour?" his father asks.

"Sweet!" shouts Josip, jumping into the air.

The father smiles as he watches his son carefully loading the round white stones into his pockets. When that is done, they head up to the road.

They walk along it for a time, Josip rattling and clicking with the sound of the shore in his pockets. A horse-drawn cart comes clipping and clopping out of the south. The driver, an old man with silver moustache, stops and offers them a lift. His face is dark brown, his eyes as blue as the ocean. The tips of his moustache are so long they touch his chest.

"It's twenty-five kilometers to Split, if you're going to Split", says the man. "Do you intend to walk all that way?"

"We are going to Split", the father replies with a smile. "And to ride with you, sir, I can see would be a great pleasure."

The man chuckles, an entire face full of wrinkles, and says, "Come up, then!"

Josip asks for permission to sit among the boxes of vegetables on the flat open back of the vehicle. His father and the driver agree, after eliciting promises that the boy will not run around or eat any vegetables. His father sits in front beside the man. Josip lies back on a heap of straw between crates of turnips and onions, listening for any conversation that might develop.

The discussion is vague at first, as if his father and the driver are feeling their way through treacherous territory. Both are Croats, but it seems that his father is more careful in his speech with strangers. There is mention of the Italians, the Germans, and the British. Josip has heard these words before and has seen a German soldier. More than a year ago, one passed through the village alone on a motorbike, stopped, opened a map, and asked directions. Josip's father, who speaks some German, informed the soldier where he was. Rather, where he was not, for the cart track leading to Rajska Polja threads its way through an unimportant range leading nowhere. This barely passable route ends in a mountainous cul-de-sac and is of no strategic importance whatsoever. The soldier shook his head, gunned his motor, turned the bike in a half circle and, after disappearing through the mountain pass, was never seen again. The people of Rajska Polja refer to this incident as "the invasion".

Josip understands that foreigners have armies on the soil of Yugoslavia, and that some of their soldiers have penetrated close to the fields of heaven, but no farther. He knows that the Germans and Italians are friends with each other but sometimes quarrel, and that they hate the British and another enemy called Americans. As the cart rumbles along toward Split, Josip learns as well that the Chetniks are not wolves but men who hate the Germans and Italians and who also hate the Croats and Muslims, and that the Ustashe hate the Serbs, and that most of the Chetniks are Serbs. The Partisans are Croats, Slovenes, and Serbs, and all want a free Yugoslavia, but each in a different way. The Communists are a different kind of trouble altogether, though some of these are Chetniks and some are not, and some are Partisans and some are not. Most Croats do not approve of the Ustashe, who are very cruel to their enemies, but they feel that the Chetniks are a greater menace. The Ustashe want a separate nation for the Croats, but they work with the Germans and Italians, who occupy different parts of Yugoslavia. Most Croats want an independent nation for Croats, which has been declared by the Italians, but it is no more than a puppet state.

What is a puppet state? Josip likes puppets; his father makes them with him out of his mother's spare cloth and large oak nuts, and Josip paints the faces on them. The old man says that some people want the united kingdom of the Serbs, Croats, and Slovenes to be restored, and it is not difficult to tell by his tone that he thinks this may be a good idea. His father replies that even if it were revived, it would not really be a natural kingdom, it could never hold together and be a true democracy, considering the nature of Serbs, who always work to dominate everything. The old man agrees and points out that it was the Austrians who caused all the troubles, long ago, when they started that other war because a Serb killed one of their princes. Why start a war over a madman? he wonders. Very strange.

His father speaks about a place called Versailles, of which the old man has heard nothing, and about the need for a Catholic democracy in Croatia, and how nations can thrive when people respect their differences and do not kill to solve their problems. He adds that it is possible here, and they must all work for it. The old man isn't quite so sure about that, but he admits there are a lot of things he doesn't understand, because he is a farmer and all he knows is the bit of soil that's his own.

"That's kingdom enough for me", he jokes, and Josip's father laughs, claps him on the shoulder.

Though their conversation is extremely confusing, his father seems to understand it all, and this surprises Josip greatly, for until this moment he had heard nothing of these matters.

Split is a mighty city, enormous. If Mostar is a hundred villages pushed together in one place, this is a thousand villages. Its streets are hard and flat, paved with cobblestones or concrete. There are many motorcars and trucks, countless people milling about in all directions. And here too Italian soldiers patrol the streets.

The cart must stop for a few minutes, blocked by a traffic jam of army trucks and horse-drawn carts. A group of German officers strolls along the boulevard in conversation with a single Italian officer whose black uniform is decorated with medals and braid. Behind him, two other Italians in simpler uniform are smirking and gesturing to the young women they pass on the sidewalk.

"Look at them flirting with the girls!" says the farmer. "What an army! Do you know what the Italian word for retreat is?"

"No", father shakes his head.

"*Avanti!*" and the farmer goes off into peals of laughter. His father smiles. Josip has noticed the frequency of his father's smiles and laughter during the trip. Clearly, he is enjoying himself very much. The knot of traffic untangles itself, and they move on. The farmer drops them at a marketplace by the waterfront, where many sea-going vessels have crowded into the small harbor, fishing boats and ships of war with cannons poking out of them in all directions. Here there is no beach, only cement quays.

Facing the long promenade is a huge old building that his father says is a palace.

"Is that where the king lives?" Josip asks.

"No, the king lives in Belgrade, or he used to, before the war. The emperor Diocletian built this palace and lived here in the fourth century, more than sixteen hundred years ago."

"It is very old."

"Yes, very old. Come, let's see it."

So, they pass through a gate and into a tunnel underneath the palace walls and up some steps into an open square surrounded by Roman buildings, his father pointing out details and explaining all the way. In the center is a building with mighty pillars capped by a dome.

"This is the cathedral, the church of the archbishop of Split. It was built by Diocletian to be his tomb. Christian slaves built it. All day they worked like animals to lay its stones, and at night they were locked into the cellar beneath it. Now it is our Catholic cathedral. It is also the tomb of the bishop of this region who was martyred by Diocletian. No one knows where the old emperor's body ended up."

"That is very, very interesting", says Josip, with furrowed brow and distant look.

"What are you thinking?" his father asks with mild amusement.

"I am thinking that God has the final word."

This is a saying of his mother's: *God has the final word.*

"The emperor should have been nicer to the slaves", Josip adds.

"Well, he wasn't. He killed them all after they built this fine resting place for him."

"That is hard to believe", says Josip with a look of disgust, though he does believe it, because his father has told him.

Now it is his father's turn to furrow his brow. His eyes grow distant as he looks to the mountains towering above the city, beyond which lies his home.

"Tomorrow I will take you to Solin, the ruins of the Roman city just outside Split. There we will see the place where the martyrs died."

Profound feelings fill Josip, solemn and silent, as if the rhythmic swell of the ocean has been suspended and all motion in the surrounding city has ceased. He is looking at the sky, up beyond the pillars and dome of the cathedral, beyond the peaks of the mountains. He is brought back to the earth by the cheeping of small birds, which he notices have made mud nests in the cornices of the pillars. They are swallows, and it seems to him that they must surely recognize him, because of his name, but also because yesterday their emissary made a visit to his fingertips, and they will surely know this. Their sounds grow boisterous as his father shakes his shoulder and says, "Let's go in and pray."

But the big doors, which are covered with wooden carvings of the life of the Savior, are locked.

Father kneels down on the steps. Josip kneels beside him. Father presses his forehead against the door. He prays silently, his lips moving, his eyes open. There is worry in the eyes, and also something Josip has never before seen in his father's face— fear. The exhalation of the man's breath trembles, and a vein in his neck pulses rapidly. Then his father gets to his feet, smiles broadly at his son, and says in a cheerful voice, "Now we will go to see your aunt."

For the first time in his life, Josip realizes that his father shields him from many things, with a confident manner that he does not always feel. This is a revelation so unexpected, so absolutely clear, so undeniable, that it leaves him stunned. He now sees his father's true strength, his greatness. Miro Lasta is a man shorter than many in Rajska Polja, nearly bald, not as lean as most fathers, not as physically strong. His face is not handsome, and he wears thick eye glasses when he reads. He is respected by all, yet he is not admired in the way that men of better appearance are. Now, however, Josip understands that his father *is* Odysseus.

They walk many blocks and enter a street filled with big houses. One of them is the convent where his mother's sister lives. They ring the bell at its iron gate, and a nun comes and lets them into the front garden. She is dressed all in white, not

like the brown Franciscan Sisters who every few years come to
Rajska Polja in summer to teach catechism. She takes them up
the marble steps of the old house and into a hallway that is
shining with a light Josip has never before seen. It is like gold,
but darker, less yellow. Their shoes tap loudly on the stone
floor, and the air is full of a scent that is like the incense Fra
Anto uses at Easter. At the end of the hall they come to a big
statue of Jesus pointing to his heart. His father and the Sister
bow to it, make the sign of the cross. Josip does the same and
follows them into a room that contains a polished wooden table
and several chairs upholstered with fine cloth. A purple rug
softens the sounds of their steps. On the wall is a single picture,
a painting of the Mother of God with many swords in her
heart. Josip stares at it, then walks about the room keeping his
eyes on hers. Her glance follows him everywhere. She is sad,
but it's plain to see that she likes him. The sister leaves, and
father sits down with a sigh, staring at the floor.

"Tata, is my mother's sister nice?"

Father raises his eyebrows and nods. "Yes, she is. All the
Sisters are very fine women. Are you nervous? Don't be. She is
our family and much like your mother."

"Still, I feel shy. What will I say to her?"

"Don't worry about what to say. You have met her before."

"I have never met her before!"

"When you were a baby we brought you here to show you to
her, and to consecrate you at the shrine of St. Josip."

"Ah, then she has seen me before."

"Yes."

"But I no longer look like myself."

Father pauses and furrows his brow, because embedded in
Josip's statement are philosophical subtleties. He is about to
reply when a little bell rings on the other side of a window in
the wall, a window that opens to the interior of the convent. Its
wooden cover is drawn aside, and the smiling face of a woman

in a white habit cries out in greeting. Josip gasps, for it is the face of his mother. He knows that this woman must surely be his mother's sister, but still, it is a surprise. As she and his father take each other's hands and exchange warm greetings, Josip observes that she is unusually beautiful. He remembers his mother's face and realizes her beauty for the first time. There are tears in the nun's eyes; she laughs and cries at the same time. Mamica does that, too.

"And this is Josip", she turns to him. "Oh, he is the image of his mother!" says the nun, offering her hands to him through the open window. Josip steps forward and comes to attention manfully. He gives one of her hands a single shake and nods his head, once, like a gentleman. This makes her laugh. Her eyes dance, her cheeks shine and flush red—as red as his mother's do when she has had a little wine after Midnight Mass at Christmas and Easter.

"This is Sister Katarina of the Holy Angels," his father says, "your aunt, your mother's sister."

"I am very pleased to meet you, Josip Marian", she says, adopting a formal manner herself, though she is smiling and does not let go of his hand. Indeed, she takes it in both of hers, making him feel a little uncomfortable, for she is, after all, something of a stranger. She tousles his hair. "His grandfather's color", she says fondly.

"Yes," says his father, "and we can thank God that he has inherited his looks from your side of the family."

"Oof, Miro," she scolds him, "Marija was lucky to catch you."

"I caught *her!*" he declares in the gruff emphatic voice that is the tone he uses when making a silly joke.

"Yes, yes, that's right. Marija knew the great secret of all good marriages. You must chase a boy in such a way that when you have caught him, he will think he has caught *you!*"

His father and the Sister are still laughing and wiping tears

41

from their eyes when another Sister brings a tray to the window, loaded with cups and things to eat.

Josip swiftly seats himself at the table.

There is tea for him, coffee for his father, a plate of sweet baked goods, bread and butter, a bowl of raisins and dried figs. Josip cannot believe his good fortune. All reticence simply dissolves. He loves this nun. He will love her forever.

"Let us eat", she says. They pray grace and then eat.

A single square of chocolate sits in the exact center of the plate, surrounded by sweet biscuits. Josip stares at it with yearning. He can smell it. His nose twitches, and his mouth begins to salivate. In another second he will drool. He might even lunge toward it and gobble it down before they can stop him, and he would be quite willing to live with the consequences. However, Sister Katarina of the Holy Angels says, "The chocolate is for you, Josip. Please take it."

He obeys. It is gone.

"Let it melt slowly," she advises, "then it will last longer."

But, too bad, it's already in his stomach. It has left a streak of ecstasy down the back of his throat.

"Chocolate", says his father. "Where did you get it?"

"It's Swiss chocolate", she replies, her expression flowing subtly into the kind of evasiveness that only the holy can accomplish without approaching the borderline of falsehood.

"Swiss?" his father says, with raised eyebrows.

She sighs, and her defenses collapse. "An Italian soldier came to the convent last December. He was not a bad young man; you could see in his face he didn't like being an invader, and I thought too that he didn't like being in the army. He asked to see the Mother Superior. That was very hard for her because her brother in Zadar was in the Molat concentration camp, and no one has had word of him since he was arrested. He is a priest who spoke against them from the pulpit. But she agreed to see this boy. When they met he begged the prayers of the community for his mother who is a widow in Italy and has no other support than him. He said he did not want to do any evil and asked our prayers that he would not be killed so he could go back home and look after his mother. Mother said the whole community would pray for him. This was hard for the Sisters because the Italians have taken away so many people, thousands, and we know some of the missing. But we all did pray for him. He returned a week later and told us he was being transferred back to his homeland within a few days. He brought us the chocolate, enough for a square for each of the Sisters. He knelt down on the floor and asked Mother to bless him. She did. Then he stayed on his knees and could not raise his eyes to us. In a voice like a little boy, he asked us to forgive his countrymen for the wrong things they were doing in our land. Then he went away. We never heard from him again."

"So, this is your piece of chocolate", Josip's father says.

"I saved it from Christmas," she replies, "hoping that you would come this year. It has been so many years since we were all together. Marija's letters, and the troubles . . ." She pauses and searches his eyes. "Have you had difficulties?"

"No more than the usual", he answers as if the *troubles* are a minor matter. "Rajska Polja is of such little interest to anyone; we are well protected."

"Protected by the mountains and protected by God. Every day I pray for this. News from the interior reaches us from time to time. The Italians—are they very harsh? They have done terrible things here, though as I told you some are better than others, like that boy Emilio."

"Since 1941 they have come to the village three times with the Home-Guard and searched every house. But no one was arrested. Recently the Italians have been undermining the *Domobran*, taking over everything in Herzegovina, breaking all their promises to the NDH and supporting the Chetnik rebellion to make things even more confused. The Partisans are growing in numbers too, and most of them are Communists. In the mountains madness is growing among our own people. To the east of us for the most part."

"We have heard. The Chetniks . . ."

Both his father and Sister simultaneously flick their eyes toward Josip and back to each other.

"Your letter said you will be searching for work here in the city. Is it so?"

"This is my hope. I must try. In Herzegovina things are becoming more unstable every day. Italian officials control all education now, and our school inspector works for them. But no one has made real trouble for us. I do not think they will be here forever. The war will end someday."

"Yes, it will end. But will there be other troubles on its heels? Croat against Croat, Serb against Croat. And the poor Muslims. Terrible things have reached our ears. Even women and children."

Her face is now anguished.

His father and Sister Katarina once again speak without words. Josip sees that their eyes are saying they must not allow him to know what they are talking about. Something terrible. He swings his legs back and forth and glances at the Gospa with the swords in her heart. He eats a biscuit and pretends he is not listening.

"Teachers in Split come to the convent asking us to pray they will find jobs", says Sister Katarina. "Sometimes an answer to prayers comes swiftly, though mostly not. It is a hard time for everyone."

Again they look at Josip.

"The Gospa will watch over your family", Sister Katarina says with finality. "She will carry this boy through these evil times, and one day, yes, one day there will be no more fear." She wipes her eyes. "May he grow old, a good, good man. May he grow old . . .", she trails off.

Josip is now entertaining a few doubts about Sister Katarina of the Holy Angels. To grow old is unthinkable. He knows well enough that people grow old, but in his heart he *really knows* that old people were born old. They have always been that way, and children have always been the way they are: they expand from extremely small, inarticulate sprouts in the belly to fairly large-sized children who can argue with their parents (always a dangerous activity). But they don't turn into old people just like that. Of course he realizes that his summation of the matter does not make sense. Though in a strange way, he is sure, it does.

He eyes the plate of bread and, with a nod of permission from Sister, finishes it off.

They sleep in the guest house on the grounds of the convent. It is a hut at the side of the garden up against the high stone wall surrounding the convent grounds, beneath some palm trees that sway in the night, sighing, sighing. The room contains a bed, a little table and wooden chairs, and a kneeling bench for prayers before a crucifix. The floor and walls are made of white bricks; the tiles above the roof beams are red. Father and Josip say their night prayers by candlelight, tumble into bed, and sleep deeply.

The next morning Josip begins to reload his pockets with the stones from the beach, but his father tells him to leave them in a pile in the room. It is to be their home for the next two or three days, and no one will steal the stones; certainly the Sisters will not. Reluctantly, Josip obeys.

They walk a few kilometers to the west of Split, cross a small river on a foot bridge, and enter the ruins of Solin. Much of it is buried deep beneath the soil. Yet the foundation stones of the first cathedral are visible, and the remains of the Roman walls, even a city gate and the paving stones of the street that runs through it. His father explains that the two ruts in the stones were gouged by chariot wheels. The most exciting place of all is an amphitheater. Its stones are almost black, not like the pictures he has seen of the huge coliseum in Rome, which is gray, nor like the white coliseum in Pula, for both of these look almost as good as on the day they were built. Solin's amphitheater is buried halfway to its uppermost stones by countless centuries of living and dying. His father and Josip climb a slope of grass to the top and gaze down into the bowl of the arena. At the bottom, sheep are grazing where gladiators once fought and Christians once died. Among the sheep is a group of boys his own age kicking a ball around and scattering the witless sheep that get in the path of their play.

"This is a better sport", his father says with a half smile, seating himself on the cap of a pillar.

Josip slides down a heap of rubble into the arena and ambles toward the boys. He says hello, and they greet him in a friendly way. He enters the game, just as he does in Rajska Polja. They are not exactly like the boys of his village. Their accent is Dalmatian, same words, but different sounds. Their clothes are those of city people, though ragged. They do not wear shoes. Their feet are black with dirt. Their hair is long. Maybe no one looks after them much.

But the game is fine, and there is a lot of laughing and shouting, and no one gets angry. The ball is a bundle of rolled rags bound by string, not as heavy as the sheepskin ball the boys use at home. It takes some getting used to because the kicks and foot moves have to be different for a ball like this. He adapts swiftly. Then his father shouts to him and beckons that it's time to go. Josip waves good-bye to his teammates. Maybe they will never see each other again. That's all right. It was fun. As his father and Josip climb back up the heap of rubble to get out of the arena, a boy runs after them and pulls at the father's coat sleeve. Josip's father stops and looks down at him. The boy's cheeks are hollow, and his eyes seem too large for his skull.

"Can you give me food?" he asks.

Father ponders a few seconds, and then thrusts his hands into his pockets. He gives the boy the hunk of bread they had saved from breakfast. It was to have been their lunch. He also gives him a coin. The boy takes it, flashes a look that is unreadable, and then tears into the bread, wolfing it down on the spot. Then he runs away. Josip's father looks after him, sighs, and he and Josip leave.

Later that day, his father visits a big office building. Josip sits on a bench outside the door of a smaller office within the building. Many people come and go in the halls: a few are Italians, most are Croats. There are stacks of books everywhere. Schoolbooks.

His father comes out of the office, shaking a man's hand, and then he and Josip go down the front steps into the street.

"Was it a good visit, Tata?" Josip asks.

"Not such a good visit", his father says, though he quickly smiles and claps Josip on the shoulder. "Let's go back to the Sisters' house."

Two more days are spent in this way. Father is visiting many buildings. He tells his son that he is looking for work as a teacher in the city, but he has found that there are no positions available. He wears his confident smile more and more, but whenever Josip glances at him, his father's face is solemn, his eyes haunted by the look Josip first noticed when they prayed at the locked doors of the cathedral.

The next morning, after Mass with the Sisters, there is a lovely breakfast in the parlor with Sister Katarina. Eggs, biscuits, tea. There is no coffee for father, because the single cup they served him on the day of his arrival had been a gift from a benefactor of the convent. The Sisters had been saving it for medicinal purposes but decided to give Miro Lasta their best. After breakfast all the Sisters crowd into the parlor from a side door, including the Mother Superior, who, Josip notices, is very old and bent. She is the one who has a brother in prison; she blessed the Italian soldier. That is what a saint looks like, his father says later on the homeward journey.

Before Josip and his father's departure, the Sisters sing three beautiful songs for them: one in honor of the suffering Christ, one in honor of the Gospa, and a final one that is about the personalities of barnyard animals and is so funny that everyone breaks down laughing before it ends. When it is time to say good-bye—really good-bye—Sister Katarina hugs Josip and kisses him on both cheeks. He likes her well enough, but this is a bit too much! All the Sisters are giggling as they watch, and their Mother Superior steps forward and puts into Josip's hand a little object wrapped in oil cloth. Very tiny. He is sure it is one of those religious medals like the ones the catechism Sisters give out whenever they visit the village. He puts it into his pocket.

"Open it as soon as you are on your way", says the Mother Superior with a twinkle of her eyes.

Without warning, without even knowing he is going to do it, Josip drops to his knees and says, "Please bless me so that I may return to my mother."

The Sisters grow silent; there is some sighing, hands held to hearts. The Mother Superior makes a simple sign of the cross over Josip, and then he jumps to his feet. It is time to go.

All the Sisters accompany them through the hallway, out the front door, and follow as far as the gate in the garden. Thirty pure white birds, waving and waving as father and Josip walk away down the street.

Near the waterfront, they find the autobus that will take them back to Bosnia-Herzegovina. The Italians call it Zone Two. Father always refers to it as "our Croatia". He explains that a land is where a people live; it's their home, not a barnyard enclosed by someone else's fences. Such fences cannot last, he says. Josip does not quite understand this, for he is preoccupied by something more important—the little package Mother Superior gave him. Inside he finds a single square of chocolate. He holds it in his mouth a long time, letting it melt slowly.

They travel for two hours southward along the coast, the sea always on the right, *Argo* always riding upon its shimmering blue. When the bus leaves the highway and turns east toward the mountains, Josip recognizes the very spot where they had debarked three days earlier. He gazes down the olive covered slopes to the single orange tree on the edge of the cliff. Below this, he knows, is the beach where he swam and the home of his friend, the *lastavica* who rested on his fingertips.

3

Sun beating down on the village. A strong breeze blowing from the south. In the grass behind the house, his mother is drying clothing. All morning she has washed the family laundry by hand in a tub on the back porch. She thinks herself alone and talks to the chickens, scolds the donkey, and from time to time sings snatches of song, or whispers prayers. She is happy today.

Josip watches her for a while, sitting unseen behind a bush. It is a great trick, hiding from his mother, because generally she sees and knows everything. His great love for her wells up with force, and tears spring to his eyes. He understands her now in a way that he has not until this moment: she is an exceptionally kind person, full of faith. She serves him and his father unreservedly, exacting nothing in return except an occasional kiss.

"Mamica," he whispers, "my Mamica."

There are sheets and blankets in need of drying. They have not been washed all winter and have grown musty. The mother would ordinarily drape such items over larger bushes, but today, for no apparent reason, she ties one end of a rope to a hook in the wall by the kitchen door, then unrolls it slowly as she walks uphill toward the rock and the solitary old oak that crowns it. She ties the other end of the rope to the tree. That done, she returns to the backyard and begins to hang the washed blankets and sheets on the rope. They flap furiously, hitting her at first. She laughs and goes to the other side of the rope, upwind, to hang the rest.

Josip pulls off his shoes and tiptoes toward the rope, which he notices is now like the rigging of a ship with signal flags. The sheets are white, the blankets are blue, red, green, gray. His mother has alternated each blanket with a sheet, making a pleasing pattern with which the wind now vigorously plays.

He is standing opposite her, a sheet between them. She still does not see him, does not appear to sense his presence. He steps forward, arms open wide, until the wet sheet slaps his whole body and sticks to him.

"O Marija", he sings in a high wobbly voice, which he thinks sounds ghostly.

His mother gives a sharp cry.

"O Marija," he wails, "I am the spirit of your little boy Joshko. I am here to tell you that you must give him more sweets!"

"And what will happen if I do not, O spirit?" mother wails in return.

"Your beloved little Joshko will fly away forever like a *lastavica.*"

"This I could not bear, O spirit. Tell me, what sweet does my beloved especially favor?"

"Your beloved is especially fond of sugar cakes made with butter and walnuts."

"I will make him one for supper. Tell him not to fly away."

"I will tell him. Good-bye, Mrs. Lasta."

"Good-bye, O spirit."

Suddenly her arms are around him, wrapping him in the sheet. He struggles to get free, but she holds him tight, laughing and laughing in the way she does only when she has had a glass of wine at Christmas and Easter or when she receives a letter from her sister, the nun in Split, or when Tata and she are discussing things quietly when they think he is asleep.

"Mamica, Mamica, let me go!" he bleats.

"But if I let you go, you will fly away."

"I won't. I promise. Make me a cake and I will stay forever."

"Then I will make you a cake."

She lets him go, he staggers back, trips, and falls to the ground. She comes around from behind the sheet, her eyes full of hilarity, hand covering her mouth to keep her laughs inside.

She sits down on the grass beside him, still chuckling.

"Oh, what a boy you are", she says.

But now he has begun to think of other things. "Why do you hang the blankets on a rope today?"

"Because today I want to catch the wind in them. And when they are dry, the scent of the wind will remain within them so when we sleep, we will sleep in the arms of the wind."

On an impulse, he leans over and kisses her cheek. She puts an arm around him and squeezes him. Her eyes are holding him so tenderly that he begins to feel uncomfortable. He senses that it is important for boys not to be captured by mothers, even by a mother as fine as this. He jumps up, goes to the other side of the rope, and presses his body into a sheet.

"Such a fellow you are, Josip," she smiles, "so full of tricks."

Now he is completely engaged with the sheet, which wraps and unwraps him.

"Is this life, Mamica?" he asks.

"What do you mean, is this life? Of course it is life."

"I mean," he says, reaching forward so that he is imprinting his entire form on the sheet, "I mean, do we come into the world like this, like a shape that pushes the air, fills a space that wasn't here before, and though we are now here, we are also hidden?"

"I don't understand, Josip."

"Are we all in sheets, pushing our shapes into space, trying to see each other behind the sheets but we can only see a little?"

"Perhaps it is like that", she says musing. Standing, brushing grass from her skirt, she goes to the other side of the sheet because she wants to hold him a while longer, to press him to herself, a habit he once loved and that he has now almost out-grown. But he has gone. He has flown away into the sky.

She shakes her head and resumes hanging up the laundry.

It's summer, very hot during the day, though cool at night. The snowpacks on the heights are almost all gone. This morning a single airplane flies low over the peaks. The entire village comes out of their houses to witness this amazing event, the first time such a thing has happened. Its engines make a rumble like thunder, but longer. The people stand in the lane watching its passage, hands to brows, shielding their eyes from the sun. The men in the fields stop what they are doing and look up without moving. Everyone is worried the plane will drop a bomb on Rajska Polja, but it doesn't.

There are circles on the undersides of its wings. The rumble fades slowly as the little cross in the sky disappears into the north.

"The British", father says. This remark sparks much debate among those who are standing nearby.

"Maybe he is lost", says an old man. "They are bombing Italy now."

"Can they fly this far from Malta?" asks a young woman.

"Are they in Malta? I heard they are in North Africa", says another.

"No, in Sicily. The Americans too."

Josip's best friend, Petar, hits him on the shoulder and says, "Let's go up to the castle. Maybe more planes will come."

"We can watch them from high up", Josip nods. "We will wave to the pilots."

"What is a pilot?"

"The one who drives it."

"Ah."

They each run to their homes to fetch bread, water-skins, and various implements they will need for whatever adventures present themselves to their minds. Petar returns to the Lastas' house first and barges into the kitchen without a knock, carrying his hatchet. Josip straps a sheathed knife to his waist. Bang, they are out the back door and galloping up the hill toward the trees.

It takes a while to get out of sight of the village. Not a single mother spots them, not a cry calls them back. Grinning, they reach the fringes of the oak forest. They are winded, going slowly now. They kick aside sheep droppings and the hard balls of the acorns and throw themselves down onto the grass. Most of the nuts are old and brown, but some are new and green, the size of a dove's egg.

Neither Petar nor Josip has brothers or sisters. They are like brothers to each other. Petar is a year older, though they are the same height, and both are altar boys at the church. Josip is not as good at soccer, though better at studies.

Petar picks up an acorn and tosses it at Josip. Clunk, it bounces off his forehead.

"Ouch!" He throws one back, missing Petar's skull by a millimeter. Petar opens his mouth like a wooden doll, and he makes a squeak like a startled mouse. His black hair always pokes out in all directions. This, added to his clowning, makes Josip throw himself back on the ground guffawing.

"Stop laughing at me, *lastavica*!"

"You are a wild man. Look at your h-h-h-hair!"

"What about my h-h-h-hair", Petar mimics. "Look at yours, just like straw." He tears up some dead grass and throws it at Josip. "Come on, let's get going!"

They heave themselves upright and begin to climb, the ground underfoot becoming more rocky with each step, the terrain pitching sharply. It takes a long time to reach the plateau halfway to the peaks of Zamak. They are sweating and puffing heavily. The final ascent must be accomplished by pulling themselves upward, grabbing onto the branches of the trees.

One slip of the foot and they would tumble downward a hundred meters. They are on their bellies as they drag their bodies over the crest onto the plateau.

It is not a large place, this relief from the vertical walls of the mountain all around them. You can throw a stone from one side to the other; the same along its length. The floor is covered with rubble. Half of the space is occupied by the crumbled ruins of the Turkish fort that for centuries overlooked the valley. It is from this structure that the mountain derives its name, *Zamak*—castle. It was not a true castle, for few men could have crowded into this narrow space. All that remains of it is a broken cistern made of cement, and the foundation walls, no more than a foot or two in height. The people of Rajska Polja—Petar's ancestors in fact—dismantled it sometime during the previous century, hurling its stones down into the valley, where they have sunk into the soil of the forest. In its place they erected a hand-hewn stone cross as tall as a man. On clear summer days it can be seen from the village as a white speck. In winter it is invisible because of the snow.

"Do you think we will see another British bomber today?" Josip asks. Petar often knows about things Josip's parents neglect to tell him. It is a custom between them that Josip will ask for useful information and Petar will ask for help with schoolwork. This is a perfectly satisfactory arrangement that neither of them feels demeaned by.

"Yes, maybe today. And soon there will be more. More and more and more. I hope they drop lots of bombs."

"People could get hurt."

"Yes, but they are smart, the British. They will drop them on the Italians and the Germans. They won't drop them on our people."

"My father says someday we will have a real Croatia."

Petar shrugs. "My father says he doesn't think so. The British will rule us just like everybody else tries to."

"Maybe the Ustashe and Chetnici won't let them", Josip says timorously, because he has already sensed the confusion and delicacy of this matter among adults.

"Maybe Partisans won't let them", Petar says, staring out across the valley.

"They all kill people", Josip muses. "Why do they kill people so much?"

"I don't know", Petar says, staring at his feet dangling over the edge. "They are angry."

"Fra Anto says we must not do what they do."

"He's right. But when they try to shoot you, what can you do? You shoot back."

Josip absorbs this. "We have no guns."

The Italians and Home-Guard took away all the guns in the village, on the day they first came to Rajska Polja. It is no longer possible to protect the flocks from wolves or to hunt deer in the mountains.

"My father has a gun", Petar says. "Don't tell."

"I won't."

"You won't tell your father, not even Fra Anto?"

"I promise. No one."

"It's for Chetniks. If they come here, he will shoot them."

"They will never come here."

"Last year your father said the British would never come here. Today a British bomber flew over us."

"But it did not drop its bomb."

"This is true. Still . . ."

Petar leaves his thought unfinished. He resumes gazing out over the valley. It is a peaceful scene. Threads of smoke are rising from cook fires in the houses far below. A dog barks, and now and then the noises of a goat, a rooster, a human voice are carried up on the warm breeze. The pastures are lush in the narrow slopes closest to the creeks that drain Zamak. Here and there the sheep move in loose clumps over the ground.

"Look, we are above the clouds", says Josip pointing to one of the flocks.

Petar grins in agreement but says no more.

For a time they are content merely to look at the world. After they eat some of their bread and drink from their water flasks, Petar gets up and begins to stack a few stones at random onto the walls of the fort. Josip joins him. They work together for a while in this way until Petar stops and stares into space.

"Your father says the Chetniks will never come here because no one is interested in this valley."

"Yes."

"Joshko, why did the Turks build a fort here?"

Josip can think of no reply.

Later they cut some brush with hatchet and knife, and spark a small fire with Petar's flint. They don't need a fire, but it's always essential to make one. This is something they have done many times before. They throw a few pine cones onto the flames, just for the smell—so nice, like Mass on Sunday. By late in the afternoon, the sun has moved around the mountain and is beating straight into the plateau. They have drunk all their water. So, by wordless agreement, they know it is time to go. They stomp out the fire, then slide themselves over the edge of the crest.

There are a few tumbles going down the mountain, another acorn war, and some good jokes. But uppermost in the minds of both boys is the mystery of the fort. They part company in the village street, after washing their hands and drinking deeply from the creek that runs past the church. And by the time they reach their homes, their fathers are coming in from the animal sheds, and their mothers are placing meals on the tables.

It is Sunday morning. After the Gospel reading, Fra Anto speaks about the British bomber.

He is a very tall man, lean and sturdily built, black-haired, lots of muscles. Whenever he plays soccer with the boys in the field behind the church, he does not wear his Franciscan habit, only his black trousers and white undershirt. He wears a big crucifix under this shirt, and Our Lady's scapular. He is really strong and so good at soccer that it is unfair if he plays for one side against another. He helps both teams, just to keep it even, and they never know when he will switch sides. It's part of the fun, never knowing when Fra Anto will fool you. He plays in bare feet. His feet are enormous and are usually cut and bruised, with a bandage or two. He wears his sandals only when the first snow has fallen, though without socks. When he gallops down the field toying with the ball between those feet, you don't get in his way. One stomp and you're dead. Most of the boys want to be friars when they grow up. Most of them forget about this when they are sixteen or seventeen, though not all. Since Fra Anto came to Rajska Polja ten years ago three boys have left for the seminary at Široki Brijeg—a great number of vocations for such a tiny village.

Now Fra Anto speaks about the bomber. He tells the people this is a sign that the Allied forces are approaching Yugoslavia, and that the war is about to change. In the struggle for this land, many factions will be active, Allied, Axis, and our own people, who are divided and angry. Old evils might be replaced by new evils. We must all pray for peace, a holy peace, a just peace that only Christ can bring. Hatred and vengeance must not take root in any heart. This is Christ's village, he says, consecrated to the Savior and his Mother. Even its name speaks of the fields of heaven. But it must be so in more than name. The Kingdom of heaven is within, and it can be preserved only when the life within us has no death in it. Hell's spirit must be kept out of every heart if Rajska Polja is to be preserved in peace. This is a task no man can do for another. We can help each other in this, he says, but each must do the major task within his own soul.

"Satan was a liar and a murderer from the beginning", he

concludes. "Wherever there is murder, there will always be falsehood with it. For this reason we must live in the truth. It is never enough simply to avoid killing others. We must never permit the smallest seed of untruth to sprout within the heart of the soul."

All the people are silent, pondering within themselves as he returns to the altar and continues the Mass.

September. School has begun. Once again Josip's father is master of the wooden building the government built beside the church in the 1920s. His father is a kind man, but he can be stern too. No nonsense. Every child knows this. Every parent in Rajska Polja supports him in this.

His father was born and raised in Split and is, like Josip, an only child. His parents died in an influenza epidemic many years ago. Josip's mother is from a mountain village in a small pocket of Croatians northwest of Sarajevo. She shares the customs of the country people, though she graduated from high school in Sarajevo and attended one year of teacher's college in Split. That is where she met father and they were married. Father accepted the position of master at Rajska Polja, despite its very low wage, because he loves the mountains and the country people. He does not like cities. Cities are rabbit warrens, he has frequently said in years gone by.

Josip puzzles over the fact that his father now wants to move the family to a city and is frightened that he cannot.

His father's accent has a strong Dalmatian flavor. Josip's accent is in no way different from the accent of the other students of the school, though he knows more words than most. This richness of expression—which he seldom reveals outside the home—derives from his father's books, the way Miro Lasta has read to Josip every night from his son's earliest childhood onward. There are many books in their home. There are many in the school as well, some from the old government, some from his father, and others donated by people his father knows in Mostar and Tomislavgrad. There is also a box of books that was brought to the school by the Italian inspector at the start of the war. These remain always under the teacher's desk and are unpacked and displayed only for the inspector's annual visit.

So, it's back to studies again. About a hundred people live within the narrow cul-de-sac of Rajska Polja and its immediate environs. Thirty-eight of these are school-age children ranging from ages seven to eighteen. Usually the older ones leave school when they finish primary classes. A few depart for the city to find work, but most take up farming alongside their fathers. It is a good life. Before the war the spring sheep-shearing always brought in some money for luxuries like tea, coffee, cocoa, and sugar, and for essentials like tools, harness tackle, fabric for making clothing, suspenders, buttons, and belt buckles, as well as shoes, which are expensive, and once every few years, a fancy hat from the shops of Mostar. Since the war began, such items have grown scarce, though the wool continues to be taken away in carts each year in exchange for the new currency, which can hardly buy anything. Even so, the fields grow plenty of vegetables, and these combined with mutton and eggs and milk provide enough. The teacher's salary is insufficient for his family's needs, and everyone knows it, though he does not complain. Because his eyesight is not the best and he is not the strongest of men, the families of the region supplement his income with food. It works well for everyone.

It is evening, a week after school has begun. Josip's mother is making sweet-bread with the raisins someone gave her, brought from the grape harvest near Mostar. The firebox in the stove is crackling and the room is warm.

The Lastas are fortunate to have such a fine house. It is made of mortared stone and is a little larger than most in the village. The walls of its three rooms are plastered and whitewashed—

three and a half rooms, if you count the small loft above the kitchen, a cubby beneath the eaves where Josip sleeps. He has climbed up and down the ladder without mishap since he was three years of age. Before that, he always slept in his parents' bed, so his mother could nurse him if he cried in the night. All of that lies behind him, in the distant past.

The floors in the kitchen, his parents' bedroom, and the parlor (which is really part of the kitchen with no wall between them) are wooden planks. Though these are rough-hewn and unvarnished, they are better than many a floor in the region, for the people are accustomed to stone slabs or pounded dirt. The building was long ago an Austrian customs shed, used once a year by officials who came from Mostar for the tax assessments. Now it belongs to the new government and is used by the Lastas as part of father's salary.

Though there are few pieces of furniture, and these all made of wood, the rooms are comfortable enough. Some of the chairs have cushions, which Mamica stuffed with wool and embroidered with the red and white Croatian braid. On a shelf are displayed dozens of her painted eggs, which she makes each Lent. Her best ones have small hearts on them. Her first ones, made when he was a baby, have acorns and flowers and braid painted on them, but their lines are wobbly. The ones she has made during the past few years are more sure of hand, more brightly colored. Her sister in Sarajevo (whom Josip has never met) sent her a package with powdered dyes in them—twelve different colors. Mamica mixes these with egg yolk to make the paint.

On the floor are a few sheepskin rugs. On a peg by the kitchen door hangs his mother's brightest shawl, which she wears only on Sunday to church. Her everyday kerchief is usually to be seen on her head, or dangling from the pocket of her long brown skirt. It is forest green with small red hearts embroidered around the edges.

61

The walls of the parlor and bedroom are lined with shelves and loaded with books. One wall of the parlor is kept bare for the family altar, a wooden table on which stands an ivory crucifix—very old. It was inherited from his father's mother, who inherited it from her grandmother, to whom it was given by a young Austrian officer who died of a broken heart when she rejected his proposal of marriage. No one now recalls their names. At its feet are a ceramic pot containing wildflowers, an amber glass vigil light, and a pile of rosaries. Quite a few of these latter have broken links, which will need replacing when father can obtain a spool of brass wire. Behind the crucifix is the only window in the room, needing a good washing soon, the glass gray from wood smoke and fly-specks. Hanging on each side of the window is a framed print, the Sacred Heart of Jesus and the Immaculate Heart of Mary. Above the window is a little icon of Majka Božja Bistrička, Our Lady of Bistrica. Father wants to walk to her shrine near Zagreb someday, a pilgrimage, just he and Josip all the way on foot, so they can pray before the miraculous statue and ask for the grace of Josip's vocation in life.

"Whatever it may be", his father often says.

"If our finances permit", his mother adds quietly.

"If politics permit", adds his father even more pensively.

"*Everything* is becoming politics", says his mother shaking her head.

"In this country, yes", agrees his father. "Politics and war and grudges that people will not let go of."

"And what does the Gospa think of all that?" sighs his mother.

This is an exchange that has been repeated several times in recent years.

But tonight, as his mother makes bread, his father is seated at the kitchen table by the oil lamp, reading aloud from *The Odyssey*. They have read *The Iliad* twice, and now they are beginning *The Odyssey* for the second time. Josip knows what is coming, yet it is always new. He is seated in the chair across the table from his father, eyes glazed, mouth open, in a trance. He is Telemachus, the son of Odysseus, and his father has not returned from the war in Troy. Telemachus has donned his best armor and, arrayed like a golden god, is about to make a speech in the agora. He will plead for help from the elders, for the means to go in search of his father.

Just then there is a knock at the door. Josip's heart sinks, and he is ripped from Ithaca back into a valley in Herzegovina, many kilometers north of the city of Odysseus.

Father removes his glasses, rubs his eyes, sighs, and gets up to open the door. Lo and behold, it is Fra Anto! Josip's heart rises again. Miro clasps the priest's arm and draws him inside. Fra Anto kisses Marija on both cheeks, and she tells him the sweetbread will be ready in half an hour if he is willing to wait. He says he is willing to wait until dawn for her sweetbread. She is famous for this bread. She makes it with a special spice—it's a big secret, this spice.

Miro finds a little flask of *slivovica* high in a cupboard, uncorks it. The scent of plums and herbs fills the air, competing with the baking bread. The special glasses for visitors are brought, so small you can hardly fit a thumb into them.

Everyone sits down at the table. No one has yet told Josip to go to bed, so he stays. There are only three glasses, however, and from this he deduces that not all the festivities will include himself.

His father pours pale, mauve slivovica into the glasses, gives one to Fra Anto, one to the mother, and lifts his own. They make a toast. To what? To the visit!

Yes, to the visit!

Živio, živio, živio!

Fra Anto often drops in like this, for no particular reason. He and Josip's father usually discuss the books they read. His father lends the priest books. But tonight Fra Anto has brought news.

The Allies have invaded Italy. It is possible that the war will soon be over. The Italians and Germans will flee, and perhaps a decent government will arise in Croatia. Josip's parents throw up their hands in jubilation. Fra Anto makes the sign of the cross on his breast, as do his mother and father when they see him do it.

The news about the war is interesting. But for the moment Josip is pondering something else. He is realizing how fortunate he is to belong to this family, which has a friend like this.

He thinks to himself: Fra Anto is a holy man. He wears no shoes. He gives his food away to people who have little to eat. He keeps nothing for himself except what is necessary to stay alive. He is never angry, even when people are angry at him—though this does not happen often. He sleeps on bare boards with a single blanket in the room behind the sanctuary. He prays all the time. He is a saint. He is always happy.

He likes my Tata very much. Look at the way they talk; they can speak with each other about so many things, everything really, about Homer and about St. Jerome, who had a lion and a temper, and about St. Simeon the prophet, whose body has not rotted and can be seen in the cathedral at Zadar, and about a book that is a comedy by a poet from Italy, and about the little flowers of St. Francis.

"Much good has come from Italy", his father says.

"Much good has come from the holy faith that is *in* Italy", Fra Anto replies, as Josip's father fills his glass again.

"Yes, that is more accurate", his father admits. "Men are the same everywhere, the good and the bad."

"Here too, Miro", Fra Anto suggests in a musing tone.

"You mean Yugoslavia."

"I mean Rajska Polja."

"Ah, yes, but the fields of heaven are better than most places—in fact, the best."

"Why is it so, Fra Anto?" the mother asks leaning forward.

"Why are we so blessed when all around us there is so much suffering?"

"I do not know", Fra Anto replies. "Perhaps in times past this village suffered more than most. Did the Turks steal many of her children and turn them into Muslims? And did those who remained neither lose faith nor rebel against God for this horror that had come upon them? It is likely such things happened in this valley, as they did in so many others. Only God can read the history of sacrifices. Or was there a saint who stopped here one day a thousand years past and asked a villager for a cup of water? And when it was given, did this saint beg from God a blessing upon us, a blessing that would remain until the end of time?"

"Or is it because we are poor and content to remain so?" Miro asks.

"Who would desire our valley?" says the mother. "It gives to the world nothing but a little wool, and not the best quality, either."

"It gives to the world its children", said Fra Anto, staring into the flame of the oil lamp. "And they are more priceless than all the gold and lands and power of the earth."

"Yes", says mother, casting a fond look at Josip. He squirms, knowing she is about to plunge into a flood of emotion, even to hug and kiss him in front of his hero. But she does not.

Mother, father, and Fra Anto nod reflectively, then glasses are refilled and smiles rekindled. Now the bread is ready. Mother removes it from the oven, long braided loaves, steaming and spotted with hot raisins. She slathers each with butter and presents the glistening prize on a platter. They all break off a hunk and begin to nibble, trying not to burn their lips.

The conversation resumes between bites. Though he is listening to the adults with one ear, Josip is observing. He thinks to himself something that has never struck him before:

Fra Anto hears my Tata's confessions, once a week, year after year. He hears my confessions too, and this is something I wish could be otherwise, but it cannot be. Even so, he likes my father very much, though he knows my father's sins. Maybe my father has no sins. No, he has sins. I saw him empty the bottle of *slivovica* down his throat that night Mamica was angry with him, and that other time when he said a crude word after Svez kicked him, and those things he said about the inspector—oh, that was pretty bad, that was. I never knew my father had it in him. But Fra Anto likes him very much, this is plain to see. They are the same as Petar and me. And my mother loves my good Tata too, who works so hard for us and carries much inside himself that he hides from us so as not to worry us.

Josip's father gets down the tambura from the peg where it hangs on the wall beside the family altar. It has been a while since he last played it. He nests its round base in his lap. It is the *bisernica* type, "the little pearl". The tuning pegs at the end of its long neck need adjusting, then father tentatively fingers its three double strings. The sound it gives is soft, high, refined, evoking countless memories of evenings spent in the happy company of guests.

Mother claps her hands together and cries out, "Sing, Miro, sing!"

"Sing, Miro, sing!" shouts Fra Anto in his deep voice, also laughing.

So, father strums the little pearl and opens his mouth. From both of these instruments pour forth the music of his soul. Even a nine-year-old can understand this. The words are simple poetry, and the music is simple too, yet they reveal joy and grief combined, loss and yearning, hopes rekindled after a long winter, love in springtime. Though it is September, the kitchen window is open, and from it one can see the stars visible above Zamak. A neighbor strolls past the window and stops to listen. Josip's mother waves to this woman. She approaches and puts her head into the kitchen, leaning her arms on the sill. Mother pours her a glass, gives her a hunk of bread. The women eat and drink as Miro sings. Fra Anto is now singing with him. They have begun a more light-hearted piece that makes Josip bounce up and down on his seat. More people gather outside, neighbors from along the lane. A few of them join the singing; it is one everyone knows.

When it is over, a wave of applause pours in from beyond the window, and mother jumps up to open the door, inviting everyone in. More than a dozen people, young and old, shuffle inside, tipping caps and kissing his mother. The door is left open for any stragglers who might happen by. The bread disappears quickly. The singing goes on for hours, long after the bottle of *slivovica* is exhausted. Toward midnight, a shooting star crosses the sky behind the peak of Zamak, flares brightly, and fizzles out. The old people bless themselves. Fra Anto asks if anyone would like to pray the rosary; they all do, none excepted. Two dozen people are now crammed inside the house. Hardly elbow room, but no one minds. The elderly are made to sit down on the chairs, and everyone else stands or kneels or sits on the floor. As the Rosary is prayed aloud, a baby cries, and then a toddler squawks, but it is all sweet. It is the sound of life. It is the sound of the future.

Springtime, and the snow-patches in the field are shrinking quickly. On sunny days the cross on Zamak shines whiter against the white mountain. The swallows are rioting, lining up along the ridges of all roofs, where they rest from building their new nests. Everyone is glad to see them back. Where do they go for the winter? No one really knows, maybe south to Greece, where it is warmer.

In the loft where Josip sleeps each night, there is a small window—no larger than the cover of a book—set into the apex of the gable. When opened during the summer, it lets the heat of the house escape. He likes to watch the swallows from it in the morning, before his mother and father are awake. If he wets his index finger on his tongue, and squeaks it on the glass in circles, the swallows stop their chattering and turn their heads toward him, ranks of them in a single line along the ridge of Svez's shed. "Pay attention", he says, as if he is a schoolmaster and they his class of tiny students. This makes him laugh.

The round white stones from the sea are arranged on the sill. He often picks them up, the small and the large, and rolls them around in the palm of his hand, remembering. They are the first thing he sees each morning. He drops off to sleep each night looking at them.

A girl has come to live in the village. She is the niece of the blacksmith and has been adopted by his family. Her home is far away. Her father was killed by the Chetniks (the people of Rajska Polja have now begun to speak openly about them), and her mother is sick in a Sarajevo hospital. The girl's name is Josipa. There are other girls named Josipa, but none of them are like this one. The children of the village know each other very well; from birth they have seen all there is to know; nothing escapes the eye and the ear. Indeed, a lot of people are related by blood here, and even the children who are not related seem to be as brothers and sisters or cousins. You do not fall in love with your brother or sister or cousin—you do not feel anything like that for them.

But, oh, Josipa, Josipa, Josipa!

It begins as a little flame in the heart that grows and grows. He can't put it out. It's not the thing that always seizes the older boys when they begin to grow moustaches, but it must be something close to it, because for the first time in his life he cannot control his eyes, which are now always seeking her face, yearning to catch a glimpse of her, anywhere, everywhere.

Her name is like his name. Just add the letter *a*. She is not a Lasta, so she has no connection to the swallows as he does, but they are both connected to St. Josip in the Holy Family. This is no small thing. They are separated by five seats in the schoolroom. She is behind. He knows how foolish it would be to turn around and stare at her. No, he does not give in to this impulse, not once. He knows how much teasing would result. She is so beautiful. Beautiful, beautiful, beautiful. Until now he has held this word in disdain. It has become an indispensable word. He can't get it out of his mind. It is a beautiful word.

Josip is now ten years old. She is maybe two years older than he is, but he is taller. The Lastas were short people, Mamica has often said, but her family bred giants. Josipa's eyes are sad and she says little, merely hangs around the schoolyard with her cousins, the blacksmith's daughters, when she is not at home helping her aunt with chores. The other girls know how to get her interested in games. Once or twice she has smiled, but she remains so shy that no one wants to force attention on her. They all know about her dead father, the brother of the blacksmith's wife.

She has long, straight hair, blond like Josip's. Her eyes are brown, not blue like his. She has rosy cheeks and a little smile that quivers because it has not been used for a while. But it's easy to see she was once a happy person. Her eyes twinkle when something nice happens, such as the day Mamica brought sweetbread to school for all the students as a surprise. A little gray cat follows her about wherever she goes. It sleeps on the steps of any building she enters, waiting for her. She carries it around a lot, stroking it, singing to it.

He would like to speak with her. The thought of such an impossibility chokes him. Instead, he has lately taken to romping boisterously with Petar the moment they are out the school door. They wrestle a lot when she is nearby, toss acorns at each other's heads, try to make their voices deeper, and laugh like idiots at each other's stupidest jokes. She notices but comes no nearer. And it's plain to see that Petar has noticed her as well, though of course they both despise girls. Girls are too soft, too sweet, too unpredictable. If you throw a nut at them, they cry.

Well, maybe not all of them—the tougher ones will throw one back without crying, harder than you threw, and then tell their fathers. You are never allowed to wrestle with them, because one day they will be mothers and you could hurt something inside and then there would be no children. You can't punch them, even when they are clumping together and whispering in each other's ears about you—yes, just loud enough so you can hear your name. Gigglers! Idiots!

But she is *so* beautiful!

He thinks about her at Mass, and while reading by the oil lamp at night, while watching the swallows, while feeding hay to Svez in the morning. He thinks of nothing but her. It could drive him crazy. He doesn't like it. But he does like it.

No, he doesn't! Better to forget her!

Then one day, after all the snow is gone from the pastures, he strolls aimlessly toward the mountain, intending to climb alone to the cross, and of course to think about her up there. She will be the size of an ant when seen from the fort. It is easy to forget an ant. He would never step on such an ant, but it might help him to ignore her from now on, after he has seen how small she is and no different from the other ants.

As he approaches the fringe of the forest, he notices a bit of color just inside the trees. It's a girl in a blue dress, sitting with her face in her hands. He swerves to avoid her. But just as he turns in another direction, she looks up, startled. It's Josipa. She has been crying.

For a moment he is undecided. Should he leave her to her tears? Maybe she wants to be alone. Maybe she would be embarrassed if anyone talked to her in this state? The dilemma is resolved by his legs, which simply pull him toward her. He sits down on the grass beside her, not too close. If he were to reach out an arm, his fingertips would just brush her shoulder. He would not do this. Never.

"Hello", he mutters, choking a little.

"Hello, Josip", she says drying her eyes on a sleeve. She knows his name! This is thrilling.

But what should he say? She is crying for her parents. No words can help.

So, he says nothing.

For a time they look out across the valley to the mountain range opposite their own. The remaining snow on its crests is glowing pink in the morning sun. The wind rippling along the valley is warmer than it has been for months. Insects are singing, birds too. The first buds of the blue alpine flowers have appeared in the grass around them. He can stare at all of these, but not at her. She is blue upon blue. She is the creation of the color blue. He has never truly looked at this color before; its meaning has remained unexamined all these years. She is the essence of blue—that shade halfway between water and sky on bright days.

Her little gray cat is not with her today. It seems she does want to be alone.

He is afraid. Why is he afraid? He knows why. He understands that he is afraid to lose her, now that he has found her. He is afraid also of himself, because he knows how stupid he can be at times, the impulsive words and actions. If he says the wrong thing she might jump up and run away. Then this fearful bliss will never occur again in his entire life. It will be lost.

Why is it so hard to breathe? His mouth is hanging open to take in more air, and his heart is thumping in his ears. His body has sunk into the soil. He is part of it. It will be impossible to leave. Moment by moment, because he is torn between the magnetism of bliss and the repulsion of helplessness, his fingers twitch on his knees, and his muscles convulse as if they are trying to hurl him to his feet and headlong down the slope of the pasture. It is the strangest feeling in the world. This love and fear melted together into a single thing.

It is like the day last summer when the swallow alighted on

his fingertips by the sea, and poised itself there for a few seconds.

Who are you? Where have you come from? Where are you going?

These questions have answers he already knows: Josipa, Sarajevo, the future. But they are not the real answers. He knows this, knows it without language—not Croatian, not Greek, not Latin—not by any vocabulary that can be articulated in thought or speech. Josip sees all of this, though none of it materializes in his mind as actual words.

The answers are to be found beyond the appearances of things, he knows. It becomes possible to find them only when the sweet shock of the unknown appears in your life out of somewhere else, from a place you did not know existed and could not have imagined until now.

First you were not here, one presence says to the other. I did not know you existed. Now you are here. And you are perfectly silent with me, yet your eyes are gazing at me, as mine are gazing at yours. These are the eyes of the swallow.

Suddenly he realizes that they are indeed looking at each other.

"Where are you going?" she says, her voice soft, almost a whisper.

Instantly restored to the realm of boyhood, he whips his head around to face the mountain and declares in a gruff tone, "To the cross."

She tilts her head inquisitively. "Which cross? Is there a cross on the mountain?"

"Yes, up there on the castle."

"Is there a castle on the mountain?"

"No, a fort. The fort on the mountain that is called Zamak."

"I would like to see it", she says after a pause.

"It's too hard to get there", he shrugs. Then he realizes that he has really told her he thinks it's too hard for *her* to go there. Does she feel belittled by this? Has he lied to her? Perhaps, after all, it is not too hard for a girl to climb up there. Regardless, he cannot take her up there, because it is exactly where he had planned to forget her.

"I can try," she says, "even if it is hard to climb."

For this he has no immediate answer. Because he does not reply, she looks away and stares out across the valley again. Her face is sad, though she is trying to hide it.

Still he does not move. He cannot return to the valley below or scale the heights above. He is caught between two zones, trapped between the past and the future, in a place that is timeless.

Josipa looks at him. He looks at her. A current flows between them, without beginning or end, no initiator, no recipient, for both of them have given and received at the same moment. It is unlike any other look Josip has ever received or given. It dissolves all thought. It demolishes time itself. It is the strongest thing in the world. It is stronger than fire, stronger even than death. For this briefest of pauses in the many complex movements of life, and of the two smaller lives within it, there are no barriers. Only a flowing current of deep waters—waters burning with a light that is gentle and inextinguishable. In later years, Josip will still wonder what it was. He will come to understand a part of its meaning, yet he will never have full knowledge of it. He will experience it in other forms, but never again like this.

The current subsides simultaneously for both of them. He reaches out his hand to hers, which is planted in the grass and supports her body. They take each other's hands for a second or two as they struggle to rise. Then, with no more said, she turns from him and goes back down into the valley.

Time always returns. It does. You can forget it, but it never forgets you. Now the entire world, which has been sleeping in the sunshine, begins to move again. The sheep drift across the meadows, the smoke once more rises from the kitchen fires, and the branches of the oaks resume their sighing. And he, after watching her descent, turns and ascends the mountain. The climbing is now effortless, and he sees nothing of the ground beneath his feet. He is silent, without thought, borne aloft by the current, even as it slowly fades. Later, as he sits on the wall of the fort, he discovers that he will not forget her, that he no longer wants to. He knows he has been captured, and that this imprisonment is the most free thing in the world. When the sun begins to fall into the mountains like a ball of red fire, he too returns to the valley below.

4

The Italians are gone, but Josip's father is more worried than ever. He always tries to hide it. When caught unawares, his eyes are haunted with the look of fear that Josip has now come to recognize but does not fully understand. His father is often to be seen in the evenings with head in hand at the kitchen table, staring blankly at a book open before him, or out of the window at nothing. His favorite books, reread so often that he practically has them memorized, are the poems and tales of Matija Divković and the spiritual writings of Marko Marulić. But even these no longer hold his attention.

Josip knows that confusion and danger have increased throughout the country. Countless men of Yugoslavia have left their homes to join bands of fighters struggling to push out the Germans. At the same time they are killing each other. From his father, Josip learns of these matters only in the vaguest terms, with many reassurances. From his friends in the schoolyard, he gets the details, with horrifying speculations.

Even so, the general feeling in the village is that the valley is strategically important neither to the Germans, who are retreating step by step to the north, nor to the various factions that are trying to destroy each other as they fight for supremacy over the Yugoslavia that will remain when the invaders are gone.

Josip's father has a map of southern Herzegovina that he brings out and pores over endlessly, sometimes with Fra Anto, talking together in low murmurs. Mamica goes to bed by herself most nights, leaving father with Fra Anto, or with his more constant companion, sleeplessness. Month after month the situation grows worse, and the villagers learn of it mostly through word of mouth, occasionally through a newspaper. But few if any newspapers arrive in the village, and none can be wholly trusted; everyone is taking sides. Fear is now always in father's eyes; he can no longer hide it.

Infrequently, aircraft cross over the valley, going ever northward, never releasing their bombs. Josip's father believes that this occurs when the antiaircraft guns along the coast, or the weather, make it difficult for the Allies to travel their normal bombing routes to industrial centers where the Germans are still in control. They are driving the Germans back, so it is generally considered among the people of Rajska Polja that the Allies will soon be the victors. Still, not everything is clear.

Josip overhears a conversation between his father and Fra Anto one night when they think he is asleep in the loft. He has slipped silently from his bed and is lying on the floor. He removes a loose knot from a plank, and the hole permits a beam of lamplight and a flow of information to rise upward. He covers the hole with his ear.

" . . . the Allies have turned all their support to the Partisans", says the voice of Fra Anto.

"But surely Churchill realizes . . ."

"Yes, he knows that the Partisans are dominated by Communists. It's my guess that the Allied command believe that a little loss to the left will purchase a great advance against the right."

"They are naïve."

"Yes, but who can tell them anything? Certainly *we* cannot. They have no sympathy for the Home-Guard because they worked with the Fascists. They do not understand that the Domobrani are at heart only for our homeland and want neither Fascism nor Communism."

"Still they did collaborate. Are you really saying, Fra Anto, that the Home-Guard would give us a free and democratic Croatia?"

"They are our best hope at this time. They are the army of

76

Yugoslavia. Even if they compromised in the past, it was because they had no choice and did as little harm as they could under the Italians. For the most part, they are ordinary Croats, and ordinary Croats want freedom and independence. The Ustashe Croats want Fascism, the Chetniks want Serbian imperialism and the absorption of Croatia into their total control. With them we would be a puppet state, or worse, a slave state."

"But the Partisans."

"Dominated by Serbs—Communist Serbs. Though they permit Croats and Slovenes to help for a time, it will be turned against us if they ever come to power."

"It doesn't seem likely they could come to power."

"It is hard to know for certain what will happen. Churchill and Stalin are not enemies. If Churchill were to reject Communist anti-Fascists, it would create tension between the Allies. At the same time, Churchill knows that if the Soviet army penetrates south and takes Serbia, and perhaps even more than Serbia, they may never leave. Britain, and America, would not be happy about it."

"So, you're saying they've chosen a lesser evil."

"Yes. They will accept a Balkan Communism, less powerful, less oppressive than Stalin's Russia. I think they foresee a buffer zone in the new world that will materialize in the wake of this war."

"They underestimate the Soviets."

"They are counting on the ferocity of our nationalists—even our Communist nationalists. More and more Chetniks are joining them, and some of their worst chiefs have become high ranking officers in the Partisan brigades. What does this tell us about the future? I think the Communists will soon rule from Belgrade."

"But a Communist Yugoslavia! Surely Britain and America do not want that!"

"They want peace. They want the defeat of Germany."

"The Allies see us only in black and white!" declares Miro in a tone of dismay. "If they were to support the Home Guard instead of the Partisans, they would obtain more than a buffer zone. They would have friends—democratic friends."

"Don't forget, the Serbs are masters of propaganda. They have convinced the Allies that only the Partisans are big enough and sufficiently organized and disciplined to rid the land of the invaders."

"Let us pray they turn their guns only on invaders."

After which the men get up and go out to stroll under the stars.

Though all this is, of course, quite fascinating, there is something more important taking place in the world. His love for Josipa has become the light within his soul. He does not for a moment assume that this is the beginning of the usual sort of thing between boys and girls. He rejects the very thought of courtship. He is ten years old! He is a child! So he reminds himself. He is not interested in those things that seem to obsess the older youths and maidens of the village. He knows that it is how love comes into the world and families are begun. He read the booklet about it that his father gave him, and he remembers also their conversation about it, though vaguely. It does not apply to him, all that. He is sure it never will.

No, it is the flame itself that is important, moving silently between the heart of Josipa and his own heart, and back again. She feels this too, he is sure she does, for she glances at no other boys in the way she looks at him. Since their first meeting on the mountainside, they have not exchanged words, though they are continuously speaking with the eyes of the swallows.

Who are you? Where have you come from? Where are you going? Her eyes ask this of him, his eyes ask this of her, and both of them smile with the knowledge that the answers are not what they really seek. The union between them is their great secret, their great treasure. Both of them know it. Moreover, they know that they know, and they seem to know as one.

Strangely, they do not seek to be alone together. For a time it is enough to cross paths in the schoolyard and for their glances to meet. Or at Mass, or when children and parents gather by chance at the pool in the creek beside the church, dipping their wooden buckets into the water that is needed for cooking or drinking or washing. Whenever they meet in this way, the world begins anew. It is enough to keep them alive for days.

In time the language of union seeks other forms from which the radiant core may expand. He is the first to move. Before dawn one morning, he walks silently down the lane to the pool of water. He has learned that she comes at a certain hour to fill a bucket. By the big stone on which women and children stand to lean out over the pool, he lines up seven of the round white stones from the sea. He arranges them into the letter J, then he swiftly retreats to his home. From the kitchen window, he observes her in the pale light of dawn, emerging from the front door of her house with bucket in hand. She strolls along the lane swinging it, looking up at the sky. She is wearing the blue dress, which against the rose background of dawn strikes all breath from his chest and sets his heart hammering. She sees the white stones and glances toward his house. Though the daylight is not yet strong, he is sure she is smiling. She stoops, gathers up the stones, and pockets them. She fills her bucket with water and returns to her home.

Later that day, Josip barges out the kitchen door and around to the back of the house. He intends to do nothing, perhaps lie on the grass beneath the oak tree and see if chance or an angel will drop a nut on his forehead. Fra Anto says that angels guide all the forces of nature on earth and all the motions in the heavens, the sun, the moon, and the planets—from the smallest seed to the mightiest star. If an acorn falls on his forehead, will it hurt? He is curious to know. Is gravity as strong as throwing?

When Petar is not around to help test such ideas, you can figure out things in other ways. He sits down on the grass beside the rock. From the corner of his eye, he sees a flash of blue on the flat top of the rock. Looking closer he finds the blue flowers that grow only on the forest floor up the slopes. They are arranged in the letter J. A tiny blue feather caps the letter. It has not blown away, because one of his stones from the sea weights its stem.

A letter arrives from Sister Katarina of the Holy Angels. After months of disruption, the mail is running again between Dalmatia and Bosnia-Herzegovina. There is no clear government anymore. The entire land is riddled with zones dominated by this or that faction: pockets, islands, fortresses of power, their borderlines ever shifting with the movements of roving brigades—*paklensko polje*, the fields of hell, his father calls them. Some people on the coast have been wise enough to send their mail to a religious community in Mostar, a house they know is reliable. The priests and brothers move about the countryside without too much interference. They are weaponless and usually on foot. A Franciscan brother from Mostar has brought a bag of mail. Fra Anto distributes the letters to homes throughout the village.

Mamica dances around the kitchen with her most joyful expression, rips open the envelope, pockets the wax seal with the impression of the baby Jesus pressed into it, and reads aloud to father and Josip.

Beloved Marija, Miro, and Josip,
May the Holy Family bless and protect you all.

It is a great risk to write what I must say in this letter, and a greater risk to send it by our courier, who is leaving later in the day for Herzegovina. I pray it will remain unseen by those of ill will. After you have read it, please hide it carefully, for if it were to fall into the wrong hands, the hammer of Satan would fall on our Sisters.

It has been so long since I have received any word from you. I have sent three letters and a small gift (chocolate) since your visit last year. Did they arrive?

We are reasonably well, and our house has not been harmed by the Anglo-American bombers that have hit cities along the coastline and in the interior as well. Though we are close to the center of Split and the naval ships in the harbor, we have so far remained untouched. Food is more scarce than ever, however. Country folk have been generous to us, yet it is never enough. We share what we can with the poorest, among whom are growing numbers of women and children who have fled from the mountains, those whose husbands have been killed or are missing. It is not the Germans who are doing this, it is the Chetniks and Partisans. The stories these women tell us are too horrible for words. I increase my prayers for you every day.

The people of the city are courageous. We feel some relief since the withdrawal of the Italians, but we are not at all happy with the arrival of the Germans, who are much stricter in control and capable of greater cruelty. The Jews have been taken away, though we have helped to hide some of them.

In addition, this spring we harbored two Allied airmen who had fallen into the sea by Trogir. They are now gone, taken in secret to a place where it is hoped they will be returned to the Allies. Few would consider turning these pilots over to the Germans, even though they have bombed our cities and there have been deaths. The heart is often torn by conflicting loyalties. In our prayers we continuously plead for divine mercy, for a swift end to this war and a just government to be established. I am sure that the Allies will assist us in making a new and democratic Croatia.

The pilots told us that the Allies have bombed the whole region of Yugoslavia and all of Croatia this year and last, from the time they landed in Italy near Anzio, between Rome and Naples. After they conquered southern Italy they constructed a large air base near Bari. From there they strike wherever the Germans have positions of strength.

Word has reached us that in February the Allies bombed the Dominican seminary in Zagreb. Seven religious died, buried under the ruins. The seminary is located beside the railroad shunting yards in the eastern side of the city, from which German troops and weapons are sent southeastward. Seminaries in Dubrovnik, Split, Trogir, and Šibenek were also struck. Of course, they were located alongside the port facilities of these cities. Perhaps young Catholic men were flying those bombers. Such is the horror of war that decent men are turned to the purposes of evil, often without knowing the consequences of their actions.

Three months ago I received word from our sister Eva. The situation in Sarajevo is not good, because the city is deeper in the mountains and in the path of much fighting between Chetniks and Partisans. Many Chetniks are defecting to the Partisans, and it is our hope that this will bring them under military discipline and cause them to cease perpetrating their horrors upon our own people. Yet the Partisans themselves are not innocent. They too have done much evil. For the most part, they are commanded by men who are not God-fearers, many of whom are Communists. Eva's husband has joined them. Since last summer she has received no word from him, though she knows he is somewhere north of Herzegovina. She is very worried that he may have been killed. Killed by Germans? Killed by the rival parties in Bosnia or Serbia? There is no way of knowing, since the fighting is intense on many fronts and everything is confused. A friend one day is an enemy the next. Oh, what has brought this tide of evil upon us!

We must pray to have confidence in the ultimate victory of Christ. We must pray for the grace never to lose heart. This is my prayer for you all.

I long to see your faces.

I kiss each of you.

your Sister Katarina of the Holy Angels

It is a warm evening, midsummer. Fra Anto has a little talk with the boys who serve at the altar, not the youngest, just those who are ages eleven to fifteen. Josip is only ten, though he will soon be eleven. Perhaps he is included because he is advanced in his studies and is unusually tall for his age—taller than some of the boys whose voices have cracked.

A dozen village lads are seated in the front pews. Fra Anto has prayed silently, kneeling before the tabernacle, and now he gets to his feet. He has dressed himself in his brown habit. His feet are bare and need a wash. He needs a shave too. They have all just finished a hearty game of soccer in the churchyard and are still sweating. The bread he gave them has been devoured, the water downed, the satisfied feeling after a great game settles on them all.

It is a talk about purity. Josip remembers the booklet Tata gave him, and the conversation that followed. He recalls what happens when boys become youths. They go crazy. They lose all sense. They stop playing enjoyable games. They abandon their contempt for girls. They throw their shoulders back and walk about like cockerels half the time. It is inevitable. It is a force of nature. Perhaps the angels guide this too.

Fra Anto tells them that the changes in their bodies are good. These are new powers, the powers of life itself. But they must be used only in a holy way. The strength of these powers is such that a young man can easily be ruled by them, if he does not grow strong in his character.

"You study to train your mind", he says. "You work hard to build up your muscles when you work with your fathers in the field. You don't always like it. It's easier to read no books and remain uneducated. It's easier not to strain your mind and body with labor, easier to lie on the ground all day and let the birds drop boiled eggs into your mouths."

Everyone laughs.

He goes on: "So, boys, if you don't want to be a slave of your body's desires, you must be masters of your bodies. Then, when you are married someday, you will give to your wife a beautiful gift that has been saved for her alone. It will be a thousand times better than if you had already given it away. She will love you and you will love her, and from your gift to each other children will come into the world. You and she and God will give to the world its most precious treasure, a new soul for eternity."

"What if we become priests?" asks one of the boys.

"Do you all want to become priests?" Fra Anto says with a big smile that they know is his expression for half-joking, half-serious. "*All* of you! That will make the bishop very happy."

They laugh again.

His face grows serious: "I pray that some of you will become priests, if it is God's will. Usually few are called to this path. For most, it is the other holy path, to bring new life, to make families, and to build a place on earth where we all can live."

"Rajska Polja", someone murmurs.

"The fields of heaven", Fra Anto smiles pensively. "Whether it is here or elsewhere, you must carry the fields of heaven within you."

"But Fra Anto," says a younger boy, "what do you do with those powers you're talking about if you aren't going to have a wife?"

His brow furrows a little. The boys can tell he is thinking about how to express it.

"It remains within you as a strength. It is always part of what makes you a man. Yet what truly makes you a man is your moral strength—your decision every day to leave this power unused. Then this power is absorbed into your heart and your heart grows. You give it to God, and he gives back to you many children."

"How?"

"In the heart of the soul", says Fra Anto. Then, after a pause, a big grin, a glance of warm affection: "*You* are my children!"

The boys return his grin. They like this. They like Fra Anto a lot. He's not their father, but he is like a father to them. So they are like sons.

"Is it nice, having no wife?" someone asks.

"The meals aren't so great", says Fra Anto.

They laugh.

"How soon can I get married?" asks Petar.

"Give it a few years yet, Petar Dučić", grins Fra Anto.

More laughter. Petar gets his shoulders poked by the boys beside him.

"Don't you get lonely, Fra Anto?" asks one.

"Yes, sometimes. But everyone feels lonely now and then, even husbands and wives who love each other very much."

Silence, as the boys absorb this. They are thinking about their parents.

He gives them a minute or two to ponder, then concludes, "In this world are many people who do not master their bodies. Such people say that no one can tell them what to do, not even God, and they think that in this way they have no master. In the end they become slaves to anything."

"Like the Turks."

"Well, I suppose a bit like the Turks when they stole our young people and made them into slaves."

"Fra Anto," pipes Josip, "you mean we mustn't let our bodies be Turks over our souls?"

"That's right", says the priest. "You are free men. But to remain free you must work hard."

Josip is alone in the church before the Blessed Sacrament. He has knelt a long time, praying in the ways he has learned to pray from childhood. Mostly words. But there is something new: the current that has awoken in his heart. It's what he feels for Josipa. Yet he is not thinking about her exactly. The current contains her but is not *her*. This is perplexing. What does it mean? What *is* this current? He felt it with the swallow by the sea, on the mountain with Josipa, and now here alone in the church. He does not need to think overmuch to realize that it is the presence in this church, the Body and Blood of Jesus. He knows this. He has felt it before: a flash on the day of his First Holy Communion, another flash on the day of his Confirmation, when the bishop came to Rajska Polja. Now it is here again. And it is lingering, swelling, fading, rising again. And this time it is not just because Josipa is in his thoughts.

So, he gets up off his knees and simply sits in the pew, soaking in the peace of the church, gazing fondly at the red cloth covering the tabernacle, glancing from time to time at the flickering vigil light, the crucifix over the tabernacle, and the glow of colors fading in the stained-glass windows that depict scenes from St. Francis' life. He is preaching to the birds. He is opening his arms to receive the wounds of Christ in his hands. He is taming a wolf. Josip sighs and closes his eyes. *Here* is the exact center of the fields of heaven. Here is the source.

Usually, almost always, he does not stay long after Mass, or the Rosary, or other parish events that take place in the church. The impulses of his body fling him out of the pew like the other boys, and he must command his limbs sternly in order to bring them under control, to genuflect, to walk slowly and reverently to the door and out into the village street. Now he doesn't want to leave. He wants to stay and stay and stay forever. Eventually, he hears his mother's voice calling him. He gets up and goes out the door to find that it is completely dark outside. When he had entered, only moments ago it seems, the sun was lowering in the sky, but sunset was still far off. Has he been inside the church all this time?

Mamica is annoyed with him. She has been searching everywhere. He has had no supper. She slaps him lightly on the back of his head, and he stumbles forward. She catches him and kisses the spot she has slapped. Is he feeling ill? He shakes his head. Is anything making him sad? He shakes his head again. They go home with their arms around each other. He climbs the ladder to the loft and falls instantly asleep.

It is autumn now, a tide of red and yellow slowly washing across the upper slopes, the oaks tuning purple and brown. On blustery days, the wind threshes the seeds from their branches and scatters them onto the forest floor. The days are fine and clear, the evening sky is crowded with stars. There is frost at night, and the grass around the houses is covered with a film of crystals each morning. The cockerel crowing in the dawn rings clearer than it has all summer.

Josip and Petar are working in the field with Petar's father. The Dučić family owns a tract of land to the north of the village, not far from where the valley narrows and ends, sealed by the two ranges that border it. Miro Lasta is with the boys, forking hay into a cart. The hay was cut three days ago with sickle and scythe and has been drying in the sun. Petar's father will give the Lastas some of this hay for Svez's winter feed. The men are chatting as they work side by side. Josip and Petar do the same. All morning and throughout the early afternoon they work in this manner. Miro stops from time to time to drink from a water-skin, wipe the sweat from his brow, and check the blisters on the palms of his hands. He has bandaged them with rags. He does not complain. Load after load of hay is hauled by Petar's donkey cart to the barn beside the Dučić's home. The final load of the day is taken to the Lastas' shed.

Mamica has been busy with some village women, packing vegetables into the root cellar behind the house. Potatoes, carrots, cabbage, turnips, beets. Their tasks completed, Mamica has spread a checkered red and white cloth on the grass, and the women are sitting around it, eating bread and butter and sipping from glasses of red wine, which one of the other mothers has brought. It's a wonderful feeling, this sitting in the late afternoon sun with the barns and the cellars full. They are ready for winter. Firewood is stacked by the kitchen door, though they could use a little more in case the approaching winter is severe. Mamica has a fire going in the kitchen cook stove, and the breeze occasionally pushes gusts of smoke down among them. She intends to make bread later with the fresh grain that is now spilling over the top of the storage bins. For the moment she is content, working even as she rests, joking with the other women as they braid garlic stems and tie up bunches of onions that will hang from the rafters of their kitchens.

"Done for the day?" she asks Miro as he flings himself down onto the grass beside her. Nodding, he lays his head on his wife's lap. A neighbor woman fills a cup with wine and hands it to him. He takes it gingerly, because of his blisters, and sips with pleasure. There are smiles and banter all around.

Without warning, a gunshot echoes across the valley. First Petar and then Josip jump to their feet and stare toward the end of the fields—no, not precisely to the end, rather to the northeast slopes. The boys are thinking, is it the secret gun owned by Petar's father? But they do not say anything about this.

No, it cannot be his gun. The sounds are too far away, and besides, there he is, Mr. Dučić, a small figure standing at the end of the valley with nothing in his hands. He too is staring up the slopes. There are more gunshots, all distant, fading and fading. And then there are no more.

"It's just hunters", says Mamica, though her eyes reveal her worry that it is a different kind of hunter from those who seek the alpine deer.

"Perhaps", says Miro, standing now, staring toward the mountains without blinking, his body completely still. There is no more conversation; there are no more shots. The adults look away and set about gathering up the food and dishes. The tension departs as swiftly as it came, and everyone goes about his business.

Josip and Petar are left alone with their thoughts. They exchange glances, turn, and stride up the slope toward the trees. By unspoken agreement, they will visit the castle. They are halfway to the edge of the forest when a shriek comes from below. It is Josip's mother standing by the kitchen door. He has never before heard this tone from her.

"Come down here!" she cries, beckoning frantically with her arms.

"We're going to get more firewood!" Josip shouts back.

"No, come now, Josip! Petar, you too!"

Groaning, they obey. The world is ruled by anxious mothers!

When they arrive at the house, Josip asks: "What's the matter, Mamica? We were just going up to the trees to get dead wood."

"You do not go anywhere from now on, unless you first ask me or your father", she says emphatically, with a wild look in her eyes that is, again, something he has never before seen in her. This is sobering, and he nods.

"I won't, Mamica."

"Good. Now go help your father in the shed. He is trying to pitch the hay into Svez's loft with those hands of his. Petar, will you help too?"

"Yes, Gospodja Lasta", he bobs his head humbly.

"Good, and stop into the kitchen before you go home. I have a little cake to send to your mother."

This is worth a grudging smile from both boys. They head off to the barn smartly, and before they know it another day draws to a close.

Sunday morning, two or three weeks after the gunshots. Mass has ended and people are pouring out of the church. The first snow fell during the night but has melted away. The sun is shining brightly, and it promises to be a warm day.

The men have their heads together, worried. Yesterday there was a thick fog in the valley and wolves came down from the heights and attacked the flock. There are five small flocks in the village that usually graze together, guarded by a single shepherd. The families take turns watching over them. Petar was on duty. When he heard the sudden panic of sheep bells and the braying of the donkey, he knew there was trouble somewhere on the

89

outer perimeter of the flock. Gripping his staff, he strode through the mist toward the commotion and stumbled upon a dead ewe and lamb. The faces and feet had been ripped off. His donkey stood nearby, screaming with fright. Usually wolves will attack a donkey first, which is why one of these poor decoys is always with the flock.

Petar now tells the men that he saw a brown animal slinking away into the fog. Winter wolves are black or dark gray, summer wolves are brown. The men discuss this—the color indicates that the marauders came from lower in the mountains, where winter arrives later than it does in Rajska Polja. The implications are now analyzed in detail.

"Damn!" exclaims one of the shepherds. "If only we had our guns!"

Petar and his father exchange a look.

Fra Anto comes out onto the front steps, as he usually does, to chat with parishioners who linger in the dooryard. He is in an energetic mood and suggests to some of the parents that he and the altar boys take a hike in the hills. Not far, just to the end of the valley and back, through the forest rim, not on the valley floor. No one has any objections, though there is more hesitation than usual.

A walk with Fra Anto is always an adventure. Even so, today there are few young people interested. Some have schoolwork to complete, some are nervous about wolves, and some have unfinished chores in preparation for winter. For various other reasons, only a ragtag group of disciples sets out with him an hour later. Josip, Petar, an older lad named Marko, and his little brother, Saša. The latter is slightly built and not yet seven years old. Fra Anto has doubts about the boy's ability to climb with them. Saša pleads desperately, however, leaning every gram of energy into his body and facial expression, and Fra Anto gives in. He cannot bear to disappoint him, though he knows he will probably be carrying Saša on his shoulders before the day is over.

Fra Anto has packed a rucksack full of bread and cheese, also smoked sausage (gifts from people who have killed their pigs). He is dressed for a hardy trek: rough trousers, shirt, a woolen sweater, and sandals, though sockless.

So, off they go! Straight up the slope of the pasture and into the trees. Turning to the left, they proceed in a northwesterly direction through the sparse undergrowth beneath the oaks. Fra Anto has to bend not to get hit in the eye. Acorns are everywhere underfoot. Birds and small animals flee as the hikers approach, and you can hear them rustling away through the bushes. The sun bakes a wonderful smell from the ground beneath pine trees. The higher the hikers go, the more pines there are, stunted, bristling with green cones, and dripping sap.

Little by little, the trees thin out, and the going is easier. Saša asks for a break. They stop and drink water. Fra Anto passes around a bag of small candies, one for each person. Where has he obtained such a treasure! It is ecstasy. Petar crunches and swallows. Josip remembers to let it melt slowly. Marko does the same. Saša simply gulps his down and licks his lips. He takes Fra Anto's hand and stares up at him with adulation. The priest laughs and says, "You are a strong fellow, Saša! I am proud of you!" The boy beams and dances on the spot.

"Let's get going", says Fra Anto, "We have a long way to go, and I have a big surprise for you."

A surprise! Now everyone is hooked; they will not lag behind for anything.

Another hour passes during which they pick their way through a stretch of sharp white stones that have fallen down from the peaks above. The slope of the mountain is bending sharply around to the west, where it meets its counterpart. Now they have arrived at the end of the valley. Far behind and below is the little smudge of Rajska Polja resting in the green sliver of its pastures. It is hard to believe that their village is so small, nothing at all really. An airplane flying overhead could not spot it, unless it were looking for it. It seems you could toss a stone from one side of the valley to the other.

Indeed, at the spot they are now standing, they could do just that, for the mountain walls have closed in here, prohibiting passage into the interior. There is no pass, no road, not even a goat track.

"Now the surprise", says Fra Anto with a cunning smile.

He leads them through the stones and stunted oaks to the crest of a fold in the mountain. The fold is little more than a vertical ridge among other such ridges scoring the cul-de-sac.

"Look down", says Fra Anto.

Their eyes wander down to the bottom of the fold, and they see that it works itself deep into the body of the mountain—deeper than is visible at first from any other direction.

"There was once a narrow pass here", says Fra Anto. "Long ago, more than a century ago."

"But where is it?" Petar asks.

"It's here, buried beneath those boulders at the bottom. No army, no cannons, no vehicles could come this way now, but in times past it was not so. That is why there was a Turkish fort here."

"Ah", says Petar with excitement.

"Your grandfathers' grandfathers would have seen it as it was before it was blocked."

"But who blocked it?" asks Josip.

"The Turks. When the Austrians advanced and began to push them from our land, the Turkish overlords saw that they could not hold all passages to the south. This pass was never important, not even before the invasions, but it was a danger to the Turks because it was a backdoor into their territory. I should say, it was a backdoor leading to another backdoor. The main routes were well guarded, but in the end, as they lost ground, they tried to seal all gates. So, they brought their cannons here and blasted the mountains above the pass until it was filled with rubble."

"But why have our people not remembered it?" Petar asks with a frown.

"I do not know why they have forgotten, but it may be because the pass was rarely used at any time in ages past. Then the Austrians took it all into their empire, and peace was enforced. The Turks, our greatest enemy, were cast out. There had never been much need for the people of Rajska Polja to take this route, for there are thousands of kilometers of barren hills in this direction, while the paths to the city were open at the other end of the valley." Fra Anto goes down on his knees and withdraws a map from inside his shirt. He opens it on the ground, and the children kneel to hold it flat against the breeze.

"See here", he says, pointing to a hairline among a sea of wriggling lines that represent the mountains and ranges of Bosnia-Herzegovina. "This is the valley of Rajska Polja. Beyond us there is little human habitation. But there are routes, leading to other routes, that will bring your feet to roads a hundred kilometers north of here, and from there into Slavonija, and beyond into Austria and Hungary. If an army had a map, or a guide, many soldiers and horse-drawn cannons could be brought quietly this way, close to the cities of the south, without the Turks knowing it."

"That is why the fort is here", murmurs Petar.

"Yes, though it was really no more than a watchtower. All of that ended when the Turks withdrew."

"Before he died, my grandfather once told me there was a way into the north from Rajska Polja. I thought his mind was failing."

"His memory may not have been clear, Petar, but what he told you was true."

Fra Anto folds the map and stuffs it inside his shirt. Standing, he smiles with satisfaction: "Well, should we go down and see the pass that does not exist?"

It takes a good while to descend because they must step

carefully among the boulders and the sliding scree, added to the fact that descent is always harder on the legs than climbing. The slope eventually spills them out onto a roughly horizontal gully, level with the valley floor. Turning to face the wall of mountain, they find that in the shadow of a ravine deeper than the others lies a tumble of huge rocks. Fra Anto leads the way into the shadow and comes to a stop against a pile of boulders. The rubble blocking the pass is about ten meters high. Clearly no horse or military equipment could be brought through here. Even so, a man could climb. This they now proceed to do— even Saša, who is half carried up and over some treacherous spots by his brother. He asks to be put down; he can do it himself, he says.

Reaching the top, they progress along the ravine a hundred meters or so, stepping from boulder to boulder. In a sense, it is a pathway, though at all times uneven. In many places, it is possible to go only in single file. Soon the boulders are fewer in number, and they begin to descend. It is like a staircase now, leading them downward to the other side. When they reach the bottom, they find themselves standing in a narrow stretch of ravine on the north side of the barrier. The ground underfoot is flat, covered with natural pebbles and light debris that have slid down from the mountain slopes. Dusty bushes grow here and there. The soil is parched and hardly anything is growing in it, except for some prickly shrubs and tufts of sallow grass. It might be good enough for goats to live on, but not for sheep, and certainly not for men.

"Well, should we go back?" Fra Anto asks with raised eyebrows, waiting for their response.

"No, no!" come the unified cries, "Let's go on! A little farther!"

And so they go on. The walking is fairly easy now, after all the climbing. The ravine never changes in appearance, though the route twists and turns sharply or meanders gradually, only to return to its irregular pattern. Whoever traveled here in times past would need to have much patience, for this is not as the crow flies. After half an hour, they stop to drink from their water-skins and eat some bread and sausage. Their appetites are keen, and most of the food is soon gone.

"Should we go back?" Fra Anto asks. This time there is some indecision. Saša and Marko are worried about reaching home in time for supper, though they are willing to go on a little farther.

"Half an hour more", says Fra Anto with a smile. "There is another surprise."

That settles it. They continue on their way, the minutes seem to fly, and not long afterward the ravine widens to about twice its prior size. A miniature valley lies before them, about fifteen meters across and just as long. At the far end, it narrows again and resumes its former course. The glen is covered in thick blue-green grass. Scattered here and there are a few late-blooming alpine blossoms that have escaped the frost. In the middle of the glen lies a pool of clear water, fed by a trickle that falls down from the cliffs above, making a spray where it strikes a rock beside the pool. In the spray is a rainbow.

"The water is good", says Fra Anto. "You can drink it."

The young people run forward and throw themselves onto their knees. Then they lie down and thrust their lips into the pool. It is about three meters in diameter, a meter deep. The bottom is white stone, clean, with no weeds or slime. The water is cold and flavored pleasantly with minerals. The pool is ringed by grass with a rim of damp gravel. As the young people continue to drink at the pool, Fra Anto happens to glance down at a strip of gravel. He sees there the prints of deer. Then he sees the imprint of a boot. He stares at it for a minute or two, then he says in a quiet voice:

"Let's go home."

BLOOD

5

The snow lies thick on Rajska Polja. Christmas has come and gone. The festivities have been unusually merry this year, with generous gifts exchanged between families throughout the twelve holy days. People sense the war will soon be over and peace restored in the land. Though there is still some concern about what kind of peace this will be, they are praying for the Allies to establish a free Yugoslavia. In their most hopeful moments, they think it possible that an independent Croatia will emerge, a new country composed of all the regions where Croats are the majority, including Herzegovina. This nation existed in times long past and more recently in artificial forms under Austrians and Italians. Why not again?

It is the last day of the year 1944. A group of men are standing together in the lane outside the church. The women and children have all gone to their homes to prepare meals. A few older boys have been permitted to hang on at the edge of the discussion. Josip, unseen, is among them.

Miro Lasta cautions that it is optimistic to hope for a democratic Croatia at this time because the Partisans have now grown to such strength of numbers that they have organized into a regular army and call themselves the legitimate army of Yugoslavia. Rumors have filtered south that this Partisan army is slowly pushing the Home-Guard and remnants of the Axis ever closer to the borders of Austria. They are heading for Zagreb, though they are meeting much resistance along the way. If they win, they will make a new government in Belgrade.

The other men of the village are certain that when the Allies come, they will stop the Partisan and Chetnik outrages and throw all the perpetrators into prison. Fra Anto says this will not happen because the Allies are supporting the new army.

"Support the Communists!" the men reply. "They would never do that."

"They are already doing it", says Fra Anto with a dark look. "And where it will end, none can tell."

Josip makes a Christmas gift for Josipa. On the feast of the Mother of God, he will give it to her. It will be late because some of the skills needed in its making are difficult. He borrows Mamica's paints and in the privacy of his loft, by candlelight, brushes a face on the largest acorn he can find—very pretty. He gets Mamica to teach him how to braid strands of blond hairs plucked from Svez's mane. "For what are you learning this, Josip?" she asks him with a laugh.

"I will help you braid the garlic next autumn", he replies with a masked expression. Of course she knows this expression well and can see right through it, but she decides to leave it alone.

Using a paste of chalk and gum from boiled rabbit skin, he glues the braids onto the doll's head. Then, after the braids, a body and arms of oat straw tied into the right shape by twine. A twig is inserted into the head; then it is popped into the bundle of straw and secured by a dab of glue. Finally, a remnant of blue cloth from Mamica's sewing basket, not quite like Josipa's dress, but close. A borrowing of needle and thread, and the masterpiece is complete!

He goes to the church early on the morning of the feast, the first day of January. No other people have arrived yet. He knows where she always sits with the blacksmith's family for Mass, the exact spot on the precise pew. He has wrapped the doll in an old newspaper and tied it with red thread. He has painted her name on it. He leaves it in the place where she sits, returns to his family's pew, and kneels. He can feel the current, but whether it is Christ or purely the thought of Josipa, he does not know, does not ask.

She arrives with her aunt and uncle and cousins. His eyes hurt with the effort of watching her without turning his head. She sees the package, her face lights up, and her eyes instantly flicker toward him and smile. The glance of the swallows. She holds it against her chest throughout the Mass, even when she goes up to receive Communion. As she returns to her seat after receiving, she does not look up. Her face is reposed, looking inward, though her arms press the package close to her heart.

After Mass they do not meet, do not have a chance to speak, not even with the eyes.

Late in the afternoon, as Mamica is preparing a chicken to go into the broiler for supper, cutting vegetables for the pot, and sprinkling her secret spices, there comes a knock at the door.

Josip's father closes the Bible he has been reading, removes his eye glasses, and gets up to answer it. Standing there on the porch is Josipa.

His voice booms with hearty greeting, "Ah, Josipa!"

Up in the loft, Josip hears this and his heart begins to hammer. Suddenly, he can hardly breathe. He has been lying on the floor reading a book about the creatures of the sea. Now, without thinking, he slides toward the ladder and scrambles down it hand over hand, flipping near the bottom, and landing on his feet. Fortunately, no one has seen this extraordinary behavior because Mamica has bustled to the door and is brushing snow from the shoulders of Josipa's coat, whisking off the girl's kerchief, and sweeping her boots with the twig broom.

"This is so nice, such a surprise!" exclaims Mamica. "Come in now and have a bite."

Wordlessly, Josipa smiles, bobs her head, and seats herself at the kitchen table. Josip's father is standing near her and is asking if she has finished reading the book he gave her. Since last autumn he has been lending Josipa books to take home from school to read. They are his own books, and they have developed a habit of discussing each one after classes while Josip and Petar are wrestling with other boys out in the snow of the school yard.

Josipa says shyly that she likes the Austrian fairy tales very much but thinks the Croatian ones are better.

He asks her why she thinks this.

She explains, and adds that she does not like the tales by the brothers Grimm.

Mamica is rummaging about in the cupboard in search of the remains of the Christmas bread, with raisins, dried cherries, and sugar dust on top. She is slicing it now to bring to the table. Then a dish of butter, a jug of goat's milk, and a glass.

As Josip's father and the visitor talk about the book—which she has brought to the house to return—Josip remains paralyzed at the foot of the ladder. He does not reflect on what he must look like to the others. He is merely there—a consciousness. His mouth hangs open, his chest is heaving, his eyes are moist, and his hands dangle by his sides, with arms spread a little as if on the verge of flexing and carrying him into the sky. He is aware of nothing regarding himself, save for a heart banging so hard it threatens to shake all of him into pieces.

"Josip!" his mother exclaims. "Don't be rude. Come and greet our guest. You know each other, don't you?"

Of course they know each other, of course—as no other souls on earth know each other. This, above all other truths, must remain unspoken.

Josip moves his legs woodenly toward the kitchen and slowly seats himself in the chair opposite her. He scrapes the chair forward. By an act of the will, he is able to fold his hands on the table top and nod a greeting. As if he is indifferent to her presence.

She nods in return.

"Josip, close your mouth!" says Mamica.

He closes his mouth.

"Lost in the clouds", she explains to Josipa. "What were you reading up there?'

"Ab-bout the-the-the s-sea", he stammers.

His parents glance at him curiously.

"Have some bread, Joshko", says father with a small smile.

Josip's parents and the girl eat and chat. Josip says nothing. Josipa says little. She finishes her bread, drinks a glass of milk, and then rises.

"I have to go back to my auntie", she says with a smile. "We are bathing the baby tonight."

"Ah, good", says Mamica. "That is a fine baby. Your aunt and uncle are blessed to have a houseful of such beautiful girls."

Josipa smiles again and dons her outside clothing. Mamica wraps the last of the Christmas bread in a cloth and gives it to her to take to her aunt.

Josip's father and mother accompany the girl to the door. Josip is still frozen to his chair, and his mouth has dropped open again. The door is now open. Outside it is dark and heavier snow is falling.

"Josip," says his father, "go along with Josipa. It's hard to see in this dark, and it would be easy to slip on the icy patches. Besides, I have books to lend her, too heavy for her to carry."

"Too heavy?" says Mamica, with a raised eyebrow.

Josip's father goes to his bookshelves and selects three volumes. Josip has now put on his boots and his outside coat over his sweater. His father gives him the books to stuff inside his coat, so the snow will not stain the covers.

The little gray cat is sitting in the snow, waiting, mewing plaintively. Josipa scoops it up in her arms and the two young people set out, side by side into blinding snowfall. Their feet know where they are going. They are silent. The glance of the swallows is impossible in the dark, nor would they dare the brush of an arm against arm, yet Josip feels the presence of her soul. She feels the presence of his. They both know this, and know it as one.

Who are you? Where have you come from? Where are you going?

They already know the answers. The questions are merely a trusted form through which the more real thing can pass between them.

No longer do I see you, Josip thinks without words, *but you are here.*

If you were to speak at last, what would you say? she replies. *And if I were to speak at last, what would I say?*

I am here, his soul cries, *I am here, I am here.*

There is no need to say this; it is already spoken.

On the doorstep of her home, he gives her the books. She removes a package from within her coat and gives it to him. Then, at the same moment, they turn from each other and part.

Upon returning home, Josip carries the package unseen to the loft. He notices that his name has been penciled on the paper. Carefully, he unwraps it.

Inside is a twig about six inches in length. He turns it this way and that. It is a thin stem of wood with two smaller branches rising at an angle from it, like a tiny body with raised arms. Looking closer, he sees that she has scratched the shape of a man onto it. There are holes in the hands and the feet and the side. Now he understands what it is. Tucked horizontally between the arms and the center pole, crossing behind the head, is a brilliant blue feather.

He drops to his knees and rolls over onto his back, accidentally kicking over the candlestick. He pays no notice. Its flame snuffs out, but the flame within him flares. He rolls around on the floor, holding the gift to his lips, kissing and kissing and kissing Jesus, Josipa, the swallow.

A month has passed. There have been killings in villages to the north and to the east, mostly in regions beyond Sarajevo and Mostar. Word has reached Fra Anto that Partisan brigades are responsible. In addition, they have been firing their rifles and, occasionally, mortar shells at the great shrine of Široki Brijeg, from which all the students have been sent home. The Franciscans remain, though their provincial in Mostar has encouraged them to consider coming into the city, where there is some protection. He has suggested that the seminarian friars return to their families, but none have chosen to do so. Even so, there have been raids in Mostar, political assassinations, and isolated atrocities. Though the war appears to be nearing an end, vicious fighting between rival groups has not abated in many regions of Yugoslavia. For the most part, the factions have merged with the Partisan army, yet they continue to terrorize all the countryside. It is impossible to know where they will strike next.

It is now the first week of February. A difficult birth is taking place in the village. A woman who lives in the house beside Petar's is delivering her first child. She is young, married to an older man whose name is Josip. Close to forty years of age, he is a farmer, and one of the most devout people in the village. When he was a boy, it is said, he wanted to become a priest but did not have the intelligence for it. He remained a bachelor until last year and even now is considered to be something of a home-grown saint, for never has an unkind word crossed his lips, though it must be admitted that, on occasion, a sip of *slivovica* has crossed those lips. He is liked by all, and everyone rejoices that he and his wife have been blessed with a child. His wife—whose name is Tereza and who is a cousin of Petar's family—is from the next village beyond the end of the valley, a place fifteen kilometers away along the trail to the south. The couple has been very happy together this past year. Yet the baby is coming a month early, and the woman has begun to bleed.

Her screams can be heard throughout the village whenever a contraction comes. Some of the men decide to take a stroll in the forest despite the depth of the snow, and they invite the worried husband to go with them. They tell him: What can you do here! You will worry yourself sick! But the man refuses to leave his wife's side. Mamica and Petar's mother are in the couple's bedroom, stroking Tereza's forehead, rubbing her belly gently, and whispering reassurances. A few old women are also in the room, among them one who was the village midwife for two generations until she went blind. Though her blindness is not a great impediment, she must rely on what the other women describe, or what her arthritic fingers can feel.

"It does not look good", she murmurs.

The others can tell very well that the situation is not good because the bleeding does not stop, no matter how many cloths full of ice chips they place on her belly and beneath her lower back. So far, there has not been a great loss of blood, yet it steadily increases over the passing hours, and the baby is still no lower in the canal. It is alive, the old midwife declares. She can feel its tiny heartbeat through her fingers; it flutters like a bird, she says, as her eyes stare into space with two white moons in them, her fingers seeing better than any eyes in the room, blind or otherwise.

Petar has retreated to Josip's loft where they are working on their mathematics problems, trying not to hear the screams from the other end of the village.

"It's hard to be a woman", Petar sighs at one point and throws down his pencil.

Josip nods. They lock eyes.

"The fort?"

"The fort."

Petar straps his hatchet onto his belt, Josip his knife onto his own. They are just getting into their outdoor clothes in the kitchen when Josip's father opens the door, stomps snow from his boots, and steps into the house.

"Boys, I need your help."

Instantly they are alert, springing to attention. Yes! Anything!

"Tereza is bleeding more than before. Josip cannot leave her. In her home village lives a woman who is the best at delivering babies that are not born easily. Can you go to Tereza's mother and tell her that she and this woman are needed?"

Of course, they nod.

"Can you run?"

Yes, yes, they will run. All the way!

They charge for the door, but he stops them and makes them take a moment to drink water. He gives Josip an extra water flask.

"Do not eat snow", he warns. "Though you have thirst, it would chill you and make you more thirsty than ever." He stuffs black bread into their pockets.

"Run swiftly, now. A life depends on it. Maybe two lives."

They are out the door and galloping along the track to the southern end of the valley. The route is only a footpath during winter, yet it has been traveled in recent days, so the surface is firm. Because the snow on both sides is soft and deep, they go single file, Petar ahead, Josip hard on his heels. Their boots drum the surface, their breath whistles in and out. The sun is overhead, but a bitter wind is blowing at their backs from the north. They stop for a moment to button down the flaps of their fleece caps and to pull their trouser cuffs over boot tops, lacing them with thongs to keep snow from falling inside. Then they run again.

Petar is thirteen years old and strongly muscled. Josip is eleven, slighter of build and leaner, but a few centimeters taller than his friend. Each has his strengths and weaknesses, yet they both possess robust constitutions that are the fruit of endless racing up and down the pastures and the mountain side. Their lungs hurt from the sharp inhalations of frozen air but will not burst.

They say nothing, merely run and pant. They enter the pass and leave the valley of Rajska Polja behind. One, two, three kilometers, four, five, six. They stop and catch their breaths. Their tongues are now dry, for a lot of vapor has been blowing out of their mouths. They take a drink from the water-skin, passing it back and forth. Then they run again. Seven, eight, nine kilometers—more than halfway!

They stop again, a one-minute break. A few more sips, a bite of bread.

Let's go!

Now Josip takes the lead, his longer legs falling into a pace that is best for him, a lope that eases his lungs a little without slackening their speed. Petar is pounding along behind but is not allowing any gap to spread between them. The trail is still single file, descending gradually, but the pass has opened up and has become another valley, swinging around to the southwest. There in the distance are a few wisps of smoke beyond a stand of trees, the kitchen fires of Pačići—named for a pond where the people of this place raise ducks. Josip thinks the name is amusing. A town called Ducklings. It is not in fact a full village, being no more than a cluster of five or six houses belonging to branches of a single family, whose name is Dučić. Petar is related to them all. He now leaps past Josip and takes the lead, putting on speed. Both boys round the edge of the naked beech woods within seconds of each other and slow to a trot as they enter a barnyard, scattering geese, ducks—an enormous black pig is galloping in circles, and a donkey tethered to a corral begins to bray and kick its hind legs in the air—all of which sets off a frightful clamor of animal noises. The door of the nearest house opens, and a man in shirt sleeves steps out just as the boys stumble to the finish and collapse at his feet.

"Petar! What—!?"

"Uncle," Petar gasps, "Tereza's baby is coming early. She is bleeding. The women have sent us to fetch the midwife."

The man's face clouds with worry. "Is the midwife in Rajska Polja not enough?"

"It is she who asks for help."

"But Baba Jela and Tereza's mother are not here", he says, pulling the boys into his kitchen.

"Where are they?"

"They are assisting a birth, at a farm—over there." He gestures to the mountains farther south. "They went away two days ago. If all goes well they should be home soon."

"But they must come now!" cries Petar.

"I know, I know", says the uncle, putting a hand on his nephew's shoulder. "Sit down, boys, sit down here." He closes the door, and paces about his little kitchen. Two live chickens are sitting peacefully on the table. A gosling is craning its neck through the slats of a wooden box behind the stove. The black pig is staring in the window, its two front trotters clacking on the sill. The uncle pours the boys cups of tea. They gulp it, burning their throats. He pours another and another.

They are calming down now, their heartbeats slowing, breath returning to normal.

"When will they come?" Petar asks, his voice hoarse.

"Soon, soon", says the uncle, rubbing his unshaven chin. He sits down beside them and stares at the floor.

Petar and Josip are perched on the edges of their chairs, tense, scanning the man's face. They can tell he is thinking about what to do.

"Look", he says rising and throwing on his coat. "One of you must go back and tell them that Baba Jela will come. Let them know it could be a while, but she *is* coming. I will go to the farm and see if I can hurry them up. One of you should stay here in case the old ladies return by a different route, for they said they might go to visit a sister on another farm to tell the news of the baby. That is on a different trail, in the other direction—" He points vaguely out the window. "We could easily miss them."

Petar jumps up and buttons his coat, then crams his hat down over his ears. "Joshko, you stay here in case the Baba comes when Uncle is gone. I will go to Rajska Polja to tell them she'll be there soon."

This makes sense. It is, after all, Petar's family that is in trouble, and he is as good a runner as Josip.

So, it is agreed: If the Baba arrives with Tereza's mother before Uncle returns, Josip must bring them to Rajska Polja by donkey and sleigh. The women will sit on the sleigh, and Josip will lead the donkey at a fast clip, hitting the donkey on the nose with a stick if it gets lazy. It's a stubborn donkey, but it understands a stick. Can he do this?

Yes, of course he can do this, Josip nods in the affirmative, throwing his shoulders back. He has never before hit any living thing with a stick. Svez is lazy enough, but the Lastas have never been ones to rush things.

Uncle goes out the door and walks briskly away toward the south. Petar goes out the door, stops, turns back to Josip, and withdraws something from his pocket. He grins, throws an acorn, which bounces off Josip's head, and breaks into a gallop toward the north.

So, there he is, sitting in a kitchen belonging to people he does not know, staring at their chickens and their gosling who has begun to peep. The pig tries to get in the door, it knows how to jiggle the latch. Josip forces him out again with the chair, and slams the door shut. The pig gives up.

An hour passes, then another.

It is not easy to wait there doing nothing. The pail on the stove has stopped simmering because the wood in the firebox is burning low. He throws a stick onto the embers, lifts the pail, and gulps down the last of the tea. He eats the remaining black bread his father gave him. It takes the edge off his hunger, but not by much. Would the uncle mind if he took some of his bread? No, he won't do this. The uncle probably wouldn't mind, but, well, food is serious business these days. Maybe they don't have as much food here as they do in Rajska Polja. He can wait until he gets home.

He ponders the pictures on the walls. A Sacred Heart, so brown with wood smoke that it seems to have no colors. An Immaculate Heart, the same. An old calendar from 1939, with a photograph of the cathedral in Zagreb. St. Stephen's. He didn't know its name. This is interesting. You learn something new every day.

He sits down again and swings his legs back and forth. His legs are sore. That was a long run. Now he is really hungry. Still he won't give in, he won't steal. No, better to say he won't borrow without asking. Is it the same thing? He's not sure, but one thing is for sure: he wouldn't enjoy telling Fra Anto about it in the confessional.

He falls into a light doze. When he startles fully awake, he finds himself still seated, with head in arms on the kitchen table. He cannot tell how long he has been in this state, but it seems by the light in the window that the morning became afternoon while he slept, and is now creeping toward dusk. The animals are raising a ruckus. There are men's voices out in the yard. At last!

Josip stands, puts on his cap and mitts, and opens the door. He is surprised by what he sees. There are more than a dozen men out there, looking around at the houses, and a few stragglers are arriving behind them. Maybe eighteen men. He does not recognize them. They are dressed shabbily, most of them bearded or needing a shave. They all carry rifles. Josip's mind goes blank, and he simply continues to stare at them.

They stare back for a second, until one in the forefront strides forward, grabs Josip by the collar of his coat, and drags him into the yard. A stab of fear constricts Josip's heart. In his entire life he has never been treated so rudely. As the other men scatter to every house, throwing open doors, and pointing their guns inside, Josip stands before his captor, quaking in every limb and uncertain about what to do. The man lifts the hem of Josip's coat, pulls the boy's knife from its sheath, and hurls it across the yard. A gunshot explodes from one of the houses, followed by another in a different house. Josip bursts into tears and covers his face with his hands. His captor hits him hard on the side of the head, and he falls to the ground.

"Where is everybody?" the man shouts.

Josip shakes his head. The man grabs him by the collar, pulls him to his feet, and hits him again, a hard slap on the face. His nose begins to bleed.

"Tell me, now, boy, or I will shoot you."

"I-I-I d-d-d-don't know."

"Did they hear us coming? Which way did they run?"

"I-I-I d-d-d-don't know", he sobs.

The other men come out of the houses and gather around. Their faces are unlike any Josip has ever seen before. The look in their eyes especially. Their trousers and the arms of their coats are soaked in blood. So much blood. They look at him as if he were a duck and they wanted to cut his head off.

"M-m-m-Mamica", Josip whimpers.

The men laugh.

"Shoot him and get it over with, Jure", says one of them to Josip's captor.

"Not so fast. He knows something."

"Who cares. If we go now we can still make it to Mostar by midnight."

A big discussion breaks out among the men, as all the while Josip's captor continues to stare at him.

"No, let's stay here", says another. "Make a feast. Roast pig, duck, chicken."

"Let's go!"

"Let's stay!"

"If any come back, we pick them off—*ping, ping, ping*—one by one."

"Right, I'm tired. Ten days in the snow."

"In Mostar there will be booze and women."

"Haven't you had enough?!"

"Never enough for me!"

More laughter.

"Shoot him, Jure, and let's get going!"

"Why waste a bullet on this little scum?" replies Josip's captor, fingering a hatchet hanging from his belt.

"Right! Ammunition's low."

"Come on, the sun has set. We should move on."

"Let's stay", says an older man, waving a pistol in the air.

"No, the road to the city is clear. The others are coming from the north and the south."

"They won't need us tonight."

"Still, I want to be in on the fun at Mostar!"

The men turn their attention to each other and the discussion becomes an argument, growing hotter, with some shouting. Only Josip's captor continues to watch him. His back is to the others.

"What is your name?" he murmurs.

"J-J-J-osip", he chokes out.

"Your family name."

"L-L-L-asta."

The man's eyes do not blink. He continues to stare at Josip as if the boy is already dead.

"Run", he whispers.

What does this mean? Where should he run to?

"Run", the man mouths, and removing a finger from the

trigger of his rifle, points it in the direction of a nearby shed standing against the edge of the woods.

Josip turns on his heels and trots toward it.

"Hey!" shouts his captor, and curses.

Something whizzes past Josip's ear, followed in a split second by the crack of a gunshot. Another whiz and another explosion. The other men have stopped their arguing and are laughing at the sport.

"Your aim's off today, Jure!" they roar.

"I'll get him!" Jure barks, and charges after the fleeing boy, who has just disappeared around the back of the shed.

It takes no more than a few seconds to run Josip to the ground. The captor snags him by the back of his coat just as the boy is leaping into the deeper snow of the woods. He punches Josip hard on the spine and throws him down. Lying on his back, with the man's boot on his chest, Josip screams. The man raises the muzzle of his rifle, points it at the sky, and pulls the trigger. Then he fires a second shot. He kneels quickly and covers Josip's mouth with his bloody mitt.

"Be silent", he says through gritted teeth. "You are dead. Lie here and do not move until we are gone."

He wheels and goes around the corner of the shed.

Josip is paralyzed, alone with his racing heart, expecting to see at any moment another man come to shoot him. For a time, he hears noises from the barnyard, shouting, arguing, animals panicking, and the sound of smashing glass in the houses. No more shots are fired. Night falls before there is silence.

The sky is full of brilliant stars, casting a pale glow on the earth. Because he is shaking uncontrollably with chill, or terror, he picks himself up and stumbles to the back wall of the shed. Peering around the corner into the barnyard, he sees no figures walking or standing there. No light shines in any of the houses within his range of vision. He steps carefully through the snow, keeping to the backsides of the buildings until he is near the head of the path to Rajska Polja. He cuts across a bit of woods, the snow muffling all sounds, and strikes the path about a hundred meters north of the barnyard. It is a gray ribbon unwinding into the north. He walks slowly at first, because his body is aching in several places—especially his back where the man hit him, but also his head, his nose, and his legs, which are very sore from the long run earlier in the day. Nevertheless, he breaks into a slow jog, whimpering all the way.

Thinking is hardly possible, yet he is aware that the men have gone in the other direction because they are heading for Mostar. He must bring the news to Rajska Polja that bad men have been to the village of Petar's family and that they may have killed some people in the houses. Petar's father has a gun, and he will come back here to protect Pačići. Also he must tell them that he is unable to bring the midwife. He worries about the baby and its mother. Has he failed? Should he go back and wait for the midwife and Tereza's mother? But what if the bad men return? . . .

His legs keep carrying him north.

His entire body is a mass of pain now. The muscles of his legs give out at times, and he stumbles. Again and again he trips because it is hard to see in the gloom. His feet miss the hard-packed trail and sink into the softer snow beside it. Yet he always gets up again, stifling his sobs, and presses on. His lungs are aching, his throat is raw, and the wind from the northeast is more bitter than ever. He wants only to lie down in the drifts, curl into a ball, and sleep. Yet he is propelled by the dual drive within him—fear lashing from behind, the need to find help pulling him forward.

Hours pass. He is walking more slowly, stumbling more often. One foot after another, each step purchased with a stab in his lungs, a stab in his thighs. He is about to give up at last and drop into a snow bank, as soft and comforting as a goose-down mattress, when his will is strengthened by a glow in the distance. Yes, there, just ahead is the place where the valley opens wide into the fields of heaven. The moon is rising to show the way. It is still low and red, like a moon in autumn, when the wood smoke of kitchen fires lingers close to the ground. He has always loved that time of year, when the beech and oak leaves in the forest have been taken by the wind, the pines whistle and the harvest is in the barns; when houses are warm and cakes are made with walnuts and raisins. On such nights all souls are quickened, heaven and earth meet, and mortality and eternity are as one.

Josip rounds the last bend in the trail and enters his home valley. He comes to a halt, catching his breath. There is no moon. It is not in the sky where it should be. Then, with a start, he sees that a building is on fire, a house among those nearest this end of the valley. He cries out and stumbles forward.

Rajska Polja consists of only a handful of buildings: two rows of houses scattered haphazardly along its central lane beside the creek, which is frozen over now. Josip's home stands close to the southern edge of dwellings, while the church and school are at the north end. That is where Petar's home is too, and the home where the baby is being born. Mamica will be there. Perhaps Tata is closer, helping put out the fire. But as Josip passes the first house, he sees that there are no lights in it, nor are there any in other windows along the lane. The village is illumined solely by the glow coming from the burning house, the fourth from this end. Then he knows. It is his own.

Josip stands before his home and stares through its open doorway into a sea of embers. The heat is great, for all the books are burning. Poor father will feel so bad about this. He must find him.

Proceeding up the lane toward the north end, he finds that all buildings along the way are standing, yet black stains from smoke are above every window. The roofs have fallen in on most, though the thick stone walls are erect. He sees a shadowy human shape lying in the snow. He goes to it. It is someone, a man, he thinks. Josip goes down on his knees and shakes the shadow's shoulder, pleading. "Where is my father? Where is my mother?" It may be he only thinks these questions, for his throat is making choking noises.

Did the bad men come here? Has everyone run away into the forest? But what about the mother giving birth? She could not have run away. He must find her and her husband and ask if they know where everyone has gone.

Step by step he goes along the lane. Another sleeping form in the snow, an old woman. He shakes her, but she will not wake up. Farther on there are three more shadows, a man, two women. They will not wake up, no matter how hard he shakes them. Whimpering, gazing in fright at the passing houses, he sees that each has been gutted by fire. Because most are made of stone and earth, with slate shingles, there is no longer any fire in them. A few sparks burst from within their doorless entries, mouths waiting to swallow him.

Next comes the house belonging to Tereza and her husband. Unlike the others, it is not burnt, though its door hangs open. He steps hesitantly onto its porch and goes inside. He has visited this house many times in the past. He remembers that there is always a candle and a box of matches on the window sill next to the door. He feels about in the dark and finds them. The candle has been knocked over. He sets it upright, strikes a match, and puts it to the wick. The flame of the candle rises, illuminating everything within the room. It is the kitchen. Furniture has been smashed and tumbled into a corner. Some of it has burned but is now cold. There is a puddle of water on the floor. Someone has put out the fire.

He jumps at the sound of a sudden noise that comes from within the next room. Squeak-squeak. Squeak-squeak.

Carrying the candle with him, he peers carefully around the doorframe and sees the old midwife, sitting in her rocking chair in a corner. She is staring ahead, the white moons in her eyes. She is wrapped in a blanket. She sighs like a whistle, and moves the chair a little. Squeak-squeak. Squeak-squeak.

Josip goes to her.

"Who is there?" she whistles.

He swallows and whispers, "Josip."

She turns her head toward his voice.

"Are you alive, after all, Josip?"

"Please, where are my mother and father?" he asks.

"Ah," she breathes, "ah."

"Do you know?"

"Come here, child, come closer." She reaches out a spotted claw to him, which is gnarled and blue with the cold.

He touches her fingers with his own.

"Sit with me", she says.

"I cannot. My house is burning and I must find my parents."

"Sit with me", she says again, tears rolling down her old face.

He does not know how he can comply with her request, but he moves closer.

He begins to cry. He is ashamed even as he feels the release of tears. She reaches up and gently pulls him to herself. He kneels on the floor and lays his head on her lap. She strokes and strokes his forehead, his hair, his cheeks. At first he is repulsed by this, then succumbs, and lets her go on. He cries and cries, not like the weeping when the man slapped him, nor the sobbing of his long walk home; it is something else, a kind of crying he has not done since he was very young.

She puts her other arm around his shoulder and rocks the chair.

"You are tired", she says at last. "You have come from afar."

He nods without speaking.

"Rest", she says. "Rest a little, for you still have far to travel."

"I want to go home."

She does not reply, and in her silence he remembers that he no longer has a home.

She lets him cry a long time, stroking and rocking and holding him to herself.

Pale gray light grows in the bedroom window. His feet have woken him, they are very cold. He still wears his coat and boots, and a blanket is around his shoulders. His cheek is resting on a shoulder.

Where am I?

Then he sees the old woman's face next to his. He is surprised to find that he is sitting on her lap, her arms around him. Coming fully awake, he straightens up, feeling very embarrassed. He is too old for this! Uneasily he slips from her lap and stands looking down at her. Her eyes are open but no whistle breath comes from her mouth. On the floor, spreading from beneath the chair, is a pool of purple blood that has frozen in the night.

Startled, he steps back and bumps into the bed. Turning, he sees that Tereza is lying on it beneath blankets and sheet. There is a newborn baby in her arms. Beside her on the bed, her husband, Josip, sleeps with his arm around her waist, covering the newborn as well. Everyone is sleeping.

They are asleep as the entire village is asleep. The husband sleeps with a large hole in his back, from which blood has ceased to pour. His wife sleeps with a small round hole in her forehead. The child sleeps with a hole in its chest.

Josip steps backward out of the room. In the kitchen, he turns and then hurries through the doorway and out into the lane. A light snow is falling from the overcast sky. A few steps beyond, toward the church, two figures lie on the ground, white with a dusting of snow. Josip goes to them. One is Petar's father, lying on his back, asleep. Beside him is an old hunting rifle, its barrel bent at an angle, the butt of its stock smashed to splinters. Lying face down is Petar, also sleeping. His face is turned to the side, as if he is dreaming deeply with open mouth. The back of his skull is split and is locked in a pool of frozen blood. His outstretched right arm has no hand, only a severed stump. When Josip sees this he screams and runs toward the church. Smoke is rising in wisps from its broken windows.

On the steps he finds another body—a man. It is lying on its back, without clothing. It floats in a sea of frozen blood. It is difficult to know who it is, because the face is a mass of pulp. The arms and legs are outstretched. There is a great wound in the side. Another part of him has been cut out, for in the most private place there is a gaping hole. Bullets have been fired into the hands and feet. Josip then sees the feet, which are huge, bruised, with a bandage or two.

He vomits, screams, vomits, gags, vomits again, and then when his stomach can turn out nothing more, he runs into the church through its open doors. At the entrance he stumbles over a heap of brown cloth. It is Fra Anto's habit.

"O-O-O-O", he moans, stumbling toward the sanctuary, "O-O-O-O, Jesus—"

A terrible emptiness reigns in the church, for the tabernacle door is open and there is nothing within it. Entering the sanctuary where he has so often served Mass, he finds the sacred hosts strewn about on the floor. Some are muddy, some bloody, and the large host from the monstrance bears the imprint of a boot. He drops to his knees and scrambles around, cramming the hosts into his mouth. He does not think about this, does not question it, but merely does it. He tries not to vomit, and succeeds in keeping the hosts down. When everything has been consumed, he runs out the front door, past the body of the priest, and back along the lane toward the schoolhouse.

By the light of day it is possible to see more bodies scattered here and there, in the side lanes and yards. Petar's mother lying beside the creek, Marko and Saša lying across their doorstep, Marko's arms around his brother.

Clomping up the front steps of the school, Josip sees the little gray cat, dead on the porch. The door has been blown open, disintegrated—blast marks all around it. Stepping inside warily, he hopes he will find his father alive, his mother as well. Instead there are only lifeless bodies. Josipa is among them.

He stares at this for a moment, unable to move, all thought seared from his mind by what he beholds—so vast and dark that to gaze at it any longer would be to fall headlong into hell forever.

He runs outside and down the lane toward his home. He comes to a brief halt before its ruined stone walls, only long enough to see that all the embers have settled down to ashes, and that two human skulls are within the ashes.

Then he runs again and does not stop running.

6

Be silent! You are dead!

The sun rises beyond the eastern range of the mountains, breaking though the thin overcast. Josip stops once at the head of the pass to look back at Rajska Polja. The snowfields of its western pastures are bathed in rose and gold, its houses appear to be normal, as if life goes on within them. He turns away and resumes running along the path. He is without thought, without feeling.

Be silent! You are dead!

He is unaware of how long he runs and of what he sees along the way. There is stumbling at times, slowing of pace, resuming of pace, hastening, faltering, but always the headlong pitch of the disconnected body. The pain in his lungs and limbs is not pain, because the body is not his. He passes through Pačići, pausing only to drink from the water-skin that is still hanging about his neck. Bodies lie in the barnyard, but he does not look at them. All doors are open in the houses, no smoke rises from the chimneys. There are no animals, only a few chickens, ducks, and a single gander, which hisses at him and strikes at his shins with its beak. He does not feel it, and walks without haste across the bloodstained snow of the barnyard.

Entering the footpath at the south side of the dwellings, he continues on as he has done until now. Little by little the path slopes downward, turns and twists around hillocks, around mountains, enters other valleys and goes ever on into nothing, into the nothing beyond nothing. Yet he senses that the nothing ahead is where he must go, because the nothing behind is the annihilation of everything. There are no tears, no cries, only a dull consciousness carried forward by this body, which is connected to it, yet does not belong to it.

Though the sky is now deep blue without a cloud, there are no colors in the world. Birds have begun to call and swoop from pine to beech, yet there is no music in the world. There is no sound or motion other than his trajectory. Terror has dissolved, leaving only the gray consciousness into which there stabs from time to time the words *Be silent, you are dead*. He senses a little eruption of fear whenever these words enter, but the feeling evaporates almost immediately, because when you are dead there is no fear.

He is walking now, for he can run no longer; the body will not let him. The sun crosses the sky as he goes ever downward. It lowers in the west toward the crest of a range he does not recognize, could no longer recognize even if he had seen it countless times and knew its name, for names no longer exist.

As dusk begins to settle in, he arrives at the end of the trail, which meets with a wider path through the snow. It is like a road, for the marks of sleigh runners are upon it, as well as the prints of donkeys and men. The heels of the boot prints are on the left, the toes are on the right. These may have been made by bad men or by good men chasing the bad men, but none of this really matters. He turns to the right because that is where people are going, leaving the world emptier and emptier behind them with each step.

He follows the road until night has fallen completely. He can no longer force the legs of the body to obey him. He is about ready to fall into the snow and sleep as Petar and the baby sleep, as Fra Anto and Tata and Mamica and Josipa sleep, when he hears a goat bleating nearby. It is standing on the road just ahead. As he approaches, it naaahs at him again and jumps into the snow beside the road. The goat sinks into it and tries to get out, but the snow is too deep. Josip stops and watches its struggles, then notices that beyond it stands a stone shed cutting

123

into the side of the hill. Beyond that is an empty house, a black square against the charcoal snow, with a black chimney from which no smoke rises.

He jumps into the snow and catches the collar of the goat. Together they lunge toward the shed. The goat escapes him and trots inside its wide-open doorway. He stumbles in after it and falls onto a pile of straw. Though it is cold inside, he can smell hay and the animal's droppings. For a moment, this invigorates him, but then it quickly fades, as his mind registers no more smells. His eyes close, yet he cannot sleep immediately. Fire and blood fill his thoughts, while a gnawing pain grows in his belly. The goat trots all over him, naahing and naahing, hurting him with its sharp hoofs. Its distended bags slap him on the face. He reaches up and grabs the udders and squeezes. A jet of warm milk splashes his cheek. He opens his mouth and a stream of milk fills it. He squeezes and squeezes. The bags are very full, the milking is long overdue, and the goat is desperate. He empties its udders squirt by squirt into his mouth, choking and sputtering, losing a lot of it down the sides of his face, into his eyes, his collar, his jacket, his cap, until he is soaked from the chest upward and his belly bloated. Then the goat goes away. He pulls straw over himself, and the gray consciousness fades.

The goat wakes him just before dawn. It trots on him again, forcing him to scramble around on hands and knees, bunting and butting him until he falls flat on the ground. It steps over his body, braces its legs, and demands another milking. Lying on his back, eyes tight shut, mouth wide open, he empties its life into his own. That done, he gets up and returns to the road.

Within an hour or so, the snow underfoot becomes slush, and patches of wet gravel increase in number. The sun rises in an empty sky. By the time it is overhead, the entire road has become mud and gravel, deeply rutted and revealing the prints of animals and humans, all of them bearing onward in the direction he is going. The road is falling more steeply. Gradually it becomes drier, and now there are only patches of mud, though the woods on either side are still buried in snow. The air is growing warmer.

In time the road comes to a bridge over a river. He crosses it and arrives at the intersection of another route. Because at all moments of choosing his feet have carried him to the right, he turns right once again. Now he is walking down the center of a gravel road that is flatter than the one he has left; it twists and turns as it follows beside the river.

During the first hour, he meets no one. He passes three large rocks beside the road, and shortly after spies a dark form walking toward him. As it approaches, he sees that it is an old woman, leading a pig by a rope. It is a small pig, spotted brown and pink. She moves along slowly, bundled in a heavy felt coat, her head bound by a shawl of blanket cloth. When she notices him, she slows a little and stares at him, hisses and raises her walking stick.

"Don't!" she cackles. "Try to steal my pig, and I will break your head."

She walks on. He remains motionless, gazing after her. Then a rumble increases in volume from that direction. An open-backed army truck, carrying soldiers, appears around a bend in the road. One of the soldiers stands as they go by and points his rifle at the boy by the side of the road. He is a strange looking boy, his wet clothing filthy with mud, staring at them with an open mouth, hands dropped to his sides, arms spread a little. The other soldiers laugh and pull the man with the gun down to his seat. After they have gone, the smoke of their cigarettes and a cloud of exhaust hang in the air.

He continues to walk, going nowhere. Now and then, distant rifle fire echoes against the walls of the valley through which the river passes. These sounds are far away, far, far away.

It does not matter, near or far does not matter. When you are dead, it does not matter.

Even so, as the sun crosses the sky again and falls silently toward the west, houses appear at random beside the road. Sometimes a person or two, farm people or mountain people, look down from their stone cottages or their animal sheds to the figure passing beneath them—a boy without weapons. They always return to what they were doing and do not trouble him.

Another truck passes with soldiers in it. None aims a rifle at him.

He sleeps that night in an abandoned shed, under a heap of straw. His hands shake continuously. He is so thirsty that he wakes in the dark and crawls on hands and knees toward the sound of water. It is a dribble running off the hillside beside the shed. He sucks at it until he is full, and then crawls back to the shed and sleeps.

In the morning, he stumbles down to the road and walks on. All day long, his body drags him forward. He sees nothing of the passing scenery, only his feet. In-out, in-out, in-out. A blur of feet belonging to someone. His boots are soaked, cold in the morning, hot by afternoon, and whatever is inside these boots makes squishing noises to accompany the clip and clop and clip and clop that is without end.

A horse and cart come trotting along the road behind him. On the driver's board sit two white-haired men with a black-haired boy between them. All three of their faces are anxious. They are moving quickly, and the boy on the road steps into the ditch to avoid being hit. As they pass, he notices the cart is carrying a scanty load of hay. Tethered to its staves are three brown goats and a white one.

There are more and more houses now along the road. Soon the road becomes a cobbled street leading into a village. No, it is a hundred villages pushed close together. He senses that he has seen this before. Down in the middle of this place, he arrives at a bridge. It is an ancient bridge, flanked by two high towers. This too is familiar, though it does not matter.

For no reason whatsoever, he climbs the steep arch of the bridge and stops at its crest. He gazes down into the water of the river. This is familiar also, the feeling that narrowness and wideness were once somehow important to him, but not any longer. A flag flaps on a pole on top of the tower, a flag he does not recognize. For a brief moment, he sees a boy beneath the flag, waving a sword that flashes in the sun.

He wheels around and quickly returns to the street from which he has come. He turns right because his feet know he must always turn to the right. On he walks for a time, seeing none of the people who look at him from windows or who stare at him from the corners of their eyes as they pass him by. His water flask is empty, and he must drink. Hunger has returned as well, but it is thirst that drags him off the street and through an alley to the edge of the river. It is a chilly day, but the skiffs of snow are thin. After slipping and sliding down to the muddy bank, he kneels and plunges his face in. The water is very cold. He shudders, and opens his lips, sucks it in, chokes, sputters, and lifts his head. His body makes him do this. It wants to breathe, though it does not matter to him if it does or does not breathe. Yet because the thirst is strong, he pushes his face underwater again and sucks and sucks, until his teeth ache and his lungs demand that he breathe again.

He sits back on the bank and stares at the water. A black sack slowly floats by in center-stream, pulled along by the current. Then another. Followed by a third. A fourth drifts closer to the shore and an eddy rolls it a little. There is a human face at one end, a man. The man's body is bound by wire, and the black sack is in fact brown, darkened by the water. It is a robe. It is the same as the robe worn by someone he once knew, back there in

the place he has come from, a long time ago. The face sub-
merges and the sack is pulled onward. Three more bodies, each
like the others, float by.

He gets to his feet and climbs to the street. He turns right
and walks again. Night is falling by the time he leaves the last
street and continues on the road. He is going forward to another place that does not matter. He walks and walks. Now his
body is complaining about hunger, and his limbs are growing
weak. Nothing moves on the road for an hour, then another
hour. The stars are out in force, and the whisper of the river is
strong in his right ear.

He sleeps in another abandoned shed that night, without
dreams, for the exhaustion of the body will not permit even the
slightest refusal of its craving for rest. In the morning, he goes
down to the river and pushes his head under again, after checking to see if more sacks will float past. There are none. Then he
goes back to the road and continues his journey. All day he
walks. He is dimly aware that people in vehicles, on foot, or
riding on animals pass him, going in both directions. No one
gives him trouble. He does not concern himself with this,
because he is alone in the world and they are only shadows. The
river leaves the road and swings away into the eastern mountain
range. The track beneath his feet begins to rise steeply. Now he
is sweating heavily under the sun. Now he is chilled as it hides
behind the mountains. Now he is shivering again as the stars
come out. Now it is snowing again.

Higher and higher his feet take him. He cannot find another
shed in which to sleep, so he continues to follow his body long
into the night. There comes a moment when his thirst commands him to stop. He tries to drink from his water flask, but it
is empty. He did not fill it back there at the river. He takes a few
more steps forward. He turns to the river, but it has disappeared.
He turns back toward the city, but it is also too far, no glow in
the sky where it should be, no glow ahead. Nothing. The snow

has ceased falling, and the thick clouds part, revealing stars. Yet the road remains. It is there.

His head is burning, his eyes are burning. He is a skull in a heap of embers, he is a pool of blood. He is silent. He is dead. A few more steps, and he pitches forward and falls unconscious onto the road.

A foot presses into his chest. As his eyes burn and burn and flutter open at last, he sees only a shape bending over him. The presence is not a presence but an absence of light surrounded by stars. There is no foot on his chest, but rather a pressure inside his ribs pushing for release.

He feels his body being lifted, his head and arms flopping backward. The arms that carry him are as big as the world; they are the monster of the sea that will pull him down into the deep currents of devouring. He can no longer resist anything. He wants to put on his burnished armor and stride into the agora to plead for the means to go in search of his father. But he can do nothing, for all words collapse into fire, all ships burn, all towns and cities burn—and people burn inside them—all words fail to change the minds of elders, the good and the bad. This does not matter, because good and bad have now dissolved.

The sky throws enough pale light for the boy to see that he is riding on the back of a moving animal. It clips and clops slowly forward, and its long ears twitch at every sound in the surrounding dark. It is snorting puffs of frost into the air. He reaches out to pluck a hair from between the ears, because he must braid it into a gift. He will braid the garlic so it won't be spoiled by frost, or else Mamica would be angry with him.

The word *Mamica* has power. As it rises to the surface of his mind, he whimpers and then begins a low, low, dark moaning that does not cease. He wants to vomit, but cannot because the holy is within him. He must not waste it, no sacrilege may pass his lips, but he cannot remember what this means.

"Ooh, ooh", murmurs a deep voice behind him, a voice connected to the arms that are around him. A mouth clicks and a leather strap crosses the boy's lap, pulling to the right.

He is riding with a man on a donkey, going along a road into nowhere. The man knows where they are going, but it does not matter.

"Sleep, sleep", murmurs the man. "Soon we will be there."

He sleeps again and burns and burns; his lips are cracked and his tongue scrapes the roof of his mouth. When he opens his eyes, light is everywhere—green upon the eastern side of the valley, rose and gold upon the west. There are houses along the way, here and there, some in the hills above the road. A human voice calls from a forest. Cocks are crowing.

His body is too sore to turn around and look at the face of the man behind him, whose body is close and warm and whose arms keep him from falling onto the road. The donkey is white. It is still puffing frost and flicking its ears.

Now they have come to a village. No, a thousand villages pushed together into one. Along its skyline can be seen tall spires, like needles. These are familiar to him, though he has never been here before. They are pictures in a book, he is a boy in a book, the story is full of blood.

"I—", he croaks.

"Ah, you are awake", says the voice of the man. "Good. Soon you will have food."

How can he speak to one who has stolen him? He will not speak, he will be silent. He is dead.

"What is your name, boy?" The man asks, as they enter a long street full of countless houses.

I have no name, the boy thinks.

"No answer? Tell me, boy, why were you lying on the road in the middle of the night, far from anywhere?"

It is important to stare straight ahead, for the opportunity will present itself for escape. He will run. He will not stop running, and never again will he permit another to catch him.

"Did you fall off a truck, a wagon? Did you run away from home? Did your Papi beat you?"

Now the boy turns a little and sees the face of the man for the first time. He is dark-skinned, blue-eyed. The eyes are gentle, worried. His hair and moustache are black, with threads of gray in them.

"Me, I am Alija. If you tell me who you are and where you have come from, I can return you to your family. Do you have a family?"

No longer is it certain that children have families. Once there was a world where children had mothers and fathers, and those few who did not were taken in by relatives. That world has gone.

"You do not answer", says Alija. "Are you afraid to go home? Did they not treat you well?"

Now the man's voice falters.

"Or are they . . . ?" He asks no more questions. He turns the donkey's head into an alleyway that climbs the slope of a hill filled with crumbling houses. Some have bullet holes in their walls. One has been gutted by fire. From there, the donkey is guided into a smaller alley, narrow, shadowed, and stinking of urine. The sweat of the donkey. The scent of tobacco in the man's coat. Only such smells have returned to the boy. Nothing more.

By a door at midpoint in a series of doors, within a single long building from which plaster has fallen, the donkey comes to a halt. The man slides off its rump, lifts the boy from its back, and puts him onto the ground. The boy's knees buckle, and he begins to fall, but the man grabs his coat and holds him upright. He shouts a name, and the door opens. A woman steps out into the alley. Small children are hanging onto her skirts, peering cautiously from behind the fortress of her body.

"What is this!" she cries in alarm.

"I found him lying on the road in the night", replies the man.

"And you bring him *here*!"

"He is—" Alija does not finish his thought. "He has nowhere to go, I think."

The woman shakes her head, anxious, irritated, staring at the boy with disapproval.

"Who is he?"

"I do not know. He does not speak."

She shakes her head again. "You risk your life to find a handful of food to fill these little mouths, and you bring home no more than another mouth!"

"I have brought food", mumbles the man, pointing to two sacks dangling from the neck of the donkey. "Beans and corn meal."

When the man reaches for the sacks, the boy remains standing and stumbles back a step or two. Then he turns and staggers away down the alley.

"Come here!" shouts the man, who is about to follow and bring him back. "Where are you going?!"

But the woman seizes Alija's arm. "Let him go!" she cries. "What can we do? There are so many. You have your own to feed!"

So, he staggers onward. As blood pumps through his limbs, the muscles begin to work properly. Though he stumbles on cobblestones, he can walk now. Going nowhere. Back down the hill toward the maze of streets. At a corner of the main alley, his feet turn to the right. Like the donkey, they carry his body along; they know where to go, though he does not.

Now he is in a wider street, where people are hurrying to and fro, hunched inside their coats, heads down, eyes strained with fear. He turns another corner and enters an open square. Along one side of it stand a dozen market stalls filled with vegetables for sale. Old women sit on wooden crates beside each stall. A few carry hatchets or large knives in their hands. As he passes them, their eyes observe him cautiously. One lifts her knife in an abrupt gesture, warning him away.

He goes on and finds himself caught in a flow of people crossing the square. Where he is going he does not know. He is going with them, that's all.

A gunshot cracks the air and echoes against the surrounding buildings. Women scream and run toward alleys and doorways. Men grab women and children and hurry them away to cover. Another shot rings out.

The boy is standing alone in the open square. He is silent, he is dead, so it is not necessary to run, though he senses he should do something. It is impossible to think about what it is. And for once his feet will not show him the way. So, he looks up at the sky, where it would be possible to fly if his arms had feathers. A flicker of wings that no human eye can follow, and he would soar into the high places where no man can go.

He lifts his arms and closes his eyes. Yes, it is possible to go up, and perhaps a bullet will send him there, or something else, he doesn't know what, but he will wait for it. It will come.

Another shot. It whacks and pings beside him, chips the cobbles, and a splinter of stone tears the leg of his trousers. It does not hurt. He looks down at his leg and watches as a tiny droplet of blood on the cloth slowly expands.

Children are crying, a baby wails, men and women are shouting at him.

"Run, run!" and "Lie flat!"

These are the voices that can be heard on the edges of storms when the breakers of the sea rush up from their prison and devour the land, when birds are ripped from the air by black wind. Sometimes these voices lurk under dangerous waters, between two monsters, the monsters on all sides, the monsters behind and ahead and below, and only above is safety to be found, though even this does not matter.

A woman's voice is screaming more loudly than the others. He sees her running toward him from the shelter of a shop door, her coat flapping, her eyes wild. Another whack-ping—explosion! She has him now, and she has stopped screaming. Her mouth is a tight line, her eyes are like fire, and she enfolds him in her coat as she drags him from the open space toward shelter. Reaching the alcove of the shop, she throws him onto the steps and covers him with her body.

Soon the gunfire ceases. People wait. Then after a time, one by one, they come out of their hiding places and go on with their business.

The woman stands and pulls the boy to his feet. She holds him by his shoulders. Her face is gaunt, gray-skinned.

"Go home", she says. "Go quickly to your mother. It is too dangerous to come here."

He says nothing, can only look back into her eyes from the pool of his emptiness. She pauses and peers more closely, her eyes flickering all over his face, his hair, his cracked lips.

Suddenly, she begins to blink rapidly. "What is your name?" she asks.

He has no name.

"What is your name?" she asks again, shaking him.

He opens his mouth and cannot close it. Nothing will come out of it.

Tears springing to her eyes, she whispers, "Are you from Rajska Polja?"

So it is that he arrives at a place where he may rest for a while. She lives on the third floor of a large old building in which there are dozens of flats. The building is a block long and much in need of repairs. She has two rooms. One is a bedroom, the other is a place for sitting, cooking, eating. In it are a single soft chair with a white lace cloth on the back, a bare wooden table and chairs, and a little cabinet filled with glasses and china cups.

Above the table is a window, and on its sill sits a potted plant with purple flowers. The walls are covered with peeling green wallpaper. In one corner of the room, behind a screen, a tin pail serves as a toilet. After he has slept off and on for three days, lying on a mattress that the woman put in the corner of the main room for him, and has swallowed the soup and bread she continually forces upon him, and drunk gallons of water, he is able to sit up with his back to the wall and to observe.

He knows that her name is Eva and that she is his aunt. This does not matter.

For two or maybe three weeks, he lives with her in this manner. She goes out most mornings because she works in a factory, though some days the factory does not open. At such times, she remains at home or goes out to buy food or simply is elsewhere. From time to time, she asks him questions, though whenever she does he closes his eyes and sits motionless on the floor with his head against the wall. If she asks questions that come too close to what must never be recalled, he simply drops his head between his knees and remains in this position for hours. In the beginning, this made her angry and then frantic with pleading, because she wanted to know something desperately. At other times she would sob uncontrollably, as if she had read everything in his silence and had extracted from it far more than he himself knew, which was nothing, really. Now she has become quieter and asks infrequently.

She dressed the cut in his leg, and it is healing. It was infected for a time, but she cured this with stinging salt. He loathes the pail behind the screen, though he is forced by necessity to use it. An indoor toilet is unthinkable, very disgusting. He has never heard of such a thing. When he is able, in the third or fourth week, he leaves the apartment for the first time and finds at the back of the building a heap of garbage and blasted bricks behind which it is possible to meet his bodily needs unseen by any eyes. At that time, also, he begins to wash his hands in a tin bowl at the kitchen table. Until then, she has done it for him, his hands and his face. Once, after she goes off to work, he undresses and washes his body, especially his feet. Then he dresses himself again, learning in the process how bad he smells, that he has become as low as a donkey or a goat—worse, for the animals are clean in their stench, while he is not. He understands this. It can take hours to see such things, even the simplest. The smell is due, in part, to old blood, someone else's; he won't think about that. Also the goat milk that soaked him, now gone sour, and also the sweat, his own and the donkey's mingled.

It is impossible to look into the little mirror on the wall beside the kitchen cupboard. He is very afraid to see what is in it.

He can look out the single window in the rooms, but the view is of a brick wall. Sometimes the window is bright, sometimes dull, sometimes black. He sleeps and wakes and sleeps again.

She comes home, feeds him, goes away again. No one visits his aunt. Only once, a neighbor woman living down the hall knocks on the door asking for a bit of flour to make bread; she does not want to come in. His aunt has only a sack of meal for pancakes. She lends a little, and afterward complains to the silent boy that she has been foolish to give away food now that there is twice as much need.

Every few days she brings home vegetables. Once, an orange. She kneels beside his mattress, peels it for him, and feeds it to him sliver by sliver. It is sour, but when it is in his belly he feels his body's strength return a little, and it does not take so long to see things.

In the fifth week, she brings home some clothing for him: a shirt and trousers and underclothes, also two pairs of socks. They are all well-worn by their previous owner, but are clean.

One day when she is away, he examines a few framed photographs on a shelf above the kitchen table. Old men and women. A young couple in wedding garments—his aunt, very pretty, and the uncle he has never met, strong and handsome. Beside it is a photo of Sister Katarina of the Holy Angels as a young nun, very beautiful. It is not possible to feel beauty, but he recognizes it, knows what it is. Beside this is a photograph of a boy.

He recognizes this face, though he cannot remember when he saw it—long ago, back there in the world that is now gone. He takes the photo from the shelf, sits down on the mattress with his back to the wall, and holds it before him. He gazes at the image for a time, straining to recall who it is. It is a strong and solemn face, yet kind and gentle. Though the mouth is set firmly with resolve, the large eyes are dancing with humor. This is a person whom he would like as a friend, if they could know each other. But who is it? Surely they have met before.

For the first time since he has come here, he tries hard to understand a thing with his mind. The strain is too much, and after a while he lies down with the photo in his hands and falls asleep. When he awakes, his aunt is standing by the hotplate, stirring something in a steaming pot. She looks at him and smiles. It is her first smile since they have met.

He sits up. She nods in approval.

"So, you were looking at the photo", she says. "Yes, that is how I knew you."

What does she mean?

Seeing the confusion in his eyes, she sits down beside him on the mattress and looks with him at the photograph.

"It's old", she muses. "See here, written on the back, 1892. It must have cost a lot to have it done in those days." She looks at the boy. "Do you know who he is?"

He does not respond.

"This is your grandfather."

Suddenly she jumps to her feet, goes to the kitchen area, and returns carrying the small mirror in her hands. Seating herself beside him again, she turns the glass toward him. The mirror and the photo are side by side.

With his heart hammering, he slowly looks into the mirror. He is paralyzed by what he sees. The face is the same as the one in the photograph. Not quite the same, for the eyes of the boy in the photograph are laughing.

His aunt touches the frame of the mirror.

"It is you", she whispers.

He cannot close his eyes now, though he desires to do so. He can only look from one to the other and back again. A whimper rises in his throat, followed by the moans of a dying animal.

"Josip", she whispers, stroking his head with her hand, tears running down her cheeks.

Then it is possible to see farther—not much, just a little. Yet this opening of the interior prison-gate permits a sudden inrush and outrush of feeling. His chest heaves and he begins to pant; then a sob escapes his lips.

His aunt is sobbing openly now, and his crying blends with hers. When it is over, she says again his name.

"Josip."

He does not bury his face in his knees. He merely continues to look into the mirror. The eyes are red and wet, the mouth is buckled with pain. Still, it is now a living face, and he understands that this is better than what it has been.

"Josip", says his aunt. "Are they gone?"

He nods in affirmation. His first word. She holds him tightly in her arms and he buries his face in her shoulder.

So, with time and love, words return to the world. And with them comes the resumption of action. He remembers who he is. He knows what has happened to his past, though it is unbearable most days to think about it. At night he frequently dreams of the blood and fire. He is always running through fire or swimming frantically in blood, drowning in it, for he has never learned to swim. He wakes choking in the dark. It is terrifying, but it seems better, somehow, than nothing.

Each day he empties the toilet pail into the sewer hole at the end of the alley, washes the dishes and pots, waters the plant on the windowsill. Once a week, he goes out with Eva to shop. German soldiers patrol the streets, and sometimes shots ring out. Eva tells him that Partisans hiding in the city are sniping at Germans, that their army is drawing closer, and the Germans will soon be gone. She sells her china cups to a woman who lives in a wealthy home higher on a hill of the city, and this augments her meager supply of coins. Josip carries home the bag of potatoes, the sack of beans, and the half cabbage that they are now able to purchase.

On a Sunday, they walk beside the river, which is now swift-flowing and jade-colored from the mountains. He is afraid to look at it, because at any moment black sacks bound with wire might float along. Once, they pass a church, and his feet turn toward it, to the right. But he winces, for it seems that in his mind he will always see a naked body on the steps of churches, with its face smashed and its flesh mutilated and holes in its hands and feet and side. So, he tells his feet that it is ridiculous to turn always to the right and makes them go left. His aunt observes this struggle, follows him without a comment. Later, she purchases a loaf of sweetbread at enormous cost, for there is still some money remaining from the sale of the china. They even find a place that sells small satchels of tea. For supper they feast on boiled cabbage and fried potatoes sprinkled with finely chopped smoked sausage. Afterward, the sweetbread and tea. Josip cries a little, wordlessly, without explanation, as he slowly eats and savors each bite of the bread. He lets the currants and buttered pieces melt slowly in his mouth. His aunt asks no questions about this, though she observes it all with a look of profound sadness. She uses his name often, more than people usually do with others. Yet he is not unpleased by this, for now that he has found himself again, his body and his mind reunited, he *is* Josip.

"Josip, did you like the supper?"

"Yes", he nods. Then nods again and looks up into her eyes with a swift glance of gratitude.

Later in the evening, she chatters about inconsequential things, hums songs, shows him a book that she brings out of her bedroom. It is a tattered picture book with colored photos of the Adriatic. He spends hours going through it, lingering long over each picture.

"Do you like it?" she breaks in at one point.

"Yes", he murmurs.

They have begun to speak together, now and then. She does not ask much in this regard.

Some days it is: "Josip, take the garbage to the back and burn it."

"Yes, Auntie."

Or: "Josip, did you wash this morning?"

"No, Auntie."

"Then do it now, you smell like a dog in a rainstorm."

"All right."

"And don't forget to wash behind your ears."

"I won't."

One, two, maybe three words at a time. Little by little, nothing that plunges him into the sea of memory, in which he is not yet ready to drown. It is there, and he knows what is in it. But he will not rush into it as he did as a child on the day a *lastavica* perched on his fingertips.

Strangely, the memory of the swallow is calming. He does not think about it, merely closes his eyes and lets it perch in his mind.

"Josip, what are you smiling about?" asks his aunt with a chuckle.

His eyes snap open. "I don't know."

"Come on, it was something. What was it?"

"A bird."

"Ah, a bird", she sighs and returns to her sewing. She is darning his old socks, the ones in which he walked from the mountains. But he cannot think of the mountains, so he returns to the sea.

That night he crawls under his blanket and as usual curls into a ball, preparing to fall into bad dreams. Eva comes to him and kneels by his mattress. She strokes his forehead.

"Today you smiled again", she whispers. "You will be well."

She opens his clenched hand (now he realizes for the first time that his hands are always clenched). Into the palm of his hand she puts something. It is soft and round. She turns off the light and goes away into her bedroom. He hears her move about in the room and then lie down on her bed. The springs squeak while she tosses and turns, as she always does. Then he knows by the sounds of her breathing that she is asleep. He sniffs what is in his hand, pungent with the scent of fruit. It is a fig. He puts it into his mouth and chews. His entire mouth, his tongue, his lips are flooded with sweetness. He holds it in his mouth as it turns to mash, then melts, and is absorbed by his body. Then he weeps silently and, without knowing it, falls into a dreamless sleep.

7

Josip has lived with his aunt for more than four months. During this time most of his hair fell out in long wisps, leaving his skull half-bald, a red scabby patchwork. Thick blond bristles are growing in again, and the scabs are gone. His fingernails softened and loosened as well, separating from the base, and then peeling off toward the tip. For several weeks he was fascinated by the red corrugated skin that lay underneath, fibrous and sensitive. The nails are growing in again.

Now he can work at his aunt's factory. This is a cement-walled building inside a fenced compound. It is located on the edge of the city in a section called Novi Grad, a half hour's walk from their flat. They go there at dawn most mornings. Eva works in the company office, tapping on a typewriter or filing papers or making check marks on a list that tracks shipments in and out. Josip can see her through the window that divides the office from the shop floor, as he runs back and forth among machines that make nuts and bolts and other small metal items. Seven men work on the ten machines, and they are always pressed for time, except when a truckload of metal fails to appear from the coast. Josip is not strong, yet he is able to accomplish his minor chores: carry buckets of bolts here and there, fill wooden boxes with them, hammer the lids closed, replenish the long-necked oil cans that lubricate the machines, check the level in the big oil barrel. He also fetches drinking water for the men, sweeps the floor of metal tailings at day's end, dumps them into the scrap bin for melting, carries firewood to the small smelter outside in the back lot.

It is dirty work, but he is grateful to have it. He is helping to bring in some income, is no longer eating away so much of his aunt's wages. The men treat him well; they don't want to lose him. There are a lot of people without jobs right now who would eagerly fill any opening, but they would demand higher wages. Josip works ten hours a day and receives a quarter of a man's wage. It is the first time in his life he has earned money. He is proud of this, conscientious in his labors, and he learns from his mistakes. Besides, a life of constant action has distracted him from memories of his recent past. He drops onto the mattress each night after a hasty supper and falls asleep within minutes. He does not awake until his aunt calls him in the morning, and he seldom remembers his dreams.

Still, he is thin. His cheekbones stick out too far, and all his ribs are visible. This is meaningless to him, but not to his aunt, who pushes whatever she can into his mouth. Generally he feels continuous hunger, yet he holds back, pats his concave belly, tells her he is full. She is thinner too, paler than when he first met her, with dark pouches under her eyes. She is only thirty years of age, she tells him, but he thinks she looks like a woman of fifty. Her hair is completely gray.

Why is she so good to him when he gives so little in return? She is as generous as Fra Anto. Most people in the world, Josip knows, have faith in God, yet his aunt, it seems, has none. She does not go to church, even though there are churches everywhere. The city rings with bells and the calls of muezzins from their minarets. There is no crucifix in the apartment, nor are there any other religious images. There is no Bible or catechism, no prayer books or rosaries. Her sisters are very religious, Mamica and Sister Katarina, but why Eva is not is a subject they never discuss. He thinks of Mamica from time to time—that she still exists cannot be questioned. He knows she has died but feels she has not. This is reinforced by the presence of his aunt, who, if no longer as beautiful as she was on her wedding day and never as beautiful as her sisters, still shares many of their mannerisms and qualities, including a kind heart, much like Mamica.

Josip does not pray with words. He does not think about all that. Whenever he sees a church, he feels both drawn to it and afraid of it. He never enters one. He works and sleeps and when he is not doing these, he simply rests. He believes that this speeds the growth of his hair and his fingernails. He hopes, as well, that it speeds the growth of his muscles. Strength has become very important to him. If you are strong, you can work. If you can work, you will eat.

One evening, as they eat a meal of boiled potatoes, his aunt is excited, chattering animatedly about the end of the war. Since April, Partisan flags have been flying from the roofs of government buildings. It is like the old flag of the Kingdom of Yugoslavia, but it has a red star in the white center bar. Eva thinks that it will become the national flag because the Partisans are now the official government in Belgrade, ruling over all the peoples of Yugoslavia. The old puppet regime of Croatia has ended. Its army has been conquered, and its soldiers have fled to Austria. Something new and wonderful is being born. She hopes, moreover, that her husband may soon return. She has not seen him or heard from him for more than eighteen months. He is in the Partisan army. She will not consider for an instant the possibility that he has been killed. She will admit the slight possibility that he may have been wounded and is recovering, perhaps in the north, in Belgrade, because the capital has fine hospitals and good physicians, both Serb and Russian.

"But we are Croats!" Josip says to her during one such musing. He is unsure why he says it. It just jumps off his tongue.

"Your uncle is half-Croat", Eva replies with a thoughtful look. "His mother was a Serb from Banja Luka."

"Is my uncle a Chetnik?" Josip asks.

"No", she shakes her head abruptly. "Never that. But the Chetniks have come into the army, and they all work together to make a new country. The Partisans have given us a democratic Yugoslavia, a free republic."

"What is a republic?"

"It's a government by the people."

"No king?"

"That's right. No more kings, no more tyrants."

Another day, he asks her, "Will there be more food now that we have a new government?"

"Yes, of course. They will organize things properly, and our country's riches will no longer be siphoned off by European capitalists."

This begs more questions, but he is too tired to probe further.

"Josip", she says. "Would you like to catch us some fish?"

"How will I catch them?"

"It's not hard. I can show you."

"Do you have a net?"

She laughs. "You catch fish from the sea with a net. You catch fish from the river with a line and a hook. Do you think you could try?"

"Yes", he declares, lifting his chin and throwing his shoulders back. She smiles fondly at him and pats his shoulder.

From somewhere she obtains a hook and a spool of heavy black thread, more like thin cord. On their next day off work, they go down together to the Miljacka and throw it into the water. Not much happens. Nothing really, except a lot of waiting. Eva pulls it in, hand over hand. Up it comes, their fish—a bare hook with a bit of green slime dangling from it. They throw the line in again. Nothing. Again and again they try, and after a few hours they give up. There are other people along the bank tossing in their lines and a few standing on a nearby bridge dangling long strings that they jerk up and down. Now and then a wriggling sliver is pulled up.

He would like to try again in the evenings after work, but then it is dark outside and too dangerous. He might get shot, his aunt warns. So, he waits for Sunday, when he can teach himself to fish without fear of being shot.

On the next free day, Josip walks toward the river along a street named *Ante Pavelić* and sees soldiers tearing down the old street signs and putting up new ones: *Marshal Tito*. An army truck passes, with a big red star painted on its door. In its open-topped back, several men are standing and rocking with the motion of the truck. Josip stops in his tracks to watch them go by. The men are not soldiers. Their hands are bound in front of them, and their faces are bruised and bloodied. Their hair is disheveled and their clothing rumpled. They are burly workers, stout businessmen in shirts and ties, and even a friar in his brown robe. Four soldiers guard them with bayoneted rifles. In a glance, Josip sees that the faces of the prisoners are bleak with dismay. He feels sympathy for them, though they are probably criminals. But surely the priest is not. It is confusing. The faces of the soldiers are hard with contempt. It seems to him that he has seen such expressions before, somewhere. Then he remembers the men who came to Pačići—their eyes. In the eyes of these soldiers is the same expression.

All of this occurs within a few seconds, yet it is sufficient to impress upon Josip a sense of the architecture of his new world. It will be months, and in some aspects years, before he deciphers it all, but now he understand the basics. The Partisans are the government, and the Partisans killed his past, and thus the new government is his enemy. He realizes at the same instant that he must never speak of this—not to anyone, not even to his aunt. And certainly not to his uncle, if his uncle ever returns.

That day he catches his first fish. He has rubbed the hook with a bit of grease, saved from their last sausage. When the fish takes the hook, he thinks he has merely snagged a rock at the bottom of the river. Then the line jerks in his hands and zigs and zags, disturbing the surface of the water. A thrill quivers upward along the line and penetrates through his fingers into his whole body. Gasping, he resists. Hand over hand he pulls it in.

Fish, like men, are fond of sausage. This is important to know. You learn something new every day.

It's not all that big; not quite as long as his shoe. But it's a healthy brown trout, spotted with colored dots. It thrashes around mightily on the pavement, gasping for breath. He tries to carry it home on the string, but the line breaks. So, he has no choice but to stick a finger into its raspy gill and to carry it this way. A strange feeling, sticking your finger inside the body of a living thing that hates what you are doing to it. It makes him sad, but not so sad that it can dispel the glow of triumph. Since he came to this city he has not until now felt this happy. There are hours each day, whole passages of days, in fact, when all energy melts from him and he is merely a sack containing a ball of sorrow that must not be closely examined. He often feels like crying, but he is learning not to give in to the feeling. It can stay inside, he tells himself. All inside, pushing farther and farther inward, into a cellar from which it cannot escape. There are harder moments, when colors fade, when sound goes too, and he can only put his head between his knees and stare at the floor. There are times when he still curls into a ball on his mattress, with a knife turning and turning in the center of his chest. These moments have become less frequent during the past month.

The fish has completely dispelled all gloom. It is flashing in the sun, covered with jewels, silver, gold, its pale eyes reflecting the sky. He runs all the way home with it. Stamping swiftly up the stairs to the third floor, he stifles a cry that would alert his aunt to the coming good news. He flings open the door and bursts into the kitchen. She is seated at the table, cutting the top

147

off a single rubbery carrot. Her face lights up with astonishment, the gray flees from her skin, her cheeks flush red, and her
eyes sparkle!

She hugs him, takes the fish from him, and lifts it high in
wonder.

"A kilo at least!" she exclaims. "Oh, *Josip!*"

That night there is a feast. They eat it all, except for the
intestines. Head, tail, eyeballs, organs—everything.

"Tomorrow I will catch another", Josip declares in a manly
voice.

Of course, the next day she won't let him try because he has
to work at the factory. And she does not want him out after
dark, when he could be arrested or shot. But the following
Sunday he returns to the river. He does not forget to grease the
hook and also adds a bit of gristle to the barb. That day he
catches another brown trout, not as large as the first. Then
another. Between them, they add up to the weight of the first.

The following Sunday he catches a fourth fish, larger than
the three previous ones. It is not a trout but something fatter
and wider. An old man tells him he is lucky to have caught such
a fine carp, and after offering this observation begs the head,
tail, and entrails. Josip lets him gut the fish and take the nones-
sentials. Though this will deprive Josip and his aunt of certain
nutrients, the praise is worth the loss. Besides, the old man is
very thin, and when he swallows the raw liver on the spot, Josip
does not regret his moment of generosity.

The carp must weigh more than three kilos. As he is walking home with it in his arms, carrying it like a baby, three boys
his own age come out of an alleyway and pull him into the
shadows. They pummel him with their fists, bloodying his
nose and closing his right eye; one seizes the fish, and then
they all run away with it. Josip takes a few steps after them, but
they have disappeared into the maze of alleys, and now it is not
so easy to walk steadily because he can see only with one eye.

Downcast, he shuffles home, trying to suppress the ache in his chest, the choking feeling that comes when he is drowning in a dream.

Yet he does not give up. On the following Sunday, he brings to the river a rusty iron rod that the foreman at the factory let him salvage from the scrap pile. He catches another trout. Not so big, but a meal in itself. He wraps it carefully in a cloth and stuffs it inside his shirt. He returns home by the ordinary route, using the rod like a walking stick, clanging its base on the pavement stones all the way. He spots the three thieves waiting at the mouth of the alley where they stole his fish. They look at him, he looks at them—they wheel and run away. This is interesting. You learn something new every day.

There is a loud knock at the door of the apartment one evening. Eva opens it cautiously, and two men step inside without being invited. Josip is sitting in the comfortable chair reading the book about the sea. He looks up with curiosity. As the men talk with Eva, a wave of dread washes through him. They are government soldiers. The enemy has come. He looks down at the book and pretends to read. His heart is crashing within his chest, his blood racing through his veins, his hands threatening to tremble. But he brings himself under control without this being noticed. His body remains perfectly still.

The soldiers are not behaving in a threatening manner. They are merely asking questions. His aunt does not appear to be troubled by the arrival of such visitors. Indeed, Josip can tell by her face and the tone of her voice—and they surely can see it as well—that she is a friend of the new order. Even so, they want to know where she works, whether she has registered with the workers' organization, what her religious affiliation is, what she thinks of the end of the war, and her opinion of General Tito. All her answers are satisfactory.

"Your son?" one asks, nodding toward Josip.

She crosses her arms, and replies somewhat nervously, "My nephew."

More questions about Josip. They want to know who his parents are, where he lives.

"The parents are dead", says his aunt. "He lives with me."

"When did they die? Who killed them?" The soldier's tone is cooler now.

"I did not say they were killed. They were mountain people, they lived up there", she points lazily toward the hallway. "Influenza."

"When did they die?"

"Last year", says Eva with an offhand gesture that contains a simulation of sad indifference.

"What did they think of the Partisans?"

"I don't know. They weren't political people."

"And you, boy", says one of the soldiers gruffly. "What do you think of Partisans?"

Josip looks up from his book, chokes, and tries to rasp out a few words.

"Speak up!" barks the other soldier.

"He has a cold in his throat", says Eva.

"So? He can talk, can't he? Answer my question, boy!"

"He works at the factory", Eva goes on. "He's a good boy."

They push her aside, and tower over Josip.

"Answer", says one.

"Th-there w-will be more f-food now", stammers Josip. "The new g-government will let us keep our country's riches."

"Right, and what's the name of our country?"

"Y-Yugoslavia."

Satisfied, the soldiers nod abruptly and turn to leave. Eva follows them to the door.

"My husband is with the Partisans in the north", she says in an anxious tone. "For two years I have not heard from him. Will the men be returning soon?"

Now their attitude grows more respectful.

"Do you know the name of his brigade?"

She shakes her head. "He never told me. It was a secret. He is very loyal."

"The country is being reorganized", one says. "Loyal men are needed everywhere. You will see him when the time is right."

They tip their hats to her and go on to the next apartment along the corridor.

Bang-bang-bang.

Eva closes the door, leans her back against it, and exhales loudly.

"You answered well, Josip", she whispers.

With his face buckling, his chin falling to his chest, he says, "We spoke lies, Auntie."

"Not really", she grumbles. "It was just to make things smoother. They could make trouble even for people like us."

He is about to ask her what she means by *people like us*, but he knows somehow that this too would create problems. It is better to be silent. Though he is not dead anymore, he must be silent. If he wants to live, he must remain silent.

The schools in the city have been closed, but they are now re-opening. Josip cannot leave his job at the factory because he and his aunt need his small income in order to survive. But some classes are held in the evenings. To obtain permission to attend them is complicated. There are necessary documents to be applied for, filled out, submitted, approved, followed by other documents. This way he won't be shot or arrested.

Josip does not want to attend the classes, but Eva insists that he must learn, he must grow. He is smart like his father was, she says, and has a future to think of. Three evenings a week, he attends a class in the high school. He is placed in a group of city youths, two dozen boys and a few girls, all about his own age.

The subjects are grammar and spelling, history, and political formation. The history is not taught from books, because the books have not yet been written. The political formation is clearer, prepared by cadres of Communists who know the power of education and have long prepared for their moment. Josip cannot focus on any of it. He is very tired after a day at the factory, and he is always hungry.

One Sunday morning in November, he wakes from a deep sleep and lies for a while on his back, staring at the ceiling. The window above the kitchen table reveals that the brick wall is sunlit. It will be a nice day. Rolling over to catch a few more minutes of sleep, he finds on the mattress beside his head three ripe figs. He smiles. His aunt has left them for him as a surprise. He feels a wave of affection for her. He chews two of them rapidly. The pleasure and energy they give are great. He jumps into his trousers and shirt, pockets the third fig, and tiptoes to the door of the bedroom to see if she is awake. If so, he will thank her for the gift.

The door is open a crack. Peeping through it, he can see a figure on the bed. It is not his aunt, it is a man sprawled among the bedclothes. He is asleep, snoring with his mouth open.

Josip takes a step back. Where is Eva? Perhaps she has gone out to find food. Who is this man? Is it his uncle? Yes, surely it is his uncle returned from the war.

Josip knows he is a Partisan soldier and is not happy about this. Yet they are related to each other by marriage; they are family, and thus it is to be expected they will have little difficulty living together. Curious to see what his uncle now looks like, Josip pushes the doorway open a few centimeters. It creaks on its hinges, but the sleeper does not stir. The man on the bed bears little resemblance to the uncle in the wedding photograph. His face is turned away from the door, and what can be seen of it is bearded with weeks of growth. His blond hair is long and greasy. His open mouth reveals missing teeth.

The smell of animals is in the room. A heap of shucked clothing lies beside him on the floor. A rifle leans against the wall beside his head. Josip tiptoes backward and quietly closes the door.

Because it is Sunday, he decides to go fishing. With hook and line, and a chunk of bread for himself, he goes down to the river. He whiles away a few hours there and catches nothing. It is better, he thinks, to give his aunt and uncle some time to be alone together. He does not want the uncle to resent the presence of a nephew who must be fed. During recent months Josip has grown canny about survival, and he knows the complications that can arise when people are poorly fed. Money does not always guarantee that food can be obtained. Yet if he can bring home a big fish, this will make things easier.

Indeed, in the afternoon, an extra dab of rancid lard on the hook brings in a fish. It's a good little carp, fat and shining and flapping. More than a kilo in weight, he estimates, certainly enough for three people.

With a mixture of eagerness and trepidation, he enters the apartment. His aunt comes forward to meet him, and exclaims her surprise and gratitude over the fish, which Josip presents to her with a smile. She turns with the fish and says, "Jure, look!"

His uncle is seated at the table. The man shoots a glance at the boy, then turns back to what he has been doing. He is wearing only trousers. His face is soaped, and he is leaning over a bowl of water, shaving with a bone-handled straight razor. The mirror is propped up on the table top, and he is peering into it as he scrapes and scrapes.

Eva pulls Josip over to the table so that man and boy are now facing each other.

"This is Josip, my sister's son", she says. Josip wonders about the high artificial pitch of her voice, the strained smile, as if she must work hard to convince the man of how fine is this boy now living in their home. "He has brought us supper!"

Her fingers play nervously along Josip's shoulders, distracted, not realizing what she is doing, squeezing, trembling, fluttering. He doesn't like it.

Still less does he like the grunt his uncle gives in reply, not really looking at Josip, as he scrapes and scrapes.

"So, cook it", he growls through the soap bubbles.

"Yes, yes, I'll make it now. Here, Josip, give me a hand. You cut the rot out of these potatoes. Your uncle has brought us butter and cheese too, such a treat!"

Josip knows that he is the cause of the tension between his aunt and uncle. The man is not pleased by his presence, and the woman is trying to make things nice, peaceful, a good encounter of first impressions as they get acquainted. Josip sets to work cutting the rot from the last of the potatoes while Eva guts the fish. His throat is closing, and his eyes are wet. He should find another place to live, he thinks to himself. He can always visit his aunt whenever uncle is away soldiering. As the potatoes boil in a pot of water, and the chunks of carp boil in another, Eva keeps up a stream of chatter. Josip has never seen her behave like this. She is both happy to have her husband back, safe and well, and is also worried about something. Of course, it is the issue of the unexpected orphan. The husband had no say in the adoption, and he is irritated.

The uncle goes into the bedroom to dress, wiping his face with a cloth. He still has not looked directly at his nephew, has not said a word to him. More than ever, Josip wants to cry, wants to leave and not come back. But where would he go? Night has fallen, and it is not uncommon to hear gunshots in the city at this time of evening. The uncle returns to the table, and all three sit down to their meal. It is a better meal than any they have had so far. The fish has guaranteed that it will be good, but the butter dripping down the gray potatoes, a pinch of salt, and of course a slice of cheese on each plate are all delicacies. Josip cannot look at his uncle. He can only raise his eyes as far as the rims of the pots. Auntie continues her chatter: two years of news to catch up on. No one mentions the boy, the cause of his presence, or the brief history of his residency in the apartment. Uncle, too, is sparing in describing his battles. He restricts himself to generalities uttered in the briefest of words, all in a tone of bitterness.

"You must have seen many comrades die", says Eva, putting a hand on his forearm. He moves his arm away. He concentrates on rapid, steady consumption of the meal.

"Many."

He drinks from the bottle of *slivovica* that he has brought from the bedroom. He pours a little into Eva's glass. She sips from it delicately.

"And now you have won."

"Now we have won."

"It's time to forget, time to build what you have fought for, the new Yugoslavia."

"Time to forget", says Uncle, tipping the bottle up and emptying it into his throat.

"Will you stay with the army?"

He shrugs.

"You have sacrificed so much, Jure—we have sacrificed so much. The government will reward you."

Again the man shrugs.

At the name *Jure*, which he now hears for the second time, something awakens in Josip. He glances surreptitiously at his uncle's face and sees it nakedly, fully, for the first time. He freezes, and the bottom falls out of the universe. He cannot move; he cannot jump to his feet and run. He cannot cry out. His mouth is hanging open, his throat closing in a whimper. But his aunt's chatter distracts from this. Anyone looking closely might see no more than a boy entranced, fascinated by a war hero.

The face is different from the one in the wedding photo,

older by ten years and leaner. It is the face of the man who hit him in Pačići, who told him to run, who put a boot to his chest, fired his gun, and mouthed the words, *Be silent, you are dead.*

Were the terrors now ripping through every portion of his being not paralyzing him, Josip would run. He would scream and bolt for the door, racing down the flights of stairs and out into the night of Sarajevo. He cannot.

Jure now turns his head slowly, chewing a mouthful of fish, and looks directly into Josip's eyes. There is no change in his expression. Eva's questions and chatter continue. Jure answers with single words, but all the while he is peering straight into Josip's soul and telling him that if he speaks a word he will be truly dead.

Wiping his mouth on his sleeve, he interrupts his wife, leans back in his chair, and says, "Get me more to drink."

"There is nothing in the house, Jure. Nothing."

Without taking his eyes from the boy, the uncle pulls paper money from his trousers pocket and slaps it on the table.

"But the curfew—"

He gives the woman a slip of paper. "If anyone stops you, show them this. If it's not enough, tell them Desetar Wolf sent you."

"Wolf?"

"Wolf of the Zenica Shock Battalion."

She pockets the money. "So, that is who you were with. I thought you were in the north."

"In the north, in the south, here, there, everywhere."

Eva throws on her coat. "In the mountains between Bugojno and the river?" she asks hesitantly.

Uncle blinks and breaks the mesmerizing gaze that has held Josip captive. He turns to his wife and says, "No, we never went there." He smiles. It is a normal man's smile of reassurance, yet his eyes remain those of a wolf—the wolves who destroyed Pačići.

"Ah, of course not", she says and swallows noticeably. "There was fighting in so many places. How brave you all were."

"Brave", nods Jure. "Yes, we were brave."

"I'll see what I can find", says Eva. going out the door.

"Bring *rakija*", he shouts after her. "It's too long since I had brandy."

She tells him she will try.

Alone together, Jure and Josip remain without moving. Josip betrays no emotion but cannot raise his eyes. His uncle regards him with a frown, staring at the boy until the force of his eyes commands him to meet his gaze.

"You remember", he murmurs in a quiet tone.

Josip can neither blink nor nod nor answer with words.

Jure leans forward and slaps the boy lightly on the cheek. "Speak."

"I r-r-remember."

"I saved your life. Never forget it."

Josip shakes his head.

"If you forget it, I will kill you this time."

Josip nods up and down.

"You will never speak to Eva about what happened."

Josip shakes his head.

"If you even hint at it, you will drown in the river. You will have an accident."

Now tears leap to Josip's eyes.

"If you tell her and run away to escape me, I will find you. Then you will die more slowly." Jure removes his straight razor from his back pocket, and then opens it. Opens it and closes it. Opens it and closes it.

"Do you understand?"

Josip nods and wipes from his cheeks the tears that have begun to run down them.

Jure strikes Josip's face again, a little harder, not enough to leave a mark.

"You will never again cry in this home. If you cry, your aunt, because she is a woman, will want to know why."

He nods.

"I am going to find a place for you to live with others who have no family. This will take time. Until then, when I command you to do something, you will do it. You will stay out of my way, and you will be silent."

You are dead.

Upon command, Josip washes the pots and pans, empties the toilet pail into the sewer down on the street, returns to the apartment, and stands in the middle of the room, not knowing what is permitted and what is not. Uncle has left the room. The springs of the bed can be heard whenever the man turns from side to side. Josip sits down on his mattress, picks up the book of the sea, and turns to the page where there is a photograph of a swallow. He gazes at it with longing. It comforts him a little, tells him it is possible that his uncle only threatens to kill him and that he would not actually do such a thing. Until he has been sent away to a place for children without parents, it will be possible to survive in this apartment, as long as it does not last long. Or perhaps his uncle will go away soon. He tells lies, so it may be that nothing he has said is reliable.

Even so, when Eva returns with a triumphant look, carrying a bottle of *slivovica* in one of her coat pockets and a bottle of herbal *loza* in the other, Josip greets her with a forced nod, and pretends that he is absorbed in the book. Women, of course, can read atmospheres, faces, thoughts, anything.

"Did you get along together?" she asks in a low voice, offering a hopeful smile.

Josip returns the smile—entirely artificial—and returns to the book.

"Good", she says with a note of relief. "Good."

It is impossible to sleep. After the lights are turned out, and the door to the bedroom is shut, Josip curls into a ball, begins to whimper, and then to moan. The squeaking bedsprings are so loud he is forced to put his fingers into his ears until it is all over. Then the mumbled conversation of his aunt and uncle resumes.

They are talking about him, this is certain.

Eva is describing Josip's excellent qualities, his hard work at the factory, his habit of fishing, the quietness of his demeanor—the boy will be no trouble, she assures her husband. He mumbles a reply, in the tone of a mildly disgruntled man who is, after all, kindly of heart and willing to sacrifice.

The squeaking resumes. Fingers in ears, his mouth opens wide in screams that cannot be allowed to vibrate the air and penetrate the walls of this prison. Perhaps he sleeps, perhaps not. In the morning, he cannot remember falling into dreams, though he must have at some point because there was blood and fire in the night, and an old woman's chair rocking and squeaking, rocking and squeaking.

Eva rouses him before dawn. Uncle is sleeping, she says, he emptied both bottles last night—well, they both emptied the bottles, she laughs. But they must be off to the factory now.

As usual, they walk to work. He is completely silent. Even when she asks him the usual questions of no import, he cannot speak. He nods or shakes his head. She stops in the street, and feels his forehead.

"You're burning up", she scowls. "You can't work in this condition."

At the factory office she obtains permission for time off, in order to search for a doctor who can tell her what is wrong with the boy. They find the clinic of a doctor down near the market where Josip was almost shot, that day she saved him from the sniper. There are no Christian images in the outer office, no Islamic symbols either, nor is there any indication of political interest. Eva and Josip sit on the floor among a crowd of other people, most of whom are Muslims. Hours later, when they are admitted to the surgery, they see that it is a bare room, containing only trays of instruments, medical books, and an examination table covered with a green sheet, its old bloodstains washed and rewashed. The doctor is a thoughtful man in his sixties, a secular Muslim, very thorough in his approach. When he has finished his examination and Eva has told him what she knows, he informs her that the boy may have typhoid. More tests are needed. Typhoid is highly infectious, and thus he must be admitted to hospital for observation.

By now, Josip's body is throwing off a lot of heat. He has become the embers of civilization in the house of annihilation. He is incapable of thought or word or action, yet even in his semidelirium he feels a faint return of hope: the promise that he will soon die far away from his uncle. He will at last go upward on his wings.

Unfortunately, his escape is not so easy. Everything that happens after that is erased from his memory because it has not really been imprinted on it. Three days later he becomes aware that he is lying inside a box—or as it slowly reveals itself to be, a cement-walled chamber. He is lying on a mattress on a damp floor. He is naked under a dirty sheet. His head hurts badly, and every part of his body is aching.

A single light bulb burns in the ceiling; it hurts his eyes. He thinks, at first, that he is in the factory, but no machines are present, no sounds of whirring motors and screaming metal. The walls are painted dark green and sweating moisture. At the far end of the room are metal tables like trays, drained by hoses into buckets. Though the door of the room opens onto a hallway in which there is a faint yellow glow, no other people are present, and no sounds can be heard. He has never seen the inside of a hospital, yet he is sure from his reading of books that such places are always clean, full of light, and bustling with good people who minister to the sick.

Perhaps this is his new home, the house of orphans. He will live here and never again will he meet his uncle, the wolf of Pačići. He will get better and will return to work. He will purchase his own food, and he will fish in the river. And if this house is too lonely, damp, and dirty, he can find a place to sleep at the factory, be a night-watch maybe. There is a cubbyhole behind the smelter, a few blankets and a sheet of tin over it would turn it into a good apartment for a boy.

He sleeps.

When he awakes again, the doctor is hovering over him; Eva is there, too.

"—not typhoid, just influenza, though a bad one. He cannot be moved until the worst is over—"

He sleeps again. When he wakes up, he sees the book of the sea on the floor beside his head. His skull pounding, he rolls onto his side and grabs it, opens it, finds the swallow, talks to it, listens to it, lets it perch on his fingertips.

Who are you? Where have you come from?

They ask this of each other, again and again, until the flames consume his body and his mind falls away like the curve of a wing's tangent, back to the earth.

"Where are you going?" he cries.

Back to the place of our labor, sing the eyes of the *lastavica, down to the heaving seas, the swaying forests, the dark sleeping fields, the cold mountains, the blossoming trees, and the consuming fires.*

"I can't see you!"

I am here,
I am here,
I am here.

Now he sits up. A beam of sunlight pours through a small window at the top of the wall. An old woman is spooning soup into his mouth. When she has finished, she moves on to three other bodies lying on mattresses along the wall and tries to feed them, one by one. A man is lying on the mattress closest to Josip's. He is tossing and turning, sobbing loudly, groaning, sobbing again. His body is bandaged in several places. The old woman goes to the 'door and calls for help. Two men come in and kneel by the bandaged man.

"He's going to burst his stitches, the idiot!" says one.

"Let's tie him down. Better than bleeding to death", says the other.

"He won't make it anyway—those wounds, and the sickness on top of it."

They force the man down flat on the mattress, and secure his body with strips of canvas so that he will not thrash and open his wounds.

Josip watches this for a time, until the two men and the old woman go away. Then he returns to his book.

Now the swallow tells him to get up and go to the bandaged man and speak with him. For the first time in many days, Josip stands upright, his legs wobbling underneath him, his head spinning with dizziness. He wraps the sheet around himself and shuffles toward the figure on the mattress. He kneels and puts his hand to the other's forehead. It is very hot. The eyes are bandaged, blood has crusted there. Have his eyes been taken out, or are they only hurt?

Josip is not afraid. The man is, after all, bound by webs. Bound more by his weakness.

"Who is there?" cries the blind man.

"Josip", he croaks.

"Who?"

"The *lastavica*."

"Who are you?"

"The *lastavica* is coming to you. He would speak with you."

Now the man has stopped thrashing and sobbing. He is not dead, he is listening.

"Is it you, is it you?"

It is difficult to know what this question means.

"Yes, it is me", Josip replies, stroking the forehead as Mamica used to do whenever he was ill.

The blind man sighs, and his body becomes completely still.

"I knew you would come."

"I am here, I am here, I am here."

The blind man dies in the night. His body remains motionless throughout the morning, until it is taken away. There are now five sick people in the room. More people come and go—visitors, doctors, nurses, patients. Another man dies, and he is taken away. A family comes in, kneels on the wet floor: father, mother, brothers, sisters, grandparents. They talk with a youth whose chest is crossed by bleeding bandages, half of his face is gnarled by burns. He is sitting up with his head on his knees, crying. The women are wailing. The father tells them to leave him alone with his son for a minute. He is not weeping, but his face is contorted with anguish. After the others go out, he leans forward and embraces his son, says nothing, merely holds him. The son lifts his arms to return the embrace. He does not die, but the following day he is taken from the room to another place.

Eva brings food. The hospital cannot supply all the needs of the patients.

"Your uncle asks after you", she says with a smile. There is color in her cheeks again, and she is not so thin. "He hopes you will recover soon."

Is she lying? Is she trying to make things work properly between her husband and nephew by pretending the situation is normal? Or has the uncle actually sent this message, in order to hide his life as a wolf? If so, the lie is his, not hers.

"Will I soon go to the house for children without parents?" he asks.

The question makes her uncomfortable.

"I do not think you will go to live with the orphans. You and Jure will get used to each other. In time he will understand that it is better for family to remain together."

"He wants me to go."

"No, no, he doesn't want you to go. He is a good man. He has—well, he has been through so much suffering, so much fighting for our country, and now he needs rest. When he has rested, and you are well again, then you will see. He will be a father to you, as once Miro . . ."

The name breaks open something, crashes through the walls of Josip's terror of his uncle. Tears spurt from his eyes, and he begins to sob uncontrollably.

"I know, I know", his aunt croons, soothing and soothing, stroking the wisps of hair from his forehead. "It is hard. It is so hard for you. But they are in heaven."

He wants to believe this. He needs her to believe it too—to believe for him.

"Do you believe in heaven, then, Auntie?"

She frowns. "No, Josip. But you do."

And with this he learns that even the best of people, in their good intentions, can damage you. He understands that she has told him only what he needs to hear, yet at the same time she has denied what he needs to hear. Thus, everything is unreliable, in contradiction. You may comfort the blind, but in the end they die. Human life is a man bleeding to death, with no eyes in his sockets, leaving only the mind ticking away with whatever has filled it before the removal of the eyes. The eyes that he thought were his own are, in fact, blind. And now she is saying that she sees farther than his blindness, broader and higher than his childish beliefs; she will try to comfort him with them, though she thinks they are untrue. Thus, there is no solid true and untrue, only what the blind need at this moment or that moment; it does not matter, it makes no difference.

So, in the end, all words must dissolve into the realm of silence.

He dries his eyes. He says no more. Soon she kisses him and leaves.

Because she has destroyed paradise, he is unable to move that day. He curls into a ball and stares into blackness.

The next morning, the blackness has receded a little. No light has replaced it, yet this darkness, he feels, cannot be everything. He senses it, hopes it is true, but frequently wonders if anything is true.

More days pass, during which the desolation slowly declines. His appetite begins to return. The old woman gives him more soup and crusts of bread. She does not speak with him. There are so many she must feed with her scraps. He is restless now. Though he sleeps off and on throughout each day, he is up and about too. This is not as embarrassing as it was in the beginning. A nurse has given him a set of hospital pajamas, too large for him. He must keep the cuffs rolled up and the waist tied tightly with a string. There are a lot of stains on the cloth, though it has been washed. He likes to amble from mattress to mattress, looking people in the eye, those who have eyes, those whose eyes are open. None of the eighteen people in the cellar are talkative; most are in pain. But he has learned that many of them appreciate a delicate perching on the fingertips of their minds. You cannot touch them in any other way, cannot sit on the end of the mattresses because of the risk of infection. But you can look, and this is a form of touching.

Once, he tries speaking with his voice to a man lying on a canvas sheet, for there are no more mattresses available. Josip asks the man where he has come from. The eyes answer without words: I have come from a place of pain, and am now in a place of pain, and soon I will depart for another. From then on, Josip no longer asks questions with his voice. He speaks only with his eyes, and it is a wonder to him that so many—though not all—understand a little of his new language. His task is to remind people that, as they take flight, they are going upward to an open and light-filled place without sorrows. As high as the sea, as deep as the sky—yes it is like that, not the other way around. Whenever it is right to do so, he speaks in this way to people prostrate on their bloodied and fouled beds; he also senses when it is not right to do so. The swallow is sometimes with him, sometimes absent, for he cannot make it come or go at will. But when it is present, he may speak. He speaks to all the sufferers in this way.

He forgets about infection, forgets the rule of the hospital, because it does not matter. Now he dares to touch some people with his hands, taking their hands tentatively, without force, as a bird might alight for a moment before the flicker of its eye, flicker of its wing, carries it away on the wind. Those whose hands he touches invariably grow still, look at him curiously, and then gratefully begin to weep. This is true for the old and the young, the weak and the strong.

He does not ask himself why he is doing these strange things, why it is so important to explore this new way of speaking. He simply does it. It is a state in which fear evaporates, and the distance between himself and other souls diminishes almost to nothing. Yet there always remains a gap, for complete communion has occurred only with Josipa, who is gone, and cannot be replaced by any other. Perhaps he is seeking comfort for himself, trying to feel a hint of what he felt long ago when the communion flowed. He can recall those times as an undefined light, though always surrounded by the walls of memories that came later, the blood and the fire. Whenever he approaches the walls, his mind and body flinch and quickly turn away. Yet a swallow may fly over a wall, and thus the core of love remains open to him.

He does not think much about this. It is just a way of knowing—knowing where one can go, where one cannot go, what one may see, what one must never see.

Then there is a meeting unlike any of the others. One morning, Josip awakes and discovers that a new patient has been brought to the cellar. Three have died while he slept, and now there are enough mattresses for everyone. The new patient has eyes, but no arms below his elbows. The stumps are bound by bandages. One of his legs is broken and is bound by splints. He is sitting with his back to the wall, staring at the bar of sunlight that enters through the small window at the ceiling, hits the opposite wall, and moves slowly at an angle across it. He observes its progress without shifting his body or altering the direction of his gaze.

The day is hot, the walls are sweating, the cellar is dank with thick humidity. The stench of decaying blood and other matter is growing stronger. Two hospital workers pour buckets of water onto the cement floor, none too careful about splashing the mattresses, and then with their straw brooms they scrape the resulting soup toward a drain hole.

Josip wobbles unsteadily to the new patient and kneels at the end of the man's mattress, taking care not to block his view of the beam of light. Because of the heat, the new patient is wearing only canvas shorts. He is about forty years old. His body is one that has known a life of labor, very strong but now defeated. Perhaps he is a farmer. His brown face indicates constant exposure to the sun. He is clean shaven, and the hair on his head is black, cropped short. His eyes are brown, and thus it may be that he is a Muslim, though this is uncertain, since the eyes of some Croats are brown, though most are blue. Some

Muslims also have blue eyes. The man seems to rest in solitude. A terrible loneliness hangs about all patients, but it does not seem to be around this man. His solitude is composed and peaceful, despite what has happened to him.

His eyes flicker, acknowledging Josip's presence.

Josip senses the swallow within himself. He speaks with his eyes to the man without arms. It is the message he usually delivers. He senses also that with this man it would be permissible to touch hands, though the man has no hands. So, he rests his fingertips on the toes, at the end of his good leg. With this contact he becomes fully the *lastavica*; all motion dissolves, all noise fades, and there is only presence. The man's eyes slowly register the fingers on his foot, then they rise to meet the gaze of the strange boy who has arrived, out of nowhere it seems, at the end of his mattress. For a time, he looks at Josip in the same way he has regarded the progress of the light.

There is, of course, no speaking with the mouth. Even so, the gap is very small, the distance between them narrower than any Josip has experienced with other patients. He does not analyze this, nor does he question its purpose. It begins as the silence of the *lastavica* and swiftly becomes the shared silence of two *lastavice* twining the path of their flight as they rise on a current of air and light that has no beginning and no end.

"Who are you?" asks the man in a quiet voice. His voice is deep, just above the silence.

"Josip."

The man smiles—a gentle smile. His eyes are smiling too.

"You are Josip."

"I am Josip", he replies, as if this confirmation has been too long overdue. His aunt began the process, and now this man completes it with an authority the boy did not realize existed anymore in the world.

"Yes, you are Josip. And where have you come from, Josip?"

"From the fields of heaven."

"This I have already seen."

"Where have you come from, sir?"

"From the sea."

"Upon the waves?"

"Yes," nods the man, "and from beneath the waves also."

"Will you return there?"

"I will."

"When will you go?"

"When the wind takes me."

"Then it *is* you!"

"Yes, it is me."

"You are the swallow who once landed in my hands."

A look of curiosity fills the man's eyes.

"It is you who have landed in my hands", he says, raising his stumps.

Though Josip understands that the other is speaking with humor, he knows also that it is true.

"Though there is no holding and keeping", the man adds.

"I may fly as I will?"

"You may fly as you will."

"This is the way of the *lastavice*. It is the way we must be."

"Yes, Josip, it is the way we must be."

"Why did you come to me?"

"It is you who came to me."

"But you came to me beside the sea, that day. When we first met on the beach of white stones, by the cliff where the *lastavice* live."

The man says nothing. His smile has returned, and he continues to gaze at the boy curiously.

"Do you not remember?"

"I remember", says the man.

"I did not want you to fly away."

"But we all must fly away."

"Why must we?"

Now the man's face saddens.

"It is the way of the *lastavice*. You know this."

"Because this is not our home?"

"Yes, because this is not our home."

For some time they say no more, simply regard each other without discomfort.

The man is the first to resume:

"You are from the mountains."

Josip nods. He does not want to think about the mountains, back there—all that is behind him.

"When I was your age, I would go out to sea with my father. I loved the sea, though many drown in her. I loved her, and still to this day I love her. Often did I stand on the prow of our boat and look east toward the white peaks of the Dinarics."

"Did you go there?"

"Never have I been there."

"Yet, here you are, in the mountains."

"No, I am standing on the prow of a boat. I am upon the sea."

Now it is Josip's turn to fall silent. He does not understand what the man has said, but knows it must be true.

"I am not upon the sea", he whispers, hoping this will prompt an explanation.

"You are upon the sea, Josip", replies the man.

"Are we not in Sarajevo?"

"Sarajevo, too, is within the sea. Though these hills are waves, they are not the highest."

Another long silence follows.

"What is the highest?" asks the boy.

"The highest is within you. It is a country of mountains and valleys, the beds of alpine glens, the crevasse and its fall from which there is no return, and the summit from which one does not wish to return."

"Is that where you are?"

"No, I am upon the sea, as I said."

"I do not understand you."

"It is not necessary to understand me."

"Why is it not necessary?"

"Because you will remember my words, and when you have grown old you will understand them."

"Will I grow old? I do not want to. I would fly away."

"You must not fly away before the appointed time."

"How will I know it is the right time?"

"How do you know when to be a *lastavica*?"

Josip shakes his head; he does not understand.

"You will know when it is time for you to know", the man adds. He closes his eyes. He is fatigued with the effort of speaking.

"Will you bring me water?" he asks.

Josip goes out to the hallway and searches along it for a source of water. He finds a barrel with a dipper hanging at its side. He fills the dipper and returns to the man of the sea. The eyes of the man thank him, as Josip tips the dipper and lets the water pour slowly into the open mouth.

"I must sleep now", says the man to the boy. Josip nods and goes away.

The next morning, the doctor wakes Josip, says that he is recovering well, informs him that tomorrow he will go home. This news prompts the return of dread; and after the doctor leaves, he looks along the row of mattresses, hoping that the man of the sea is still there. He is there. He is sitting up, back to the wall, observing the bar of light on the opposite wall. Josip goes to him. The man smiles and says:

"You did not fly away."

"I did not fly away."

The dread recedes, almost all of it. In this presence, there is little fear, and within seconds none remains.

"Did you sleep, Josip?"

"Yes."

"You are no longer very ill."

"Soon I will leave here. Then we will not speak together."

"We will speak together, always."

"Who are you?"

The man thinks about the question a moment before replying.

"I would like to tell you my name. Yet I would also prefer not to tell you my name."

"Why?"

"Because then you will remember what is important. This way of knowing will remain open to you if you do not know everything."

"I do not understand."

"In time, you will understand."

"Can you not tell me your name?"

"I can tell you my name, and I will tell you if you choose it. But I ask you to choose a higher way."

"Why is it higher?"

The man lifts his arms—the stumps performing their task instinctively.

"It is higher because it will take you upward."

"To where the *lastavice* fly?"

"Yes."

"You do not have to tell me your name. You have already done so."

"I have already done so? Tell me, Josip, what is my name?"

"You are the Lastavica of the Sea. I am the Lastavica of the Mountains."

"Yes, you have understood. But you are more: you are the Lastavica of the Fields of Heaven."

Later that evening, he returns to the man of the sea and sits on the end of the mattress. He feels the sadness of impending departure. Though their eyes greet one another, for a time they say nothing.

"You wish to ask me something", says the man at last.

Josip nods.

"But you are shy to ask it?"

"Yes."

"You need not feel shy. You may ask."

"What will you do without arms?"

"The *lastavice* do not have arms. We have wings."

"Did you lose them in the war?"

"I lost them in a war, but not the war you think of."

"In which war did you lose them?"

"The war that will last until the end of time."

"Will I see you again?"

"That is for the wind to decide."

"I hope we will meet again."

"I too hope for this."

"Do you have a family?"

"Yes." For the first time, the man's face registers pain. He closes his eyes.

"Are you seeing them now, as you stand on your boat."

"I am seeing them now."

"Are they dead?"

The man opens his eyes and looks long at Josip.

"She stands with me upon the sea, though not on the land. She is above. So, too, my daughter, and so, too, my son."

"What are their names?"

"They are forever the family of the Lastavica of the Sea. That is their names."

"If we meet again, will you tell me their names?"

"I will tell you, if the wind decides we are to meet again."

"What if it doesn't?"

"It is not our task to question it."

"I do not trust it."

The man sits upright, leans forward, and speaks intensely:

"Josip, above all things you must trust it. Trust where it will take you."

Josip covers his face with trembling hands.

"Are you afraid?" asks the man.

"Yes."

"In your life, Josip, you will have much to fear. In time, you will come to a length of days, and wisdom, and goodness. You will suffer, and this suffering will bring much good to others."

"I do not understand what you are saying."

"You do not need to understand. Only remember: you will be afraid. But do not be afraid."

"What can this mean! Tell me what it means!"

"You will be afraid. But when you are afraid, do not be afraid."

Josip is choking back his sobs; he is no longer the Lastavica of the Fields of Heaven. He is only a boy with nowhere to go, other than a place where a wolf wants to kill him.

"Look, Josip", says the man of the sea. "Look at the wall."

With his one good foot he nudges Josip, pushing him gently, making him turn to face the opposite wall. The bar of light is climbing higher now.

"Do you see?"

Josip shakes his head.

"Surely you see", says the man.

"I see the light, but the walls imprison it."

"The light has entered the prison. Nothing can keep it out."

"If there is no window, the light cannot enter."

"If there is no window, the light enters within you."

8

Eva comes for him the following afternoon. With his eyes Josip says good-bye to the Lastavica of the Sea, and the man does the same to the Lastavica of the Mountains.

Dressed in his ordinary clothes, his book under his arm, Josip walks with his aunt from the hospital to the apartment. His legs are unsteady, his head still dizzy, his eyes blinking at the too-bright sunlight, but he is no longer burning. It is only weakness. Instead of sickness, he must now deal with a growing feeling of dread.

Eva walks along beside him, an arm draped over his shoulders, ready to catch him if he falls. She is chattering, telling him disconnected things, preparing the way for reunion with the uncle.

"He has been drinking a lot lately, Josip. Soon he must report to his battalion, and he does not want to go back. But what else can he do? There aren't many jobs yet, even if they let him go. He sleeps through the morning and goes out at night, so only in the afternoons will you be together. Do not mind if he says harsh things. He is angry with me too, sometimes, though he would not harm a mouse. He was always like that: a bit of a temper, but basically a good man. With everything he saw, all that killing, his comrades dying all around him, it has made him sad, and he does not like to talk about it. You won't ask him questions, will you? He doesn't like questions, because he is trying to forget." She sighs and catches her breath. "That's why he drinks so much. It eases his pain. He lost friends, brothers-in-arms. But he is irritable too, so don't bother him if you can help it. Do you understand?"

Josip nods, *I will be silent.*

"In the afternoons, he just sits at the table and looks out the window; not that there is much to see, with the brick wall. He says we should move to another apartment soon, maybe closer to the center where there is a view of the river, after we have—"

She stops herself, glances at the boy with a worried look, then continues.

"He has spoken with the committee for the orphans, but they say there is not enough room for you, not even for a boy whose uncle is a war veteran. Soon the government is sending money for construction of a building and for staff to look after the children. But the youngest will have first place, because they are in greater need. I'm sure boys of your age will have a place with them as things improve. You'll be happier there, with other children your age, better than our place, with two people who are very tired and have been through so much, and with never quite enough to feed us all. You'll see, Josip, everything is going to get better, now that the bad times are over."

Uncle is not in the apartment when they return. Josip collapses onto the mattress and goes to sleep.

It is night when he awakes. No house lights are on. He has slept for hours, and during that time the life of his aunt and uncle has continued around him. Now they are in their bedroom, talking in low voices. Josip cannot hear the words, but the tone is certain. His aunt is pleading, his uncle is growling. Josip curls his body tightly, fists clenched between his knees, ears toward the bedroom wall, eyes wide open like a forest mouse listening for a hunting owl.

Now, as voices are raised, he is able to pick out words.

"But why? He is my own flesh."

"Your own flesh! He is another mouth to feed. We don't have enough money!"

"We have enough money for drink, so why not enough to feed a boy who has lost everything."

"Don't start on me about that. The drink helps me—"

"It does not help *us*."

"Who is *us*?"

"You know what I mean. The boy—"

"Damn that boy! Damn him! Why didn't he die with his parents?"

Auntie is sobbing, "How can you say such things! I lost them too, my beloved sister and her family. And maybe Katarina down in Split—who knows where she is?"

"Belgrade is going to do something about those nuns and priests. They're all parasites!"

Sobbing and shouting, squeaking springs, feet stomping back and forth on the floor. Neighbors pounding on the walls.

"He's going", uncle roars. "One way or another he is going!"

"What do you mean by that! We can't just throw him out into the streets."

"Why not! Take a look at the streets. Kids like him are everywhere."

"And why, why if the new order is a better way, are there so many kids like that?"

"Be careful—watch your mouth", says uncle in a lower voice. "Don't bring trouble on us."

A sob, a sniffle, a nose blowing. "I won't", she says in a conciliatory voice. "I won't bring trouble on us. I'm not stupid."

"You're not stupid, Eva, but you don't know anything."

"I know what I know."

A cold laugh. "You know what you know."

"I knew you were brave, Jure, but I didn't know you were cruel."

"I've grown up. I've learned a few things."

"Have you? Tell me what you learned, then. I'd like to know."

"You don't want to know."

"What do you mean? Stop sucking on that bottle and tell me what you mean."

"Get me another bottle, and I'll tell you what I mean."

Squeaking-squeaking. His aunt opens the bedroom door and by the pale light filtering between the apartment blocks, Josip sees her shadow cross the window. A cupboard door opens, glass clinks, she tiptoes back into the bedroom and closes the door. She has pushed it shut, but not firmly enough because with a faint squeal of the hinges, it swings open behind her, invisible in the dark.

A cork pops and rolls onto the floor. Silence for a minute or two.

"You don't know what I've seen", says the uncle. It is his quietest level of speaking, but because the door is open, the words are audible to the boy on the mattress, no more than a meter or two away from the mouth of the speaker.

"You should tell me, Jure. There should be no secrets between husband and wife."

Another cold laugh.

"Tell me."

"All right, I will tell you", he says in the bitterest of tones, slurring his words a little. "But you will not thank me for telling you. You will say there *should* be secrets a man does not tell his woman."

"I am your wife, not your *woman*."

Jure laughs again.

"Maybe not for long—after I tell you."

She does not reply. Then the uncle speaks:

"We were in the south, east, everywhere, cleaning up pockets of Germans and Home-Guard. Then the chiefs in the east commanded a big push because the Germans were in trouble, losing ground. They're tough, but we were tougher. Last October we took Belgrade, and in March Tito declared the new government of Yugoslavia. The end of Croatia was near, and the Fascists were retreating northward. In May they abandoned Zagreb and went toward Austria, a mass exodus toward the passes. We hit them from behind, and from both sides, but they were well organized, hundreds of thousands of them, maybe two hundred thousand troops and about as many civilians. Whenever we caught Ustashe bastards, we butchered them. The Home-Guard not so much—a nice clean bullet for our countrymen, out of respect for their stupidity, and because they were just dumb puppets, country boys like us, but on the wrong side. There were so many sides at first, in the early years, Partisans all the time fighting everyone—Germans, Home-Guard, Ustashe, Chetniks. Then the Chetniks joined us, and we stopped killing them and they stopped killing us. Battalions had old Partisans and new Partisans, Croats and Serbs fighting side by side."

"You know Chetniks?" Eva interrupts.

"Many. There I was, side by side with my new comrades, the ones who only a year ago would have slit my throat. But they know where the future is. The Red Army coming down through Romania and Bulgaria, the Allies gobbling up Europe, the Reich shrinking, islands of Fascists shrinking everywhere. So, everybody gets on board with the Partisans and starts to push north. No more killing each other, the bosses told us. Just kill the Fascists, do whatever you have to do. So we did."

"Here in Bosnia?"

A pause.

"In the beginning, yes, here in Bosnia and Herzegovina."

Silence.

"Was it in any place we know?"

"No", Jure growls. "I told you that before."

"Did you kill people?" Eva asks in a quiet voice.

"What do you think soldiers do? Of course I killed people."

"Women and children and old people?"

179

"Never. Only Fascist soldiers."

"Oh", she sighs. "That's good."

"So, there we were, after we went north to join the new JNA, driving the enemy hard through Slovenia. Along the way, we caught tens of thousands and shot them. But most got through to Austria because they wanted to surrender to the British, not to the Soviets, and certainly not to us. They were terrified of us. We were always finding bodies of people who had killed themselves when they couldn't keep up with the rest. Most made it into Austria, and when they got there the British told them to come on in, you're safe now. So, there they were, hundreds of thousands crowded into a little valley, like ducks at slaughter time—"

Jure pauses. He is drinking from the bottle. Josip knows this because a moment later the bottle is hurled to the bedroom floor and rolls around.

"There they were—just like ducks. Ducks nobody could feed. So, the Brits and Americans guaranteed their safety, if they surrendered to us. They ran up white flags and we 'accepted'. Then we just shot into the crowds, all bunched together, the idiots, and we emptied our guns into them. They had nowhere to go, and they didn't shoot back because they didn't have anything to shoot back with."

"You shot too."

"Who wouldn't shoot! That was Bleiburg, a little place southeast of Klagenfurt. It was great. The Brits just stood by, watching it all. Didn't stop us. Just watching. Good old Brits. Our new Allies. At Maribor it was better. We finished off about forty thousand there. Whenever we ran out of ammunition, we used knives and truncheons and hatchets. After that, we loaded everyone that was left onto trains and shipped them back across the border."

"What happened to them?"

"That's what you don't want to know."

"You can tell me."

"No, I can't. Orders. Nobody is to know."

"You killed them too, didn't you. Men and women and children. Soldiers and non-soldiers."

"The Ustashe killed thousands in their camps. Now it was our turn."

"You took all those people to camps?"

"Don't ask me again. I told you, no one is to know." Another bitter laugh. "You can't even begin to guess."

"If you don't tell me the truth, you will never see me again. I can't live with secrets."

"All our married life you've been living with secrets."

"What do you mean by that!"

"You don't want to know."

A loud slap.

"Do that again, Eva, and you won't see me again. Or anything else."

"You'll kill me, like you killed those people?"

"Those people were class enemies. It was war."

"War? An army of civilians without guns? That's war? Is that what we sacrificed for?"

"Sit down. Shut up."

Squeaking bedsprings.

"It's time to choose, Eva. You can grow up, or you can pretend it's all going to be nice and safe from now on. What happened at Bleiburg and Maribor was commanded by the people who control our future. This is *their* country."

"But you helped them."

"I started to grow up. It's a hard world. Everyone dies in the end, some sooner, some later. And it's better for some to die early so that the rest, the majority, have a better life."

"You're saying you can do anything, as long as it helps the majority?"

"That's correct. Call it a democracy."

Silence.

"I don't believe you. You're making this up. It's propaganda."

"I was there. And at other places. We went back with the trains. British troops helped us strip the Croats and Slovenes. Underwear only. I wish you could have seen all those nice boys from England with plundered wristwatches from wrist to armpit, guarding the trains as they went by, making sure nobody jumped out. Then, when we had the ducks back in our territory, we unloaded them and marched them into the forest. In the forests there were pits we'd prepared. For days and days we executed, filled the pits, covered them over. Then more pits. Pits upon pits, a great harvest. I was at one cave where we threw in thirty or forty thousand bodies. After a while you lose count. After that, we marched the survivors farther south to camps. Most died on the way. We shot villagers who tried to give them food or water. We shot anybody who got in our way. We killed anyone we wanted to kill. And we're still doing it."

Eva's voice is choking, shuddering. "The people will not let you go on with it."

"The people don't know about it. People are blind. And no newspaper is ever going to write about this, because anyone who talks about it is going to disappear. Besides, law and order has come to Yugoslavia. Now the police, the courts, and the prisons will clean up whatever remains."

After that, no more words. Just a man's curse, and the faint sound of his aunt sobbing into her pillow.

Josip does not sleep. He is frozen, unable to run. He sees blood and fire now, even though he is not sleeping.

Perhaps from exhaustion he dozes a little toward dawn. He hears his aunt getting up, going out to work. She is sniffing and groaning. She does not try to wake him because he lost his job at the factory during his month of illness.

He is alone with his uncle. Jure is snoring in the bedroom.

How can a man who has killed so many people sleep so deeply? Does *rakija* drug him beyond the reach of nightmares? It must be so; it must be why he drinks so much.

Josip gets up as quietly as possible, dresses, but does not put on his shoes. He can't find his socks in the dark. The floor is cold but bearable. He stuffs the book about the sea inside his jacket and tiptoes to the doorway of the apartment. Now he will fly. Now he will escape the terror that has afflicted him for many weeks and the dreams of blood and fire that the terror has reawakened. He does not have any idea where he will go. He knows only that he must go, lest he be shot and thrown into a pit, a river, a cave, a hole, because all life is now valueless, leaving only the rights of power. Of power he desires nothing. He wants only to live a little longer; he does not know why, but something within him will not permit him die. If he can fly, he will not cease to be. The Lastavica of the Sea has helped him know this in the heart of his soul, though his thoughts and feelings are rioting.

Can it be true what he heard in the night? Can a man really do such things? Though his uncle is a cruel and angry person, and he perhaps killed people at Pačići, it is nearly unthinkable that he has really done the things he says he has done in the north. After all, he did not see his uncle kill anyone at Pačići—it was the others who did the killing. And his uncle spared his life.

Faces always reveal something of what is inside. He will look at the face of his uncle, and he will know the truth about what is inside. He tiptoes back to the bedroom door, which is open a crack. He pushes it wide and steps inside. Jure is still snoring. His clothes are heaped beside the bed. Josip stands a pace or two from the bed, examining the face. It is an ordinary face. Though there is darkness in it, he is sure it is not the darkness of a monster. His uncle did not do those things he said he did. He must have said it because he was angry, wanted to make Eva fear him or respect him, though it did not work. His uncle tells lies. Thus, he may have lied about everything.

There is the gun leaning against the wall. There is no blood on it. His ammunition straps are rolled up neatly beside it on the floor. Beside these, leaning against the wall, is a hatchet. Josip remembers that in Pačići his uncle wore a hatchet hanging from his belt. That day there was blood on everything, but so much happened at once that he had not looked at the hatchet for more than a split second.

He knows this hatchet, in a way that reaches beyond Pačići. He kneels and peers closer. He picks it up and turns it over in his hands. Again and again he turns it over, even after he knows where it has come from. It is Petar's. The blue stripe on the handle, the initials "PD" scratched in the steel. His chest heaving, Josip gasps and attempts to rise, accidentally dropping the hatchet to the floor. He picks it up without thinking.

"So, try it", says the deep voice of a man. "Kill me. It's what you want to do."

Jure is awake, observing him, his eyes all wolf, his mouth sneering with contempt.

"Go ahead, try."

"My Mamica, my Tata", Josip whispers.

Jure utters a single cold laugh.

Josipa. Petar. Fra Anto . . .

Josip is too stunned to cry. All thought is erased by the shock of knowledge.

"We came through the old pass out of the north", Jure murmurs drowsily, still smiling. "Down into Rajska Polja. At first, I did not know what place it was. Because it was small it had no name on maps, it was just another village of Catholic Croats. Many men of my *ceta* were Chetniks, sent down to join us, with a chief among them. We were the remains of three *cetas*, fused into one, and not easy in each other's company. I had to prove myself. By the end, I knew where we were, after we had our fun."

Jure closes his eyes, still smiling. Josip has never in his life seen such a smile. It is terrifying in its calmness, its acceptance of all that is behind the eyes.

"You can kill me. A blow to my skull will do it."

Josip's grip closes around the handle of Petar's hatchet, and a black surge of vengeance rushes through him. He sees his friend's amputated hand, sees the skulls of his parents burning in the embers of his home.

"Go ahead. I won't stop you", says his uncle.

Josip's teeth are bared. Then his teeth bite into his lower lip, and it begins to bleed.

He drops the hatchet and runs. All the way down the stairs his uncle's laughter chases him, until he is out in the street and flying away.

For three days and nights he lives in the alleyways of Sarajevo. He eats nothing, drinks once each night, bending over the river and sucking at it like an animal. He is visible to other human beings only as a fleeting shadow after sunset or before dawn. A shadow among shadows. He is barefoot because he left his shoes behind in the apartment. It is now late autumn and winter is approaching in the mountains. He crawls into cracks between apartment buildings, where no light enters and no eyes peer. A little heat radiates from the bricks, and the wind cannot enter. He shivers and dozes and wakes in terror, only to shiver again. His uncle will search for him and find him and then he will die slowly under the razor.

One evening, he is caught by a gang of alley boys who, like Josip, have no home. They pummel him, take his book, and knock him to the ground. They would strip him bare, too, except that he fights back with rage, hurls splinters of brick and concrete at his assailants, and smashes at the shins around him, the feet kicking him. Then he scrambles upright, punches and draws blood, and with a cold and desperate fury continues to punch. He does not relent, does not give way under their blows, giving blow for blow with the last milligrams of his strength until, one by one, they run off in search of easier prey. He has kept his clothes, though he has lost some blood. He licks the blood from his hands, swallows it. With the palms of his hands, he wipes the blood from his face and licks it down too. Is it theirs, is it his? He does not know.

Throughout the fourth night, he forages alongside cats for scraps of food thrown out by people into the back lots of apartment buildings. These items are few indeed, and mostly rotten, but there are bits and pieces that can sustain life: potato peelings, carrot tops, fish heads, bones with sinew on them—once a thick bone with marrow inside. It smells bad and gives him trouble in his gut, but it also increases his energy a little. It will give him strength so that he can fight again, if attacked. Gradually, he learns that the pickings improve as he forages higher in the hills of the city, where there are better homes. It is also more dangerous there, with watchdogs and watchgeese, and sometimes a human guard who is quite willing to shoot blindly into shadows.

The following night, there is a sprinkle of snow, so cold that it freezes Josip's toes, even within the rags he has wrapped around his feet and secured with twine. Realizing that he could die in this weather, he makes his way by stealth to the factory, where he knows there will be warm coals glowing in the smelter behind the main building. Though there is a risk of being captured, he will sleep at last, and he will command his mind to wake him up before dawn, in order to flee back into invisibility.

Josip knows where the hole under the fence is to be found, and it lets him into the compound. No adult could enter this way, but he is just skinny enough to slide under, scratching his back on a wire. No matter, he will be warm for the night. The front vent on the smelter furnace reveals a quiet inferno inside;

though dying down, it will radiate heat until morning. Behind it is the cubbyhole, and into this shadow-within-shadows he crawls, curls into a ball, and falls asleep.

He is yanked brutally into light and terror. A hand grips him by the collar of his jacket, swinging him in the air, his feet dangling inches above the ground. It is the foreman, a burly man of great strength who can toss a sheet of steel without help and without sweat. Now he holds a bird by its neck and is growling at it, demanding to know how the boy got in.

Josip's collar is choking him; he can only open and close his mouth; nothing comes in, nothing goes out. The foreman, seeing this, throws him upward a few inches and lets him fall to the ground.

"Lasta!" he snarls. "You good-for-nothing! What are you doing here? Your aunt has been worried sick over you all week."

He gives Josip a kick in the hind end for good measure.

"Answer!"

He cannot answer. *My uncle killed my family and my friends, but my auntie does not know and soon my uncle will cut me into pieces, and nobody will know.* This cannot be said, and the soundless scream crams the words farther down inside. The foreman curses, grabs the boy by the scruff of the neck, and pulls him upright. He hauls him across the back lot, throws him inside a storage shed, then closes and locks it.

"Stay there, and don't move!" he yells, banging on the metal door with his fist. "Don't even think of trying to get out. When your aunt arrives for work, she'll give you what you deserve, running off, not letting her know where you went. You made her crazy, and not a lick of work have we had from her these past five days. She sits at her desk crying. Crying, I tell you! All day long she cries. What kind of boy are you, wretched ingrate, breaking a woman's heart—"

And so forth. Josip is so sore in body and numbed in mind that his emotions do not register the insults. He sinks down and sits in the dark with his chin on his chest, forehead on knees. In fact, he dozes.

Eva does not come. He knows the day is passing because the crack of light at the bottom of the door slides sideways. He watches it move, hour after hour. Then it slips outside entirely, leaving only a faint glow. Then nothing.

Now the door is unlocked. The foreman throws it wide open, and shouts, "Get up!" Josip cannot make his legs obey. Once again, the man lifts him by his collar. It is dusk outside, and under the yard-light men are heading homeward through the open gate.

The foreman shakes him and says, "Well, she didn't show. No doubt she's sick in bed because of you. Well, I'm not going to miss my supper."

Fist on the boy's collar, he half drags, half leads Josip out onto the street and stomps along it in the direction of the apartment where Eva lives. Josip's feet barely touch the ground and spin like wheels trying to keep up.

"If she's in bed, your uncle will deal with you", growls the foreman, so angry about wasting his free time over this runaway that he cannot resist an occasional shake.

Now the apartment looms, and Josip is in agony, paralyzed with the dread of his impending death. One strong man will hand him over to another, and the other will take him away by force to a very private place and slice pieces from his body, until every part of him is meat.

Josip is howling with wide-open mouth, though these are not sounds that can be heard by any ears. His eyes are crazed, and he cannot even struggle to escape. The foreman drags him up three flights of stairs and comes to a halt by the apartment door. He kicks on it with his shoe.

No one answers from inside; no one opens the door.

"Poor Eva", mutters the foreman. "See, she's so worn out she's gone to bed. And where's your uncle? No matter, he'll soon be back, I wager."

He waggles the door handle. Finding it unlocked, he pushes the door open and steps inside, pulling Josip along.

"Eva! Wake up! Look, I've got your boy. Come and get him, I can't stay and babble."

The room is dark, but a dim light comes from the open bedroom door.

"Eva? Wake up, girl, I haven't got all night."

They enter the bedroom, and by the light of a bedside candle they see that she is there, awake, sitting at the foot of the bed, with her back to the door. She is rocking her body forward and backward.

Jure is there too, sleeping on his back, eyes closed, arms by his sides. Eva is holding one of his hands. Jure's mouth is wide open. The muzzle of his rifle is inside his mouth, the gun lying lengthwise from his chest to his groin. One hand droops over the firing piece, and a finger lies limply on the trigger.

"Oh, God", groans the foreman, and lets go of Josip.

The top of Jure's skull is gone, the thick blond hair at the crown is a mass of gore. The wall above the bed is splattered. The pillow is entirely red; the bed also is soaked with blood.

Memory erases from the mind of the young certain details that in old age they strive to remember, if they live to old age. Ever afterward, Josip will be unable to recall a single detail of what occurs during the following two or three days before his uncle is buried. It does not matter. The moment of knowledge was enough. The killer is dead. Killed by what hand is uncertain, though all the evidence points to suicide. Years upon years of analyzing the details observed that night extract from the single searing image nothing more than what is seen. How the death is explained, what his aunt says, if anything, what is done with the body, when the bed and walls are cleaned, when or how it is decided that Josip will return to live with his aunt—all is gone. Not a trace ever again surfaces.

There is a funeral. Dozens of men and women take part in it, some in uniforms, some in rough clothing, all with guns firing a salute into the sky as the body is lowered into a hole dug from the frozen soil by pick and axe. There are orations. Then the soil is shoveled into the pit. Josip will always remember the sound, the thumping of hard chunks of dirt on a hollow body wrapped in a sheet, but later he can recall little of what is said that day.

He stands beside his aunt throughout. Her skin is gray and her eyes are without tears, staring straight ahead. He cannot read her face. Perhaps beneath her lack of expression lies a sorrow so profound that it is beyond emotion, perhaps it is something else. To all eyes she is the epitome of courage. Jure is a war hero; she is his widow. She listens without visible feeling as veterans give accounts of her husband's bravery under fire. No mention is made of certain events in the north, which, of course, have not occurred. There may be wolves of Pačići present, but the boy does not recognize any faces.

On a pole by the grave, the new flag of Yugoslavia snaps and ripples in the wind. More than he observes the soldiers and their rites, Josip watches the flag, ponders its bars of color and its star. The order of colors is reversed. He recalls the flag of Croatia that his father kept in the parlor drawer beneath the altar of the crucifix, rolled up and waiting for a better day. It bore a red bar on top, white in the middle, and blue at the bottom. Rolled beside it was an older flag, which had a checkered white and red crest on it.

The new flag bears the blue on the top, red on the bottom. Josip wonders at this—the first stirring of thought since the death of his uncle. Why have they not put the red on the top?

After all, red is the color they love, is it not? Do they not think that this red reigns supreme over all the country?

Then he understands that the red star is central, floating on an ocean of blood, swelling and swelling as it sucks from the blood of the peoples of Yugoslavia.

Blood dries in the soul, yet leaves its stains. There is no trace of it in the apartment. Everything has been washed down, scoured. The bullet hole and the lesser holes blasted into the wall by fragments of skull have been filled, the wall above the bed repainted. It's all fresh now, as if nothing unpleasant happened here. Even so, Eva has moved the bed to another wall. She is restless at night. Her light is always burning when Josip falls asleep on his mattress. It is still on when he awakes in the dawn. She is a ghost of herself; she never smiles, never cries, speaks only of inconsequential matters, goes to work with resolve every morning, and in the evening stares out the window at the brick wall. On her days off, she darns his socks, ferrets through the city in search of clothes for him: a new pair of trousers, a new shirt, new shoes that are not falling apart. *New* is any article of clothing he has not seen before, however much it may have been worn by others, discarded, or sold for a pittance. She forgets to make meals sometimes, and she lives with him on such days as if he were not there. These are the days when he wonders if his aunt is losing her mind, even as he is regaining his.

He fishes frequently from the Miljacka and catches enough to supplement their diet. He has not yet found work. The factory will not have him back. He earns a few coins by running errands for people in the nearby buildings or by performing odious tasks, such as carrying the toilet pots of the elderly down to the sewer hole on the street, then emptying and washing them. He no longer gags when he does it. Sometimes the old people give him an extra bite of bread too.

He has returned to the evening classes. He tries to ignore the political indoctrination. He has learned how to present himself as an exceptionally slow learner, deficient in wits. His first moment of pleasure since the death of his uncle occurs toward the end of winter, when he is called upon in class to define the word *cadre*. He makes his eyes glaze a little, lets his mouth fall open, says, *uhhh, ahhh*, and even produces a bit of drool. The drool is particularly effective.

It is more difficult to maneuver in history class. His mind leaps into the subject like a starving dog lunging at poisoned meat. He cannot be held back, even though he knows what they are feeding him. This new version of history is so different from what his father taught. He hates it, but he thinks about it a lot. He worries, too, that it will imprison his mind by repetition, combined with the gradual disappearance of truth.

There are times when it is hard to resist the world that is so rapidly changing all around him. It takes energy to resist, even if only within the privacy of his thoughts. When he is alone, exhaustion can hit him without warning, and the lack of substance on his spindly frame takes its toll. Then he cannot stop himself from weeping for his mother and father and for the others he has lost. He is unable to think about them much, and certainly will not allow himself to dwell on his last memory of Rajska Polja. Yet he can grieve over the void in his life, and these moments are followed sometimes by a peace.

From time to time, his aunt cuts his hair with rusty scissors, or tells him distractedly to wash behind his ears, or to change his socks. A twitch of a smile crosses her face whenever he enters the apartment triumphantly with fish in hand, though it never lights up her eyes. She receives no personal visitors, and few people come to the door. Once, the factory foreman knocks and invites her to have a meal with him, but she declines. Perhaps it is because Josip is not mentioned in the invitation. Later, he asks his aunt if the foreman blames him for uncle's death. She replies with no more than this: "People are strange; they always have excellent reasons for their resentments."

An official knocks at the apartment door once a month and hands her an envelope with a bit of money inside, her pension as the widow of a hero. She buys extra food with it, things a boy needs, a sausage, a cube of cheese, a wizened last-year's apple. Through these gestures, he learns that she does not in any way hold him responsible for the death. He feels immense relief when he is finally convinced of this. He does not mind when she scolds, because it is better than her silence, which sometimes returns and blocks him temporarily out of her world.

Each night he dreams of blood. He is either running from it, wading in it, choking on it, or drowning in it. And when he is not, he is licking it from his hands—is it his blood or other people's blood? He does not know. Blood strengthens him and makes him want more. He wakes from such dreams gagging and horrified by himself.

He washes his hands so often that his aunt begins to notice. She tells him to stop all that nonsense, says it's wasting the precious bit of soap they own, the little brown chunk that shrinks and shrinks so swiftly. Where will they find another to replace it! He tries to stop, but can't. Ten, twenty times a day, for no reason, he will bolt toward the sink on an impulse and scrub his hands, his nails, his forearms. His nails have grown back in, but he can see the blood pulsing beneath the translucent shells.

He will at times, though not often, drift off to sleep at night lying on his back, arms by his sides, mouth wide open. If he is especially tired, he pokes the forefinger of his right hand into his mouth and with his left pulls a trigger.

"Bang", he whispers.

He dreams of fire and blood only in connection with Rajska

Polja, which is always burning. He dreams of drowning in blood only in connection with Sarajevo, which is always a cement box in which people's arms are severed, their eyes gouged out, the tops of their heads blown off—and always there is blood running from the wounds, filling up the box from floor to ceiling. Memories and hallucinations blend, mutate, cavort: an ever-changing panorama of descent into darkness, above which a red star sucks and swells ever larger.

He learns to steal. His first crime occurs in the market square one morning, when he passes a table guarded by an old man of the countryside who is sitting with closed eyes on a crate beside the table. He wears a long knife at his belt, the kind used for slashing brush in the forest. No gun or other weapons. Josip stops by the table and spots a row of brown bars on it, bends over them, and sniffs. It is a fine smell, a mix of pig tallow and the acid made from wood ash. He knows this smell as he knows the pungencies of his goose-down bed in the loft at home, or the scent of fresh-cut hay in Svez's shed; this is the smell of autumn when Mamica makes soap for the year. He seizes one and breaks into a gallop, running away as fast as he can. The old man wakes and shouts after him, but he does not give chase. Thus Josip learns from whom to steal. If they are old and alone and have no serious weapons, they are the right ones.

Bloated with glee and shame, he heads toward the river through a maze of alleys. Arriving there, he drops to his knees and washes and washes and washes, though there is no need for this, his hands are always clean. By the time he lies down in the dark that night, the glee has evaporated, the pleasure declined to almost nothing, and the shame is now so great that he cannot sleep. A new horror has arisen within him—horror at himself— he is not only a person who drinks blood, he steals from the helpless.

He continues to steal. However, in order not to be devoured by shame, he catches fish in the river, runs to the market, throws them on various tables from which he has lifted items in the past, and runs again. He does not think to offer a trade. Perhaps he believes that no one would part with so precious a thing as a bar of soap, not even for a large and healthy fish. Before long his face becomes familiar to the merchants. They eye him warily: there is a mad boy about town, and this tall skeleton with furtive eyes fits the description perfectly. Of course, there are many such children on the streets, scrabbling for objects of peculiar need, food mostly, and sometimes inexplicable items.

One evening Eva does not return from work. Josip remains awake all night, listening for steps outside in the hallway. Two days, three days, four days pass. She does not return. He does not leave the apartment. His fear grows and grows. She has been taken away in a truck with a red star on its door. No, she has taken herself away into the state of mind that blocks all things out. She has pulled a trigger. She has gone, he is sure, because she can no longer bear to live with a boy who drinks blood.

Now the blood is constantly in his thoughts. He does not want to drink it when he is awake, but it cannot be washed from his mind. Once, he makes the mistake of looking into the bedroom in the hope that he will find her there. The bed has not been used. A splatter of blood appears on the wall and spreads across the plaster, as if the building were bleeding internally. He blinks and it disappears. Blinks again and it returns. He slams the door shut and does not go in there again. With the last of the stolen soap, he washes and washes his hands, over and over and over.

To escape from himself, he returns to the night classes. He is reprimanded for his absence during recent weeks. In order to explain it, he lies: He has been very ill. He was hit by a truck. He fell down a hole and hurt his leg. He was away on a journey.

In his absence, a new subject has been introduced. The

teacher gives him a book about it—mathematics. There is nothing in mathematics that bends the past or the future. He flips through the pages, recognizing old friends in these squiggling numbers and symbols. Yes, he knows all this, it is awakening again, though at a level below what he once learned. Even so, this is good. You take one step back in order to take two steps forward. You learn something new every day.

Eva returns the next afternoon. She blows into the apartment with color in her cheeks, a big smile, a pink scarf at her neck, and packages in her arms. Josip is seated on his mattress, back to the wall. He stares at her and does not return her cheerful greeting. She kisses him and exultantly unwraps what she has brought. Loaves of bread, butter, *rakija*, a package of tea, a turnip, a radish, a green onion, new socks for him, a dress for herself. She chatters without ceasing, explaining that when she was at work last week an unannounced visitor from the Workers' Commissariat arrived at the factory, and all senior employees went away with him to a meeting. She had to go too, for she is the boss's secretary now. Labor is being reorganized, the new policies will be enforced everywhere, and it will make everything so much more efficient, so much more productive. This is what they fought for, sacrificed for. She is sorry she didn't have time to let him know—she had no idea how long she would be away, and after all, he is capable of looking after himself. How was his week? How were his classes? And what is that book he is reading? Ah, excellent. It's nice to see you studying, Josip. Good boy. Then she flies into the bedroom, closes the door, and begins singing to herself.

Josip drops the book onto the mattress. For a time he stands in the middle of the room looking at the closed door. A curtain of blood descends between himself and the door. Blood sprinkles across the floor and creeps toward him, drop by drop.

He wheels and goes out into the hallway. By the time he

reaches the street, he is running. The afternoon sun is warm, and flowers are appearing in the vacant lots, poking up from the rubble. Down by the river there is more grass, more flowers. The trees along the banks are flowering too. He is sweating from the run, his body prickling with heat, his breath tearing in and out. He turns to the right and races along the shore toward something that he does not define to himself. He can sense it only as a place he must go in order to leave everything behind, everything, for the blood is back there behind him. But it cannot be left behind, it always follows, and it is following still. He feels it catching up. It is on his heels, the ocean of roaring blood reaching for the well of stolen blood within him, trying to swallow him so that everything will swirl down into the sewer hole.

With a burst of speed, he passes the last houses of the city. Then the solitary farmhouses begin. He is pulling ahead now, farther and farther from the ocean, going deeper into the mountains, always beside the river. Finally, he is spent; there is no more fuel to drive his legs. He stumbles to the side of the road and collapses onto the grass. Quickly the ocean tide sweeps up to him and pushes him down the bank to the river's edge. At this spot there is a shallow full of water weeds and brown stones. He wades in up to his knees, gasping. The water is so cold that he shouts when the shock hits him.

He will wash everything off, all the splatters of blood and bone on his shirt and trousers and shoes. He tears all clothing from himself, and the current tugs it under and toward the shore. His teeth chatter, the flesh of his hands and arms and legs turns red, the skin rises in bumps like a plucked duck, and soon, unless he hides beneath the water, his head will be severed with an axe.

He plunges under. It is all yellow and brown down there, with swirls of green murk stirred up by his feet. His legs push him out farther, and the mud slopes into the depths. He will wash it all away, the blood on his hands, the blood in his mouth, the blood that is falling and falling like ceaseless rain upon the mountains all around. He will wash it all away in the river, for the river has not yet turned to blood.

Knowing that no large hands will pull him up and carry him to shore, he understands that he has come to the end. He will sink into the pit as so many others have sunk into it. Yet he will go down naked and free and cleansed at last. All murder and theft and falsehood will be washed out of him, all fear and shame.

Now it is up to his neck, now it covers his face and his hair. Now he is sinking. He is screaming, his mouth open wide, blood spewing out from within.

Now he is choking, his arms lashing, his legs kicking. Up he rises into the rain of blood, then down again. Lashing and kicking, his arms and legs and lungs refuse to obey him, and they will not let him go down. He hates them, forces them to stop, and sinks again. But their power is greater than his will. They do as they wish and force him up again. Now the current has taken him into center stream, where it is deeper. Sinking and rising and bobbing along, sinking and thrashing, and rising again. Slowly, slowly he is cleansed. Slowly, slowly, he realizes that he has learned to swim.

THE PALACE BY THE SEA

9

He is standing on a rock, smiling to himself, soaking up the light. The Adriatic has never been so blue. Of course he feels this whenever he jogs through the park and the woods to the topmost height of the Marjan. Bluer and bluer the sea becomes—always. Among the many fine places to be found in and around Split, this is the best because from here it is possible to survey the entire world. To the south lies the old part of the city, its white buildings capped with red tiles and the bell tower of the emperor's palace. To the west the bay, and to the northwest the island city of Trogir, built by the Romans and Venetians.

The crest on which he stands evokes the latent sense of proportion. The flatness of the world shifts in the mind's eye and becomes an orb revolving slowly on the sea of infinity. The islands beyond the bay become amethyst clouds floating above the hiatus where water and sky merge. Here, everything about life that he finds burdensome or disgusting or boring falls away. He admits a single exception to this illusion of supreme vantage—the wall of the Dinaric Alps looming behind him, blocking out his past.

Saturdays are his day for making love. This is how he thinks of his affair with sea and sky, his only passions. The act of running from his residence near the university down through the streets toward the hill of the great park is a headlong race to his trysting place. Prancing like a race horse up the slopes, charged and exalted by altitude, sole master of his sweating, oxygenated body, he is fully himself. And upon his arrival at the top, he becomes, for a time, accountable to no one. A week without this rejuvenating event is a dull one, and sometimes a dispiriting one.

This morning is one of the finest since last autumn. The light is stronger after the short winter, the air still cool, and in his backpack he carries a wool sweater, a flask of water, and some bread and cheese. Beaming with pleasure, he spreads his arms wide and sings in a baritone voice, *O More Jadransko, O Jadransko More, O Adriatic Sea, my beloved, my beloved.*

He laughs at himself and wonders if anyone suspects his secret passion. A mathematics major, member of the swim team, sweeper back on the soccer team, a man of few words who moves among the crowds of students as if he were a giant. So tall, so remote, that the affairs of mortals cannot touch him. Yes, a towerer, defying gravity, striding higher and higher through the forest of Communist beeches, religious oaks, and the simply atheistic birches who are good at heart and declare their independence of all ideological loyalties. Like these latter, Josip the ever-striding adheres to a politics whose sole aim is to contest the limitations of his flesh, expanding its capacities in tandem with those of his mind.

But what am I striving for, my beloved? he asks the sea. *Where am I going? And what am I, really? For I am neither a giant nor a swallow, though my companions tell me I am a giant, and voices from the past tell me I am a swallow.*

But the sea does not reply in words comprehensible to man, for the sea informs its devotees by swelling and receding in cyclic rhythms without ceasing, its waves spreading toward the outermost reaches of the world until the end of time. It will permit neither analysis nor mental capture, for, as he knows full well from his studies, a dot at the exact center of a circle cannot enclose the circle.

Such musings, among countless others with which he entertains himself, are pleasurable. They are never fully conclusive. It is enough to enjoy the presence of the elements in fathomless forms and volumes, to savor the way they stimulate states of consciousness in which such ponderings float to the surface and give him release from the realm of the specific, precisely because they are not logical.

Do you know that I love you? he asks the sea. *How can one not fall in love with one's liberator! Is your determined pattern an equation properly stated? Is love itself the liberator, or are the messengers of love mistaken for the one who sends them?*

He shakes off the thought. In that direction lies the return of sentiments, doubts, and loneliness. He loves solitude. He loves the interior. He dislikes intensely the habits of mind and emotion that dominate his fellow students. It seems that he is immune. Yet for all his dislike, he will not take issue with their beliefs or nonbeliefs—to do so in this country is a futile exercise—he simply avoids it all.

Josip now removes his socks and running shoes, and stretches out on the rock and closes his eyes. The radiant sun rises from its base in Bosnia, over the crests of the mountain range, and floods the city. Sweat has soaked the jersey and shorts of his soccer uniform. He shivers a little, though within minutes the combat between the sun and the sea breeze is over, and the sun has won. It burns his cheeks and warms his limbs, the bare arms and legs and wiggling toes soaking it up hungrily. His body stretches luxuriously, the heartbeat is slowing now, the heaving of his chest subsiding.

How does one put an end to all this growth! It is conspicuous to be so tall. People notice and want to see what is inside; they especially want to probe what is in the mind.

During his first year he could hardly focus on his studies. All the beautiful, beautiful girls, everywhere around him. And so many interested in him! His metamorphosed appearance, no doubt, transformed by those years of swimming during high school, the summer work as a laborer on the Jablonica dam, the muscles, his clear skin and golden hair, perhaps even his diffidence—a persona onto which the lonely can project anything they like. People always seem to fall in love with an image first, never the substance, for to know the substance of man would spell the end of the human race within a generation. Well, perhaps not. But certainly the end of marriage, and not long thereafter, the end of civilization.

Hard to say if this surmise is true or not. The only certainty is that people simply will not stop falling in love, and he is as guilty as the rest of them. During that first year and well into the second, there were three girls: a Communist, an unaligned atheist, and a Catholic—all beautiful. The first and the second were interested in going to bed, and then maybe afterward to the state ceremonies that would have chained him to their beds indefinitely. As much as he yearned for the former, the threat of the latter corollary kept him chaste. The third girl, Suzana, was different: nonpredatory, intelligent, and even humble, a student of literature. He really liked her—no, to be honest, he was intoxicated and obsessed with her for months. Neither he nor she was completely dominated by desire for sexual expression, for they both were certain that their feelings for each other were absolutely the most singular outpouring of mutual human love in the history of mankind—to consummate it prematurely would weaken it. They had kissed a few times. So unexpected that pleasure. Well, they had respected each other right to the end, she for religious reasons, and he because, well, because he was torn with longing for the union but repelled by what it might cost. Human love always brings ecstasy and anguish, he told himself at the time. The ecstasy is the bait, the anguish is the snap of the trap. In the end, they parted because their differences were hurting them too much. He told her he could not go back to the ways of his childhood, and she told him with copious tears that in her heart of hearts she could not marry a man who did not love Christ. This was startling, shocking really, but it was good that it resolved the dilemma.

Since then, for a year and a half, he has not fallen in love. He repels all probes, makes none of his own. Early warning signals of potential love slam into the wall of his apparent distraction. His face registers nothing, responds neither appropriately nor inappropriately. It is as if he has not noticed the overtures, and in this way he remains the catalyst of small disappointments but never the cause of offence. He is the quiet guy, the strong and gentle, smart and disconnected guy who seems to wish everyone well as he lumbers down the faculty hallways with a goofy look and a stack of books wedged under his armpit. Only occasionally is another tactic needed: with commissars pressuring students to join the Party, it is necessary to glaze his eyes, drop his jaw, breathe noisily through his mouth, and in the worst cases, drool a little. The drool always works.

Total isolation is kept at bay by camaraderie on the soccer field with his rowdy teammates, and also with a smaller fraternity of swimmers, some of whom are like him in temperament. To this must be added the fascinating discussions with impassioned math majors, who are stimulated not so much by sports or sex but by problems in quantum mechanics. Though Josip is not a humorous person generally, the soccer guys have taught him to banter and to play, the swimmers have given him a quieter community of fellow solitaries, and the math people have enabled him to foresee a future in which it is possible to function successfully without political or emotional commitment.

Now the breeze stiffens, the sun is directly overhead. The day will be hot, and his clothes are drying. He sits up and gazes out beyond the tip of Čiovo, toward the larger and more distant islands of Šolta and Brač. Today there is a yellow-orange haze on the water, and the islands float on it like purple ships. In the middle distance, a tiny vessel coasts northward; only its sail is visible, a white triangle cutting through the saffron.

In that instant, he recalls the journey he made with his father to the sea when he was a child. He was eight or nine years old at the time. It was during the war, the Italians were still here, the Germans were still in the east, and the Partisans were still an unthinkable specter of the future. This memory never fails to elicit a constricting of his throat, a moistening of the eyes. He tries not to recall it in detail and permits only a brief replay of a vague sense of ocean and vast spaces, the golden light beneath the waves, two mighty hands pulling him back to the realm of open air, a bird that landed on his fingers for a second or two, and a sailing ship—commanded by Odysseus, he was sure.

Enough! He slips on his shoes, ties them with trembling hands, which he soon brings under control, steadies his thoughts, and jumps to his feet. Saluting his lover the sea, he turns and runs back down the mountain.

The following Saturday: he awakes with a feeling of affection for his little cell, which is situated on the fourth floor of a concrete tenement on the uphill side of Velebitska. He would like to take a shower, but usually at this time of day there will be a lineup for the bathroom down the hall. The crucial plumbing is shared by the residents of the eight apartments on this floor. Despite its limitations, he loves his room, three meters wide and four meters long. It contains the usual items: a cot and mattress, sheets and a pillow. A sink and tap. A wooden desk and chair, a hotplate and kettle. His few articles of clothing are hung from nails on the door. He has not yet been able to purchase planks for proper shelving on which to house the growing collection of books, which are stacked along the walls and in little piles here and there. A striped goat-hair rug, orange and white, relieves the gray décor with some color, augmented by magazine photos taped to the walls—mostly scenes of the Adriatic islands. The single window opens onto the docks of the inlet behind the city. Across the water he can see the miniscule amphitheater of ancient Solin, where he once played soccer with a group of street boys.

He has been reading Aristotle since dawn. The integration of science and philosophy is intriguing. Modern thought divides them. Why? Is a philosophy of mathematics possible? Needed? If so, why? If not, why not? Thinking about these intricate problems, he hops about the room on one leg trying to get the other leg into his running shorts. Mind and body—are they possessions of the self, or are they the self?

Dressed, he ties his running shoes, bolts out the door, thunders down the staircase, and bursts onto the street. Turning left he begins to trot, and then he breaks into a gallop, feeling the familiar exhilaration flood his body, his chest expanding, his lips pulling back into a grin. He waves at students he knows and excuses himself as he swerves around the matrons and elderly people trudging toward the markets.

He likes to vary his route to the base of the Marjan, and this day he decides to pass through streets that will offer him more challenges: a maze of narrow cobbled lanes within the palace complex, where there will be less space, less predictability, and more people, all of which will demand instant reflexes at high speed; in short, not only animal power but intelligence. So, through the north gate he plunges, hitting no one in passing, though there are a few near misses—people, unless they are deaf, tend to move to the side at the sound of galloping hoofs. It is the sharp turns into side streets that offer the best perils, because you never know what you will meet, be it man or beast or myth.

He turns left, right, left again, heading in a more or less constant direction toward the east gate, which will bring him to the great market on Zagrebačka Street. From there he will turn onto the waterfront promenade and break into top speed toward the base of the Marjan. And then, running uphill, accelerating even as he must ease his pace, he will arrive at the highest point of the city, from which he will once more survey the entire world in a state of exultation.

Before he has reached the east gate, however, he turns into one last side street, only to find his way blocked by a cluster of old women who have their heads together over an article of baby clothing that one of them has knit and is proudly showing to the others. He screeches to a halt and waits until they notice him. They can hardly ignore him! He is a massive slab of presence, sweating and huffing and puffing, hands on hips, pawing the cobblestones with his hooves. He will not push past them, frail and deserving of respect as they are. His clearing of throat and request for passage through is ignored, perhaps not even heard. These women can focus! A flash of yellow catches the corner of his eye. He glances at it.

In a shop window, by his right arm, stands a display of antique items and folk art. On a shelf in its center is a toy sailing ship. Its hull is painted bright yellow, its bow and stern carved in the bold curves of Dalmatian fishing boats. Its sails are made of white cotton, and its rigging is fashioned from red thread. A miniature black net is coiled on its deck. A wooden fish lies beside it. A tiny captain stands at the wheel, his face turned to hail passersby.

Josip stares at it a few moments. Then he bursts into tears. Covering his face with his hands, he sobs loudly and uncontrollably. The old women fall silent and stare at him with open mouths. They part to let him pass. He does not see them. He wheels and runs straightway back to his room.

It is the kitchen at home. The time is a few months after his first journey to the sea. Snow is falling in the dark outside the window. His mother is baking bread for the coming Christmas, bustling around the room, muttering about the wet firewood that they forgot to cover after the sunny day was over, little realizing that a heavy snowfall was about to ruin things. Now the wood that should be dry has become wet, and the heat it produces is not quite right. Don't fuss, says his father, your bread is so great and unique with its secret spice that no man would refuse it even if it turned into charcoal. She kisses him on one cheek and pinches the other, and then they laugh together. His father is seated at the table, drawing something with pencil on a sheet of paper.

"What are you doing, Tata?"

"A secret, Josip", says Miro, covering the paper with his forearm.

"Is it a Christmas secret?"

"Yes, it is."

"Is it a secret you wish to keep from me?"

"Yes, certainly", his father smiles. "What else!"

"And that is why you will not tell me what you are doing on the paper?"

"You have deduced correctly."

"Oh, my Tata", the boy croons, sidling up to his father, rubbing shoulders, and rolling his eyes in a way that is considered charming and irresistible. "Oh, *please*, please tell me, my Tata!"

"Never!" barks his father, though it is his joking bark.

Early the next morning, Josip climbs down the ladder from the loft. His parents are still sleeping. He lights the candle in the dawn and goes prowling though the parlor in search of the secret. He feels a little guilty about this, but he is desperate to know what his father was doing last night. A piece of paper cannot be a Christmas gift, so it must be *thoughts* about the gift. To know these thoughts would not entirely ruin the surprise. It might even increase the pleasure—so he justifies it to himself.

Under a stack of his father's school papers, on the floor beneath the family altar, he finds the piece of paper. It is a drawing of a lovely sailing ship. Tata must have used Mamica's egg paints to color it. Its hull is yellow, its sails are white, and a small captain stands at a wheel. Written at the bottom of the sheet is: *This year or next, for my Josip. In memory of our journey to the sea.*

Beneath this, the words: *"My father, time will show you what my spirit is." The Odyssey. Book XVI.*

This is very nice but somewhat puzzling. He hides the paper again and never mentions it. That Christmas, Josip is not given the drawing as a gift. Nor does he receive it on his feast day, March 19, nor at any other likely celebration. From time to time, it comes to his mind like a fine idea that has been abandoned. *This year or next* could mean anything. Perhaps his father intends to take him on a second journey. Perhaps it means something else that cannot be understood until it has happened. The mystery becomes clear one day in January of 1945, when Josip is rummaging through the house in search of a missing sock. Perhaps Mamica has stuffed it into her sewing basket and intends to darn it with wool when she has a free moment. She usually keeps the basket beneath her bed. On hands and knees he peers under, finds no basket and no sock. However, he spots a wooden box on father's side of the bed. He has never seen this box before. Crawling farther under, he tips the box sideways so he can look inside. It contains a little wooden sailing ship, the carving of its hull nearly completed, unpainted, not yet smoothed of splinters. There is also a spool of black thread, a wad of white cloth, and the old drawing. Josip crawls out from under the bed with a smile on his face and says nothing to anyone about his discovery. Three weeks later, the Partisans come to Rajska Polja.

Recurring sorrows, memory erupting into consciousness. He understands why it happens. He is not entirely its victim, for he recovers from it more quickly than he did during his younger years. Even so, it can still afflict him when he least expects it. It is triggered by certain colors or a strand of song floating on the night wind, the strum of a bandura, the sight of a mother and father and young son walking side by side on the promenade, anything too close to what once was. In such moments, the blow of a hatchet splits his rib cage, and agony pours from the severed arteries. Whenever this occurs, he is able to bring it under control by changing his thoughts, and then he is slowly able to change his emotions. It passes. Such incidents are becoming less frequent as years go by. Life goes on. It must. That's the way with human beings, and like it or not, he's part of the species. Besides, others have suffered far worse than he has.

After he left Sarajevo to enter the university in Split, he returned for only a single summer to live with Aunt Eva. Before that, they lived together for six years in the same dingy apartment, though Josip helped to make it less desolate as he grew older. Salvaged wood and cloth turned a part of the main room into a bedchamber for him. Its walls gradually filled with photographs clipped from newspapers and magazines. Pictures of the Adriatic islands, fish and birds, sunlight and seagoing ships—emblems of escape and transcendence. The badges from his school swimming club, which Eva displayed proudly to anyone who came calling. His graduation certificate from high school. The letter announcing his scholarship to the university.

The death of his uncle was never mentioned again. Numerous were the times, after Josip's sanity returned, when he pondered the single burning image that could never be erased: Eva, seated at the end of the bed, rocking her body back and forth; Jure, lying as if asleep, his finger on the trigger, the barrel in his mouth, the top of his skull blown off. Has he destroyed himself, this man of laughing callousness? Or has she killed him? Has she grown frantic about Josip's week-long absence and come to believe that her husband disposed of the boy permanently and is lying about it? He has killed many people, told many lies—thus, why would he not eliminate this interloper whom he hates so much? Did she come upon her husband as he was sleeping, drunk and open-mouthed, insert the barrel of the gun gently into the unsuspecting mouth, and pull the trigger? Did she calmly arrange the gun, the arms, and the finger, so that she would not become the third victim?

Guilty or innocent of murder, she must have been shaken by Josip's return nearly as much as by the death of her husband. Nevertheless, both she and the boy make an unspoken agreement that Jure will never again be mentioned. He did not exist. What happened has not happened, as so many other events have not happened. In order to continue living, they must forget the past with an absoluteness that permits no conjecture. Truth and falsehood alike must serve the necessity of survival.

And so it is. The first three or four years are hard, cold, hungry, and full of fears, especially in the period before Tito's break with Stalin, before the beginning of reforms. This is the time when silence is added to silence, when Josip learns never to speak about matters beyond the immediate and the physical, nor to infer them either. He is a poor student in the fields that are the most important to the new order, that is, politics and history. This might have ended any hope of advancement in education, yet so brilliant is he in the field of mathematics that the state decides his abilities may someday prove useful to the country. He is not exactly an *idiot savant*; rather, he is somewhat lopsided in personality and missing a component of his mind, the part that is so crucial to governments. He is simply not interested in those matters, and thus in the files of anyone to whom Josip's life is a concern, the boy, the youth, and the young man are officially harmless.

During those years in Sarajevo, his chief pleasure, after fishing, is soccer. The physical exhilaration pushes out despondency and can even banish certain thoughts for a time. Swimming is a deeper matter, a private one, yet it seems to hold his interest more than anything else, save mathematics. Thousands of hours are spent in midstream of the Miljacka and the Bosna, pitting his limbs against the force of the rivers with exterior calm and inner ferocity. Year after year he grows stronger, no longer skeletal but muscular and lean. It is now easier to obtain work with such strength. Mostly physical labor at construction sites. Later, he has the job at the Jablonica Dam, which he obtains through Eva's influence. He saves every coin he earns, after subtracting what he gives to his aunt as a contribution for their food and rent. Not that she needs it, she assures him, not with her new wages, since she is rising in the secretariat and is a consultant on labor matters to the Ministry. She forces him to stop giving her his wages. Save it for the future! You have your future to think of! You *are* the future!

He loves her and fears her. Or perhaps it is not she whom he fears, but the secrets she holds within herself, the events in which she played a central role and that cannot be spoken of, for they did not happen. There is a grayness that, at unexpected moments, can return to her skin and her eyes, and during those few days he is shut out. Nothing will reach her, she will not acknowledge his presence. This seldom occurs, only two or three times a year, and hardly at all during the year before he departs for Split. Occasionally, she is flushed with happiness, an animation that has its cause in places other than home. She has men but sees them elsewhere. She is like a true mother, very good to him, and she asks nothing in return. For this he is grateful, but still he fears her.

During those years, physics and chemistry begin to interest him, too. Also astronomy. Without knowing it, he is integrating the disciplines of astronomy, mathematics, and physics into a zone of astrophysics with metaphysical innuendos. When he is able to jot down on pieces of paper his intuitions about this emerging sense of reality, they manifest themselves as phrases that, even to their author, have a certain beauty. He would not dare to call them poems. They are not poems, and he certainly no longer entertains any interest in a world beyond this one. Yet he does not dismiss these fragments out of hand. He feels that they may at some point in the future find their place in a purely physical cosmology that he hopes to develop. First, he must learn more.

He is, without doubt, the city's most outstanding student, a distinction that means nothing to him but does not go unnoticed by educators. He is observed and considered for various avenues into a brighter future than the one available for him in the capital of Bosnia. He gives all the right answers in the sciences, yet so many wrong ones in sociopolitical studies. Not suspiciously wrong, just off the mark, and never reactionary, but usually just plain stupid or vapid, enough to indicate to concerned officials that he is a pleasant fellow with some potential for mainstream life in the new Yugoslavia. He will neither sink to the dangerous bottom nor rise to the dangerous top.

During Josip's second winter at university in Split, Eva married the foreman from the factory, who had recently divorced his wife. They had thereafter become influential in the endless maze of workers' committees and moved to Belgrade. Eva explained it all in a letter, but it seemed meaningless to Josip, who, strangely, felt some relief at the departure of his aunt to a region of the country where it would be difficult and unnecessary for him to go. He and his aunt wrote back and forth several times, always with avowals of fidelity and gratitude. She had saved his life more than once, and perhaps he had saved hers as well. In the end, the letters became fewer in number, and now he receives a card or two per year, filled with scribbled generalities, usually dated the first of May or November 29, the anniversary of Tito's proclamation of the People's Democracy.

At one point during the first years of living on his own, he located the convent of nuns that he had visited as a child. All religious insignia had been removed or defaced and the building transformed into an office for functionaries of a federal ministry. The secretary at the front desk knew nothing (she assured him) of the whereabouts of the former owners. His persistent questions earned him a cold look and a hand on a telephone. He fled from the place and never returned. Every subsequent effort he made to locate Sister Katarina of the Holy Angels turned up nothing. In his second year, he chanced to overhear a muffled conversation at a stall in the market: two old women huddling with hands on their breasts, bemoaning the loss of many religious throughout the land. One told the other how much she missed visiting her dear friends, the Sisters on Stanislavska Street—the very convent where his aunt had lived. "They were all arrested or scattered", said the other. "I watched them being taken away, and none have returned."

Thus he is alone in the world. During the past four years, Split has been his home. From his residence, it is a twenty-minute run to the faculty of mathematics, a fifteen-minute run to the library, a half-hour run to the top of the Marjan. In the summer there is always employment at the university. Combined with his scholarships, his wages permit him the extravagance of solitude. Few non-Communists are as privileged as he is, and few are as alone. He does not mind this aloneness. He prefers it. The life of the mind, the dreams of the sea, and the little black notebook filled with his intuitions and questions—which he has titled *Fragments*—are enough for him.

He has begun work on his graduate degree. He has dropped soccer because there is not enough time to do everything. Swimming cannot be abandoned, however, because it is essential to the foundation of his consciousness. It *must* not be abandoned, even if he were to feel like doing so. It keeps him physically healthy and balances the mental abstractions. Besides, there are those infrequent discussions with fellow solitary swimmers that he is slowly coming to value. From time to time, he inscribes random thoughts and dialogues in his notebook:

Fragment:

Today, in a shop window, I saw a most beautiful thing. It was a large seashell, cut in half so that its spiral interior is exposed. It is called the "chambered nautilus". Nature's powers are so endlessly ingenious that one must take care not to assume one knows where its outermost (and innermost) frontiers are located.

Fragment:

Ivan Radoš at the biology faculty recently urged me to put my eye to a microscope. There, below the strata of human vision, is a realm of astonishing complexity and order. "They're diatoms", says Ivan in my ear, breathing the words as if he were an Old Testament prophet delivering a revelation. Well, I must admit it is a revelation. One that prompts a question: Are there other realms within realms within these realms? Why, moreover, do such marvels strike human consciousness as beautiful?

Fragment:

Theorem: If beauty is cleaved from immortality, will not the materialist devaluation of human love extract a dreadful price?

Corollary: If love is cleaved from immortality, will not the materialist devaluation of beauty also extract a dreadful price?

Conclusion: Without the eternal, all things, all beings, are devalued. Yes, but is immortality real? If it is real, then our present condition in this land seems more horrible than ever. If it is not real, then there is only survival, pleasure, and betrayal.

Fragment:

Is there a primal injury? The injury of mankind? The injury of my own life?

Fragment:

I have been thinking of Telemachus today. The Greeks, as far as they were able and considering the times they lived in, seemed to understand the relationship between heroism and weakness better than we do. The young prince is suffering on two fronts, exterior and interior. His father has been missing since he sailed off to Troy. His mother is besieged by callous suitors, each of whom desires the queen only for the sake of taking the king's property for himself. Telemachus realizes he is too young to protect his mother and his home adequately, and thus he decides to sail off in search of Odysseus, to bring him back to defend his family and his throne. For this, Telemachus needs help from the elders of Ithaca. He dresses himself in dazzling armor, arms himself with a bronze spear, holds his head high, and strides to the agora, where he intends to deliver a stirring speech that cannot fail to rouse support for his quest. The crowd is impressed by him. He begins his impassioned and eloquent pleas—then bursts into tears! His sorrows, frustration, and anger have overcome him. The crowd is no longer impressed with this sobbing boy, whom they had at first taken for a god. Such is the judgment of men. They are never to be trusted. One must never invest hope in their nobler qualities.

Fragment:

Three theories of the material cosmos: the solid state universe, the perpetually expanding universe, the oscillating universe. The latter model, an endlessly repeated cycle of collapse and expansion, appeals to the fatalistic mind. Well, I admit it appeals to me. At the same time, an inner note of caution: something warns me not to jump to conclusions. There may be more models to come, ones that human intellect cannot yet conceive.

10

Today, as Josip is drying himself after the practice swim for next week's meet, Antun Kusić snaps his wet towel at him. Josip gives him the same in return, and makes him howl.

"Lasta", says Antun, "I'll pay you back for that. Or I'll take my dues in your valuable time."

Antun is his match in the hundred meters and a better diver. He is a good fellow. Josip trusts him—as much as he is able, considering the times they live in.

"Make your offer, Kusić, but I don't promise I'll pay."

"Come with me for coffee. I need to talk with you."

This is new. They can talk anywhere, so why a special invitation? They go to the bistro on Partisanska where the poets and *rakija* addicts hang out. He has never been there before, but it seems Antun is an old familiar. He finds a table in a shadow, where no ears are close enough to make trouble. They drink tiny cups of coffee so strong that Josip knows he will not sleep for forty-eight hours afterward. But he is curious. Has Antun lost his mind over a girl again? The last one broke his heart, and now it appears to have mended completely, within days.

"You're in love again", Josip says.

"In a sense."

"With anyone I know?"

He shakes his head. "No, it's not a person."

"Not a person", Josip laughs. "What then?"

"With a way of . . ."

Ten seconds, twenty seconds, thirty seconds . . .

"Come on, tell me. You can't leave me hanging in space like that."

Antun leans forward earnestly. His narrow swarthy face and bristling black hair, cut short for gliding through water, remind Josip of Petar Dučić. His eyes are jet black. Today they are not laughing as they usually are. He is in his intense mood.

"Can I trust you?" he whispers. Josip hates it when people whisper to him and hates it when he is forced to whisper to them. If you're whispering, he believes, you're making a mistake about something or other.

"No, Kusić, you *cannot* trust me!"

"Good, now I know I can trust you."

"What's the secret?"

"Shhh," he puts a finger to his lips, "for heaven's sake, don't shout!" Josip was of course speaking in his normal voice, not shouting at all.

"So, tell me."

"Lasta," he says looking Josip in the eye, "do you believe it is possible to speak a language other than one's native tongue."

Josip bursts out laughing. "Without a doubt."

"I don't mean German or Italian. I mean—"

"Oh, you mean sign language? Just now you put your finger to your lips, Kusić. That was an item from a vocabulary."

"Nonsense, it's a universal symbol. Stop distracting me. I mean is it possible to speak an undiscovered language?"

"What do you mean? How can you speak an undiscovered language if you have not discovered it?"

"Exactly."

"What do you mean by *exactly*? Be more specific. Define your terms."

"Aaargh, you scientists!"

"Well, thank you for the coffee, I must be going now. I won't hit you with the towel again."

"Sit down, sit down. I want to talk."

"Is our discussion not yet over?"

"It has not yet begun."

Intrigued, Josip continues listening. It turns out that Antun has been watching him for three years. Not the political observation they must all endure, but something different. Maybe the assessing of personal reliability and unreliability that everyone makes about others in the privacy of their thoughts.

Antun says that he has known for some time that Josip is not sympathetic to the regime.

Josip replies with dead silence, completely masked. Where is Antun going with this? Is he the cleverest trap of all?

"I hate it", Antun declares. "I hate everything they do to us."

"What are they doing to us?" Josip asks with a small smile and a neutral tone that commits nothing. Still, poor Antun cannot stop himself.

"Look, Jozo," he says, leaning closer and moving to a new level of intimacy, "when you lose your place in the continuity of time, you become extremely dependent on the social."

This is quite an insight from his locker-room pal. A Literature major he may be, but Josip thought he studied Goethe and Gorky and the more anti-imperialist novels of Dostoevsky.

"What do you mean by the social?" he asks, in no way convinced that Antun is genuine. Perhaps he has political troubles, social debts of the more dangerous sort, and is paying them off by informing. Is it a routine fishing expedition or something more serious?

"We forget our history", he continues. "Maybe we never learn our history, like these kids they're teaching nowadays. You and me, at least, we learned a few things before the—"

"Before our beloved Marshal Tito liberated us?"

Antun sits back, his cheeks flushing. His mouth twitches, he clenches a fist and thumps it soundlessly on the table top. His eyes now blink rapidly, close to tears.

"Beloved you call them", he whispers. "Do you love them too, Josip?"

Love them? While it is possible to evade, it is not possible for Josip to lie directly. He lowers his eyes and shakes his head.

"They killed half my family, you know", Antun goes on. "In death pits, in the north. No one has ever heard about that, but I heard about it because an uncle climbed out of one of those pits and left a trail of his blood across Slovenia and as far as Zagreb. There he told his story before he died."

"People say many things", Josip murmurs, growing more afraid and ashamed with each passing moment. He is choking, but he cannot let the other see this. What if the police are searching for leaks about the great slaughter. They know that Jure was one of the executioners, and they know Josip lived in his apartment before his death.

"I was in the room when he died", Antun declares. "Do you think a dying man would cling to a crucifix and lie through his teeth?"

"I don't believe in heaven", Josip tells him.

"But my uncle did", Kusić breathes vehemently. "My uncle did!"

"Look, Antun", says Josip in a conciliatory tone, opening his hands wide on the table top. "Whatever happened back there in the past, there's nothing we can do about it."

"You're wrong, Josip, and moreover you know you're wrong. And moreover still, you don't have to worry about my being an informer. I'm not. I'm clean and I'm safe. And as far as *they* are concerned, I'm just an average guy who's pleased about the state of the country. The uncle who died was Domobrani, but another one, who is very much alive, was Partisan. A Communist uncle in my dossier gives me some protection."

"I have one of those, too. A hero."

"A hero", Antun bites off the word so bitterly that no one could ever mistake it for a performance. Suddenly Josip is sure—though he does not know how he is sure—that this is not a trap.

"We should go for a walk", he whispers. He does not mind whispering now.

Out on the street, he whacks Antun on the back. But his friend is in no mood for play fights, and he says nothing for a block or two as they idle their way over the city hump toward the old town core. No one is following them.

"The continuity of time", Josip says, trying to get things moving along. "What did you mean by that?"

"I mean they've erased our history and are rewriting what remains. I mean, as well, that whole zones of literature are now forbidden and are disappearing from libraries. And who knows what else is missing. The entire field of newspaper and radio is their toy. Toy? No, it's their weapon! They fill our minds with whatever they want us to think."

"The older people remember."

"Yes, but most are frightened. Hundreds of thousands of people have disappeared. And before he disappeared, a man whom I trust, a professor in Zagreb, told me that a quarter of a million Croats are either in prison or facing trials. The cardinal of Zagreb is in prison, too."

"They can't really do that, can they? A cardinal in prison?"

"They've done it. A big political trial—he was archbishop then—lots of false evidence against him. He spent five years in a jail cell, and then they commuted his sentence to permanent house arrest. They will probably kill him. He is a brave man. Don't believe the papers when you read that he's a Fascist criminal."

"But how can we know what is true and untrue?"

"Exactly—how can we know? And we are knowing less and less with every passing day. But of this man you can be sure, he is the best, and what they say about him is untrue. He is the real Croatia. He is one of the true heroes."

"His name?"

"Stepinac."

The name is new to Josip. But then he does not read the regime's vile newspapers or listen to their vile radio programs.

"I don't recall having heard of him."

"You see—erasure. Erasure! You, a mathematician, will understand the concept of a negative as positive function, right? You will understand, at least, the power of subtraction."

Josip is beginning to realize there is a lot more to Antun than he had supposed.

"I too lost family", he whispers as they round a corner onto the waterfront.

"Who killed them?"

The question that is always asked: Who killed whom? The answer identifies you fairly accurately, and it locates your place in the political continuum.

"Partisans did it", says Josip. "They killed everyone I loved—everyone."

"But—"

"By an accident of fate, my Communist uncle—no, I cannot describe all that. It's too complex and too insane. You wouldn't believe me anyway."

"Josip, there is no need to explain. I know how things go. It is *all* too complex and insane, those times—"

"And now we have a new insanity."

"Yes, and that is why we need a new language."

"What exactly do you mean by a new language?"

"I mean new ways of communicating the truth. Not just data, not just information—Truth!"

"Yes, but what do you mean by truth?"

"That has been asked before, you know."

"Let's stay on the topic. Are you suggesting we need a black-market history to hand out to every student in Yugoslavia?"

"That's not a bad idea, but it's not what I'm thinking of. I believe that in our times the control of all public communications, all education, and all public culture is creating a new consciousness in our people, and as a result they will become less and less able to comprehend the truth, let alone remember it. Our strength in the future will depend on those with faith, especially the ones who remain in their churches, as they always have. But not everyone is a believer. In fact, the state is making it harder and harder."

"Are you a believer in Christ?" asks Josip, eyeing him carefully.

"Yes," he nods, "but I must remain quiet about it. Not everyone is quiet about it, and they are heroes too. I am not a hero, Josip. I hope someday to be a writer, but I am damned if it's going to be poems about tractor production and novels about life on the collectives!"

"Lower your voice, Antun."

"Sorry."

"So, you're saying that—"

"I'm saying that through genuine culture man can know himself, even in nations where his identity is denied."

"But what do you mean by *genuine* culture?"

"The beautiful and true! In music, in poetry, in literature, even in novels without political or historical references, we can apprehend what is not immediately known through rational thought or the accumulation of objective facts."

"Antun, you're investing too much faith in culture. Does culture have the power to liberate man from overwhelming historical forces?"

"Culture is the last refuge, the sanctuary, the human place in the midst of the surrounding dehumanization. Through the arts man is able to know himself, even if only on the intuitive level. He senses his own worth, even when he cannot articulate it."

"Can a poem or a song defeat a tyrant?"

Defeat a killer, defeat atrocities, defeat the bottom falling out of the universe when you least expect it?

"Yes. Yes, it can, given enough time. When a work of art is

both beautiful and true, man's freedom is strengthened by it—both his interior need for freedom and his capacity to seek a rational understanding of it."

"You hope for a lot."

"Yes, I hope for it. And if I didn't, I would die of despair."

"You are a person of extremes", Josip says, not unkindly.

"Am I? I suppose so. But which is more extreme, a man who desires to speak the truth in a season of lies or a tyrant who creates the lies that engulf an entire people?"

Josip nods in agreement.

"Why are you telling me all this, Antun? I respect you, and to tell the truth, I like you a lot, I always have, even though you're pretty fast with the wet towel, but I do not see what I can do about it."

"You are a poet, Josip."

Josip stops in his tracks and laughs outright. A poet? That is ridiculous!

"A *poet*?"

"Yes, you are a poet. Regardless of what you think." Antun pauses, and looks at Josip somberly, a world of grief and hope within his eyes. "You are."

Later, Josip forgets much of what they talk about after this stunningly erroneous statement. Suffice it to say that at various times during the past few years Antun has overheard him discussing with others any number of subjects, ranging from stellar constellations to oceanography to theories of wave motion. He has mistaken Josip's cryptic minimalism for poetic inspiration. They argue this for an hour while sitting side by side on a cement wall at the harbor front, their legs dangling over the water. Josip defends himself vehemently. Antun asserts ferociously, defining *Josip* to himself, of all things!

Demanding proof of Antun's theory, Josip makes him regurgitate some of his memorable sayings.

"Two years ago, you were talking with a professor in the

225

hallway outside the science lab", says Antun like a trial lawyer. "Remember?"

Josip shakes his head, frowns.

"Sure you remember. I'd come to pick you up for the practice swim, and you made us late. You told the prof that the sea is a cosmos and the cosmos is a sea."

"So? Einstein suggests something similar in his theory of—"

"Yes, but Einstein didn't say it the way you said it."

"A fluke, an accident of speech."

"A stroke of poetic intuition."

"Please, enough!"

"Then at the party Suzana brought you to last year, you went head-to-head with that idiot from the history department. I thought you were being quite rash that night, taking him on, but then I remembered that you have the mantle of science to protect you and are widely known as a nonpolitical cretin of the first order."

"Thank you so much, Antun."

"You didn't say anything you could be arrested for. But I knew what you were saying, and a few others knew too, and it electrified us. We were frightened for you, and at the same time we were in awe of the beauty of your words. No mole with his head buried in Pythagorean theorems could come up with phrases like that."

"What on earth did I say, if it was so earth-shattering?"

"Don't you remember? The idiot was babbling about monetary policy, and a professor from the faculty of economics was sitting right beside him, and they were both knocking back the *slivovica*. It was pretty loud in there, with everyone singing, dancing, and the radio blasting. The economics parrot was agreeing with the history parrot, both of them looking after their own hides, you can be sure. And you just kept listening to them, staring into space, your eyes glazed, and when they'd finished their song and dance in praise of Tito's reforms, you said, 'Words are gold, split and shared as coinage, small pebbles, emblems offered back and forth—given, received; given, received—expanding the vocabulary of the soul.'"

"I said that? I don't recall saying that."

"You said it. It came from your very own mouth."

"I was probably quoting something I'd read."

"No, you weren't."

So the discussion rages on, with Antun supplying more of the golden ambrosia that apparently drips like warm honey from Josip's lips.

He begins to recall the night of the party more clearly. The words did just spring to his lips. Who knows where they came from, from what dusty corner of his mind? It does not matter. He is not a poet!

At the end of their Marathon conversation—or is it Thermopylae?—Antun invites Josip to become part of a small, "intimate and private" group of people who hope to produce an "alternative culture", as he phrases it.

Josip declines. He says he admires them for it, but it's not for him.

Fragment:

> He pushed hard to get me to join them. But what is all this pushing, all this desperate intensity! Should poetry push itself into the agoras of the world? No, poetry does not push. It simply is present, radiating its virtues. By the same token, is a word more than itself? Is a symbol both itself and what it signifies? A chambered nautilus and a diatom are integrated and compact in themselves. They are what they are, yet they remain as presences in the world and may point to some larger cosmology, despite their small stature. Subtract them from existence, and the world is poorer. Perhaps this applies to individual people as well. Antun *is* who he is, yet he may

point, without knowing it, to something greater. Not so much by what he believes or says, but rather by what he is. I must think more about this.

* * *

Memories continue to afflict him from time to time. Often the worst, and not so often the best. Between these two poles there are others, the inexplicable:

It is nine or ten years ago. In Sarajevo the winter has come and gone. He and Eva are hungry all the time because, even though her wages have increased, money is numbers on paper. Then and now, food is real currency. It always has been and always will be.

He has come up out of the river on a spring day. The valley bottom is warm, though the heights of the surrounding mountains are still white with snow. He dries himself off, gets dressed, and then walks from the river into the lower hills, hoping he will find a field where a farmer might have forgotten to dig up every potato plant. The pastures are dotted with isolated hay cones; black from the spring rains, they stand like ominous sentinels above the city. Then he comes upon a plowed field, the soil wet, rust-colored. He takes off his shoes and slowly crosses the field, searching for dead stems of potato plants, beneath which a few tubers might still be sleeping. There are none.

He stops in the middle of the field, enjoying the feel of earth beneath his bare feet, the mud oozing up between his toes. As he watches it slip and curl and rise toward his ankles, the sun comes out, and the rust turns to red. Suddenly, he sees that his feet are sinking in bloody gore. He knows it is only soil, but he shouts in terror and tries to pull his feet out at once. This trips him and he falls backward. Then the weight of his body pushes him into the blood, and it begins to suck him down. He flips over onto his belly and scrambles on hands and knees to the edge of the field. There he lies on the grass and sobs uncontrollably.

Why can he not forget? Why do these memories return? Are they pushing for resolution, explanation? Or does a consciousness higher than his own try to show him important things— even those he would rather not see?

Sarajevo again. He is sixteen or seventeen years old. That year, the gymnasium is given a single telescope. One small instrument for two or three hundred students. The time allotted for each is not much, but those few moments at the lens are worth years of waiting. He spends days preparing for his brief glimpse into the universe, reading star maps, devouring books on astrophysics, lying on the apartment roof for hours in the dark, staring upward. Finally, the night arrives for his class. Each student is given two minutes at the telescope. They can point it anywhere in the sky they want to look.

When his turn comes, he knows what to do. He turns the barrel to Andromeda, a spiral galaxy countless light-years away, the closest major galaxy to our own. For the first time, he sees infinity with his eyes, almost feels it in his flesh. The light from that spinning wheel of fire pours through the glass lens, inverts through the organic lens of his eye, burns an image into his brain. Then, with only half a minute remaining, he turns the telescope to the constellation Pegasus. During those final seconds of seeing, he hears galloping hooves and feels himself rising on the back of a white horse. Then a hand grabs the instrument and barks, "Next!"

The following morning, he is wandering in a woods north of the city. There is no school that day. It has rained heavily before dawn, and now it has stopped. Fog covers the valley bottom and stretches partway up the slopes. He meanders without purpose through the mist, picking his way slowly among bushes and rocks dripping with moisture, knowing that he is probably getting lost, but not worrying about it. Eva was in a mood at breakfast, and he knows that during the night she had been thinking about her husband. In those years, he still experiences, from time to time, small hallucinations in which the walls of her bedroom seep blood. Thus, he is glad to escape the apartment for the day, desiring to be alone and to retain the sense of wonder he had felt the night before.

The fog thickens, as if the layer over Sarajevo is rising into a new cloud, engorged with rain. Yes, he is inside a cloud, and it is carrying him upward to the heights, rising above all the unhappiness of mankind.

Suddenly, the bushes seem to part and he finds himself walking unimpeded across a sloping grassy meadow. Without warning, he hears the pounding of feet—like the boots of mountain terrorists descending into an unguarded village. He freezes, motionless, hoping that the fog will hide him. His throat swells with fear, his heart skips beats, and his hands clench into fists. When a shadow appears in front of him, he stumbles backward away from it. And there before him stands a great horse. It is white. He is certain it is Pegasus descended, though its wings are invisible. Breathing in silence, they regard each other solemnly.

Never in his life has he ridden a horse. He knows how to bounce along on a donkey, but on Svez his feet were never far from the ground. A fall from his back would bruise you, but not break you. Now this immense marvel of beauty and power commands him to ride upon him as his guest. He could toss a rider into the air to shatter on the rocks. He could annihilate with one kick. His hoofs thump the sod like the booms of a drum. He steps sideways, turning a little as if to say, get on!

Josip grips the mane and jumps, his belly across the horse's back, then swings a leg over. Now he is sitting. Now he is trembling upright, straightening his spine. The fog is so thick he can barely see his hands on the mane. Pegasus moves forward, high-stepping and sure, slowly, slowly, slowly increasing his gait until they are clopping in circles around the wide pasture. Little by little, fear is replaced by exhilaration.

The horse breaks into a full gallop, and Josip's fear returns. The fog whips his face, yet he is laughing and laughing in his fear, cries of happiness leaping from his throat. He does not ask where they are going, does not think of it. He is being carried higher into the cloud, and the cloud rises with them as they ascend. Now they are entering the sphere of the constellations; the stars are invisible, but they are singing all around: *We are here*, they chant, *we are here!*

Then the horse and boy plunge downward, headlong into the unknown. Is it to earth they return or to the depths of the sea? They are galloping beneath the waves now, the cloud raining within itself, soaking them, the horse swimming even as he runs. Now they rise again, and Josip bends his neck to see what the hoofs are striking upon; it is a path beaten by many feet, but of man or beast he cannot say. Is it seafloor or mountaintop, he does not know. Onward they run into a field higher than the other. The boy yearns for the ride to go on forever—never, never, never to stop! He wants to go upward always, far from the cities of mankind and the enclosures of the self with their bleeding walls. Then he weeps with the memory of what he is fleeing, and the horse sobs with him, for their tears are streaming out behind them as one.

The horse slows to a canter and comes to a stop, his great sides heaving. He wheels and breaks into a gallop again, taking the boy back to the place where he found him. The horse tells him this without making any sound, in his own language, and thus Josip learns that there are other unknown tongues besides the *lastavice* speech and the heart-soul speech of humans.

Why now? Josip cries in that language. *Why, when the ascent has just begun, are you taking me back?*

Then Pegasus answers:

You must live in the place that is the station of your labor and your love. Down there in the swaying forests, the dark sleeping fields, the cold barren lands, and the cities of man, where the indestructible, the faithful, the true are needed.

"No!" the boy wails. "Do not take me back there!"

The ride abruptly ends. Pegasus halts in the center of the pasture and tells him he must get off, must put his feet onto the earth and live in the rank of being that is his own.

Josip is blinded with tears as he slides from his back.

You will ride upon me again, and I will come forth with all the white horses in the armies of heaven. In battle array shall the armies ride, for the One who is Faithful and True is coming upon his white horse, and it is he whom we follow.

"Who is he?" Josip cries out with his voice.

He is coming! He is coming! He is coming!

And though Josip does not understand anything of these words, this much he retains: the horse upon which he has ridden is not Pegasus, but something greater. And even in its greatness, it is but one of the many who will ride forth in the armies of heaven. Then it gallops away into the fog and never again appears.

So memory fades, and life resumes. Now he is a man; now he lives in Split. It is an ordinary Saturday. Josip's term examination is over, a major paper handed in, he is confident of the results, he has had a good breakfast, and last week his team won the university swim meet. Soon they will take on the city. After that, maybe the whole country. Who knows, maybe someday the Olympics! It's a great feeling, this. And today the weather is the finest—high blue skies, cloudless, with a cool *mistral* breeze blowing in from the northwest, bringing with it the salt smell of the ocean.

Josip decides to stroll down to the harbor. A week of dusk-to-dawn studying has left him more tired than usual. A walk will warm him up for the big run to the height of the Marjan. He can afford to while away a few hours looking out at the Adriatic, which he knows will be unusually turquoise on such a day. He walks past the imperial palace of Diocletian and proceeds along the promenade toward Trumbićeva, which will take him to the street that leads to the park.

As he approaches the spot where he should begin his ascent, he happens to glance down at the last wharf on the bay. Near it is a smaller quay, lower to the water, where little boats can tie up. Indeed, there is a boat there now, a red and green open-top craft, bobbing up and down. Crouched between the seat boards, a girl is untangling a black squid from her net. She pulls it out and thwacks it down on the bow. It's not a big one, but it's enough to make a meal for a household. The few times he has eaten this delicacy have made him want more. He could pretend to himself that the squid attracts him now, but it is the girl's presence that draws him closer. She is dressed in sea gear: a green rubber slicker, rough trousers, black boots. Her blond hair is flying in the breeze. She moves briskly, with a subtle smile of internalized victory, for she has caught a monster of the deep and now someone will eat it—her family perhaps? Or will she sell it? She is in her late teens or early twenties, rather pretty. The university is crowded with such beauties, a good number of them more attractive than she is. In his experience, female students are more open to conversation than working girls. Perhaps working men find working girls more open than students. As always, it depends on your loyalties, your familiarities. The city is a collection of villages. Even so, he approaches, if only to admire for a moment another way of life.

Arriving at the steps leading down to the water, he notices another figure there, a man standing alone by the edge of the wharf, looking out at the shimmering sea beyond the harbor mouth. The girl lifts the squid, steps from the boat, and passes by the man without a word. Carrying the squid before her as she comes nimbly up the stairs to the street, she passes Josip without a glance. He pays her no notice now, for his attention is fixed on the man below.

Wearing peasant clothing, woolen trousers, dusty shoes, a brown jacket, and a small black cap on the crown of his head, he is average in height. His hair is gray, and his face is darkened by long exposure to the sun. By his feet lies a burlap sack, fastened at the top by a loop of rope. As Josip watches him, a feeling grows that has no clear cause. It is as if he knows this man, though in what portion of his past he cannot begin to guess. Perhaps he has never met him before, and it is merely something about the way the figure holds his body. The tilt of the head, the arms dangling straight down at his sides, the stillness—nothing remarkable, yet somehow familiar.

Josip goes down the steps and halts a few paces from the man. A swift glance at the side of the other's face produces no sharpening of memory, no recognition. Yet there is cognition on another level. He does know him, but from where?

The man, noticing Josip's presence, turns to face him.

For a long moment, they study each other. Then the man smiles.

"Ah, Josip", he says in a voice that is deep, yet so quiet that it is just above the surface of sound, as sea-swallows in the evening will skim the waves.

"Have we met, sir?"

"You did not fly away", says the man.

Then Josip steps closer, his mouth dropping open.

"It's you!"

"Yes, it is me."

"S–Sarajevo!"

"Yes, Sarajevo.

"It is so long since that time."

"Many years. Is it ten?"

"But how did you recognize me?"

"How did you recognize *me*?"

"But I was young. I looked different then."

"I too looked different."

Josip glances down at the arms. The hands at the end of them are gloved, the thumb and forefinger on each hand have been cut away, revealing hooklike clamps.

Again the man smiles. "You see, the wind decided."

It was indeed the wind, the allure of the *mistral* conspiring with the sun.

"But, how did you recognize me?"

"Do you think I would not recognize the Lastavica of the Mountains?"

Josip laughs, though still somewhat in awe. "You remember that? All this time and you remember?"

"I remember. And you—do you remember?"

"Yes. You are the Lastavica of the Sea."

The man's right arm lifts a little. "I would shake your hand, if I could, but as you see I have not grown new arms. These are made of wood and wire."

"Yet it seems to me that you still fly, for you have wings that none can see."

Now the man of the sea gazes fondly at Josip.

"And by those words I know that *you* still fly, Josip, and that you too have wings none can see."

Josip drops his eyes.

"I don't know", he shakes his head. "Maybe—"

"The wings are there."

"Are they?"

"They are. Have you forgotten?"

"There were times when those days in the cellar were more real to me than anything else that followed. But less and less, it seems, as I grow older. When I am alone—when I feel entirely alone in this world—I think of what we spoke about. It has faded a little, yet it always returns. But now my life is full of other things."

"Your mind is full of ideas. You are a student."

"How do you know that?"

"It is in your face. Still, your eyes have remained the eyes of the *lastavica*."

"Is it so? Is this true?"

"It is so. It is true."

Josip can think of nothing more to say. Nearly half the length of his life has been lived since they last met. But what has filled those years? He sees all of it in a flash, in its richness and complexity, its terrors and consolations. Yet to describe it might widen the space between himself and the man of the sea.

"Would you like to walk with me?" asks the man. He bends at the waist and with a metal finger hooks the rope of his satchel. Directing his wooden arms by a jerk of his body, he deftly swings the sack over his shoulder.

"So, shall we go?"

Josip nods, and together they walk up the steps to the street.

There are so many questions to ask, so much information he desires in order to fill out the space within himself that he has kept clean and waiting for the *Lastavica*. Now he has returned. But is it necessary to know such details? Much can be deduced from his clothing and manner.

"Tell me about your life", says the man, solving the problem for both of them. As they walk toward the promenade, Josip describes what came after their first meeting. His aunt, the factory, school, swimming, fish, soccer, running, university, and finally, a walk in the *mistral*, which has brought him to this moment. Omitting unnecessary details, especially avoiding the topic of his uncle's death, he describes everything with utmost simplicity, so as not to complicate their way of speaking. And all the while, he is aware that his voice is as deep as his listener's and that he is a head taller. He wonders if these changes seem odd to the man, for when they last spoke Josip was a child and somewhat insane. Now he is robust and confident. If life is still dangerous, at least he has learned how to survive.

"And you?" he asks when finished. "How do you live?"

"I travel here and there."

"But how do you earn a living? Do you have a home? Does the government help you?"

"The government no longer knows of my existence."

"But how do you eat?"

In front of Diocletian's palace, the man of the sea stops by a bench overlooking the water. He and Josip sit down on it.

"Can you open my sack? It is easier if you are my hands."

Josip unties the knot and opens the top. Exploding upward from inside come marvelous smells and colors.

"You may look."

Josip thrusts his hands inside. The sack contains packages of yellow and green and red and turquoise and pink and purple paper tied with yarn.

"What are they?" he asks.

"Open one."

The package contains a little wooden fish, painted bright colors. It is very pretty.

"Now, another."

The next contains a handful of dried lavender. Josip inhales the scent, closes his eyes, and sighs.

"Another, if you wish."

The next contains sage.

"Do not be shy."

Finally, a carved wooden horse. The horse is white, and it stirs a memory. Josip strokes its back with a finger. He once rode a horse like this—years ago in Sarajevo. The horse spoke to him. Or had he imagined it? He was still sometimes crazy in those days.

"You sell these?" he asks.

The man nods.

"But how do you make them?"

"I cannot make them. Along the shore of the sea are old people beyond numbering, in whom such beauty has not died. They give me these carvings, and also their flowers and herbs. On the islands, herbs grow with great potency and purity of color. I take these things out into the world and sell them. Then, with the money, I buy paints and wood and threads and paper and tools, and when I return to the people, I give them what they need to make more, and some of the money. I purchase food for myself along the roads where I travel, but more often I am given enough to eat, a meal, a blanket, a room on a cold night. It is a fine way to live."

"But you have nothing."

The Lastavica turns his eyes to Josip and says, with great seriousness. "No, Josip, I have everything. And more than everything. Have you not yet learned this?"

Ashamed, Josip looks away.

The man of the sea stands and says, "Shall we go on?"

It's not certain what exactly he means. Go on with the discussion, continue walking, resume their friendship?

"Of course", Josip replies to all three possibilities.

He re-ties the packages and puts them into the sack. The older man hoists it to his shoulder and begins to walk back in the direction of the little wharf.

"Where are we going?" Josip asks.

"Where have we come from?" replies the man with a smile.

"We know where we have come from," Josip replies, "but where are we going?" By ignoring the other's inference, Josip is insisting on a routemap, and saying at the same time that he is no longer a boy, no longer confined to the cryptic language they shared so long ago.

"We will go where the wind takes us", replies the man of the sea, refusing to be drawn into this. "For to act with our own purpose, though not wrong, is to limit the actions of life. And for purpose to be true purpose, it must be contained within submission."

"Is not all choice a limiting of possibilities?"

"Yes. This is necessary. We cannot do or be all things. And within the identity that is our own there are a multitude of choices."

Without warning, certain advanced equations spring to Josip's mind, and he wonders if his old friend—so mysterious, so quintessentially a wanderer-mystic of some kind—is also educated.

"You are a philosopher", he says, with a whimsical smile.

"You think I am a man who sells toys and herbs, and you *wish* I would be a philosopher."

"No—well, maybe. If so, I suppose it's the university. It gets into your blood. Everything becomes knowledge after a while. I am a mathematician."

"You are not what you *do*, Josip. You are what you *are*."

"You are a philosopher, that is plain to see."

"These terms—"

"I'm sorry, have I offended you?"

"No, it is interesting to see your mind work, and for this I am grateful. Yet I wonder—how easily the important thing gets lost."

"In me, you mean."

"In everyone."

"Even in you?"

"I remain with nothing in order not to lose the riches that have been given to me."

Josip notices that they have come to a halt before the little church of St. Francis. Its name is the same as the church of Rajska Polja. He looks away. It is better to forget all that. During the few seconds that it takes Josip to stop the rapid blinking of his eyes and to turn toward the street, his back to the open doorway, the man of the sea regards him thoughtfully.

"Let us go inside", he says.

Josip stuffs his hands deep into his jacket pockets, his fists clenched. He shakes his head.

"Only for a moment", says the other.

Josip hesitates, might even follow him up the steps, but his lungs begin to ventilate rapidly, his heart pounding with sudden terror. Lying on the steps is a naked giant with holes in his hands and feet, his bloody face obliterated.

"No", he gasps. "I cannot."

"Why can't you?" asks the man, with a curious look.

"I . . . I . . . because the watchers will see. They report everyone who goes to church. My studies, my future."

"Very well", says the man of the sea. "We do not need to go in."

They slowly walk on, side by side, as Josip's breathing steadies and his heart calms down. The man of the sea asks no more questions.

Now they are crossing Trg Republike, the big square devoid of republican activity but crowded with old women, selling flowers, and a few younger ones sitting on the flagstones beside open bags of black-market wares, mostly vegetables and sea-shells—in full exposure to the eyes of the state. Their boldness stems from desperation or perhaps from a misplaced optimism about the "Visible Hand" reforms. Doubtless, these furtive capitalists believe that the eyes of the watchers have turned elsewhere. They know themselves to be small fry, not worth the trouble of harassment or imprisonment.

Through a maze of side streets they come to the old Roman "golden gate" and enter into the walled compound of Diocletian's palace. Without knowing where the man of the sea is leading him, Josip simply follows. He then sees that they have arrived at the peristyle and are standing before the emperor's mausoleum. It is also, he recalls, the Catholic cathedral. Bells are ringing in its tower.

The man of the sea makes no move to enter or to leave. Josip looks up the stone staircase to the big wooden doors, which are covered with carvings of the life of Christ. He remembers what he has not thought about for many years—his father kneeling before those doors with a look of fear in his eyes—a look the child Josip had never before seen in them.

His heart beating wildly again, hands in pockets, he turns away and leaves the peristyle. Oblivious to his companion, he goes quickly through the tunnel under the walls and bursts out onto the open promenade by the waterfront. The sun is shining brightly there, the breeze is fresh, the palm trees are swaying. He stops to catch his breath and calm his heartbeat. The man of the sea, he notices, is beside him.

"I-I-have to go", Josip stammers.

"Where are you going?"

"Back to the university. I . . . I must study."

Though he has throughout his life guarded himself from telling lies, failing only during the most dangerous moments, he has never before lied to an honest man. Most terribly, he has now lied to the very person with whom he has shared the language of truth in its highest form. Josip is shaken by his own behavior, which has erupted without warning from within. He wishes only to flee from the face before which he can feel nothing but shame.

"I have a gift for you", says the man of the sea. "In my coat pocket."

Hesitantly, his face strained with remorse and confusion, Josip reaches into the pocket and takes from it a package wrapped in turquoise paper and tied with red yarn.

"What is it?" he asks, because it is necessary to fill the void that has opened in the very center of his chest.

"Unwrap it when you have returned to the place where you live."

Josip stuffs the package into his pocket, nods his thanks, murmurs good-bye, and hurries away down the street.

He knows he is running away, running from what he has remembered, what he has loved. And he runs, most of all, because the resurrected presence has proved to be a gate into an ancient ruin.

Later that day, after an irritating discussion with a political toady who lives in his building, a distracted hour or two rummaging in the library, and a supper that sits in his stomach like a stone, Josip returns to his room. In his absence, it has become hollow, dark, cold. He closes the door behind him, jumping at the sound. For a few minutes he paces back and forth, back and forth, in the enclosed space.

He recalls that when they were in the cellar together those many years ago, he had asked the man of the sea to tell him his name, and the names of his wife and children. And the man had promised that if he and Josip were ever reunited, he would tell the names. Now they have met, and Josip realizes that he did not think to ask. How could he have forgotten to ask! Was it because he was in haste to escape from the man? Or was it, on the other hand, a subconscious desire to retain the cryptic quality of what they had shared in that time of suffering? And even if he had remembered, would he have absorbed the specific data—so vital, so personal—and then shelved it like a book that has been read and is soon forgotten? Or would he have been afraid to find out what is in the book? He does not know. He cannot explain any of his behavior.

When he is able, he sits down at his desk and opens the package. Inside he finds a wooden carving of a swallow. It is perfectly formed, its wings folded, head tilting up with humble composure. Its coloring is not that of the sea-swallows; it is a swallow of the mountains.

Josip is blinded with a stab of anguish. As he holds it gently in the palm of his hand, it grows warm and remains without flight.

Three days later he tracks down Antun Kusić and invites him to go for a practice swim in the university pool. They do laps for an hour, then shower and towel off. Antun snaps his towel. Josip returns the gesture. They laugh but say little.

Josip walks him back to his residence. At their parting, Josip hems and haws for a minute, and then says in a low voice, "Will you introduce me to your friends?"

Antun's chest inflates with emotion, and he fiercely shakes Josip's hand.

11

Now it is August, so hot and windless that even seasoned Splitophiles are sweating day and night and complaining about it too. Josip, who has endured much cold in his life, loves the heat, loves sweating, does not mind waking up each morning in soaked sheets. *Give me more!* he declares, as he stands at the window smiling a welcome to the ball of fire rising over the Dinarics. *Give me more, give me more, more and more and more!*

Today, as he has done for the past three weeks, he will help Ivan Radoš in the biology lab. They will catalogue his photographs of diatoms, which have been obtained with great effort through a high quality camera and a powerful Czech microscope. Hundreds of crystal clear, black and white images of the infinite microcosm.

"Bacillariophyta", says Ivan. "Photosynthetic. They live on light. They're silica-based single-cell organisms—a kind of living glass."

Josip raises his eyebrows. "Living glass."

"You can find them in any water on the planet, and they're more numerous than all the grains of sand on all the beaches of the sea. There are thousands of species, in every shape imaginable."

"Like snowflakes", Josip suggests.

"Snowflakes are two-dimensional crystallographies and quite impressive. But these have a much broader figurative spectrum. They're three-dimensional, and they live and move and surprise you. The floating diatoms are spectacular for their qualities of light; their adaptations allow them to live near the surface. But my favorites are the heavily built sessile marine species. There's more elegance, more symmetry, with no loss of complexity."

"Ah, I see."

Beneath the data of Ivan's lecture, Josip hears the fervent outpourings of an enamored man. He's in love with these little things, though he disguises it with scientific terminology.

"You're a poet, Ivan."

The scientist jerks his head up from the lens he has been peering into and laughs.

"Poets are dreamers, Josip. They scribble their subconscious onto paper in order to connect to food sources."

That evening, Antun comes by Josip's room to pick him up for the walk to the first meeting of his alternative culture friends. Antun is dressed in a fine black blazer, flawless black slacks, shining black shoes, white shirt, and black tie. His black hair is slicked and combed. The shadow of beard on his closely scraped chin is black. His eyes are liquid black, as if he were a sable otter that has just heaved itself out of the water, exuding a mysterious and admirable swarthiness. Yet all of this mono-chromatic effect disguises a rather guileless personality.

Sweat is running off Antun's brow, but you can be sure he will not remove the jacket and roll up his sleeves, which would ruin the splendid impression he hopes to make this evening. He is a visual exclamation, the most significant of punctuation marks! He wants both himself and his friend to be signs of vigorous youthful resistance, and stylish ones at that! He harangues Josip into changing out of the dingy trousers and shirt he had planned to wear and browbeats him into putting on his blazer, cleaner trousers, and a tie. This tie, Antun tells him, is good only to be buried in. But what can Josip do, it's his only tie! And his brown leather shoes are so worn that the heels are beyond all hope, though spittle and candle wax improve the shine. And the hair! Antun insists that Josip must shove that stack of hay under the tap, and then try to get some order into it. He even lends his comb, and fastidiously washes it off after Josip has used it. When the tormentor at last gives his half-hearted approval, they set out on their perilous adventure.

They walk around to the other side of the hills, at the center of the spreading city. Above the sparkling crown of its topmost buildings, the sky is deep purple. A few blocks from the imperial palace, they turn and begin the ascent into the more refined streets of the Manus district. The buildings along the tree-lined sidewalks are older and larger, the homes of the upper middle class and the wealthy of the pre-Communist era. Hard to say who lives in them now, probably people in good standing with the regime. So, why is the underground launching itself from this unlikely place?

Antun knocks on the front door of a three-story house that surely must have been at one time the residence of a high Austrian official.

"Who lives here?" Josip asks.

"Dr. Horvatinec", Antun replies. "Don't ask so many questions."

"I only asked one. A reasonable one, at that!"

"Shhhh."

The door is opened by a pleasant-looking woman in her late fifties. She smiles and welcomes them, examining the visitors' faces with interest as she brings them inside and takes their jackets in the entrance hall and inquires their names. They introduce themselves as Antun, a doctoral candidate in literature, and Josip, a graduate student in mathematics. She is Madame Horvatinec, wife of the doctor. She simultaneously takes their hands in her frail arthritic fingers and holds them—a familiarity that disarms both of the young men, who are feeling somewhat nervous. Her tailored clothing is without ostentation, though cut from expensive cloth. Her manner, like her dress, is relaxed and gracious, neither formal nor informal. She explains that she was once a concert pianist and studied in Vienna as a young woman, but she has lost the dexterity she once had in her fingers. Still, she assures them, her interest in what they are doing is undiminished by her inability to participate directly in the arts.

"Please come into the parlor and have a seat. Simon will be down in a minute."

Leaving them to perch on fragile embroidered chairs, she goes off in the direction of a kitchen, from which come the sounds of cupboards opening and dishware clinking. Food and drink are being prepared.

The large parlor is floored with Oriental carpets, and at the end of the room is a marble Renaissance fireplace. In the corner stands a rosewood grand piano, against walls that are crowded with overflowing bookshelves. Scattered about the room are deep armchairs, a long settee, the more delicate chairs on which the visitors are sitting, a brass coffee table, a silver samovar and a blue Chinese urn containing dried flowers. Hanging on the wall above the mantelpiece is a large painting of a naval battle. Antun leaps up and reads the brass plate on its frame.

"Lepanto", he whispers and hastily sits down again.

"A good sign", Josip whispers in return.

"Shhhh."

A moment later, a man strides into the room, and both visitors rise to meet him. They know instantly that this is Dr. Horvatinec. As introductions are made, keen blue eyes behind wire-rim spectacles examine the faces before him. His bearing is that of a younger man who was perhaps an athlete in his youth. His handshake is firm. His fine charcoal suit, striped aqua tie, and ornate black shoes of nonindigenous origin (Italian, maybe) so distinguish him that Antun begins to feel shabby by comparison. Still, there is no arrogance in their host's demeanor, and his dignity seems entirely a product of moral character, unlike many at the university who display such status. Rare are the men like this doctor.

He bids them sit down and takes a seat for himself in an armchair facing them. He crosses his legs at the knees, and in a Croatian dialect that is Dalmatian of a rarefied sort, inquires about their studies, their interests, their origins. His voice is deep, rather quiet, without affectation, but clearly accustomed to speaking with authority. His eyes linger a little over Josip's minimalist responses. Antun is eager to tell what he may. Josip is somewhat tense with the effort to hold back details that could so readily pour out in the company of such a man. The doctor does not probe.

A few minutes later comes another knock. A woman in her forties has arrived at the door. Madame Horvatinec greets her in the hallway with enthusiastic exclamations, which are returned by the newcomer, followed by kisses. She enters the parlor. The doctor gets up and kisses her as well, then introduces Antun and Josip. Interestingly, she is a Serb. A wide-shouldered woman in a long green dress, she is obviously cultured, though her mannerisms are a little affected. However, within minutes it is plain to see that beneath her temperament and her origins she is humble and sincere. She is visiting from Belgrade, where she teaches literature. Her name is Tatjana, and she is a published poetess. She wears at her throat a tiny Byzantine cross. Josip wonders if she wears it in Belgrade, or only away from home.

Next arrives a man in his seventies, whom the doctor embraces, and Madame Horvatinec greets with a cordial shake of the hand. Has she not met him before, or does she have reservations about him? His name is Stjepan, and he seems loath to disclose any further personal information in a room that is becoming increasingly full of people he does not know. The doctor informs the group that the man has written three novels, none of which are yet published, all of them of the highest quality.

"What are they about?" Antun asks, disingenuously.

The novelist appears to be troubled by the question and glances at the doctor. "Simon?" he murmurs.

"It's all right. You are among friends", replies the doctor. Turning to the others, he says, "Stjepan's books—though fictional—are about the lives of ordinary people who have suffered through what has come upon our country."

"Do you mean Croatia or Yugoslavia?" asks Tatjana, uncomfortably.

Madame Horvatinec, who is sitting beside the woman, puts a hand on the other's bare forearm and says, "His stories are about what has happened to *all* of us."

"I'm sorry, Vera," says the poetess, "I didn't mean it to sound like that. It's just . . . you see . . . am I really the right person for a gathering such as this?"

The doctor's wife flutters her hand on the other's arm. "You are exactly the right person for this, and, with your permission, I will later on read to these dear people one of your poems."

"Certainly not!" says the poetess, though she is clearly gratified by the suggestion. Vera Horvatinec links arms with the woman, whose eyes are brimming with tears, and they sit this way throughout what follows.

Shortly after, there is another knock at the door, and a round little woman with close-cropped gray hair enters. She is about the same age as the poetess, but she wears a gaudily flowered dress and a frayed sweater. Her shoes are almost as decrepit as Josip's. Her name is Iria. Raised in Mostar, she was born in Lisbon, the daughter of a Portuguese mother and a Bosnian father—a merchant seaman. Now she is a music teacher in Split, private pupils only. She also writes her own piano compositions and collects traditional folk songs of the Bosnian Croats and Muslims. All of this is explained by Simon as the woman blushes. It is difficult to connect her appearance with her art. Vera pulls her down onto the settee, Lisbon on one side,

Belgrade on the other. Three categorically diverse women linked together as sisters.

"She is our very dear friend," Simon concludes, "and more gifted than people realize."

She and Josip are the only two people in the room who have managed to say nothing throughout the proceedings.

Another knock, and in comes a lanky, bearded fellow about thirty years old, dressed in dirty slacks and sweatshirt, with sandals on his not very clean feet. Antun begins to feel better about his own appearance. Dr. Horvatinec introduces the newcomer as Vlado, a sculptor. He is a swarthy Macedonian who looks as if he has just returned from slaughtering, single-handedly, a Persian army.

"You might as well be honest, doctor. I am Vlado-a-sculptor, as you say, but I am also Vlado-a-nihilist, and I think you are all crazy even to talk about this."

"If we are all crazy, Vlado, then you will find that your nihilism is compatible with our delusions", smiles the doctor.

"We'll see", says the nihilist sitting down on the floor, folding his arms and crossing his legs, and glancing suspiciously about at each face.

"He is not a dangerous nihilist", says the doctor to the others. "He is angry as we all are angry, yet he is the only one among us who will admit it. He studied under Meštrović for a time."

"Too much realism", Vlado interjects. "I go my own way now."

"That you do, and we are glad to have you with us."

"Why did you come here tonight?" asks the novelist, with his own brand of suspicion.

"Because you are doomed to failure", Vlado snaps back. "Because it is impossible to create an alternative culture, even if it is organized by Simon. No one in this room fails to admire you, Simon, and you know that our instincts are to follow you wherever you would lead us. But this is pure folly. Suicide. I have come here tonight, perhaps for the only time, to warn you that an individual mole or, should I say, a dozen individual moles, all burrowing under the walls of the prison, unknown to each other and operating in isolation, are more effective than a herd of moles galloping blindly *en masse* toward the wall. Feeling reassured by such good company, confident and consoled that you are not alone as you race toward the wall, you will smash into it all *together*, at once! Yes, sooner or later, you will be smashed."

"Then come along, be smashed with us", says Antun with an ironic laugh.

"Who are you?" growls Vlado, turning a stormy look on him.

"Antun Kusić, master of literature, associate professor of aesthetics."

"Let me jot that down, Antun Kusić, so that I may report you to the UDBA. It will save you a lot of wasted time and energy."

Most of the people in the room stiffen, shift in their seats. Dr. Horvatinec chuckles.

"He is joking", says the doctor. "Our friend the nihilist would be the last person on this planet to contact the UDBA."

"You're sure of that?" says the novelist.

"Yes, I am sure."

"The nihilists, in my experience, are the first to collaborate."

"Not this one."

"Well, Antun Kusić, aesthetician," says the sculptor, ignoring all of this, "you are a hero; that is plain to see. You have real courage, which is also plain to see. There are many like you in Croatia, maybe everywhere in this prison land. But, I tell you, guys like you are always the first to be hauled away."

"I don't worry about that", Antun shrugs.

"You had better worry about that."

"Come, come", says Vera, getting unsteadily to her feet. "Let's have some wine. We've broken the ice very nicely, and now we all agree on things." Everyone in the room chuckles or smiles ruefully. The character she is playing is universal in the land, the peacemaker mother, the scolder, the authority on domestic politics, who knows very well how to handle squabbling children.

After the wine glasses are filled and food is served—almond biscuits, sweet cakes dribbled with liquid chocolate, and home-made pastries—people thaw out another degree or so. The discussion begins in earnest. There is agreement that this meeting and all subsequent meetings will not be mentioned to people outside the circle of new friends. It is also agreed that each will, with utmost discretion, keep his eyes open for other people involved in arts and letters—in culture generally—who seem unhappy about the current state of affairs, are reliable, and might be willing to participate in a project, perhaps even to join the group. A delicate balance—secrecy, with the door open a crack.

It is decided that no preemptive activities will begin for a year. Within the coming twelve months, they will consider ways in which a journal of culture can be published. It would, of course, be illegal to publish such a journal, free of censorship, bypassing the official permission of the state. They certainly risk the loss of their jobs, and possibly imprisonment. Each will contribute what he can in terms of writing. They will use pseudonyms. They will print and distribute by hand.

Simon assures the group that printing will not be a major problem, because the journal will be, in its physical aspects, an unpolished product, on the cheapest paper, stapled or stitched. Perhaps there will be no more than a few hundred copies of each issue. A quarterly would be best. Detailed planning will be needed to bring it off without observation by informers or entanglement with the police. Anonymity and strict self-discipline will be the rule at all times. He and Vera will fund the enterprise, but the real work will be in the realm of creativity. Through the arts the voice of the people will be articulated—and through the journal the voice will be heard.

Antun mentions that he has already written an essay on the geo-psyche of Croatian poetics. He then qualifies himself pedantically by saying it is also about the poetics of the geo-psyche. He is forced to explain. People digest it, warm to it.

"There will be room for academic essays in our journal," Simon goes on, "and this is surely important. Yet there is a difference between insightful commentary about culture and the actual creation of culture. For both, we will need to create a community of people drawn from many walks of life, from here, there, and everywhere. It will be difficult and dangerous."

"It will be impossible", says Vlado darkly.

"The most problematic contribution may well prove to be yours, Vlado", says Simon. He goes on to explain that, because the sculptor is well known in Dalmatia, his work would be immediately recognizable by the police.

Vlado now offers to sculpt something in a different style. How about a piece titled *Freedom* for the first issue? Simon emphatically supports this idea, but wonders if Vlado really wants to abandon his adamant antirealism.

"My work is not *anti*-realist," Vlado shoots back, "it is *meta*-realist. But I can bend a little in the direction of cognitive expressionism."

"Excellent", says the doctor, while everyone else puzzles over the term. "It can be photographed and reproduced on the cover, but you realize it can never thereafter be exhibited in public. It should be safely stored away, somewhere other than in your apartment-studio."

"May we purchase it, Vlado?" asks Vera.

"Of course, if it ever sees the light of day."

There are other matters discussed that evening. Simon asks Iria if she would be willing to write a composition—music and lyrics that would embody the spirit of the people. Iria agrees with a nod, her cheeks flushing bright red.

"It should be called 'Song for the Homeland'", declares

Antun. This sparks a debate. Is the homeland Croatia alone, or is it all of Yugoslavia? Clearly the Croat majority in the room prefers the title to mean the republic within Yugoslavia. Tatjana and Vlado have reservations. Simon maintains a neutral stance in order to moderate the discussion. Soon their thoughts about the central goal of their project spin off in tangents about nationalities and ethnic loyalties within the larger imposed state. It goes on for some time, and because these questions are vital and complex, no one seems able to draw the discussion back on course.

Josip clears his throat. "Could it be titled . . ."

Because he has not yet spoken, and perhaps also because this extraordinary model of humanity has sat motionless for three hours like a bronze god parked in the corner, all voices fall silent.

"Could it be titled 'In the Homeland of the Soul'?" he asks in a low voice.

Instantly, he regrets that he has broken his silence. It seems his silence has bred more silence in the others. Then, to his surprise, one by one they nod. Murmurs of agreement follow: Yes. That's good. It says it all. What do you think, Iria?

Iria gives one of her smiles.

Then Vera begs, "Play something for us, Iria, would you? Please? One of your own?"

So, the little round woman, who looks as if she should be selling black-market flowers on the promenade, gets up and crosses the room, seats herself at the grand piano, and flutters a few keys. She closes her eyes and begins. Slowly at first. It is simply classical, yet a piece no one recognizes. It gathers strength, the central current growing complex with alliances, themes blending and parting and reuniting again, and all the while it remains meditative and melancholic in the Slavic way. Though it is unlike anything else they have heard before, they recognize in it the faintest residue of the Orient and the cool northern exultation of Europe, followed by the heat of the Western Renaissance and the dread suction of the Turkish tide rising from the south. Then, in the final movement, when the tide is repelled at last by valor and faith and passionate love for what must not be lost, they hear what has been purchased by immeasurable sacrifice. The entire concerto is about the crucifixion and the resurrection of a people. How she creates it no one can guess. Why it should pour from this most unlikely of persons is another mystery. Everyone in the room stops guessing, leaves behind all thought, and rises with her into a realm that is never seen with the eyes, and is only rarely felt in the homeland of the soul.

When it is over, not a sound can be heard in the room. No one speaks. One by one they get up, shake hands, embrace, kiss, and take their leave. In the hallway people are milling about, whispering to each other about the next meeting, when, where? It is not at all a secretive sound; it is the whisper of reverence.

Because Josip has listened to the concerto with closed eyes throughout, flying somewhere within himself as the Lastavica of the Mountains, and at certain moments alongside the Lastavica of the Sea, he does not notice the departures. Antun is in the hallway, deep in discussion with the old novelist, their voices low and intense, and mutually excited by a literary question. Josip remains seated in the corner, eyes closed, his head thrown back against the wall, hands folded in his lap, breathing lightly though his parted lips.

When he opens his eyes, he sees that he is not alone. Seated across the room from him is a young woman in a long white dress that reaches nearly to her ankles. Her feet are bare. Her recollected face is extremely still. She is looking at him with wide open eyes. Her hands rest on her lap, and cupped in them is a chambered nautilus.

255

12

The young woman lowers her eyes. Without looking again at Josip, she gets up and leaves the room. Beyond the parlor is a dining room. There she pauses and picks up a stringed instrument that is lying on the table. From the distance of a few meters, it appears to Josip that the strings are vibrating, as if she had put the instrument down only moments before, picked up the seashell, and come into the parlor, where she had silently observed him sitting, immobilized in his solitude. Now she is departing as swiftly as she has come. She puts the shell on the table and, cradling the instrument as if it were an infant, vanishes into another room. A door is closed.

Antun calls to him from the hallway. "Time to go, Josip!"

He gets up and says his good-byes to the doctor and his wife.

"Will you come again?" asks Simon.

"We hope you will", says Vera, putting a hand on his arm. "It was lovely what you said tonight, about Iria's song—the way you said it."

Simon shakes Josip's hand. "You are a man of few words but many thoughts, I believe. Is this a work you wish to be part of?"

Josip nods solemnly. "Yes", he says. "It is."

"We can use a mole who can count to a hundred", Antun jokes. "One who can keep his lips sealed too."

Josip smiles, and the others laugh. He and Antun leave.

They cross half the city before Antun is able to penetrate Josip's thoughts.

"Thanks for agreeing to join us. It's going to be interesting. And don't look so worried."

"I am not worried."

"Then what's the matter with you?"

"Nothing is the matter with me."

"Yes, there is. If I pushed you into a pool right now, you'd continue walking under water and not even notice."

"Who is that girl?"

"What girl?"

"Did you not see her? She came into the room as everyone was leaving."

"I didn't see anyone. You were imagining it. An enchanted evening, especially the music at the end."

"She was there. Only for a few seconds."

"Maybe a maid."

"Do they have servants?"

"I don't think so. No—they wouldn't."

"Do they have children?"

"I'm not sure—wait, yes, I heard they have a daughter. She's a student at the university. Music faculty, I think."

"Do you know her name?"

"Know her name? Of course not."

"When is the next meeting?"

"Of the ACU, you mean?

Josip looks at Antun blankly.

"Too stunned for acronyms tonight, Josip? The Alternative Culture Underground—my name for it. It has a nice ring, don't you think?"

"Where is the faculty of music?"

"Music? Oh—I see—the mysterious girl. You're sure she's real, are you?"

"At this moment, I'm not quite sure."

Alone at last in his room, Josip does not turn on the light. He throws open the window and lies down on his cot, looking at the stars over the Dinarics. He can feel his heart booming

257

slowly and relentlessly, his eyes swimming with wonder, his arms reaching into the air like a child desiring to be lifted.

Into what zone does he wish to rise? No longer is there any longing for escape. Now he reaches for some new thing, which is waiting for him. It is simultaneously above and within him.

Who is this woman? She has appeared out of the unknown, the realm of theoretical nonbeing, only to reveal in a flash of light that she exists; she has lived for years, and he did not know of her existence. Now he knows. She is here. Her white dress, her silence, her very great beauty and composure, the musical instrument in her hands—all of these show him that she is entirely present and entirely miraculous. This certainty is consummated, above all, by the chambered nautilus. For its intricate unfolding of rooms within rooms is replete with meaning—the spiral genius of pink and white enclosures within the household of its exterior form.

"If I die now, at this very moment," he declares to the stars, "it has all been worth it. For I have seen that she exists. She is on the earth with me."

He does not need to know her, still less to direct the trajectory of his obscure and painful life toward her luminous life. It is enough to know that there is one like her.

Now the little wooden swallow is in his right hand. His arms are raised, playing with it, making it soar back and forth. He laughs, laughs at this playing, this unabashed childish joy, as streams of water run down his cheeks, his happiness so close to sorrow, yet infinitely above it. The sorrow is the lower air through which the bird must pass to reach the higher winds. A flicker of wings and it soars upward, arc after arc, rising and rising into the dark until it is seen no more. He goes with it, because he is the Lastavica of the Mountains.

October. The second meeting of the group is scheduled for this evening. Josip awakes before sunrise in a state of nervous anticipation. Because it is a Saturday, he wants to run to the top of the Marjan as usual. He needs to burn off excess tension, but he cannot fix his will on anything. He paces back and forth in his room, unable to concentrate. She is always in his thoughts, her chambered nautilus as well. For two months she has taken up residence in the exact center of his soul. Does he believe in the eternal soul? Perhaps. He does not need to think about this; his only certainty is that paradise is possible and that if he does not see her again he will be shut out of paradise.

He has not seen her again, despite three or four separate incidents when, impelled by ardor and longing, he has lingered around the music faculty at the hours when an apparition is most likely to materialize. He has learned through complex negotiations that her name is Ariadne. The joy of her most beautiful name compels him continuously to write messages to her in his mind, which is alternately exalted by the certainty that she is an incarnation of all that is truly feminine, heroic, and sacrificial, and deflated by the equal possibility that she is no more than a dream.

Fragment:
> I have beheld you walking in your grace,
> containing your mystery like a secret crown,
> your royalty like a serving maid,
> the inland sea of future generations
> and the beating heart reserved for me.
>
> My life, which until now has been a desolation,
> is suddenly a sun-struck winter garden
> aburst with flowers, promising full fruitfulness.
> I am drugged by perfumes and visions,
> and am more awake than I have ever been.
> Though you do not know me, and I do not know you,
> still I know you and you know me.

Tonight at the meeting she might come into the room. If he were still in the habit of praying, he would beg God for this. Instead, he possesses only his yearning to meet her, a force so immense that no power on earth can resist it. At first, he believed that it was enough to know of her existence. Though their encounter lasted only a few seconds, the image it burned into his memory is the strongest of his adult life, stronger even than death, and thus he now feels that if he were to lose her, death would win, and this would mean a lifelong sentence of living death.

Even so, he is not entirely bereft of reason, nor of an overarching sense of proportion. He knows that he cannot engineer a meeting and willfully bring about the bliss that might come from it. It must be a mutual step, simultaneous and miraculous (now he even begins to believe again in miracles and paradisiacal illuminations).

On the other hand, he wonders whether he should employ every strategy developed throughout the long history of courtship in order to win that which he must win if he is to survive. But where would he begin? He knows nothing about such tactics!

No! No, he will not! If this love is real, if it is for life, perhaps even for eternity, it will not be dependent on human strategies. It will speak to both hearts at once, and it will accomplish what human limitations cannot.

He climbs into his running gear and goes out onto the street, then turns toward the green mountain of the Marjan. He will run off the madness, he tells himself, but still retain the reality. He gets no more than a few blocks before turning around and galloping at a headlong pace back to his apartment.

Arriving there, he opens the window, kicks off his shoes, and throws himself down at his desk. Still huffing and puffing, he takes pen and paper in hand and writes.

To You,

I write this as the overflow of a soul that cannot contain its excess of wonder. I will not deliver this letter to you, for to do so would reduce what has occurred to the linearity of communication. Yet I may write it to your soul.

I can say nothing to you, for I know nothing except this, and even this I do not know for certain: your name is Ariadne, you play the violin, you are the daughter of two courageous people, and you held the chambered nautilus in your hands as you would hold a beloved child. Are you the sea, Ariadne, and the nautilus your work of art?

I have seen you with my own eyes, though this does not necessarily mean that you exist in any realm accessible to me. Are you real? Did you see me that evening as I saw you?

I do not wish to compromise the purpose of the cultural group, to use it merely as an excuse to enter the palace where you live. Yes, your father's house is now a palace. To do so would be dishonest of me, at the least a mixed motive. For you I must have only the purest motives, even though it may cost everything, indeed the consequence of never again seeing you in this world.

You are here (whether in this world or not).

I am here.

I will say no more.

Josip Lasta

He is determined not to send this letter to her; it is penned strictly for the purpose of relieving the anguish he feels over the possibility that they will never speak to each other. Though he dresses in his ordinary clothes, and throughout the remainder of the day performs the necessary functions of a normal human being, he is not entirely on this earth. The single sheet of paper is folded, with her name penned in fine script on the back of the sheet. It is inserted beneath his undershirt, next to his heart. The words will be absorbed through the skin, the paper too, and they will become part of his body so that her name can flow as molecular light through his veins and pulse within his heart.

Antun Kusić knocks on his door an hour before the meeting is to begin. He has given himself a margin of time in which to groom his friend Josip. Tonight he enters the room and throws up his arms in surprise.

"What happened to *you*!" he exclaims.

For there, before his very eyes, stands a man transformed: Josip in a pressed white shirt, black trousers without wrinkles or debris, a fine new blue tie, and a brown blazer that is not missing its elbows. Even his black shoes are shining.

"Where did you get those?" asks Antun, pointing at the shoes with a laugh of disbelief.

"At the market. They had previous owners but are still presentable, don't you think? I darkened them with ink."

"Let's hope it doesn't rain. And who cut your hair?"

"I did."

Walking slowly around Josip, the inspector frowns, but murmurs a guarded approval. "Not bad. Nice to see you've parted your hair for once. Of course, there are a few over-enthusiastic patches here and there, but they're at the back of your skull. Just keep your face toward Ariadne at all times."

"Toward whom?"

Antun snorts and grins. "Just do what I tell you."

"Will she be there, do you think?" Josip asks in a low and somewhat shaken tone.

"Who knows?" Antun shrugs. "My guess is that Simon and Vera would prefer their daughter to keep a distance from illegal activities. Or maybe she's not interested."

"But music *is* culture!" Josip bursts out with rather too much intensity.

Antun laughs and says, "Let's go."

The Horvatinecs' living room is crowded. All those who attended the previous meeting have returned, and most have brought one or two newcomers with them. Ariadne is not present. Josip sits on the floor in a corner that he has chosen for its view of the dining room. There are a lot of interesting people here tonight—more writers, poets, a playwright, and three musicians, as well as a scattering of students.

Despite Simon's and Vera's gentility, the evening does not begin well: Vlado has brought along another sculptor, a woman in her thirties who asserts her presence in an unpleasant manner. Without waiting for the hosts to guide the discussion and ease the introductions, she declares to all and sundry that she is a "Euro-marxist" and adds, with an aggressive out-thrust chin, that she is a Marxist who despises totalitarianism.

"A contradiction in terms", declares Antun.

A big argument ensues. The woman storms out, slamming the front door behind her.

Vera uses her best mother-placater skills and settles everyone down. Vlado apologizes for his guest and admits she is more unstable than he had supposed. Simon asks him how much the woman knows about the purposes of the group.

"Almost nothing. She thinks we're one of those effete culture clubs that want to have European-style salons. She says she's a Marxist, but she's really just a baby with intellectual pretensions, the romance of revolution and all that. But don't worry, her romance, I assure you, has no prisons or torture cells in it."

"What about the romance of nihilism?" Antun shoots back. Vlado ignores him.

"Why did you bring her?" asks the novelist Stjepan.

"I thought it might help her to grow up", says Vlado.

"You might have destroyed us all", murmurs Stjepan, rising to his feet and preparing to make a departure.

"Please, please, please, everyone", says Simon. "Please, Stjepan, sit down. We must not be so easily shaken. There will be dangers in our work—this is inevitable. And certainly one of the dangers will be the risk of informers coming among us. Can this be avoided entirely? No, it cannot. So, I suggest that now is our moment of choice, not unexpected but arriving somewhat early in our discussions. I suggest that those who wish to continue must seriously consider the possibility of imprisonment. Let us face it now and during the weeks to come. I suggest that we all go home and think about this risk, and each must ask himself in the solitude of his private conscience if he is willing to accept it. Our first task is to face the fear within our own hearts. This fear is our greatest enemy. In my estimation, the young lady who departed so abruptly this evening is a great help to us, for she is the catalyst of an important factor in what we become."

"Do you mean, darling," asks Vera, "how we develop and how effective our work will be?"

"Yes, but more than that. We must not see the journal and our little gathering of people as a conglomerate of parts that are loosely connected under the term 'culture'. We must understand that the world is neither individualist nor collectivist."

"You're saying there's a third way?" asks Tatjana, the poetess from Belgrade. "What is your conception of it?"

"When people of like mind and heart come together, a community is formed. This community is greater than the sum of its parts. It's a reflection of an ideal communion that exists beyond this world."

"You're a Platonist?" suggests an eager young man, perched on the marble base of the fireplace.

"Not exactly, Zoran. Plato saw a truth that he articulated within the limitations of his times. Read beyond the classical philosophers and when you arrive at the medieval scholastics, you will understand the fuller meaning."

"Medieval philosophy has been stripped out of the library", the young man murmurs.

"I will lend you my books", says Simon.

"You're still a Christian then, Simon?" asks one of the poets.

Wrapped in his own thoughts, Dr. Horvatinec stares at the floor and does not answer.

Tatjana interjects in a tone of dry irony. "Isn't it tragic that only ten or fifteen years ago such a question would not have been asked of a man of good will? Was not all this land Christian?"

"A rather simplistic summation," says Stjepan, "but in a sense it's true. It is symptomatic of our times that we cannot assume as much of the younger generation, who have been subjected to indoctrination."

"You underestimate us", says a young woman. Like a few of the others in the room, she has not yet introduced herself. "Excuse me, I am Ana. I am studying medicine in Zagreb and am here visiting my brother." She points to the philosopher Zoran. "It is true that we were only children or youths when the Communists came to power and our so-called education began. But we have been blessed with parents and friends who remember what life was like before they took over. And though some are dead, many still speak. Though our true culture is going underground as if into a tomb, it still lives."

"It is more alive than the public culture", declares Zoran emphatically.

"I think we should be careful about despising all public culture", says a young man sitting on the floor by the piano pedals. "I am Ivan, from Livno. I study music here in Split. I believe that music is capable of retaining the spirit of truth, even when the state seeks to distort or bury it. Truth is always embedded in beauty."

"Can beauty *be* beauty without overt truth?" counters Antun.

A new tangent spins off this question and goes on for some time. The poets in the crowd defend the absolute rights of beauty, while the more religious literary people defend the rights of prudence over beauty. The elders in this bloc advocate an integration of both, with truth as the higher arbiter. Not everyone in the room can follow the discussion. The pianist, Iria, closes her eyes and falls asleep, her head leaning on Vera's shoulder.

One of the poets raises his voice and declares, "I *despise* those English romantics infatuated with Italian decadence!" Another retorts, "What about Benedetto Croce, eh!"

Others join the debate, a quintet of academics:

"Idealism without sufficient awareness of its political consequences."

"No, no, no, he was merely saying that an artist's mental images are transmitted by physical artifacts, which the unenlightened call works of art."

"And so they *are* works of art—regardless of who is enlightened or unenlightened!"

"Art historians too often minimize the history from which the art arises."

"Ha! All historians do that. They also minimize the cultural subjectivities."

"Yes, but because historiography is an *interpretation* of the past, it too is an art form."

"I don't think that's a good thing. History is facts, therefore historiography should be factual."

"That's impossible to achieve! Any study of history is a culmination of particular philosophies!"

"Culmination? There's our problem, isn't it? Social philosophy or political philosophy always want their culminations. And that is measured in dead bodies."

"Always? You're being extreme."

"No, he's being a poet in search of a cause!"

"A poet transcends these categories."

"You're wrong—you're dead wrong. A poet is true to the degree that he is rooted in *immanent* reality."

"A partial truth. Lyrical intuitions must not be enslaved to random social infatuations. They demand discipline."

"Of course. But be careful about sliding into Hegelian traps. In that direction you will soon enough find yourself declaring that poetry must be replaced by philosophy."

"Plato says that philosophy is born of wonder. Is not poetry also born of wonder?"

"Yes, but watch out or Hegel will kill them both!"

"You're just mad at him because he gave us Marx."

"Nietzsche gave us Marx."

"No, he gave us Hitler."

"No, Satan gave us Marx and Hitler."

"And Churchill gave us Yalta!"

"Ha! Satan gave us Yalta."

"Then Satan gave us Churchill."

"You're forgetting Roosevelt."

"All right, Satan gave us Roosevelt, Churchill, Stalin, Hitler, and Tito."

"Anyone else you can think of?"

"The list is too long."

"And what about us? Look at our own *cultural* strategists, the newly famous. All the splendid art produced by legal sources!"

Zoran interjects: "Your question brings us full circle, back to beauty and its relationship to truth. Don't you see how art reinforces tyrannies to the degree that it obeys the diktats of social pressure, gnostic myths, or political expedience?"

"And undermines tyrannies to the degree that it refuses to obey the diktats", says Antun.

"If I have to march in a procession in honor of Tito's birthday one more time, I will shoot myself", declares Vlado.

"*Tito, Tito, you are a beautiful flower!*" someone sings in falsetto.

Everyone laughs.

Simon stands up in the middle of the room with a broad smile and claps his hands for attention. Iria wakes up and blushes. Vera leaves for the kitchen to make preparations for food and drink.

"This is very good, all this discussion", says Simon. "I am delighted. This is what a healthy community does. It is neither passive nor aggressive. It is a mind alive."

"And a heart alive", murmurs Ana, precipitating nods of agreement throughout the room.

"Yes! Minds and hearts alive", Simon continues. "Here, we can struggle and debate and disagree because we are free to speak in an open forum. We are fighting and thinking because we trust one another."

Food and drink are brought into the room by Vera and Tatjana. People shake themselves, get up and stretch, sip wine, and engage in several sub-discussions that meander off into other rooms. Josip alone remains in silence. He is sitting with his head back against the wall in the corner, gazing without blinking in the direction of the dining room.

Why doesn't she come? Is she in the house?

Fifteen minutes later, Simon calls everyone to order and the meeting resumes.

"To business", he says in a voice of authority. He thanks all those who have come tonight and suggests that a third meeting be held in mid-November. He reiterates the agenda from the first meeting, the steps taken toward an inaugural issue of the journal. A printer has been found who is willing to produce it secretly. Those present should not lose sight, in their enthusiasm, of the dangers of a false sense of security. They should exercise maximum caution in drawing others into the "community". Cultural interests are not necessarily indelible signs of a person's suitability. Nor is religious fervor, because a person of strong faith can still be lacking in discretion, just as a person of little or no faith can be lacking in conviction and perseverance.

"But what shall we call ourselves?" asks Antun. "How about the ACU?"

"ACU?" Simon smiles.

"Yes, the Alternative Culture Underground!"

"Ugh", grunts Vlado. "ACU sounds like a political party."

"Well, it is, in its own way."

Josip Lasta clears his throat and says in a quiet voice, "I think . . ."

As on the night of the first meeting, everyone falls silent. Why does this happen? In any event, every eye in the room has turned to him.

"I think we are the *Dobri Dupin*."

Blank stares give way to awareness in numerous faces.

"Ah, I see what you mean, Josip", says Simon. "Yes, we are like the dolphins."

"It's good", says Vlado. "We are made for the sun and the air, but we move swiftly and surely above the water or below it."

"Now you see us, now you don't", laughs Antun.

"It's perfect", says Ana, echoed by her brother Zoran. "The dolphin is the friend of man, but he is not easily captured."

"I like the sound of it", says Stjepan. "If anyone hears of us, we're just another aquatic club."

"It could be a useful name if word of us leaks beyond the group", suggests Tatjana. "Perhaps we could go swimming together sometime just to help the image."

Everyone laughs or chuckles.

"Not with my belly", says Stjepan.

"Not with my aversion to sharks", says Vlado.

"You mean your aversion to contact with water of any kind", says Antun.

More laughter. For the first time the adversaries Vlado and Antun exchange crooked grins.

"Well, the name seems apt to me", says Simon. "Shall we vote?"

All hands are raised in confirmation. It is settled. They are The Dolphins.

Vera asks Iria to play the piano. As on the night of the first meeting, Iria seats herself on the bench before the grand piano as if she were a child at her first recital. She closes her eyes, and her fingers move, improvising as they go. This piece is unlike the passionate-melancholic concerto of the previous meeting. It is playful and not as complex, and before long everyone realizes that it is about the happiness of dolphins as they play in the sea, as they dive into the deep blue shadows beneath the waves and rise again in leaps that defy gravity.

When it is over, no solemn silence remains in its wake. Instead of reverent awe, there is joy. In this school of Dolphins there will always be room for both.

One by one, people make their departures until only Josip remains in the room, still seated, head tilted back against the wall, eyes half open, gazing with absolute stillness toward the dining room. But Ariadne does not come.

At last, heartsick, downcast, he inhales deeply and gets to his feet.

He can feel the letter pressing against his chest. The paper is damp with his perspiration. Perhaps it is inevitable that inaccessible souls can be known only through their fleeting appearances and their names, and that their role is to be forever remembered in the minds of others as glimpses of glory. And, as such, they really should not be fully known or embraced. It is enough to feel the frail words of his letter, which includes her name, imprinting his flesh. He understands, too, that he is no less a romantic than the despicable English illusionists who worship the pagan goddess Beauty with no other thought to reality. He understands and laments it, and knows too that he will outgrow it. Yet he feels that it would be better never to outgrow the burning moment when he saw her. That glimpse offered a promise of restoration—the return of something he had thought long lost. That it will lead nowhere is beside the point. He will always have it to turn to in times of darkness.

Out on the walkway leading to the street, Antun is waiting. The student Ana is with him. Antun tells Josip he is going to walk her to the place where she is staying, to make sure she arrives safely. Her brother the philosopher has become invisible, doubtless walking his own companion home, to make sure that she also arrives safely. So it seems that several people are returning to wherever they go, accompanying others whom they have just met. Very interesting, Josip thinks, as he stands alone on the sidewalk watching Antun and Ana stroll away, already arm in arm. Amazing, the swiftness of otters.

Josip does not mind walking home alone. Before doing so, however, he looks back toward the house and peers up at the windows on the second and third floors. None are lit, none contain the face he hopes will be there. Sighing, he turns toward the street and takes a step. Abruptly, he halts.

A woman's form is standing by the open gate, an arm extended to close it, or perhaps she has just opened it. The faint glow of the parlor window bathes her features. Under her arm is a violin case.

For a time that seems measureless, they neither move nor speak but simply regard each other. Her expression is just as it was on the night of their first meeting.

Simultaneously they take a step forward; simultaneously they are startled by this coincidence. Then both return to the inexplicable mutual attention.

She is the first to speak—a whisper: "Josip."

"Ariadne."

That is all. Yet volumes are spoken in the realization that they know each other's names, have learned these names from sources separate from each other, and have remembered the names out of all the other names they heard in the house.

Now she lowers her eyes and moves past him toward the front steps. He turns and follows her. She sits down on the steps. He sits beside her. At this fulcrum of the past and future there is total potential and total danger of loss. With a word, the future will be propelled in one direction. A different word and it is jettisoned in another.

Silence. I have beheld you walking in your grace and have hoped for everything and counted on nothing. Now I behold you sitting beside me, with me, waiting.

Because he knows there is nothing he can do to make anything happen the way he wants it, and because he knows as well that he can give her nothing but his poor self, he reaches inside his shirt and extracts the sheet of paper onto which he has penned her name and poured out his soul. He gives it to her. This is not so much an act of hope or desperation as it is an act of abandonment. She takes it in her hands and holds it as she held the chambered nautilus. Then, she reaches inside her coat and extracts a folded piece of paper. She puts it into his hands. He looks at it in puzzlement and wonder.

She stands abruptly, then runs across the porch and enters the house, softly closing the door behind her.

Josip walks home in a dream. The paper is warm in his right hand. He can smell a natural perfume on it, like herbs, perhaps a mixture of lavender and honey. Her fingers have touched this paper, and it is as if he can touch her hand through it. He puts it inside his shirt and carries it there all the way back to his apartment. He notices nothing on the way. Not even the two policemen who stop him and demand to see his identity papers. Not even his mechanical presentation of the papers. Not even his smile of benevolence upon them, nor their dismissal of him—"Drunk!"

Back in his room, he lights a candle by the open window. Over the Dinarics constellations revolve, galaxies spiral, and comets shoot from north to south. The earthbound stars of the city shine and dance. When he can overcome the intolerable anticipation, he opens the sheet of paper and reads.

Josip Lasta,

My father tells me this is your name, the name of the man who sat in the corner of our parlor this evening. He tells me you are a person of honor.

It is only a few hours since you first entered our home, and now my life is changed forever. I cannot sleep. I am sitting at the desk in my room, by the open window. A warm breeze is flowing in from the ocean. I have a beautiful seashell before me. It weights the paper as I write to you.

I will not send you this letter. I will keep it next to my heart until the path into the future opens or closes. It will neither be delivered to you (the one whom I long to read it) nor be put away in a trove of private memory (if it proves unnecessary for us to know each other), until it is certain what is to become of us. I write "us" because this is how I now think of you and me, as one, though we have not yet spoken.

These are the words of my soul, the kind of words that are closest to music. I love music more than anything else in this world. Do you know music as a language of the soul? I think you do. When we met (yes, Josip, we met), I was in a corner of the dining room where no eyes could see me. Not wanting to disturb the guests, I remained there in order to listen to Iria's composition without intrusion. When it was over and everyone had left the room (or so I thought), I went in to sit beside the piano, to absorb the resonance of the concerto, which still radiated the room. I did not see you at first because my eyes were full of tears.

Then I saw you. Then music became flesh, light became form and place. Then, too, time disappeared.

Josip, do you believe, as I do, that every person carries within his soul a hidden image of the one he loves? Is it just attraction to the beauty of the other? I do not think it is this, for women first love the character of a man and then his appearance. We love best in another what is best in ourselves, yet we also love what is not in ourselves.

To love an ideal human being is not realism, for no person is perfection itself. Yet we can see what is truest in the other, be it only his potential, or be it fully grown. How does it come to us, this knowing? How is it that throughout my entire life there will never be another? There is only you.

How can what I have just written fail to seem no more than a girl's infatuation? Yet I know it is not. I knew immediately on seeing you that I loved you completely and eternally.

Do you doubt me, Mr. Josip Lasta, with whom I have never spoken and whom I may never see again in this world? Do you doubt me? Do not doubt. It is true what I have written.

Please do not suspect a shallow attraction. Many young men have been interested in me, some more handsome than you are (though I now think this is scarcely possible). I have liked them and have been friends with some, but none have I loved. When we hear a certain piece of music for the first time, we either drown in it with joy, or we are indifferent to it, or we are interested, yet detached, or we struggle to swim, to escape it. In all cases, we judge it by the music we have already heard in our own hearts.

Now I have seen the most beloved music living. I have seen it with its closed eyes, its breathing body, its beating heart. I have seen the soul and the mind of this music, which is you. I have seen the music open its eyes and look back at me. And in that moment there was no distance between the composer, the musician, and the one who hears the music. Only for an instant was this given to us, and I will not seek to make it happen again.

Life is now splendid because you exist. It is not essential to know you, though I will admit I hope to know you. You are the incarnation of everything I love. Do not ask me to explain this. It is simply that you are the one whom I have always known would come, though I was willing to remain forever without you. If we meet again and if we are free to speak with each other, then I will perhaps give you this letter. Or it may be that Life will ask us not to speak, and that I will keep it private always. The future opens ahead of us as a great mystery before which we can only kneel in reverence.

Will it be that I shall read this to myself when I am a very old woman? And will I smile over that moment long ago, when I met a young man who was all that my heart ever desired, to whom I desired to give my whole being? And will I feel no more than a mild regret that he was here for a moment only, and then he passed on and disappeared out of my life? Or will it be that he becomes my life? If you read this at some point in the future, if you read it when you are young or when you are old,

or read it unbeknownst to me, or never read it, Josip, you will
not fade from the sanctuary of my soul, neither in this world
nor in the next.

Ariadne Horvatinec

13

November, a stormy evening, hard rain and cold wind rattling the windows of the Horvatinecs' parlor. The third meeting of the Dolphins. A few people have dropped out, but all of the original members have returned. Josip is in his corner, incapable of thinking about anything. Behind his closed eyes, he sees only her face, each phrase of her letter flaring like a torch in the darkness of his solitude. Will she come to the meeting? Will she appear with her seashell afterward, or will she be standing outside beneath the thrashing leaves? Will she retreat as the inhabitant of a nautilus dwells entirely within, unless caught unawares? Or will she stand forth exposed and waiting for him?

It is a stormy evening inside the house too. Vlado is speaking: "We have gone about it the wrong way, Simon. Too many people know about this. Who are those people, really, the ones who were here last time? What are their political vulnerabilities? Who will they talk to? People are so stupid. They can't keep secrets."

"We have protection that you're not aware of, Vlado", says Simon. "As long as we are not blatant about our activities, certain eyes are turned the other way."

"What do you mean?"

"I cannot say."

"I think you mean spiritual protection from God and the Gospa", says Tatjana.

Simon's eyes grow distant, absorbed in a private qualification: his face, so complex and intelligent, becomes thoughtful.

"If that is in fact the truth about the world, then there will be some protection from above. Yet the world is a zone of war, and always has been. In this war, there must be human strategies. I have a strategy that offers more than spiritual cover . . . friends in the Party."

"Hopefully you have friends in the UDBA."

Simon looks at Vlado intensely but says nothing.

"Have you ever seen a dead dolphin?" the sculptor goes on. "I have. They get tangled in fishermen's nets sometimes. And after a bad storm, occasionally you will see them beached."

"We all know the risks", growls Antun. "Why be pessimistic about it? Do you want us to give up before we've really begun?"

He is in a mood tonight. Ana has returned to Zagreb, and he is brooding and despondent.

"No, I do not want us to give up", snaps Vlado. "But I do not want to see this school of jolly dolphins playing in the sea as if there were no real danger, as if the thrill of our clandestine counterrevolution were a boy's adventure."

"Simon is a bit more than a boy", scolds Vera.

Simon chuckles, but lets the argument continue.

"I know, I know. But what if this 'cover' he refers to is not enough? Do you really think the regime will tolerate what we hope to do? Remember what happened to *Narodni glas*, the people's voice, indeed. One issue and a bomb exploded in front of their office. And that was before Tito really clamped down. If they spot an issue of our magazine, they will leave no stone unturned in Yugoslavia until they find a thread that connects to us. And then we are all dead dolphins."

"First you called us moles, now you admit we are dolphins", says Stjepan. "Thank you for promoting us to a more advanced class."

"Both metaphors remain applicable", says Vlado, clenching his fist and pounding the air. "Look, all I'm trying to say is that the pleasure we take in each other's company may exact a terrible price. If we keep the door wide open the way we have, strangers will just keep coming in on the arm of people we barely know. Some merely curious. Some suspicious, and some—I am sure they will eventually come—some who believe in nothing and only want a bit of information, coinage to trade with the regime. People aren't what they used to be. They're changing, and most of you don't even know it."

"Yes, people are changing," says Simon, "but it's not because of ill will; it's due mainly to ignorance and indoctrination. That may be one of the purposes of our group, Vlado, to help such people."

"You hope for too much, Simon. You think too highly of mankind. Scratch beneath even the noblest character, and you will find the seeds of betrayal. People always can rationalize their betrayals."

"This is true," Simon replies in a pensive tone, "yet should we permit this reality of human nature to overpower our higher qualities? Should we capitulate at once, hand over everything to the enemy, simply because the seeds of the enemy are also within us?"

Vlado shakes his head. "No, I'm not suggesting that."

"Then what are you suggesting?" demands Zoran the philosopher, who has until now remained silent.

"He is just expressing his fears", says Tatjana. "The fears we all feel."

Vlado hangs his head. "Maybe it's no more than a feeling. Maybe. But I still sense we are overlooking reality here. Yes, we are dolphins. Yes, we must continue and not capitulate. Yes, we must overcome fears. But have you ever looked at the face of a dead dolphin? Even in death his lips continue to smile."

Ivan the musician interjects: "You're saying the dolphin is a naïve child. He plays in the sea and doesn't understand the threat of death. You're saying that we too are naïve."

Vlado nods. "And someday, perhaps sooner than you think, you will be caught in a net. You will be dead or dying and in pain, and you will have smiles on your faces because you printed a few poems and pictures on paper and handed them out to a few people who won't even understand what they're reading, or even guess the cost of producing them—the cost in terms of human sacrifice. But you—*you* will have your smiles."

"*You?*" asks Antun.

"Yes, *you*. I will be there in the net with you, but I will not be smiling."

"Come, come, now", says Vera, getting to her feet. "We're being so serious this evening. Let's have some wine and a bite of something. I wish Iria were here to play for us, but she's sick in bed with a bad cold. Nevertheless, she sent us a great surprise, and I'll tell you about it after we all cheer up."

After the break, Vera stands in the middle of the parlor and rattles some sheets of paper before her.

"Iria has completed her new composition, 'In the Homeland of the Soul'."

Spontaneously, everyone bursts into applause.

"But who will play?" someone asks.

"I could try", offers Ivan.

"Good, Ivan", people murmur, and clap again. In everyone's thoughts, however, is the realization that he is young and surely not as accomplished a pianist as Iria. They worry that he will mar this first performance, yet they cannot bear to leave it unheard.

"I will ask Ariadne to accompany you", declares Vera. "It's for piano and violin."

Simon frowns. "Vera . . ."

"Don't worry, darling. After all, it's a musical evening. If the watchers are keeping an eye on the house, it will be better if they hear some music."

"An aquatic musical group", Stjepan shakes his head. "Unique. And perhaps not quite credible."

"In any event, I will go ask her."

"I am here, Mama", says a young woman, stepping into the parlor from the dining room, a violin under her arm.

In the corner Josip is paralyzed with wonder. Ariadne goes to the piano and leans over the music sheets Ivan has propped above the keyboard. The piano is positioned so that both of them are facing the audience. Side by side, they read through the sheets silently, turning pages every so often, familiarizing themselves with the work.

She is slightly built, but not small. Her dark brown hair is pulled back neatly and hangs in a French braid down her back. A gray sweater covers her white blouse, and her skirt is gray also, the hem near her ankles. Her feet are in pink slippers. Josip is breathing shallowly now through his parted lips; his face is flushed, and his heart is pounding with a mixture of agony and joy. The sound of it must be audible to others, it must be shaking the walls of the room. But no one seems to notice. Ariadne does not look in his direction, not even a flicker of her eyes. She is reading the notes swiftly, her brows lightly knit. Her lips are without tension, and her entire expression is poised and thoughtful.

Ivan glances at the girl, and she nods.

The performance begins with the piano's bass notes, repeated in monotone until Ariadne lifts the base of the violin to her chin and draws the bow across the strings, making a long bass note that is slightly higher than the piano's. Slowly, slowly the score gathers force, releases a swell of lamentation. At first the violin and piano work side by side, then they gradually merge, and then become one. From that point onward, the melody rises and takes all the listeners with it. Into what realm? Into what sea of memory and what undefined future? Everything is there, the world and the land and its people. Violence and pain subsumed in an eternal harmony that returns again and again. The tides of sorrow heave and lament, yet are contained within the infinite sea of harmonious order. The cries of mankind rise and are heard by the mysterious presence within the music, some vast intelligence that sees and grieves and suffers with the people. Then the second movement begins and draws the listeners still deeper and higher. Now the women in the room shed silent tears. Soon after, the men begin to wipe their eyes. By the end of the third movement, the personal pain of each one has been incarnated in the work, and their sufferings revealed as meaningful, of inestimable value.

As on the night of the first meeting, silence follows the conclusion of the performance: a solemn and contemplative repose. There is no need for words because everything has been expressed.

Gentle applause, sighs, murmured *bravos*.

People sit without moving. It's getting late, and some must leave. One by one, they stand and shake hands, embrace, say their good-byes. Ariadne and Ivan are talking quietly, discussing details of the score. Josip remains motionless, facing the piano across the room. Will she look in his direction? Will she leave without speaking to him?

Ivan, clearly, is somewhat overwhelmed by Ariadne. Her manner with him is polite and pleasant, restrained; she says little, only a few comments about the composition. He is prolonging a discussion about music solely for the purpose of speaking with her. Any subject matter would do. It is common knowledge that he is engaged to someone else, a girl from his home town of Livno. Josip detects the exact moment when Ivan recalls this, overcomes his attraction, and firmly puts it from his thoughts. His manner becomes professional, and he departs soon after. This leaves Josip alone in the room with her.

Now she looks up and glances directly toward him. By this he realizes that she has been aware all along that he is here, conscious of where he has been standing. He takes a step toward her.

"Ariadne", he says in a low voice.

She blushes and turns to leave the room in the direction of the kitchen.

"Ariadne, I would speak with you, if you wish. Your letter . . ."

She turns back to him and closes her eyes.

"I should not have given it to you", she murmurs.

"And my letter—should I not have given it to you?"

"No, no", she breathes earnestly. "It is . . ."

Confusion races back and forth between them. Each is treasuring the letter he has received, yet both are embarrassed by their candidness, afraid that the message may have ruined the possibility of knowing the other.

Has he turned her away? Is she disappointed in him? Has he been such an inarticulate fool that this fine and serious girl could not possibly retain any interest in him? Yet her letter said . . . did she mean what she wrote? Was it a passing interest or infatuation? He does not know, and for the moment he does not care. It matters only that they are here together, even if it comes to an absolute end.

"Please, speak with me", he pleads.

She meets his eyes, and nods. "I will ask my parents. Do not go."

"I will not go."

She leaves the room and shortly after returns with Simon, her arm linked in his.

"Was it not wonderful, Josip?" he asks. "Iria has surpassed herself. But of course only she will play it as it ought to be played. Even so," he bends down and kisses his daughter's cheek, "you were magnificent. How did you and Ivan play together like that, seeing it for the first time?"

"It was the music itself, Tata. It took us to itself. We did not need to master it, for it mastered us."

"Yes, exactly. Now, where is your mother. You wanted to ask us something?"

"Mama is upstairs showing Tatjana to her room. She flies to Istria tomorrow for a culture conference."

"Ah, yes. Well, I am not your mother, but perhaps I can function in her absence."

"Dr. Horvatinec", says Josip, squaring his shoulders and tipping his head forward in a gesture of courtly deference. "I ask your permission to speak with your daughter."

"Speak with my daughter?" Simon replies with a puzzled look. "No one has ever before asked my permission to speak with her. People speak with her all the time without obtaining royal approval. What do you think, Ariadne?"

"I would like to speak with Mr. Lasta", she smiles.

Simon regards them both with a thoughtful look, then his glance settles on Josip. Josip's life hangs entirely on this glance. He struggles to remain calm and dignified, a young man worthy of seeing such a daughter. Then in those aging eyes he sees that Simon understands everything.

"Of course", he says at last. "Why don't you two sit here by yourselves and talk. I must go say good-bye to Stjepan, who is trying to break up an argument between Vlado and Antun out on the sidewalk. Those boys are one and the same kind, and they do not know it."

When he has gone, Josip and Ariadne remain standing a few feet apart, looking at each other, unable to speak.

Josip clears his throat. "Should we sit down?"

They sit on the settee, a few feet apart. There are so many words that rush through the mind, questions, declarations, reassurances. As each considers what most needs to be said, they simultaneously abandon all of it. Josip is the first to speak.

"Your letter is life to me", he says in a trembling voice.

"As yours is to me", she replies.

"It is unimaginable. That we should feel this at the same time and write what we did, and give it the way we did, even though we had not met. Surely this has never before occurred in human history."

She smiles, "Probably not."

"I do not want to presume. I fear I am presuming too much. I only hope to know you."

"Then we will know each other, you and I, because this is my fear and my hope also."

He swallows and extends his hand to hers, which is resting on the cushion between them. He touches her fingers with his own, then withdraws his hand.

"I scarcely can believe it, Ariadne."

"Nor can I, Josip, but here we are."

"Here we are."

"I do not know what to say."

"Nor do I."

"But we are speaking."

"We are—without words."

"Without words."

14

The time is three months later. They have taken many walks together throughout the city, seeing things long familiar, but entirely new because they are seeing together. The meals Josip has taken with the Horvatinec family have put a little weight on his frame, which until now has been bone and muscle in its minimalist form. More meat and fish have helped. His cheeks have filled out; his color is better. The only interests he and Ariadne do not share are running and swimming. He has dropped out of the university swim team, but he continues to do a hundred laps each day. She approves of his perseverance, but she says she prefers to walk. Besides, it is impossible to hold hands properly when you run or swim, nor can you really speak with each other. When you are running, running is your primary focus. When you swim, swimming is your focus. When they walk together, *they* are the focus and need not pay attention to where they are going.

Vera scolds Ariadne for neglecting her studies. This is not so, but it is true that she no longer practices violin four or five hours a day. Now it is three hours a day, and the rest of the time is spent either walking with Josip or staring out her bedroom window, anticipating his arrival.

It is much the same for Josip. He is writing his master's thesis, but he can concentrate on it only with an extra effort of the will. Even so, in the privacy of his little cement cell, whenever he looks up from his books, he sees her face floating above the mountains. Near him or far from him, she is always here.

He looks back down to his papers, sighs, and continues to write:

The Newtonian universe, which conceives reality as a mechanism, is concerned exclusively with material phenomena: weight and mass, volume and velocities, and thus its refusal to consider beauty and faith as realities. With the advent of twentieth-century physics, the realm of philosophical speculation returns. Einstein's differential equation of gravity or Schroedinger's wave equation do not prove the existence of the metaphysical, but they no longer banish the questions that arise in human nature regarding the nature of ultimate reality (which once more may be considered), that is, dimensions beyond the empirically evident. The "intelligence" evident in mathematics, for example, cannot "prove" anything about the ultimate nature of reality, yet it can now function in an inferential manner as a signpost into the unknown. Thus—

He throws down his pen, closes his eyes.
I love her, I love her, I love her!
They have not yet kissed. They have not even discussed it. They merely know that the time is not ripe for it. Their love is so great that a single prolonged kiss might burn up the land, ignite the sea. He kisses her forehead, cheeks, her hands. She responds in kind. They are always pressing close, side by side, arm to arm. In winter it is possible to embrace through thick coats. When spring comes, they will desist. Their hands are ever in danger of melting into a single unit. They send love to each other through their eyes, reinforced by the subtlest touches of hand to face. Once a month, they attend a symphony concert together. Once a week, they walk to the top of the Marjan and spend a few hours there, resting, talking, laughing. She too has always loved the sea. Now they love it together. Sometimes she lies down on her back with her head resting on his chest, and he strokes her forehead with his fingertips until she falls asleep. At other times she merely looks into his eyes for a long time; then, on an impulse, she reaches up and puts a finger to his lips, or the palm of her hand against his cheek. He feels pain (fear and loss) whenever he returns her to her home and they must part until

tomorrow. Yet there is joy in the pain because the reunion the next day is always better than the one before.

So it grows and grows, and none can stop it, none deflect it from its course.

They have discussed many subjects together: music and mathematics, poetry and politics, love and suffering, desire and self-denial, and also their pasts.

Though love has dissolved many of the ramparts that have guarded his most devastating memories, Josip cannot tell her everything that has happened to him. Indeed he has told her only, with a choked voice, that his parents died in the war, were murdered by Partisans, and that he is alone in the world. Seeing that he is unable to tell her more, she does not probe. Instead, she kisses him on the lips, swiftly and tenderly. This happens on the topmost rock of the Marjan. He returns the kiss as gently as it is given.

Arms around each other now, they realize that this long-anticipated kiss, which has come at last, contains for the moment no carnal desire. They know as well that the longer they keep their passions in check, the deeper their soul-love will grow.

"I did not know I was so alone", he says at last, "until you came. Suddenly I discovered two things at once. I understood that I had been alone within myself—since childhood—and that I am now no longer alone."

"This is what we were made for, Josip, to find each other and no longer to wander through this world in isolation."

"I mistook isolation for solitude. I loved my solitude, and now I no longer love it."

"It was the same for me. Music was my companion and my spouse. I still love it, but it can never again be enough for me."

"Do you not fear that it will be taken away from us?"

"Yes, I fear it. But I believe we must cast out the fear. Then our love will be indestructible."

"So many people have lost love or never found it. So many are alone. So many."

"If we live our love fully, then we can love them too."

"We will love, fully." He nods solemnly.

She takes his hand just as he is reaching for hers. How is it that they seem to move as one, when they have barely begun to live as one?

"I cannot tell you what I love in you, Ariadne, because if I were to try I would not cease speaking, and then there would be no time left to live it."

"I am the same, Josip. The same", her voice trails into a whisper. "The gift we have been given is so great, a lifetime of gratitude would not be enough to repay it."

"One does not repay a gift."

She smiles, "Yes, you are right."

Her hand is a small sun resting in his. He will never let it go. This holding is life to him; to let go of it is to sink into darkness.

"Still I would speak to you", he says. "I must speak. The signs and gestures and our self-denial—all of these speak. But there are other languages that can take us higher."

"Like certain kinds of music."

"Yes, they help us rise even as we create them."

"Love is higher than mankind, Josip, but within us too. It is love who creates in us."

"You say *who*."

"Yes, I say *who*. It is very mysterious. It moves silently and without intrusion. It is a force, yet it does not force. It is a power, yet it is the gentlest thing on earth. It is a fire, its flames even brighter than the flame within your heart and mine. In fact, I believe we are within something greater that flows through us. But this is not just energy or biology. It's as if—no, I can't find the right words for it." She pauses, then continues. "It's as if you and I are alone together, yet not alone. It's as if another is with us who is the source of our union."

"Do you mean God?"

"I'm not sure. But I feel that there is more in us than ourselves. Our love is not only *our* love. I know this does not make sense, but it does to me, at this moment anyway."

"Love is a language without words", he whispers and can say no more.

"Without words", she says, then she smiles suddenly at the necessity of using words.

They lean into each other for a while, supporting themselves shoulder to shoulder, hand in hand.

"When I was a boy," Josip says at last, "I used to speak a kind of language that did not make sense. It gave me pleasure, though my mother scolded me for it. She warned me that I must not talk nonsense."

"And your father?"

"I think he understood. He never scolded me when I was being *foolish*, as my mother called it."

Sitting on the big rock beside the oak tree in their backyard, he is gazing out over the roofs of Rajska Polja and beyond, surveying the valley as a whole. His mother is seated on the grass beside the rock, cracking walnut shells that she will boil to make a dye that is useful for staining raw wool. She is humming to herself. They are both feeling whimsical and light-hearted that day.

As he gazes at the valley, Josip is learning that parts compose a whole but are not the summation of it. He is perhaps only nine or ten years old at the time, and he has discovered that parts have a kind of being in themselves, yet they can also belong to something greater. At the moment, the valley is, in turn, part of a whole called Herzegovina. It is part of the world. The world is part of the solar system, and the solar system is part of the universe. The universe is a sea.

It all fits together, and it moves in a marvelous order. This is the first time he has seen it with his eyes. Though, of course, his textbooks and Tata's lessons have already inscribed it in his mind. Now it lives. It is immense, complex, and so moving that tears spring unbidden to his eyes.

"O *cosmos!*" he gasps.

His mother turns to him curiously and smiles.

"What did you say, Joshko?"

In reply, he takes one of the white stones from the sea out of his pocket and rolls it around in the palm of his hand.

"It's so beautiful, Mamica," he breathes, "so beautiful . . ."

"Yes, it's a nice stone. Don't lose it."

He had not meant that the stone was beautiful, only that everything is wondrous and the particular harmony in the stone's form reflects the vast harmony in which they live and move and have their being. His eyes are misted with the wonder of it all, his immersion in a world that he has not really understood before.

He turns to her and says, "The sea is a cosmos, and the cosmos is a sea."

She chuckles. "Well, it's not quite like that."

"But it *is*", he says emphatically, yearning for her to understand.

She is exasperated by his speaking cryptically. He has been doing a lot of it lately. Something he said about a feather the other day, and then there was all that nonsense about the swallows—as if they could talk to a boy!

"We swim in it!" he declares.

"What do you mean, we swim in it? Swim in what?"

"The cosmos."

"Josip, stop that now. People will think you've lost your wits."

"But it makes me happy."

"How happy will you be when you're sent to a hospital for crazy boys?"

She kisses him, and tells him to go find more walnuts.

Now, all these years later, he remembers that incident as freshly as the day it happened. Perhaps it was fourteen or fifteen years ago, in a time before the world ended.

"My father was a literate man", Josip says to Ariadne. "Not in the sense of one who merely filled his mind with the contents of what he read. He understood that words of beauty and truth raise man higher than himself. No, that is not exactly what I mean. To be honest, he and I never talked about it. But I remember the stories he read to me, and I remember him smiling at me whenever I spoke in my strange tongue."

"What did you say in that tongue, Josip?"

"Little things."

The blue feather falling from the sky is sent.

"About nature?"

"Yes."

The sea is breathing.

Then, later:

The dove, soaring, sees the distant curve of the earth,
and trembles at its shape—
The sea surrounding it is deeper than fathoming.

Later still:

Rising higher, he looks down to the small orderings of man—

"I once wrote a line of poetry", she says. "It came from somewhere inside of me, but I don't know where. They were terribly important to me, those few words. They seemed to have no beginning and no end."

"What were the words?"

"*The wing's curve, the wind's curve, the earth's curve.*"

"That's all?"

"Yes, that's all." She squeezes his hand. "So you see, I too was capable of *foolishness*."

"How old were you?"

"Twelve. I remember because it was my birthday, the day we heard that my uncle had been arrested."

"The curve of a wing and the arc of the planet. To connect them is a way of seeing, Ariadne."

"Yes, but what did I see? And what did it have to do with my uncle? I was crying for him, alone in my bedroom. Then the words came. They just came, and now all these years later I still do not know why. Yet I remember them, and I know I must not forget them."

"It's strange isn't it? I have so many passages like that in my memory, and also the feeling that they must be remembered. Why are we like this?"

"I don't know," she smiles, "but I am certain of one thing: we are now like this together."

"*How will these small wings carry me?*" he whispers.

"You are speaking your language, Josip."

"Yes. *How will these small wings carry me, for the earth is so great and I am so small.*"

"The bird rises and takes us with it. Yet, as we rise, we tremble at what we begin to see."

"The curve of a wing, the curve of a horizon. Then we begin to understand, Ariadne, that we are very small."

"It seems to me that the higher we rise, the greater is the mystery of the unknown. The more we see, the more we realize how little we understand; but love shows us our greatness too."

"The world is growing cold. So much hatred, so much death, so much spilled blood."

"That is why love is needed, Josip. The indestructible love."

"And at last this love has come. You are here."

"I am here", she whispers, looking up into his eyes. "I am here."

Her arrested uncle has been missing since 1945. A Jesuit priest, he taught theology in Zagreb. Refusing to flee before the approaching Partisan army, he remained in the city to minister to the wounded. He was caught in the net. He was Simon's older brother.

"Are your parents Christians?" Josip asks.

"When I was a child, we went to church. As you can see, my mother is not exactly a typical Croat. She spent much of her life in Vienna. Tata studied surgery there before returning to Split. It's where they met. Their circle of friends in Austria was the intellectual and cultural elite of the time. I think there were many atheists among them, but no Communists as far as I can tell. As you know, they have no love for either Communists or Fascists, so I suppose you could call them liberal democrats. They do not discuss it with me."

"One may be a devout Christian and a democrat. Antun and Tatjana, Ana and Zoran."

"Yes, but that's not the case with my parents. You must understand, they are the best of people, Josip. They love each other and have been through so much since the Communists came to power. They shelter me from everything."

"Ariadne, this is one aspect of your family that puzzles me. Your father is a highly visible man, yet he is not connected to the regime, nor is he sympathetic in any way to it. And now our Dolphins put him in more danger. Why does he risk it? What does he hope to gain by it?"

"He loves our people, and he knows that what we are has been purchased by untold centuries of sacrifice. He sees what has happened in Russia and is happening now in China. He hopes for the coming of true democracy, so that we will be free to know ourselves as we really are."

"But we are Catholics", Josip murmurs, staring at the ground beneath his feet.

"Yes, this is our socio-cultural consciousness. My uncle talked to me once about this. He was an extraordinary man. The summer before he was taken from us, he and I went for a walk to the church down by the imperial palace, the little place the Franciscans have on the promenade. We went inside and prayed together. You must understand, Josip, that he was the most brilliant man, yet he could pray as a child. I loved him. I still love him."

"Yet you are not a believer."

"I'm not sure what I believe now. I love my family, and I believe in God. But I don't know about religion. Josip, you said that we are Catholics. Yet you do not pray or go to church either."

"Catholicism is our culture and our history, and for that reason it is an indelible part of our Croat identity."

"Still, I wonder," she says uneasily, "can there be a living culture without a living religion? That is what my uncle said to me the last time we saw each other. He told me that great evils were approaching and perhaps the crucifixion of the Church. Everyone would be put to the test. I thought he meant the Nazis, and so I argued that they were being pushed out. He said that after the Nazis there would come a worse evil. I would live to see it, he told me. His face was so worried, so anxious for me. He took me up to the tabernacle, and we knelt before it, side by side. He begged God not to let me fall into the evil. Later, as we walked together back to my home, he told me that the Communists would come and stay for a long time, but eventually they would lose power. After that would be the time of greatest danger, he said. A false peace, he called it, a moral void. And into that void the worst evil of all would come, if we do not recognize it and resist it."

"Did he say what kind of evil?"

"No."

"Well, we have evil enough right now. It looks as if they will never lose power."

"Yes," she nods, musing, "it looks that way. But we can still live as if their days are numbered."

"I suppose that's what the Dolphins are about. Ariadne, I am still puzzled by your father's confidence that we will not be troubled by the police."

"There are three reasons for his confidence. The first is that there is another brother. My father's younger brother is an influential member of the Party. A high official in Dalmatia. The second reason is that my father is one of the most skilled spinal surgeons in Yugoslavia, perhaps in all of Europe. He has operated on people in the resistance and on big officials from Belgrade. No one would want to see him in prison."

"And the third reason?"

"His character. As you see, he is a man of noble qualities and great intelligence. Also he is a kind of father to many people."

"Ariadne, it seems to me that great men can become the objects of envy and hatred."

"But he would harm no one! He is a moral leader among our people. His presence alone gives others courage."

"He is a moral leader, though not a religious one", Josip muses.

"It wasn't always so. When he was a boy, he wanted very much to be a priest, like his older brother. But he fell in love with Mama, and I think they were both influenced by thinkers in Vienna. He began to doubt, and then the doubts grew. He was horrified by what the Ustashe were doing, and at that time he did not have a clear picture of what a danger the Chetniks and the Communists would become. His high idealism could not bear to see our nation involved in evil, and it shook his faith to the roots. A friend of his tried to help him understand. He is an archbishop now, the cardinal in Zagreb."

"I have heard about him. A controversial figure."

"Yes. He and Tata talked a lot together when my father was going through his crisis of faith, but Tata was listening to many different voices by then, mostly intellectuals from other countries. He had known the cardinal since they were both young, and he admired him very much, even when they disagreed.

Once my father told me that Stepinac is a sign of contradiction, and for that reason he is a sign who will be rejected. He condemned the evils committed by the Ustashe, defended the Jews from the Italians and the Germans, and now the Communists call him a Fascist. He defends the civil freedoms of all men, in the face of every kind of regime, and for that reason each in turn has viewed him as an enemy of the state. I hear that when he ordains men to the priesthood he tells them, 'I am sending you into a river of blood.'"

"So, you don't believe what they say about him in the press?"

"No, of course not. He is a saint, Josip, a man of truth, and he is suffering for it. Tata says they will kill him."

"Ariadne, you believe in saints, but you are not sure about religion?"

Tears fill her eyes. "I recognize the contradictions, Josip. It's what our enemies have done to us. They have confused so many things. But you, also, Josip—you believe and do not believe."

The pain this question evokes is beyond all proportion to its subject. He swallows hard and breathes more heavily.

How can he tell her about Fra Anto's body, which continues to lie prone on the steps of every church? How can he explain that he knows the image is a wound in his mind, that there is in fact no body lying there, but that the horror blocks his entry to churches? If the enemies of God can kill a man as good as Fra Anto, and imprison a man as fine as the cardinal, and destroy families and villages and nations that follow God, where then is God? And if he exists, why does he not act, why does he not defend his children? The question is so steeped in blood that, whenever it flashes into his mind, he can sustain it only for a moment at a time. It must be pushed away. He cannot solve it, so why should he torment himself with it?

He says nothing of this to Ariadne. Their love is everything to him now. Their love is the world. It is his religion.

Another day: They are strolling along a walkway in the park below the crest of the Marjan.

"I love your name", he whispers.

"Do you?" she says. "To tell you the truth, I have never been that fond of it."

"No?" he exclaims. "Why not?"

She laughs. "My mother worships everything classical, especially the golden ages of Greece and Rome. The Greek myths have always appealed to her."

"Ah, I wondered why you have a Greek name."

"You must know the story of Ariadne and Theseus?"

"Of course. Theseus was a prince of Athens who was sent to Crete, where he was to go down into a Labyrinth as a sacrificial victim to the Minotaur. Every year this monster devoured young men and women as human sacrifice. No one who entered the Labyrinth ever came out again."

"Yes, but when Theseus arrived in Crete, the princess Ariadne fell in love with him." She squeezes Josip's arm. "Very, very much in love with him."

"And she gave him some thread."

"She gave him a ball of thread, which he attached to the door of the Labyrinth as he went in. In this way, he could find his way out if he was able to kill the Minotaur. And so he did."

Josip smiles. "And so he did."

"Remember how he and Ariadne sailed away together and were shipwrecked on another island. There are different versions of what happened next, some better than others. In the one I like best, Theseus was blown away to sea in a storm, and Ariadne was convinced he had abandoned her, so she died of a broken heart with a child in her womb. In another version, Dionysus arrived after the disappearance of Theseus and married her."

"Why do you prefer the first one? It's horrible."

"Every version ends badly, Josip. In the one I like best, Ariadne remains true to her first love, even though she dies."

"All in all, it's not a happy tale."

She laughs again. "In the beginning it is happy."

"One may defeat a monster only to be defeated by the human heart."

"In any case, I would not like to be part of such a tragedy."

"Then you, Ariadne, must make of your life a happy story."

"It is no longer my life. It is our life. I feel certain, my Josip, that together we will make a story with only joy in it."

It is spring of the year 1957. More than two dozen people are crammed into the parlor, dining room, and hallway of the Horvatinec home, gathered together to celebrate the inaugural issue of *Dobri Dupin*. Wine and *rakija* are flowing. The tables are heaped with sweets and breads and slices of smoked fish.

Iria plays "In the Homeland of the Soul", which is greeted by tears and heartfelt applause. She blushes unceasingly and says nothing. Stjepan laughs and waxes ebullient for the first time. Vlado manages a few transitory smiles, and even his cautionary notes are somewhat humorous. Antun and Ana announce their engagement; they are so publicly in love that everyone dotes over them. Stunned with euphoria, the slippery otter is practically unrecognizable. In marked contrast, Josip and Ariadne sit on two stiff chairs, side by side, in a corner of the dining room, far from the radioactivity. Their love is not public. They cast long glances at each other and briefly touch hands.

Simon presents a copy of the journal to each person present. It is a humble creation, sixty staple-bound pages of newsprint covered in a fine sheet of glossy turquoise. On the cover is a black and white photograph of a sculpture by Vlado. It is, of course, a leaping dolphin.

Most people plunge into the volume immediately, and conversation dies, replaced by quiet murmurs and general wonder that such a work has really come into existence.

Josip and Ariadne bend over their copies:

The subject matter is broad ranging. All of the authors' names are pseudonyms. There are three political essays, and it is not difficult to recognize Antun's hand in one titled *The Corruption of the Geo-psyche under Imposed Cultural Revolutions*. A long short story, *The Watering of the Earth*, about those who died during the war, doubtless written by Stjepan. More than a dozen poems in various styles. Josip says to Ariadne that he thinks one titled "Flowers in the White City" is by Tatjana. There is an essay on modern antitotalitarian fiction. Another on underground literature in Eastern Europe. Iria's musical score, with stirring lyrics by someone named "Slobodan".

There is a rather clumsy piece by "Žir" (acorn) titled "Labyrinth", which Ariadne points out to Josip and reads to him in a whisper:

In the island of the sea there dwells insatiable appetite,
The bull of Beograd in its subterranean hell
Will gorge upon its feast of human blood
And none can tell when he is full, for he is never full.

This man-devourer, muscle and sword cannot defeat;
A girl alone will weave demise, for she
with finest thread uncrypts the maze, confounds the dead.
The beast is bled and black its light.
The gods of Baalgrad fall back at sight.

Then blow harsh winds, the valiant prince
Is taken from the love that saves, the thread unwound is
    wound again.
She grieves the loss of one she wed, and a child within its
    mother-bed,

For woes both ancient and to come, no sword suffice, no
   human art:
One may defeat a monster yet be defeated by the human
   heart.

Ariadne looks up. "Josip, *you* wrote this!"

He smiles ruefully. "I'm sorry, it's not very good."

"It's strong, and the poetic sense is in it. But the rhyming and
meter . . ."

"I know. It's embarrassing. But it will stop Antun from
calling me a poet. Now he'll have to admit I'm no more than a
scientist who dabbles in poetic fragments."

She gives him a long look. Then, lowering her eyes she
says, "No matter what comes, my beloved, we will not be
defeated."

Sensing some unstated fear or sorrow in her, he puts his arm
around her shoulder. Then, forgetting entirely that there are
other people in the room, he leans over and kisses her on the
lips. Their second kiss. She begins to tremble, and silent tears
run down her cheeks. He holds her close.

Looking up at last, they see, to their embarrassment, that
everyone in the room is staring at them, and beaming with
approval.

Antun leaps across the room and punches Josip playfully on
the shoulder. He lifts a glass.

"Won't be long before another engagement!" he declares
theatrically. "And before you know it—baby dolphins everywhere!"

The room ripples with laughter. Vera jumps in with maternal
rights and powers: "Now leave the young people alone!" she
scolds. "They don't need a whole soccer stadium watching
them hold hands. Ariadne, you take Josip out for a walk. He is
looking pale."

More laughter.

"And bring me back some acorns", calls Antun, as they leave.

Simon observes it all with a slight smile that is belied by the worry in his eyes.

15

Josip awakes in his darkened room. It is the middle of a hot summer night. The window is wide open, and stars are blazing in the sky across the bay, above the mountain wall. That wall is a dam holding back the horror of his past.

Standing before the open window, he gazes at the sky—the sea above. He is aware as never before of the inner reservoir of life within him—the inland sea. Thousands of children might come from him, if time and the sequence of generations permits. To germinate untold numbers of human lives, each of them never before seen, never to be repeated. How splendid and mysterious it is. He has never given much thought to his body. Though he looks after it, feeds it, cleans it, and exercises it, on the whole he lives almost entirely in his mind. This body carries him, like a beast of burden, and if he regards it as a component of his identity, it is not central, not entirely integrated with the whole.

Ariadne is helping him to understand himself, to see the part and the whole. But how can this ever find complete expression? How can he consider the creation of a new life when the world is so full of perils, and this land one of the most dangerous? Is it not an act of cruelty to conceive a child? Will he and Ariadne become another tragedy, like Josip and Tereza in Rajska Polja, who gave birth only to see their baby shot as it took its first breaths?

He cannot bear this memory, even though the loss is another's. How, then, could he ever survive the destruction of his own child?

Josip and Ariadne have discussed this in a roundabout way: so much death, so much innocent blood spilled by men of power, and now all the land is in the absolute grip of such men.

"But we have survived", she says.

"Have we?" he asks.

"We have."

"And what have we lost?"

"Life always contains blessing and loss."

"But what has our survival cost?"

"I do not ask the cost, Josip. This is what was given to me. And what you are was given to you."

"Tell me, Ariadne," he says, in a voice of deep gloom, "what was given to me?"

"Your life was given to you", she whispers. "And beautiful is this life to me. So much, so much has been given to you, and it is given to me through you."

He ponders what she has said. He cannot explain to her the agony that he feels over the question of survival. His entire community was destroyed, with most of his family, and the only other member who was not destroyed has allied herself with the regime of the killers. He is alone in the world. How can he create a family from the foundation of such aloneness?

"You are not alone", she says, reading his mind, taking his hand. "We are together. Is it not enough?"

"It is enough", he says, because to say anything else would damage their union.

"You say one thing with your lips, Josip, yet I hear in your heart another thing."

"To marry, Ariadne, and to bring children into this world, is a terrible risk."

"Yes, but has it ever been otherwise? Life is always dangerous. It is always risk."

"I do not know if I have the strength to take this risk", he groans, covering his eyes with his hand.

"You are strong, Josip, stronger than you think you are. You suffer for your lost family—I know this is really what troubles you. But now we are able to make a new family, and through us life will triumph over death."

"Will it? I do not know."

She has never seen him weep before. She is astonished, but she is able to understand the conflicts in his heart: he is impelled by the vitality of his strength, and at the same time he is pulled down by the memory of the evil he has experienced.

"I love you", she says quietly. "And I will not leave you."

"You will be taken away. I know you will be taken away."

Now she sees that this large man, a man of so many strengths and qualities of character, can revert to the condition of a frightened boy. Many women would have been repelled, many would see such vulnerability as a threat to their future security. Instead, she loves him more than before.

"I cannot be taken away", she says, pulling the hand from his eyes. "I cannot be taken from you, because I am now, and forever, living in your heart."

He gazes at her bleakly, questioningly. She puts the palm of her hand to his chest.

"This is where I live", she says. Then she takes his right hand in both of hers and presses it to her heart.

Josip ponders this conversation again and again as he stands alone in the night, gazing at the stars. And it comes to him slowly, slowly, that written in the glory of the cosmos is both a promise of joy and a promise of sorrow. Beyond them and through them is the promise of final victory. He can feel hope now, a sense that even sorrows may become part of the coming victory. He will suffer, but he will no longer suffer alone. He returns to his bed and sleeps.

It is September of 1957. The wedding takes place in the parlor of the Horvatinec home, which is now crammed to the full with guests. As each one enters, he is presented with a tiny glass of *rakija* and a sprig of rosemary tied with a pink ribbon. Antun is doing these honors because Vera is upstairs with Ariadne putting the finishing touches on their hair. Antun is now living in Zagreb, completing his doctoral thesis, but he and his wife, Ana, have come by bus to Split for the event. The only Dolphin missing is Tatjana, who has not returned from a conference on literature in Italy. In fact, she has remained there as a refugee.

The second issue of *Dobri Dupin* has been printed but not yet distributed. The two hundred copies are hidden away somewhere in the house, because there will be people here today of questionable reliability. All Dolphins have been alerted to the need for silence about their activities. Besides, it's not a meeting, it's a wedding!

Simon has given Josip a fine suit and tie, and new black shoes as well. During the past few months Josip's admiration for his future father-in-law has developed into an unspoken affection, though he remains somewhat in awe of the man and feels quite unworthy of his daughter. Yet Simon treats him as a son, as if Josip were already inextricably and fundamentally one with Ariadne. Despite several satisfactory, paternal-filial conversations about the future, there remains a gap between them, caused in part by the many other concerns on the doctor's mind, and perhaps also by the enigmatic nature of his future son-in-law. That Ariadne loves Josip with a rare and absolute devotion cannot be contested, and the doctor knows his daughter's mind well. He trusts her discernment, but so far has little empirical evidence of what her betrothed is really like. He knows that he is reliable, intelligent, discreet (he is, after all, a Dolphin), has overcome the obscure sufferings of his childhood (as have so many others), and is now an assistant professor of mathematics at the university. He will provide adequately for Ariadne, and in all likelihood they will be happy together. For this—above all for this—Simon is grateful. Even so, as he brings his daughter into the parlor on his arm, there are tears in his eyes and a tension in his face that is lightly masked by an apparent joy.

For Josip, the surrounding world dissolves as she enters the room. He sees only her eyes uniting with his, feels the sun glowing in his breast and the light in hers as they stand together. They are already one heart, and in a few moments they will be completely one in the eyes of man and state.

The ceremony is a civil one, officiated by a clerk from the municipal marriage bureau. He does his duty and departs swiftly.

Unchecked jubilation erupts, loud cheers, laughter, embraces, the guests waving long multicolored ribbons in circles. Vera enfolds her daughter, sobbing with a surfeit of emotion. Simon pumps Josip's hand, while Antun kisses his friend on both cheeks and Vlado punches him lightly in the stomach and grins. Stjepan ponderously bestows a florid, grandiloquent speech of congratulation. Iria stands on tiptoes and kisses the down-bending Josip on his forehead and does the same to Ariadne. It goes on and on, and in the tumult, both bride and groom forget to kiss each other. They will not, however, permit their hands to be separated—these hands are welded together. Now the flowers become visible, flowers pinned to clothing, flowers bursting through the walls, flowers in vases everywhere. There are roses and chrysanthemums and hibiscus, and the pink orchid at the neck of Ariadne's white lace dress.

The windows are all open, and though it is an autumn afternoon, birds are rioting in the garden as if it were spring, as if they were in courtship, as if all creation were leaping to a new level of fecundity. Innumerable nests and homes and generations of lives are pouring from this single moment. As the noise of birds and men grows in volume, Zoran is shouting something abstract into Josip's ear, something about "co-creation". Iria is at the piano playing a Bosnian wedding song, and three or four people sing along. Ivan is strumming a bandura—evoking only the best memories. One of Ariadne's cousins is here as well, a girl from Austria. She is lovely, and Ivan is captivated by her, pulled in an ever-tightening orbit toward her. All commotion stops when Vera urges the cousin to play a wedding sonata by Mozart. Like Ariadne, she is a violinist. A member of the Vienna symphony orchestra, she comes from another world, a safe world, where culture is never a dangerous pursuit. Of all the people in the house, she is the only one who can cross borders without trouble. She plays the piece with aplomb and feeling.

Perhaps it is the music that opens a path in the tumultuous proceedings: at last Josip kisses his bride. So tender and swift, this kiss, so full of everything that is to come. None of the burdensome past is in this kiss, only the bright future. She knows it too and speaks it back to him, their eyes confirming what has been exchanged.

He will not remember the feast that follows, the marvelous food that has taken days to prepare, nor the fragments of conversation with these dear friends, whom only a year or so ago he did not know existed and who now have become like family to him. He feels a great affection for each and, as ever, can articulate it only with his eyes, a hand to an arm, or a mumbled word of thanks. They understand his diffidence and recognize all that he wishes to say, but cannot.

There are a handful of people here whom he has never met, bubbling friends of Ariadne's from the music faculty, and also a few older men and women who seem congenial enough but whose manners are reserved. Josip is introduced to the director of the city's main hospital, then to a friend of Simon's, a fellow doctor, and finally to someone named "Uncle Goran" and the woman who accompanies him. Goran is Simon's younger brother. He appears to be ten years older, and he is at least twenty kilos heavier. His manner is as unlike Simon's as could be, for his eyes are guarded and his mouth, smiling so socially, is lined with old ironies and sarcasms. He says the right things, pleasantries and best wishes, as does his companion, but Josip excuses himself from their company as soon as he is able. He recalls that this is the Communist brother.

Dancing begins, quite a feat in the crowded rooms. It spreads from room to room and out into the back garden, where torches have been lit. More than one love is sparked this evening and more engagements consolidated. They dance for hours, Ariadne graceful, as she is in everything, Josip clumsy but rapturous.

Later, when they make their departure, Josip and Ariadne go down the front steps of the house and turn to face the crowd that has poured out onto the sidewalk to bid them good-bye and good luck. Everyone talks at once, shouting farewells and advice and blessings. Dangerous amounts of food and drink have been consumed, and few, if any, of the guests are entirely sober. Vera steps forward and places into Ariadne's hands a loaf of bread with an open bottle of wine perched tipsily on top of it. She kisses her daughter, and then speaks in a voice of tyrannical maternal command:

"Now, walk to the car, my dear, and if you can reach it without spilling a drop, you will have a happy life."

Everyone holds his breath as Ariadne obeys; step by step she goes, until she arrives safely and clasps the neck of the bottle with a gasp of relief.

The crowd applauds and shouts incoherently.

Simon steps up to the groom.

"Josip, my son!"

"Yes, Father?"

"Remove your shoe!"

Puzzled, hopping a little to keep his balance, Josip removes one of his shoes.

Simon takes the shoe and gives it to Ariadne.

"Show him!" he commands.

Ariadne takes the shoe and gives Josip a thump on the arm with it, laughing.

"Now you know who's the boss!" cries Vera.

"Now you will always remember", declares Simon, "that you must never use your strength against a woman!"

The ritual completed, the entire crowd bursts into cheers. Somewhat dazed, Josip hops about and puts his shoe back on. Ariadne drags him into the back seat of the car, and the driver takes off with them down the hill toward the promenade, past the imperial palace, and onward into the south, toward the sea.

They will spend the week in a hut on the shore of the Adriatic, about an hour's drive from the city. It is an isolated place at the end of a dirt road that leads down to a little cove. The driver helps carry baskets of food and water jugs from the car to the back door of the building. The wind is blowing in off the sea, and the lap of invisible waves softens all other sounds. A night bird cries. The stars in the west are brilliant. Unseen trees stand nearby, their limbs sighing, and the scent in the air is of oranges and lavender.

When the car drives away up the slope of the hill, leaving them alone at last, Josip and Ariadne hold each other tightly for a time, listening to the wind.

"Let's go in", she says.

Josip unlocks the door, and they enter the little dwelling that will be their first home.

Striking a match, he lights an oil lamp hanging from the rafters, then a candle on the wooden table that stands by a window overlooking the sea. Hand in hand, they glance about the room. Its walls and floor are stone. In the shadows above the roof beams are red tiles. It is very small and perfect.

A white quilt covers the low wooden bed, and on the pillows someone has laid sprigs of rosemary and lavender. They look at the bed, then at each other, and they smile. How is it possible, such happiness?

They sit down on the two chairs by the table. With his fingers Josip strokes the gold band on her wedding finger. She touches the ring on his hand and strokes it. Time has disappeared. There is only quiet now and peace, caressed by the waves and by the wind.

The people who prepared the place have arranged a vase of lilies on the table and a bowl of fruit—pomegranates, yellow plums, black grapes—and another bowl of ripe figs. Josip gazes at the figs, then takes one. This movement is oddly familiar, but he cannot remember why. He is about to put it into his mouth but pauses and, with a look of great love, lifts it to Ariadne's lips. She opens her mouth, and he places it on her tongue. They hold hands as she slowly eats it.

Later, when they are ready to go to bed, Josip removes from the inside pocket of his jacket a little package. He puts it into her hands. She opens it carefully. Inside, she finds his most precious possession, the carving of a swallow.

"For you", he whispers.

She kisses it. Then, from a bag by her feet, she takes a package wrapped in turquoise paper and puts it into his hand. He opens it carefully. Inside is the chambered nautilus.

"For you", she whispers.

16

Their first literal home, after the hut by the sea, is an apartment built into the north wall of the palace compound. They love its two small rooms, which are a little cramped but spacious because of their joy. It is theirs and theirs alone. The stone hut where they first knew their nuptial love will always be the icon of their homes to come. And they must surely come, because in time children will fill each one, and more rooms will be needed, more beds, more noise and activity and laughter and crying. As many children as life will give them.

The apartment is on the third floor, reached by an exterior stone staircase that zigs and zags up to the porch by their front door. Here Ariadne keeps a terra cotta pot with a bushy juniper growing in it, and another pot with a leafy plant that perpetually sprouts bright pink flowers. She and Josip like to sit here in the evenings and gaze out over the maze of narrow cobbled streets of this city within a city, savoring its atmosphere, the Roman foundations on which were built the medieval and Renaissance additions. The latter are mostly apartment blocks, and in one of these the Lastas now live.

The apartment's sitting room has a small window opening onto a park north of the city walls. It is crowded with books, and a comfortable sofa and chair have been donated by Stjepan, who, it turns out, is a semi-affluent bachelor. Josip's goat-hair rug adds a splash of warmth, and Ariadne's violin and music stand fill the rest of the space. The walls are cream-white bricks that Ariadne has scrubbed clean and then brightened further by brightly colored landscapes painted by friends and soberly balanced by the nineteenth-century painting of the sea battle of

Lepanto, a wedding gift from Simon and Vera. In an alcove is the tiny kitchen, and beyond that a curtain hides a small bathtub and toilet. Their bedroom, off the parlor, contains a wide bed with head- and footboard carved in Dalmatian folk motif. Beside it is a desk for Josip's work, heaped with papers, journals, books. There is also a set of dresser drawers and a very old wooden armoire, in which Ariadne keeps her dresses and Josip his one good suit. The little latticed window opens onto a network of tree branches in the park, some of which have bird nests cradled in the crook of their arms. Displayed on the sill are the chambered nautilus and the carving of the swallow. Josip has placed with them a single round white stone from the cove where they spent their honeymoon.

"I will add a stone each year", he tells Ariadne.

"Good," she replies, "this means we will need to find a house with a larger window, for I expect to see seventy-five stones sitting there someday."

"Three quarters of a century! By then I will be bent and toothless and forget my own name."

"I will remind you."

"Ah, that is worth waiting for."

"And if I forget your name and my name too, our children will remind us. And their children also. We will be the quaint old couple taking walks on the promenade with our canes and our fond memories. People will not want to talk with us so much because we will speak too slowly and we will not finish our sentences properly."

"But inside ourselves, Ariadne," he says drawing her down onto the sofa and kissing her, "we will be young always."

"You will be running to the top of the Marjan—always."

"You will be demolishing my heart as you play your violin—always."

"You will be jumping into the sea as you did at sunrise on our first day as man and wife—always."

"And I will bring you with me deep into the blue and golden light—always."

"And we will laugh underwater—and conceive our baby dolphins there—always."

Here the conversation ends—as always.

The quarter where they live within the palace compound is a neighborhood of artists and academicians, bureaucrats, shop-keepers, and assorted young married folk who have procured the rather decrepit dwellings with a mixture of romanticism and Party connections.

Simon and Vera had at first encouraged Josip and Ariadne to move into the family home on the hill of Manus, reasoning that the house is too large for two aging people, and that there is more than enough space to make a separate apartment. But Ariadne insisted on a separate dwelling. They eat with the Horvatinecs once or twice during the weekdays. Every Sunday, if Simon is not in the surgery that day, the Lastas and their parents take leisurely walks together on the promenade after the midday meal, then sit in the Horvatinecs' garden throughout the afternoon and into the evening, sipping wine, talking about their dreams for the future and the situation in the country, discussing articles that have been submitted for the third issue of *Dobri Dupin*, and exchanging news of the Dolphins and other friends. They try not to stay out too late, because Josip teaches on Monday morning. Besides, they need time every night to fall asleep in each other's arms.

Though Josip slowly grows accustomed to all this bliss, sometimes during his run to the top of the Marjan he stops in mid-stride, shakes his head, and says to himself: *I am married. Yes, I am a married man. Just yesterday I was a child! Now I am married to the most wonderful woman in the world. Is it possible? Is it real? Perhaps, after all, there is a God.* Then he resumes his run. Reaching the top, he never fails to experience elation, yet, after the run back down into the city, the arrival at his home is the greater exultation.

It is their first Christmas together. In the days preceding the outlawed feast Josip helps Ariadne drag the potted juniper into the parlor, where it sits in the exact center of the room. She decorates it with straw stars and numerous small bells that she has collected since childhood. Tying walnut shells to the branches with red thread, she fills them with grains of golden incense, raisins, and nuts.

She asks him about the customs of his family when he was a child. He tells her he cannot think about all that, he does not remember much. "We had nice food. We sang too", he murmurs vaguely. He looks away from her and busies himself with moving the little kitchen table to another wall where she wants it. She regards him thoughtfully, but says nothing.

One Saturday is spent walking in the woods on the far side of the Marjan, collecting birch twigs, pine cones, and sprays of evergreen to decorate the apartment. The birch twigs are for *polazniki* (carolers), which by tradition represent the shepherds of Bethlehem. When she was very young, aunts, uncles, and cousins would arrive at the house on Christmas eve and barge in carrying birch twigs or evergreen fronds, and then run about, lightly striking all the inhabitants, warning them to stay awake because Herod would soon come to destroy the children. After that they sang a carol, were fed dry bread and sour wine, and then they all went off to midnight Mass. Since the war, Simon and Vera no longer continue this custom.

"You will not hit me too hard, I hope", Josip says to his wife during their nightly embrace.

"I will hit you very hard, and maybe with a shoe too!"

He laughs. He loves her so much: to strike each other even in jest is unthinkable.

The day before Christmas Eve, she brings up the subject of

Mass. She would like them both to attend, even if they are no longer certain of the faith. It is a custom, and people should not abandon customs too readily. Especially now that the government hates these customs and seeks at every turn to abolish them.

"I would rather spend the night alone with you, Ariadne. We will think about our future together, and about the light within us that will defeat the darkness. We will think about our children, the ones who are coming to us."

"That is a beautiful way to spend Christmas", she nods in agreement.

Even so, on Christmas Eve she puts a little crèche on the windowsill, flanked by the nautilus and the swallow. The crèche is very old, a log stable made of twigs and stuffed with moss. St. Josip, Mother Marija, the angel, shepherds, and animals are arranged, fine porcelain figures that belonged to Ariadne's grandmother. The manger is also porcelain, but empty. There is no child.

"Where is the baby?" Josip asks curiously.

"I'm hiding him from Herod." She will explain no more.

On Christmas morning, they awake to the sound of bells ringing throughout the city. This, doubtless, is illegal, but the government probably does not have the stamina to destroy Christmas utterly; they know that the people would never accept it. An uneasy truce endures for a day, with government offices reluctantly open. Drowsing on the bed, tangled in sheets, Josip gazes toward the crèche and smiles: the baby is there in the manger. It is unlike the other figures, for it is made of wax, so perfectly molded that it is almost human, delicately painted and swaddled in lace. It too is very old, from Italy, Ariadne explains.

Throughout the day, Josip does small tasks for her, such as filling a vase with evergreens, which she wants on the table, and running up the hill to borrow a cup of almond slices from Vera.

Mostly he watches Ariadne bustling about the apartment, straightening decorations, singing to herself, fussing over the dress she will wear to supper at her parents' home. She is baking a little cake, which she calls *chestnitsa*, containing a silver coin that is said to bring plenty of good luck. She also braids loops of dough for loaves of sweetbread made from ingredients purchased at the market.

"An old woman sold me a special spice—a *secret* spice", says Ariadne with a mischievous smile. "I think you will like it."

He will like it. He will like it so much that it will crack something inside him.

"I'll take a nap while it's baking", he whispers to her, kissing her cheek; then he goes into the bedroom and shuts the door. Later, after she has removed the loaves from the oven, coated them with sugar icing, and sprinkled them with the almonds, she enters the bedroom to wake him up. She finds him weeping silently. There is no need for explanation. She sees it all, understands what he is feeling on this most festive of days: the absence of his own traditions, which have been cleaved entirely from his life. Yet as she lies down beside him and holds him, she knows as well that she is recreating the traditions, and restoring, a little, what he has lost.

Vera serves roast goose by candlelight at the big table in the Horvatinec parlor. China tureens are full of steaming vegetables, steeped in butter. There are dumplings, a bowl of black rice, and the platter of smoked sea foods. Dark red wine from the islands flows. Afterward, cookies and homemade *sachertorte* and glasses of *rakija*. Stjepan is present too, looking somewhat forlorn, but restraining his loneliness. Iria is a guest as well, as are Ivan and his fiancée, a shy girl named Lucija, from Livno. Stjepan bites into a piece of Ariadne's *chestnitsa* cake and yelps.

"Ooo, poor Stjepan," croons Ariadne, "you will have plenty of good luck this year!"

"Look at my tooth, I think it's broken!" But it's not broken, and Stjepan indulges in a self-deprecating chuckle. Like the food platters, the banter and laughter are lavish this evening. Nothing serious is discussed. Hours later, as Vera is talking in a low voice with Ariadne, and the young couple from Livno are washing the dishes in the kitchen, and Stjepan is absorbed in a book he has spotted on the parlor shelves, Simon puts an arm around Josip's shoulder and invites him to take a walk in the garden behind the house. They carry their little glasses with them. Standing under a tree full of winter oranges, Simon lights a cheroot and blows smoke up into the sky.

"Your first Christmas", he says in a reflective tone. "I can see that you are both very happy."

"We are", Josip nods solemnly.

Silence stretches a bit too long. Josip asks if the spring edition of *Dobri Dupin* is nearing completion. Simon nods.

"Our situation is becoming delicate", he says, after blowing more smoke. "The printer tells me that he has been visited with surprise inspections since the last issue. He says that other printers in Split are experiencing the same. Fortunately, he is extremely careful about printing the journal only at night, and he burns all test sheets for the press run. They found nothing."

"That is a relief. Still, it does indicate an increasing threat."

"It does. There is something else that is worrisome. The other day I had a discussion with someone who warned me in subtlest terms that the journal is now known in Belgrade. Of course, we have sent copies there, as well as throughout the country. The police are turning over every stone, this person said, to find the people who produced it."

"Your brother?"

"Actually, no. My brother and I, though we maintain cordial relations, are not on great terms. He lives in his world, and I live in mine. It's a friend at the health commission, a man with connections to both worlds. Though I fear his first loyalty is to the regime, we have been friends since boyhood."

"And he suspects you are involved?"

"I hope it's no more than a suspicion. He would never betray me, and thus I think he was doing what he could, considering the circumstances of his life."

"What exactly did he say?"

"He told me that the authorities are fully aware of a quarterly journal they know to be published in Split. They consider it very dangerous. When I asked him its name, he gave me a candid look as if he knew we were both acting out of a script. He replied that surely I know its name because it's circulating everywhere among the intelligentsia. Then he said it was named for the dolphins of the Adriatic. 'Do you like dolphins?' he asked me pointedly. 'Only as mammals', I told him. 'I thought they were fish', he said, with a look that disturbed me. 'And fish eventually find themselves caught in a net.'"

"Do you think he knows about us? And do the police know?"

"I think he knows—perhaps no more than intuitively—that I'm involved in some way or other. But I doubt the police know. One of the telling signs would be surveillance, if any of us were being followed by shadows and watchers."

"Are you aware of any surveillance on your own activities?"

"None that I can see, but of course my life is rather public and not very complicated: my home, my practice, the classes I teach at the medical faculty. Other than that—nothing. I am hardly a typical counterrevolutionary."

"Yet your home is often full of people who have no love for the Communists. Surely they would know this."

"I expect they do. But these gatherings are not uncommon. The academic life naturally forms into circles of thinkers and artists. There are several on the campus. Besides, we have music as our justification. We must have more music whenever we meet . . ."

318

Simon's voice trails off into some private question that he does not share with Josip.

"They know that Tatjana is your friend," says Josip, "and she has escaped."

"Yes, she is now in America, where there is a large community in exile. That alone proves nothing, since people from all walks of life have fled, from every family, Communist and non-Communist. Which brings me to what I wanted to talk with you about, Josip." He pauses. "Have you considered leaving Yugoslavia?"

"I haven't given it much thought."

"I think you should consider it. We can expect no outside help for many years to come. Since Marshal Tito's state visit to Britain in 1953, the West thinks of us as 'socialism with a human face', as they call it. For complex geopolitical reasons, and also for reasons of international trade and banking, they do not want to disturb their so-called friendship with Belgrade."

"I do not understand them," Josip blurts vehemently, "those defenders of democracy!"

"They are first and foremost defenders of their wealth, and you need look no further than that for an explanation."

"Still, they take in our refugees."

"This is true. But the West has a divided heart. And divided hearts cannot be trusted. They abandoned Hungary during the uprising. A lot of brave young people died, and Cardinal Mindszenty was thrown into prison. No one protests—only Rome."

"If we are ever to see democracy in this land, then we must be willing to endure for a long time."

"Yes, a long time, Josip, decades I think. Perhaps generations. That is why I ask you if this is really where you want to raise your family."

"Ariadne knows the dangers as well as I do."

"Ariadne", says Simon, sighing. "But what kind of a life can you have here?"

"With my teaching and her music, we can survive. We will have a family, and our children will build the Croatia of tomorrow."

"Is that realistic?"

"You ask this question, Simon, yet you yourself are doing just that. You risk everything for it."

"I have lived my life, and I have my memories. Besides, in the time left to me I can do more here than in another country. Our Dolphins, for example. To speak the truth, even if few are listening, can achieve much. It preserves the truth and the spirit of the people for a coming generation."

"That is a praiseworthy cause, and that's why I'm glad to be part of it."

"Still . . ."

"Still, I think, Father, that you make one exception. There is only one person you would exclude from this way of sacrifice."

"I love her. I could not bear to see her hurt."

"I love her too. She is my life. But we are both willing to continue on the path of sacrifice. And because we are together in it, the darkness becomes light."

Without answering, Simon looks long at Josip.

"You have experienced much darkness in your life."

Josip looks away.

"Perhaps you know no other way of being", Simon goes on. "You have never told us about your life before you lost your family, nor have you really described how it happened. Whenever one of us asks you about it, you became vague and evasive."

Hurt by this accusation, Josip says defensively, "It's gone, and nothing can bring it back. I must look toward the future."

"Can you really see the future if you have not seen the past for what it was?"

"I see it. I merely do not wish to talk about it."

"Yet it seems you are now upset with me."

Flustered, Josip says nothing at first. Then, losing inhibition, he says in a low voice, "I do not think you are happy about the man your daughter chose to marry."

Simon takes a step back, then a step forward, and puts a hand on Josip's shoulder. "That is not true. It is not in the least true. I am worried, that's all. I worry that your qualities, your strength and your courage . . ."

He does not complete the thought.

"You are worried that my 'qualities', as you call them, might drag your beloved into torment. That is really your worry."

"Yes, of course it is", Simon replies in a subdued tone. "But this does not mean I am unconcerned about you, Josip. In fact, I do not make a separation between you and Ariadne in my thoughts. I want both of you to be happy."

Shamed, Josip murmurs, "I'm sorry."

"Do you think I fail to see what a gift you are for her? And for all of us really. But that is not the whole of life, and in these times, life itself has been devalued to such a degree that it is difficult to grasp what has happened, let alone look at the horror for more than a fleeting moment. Hell was unleashed here, and hell continues to act. In another land . . ."

"In another land, we would be safe, but would we do our part in bringing an end to hell?"

Simon shakes his head, staring at the ground. Looking up at last, he sighs and says, "Well, this is one of the reasons I love you, Josip. We are so much alike! Let's go into the house and pretend to the women that we've been discussing the weather."

So, they go in and play their roles, and after a few more hours Josip and Ariadne take their leave. As they walk down the hill toward the palace, a rare sprinkle of snow falls from the night sky.

Lying in their bed beneath the crèche, they recount their evening in drowsy exchanges. Despite his tears earlier in the day, and the disturbing conversation with Simon, Josip is at peace.

In the middle of the night, Josip bolts upright in bed with a cry of alarm.

"What is it, Josip?" his wife murmurs beside him.

"Nothing, Ariadne, nothing. Go back to sleep."

She rolls over in bed and falls back to sleep. He lies down and stares into the blackness above the bed. An hour or two pass before he gets up and tiptoes out into the parlor, shutting the bedroom door softly behind him.

Gazing out the window by the doorway that opens onto the inner compound of the palace, he sees that the dusting of snow has melted. He lights a candle beside the juniper tree, rubs his face, drinks a glass of water, and then sits down on the sofa. The dream was disturbing. He will write it out, expunge it, stop it roaring around in his head, creating havoc with his emotions.

Picking up a pencil, he writes it as a poem.

THE CROWN

In the cold dark barren land,
stars and moon and the great star
that has appeared,
puzzling the wise and the low,
scatter jewels upon the blood-soaked snow.
The grieving earth awakes to its first groaning;
and men, grown weary of toil and fear,
cynical of love and despairing of truth,
bearing lamentations as if these were their only
birthright, look up at last.

Now the star has moved on,
the shepherds return to their camps,
the kings to their cities.
The ordinary woman and the silent man
tend the turf-fire in the cave,

break the last disc of bread,
tell softly to each other their small tales
to lift hope on high
as the wind blows straight out of the
northern desert.
They pray also and make their oft-renewed covenant
with trust.

The man stands by the door
to guard from wolves and wolvish men,
the woman holding the nursing child
as if the star itself has ignited in her arms.
This boy, this boy gazes at her
and she at him, wordless they are, wordless he is.
She strokes the little feet, the hands, the brow
on which a fan of black hair as fine as thread
is spread.

Her heart is startled as the lamplight flickers
and she sees a spray of thorns—
the moment quickly passes and there is peace again
upon the uncut brow;
the child sleeps, sinking into her from whom he came,
mother and child drifting timeless while the interior angels
blow trumpets from the ramparts of the celestial city,
that no eyes can see,
chanting the songs of the many,
that no ear can hear:

She smiles, remembering the children who will come
     from her,
numberless more than Abraham's stars,
more than Sarah's countless laughs,
more and more and more until paradise is brimmed

with the impossible love.
So, she dreams, she dreams, and smiles at herself dreaming
knowing the outpouring that love insists through dreams.

Across the desert of that dark age a small horse gallops
through the silver clouds
and continues on, east to west.
Then another and another—white they are,
valiant with riders, while below their thundering feet
fire scorches the horizon, and shadows seep.
Long later she stands alone, encircled by a throng,
all faces, all the world, infested with shadows,
all shepherds, all kings, gone,
on a merciless height as swords thrust her heart.

Is this before or after the horses?—
it is hard to know, for dreams are like that.
Then the great sword, the darkest and worst
is plunged and paradise extinguished
in the threads of the blackened wick,
the flame snuffed by rivulets down the splintered wood
into wasted earth pouring, she sees
the small hands and feet and brow
within the humiliated body of her son—
though the eyes are the same, gazing at her,
and she awakes.

It is, after all, only a dream.
"Come, it is time to go", he says, the good man shaking her
    shoulder:
Rising, she murmurs, "I saw a thing in sleep."
"I too slumbered while at rest", he says,
"and saw our boy crowned king upon old Sion's crest."

324

She is silent, wrapping the child as the man unstraps the colt.
"Where will we go?" she asks.
"To a distant land," he says, "where an angel calls."
"Did he speak?" she says. "I thought he only sang."
And having heard that voice,
they say no more and go out to face the night:

It is dark, it is all darkness,
as into the land of exile and ancient bondage,
they walk,
bearing the light in their arms.

J. L.   Christmas, Split, 1957

He arrives home from the university to find the apartment dark and empty. Where is she? This is Tuesday, not Wednesday, when Ariadne has a late recital and he must make his own supper. She has probably lost all sense of time, meandering through the market longer than she had planned.

By seven o'clock he becomes frantic. This is so unlike her. He runs up the hill to the Horvatinecs' home to see if she is there. Neither Simon nor Vera has seen her since Sunday. Simon offers to go searching with him. Josip declines the offer, says it's nothing to worry about; she probably bumped into a friend somewhere and will no doubt be home shortly. He promises to let them know as soon as he hears anything.

For two hours he races throughout the downtown area looking in all the places where she usually goes—the market, the library, the music shop, the little café on Marmontova Street, where she likes to take friends for a cup of tea. A fever of growing desperation pushes his search, an ache swelling in his throat, fearing most of all that she has been careless and has said something about the Dolphins—that she has been seized by the police for interrogation and will be taken away from him forever.

As he passes through the north gate of the palace, he glances up to their apartment window and sees a light on. Wheeling, within a minute he is racing up the steps to the balconata; he throws the front door open so hard that it bangs against the wall, and he barges into the apartment. She is standing in the kitchen in a bathrobe, with a towel wrapped around her head, her mouth open in astonishment. She laughs.

"Ariadne!" he groans and throws his arms around her. "Ariadne, Ariadne, Ariadne," he whispers, "where were you?"

"Ooh, my Josip, what is the matter?" She is still laughing, rubbing the blond bristles on the back of his head, for he is kneeling now, with his arms around her waist.

"I thought I had lost you!" he cries.

"Lost me?" she smiles, her eyes frowning with concern for him. "I am so sorry to worry you, Josip, but I went to the doctor, and there was a long wait in his office."

"Why did you go to the doctor? Are you not well?" he asks, standing up but unwilling to let her go.

"I'm fine. I'm very healthy, he tells me."

"Oh", he mutters, still panting from his run. "Oh, that's good."

"And supper is late too. Today you have much to forgive me for!" Then she kisses him on the lips, and one thing leads to another.

Simon and Vera appear at the door an hour later, knocking and knocking until Josip opens to them. "She's here," he says, "she's safe."

They nod, yes, they already know. On her way home earlier in the evening she stopped off to give them the news.

"What news?" Josip asks.

"She will tell you", says Vera, standing on tiptoes to kiss his cheek.

"She's in bed now", says Josip, puzzled. "Please come in, but I think she's sleeping."

"The poor dear, of course she is on such a day. No, we won't stay, just wanted to bring you a gift."

She hands her son-in-law a loaf of bread and a bottle of wine so dark its contents are black.

"Excellent for the blood", she adds.

"Come to supper tomorrow, Josip, and we can celebrate", says Simon.

After they have gone, Josip goes back to bed and crawls in beside his wife. She is asleep. Lying on his side, he lightly strokes her forehead, her shoulders, her arms. Without waking her, he takes her hand and holds it for a time. His terror of losing her slowly dissolves, and he falls into a light doze. She wakes a short time later and, by the light of the city coming in through the window, sees the shape of her husband lying there, like a protective wall between herself and the world. Enfolding him in her arms, she whispers to him, "*Joooo—sip—*" and he awakes.

"Your parents were here", he murmurs. "They brought us bread and wine."

He waits for her to give him the news, whatever it may be. Judging by everyone's demeanor it must be good news indeed.

She takes his right hand and draws it across her belly, then presses it with her own.

"Now we are three."

"Three?" Then it hits him, a wave of wonder that makes him gasp. "You mean . . ."

"Yes, you are a father."

Even in the dark, he senses her joy. She holds his face in the palms of her hands. From these hands comes fresh love, and from his hands it is returned to her. He knows that the child within them—yes, it is as if the child is not only within her—is the bridge between his annihilated past and the future that is now so full of promise. The world is entirely different than it was a moment ago. The planet revolves slowly on its axis, and at the same time revolves in its orbit, and the disk of the sun spins like a wheel of fire across the black firmament of the heavens. They are riding on it, and the child, so safely curled within, is riding with them.

It is a spring morning. Josip has no classes to teach that day, and Ariadne is at home as well. They are reading through the latest issue of *Dobri Dupin*. The quality of the paper is better this time, and the cover is magnificent, a photo of Vlado's latest sculpture, *Sloboda*, freedom. A stone hand reaching upward from rubble and bronze flames.

There is a lot of fiction in this issue; and from skimming some of it, they can understand why the regime would think it dangerous. Yes, each issue is more dangerous than the previous one.

"I like this little acorn", says Ariadne, jabbing him in the ribs.

"Rhyming and meter still poor?"

"Very poor. But he has the poetic sense, don't you think?"

"I wouldn't know; I'm not a poet."

"Well, I will admit it's not exactly a poem, more like a prose-poem. Shall I read it to you?"

"No, please do not."

She reads it to him anyway:

TOY BOAT

Is a man's yearning for a toy boat a sign of immaturity or a
    sign of heightened consciousness? Are they the same
    thing? Conversely, are they mutually exclusive?

A wind-driven ship is a "word"—its mystique is oceanic,
    iconographic, the solid metaphor of suspension on waves
    above an abyss. Fleet of form, beauteous, the dance of
    integrated engineering within a harmonious work of art.
    The link-point between infinite water and infinite sky.

The man purchases the toy boat with the last of his coins.
He knows this extravagance will be paid for by his family's
    sacrifice,
Yet it will feed his family as no bread can feed.
This emblem will speak in the center of their home;
It will be their vessel of escape.

Can you imagine the sight of a family pursued by its govern-
    ment?
Can you see them walking on foot to the Drava River,
Toward the pass into the mythological north where freedom
    reigns?
Can you see the weeping wife walking beside the husband,
their children weeping too?
Do you see the little cart pulled by the father, the clothing
    and scraps of food, and books—and a violin—loaded on
    the cart?
Do you see the lovely model schooner (the cause of all their
    woes) perched on top?

Is this a portrait of what could happen when a dreamer loses
    touch with reality?
Or is this what happens when regimes break families,
And they must flee entirely within?
Is such flight an embodiment of failure?
Or is their flight success?
Is their flight the revenge of immanentist demography,
Forcing them to enter the land of the dispossessed within
    their native land,
to be at home only in the homeland of the soul?

Have we not all become internal refugees?
Are we not anonymous beggars hiding our tarnished crowns
Inside our bundles of rags?

O my people, find your hidden crowns!
O my homeland, find your undiscovered kings!
O my homeland, find your missing fathers,
and then you will find yourselves!

Ariadne chuckles to herself.

"Why are you laughing? Do you think this poem is funny?"

"No, it is very, *very* serious. I am just wondering if you're telling me we're going to leave for Austria."

"No," he shakes his head, "but I would *like* to leave for Austria."

"And what on earth is *immanentist demography*? No, don't tell me."

He tells her, which makes her laugh and laugh. She has been crying more than usual lately, for no reason, and also laughing at the silliest things. She throws up in the mornings and is always falling asleep when he least expects it. This can be disconcerting, especially when in the evenings he tries to proofread his master's thesis, which the university is publishing as a book. Whenever he reads a section aloud to her, her eyes glaze, droop, close. She has lost all sense of time, too, which worries him. Fortunately, she is ravenously hungry these days, so meals have become more regular.

Josip's book has been published. He is immensely proud of it, and Ariadne even more so, though she apologizes that its subject matter is, for her, impenetrable. Simon brags about it to his colleagues, gives away copies to those willing to take one from him. There are probably no more than fifteen or twenty people in the world who would read it with interest; in Yugoslavia, three or four, though one might add to their number those who happen to love its author.

A hundred copies have been printed, nicely bound too. It is a theoretical cosmology based in higher mathematics with an assist from astrophysics. Its title is *Equations Inferential of a Meta-universe.*

During one of their Sunday walks along the waterfront, Ariadne says to him, "Oh, see all these people staring at us! They recognize the author of *Metaphysical Inferences of Equations.*"

"No, they're looking at the most beautiful pregnant woman on the planet."

"No, that's not the reason. It's *you.* You're very, very famous now."

"Yes, I am. In a huge circle of about five people."

"It won't always be so. Keppler, Newton, Einstein, Lasta . . ."

"Let's go home. I know two things with absolute certainty: first, that I will never be famous. Second, that I want to kiss you and kiss you and kiss you."

"Wrong about the first, right about the second. And after that, I will play you something from Handel."

"Will you make supper today?"

"Who needs food when we have kissing and Copernicus?"

"Einstein."

"And baby Lasta."

"What will we call our baby, Ariadne?"

She pauses. and her joking mood passes. She slips into that feminine space so alien to Josip, yet so near, and ponders the question.

"She will be called Marija."

"Why do you think it's a girl?"

"I just know."

"And if it's a boy?"

"He will be Josip, of course."

He smiles.

"There will never be enough of you in this world", she adds.

So, they go home and kiss and kiss and kiss. And later they share a happy meal with Simon and Vera.

It is Saturday morning, just before dawn.

She shakes his shoulder and says, "Josip, I need to talk."

"You need to talk?" he mumbles into the pillow. "This is our day for sleeping late."

"I feel that we must talk now, or something will be lost."

He sits up in bed, rubbing his eyes, scratching his disheveled hair.

"All right. What do you want to talk about?"

"I can't describe it exactly."

"That is an auspicious beginning", he yawns.

She slaps him lightly on the arm.

"Can I lend you a shoe?"

"Don't joke. It's important. Do you remember the first morning after we were married?"

"It's the most beautiful memory of my life—I will never forget it."

"We went into the sea together, as the sun was rising, remember? The water was gold and pink. Underneath we could look up to the surface and see the morning break on the waves."

"Later you said we would always live in that light."

"You *do* remember."

"I remember."

"I want to tell you about something that happened when I was under the water with you. Never in my life had I felt such happiness. But suddenly a sorrow entered, like an arrow piercing the highest human joy that can be experienced. At that moment I felt like crying. It came and went in an instant, and then we burst out of the water gasping for breath."

"What made you feel sad?"

"Knowing that something glorious was hidden from us, but if we wanted it, all we had to do was reach up for it. It was only a sense—no thoughts came with it."

"A feeling."

"Yes, a feeling, but one that contained a meaning, like the crown in the beggar's rags. Do you know what I mean?"

"I see what you *felt*, but I don't know its meaning."

"Our part was to reach up, and then everything else would be given—from above."

"From above?"

"Josip, I think we must return to Christ."

He exhales.

"It would create problems—"

"I know. But what you said about the toy boat—about being in exile. You know, going inward. It just came to me that we should go the other way, upward."

"And if Christ is only an abstraction—what then?"

"He is real. I know he is real."

"How do you know?"

"He is here. I feel him all around us. He was in our first meeting and has been in our hearts ever since. He has been with us in a way that I can't explain. But it's incomplete."

"Am I not enough for you?" Josip asks in a quiet voice.

"Ours is the greatest human love in the whole world, Josip, truly it is. But it is not enough."

He has no answer to this. A sob is in his throat, the choking, the vision of dead bodies flashing through his mind, the burning church, the desecrated hosts, an absent God who did not save.

"I can't", he says.

"Would you not try?"

He opens his mouth and closes it.

"If he is there, Josip, as we once believed when we were children, he will do the rest. We only have to reach up. That alone is our task."

Still he cannot speak. He turns on his side to face her, putting the palm of his right hand to her belly, which is now a small mountain. His hand warms the bare flesh, and he can feel his own pulse in it. He desires with his whole being that this pulse send waves of protection to the child sleeping within.

"We cannot endanger her", he says.

"Not to reach up", whispers Ariadne, "may be the greatest danger of all. If you cannot do it for me, can you do it for her?"

For long moments, he looks down at Ariadne and their hidden child.

"We will go to God's house", he whispers. "And you will help me to enter."

THE NAKED ISLAND

The isolated shape of each memory is more or less clear, but their context is altered by a history of subsequent interpretation. Memories are reshaped simultaneously into what they are and what they are not—then pondered as actualities, which in turn are reshaped. Within this laboratory of the mind, the scientific method deceives the scientist who fails to consider that his experiment is changed by his very presence within it. The subtle arts of causality or the subtle causalities of the mind's primary artform.

Or to put it another way: From the alpine peaks of old age one peers into the valleys of the past and sees indistinct forms, highlighted only by the most monumental sub-formations— the valley is a green blur, containing serene flocks of sheep, and buildings in flames. A palace by a sea is an ivory carving, surmounted by an emerald hill, and beyond it a sheet of rippling phosphorous. Within that miniature carving, countless dramas are enacted.

Ariadne attends Mass each day and has re-embraced everything she believed in her childhood. Josip promises he will soon attend with her, but every week he finds a reason to delay. She is patient because she knows he is a man who keeps his word. For his part, he is determined to overcome his fears and is gathering strength for it. The act of stepping over a mutilated body is no small one. In a sense, it is his very self that lies spread-eagled on the steps, silent and degraded. He must rise from the dead.

He drifts into sleep with the first reawakenings of prayer.

Are you there? I cannot see you, cannot hear you. Are you there?

The following morning is their first wedding anniversary. It is a Saturday, and nothing is scheduled to happen. They will go to Mass together for the first time the next day, but for now they will simply be together and reaffirm their love. For hours they stroll hand in hand through the Marjan, recalling the first days of their courtship and chatting about their hopes and dreams. Ariadne would like to climb all the way to the top so they can look out over the sea, but Josip thinks this is unwise and makes her sit down on park benches from time to time. Neither of them wants the day to end. They eat a late supper at a café on Marmontova, linger over wine until closing time, then slowly walk the few blocks home to their apartment. Sleepy, they do not bother to turn on the lights, just head straightway to the bedroom, undress, and lie down.

Ariadne is asleep beside him. He is drowsing, though he hears his heart quietly thumping, his hand warm on the hill of her belly, which has sheltered the child for six months within the womb. Three months from now they will see the hidden face.

There will be no visual memory of the next moment, for the room is dark and the window shuttered. He will remember sounds. Into the calmness of the world, there comes a loud bang, then the splintering of wood. Ariadne cries out. He struggles upright and flings his legs over the side of the bed. A bright light appears in the bedroom door. Blinded, he stands and gropes for something heavy to strike the intruder. Something hits him on the side of the head, making his ears ring in such pain as he has never felt before in his life. Another blow strikes his eyes, and after that, nothing.

He is sitting on a chair in a cement room, facing a wall. His skull feels broken, his eyes so swollen he can open them only a crack. He tries to move his arms, but they are bound, the wrists secured to the back of the chair. His ankles are bound to its legs.

He is asleep on a cement floor. He is pulled from this hole into the darker hole of consciousness. A hand is dragging him up by the hair of his head. His face is slapped. Still, he cannot see.

"Open your eyes!" shouts a voice.

The folios of the mind, the albums of hell, display more and more pictures. The worst. The faces of wolves. He flinches, retreats into the sea—the spray of the dolphins as they leap in the sunlit waves, the soothing surf on the beach, white stones rolling under the white light, oranges dripping syrup into his open mouth, and the millions of shelters in the wall of sand where the *lastavice* live their lives.

Who are you? Where have you come from? Where are you going?

But pain negates all of this with a single blow or a shout.

Above, fly!

They will not let him fly, all those hands grabbing him, tying him, untying him, walking him from room to room, forcing a bit of bread or a slug of water down his throat. He cannot hear what they say! His nose is bleeding, and sometimes he chokes on the blood. Is it his own or another's? Because, in the end, blood is always raining down on mankind, unjust blood and holy blood—he knows the taste of both.

Yet *lastavica* is not only the name for a bird but also for a flying fish.

Beneath, dive!

They will not let him dive! He is tied by his flesh to this world.

Ariadne!

Does he say it, or is it only a constant cry within his mind? Her name, the sweetest in the world, he will cling to it, he will feel her arms around him as he enfolds her with his own. But the pain increases.

"Wake up!"

Here again are the faces of the wolves.

"Tell us about *Dobri Dupin!*" shouts one of the wolves, "And we will let you go back to your wife!"

Ariadne, Ariadne, Ariadne, where are you?

"Tell us!"

As he stumbles around inside the labyrinth of his skull, he closes his eyes, blocking out the face of the Minotaur.

"Speak!" Hard blows to the ears; first one, then the other. He feels his ears become liquid, two rivers draining away all thought.

How long does it last? A few days, a month, more months?

There comes a morning—yes, it is morning, because sunlight is glowing behind a barred window of opaque glass—when his mind, his body, and his eyes connect to each other. He is enclosed within a cement cell. Is he in the hospital? Have they cut off his arms?

No, he has arms. He has hands and fingers. Though no feathers. No feathers, no wings. No upward flight, no diving to the depths.

That day, guards take him to another room and seat him on a metal chair without strapping him to it. Facing him behind a desk, there sits a wolf in a suit and tie. The wolf smiles pleasantly.

"Your eyes, Lasta, are working again."

It is not necessary to speak with wolves.

A hand behind him grabs his hair, yanks his head back. "Answer!" growls another voice.

"I can see", Josip whispers.

"And you can hear too", says the pleasant wolf. "Now, if you wish to be released, you will tell us everything about the *Dobri Dupin.*"

Josip's head falls forward on his chest. He notices that he is dressed in a dirty cotton jumpsuit soaked with his own urine. His feet are bare.

"The *Dobri Dupin!*" prompts the wolf.

"Where is my wife?" he moans.

"Your wife will be released if you tell us everything."

"She is beneath the water with me", he murmurs.

"The *Dobri Dupin*, Lasta!" shouts a different voice.

"We are in the net," Josip groans, "and we will die with smiles."

It takes them a moment to consider this. Then he is slapped again, harder than before.

A hand shoves a photograph in front of Josip's face.

"One of your fellow Dolphins", laughs the voice.

It is Vlado, his mouth wide open. Where his eyes should be are raw sockets of bleeding flesh. There is a bullet hole in his forehead.

"He begged us to kill him", says the smiling wolf. "You will, too."

"Unless . . .", says the other wolf.

Josip vomits and chokes. He falls off the chair. Someone kicks him between the legs, and he is dragged away.

How much longer? Is it days, weeks, months?

"Horvatinec is in prison for life. We have all your friends."

"They fly, they dive", whispers Josip. This is all the resistance he can muster. That and silence.

"Antun Kusić is dead. Ana Kusić in prison. All the others, dead or in prison."

"Who was Tatjana's contact? How did she get out?"

"Did Ivan compose the song?"

"Stjepan has confessed everything. Let's hear it in your own words."

They know everything.

"Where did Vera and Iria go? Who warned them? Are they in Austria, or in hiding here?" They have just told him something valuable, a thread of hope. They do not know everything.

"How much did the CIA pay you?"

They are fishing for more, not knowing there is no more.

"My wife was not involved", he cries. "Let her go."

Laughter.

"A violinist without fingers is not a pretty sight."

"Please, the baby!"

"A shame about the baby. A baby without arms and legs—"

Josip goes mad, leaps to his feet, roaring, howling, punching anything in the room. He is struck from behind and crumples to the floor.

In the absolute dark, relieved only by the sensation of rough cement on his bruised flesh, he makes a decision. Their power is absolute. His fear for his family is their greatest leverage. They can kill him if they wish, but there is no worse threat than their promise to hurt his wife and child. They show him more photographs of people who died in agony. Among the mutilated bodies, none are Ariadne or the baby. So, he understands what they are doing—they would undermine his resistance with the tool more powerful than pain.

But how to resist? Should he tell them lies? They are too clever to believe him; moreover, he lacks inventiveness in this skill.

Truth then? Yes, the truth will confound them. Turn the language of truth against them.

"I will tell you everything", he says at the next interrogation. And he will. Everything. A unified field theory.

"At last you have come to your senses", says the smiling wolf.

"Don't try to fool us", says the growling wolf. "We will check what you tell us, and if we find you are lying, you will end like Kusić ended, only slower. Then you will beg. Oh, yes, then you will beg to tell the truth. But it will be too late."

"It need not come to that", says the friendly wolf.

He reads a list of Dolphins. It is fairly accurate, but missing a few names.

"Who else was involved?"

"Max Planck", says Josip.

They scribble the name onto a pad of paper.

"Who is he?"

"A scientist."

"Where is he?"

"He has fled."

"Who else?"

"Eugenij Kumičić."

"Tell us who he is and where he is."

"He is a novelist, author of *Olga i Lina*. He is dead."

"Go on. Names, Lasta. Give us names."

"Vatroslav Lisinski, a musician. Dead."

"Continue."

"Fra Anto."

"His full name?"

"I forget. He is dead."

They pause. The friendly wolf leans back in his chair and exhales through his nostrils.

"All dead. How convenient. You're not lying to us, are you?"

"I am telling you the truth. All of these were involved in the spirit of the Dolphins. Planck was not a Dolphin, but he would have been."

"What do you mean by *would have been*?"

"He developed quantum theory."

"What is quantum theory?

"The truth about everything."

"Don't play with us."

"The Nazis executed his son."

"So, this Planck was an anti-Fascist?"

"Yes, always. He was against war."

"Was he a Stalinist?"

343

"No."

"All right. Who else was a member?"

"Theseus."

"His full name."

"Theseus of Athens."

"That's a code name, isn't it. You all had code names."

"For the most part we used first names only."

"That's not what the other Dolphins told us."

"In the beginning it was first names. After a few meetings, we learned each other's full names, some of us, not everyone."

"Stjepan, for example."

Josip nods.

"Oh, by the way, here is a recent photograph of the great unpublished Croatian novelist."

The obliteration of much of Stjepan's face, and the bullet hole, cannot hide his identity.

"All the manuscripts are burned, too", says the friendly wolf. "He wouldn't talk. Such fools only talk on paper. Now the fool and the paper are ashes in the wind."

"You too, Lasta, will be ashes in the wind", says the unfriendly wolf.

"Unless you tell us everything", says the other. "We want to know all contacts. The smallest detail."

"What was Theseus's role in the group?"

"He was our amorphicist", says Josip.

"What is that?"

"He was a warning."

"What do you mean," snorts the friendly one, "*a warning*?"

"He reminded us of our fragility."

"Political, you mean?"

"Human."

"Human?"

"The vulnerability of conscience", murmurs Josip.

The wolves laugh. "Conscience!"

"He taught us with amorphisms."

"What are amorphisms?"

"An amorphism is a fragment," mumbles Josip, "a fragment without discernible connection to a whole. In another sense, an amorphism is that which functions as an antidote to the narcotic influence of morphine. Alternatively, it is an antidote to a dream world or dreamlike state of mind."

"You mean he kept you alert to the dangers."

"Yes, the internal and external."

"The external being the UDBA. What were the internal?"

"Our tendency to live in illusion. Also the split between temperament and character."

This puzzles the wolves for a few minutes.

"Theseus is Simon Horvatinec, isn't he?"

Josip shakes his head. "No, Theseus is a Greek."

"Where is this Theseus now? Is he in hiding?"

"He is dead."

"Again, dead."

Josip's chin falls onto his chest. His body is aching, and he is mentally exhausted with the effort to think carefully about what he says.

The nice wolf snaps his fingers. Guards return Josip to his cell. Later, he is brought food and drink. He eats it ravenously and vomits. He is given a light beating, to his body only, not to his head. Another meal is brought to him later in the day. He eats it slowly and keeps it down. The return of food sparks his hunger for more. He sits in isolation inside his cement box, gazing at a bar of light slowly moving down the wall. The tiny window, so far above his head, offers no chance to see what is outside. It is all inside, everything is inside.

To think of Ariadne is to be totally consumed by terror for her and the baby. It is to go completely insane.

He forces his mind elsewhere:

He is in a cement cellar, surrounded again by pain and death.

An armless man says to him, "In your life, Josip, you will have much to fear. You will suffer, and this suffering will bring much good to others."

"I do not understand what you are saying", says the Lastavica of the Mountains.

"You do not need to understand. Only remember: you will be afraid. But do not be afraid."

"What can this mean! Tell me what it means!"

"You will be afraid. But when you are afraid, do not be afraid."

Josip is choking back his sobs; he is a boy with nowhere to go other than a place where a wolf wants to kill him.

"Look, Josip", says the Lastavica of the Sea. "Look at the light."

A bar of light is crossing the floor.

"Do you see?"

Josip shakes his head.

"Surely you see", says the man.

"I see the light, but the walls imprison it."

"The light has entered the prison. Nothing can keep it out."

"If there is no window, the light cannot enter."

"If there is no window, the light enters within you."

The next day the interrogation resumes with a hard slap across the face.

"Max Planck", snarls the bad wolf. "You were playing with us. And if we find that the other names—"

"Easy, easy", says the nice wolf. "Look at him, look at what he has been through, poor fellow. He can't get everything right all at once. Give it time."

"No, let's cut him to pieces now."

"We know that you regret your involvement with those radicals, Lasta. We know you intended no harm. It would speed your return to the university if you were to state clearly all that

346

you know and also your political position. This unfortunate situation can be remedied quickly, and you can get back to your life without further trouble. And your wife."

"Where is my wife?"

"She is in prison. Each day you prolong her internment. Why do you do this to her?"

Josip tightens his lips but says nothing.

If there is no window, the light enters within you.

"All right. Let's begin", says the nice wolf. "There are missing names. People who attended the meetings, some dropped out, some did not give their full names. We need a few blanks filled in. There was a philosopher present."

"There were many", says Josip.

"What was his role?"

"He listened."

"Listened only? Surely he had something to say. What was his name?"

"I forget."

I will forget Zoran's name. I will forget, I will forget, O God, help me to forget!

"What was his role?"

"He taught us. Like Theseus, he taught us."

"What did he teach you?"

"He said that joy is the aesthetics of love at light-speed."

"What?"

"Joy is the aesthetics of love at light-speed."

The wolves roll their eyes.

"What else did he say?"

"Very little."

"He proposed the use of violence against the People's Republic, didn't he?"

"No one was advocating violence."

"Then for what did you organize? Why the secrecy? Don't lie to us! The others confessed about the guns and explosives."

347

"There were no guns or explosives. We never talked about that kind of thing. It was not our way."

"What was your way?"

"Culture."

The wolves snort again.

"You were planning to assassinate President Tito."

"We had no plans to assassinate anyone."

"We know that your stated intention was to destroy a legitimately elected government, which you called a tyranny."

"We believed that our art could demolish the dehumanizing power of all tyrannies to the degree that it is obedient to the universal laws."

"From your own lips—demolish tyrannies."

"Without weapons", says Josip.

"What a liar you are, Lasta! Here, take a look at this." He throws a small notebook onto the desk. "Your journal. It's all here, every seditious and traitorous thought known to man. Let me read you a few samples:

"*Art reinforces tyrannies to the degree that it obeys the diktats of social pressure, gnostic myths, and political expedience.*

"*Malevolent governments are no more than gangs of unhappy children. So are benevolent governments.*

"*In the politics of the playground is written the politics of the nation; in the politics of the nation is written the politics of the playground.*

"*Social pressure is the fascism of the democracies. Fascism is the democracy of the ruthless. Yugoslavian socialism embodies the worst of both worlds.*

"*Social engineering is the opiate of romantic intellectuals.*

"*The state of our culture will be the culture of our state.*

"*The artificial state will be brought down only by weapons used in good conscience.*"

The nice wolf looks up with a smile.

"Kiss your wife good-bye."

Josip goes mad, is restrained, and tossed back into his cell.

The Trial. It takes ten minutes. Not worth recalling though it cannot be forgotten because of the faces of men who use law to betray justice. He has never before seen such faces, and thinks they are more frightening than the wolves of Pačići, for they are not brutal men, it seems. Memorize those faces, he tells himself, do not forget what you see in their eyes. They are the slaves of the wolves. And worse, they know what they are doing. What kind of minds do they have? What goes on within those skulls? How do they live with themselves?

As Josip stands up in the courtroom, awaiting his sentence, the judge shakes his head in disgust.

"Such a pity. What good you might have done for our country. Such a promising future. You were used by others, that is why I will be lenient. You are sentenced to twenty-five years at hard labor."

Josip stares the judge in the eye and, speaking for the first time with a clear voice, he says, "Why don't you just take me out into the forest and slaughter me, as you did to so many of our countrymen?"

Hastily, he is silenced, manacled, and taken away. Back in his cell he is beaten senseless by three guards.

He hopes he is dead, but the rhythmic heaving of the floor beneath his body confirms the worst: he is alive. A thrumming motor. Metal all around. He is lying on his belly, his hands tied behind his back. Water is sloshing backward and forward, soaking his prison uniform. He is afflicted with a terrible thirst, and sucks at the water—salty, tainted with diesel oil. He spits it out.

The sound of a motor dies, and the rocking motion ceases. Above him a hatch opens with a squeal, and light burns in along with the cries of sea gulls. Blinking, squinting in the blinding light, he sees that there are other groaning bodies in the dark with him.

A man in a military uniform jumps down into the hole and drags the five prisoners to their feet one by one. Hands from above pull them up. They find themselves lying on the deck of a small boat, moored alongside a wharf below some low barren hills. There, they are permitted to rest for a minute until their eyes adjust and they are able to see.

A guard shouts a command at them to stand and line up. Wrists still manacled behind their backs, the prisoners roll onto their sides, struggle to their knees, and then stand upright. They shuffle forward. Guards escort them toward a plank leading to the wharf, where more guards are waiting for them, armed with rifles. The faces of the guards are fierce, cynical, and bored. Without warning, one of the prisoners breaks from the line, staggers to the seaward side of the boat, and topples over. The guards rush to that side and shoot their guns into the water. Satisfied, they reholster their pistols and shoulder their rifles.

"Lunch time for sharks!" says one. "The Croat bar is open!" says another.

From the wharf the prisoners are marched up a rocky path to a cluster of low cement buildings divided by a paved avenue leading into the hills. More guards are waiting there, in two lines, a dozen on each side. Many are smirking in expectation, as if to welcome the prisoners. Truncheons are in the hands of all. The pavement is splotched everywhere with old stains, bleached by the sun.

"Skin the rabbit!" shouts one of the guards. Josip is last in the file of prisoners, and he sees what is coming. One by one, each prisoner is stripped naked, then shoved between the guards.

"Run, rabbit!"

The first prisoner staggers forward. A hail of truncheon blows fall on him from both sides. He stumbles, cannot rise, and is kicked again and again until he gets up on all fours, then crawls onward under furious blows. When he is through the gauntlet, he collapses on the pavement, blood seeping from beneath his body.

"Run, rabbit!"

The next prisoner refuses to move, falls to his knees, sobbing. Immediately, the guards converge on him and beat him. Blood spatters everywhere, the thumping on human flesh does not cease. They stand back. The man is dead. Two guards drag the body back toward the wharf by the ankles.

"Lunchtime!"

The next prisoner runs—and ends like the first. Now it is Josip's turn.

"Run, rabbit!"

He is propelled toward the truncheons with a kick to his backside. Staggering forward, he feels every strike upon his body as the storm hits, sees his own blood splattering ahead of him, his blood flowing into the blood of others, all mingled.

"This is a strong one! A big one too!" Laughter.

Now his progress is slower, each step purchased at the price of countless blows. Everything is exposed, everything receives its portion. He staggers, falls; the guards step close to finish him off. He pushes himself up on hands and knees, then rises. His feet slipping on blood, he lurches forward a meter, then another.

Now he is through the lines and collapses beside the other prisoners.

"Let's send him back again."

"No, don't waste an ox like this. He'll be good for work!"

"Let's see what he can take."

"Back you go, rabbit!"

They drag him to his feet and spin him around until he is reeling from dizziness.

"Run, rabbit!"

He staggers back the way he came, one step, another step,

under a rain of truncheons and boot-kicks. He collapses onto the pavement where he began. They converge on him.

"Finish him off! A big lunch!"

"No, no, look at him. He can keep going!"

"One more time, rabbit!"

Slowly, slowly—rising on hands and knees—then wobbling upright. Again the blows rain down.

"Last lap!"

Shuffling forward, centimeter by centimeter, bending under the down-striking blows and the up-striking blows. A rib cracks. His mouth is gore—teeth are broken, and he spits them out.

Finally, he is down on his belly and cannot move—he wants the guards to complete their work, send him out of this life—*please, please kill me!* But something inside him will not permit it. He can no longer rise on hands and knees. He slithers forward through the pools of blood.

Now the laughing becomes guffaws.

"Salamander! Reptile!"

He is a steel thread of will, dragging a sack of agony.

"Enough!"

All kicks and blows cease. He can no longer move.

"What a horse."

"Bath time for baby!" a guard shouts.

Two forms with shaved heads come forward, barefoot and dressed only in canvas shorts. They pick up the first prisoner and drag him toward an iron oil barrel. There they lay him on the ground, change their grip on his body, lift him upside down, and plunge him head-first into the drum. Only the feet and shins are visible. The legs thrash weakly. Thirty seconds pass; they pull him out and drop him to the ground. He is unconscious, yet still breathing.

"Next!"

Josip sees them coming for him. He cannot move his limbs,

which are now in spasm. The two men grab him and drag him toward the barrel.

Bending to take him by the limbs, one whispers, "Courage." They turn him upside down and plunge him into the drum. It contains seawater stained with blood. From the moment his flesh enters it, he begins to scream, a scream that grows in volume until every cell of his being is screaming eternally.

18

Consciousness returns.

Buried in the folios is an abundance of material, much of it dramatic, some of it incredible, most of it banal. Why does the passage of time retain certain images in the forefront of the mind and relegate others (even the most astounding) to the background? Does the soul sift experience according to pain and pleasure, or according to its true destiny? Or does the mind do the sorting, archiving images according to a sense of destiny, however distorted this may be? There is much to ponder about this, and much that will remain imponderable.

He remembers waking up in a cement box. Always, it seems, whenever he awakes from merciless blows, it is only to find himself within cold, hard enclosures. A coffin—if he should be granted so luxurious an item—will be his final box.

Now, his eyes open upon a new world that is strangely familiar. A man is kneeling beside him, bending over him, swabbing his body with rags, which he dips into a metal bucket. Josip hopes his nurse is the Lastavica of the Sea, and for a time—as his mind blurs, then focuses, then blurs again—it is his old friend who ministers to the demolished flesh, though his wings are folded and his arms and hands have regrown. The face is the same.

Josip closes his eyes, for he has become the blind man.

"Is it you?" he cries.

"I am Sova. Don't try to talk."

Josip's mouth is swollen and aching. But he needs reassurance more than the cessation of pain.

"I know you have come to me," he raves and weeps, "as on the day when you came to my fingers."

Because teeth are missing and everything is swollen, his tongue does not make the words properly.

"Be quiet now. I must wash you. There is risk of infection."

"Though you say you are a *sova*, will you not speak to me as the *lastavica*?"

The man pauses and glances at Josip curiously.

"Is it you, is it you?" says the mouth like a cavern of gore, the body shaking uncontrollably.

"Yes, it is me", Sova replies, stroking Josip's forehead as Mamica used to do whenever he was ill.

The blind man sighs, and his body becomes completely still. He is not dead, he is listening.

"I knew you would come."

"I am here", says Sova, "I am here."

When sanity returns, as it almost always does, two other prisoners roll Josip onto his belly. His bed is a heap of dirty canvas. Because he is a mass of open wounds, he is left unclothed. Flies are buzzing around him. Birds frequently fly in through an open doorway, materialize as walking shadows then become men who turn him over. They ignore his screams, wash the wounds on his back, turn him again, lift his head, pour soup down his throat, followed by more water. More and more water. Then a mash of wet bread. (Some birds will masticate the food for their chicks before stuffing it down their throats.)

"Drink, you must drink!" the birds tell him.

Whenever they are disguised as humans, the birds are distinct individuals. One day, they make him sit up. Another day, two of them pull him to his feet and walk him from one end of the cement box to the other. His legs vibrate underneath him, and, when they collapse, the birds carefully lay him down again.

Sova is washing his body. Josip examines his face, which the owl has carefully changed into a man's so as not to frighten him.

"I know it is you", he whispers.

"Don't try to talk. You're not ready."

"Speak to me. Am I dead?"

"No, you are not dead."

"I cannot die."

"You cannot die?" says the owl, raising an eyebrow.

"I must live", chokes the mouth, now less swollen, its bleeding gums healing within the cavern, the tongue no longer a leather rasp.

"So do we all feel", says Sova. "All of us believe that we must live."

"Where is Ariadne?" Josip whispers, and then he bursts into wails.

"Shh-shhh, enough. Here, drink this."

When Josip is calm again, he says to the owl, "I have lost the sword. I cannot find the thread."

Sova frowns and shakes his head. "Rest", he says, and goes away.

During the daylight hours, the birds all fly off, leaving him alone. He sleeps, mostly. A man comes in to check on him. Like all prisoners, this man is dressed only in canvas shorts. About thirty years old, he is wiry, his dark-brown skin covered with scars.

"I went through this", he says. "You will recover."

"Who are you?" Josip asks, as the man helps him to raise his upper body in order to drink from a dipper of water.

"I am called Propo."

The others return to the cell at dusk, materialize as men, lie down, and sleep. Only Propo and Sova tend Josip's needs. They say little to him, for both are exhausted. Then they too go to sleep. Josip has dozed throughout the day and is now fully awake. Bright lights come through a window above his head; they are always on. He hears a shout, a barked command, a scream. These sounds do not waken the others.

Looking about the room, he sees that it is a rectangular cement hut with a door at one end and narrow glassless windows along the wall above his head. Within the room there are thirty or forty sleeping prisoners, each lying on a pallet of canvas. The room is unnaturally still and silent, relieved from time to time by a snore or by a cry in a dream.

Morning. Sunlight comes in through the open windows. The men (they are now always men) are sitting with their backs against the walls or are walking slowly about the room. They say little to each other, and always in low murmurs. When a guard enters with a clipboard in hand, they hastily stand to attention beside their pallets. Only Josip is unable to rise. The guard struts up and down between the rows of prisoners, making check marks on the list. He stops at the foot of Josip's pallet and stares down at him with a scowl. He makes a check mark, then moves on.

Josip is seated with his back to the wall, watching sunlight move across the floor toward his bare feet, at the end of the legs stretched out before him—legs splotched with purple and brown.

Sova brings him a tin dish with soup and boiled wheat in it.

"Can you chew it?" he asks.

Josip lifts the dish to his mouth and swallows its contents down in a few gulps.

"It is better to chew", says Sova. "It is never boiled properly."

Josip does not answer at first. He cannot yet chew food. He gives the other the empty dish.

"Thank you", he breathes.

Sova nods. "You will survive."

"I want to die."

"You cannot die. You told me so yourself."

"Yes", says Josip, and then begins to cry, for Ariadne has

357

come to his mind. He is consumed with both longing for her and shame that he had temporarily forgotten her.

Sova goes away. Propo comes.

"I think they will give you another week of rest", he says. "But try to get moving as much as you can. You must walk. Can you get up now and walk?"

Propo helps him struggle to his feet. He stands shakily, supporting himself with a hand to the wall. Propo takes his other arm, and they walk together, very slowly, from one end of the room to the other. That done, Josip lies down again and sleeps. Three times that day, Sova and Propo return and make him walk.

Toward nightfall, another prisoner joins them. He is a man in his sixties. Carrying a slice of hard black bread and a tin cup full of water, he breaks the bread into two equal pieces and dips one into the water. Without a word, he tears it into sodden bits and pushes them into Josip's mouth, then the other half.

"Who are you?" says Josip after he has swallowed.

"I am Tomislav. Here they call me Tata."

Now a fourth man arrives, very young. He too brings a piece of bread. The feeding of Josip is repeated.

"They call me Budala, a blockhead", he grins. "And it's true."

Another man kneels beside Josip, and he too gives his bread. He is in his mid-thirties, with scars on his forehead and a broken nose badly healed.

"I am Prof", he says with a keen analytical glance into Josip's eyes. "They let you live because they can see that you will be a useful pack animal. Few survive what you went through. It is because you are strong. Now you must get stronger."

Josip looks at their bodies, skin and bones. Though these men are muscled, the muscles are without any fat, and the skin is stretched tightly over every line and fold of the interior anatomy.

Another man arrives, feeds Josip his crust of bread. He is young, physically unmarked, slightly cross-eyed, and rather cheery in disposition.

"I'm Svat", he says. "This is a nice hotel, isn't it? The food is great, the swimming's great, the staff are so polite. But we're really here for the good company."

The others raise eyebrows or frown.

A whistle blows outside the window, followed by the voices of barking guards. Josip's visitors scatter to their own pallets and lie down. Josip too lies down, and for the first time falls into sleep without a knot of hunger in his belly.

He walks unaided now, if one could call it walking, this halting shuffle. Throughout that week he forces himself to go up and down the room several times each day. Whenever he whimpers with pain, he is grateful that the others are out at work and cannot hear it. As his self-consciousness grows, he is increasingly embarrassed by the whines that bleat from him unexpectedly. He knows he cannot afford any emotional or mental complexity. The simple contours of survival are the only factor. He will survive. He *must* survive. Though all odds are against him, it is not impossible that he will one day escape. Then he will find Ariadne and their child, and they will all flee into the north.

He knows this is a hopeless dream, the kind of thread that men cling to in labyrinths. But he will not let go of it. As he follows its invisible unraveling, the thread may tighten and thicken into a cord along which, eventually, he might be able to pull himself to safety.

The cracked rib gives him constant trouble; it is slowly healing but seems more painful than ever. Prof tells him it's because his other bodily pains are subsiding and the rib's protest now seems louder.

Most of the prisoners do not talk to him. As Josip observes and listens, he learns that with few exceptions they all have one or two confidants, but no one knows or speaks with all the others. Some exist as if the universe were devoid of anything except themselves. They either burn with suppressed rage, their eyes dark with animosity, or they fold their bodies and bury their heads, going inward, speaking to no one. These types are a small minority, and Sova comments that they are the ones who go first.

"Go?" asks Josip.

"One morning, sooner or later, they do not respond to the guard's command. They will not get up, though they are alive and could if they wanted to. Then they are dragged away. They make no protest, and a minute later you always hear a gunshot. Or else it happens at work. They run from the quarries toward the sea and are brought down by a bullet before they have got ten meters. Perhaps those few seconds of freedom are worth more to them than an entire lifetime of survival. Or it may be they are simply insane."

Personal loyalties are furtive. Suspicion is always in the air. An informer can obtain a bit of extra food, if he reports subversive conversation or activity. Are there any informers in the cell? How can one tell? This uncertainty is an essential component of subjugation. The atmosphere is one of constant fear and subservience, obedience and exhaustion. Humiliations are part of the day's routine. For example, the prisoners must wash their own excrement out in the yard and sort from it bits of undigested grain, which is then reboiled and eaten. All are disgusted by this practice, yet few refrain from eating the results.

"It's a degradation", explains Prof one evening. They are standing by a window gazing out at the yard as the sorting and re-cooking is in process. "They do not let us forget that we are animals owned by the State."

"Lower than animals", says Sova with a scowl.

"We are not animals", says Tata.

Gazing beyond the bucket of water where the sifting takes

place, and the steaming cauldron beside it, Josip examines the immediate environs. The compound contains several barracks grouped around larger administrative buildings in the bottom of a wide ravine, all enclosed within chain-link fences. It is surrounded by rocky white hills, not very high, but sufficient to hide it from outside view. A few stunted bushes cling to whatever traces of barren soil hide within crevasses on the slopes. Otherwise, it is a lunar landscape.

"Nothing grows here", Josip says in a puzzled tone.

"This is Goli Otok", says Propo, "the naked island."

"Nothing of what goes on here can be seen from the water", adds Sova. "Boats pass nearby; you can sometimes hear them. The islands Prvić and Rab are close."

"How far?"

"Three or four kilometers."

"And the mainland?"

"Maybe five, six."

"It could be swum", says Josip.

"It could be, if a man were unusually strong, in good health, and the sharks had not developed their habit of expecting free lunches."

"Has anyone escaped?"

"None that I heard of", murmurs Sova. "As you see, we are too exhausted. You might swim a few hundred meters, perhaps, before the guards spotted you—or the sharks. But I think it would be weakness that would finish you off in the end. No, it is impossible."

"Nothing is impossible", says Tata. "Nothing is impossible with God."

Josip lowers his eyes, stares at the floor. Everyone else turns away, abruptly ending the conversation.

While none of the thirty or forty others appear to bear him ill will, they do not try to initiate contact. Perhaps in their minds *he* is a potential informer! It is unusual, therefore, that he has been adopted by a rather large circle of six fellow prisoners. At night he ponders this, along with other questions.

Why do these particular men give him a share of their own meager rations? A piece of bread can mean the difference between life and death, yet they continue to risk doing it for him. Now, as he recovers, they take turns giving him portions of their food, one extra piece of bread a day, one extra dish of wheat soup; and sometimes they supplement this with other material: a handful of dusty herbs scavenged from the rocks, a lizard, a seabird's egg, blades of grass.

Why do they do it? They do not do this for others in the barracks, some of whom have been beaten almost as badly as Josip. Who are these six, really? In the beginning, all that he can discern about them is obtained by fragments of their behavior and minimalist conversation. As his mind continues to clear, Josip fixes in his memory an impression of each. If he survives, he will remember them. If they do not survive, they will not be forgotten. If no one survives at least they tried to think of each other as human beings.

The six are of differing temperaments, character, and background, yet all have sacrificed themselves for him.

Sova, the "owl", is a dour pessimist. He is about thirty-five, swarthy, and when he speaks it is usually in tones of bitter irony. His crime is unknown.

Svat, or "wedding guest", is a cheery optimist, even energetic, and impulsive. He is a handsome youth in his late teens, and not as gaunt as the others. His comments never contain insights, only factual observations. He is like everyone's little brother, the favorite, though he is probably unaware of this. Perhaps they see their own lost youth embodied in this good-hearted fellow. Crime unknown.

Budala, "blockhead", is a pleasant youth about the same age as Svat. He is as physically robust as the other, yet despite his age he displays little vitality. He is a quintessential survivor, a docile pleaser. The most verbal of the six, when he speaks it is usually to make an inane comment. He is so stupid they fear for him, knowing that he will one day say an innocent idiotic thing and bring destruction upon himself. Moreover, he likes to make silly jokes as if he were still playing in a carefree village square. Jokes in hell rarely amuse the other residents. Svat speaks humorously as well, but there is a difference. Where Svat evokes a general low-key affection, Budala usually provokes irritation, but he is probably unaware of his effect on others. Perhaps he is the troublesome little brother who cannot be rejected. Mysteriously, he is one of them. Crime unknown.

Propovjednik (Propo for short) is "preacher". He is in his thirties, short and bald; there was no hair on top for the guards to shave off. Burly, he has a phlegmatic's body posture, though only in the absence of guards. His flesh is wasting away, but it is clear that he was once a man of great strength. Ever ready to offer analysis, he is both clever and cautious. He was born and raised in Belgrade—an engineer. He built bridges and dams for Tito before the break with Stalin. Propo can be didactic in the manner of a man with elitist knowledge. Of course, it is impossible to maintain any illusions of superiority here, and arrogance is swiftly dealt with by guard and prisoner alike. His "preaching" is never religious; it is always about political or social matters. They listen when he speaks, but he is not well liked. Crime unknown.

Prof, the "professor", is in his late thirties, slightly built, reserved, an intellectual. His eyes and expression seem always turned to some unspoken thought. He is admired by all and liked for reasons that none can explain. It seems to Josip that there is a quiet dignity in this man, who rallies the others' dislocated qualities of character and manliness. Prof thinks before he speaks. One remembers what he says, and one ponders it. Crime unknown.

Tata, "Papa", is gentle without softness, kindly and observant of others' needs. In his late fifties or early sixties, he is the oldest of the six, yet he possesses some inner reserve of strength. Usually silent, he is the only one who has made a reference to religion. Crime unknown.

Why do they help him? It cannot be ethnic loyalty. Propo is a Serb. Sova is a Slovene. Svat is a Bosnian, though he will not say if he is Croat, Serb, or Muslim. His facial characteristics could be any of these; it is assumed he is of mixed ethnicity. Prof, Tata, and Budala are Croats, as are the majority in the barracks.

Some of the nicknames derive from temperament or mannerisms. Others, such as Svat's, may have to do with stories they have told. For example, a wedding at which Svat drank a liter of *slivovica* and was still capable of walking home. Where is home? Josip asks. Svat's face falls into uncharacteristic moroseness. "Tuzla", he mumbles and will say no more. Budala offers, without being asked, that he himself is from Lukovo, a village on the coast not far from here. He intends to sneak to the eastern part of Goli Otok one morning, he declares, just to wave hello to his grandmother.

"Enjoy it. It will be your last wave", says Sova.

The prisoners speak with each other only when no guards hover nearby, usually in the latrine, but also when they are laboring over the sifting bucket, or when side by side they blow on glowing embers of charcoal under the boiling pot. The guards have high standards. They always stand well upwind of sources of stench, which are various and numerous. Whispering at night in the barracks is less dangerous, but few are willing to waste precious time in conversation that in all likelihood would be depressing complaints or the painful reminiscing of strangers. Besides, everyone desires to plunge into sleep as quickly as he can. Otherwise, short exchanges are risked in murmurs or whispers. What do they talk about? Their lost pasts, resentments and desires, mockery of their captors, plans for escape?

Josip cannot tell for sure, though he supposes that all prisoners speak about these things.

Of his own companions, the six, there is such diversity in background that he continues to puzzle over their concern for him. Men seem to die here at frequent intervals. And always, human life is nearly valueless. If you can work, you will survive—rather, you *may* survive—but only if you are more docile than a donkey. You will be beaten like a donkey too and fed like one as well, though it must be admitted that a real donkey does not eat food passed through someone else's intestines.

"Beware of what they do to the mind", says Propo one day, after he has swabbed the last open wound remaining on Josip's body. The salty brine still stings. The gash on the shoulder muscle was deep. Propo explains that he stitched the flaps together with needle and thread while Josip was in delirium. It is not infected but still painful, and from time to time it bleeds a little. The rib is healing.

"How long have I been here?" Josip asks.

"Thirty-seven days", says Propo.

"Can it be that long? I have lost track of time."

"That's what I mean, beware of what they do to the mind. First they take away your freedom, then your strength, then your clarity of thought. Finally, when you accept the lie that you are less than an animal, they will rebuild you."

"Not me."

"Oh, yes, you. There is nothing in you, nor in any of us, that can resist a lifetime of this." Propo looks around the compound with disgust, his eyes lingering on three men crouched at the water buckets, concentrating on sifting for their reboiled supper.

What were these men before capture? Men change under pressure, and it seems that most change for the worse. Only a few are refined in the fire, and all that is best in them comes forth, solidified, yet retaining the fluidity of liquid gold.

Night. Two prisoners have been permanently removed from the barracks. Prof is now repositioned to the pallet beside Josip's. Josip is awake, listening to sounds of a roomful of sleeping men. Seated with his back to the wall, his eyes are closed. He can hear Ariadne's voice, though he cannot grasp what she is saying. Does she reach for him across the void? Is she seeking him in her dreams, or in a prison cell, or from beyond the gates of death? The agony of longing for her is greater than the desolation of not thinking about her. Then the sound of her violin. Mozart? Paganini? He begins to weep silently. Within his breast there is an earthquake of love, grief, pain.

"You do not sleep", whispers a voice beside him. It is Prof.

"I cannot."

"You are thinking of your family?"

He nods, though it cannot be seen by the other.

"What is your name?"

"Brbl."

A few of the six have taken to calling him Brbljavac, "babbler", because of his delirious ravings during the first days.

"What is your real name?"

Because one can never speak normally during an earthquake, Josip offers no reply. Yet as the tremors subside, his thoughts turn elsewhere; he realizes that a thread of humanity has been cast in his direction.

"I am Josip Lasta, from Split", he whispers at last.

"I am Vladimir Lucić, from Zagreb."

A hand brushes his arm. They shake hands.

"What was your work before your arrest?" asks Vladimir Lucić.

"I was a professor of mathematics."

"I was a professor of history."

"You are as criminal as I am, I am sure."

"Precisely."

"Why do we use these crude names? Why do we present

ourselves to each other as owl, and preacher, and blockhead, and not who we really are?"

"Do we present our names, or are they presented to us?"

"Yes, we name each other. But why?"

"I have thought a lot about this and have come to believe that we do not use our real names because we are infected with the lies that dominate everything here. To the guards we are no more than numbers. Something in us always resists this dehumanization, yet we cooperate in its spirit in order to survive."

"Survive? By reducing our humanity to a less personal level?"

"Because we feel our peril at every moment, we withdraw inside ourselves a step or two. The crude name is like a mask we hold before us or a shield to protect our true selves."

"Why would we need to protect ourselves from our fellow prisoners?"

"Because anyone can break down, betray us, curry favor with the guards in exchange for a bit of relief. You see what they have done to us, Josip? A crude name is a mask of toughness, hardness. We are beyond feeling, we say to each other. We will survive as long as we have no feeling. This is a mistake."

Yes, it is a mistake, but an unavoidable one it seems. Josip lies down and goes to sleep.

Another night: Prof shakes his shoulder.

"Let us talk, Josip Lasta."

"Why should we? We are dead men."

"We are not dead men. But we will slip closer to death if we do not use our minds."

"What is the mind?"

"You ask an excellent question. Do you have any thoughts about it?"

"None."

"Speak to me. Tell me what is in your mind."

A silence ensues. Finally Josip says, "Why do they do it to us? Why does one man degrade another, beat him to death, or throw him into the sea and for amusement watch the sharks tear him to pieces?"

"Little by little the guards chose—long ago they chose—step by step they descended into the realm of the beast-men. In their souls, they know their depravity and hate themselves for it."

"Hate themselves? No, they enjoy it."

"Do they? I think they try to escape it by being masters of it. By using more and more evil, they try to rise and only sink deeper and deeper."

"Are they evil, or are they merely ignorant?"

"At this level it is mostly ignorance, a vicious cycle to avoid despair. In the hierarchies of authority there are degrees of guilt. Above the guards is the prison administration, above it is the department in charge of prisons, above that level are the political courts, then the Ministry of the Interior and the Ministry of Justice, and above that are the leaders. Above them, Josip, one finds only spirit. The higher one looks, the greater the evil. But I am saying this poorly. The hierarchy is a descending one, and those who appear to have the most power are really at the lowest level, because under their feet is hell itself."

"Maybe it's only strata of disordered human psychology. That would account for everything."

Vladimir does not immediately reply. "No it would not account for everything", he says at last.

"Isn't it a case of men who feel powerless crushing others lower because they feel it raises them higher?"

"Yes, that's their psychology. But there is more in it than you think."

A guard throws open the door and casts his flashlight here and there throughout the room. Fortunately, Josip has laid himself flat in time. Nothing moves. The guard goes out and closes the door. No more is said. However, Josip is struck by the realization that Prof has reawakened his mind.

Since he arrived on the island, Josip has noticed the signals that pass between the six, mainly subliminal. They trust each other. What binds them together? It is not a shared past or a unified outlook on the world. And why have they congregated around him, why have they preserved him? Several prisoners have been deleted from the original number since Josip's arrival on the island. Three died from maltreatment and hunger, two were shot in the quarries where the prisoners work, others were dragged away by guards and have not returned. Crimes unknown.

"Why do you help me?" Josip asks Propo one day.

Propo looks at Josip with a direct gaze. "Because we heard about your courage."

"My courage?" Josip mumbles. What is courage? When did he last have any of that?

"No one has ever survived what you went through. Many die from a single passage through skin-the-rabbit. You survived three. I think even some of the guards were impressed."

There is nothing to say in reply.

"After skin-the-rabbit, when you had your bath, it was Svat and Budala who lifted you and put you into the barrel. They did not want to do it, but they would become skinned rabbits if they refused. They told us about your endurance. They have seen men die under fewer blows."

"So, not every prisoner is a skinned rabbit?"

"Most, not all. They are young and came here within the past few months. Their strength makes them useful. But do not despise these boys, for they hate what they do. Perhaps that is why they help you now. Svat is motivated by admiration for you, Budala by shame."

"What motivates you?"

"Each has his reasons. But I think we do it to keep from

369

sinking lower than the beasts. Animals do not sacrifice without thought of reward. Only men sacrifice in this manner. So, you help us to remain men."

"As you help me to remain a man."

"It's how we can repel their lies, each for his own reason, each in his way."

"And the guards, what motivates them?"

"The guards! They are the easiest to understand. They are the bullies we all have met in our lives. They are everywhere in this world but restrained by law in civilized nations. They who once terrorized playgrounds and neighborhoods now may terrorize defenseless men. Those sneering faces with no thoughts inside and only guns and truncheons in their hands—*they* are the less-than-men."

"Yet you are afraid of them, as are we all."

"I feel nothing but contempt for them. Do not fear what they do to the body, if you can help it. Fear instead what they do to the mind."

"You said that before."

"And I say it again."

After considering this for a few moments, Josip ventures: "What is your name, Propo?"

The latter looks away, snorts, then mutters, "Ante", as if his name were a useless and accidental ornament.

That night, Svat crawls on hands and knees in the dark to Josip's pallet and gives him a piece of damp bread. He is about to turn away when Josip seizes his wrist.

"Let me go", whispers the boy intensely. "If a guard comes in, I'll catch hell."

"Just one moment. It was you who said *courage* to me when I went into the barrel."

"I am sorry. Don't hate me. I didn't want to put you in there. But, you see, if I hadn't—"

370

"It's all right. I just want to tell you I am grateful for what you said. The word stayed with me as I went down. And maybe that word brought me up again, alive."

In the silence of a room full of sleeping men, Josip can hear the other swallow.

"What is your name?"

"I'm Svat!"

"Your real name."

The other pauses, pulls his hand away, hesitates.

"I am Kruno", he whispers. "Krunoslav Bošnjaković."

"How old are you?"

"Seventeen?"

"Why are you here, Kruno, in Goli Otok?"

"I am a criminal."

"What was your crime?"

"I threw an egg at a picture of Tito in my school."

"A terrible crime."

"I should have eaten the egg and kept my mouth shut. They were going to put my mother in jail because of what I did. But they didn't."

"And your father?"

"The Ustashe killed him when I was a baby."

"We should sleep, Kruno", says Josip, after absorbing this.

"Yes. Good night. I will see you tomorrow. Don't hate me."

"I don't hate you."

19

Two guards enter the barracks at dawn and all the prisoners get to their feet and stand at attention. Josip stands with them, a little slower than the others. After a cursory circumspection of the prisoner's body one guard nods, and the other throws a bundle of clothes at him.

"You're well enough to work", he growls. "Get dressed."

His new uniform is a set of shorts made of tougher canvas and a collarless burlap shirt. Also a set of leather boots, hanging together by its hobnails, laced with twine. No socks, no underwear. Everything chafes his still raw flesh.

The quarries are up in the hills beyond the compound. Every day the prisoners are marched there on dusty paths and down into natural ravines or artificial rock cuts, to slice from the island's body thin slabs of limestone. Thin, yes, but it takes a healthy man to lift one. Those who have not lived here forever could lift two or three at a time if they so wished, but the risk of dropping them is greater, and if you drop one and it breaks into pieces, you will be broken into pieces by the guards. They observe every movement. They are bored with watching and their boredom breeds mischief, an appetite for provocation. If they can goad a prisoner into the merest hint of rebellion, even an improper attitude, they can retaliate. The sight of blood and the feeling of power is what they live for. That, and smoking, and surreptitious sips from bottles secreted inside their uniforms. They too live with risks.

Their risk is not so great, however, that they refrain from conspiring to demolish a prisoner now and then, as sport. This diversion is a favorite pastime, a bonus payment for their life of ennui. They know that an unceasing supply of fresh prisoners will arrive from the mainland and that such labor is a disposable asset, though it cannot be disposed of too often—there must be good reasons for it, and of course there must be witnesses to justify any punitive action. Not all the guards are like this. There are good ravines where casualties are fewer, and bad ravines where the likelihood of annihilation is greater.

On Josip's first workday, his crew is in a good ravine. For twelve hours the prisoners slowly and relentlessly carry limestone slabs up a winding path to a truck parked at the crest. One stone at a time. Josip is permitted to carry the smallest pieces. A break for water every three hours, half an hour for lunch—soup and water—then another three hours before the next water break, and after that a final three hours before they shuffle back down the hills toward the compound.

All day long the guards—three of them with rifles slung over shoulders—look down without expression into the crawling pit of human ants and walk slowly and sometimes haphazardly around the perimeter. Whenever a truck drives away with a full load, the prisoners can slacken their pace a little (though never are they permitted a complete rest), and the guards sit down, exchange comments with each other, light cigarettes, and make jokes. Every six hours they are replaced. For each set of workers there are two sets of guards. Fortunately, today both sets are not entirely inhuman.

By nightfall Josip is nearly dehydrated, every muscle in his body is aching, his groin and midriff are rubbed raw by the rough clothing, his hands are blistered, and a hopeless run toward the sea has become an option he is seriously considering. On the homeward journey, Sova and Prof put their shoulders under his arms and help him walk the last hundred meters. Sova declares that it was an excellent day. No accidents, no severe beatings, no deaths. Just the usual cuffs and insults. "Puzzling", says Prof. "Maybe the thoughts of the guards are elsewhere. I wonder what is happening in the world?" All of this is in whispers. To speak aloud is to invite a blow from a fist, a rifle butt, or even the punishment of the winepress.

"What is the winepress?" Josip asks as he drops onto his pallet and curls into a ball, longing for sleep.

"If you anger the guards," whispers Prof, "they will make you carry two slabs uphill on your back. Then on your next trip it is three slabs, then four and onward. No water all day as they add weight to weight until you collapse. If you drop the stones and they break, you will be shot. It's like a game of dice for the guards. If you drop the stones and they don't break, you are merely beaten. They don't let you die, just bleed. If you survive that, they think you are strong enough to keep working. But mostly the stone breaks."

"You have seen this?"

"A few times."

"How long have you been here?"

"Two and a half years."

Two and a half years ago Josip was running up and down the Marjan and accepting a position as professor of mathematics at the university as if the entire world were operating more or less as it should. At the time, he was sure that the injustices around him were severe but temporary aberrations, which the slow evolution of civilization would change for the better. Two and a half years ago, while he was blissfully ignorant of all that was approaching, a professor of history in Zagreb was being interrogated and condemned to prison for teaching the truth.

"They banish truth", whispers Josip to Prof.

"They banish everything human", Prof replies.

Then they sleep.

So it goes, day after day, week after week. From time to time, Josip sees other crews falling under the lash or individual prisoners being chased by groups of lackeys who repeatedly drive their victims before them with a rain of blows. Often, a prisoner will be forced to run while carrying a metal box loaded with stone chips, the tray hanging about his neck by a wire loop. The lackeys beat him, *faster-faster-faster* they scream, until the victim's lungs burst or his heart bursts or his legs collapse, or the wire cuts too deep into the neck and his blood pours out onto the white stones. Going to and from the barracks compound, which is called the Wire, Josip sometimes notices dead bodies that have not been taken away, ravens perched on the skulls pecking in the eye sockets. They pass one such corpse, and Sova whispers, "He was head of a state ministry." They pass another, and Propo whispers, "That one was a poet."

It is now three months since Josip arrived. The rabbit has grown new skin and also developed other coverings. His hands are calloused and his wounds healed, though the deeper bruises are still sore. He feels less emotion than he did in the beginning. He observes every detail of their lives (he forces himself to do this, for the suction of fatigue and indifference is constant). He thinks about the personalities beneath the masks of his fellow inmates and is heartened whenever a spark shows beneath the limestone dust. He still has eaten none of the reboiled wheat. His six companions have stopped feeding him their rations. Every few days, whenever he can endure the extra hunger, he gives half of his daily portion of bread to one or another of them. They always refuse at first, and in the end the accept. Only Prof remains constant in refusal. No, there is Tata as well—a man of mysterious moral strength—his character different than Prof's, but just as strong. A puzzle, these two men. Who are they, really?

"You have been here more than three months", whispers Tata on a homeward journey not long after.

This statement of the obvious is not intended as information.

375

It is Tata's affirmation of Josip's existence. He is saying that time and identity still exist—and individual destiny. Josip recognizes this as a gift from the old man, better than bread.

"Thank you", he whispers. "Thank you."

Tata smiles. This is the first genuine smile Josip has seen since his arrest. The old man understands—understands that Josip understands.

"And you, Tata? How long has it been?"

"Four years and two months."

"May I ask what your work was before your arrest?"

But a guard has spotted them whispering, or suspects them of whispering, and shouts a warning. He is not one of the more brutal ones and thus there is no retaliation. The prisoners trudge onward in silence.

As they wearily shuffle along a track Josip has never used before, a view of the sea opens up for a few seconds. Between two hills the open water is as purple as a bird wing, the sky darker still, and an island in the distance is flaring rose from the setting sun. Josip's eyes gulp down what he sees, then the next hummock of stone blocks the view, and they plunge into the valley of the prisoners.

"They cannot banish the sea", whispers Tata.

A bird swoops down over their heads, rises upward in a fantastic trajectory of aerial dynamics, and then is gone.

"They cannot banish birds", whispers Josip.

After he has eaten his soup and bread, he collapses onto his rags, grasping for sleep, but desperate also to take the image of the bird into his dreams. He will dream that he is the *lastavica* rising over the sea.

The last thing he hears is the cry of a newborn baby. He is too exhausted to climb back out of half-sleep to cock his ears and wonder where it has come from, yet he knows that his own baby has by now been born. Yes, somewhere in this world his child has been born. Thinking about it hurts so much that in other circumstances he might have remained sleepless all night, but now he sinks and cannot awake until the harsh whistles rouse the prisoners to another day of work.

The greatest challenge is to remain mentally alert. In this way a prisoner can detect the signs of descent into total docility—then dehumanization, and then reconstruction. Most prisoners loathe the political lectures, which are held one evening a week in a building called "the school". Though everyone understands what is being done to their thinking, a few readily succumb, pretending to believe the ideology (or actually embracing it) in hope of an early release. Propo calls them the optimists. Regardless of their politics, he says, no prisoners will be released. As far as he knows, no prisoners have ever been released—except through the gate of universal mortality.

The lectures offer Josip a mental challenge. Beneath the propaganda, he can hear twisted brains ticking away with their subtle and not-so-subtle plots. Between the lines he sees the minds of the jailers, the minds of the theorists, the mind of the regime. Know this mind, he tells himself, know it as you know the eyes of the judges and the eyes of the wolves and the servants of the wolves. Every word, phrase, sentence, every theme has materialized—apparently out of nowhere—for a purpose. It has been deliberately formed for the sole purpose of reshaping your thoughts, and in such a way that it will be most effective. They have had years of practice, and that they continue to use this approach shows you that it is successful, though to what degree is still not clear. One of their tactics is the good wolf and bad wolf routine, the wolves working hand in hand to soften resistance. Most guards are brutal, but the indoctrinators at the weekly session are reasonable in tone. They speak to the prisoners as if they are men, and there is an extra ration of bread on those evenings.

After every session, the whispering in the barracks contains observations such as, "You see, they're not so bad." And, "What

377

he said about Tito tonight was true." And, "Well, at least prosperity is coming to our homeland."

Such comments usually pop out of the mouths of the weakest and youngest, and on occasion the most desperate, who are hoping an informer will report their reactions to the administration, thus speeding their way out of this hell.

No one tries to refute such self-delusions, because an informer might report the refutation and speed one's way deeper into hell.

"Poor souls", says Tata.

Prof shakes his head. "They believe that tractors fall out of the sky."

Josip listens and muses.

Occasionally, while a hundred or so men are seated on wooden benches in the "school", the commandant enters the lecture hall to check on how the evening is going. No heads turn, though all are aware he is here. A portly, sixtyish man in a fine uniform with brave medals on a brave breast, his gruff style declares that he is a decent soldierly fellow who wants no more than to see a smoothly running institution and the successful rehabilitation of sociopaths. He is no bureaucrat, and though he has personally beaten men to death, he does not make a habit of it. He was once a major in the Partisans, but he made a few mistakes along the way and that is why he is here. So the rumors go. They may or may not be true. In any event, he is known among the six as Zmaj, "the dragon". A fat little dragon with a growing belly. Whenever he throws his shoulders back and scowls and strides up and down the aisles, inspecting prisoners' faces to see if they are paying attention to the lecturer, splits of white undershirt are exposed between the buttons. Vertical smiles. A friendly dragon, this Zmaj.

His assistant, a taller and slightly leaner officer with a deep scar cut diagonally across his nose, right cheek, and upper lip, is not so friendly. He is referred to as Sokol, "the hawk". He has been known to pull a "student" from a bench and drag him outside, and then follows a pistol shot. Both men appear to be well fed. Whenever the wind is right, the smell of onions frying in butter blows into the prisoners' compound, and often the smell of cooking meat. At such moments, prisoners suck at the air as if it contained nourishment.

These hints of a meta-zone are a flaw in the regime, because the olfactory language is vastly magnified among the prisoners and becomes that much more significant, evoking a myriad of unspoken reactions. Their own zone is not so much a spot on the island as it is a psychological state. The faintest evidence of another world helps them to realize this—and to resist.

Are there more ways to resist? Josip wracks what remains of his brains to find some. One night he turns on his pallet and whispers to Prof.

"Are you awake?"

"Yes."

"I have an idea."

"Do not waste energy on dreams of escape, Josip."

"There are ways of escape that do not involve fleeing."

"What do you mean?"

"We can develop a culture within the island."

"A culture?"

"A clandestine sub-culture. Not truly subversive because it will be positive. Our captors are the real subversives because they kill. We can find ways to live as men."

"How?"

"We will have dialogues."

"Dialogues", murmurs Prof. "Do you like the taste of hemlock?"

"We can do it."

"Josip, go to sleep. I cannot keep my eyes open."

"Listen, listen to me, Vladimir."

"Enough! If we keep on whispering like this, a rat will scurry to speak to the dragon."

The next morning they are passing through the fold in the hills toward a distant quarry. For some reason, fewer guards than usual march them along, just one at the head of the line, another behind. Prof is in front of Josip.

"What kind of dialogues?" he mumbles over his shoulder.

"Anything we like. Free men can discuss anything they like."

"A recipe for destruction. They are always watching."

"We'll do it one word at a time as we go up and down the paths to the trucks."

"One-word dialogues?"

"It can work, Vladimir. It can work. Then we will have ideas in our minds, and our thinking will move again. Slowly at first, but then maybe it will gather speed."

"And with it will come the return of full consciousness. And with that will come mental anguish."

"Pain is the price of consciousness."

"It's too big a risk—"

"Let's try. For one day at least, let's try."

Now they are filing down into an artificial rock cut, about twenty meters wide and sixty long. During the previous days, another crew, using gasoline-driven blades, sliced hundreds of fine stones from the cliffs and stacked them neatly at the bottom, waiting for the beasts of burden. The crew from Josip's barracks groans and bends, and in turn each man picks up his piece of stone. They slowly re-climb the path toward the crest, where more guards have arrived and a truck is waiting for cargo. The path is narrower than most; a prisoner coming back down after delivering his load must turn sideways to pass those coming up. One false step would cause a fatal fall. Prof is among the first, Josip among the last. As Prof is coming back down, he turns sideways to allow Josip to go up.

Without moving his lips, Josip breathes, "Despair."

In a moment, Prof has moved on, and nothing is noticeable from above.

When they pass again as Prof ascends and Josip descends, the latter adds a second word: "is".

At their next meeting Prof whispers, "Despair is?" His look communicates that he is wondering if Josip has gone completely mad.

On the next pass Josip adds more: "toxic waste."

The next, Prof replies, "Despair is toxic waste?"

Josip makes as if to stumble, giving them a few extra seconds. "Yes."

A guard shouts down, "Watch it there, you stupids! Don't kill yourselves—that's *our* job!"

Other guards chuckle.

The next pass, Josip whispers, "produced by—"

The next: "internal—"

The next: "combustion—"

The next: "of—"

The next: "false—"

Finally: "assumptions."

By this point, Prof is smiling with his eyes as they pass. To smile with the mouth is too visible and would invite official curiosity and retribution.

It takes three hours. At the water break, the prisoners collapse into the limestone dust on the quarry floor, panting.

Lying on his back a few feet from Josip, Prof whispers without moving his lips, "Despair is the toxic waste produced by the internal combustion of false assumptions."

Whistles blowing, guards barking, "Get to work!"

Prof heaves himself onto hands and knees and rises, his back to the guards, his face to Josip.

"I understand. Now it's my turn."

During the three hours between water-break and lunch, Prof makes his reply:

Roman—
civilization—
fell—
because of—
obsession—
with—
gladiatorial—
games.

At lunch break, they gulp the soup and water dispensed from barrels on the back of the truck, then return to the pit and collapse again into the dust. They will have fifteen minutes, perhaps, though talking is not allowed. As before, they lie on their backs a few feet from each other.

Josip: "Roman civilization fell because of obsession with gladiatorial games?"

Prof: "Yes, you got it."

Josip: "It's hardly a reply to my part of the dialogue."

Prof: "It is. Wait and see, there's more."

Whistles blowing. "Get up, you lazy animals!"

Three hours of sweating under the ferocious afternoon sun lie ahead. But the work seems easier now because the mind is engaged elsewhere. What is Prof trying to say? In what way does it connect to Josip's sentence? And what is the *more*?

On the first pass he begins:

Carthaginian—
civilization—
fell—
because of—
child—
sacrifice.

Men are dropping because of dehydration. There are a few cursory kicks and blows, but the senior guard gives permission for an extra water-break. Lining up by the barrel, Josip makes sure he is behind Prof. No lips move, no head turns, nothing at all to indicate that men are communicating with each other.

"Carthaginian civilization fell because of child-sacrifice", breathes Josip as Prof steps up to take a tin cup from a lackey who is shouting at a comrade and not paying attention. A risk, but it works.

Prof nods as if sipping from the cup. "Yes." Then he drains the cup. "There's more."

"No more, you bastard!" the lackey bellows at Prof. "One cup per prisoner!"

Prof turns away and goes back down into the quarry.

They resume their work and their dialogue. As Prof has indicated, there is more to come on his part.

"Our", he begins, followed on subsequent passes by:
civilization—
will—
fall—
because—
of—
both.

Josip can barely contain his excitement. They now have a key to an entire world of resistance. Internal thought, a flow of human discourse among the dehumanized.

"What are you smiling at, you donkey!" shouts a guard. "No water for you at break!"

Well, it was worth it. He can do without the water, for he now has something a thousand times more valuable in his veins.

The following hours are hard and dry, yet three more sentences are exchanged:

Josip: "How will we hasten its fall?"

Vladimir: "More important: What will take its place?"

Josip: "Does conspiracy to bring down evil regimes breed counter-conspiracies that become more evil than the ones they replace?"

His head is swimming from this long thought, his eyes blurring by the time the last whistle blows, bringing another work day to a close. There is no time for a reply.

Later that night, as everyone else in the barracks sleeps, Josip turns to Prof.

"Vladimir?"

A grunt.

"Vladimir, how did you like it?"

"I liked it", mumbles the professor of history. "Let's continue. But now, I beg you, sleep . . . sleep, sleep."

During the following weeks, Josip witnesses several beatings of clumsy or insufficiently servile prisoners. One shooting of a madman who makes a run for the sea. Pistol shots at night, fewer in the daytime. Screams at any hour. A truck that passes with several corpses on it. Whatever he feels, he has learned to keep a mask firmly on his face.

Tata has joined the dialogue. It can get confusing holding two conversations at once, holding two threads as he wends his way through the labyrinth. So, they decide to have just one dialogue per day, like a hoarded piece of chocolate held in the mouth, melting slowly.

Tata is dialoguing with Propo now. Sometimes they switch, Josip with Tata or Josip with Propo. The four conspirators compare notes at the end of each day, but they are getting worried that all this nocturnal whispering is going to attract attention, get them dragged into interrogation rooms. Even so, a few fragments of gold appear in the debris.

From the mental archives:

Tata:

Western civilization survived the Dark Ages because of
Christian monasticism.

Monasticism was founded on prayer and work and art.

Work is the plastic artform of love.

Prayer is the soul's song of love.

Josip:

Children are the fruit of love.

The natural habitat of children is the family.

A human civilization is a community of such sanctuaries.

Our civilization will be reborn only as a community of
sanctuaries.

Propo (surprising the other three because he seems such an
unreflective man):

There is nothing more intimidating than a village clerk
infatuated with the powers of his office.

There is nothing more benevolent in appearance than a
dictator who perceives himself to be a humble
philanthropist.

Both are dangerous, but the village clerk is more so.

Prof:

Humor is the delight of suddenly expanded perspective.

Humor is the transformation of linear vision into the
multidimensional.

Humor is not logical. Neither is it illogical. It is in the realm
of meta-logic.

Humor, like art, liberates, for it can affirm the prisoner in his
ultimate identity.

Between Propo and Prof:

  Prof: "Are you still a Stalinist?"

  Propo: "Certainly. Are you still a Revisionist?"

  Prof: "I was neither."

385

Propo: "What are you?"

Prof: "A rabbit with a Ph.D."

Propo: "Your jokes will not liberate you."

Prof: "They have already liberated me."

Propo: (no reply)

Prof: "Stalin has a thousand Goli Otoks throughout the Soviet Union."

Propo: (no reply)

They remain undetected. They remain physically unharmed. Josip's strength grows. Then he is infested with lice, shaved bald, and cured by a bitter powder. Not long after, he sickens with dysentery and spends a week in an infirmary that is worse than the cellar-hospital at Sarajevo. There are no sea-swallows here, only infirmarians and guards who like to insult prisoners continually. It is bearable, and he slowly recovers. As he rests— if one can call it rest—he thinks of compacted sayings that may be transferred to the others. He misses the dialogues and feels a certain loneliness for his fellow conspirators. He tries not to think about Ariadne and the baby. That would immerse him in endless hell. He must not indulge in it. He will get out some-day, he will find them, and together they will escape to free-dom. Until then, he cannot afford any self-pity. Rage and discouragement alike would rob him of what he needs.

So, he turns his thoughts again and again to the dialogues. Sometimes to little poetic passages, though he knows these would not be of interest to Prof and Tata and Propo. Stop, he tells himself, you must not slide back into that sort of naming! Their names are Vladimir and Tomislav and Ante! Maybe Sova should be brought into it too. Sova is a thinker of some kind, and he would broaden the spectrum. But what is the owl's name?

Returning to the lime quarries, Josip finds that his muscles are a little weaker, but he is also stronger because he has rested and slept properly for the first time in months. During his absence, Sova has come into the dialogues, but he is not really much interested. His one contribution is something caustic about Communism, then he lags and refuses to continue. A pessimist, he is certain they will be detected and punished. It's not worth it, he says.

Unfortunately, young Svat—Krunoslav—has wriggled his way into the conspiracy as well. He has put two and two together and deduced the rest correctly. A bright lad, but without prudence, he is excited about it—too excited for safety. The others repeatedly warn him to guard his mask, to watch his manner and his mouth at all times. They permit him a simple exchange as a test.

His first utterance: "Are there any girls on this island?"

His dialogue partner, Propo, merely rolls his eyes and ends the discussion.

That night he warns the others that Svat is too immature, too optimistic, and lacks the necessary caution. He will forget and make a slip and pull them all down with him. This little brother is likeable, but he is also a deadly peril.

"Give him a chance", whispers Sova. "We were all young once."

"And lived to tell of it. And what's this—are you still involved, Sova?"

"No, no, I'm out of it. But can't you see he's going to kill himself through some stupidity if he stays here long enough. The dialogue could help him grow up, learn to think on his feet, give him something to live for."

"He's living for the very thought of girls, and that's all."

"Give him another chance."

"All right, I'll take him", says Prof.

The next day, this dialogue between the two as they teeter up and down the quarry path:

Prof: "Svat, pay attention."

Svat: "Speak, professor!"

Prof: "It's time for you to start thinking."

Svat: "I'm always thinking!"

Prof: "There will be girls enough if you survive. To survive you must begin real thinking."

End of day. In order to continue, they need another day.

Svat: "What is life without women?"

Prof: "I agree. But you must stay alive if you want to appreciate them."

Svat: "I'm going to escape."

Prof: "Unlikely. You need to survive long enough for that.

Svat: "I'll survive. What is a kiss like?

Prof: "Shut up, idiot."

Svat: "I would die for a girl's kiss."

Prof: "That may well happen."

Another month passes without detection. No one will dialogue any further with Svat; he is too great a risk. Because he and Budala are naturally allied by their youth, and also in the shameful task imposed upon them of bathing new prisoners whenever a boatload arrives, they remain close to each other. They are alike in temperament and differ in character—the good brother and the bad brother—though of course neither one is entirely good or bad. Inevitably, Svat brings Budala into the conspiracy. It seems to spark something in the blockhead, and he appears to be more cheerful as a result. They are dialoguing together in the quarries each day, though what they talk about is anyone's guess. Girls, no doubt, and perhaps naïve escape plots.

The days are growing shorter, and now artificial lights are used during the final hours of each day's work. The truck parks on the crest with its nose pointed toward the pit, its headlights augmented by the guards' flashlights. In some ravines and quarries the poor illumination, combined with the prisoners' fatigue, has caused more accidents. A few men have been shot, not for disobedience but as horses with broken legs are shot.

The men of Josip's barracks are moved to a quarry at the east end of the island. They are higher in the hills here, working near the base of the highest point of Goli Otok, a peak named Glavina, which offers a better view of the water that separates it from the mainland. In the near distance, the mighty wall of the Dinarics can be seen. Vistas of transcendence, a zone promising other worlds. All minds muse more painfully on escape because it is now a visual possibility. Perhaps the administration senses this or understands the psychology of prisoners all too well. Tougher guards, and more of them, are assigned to the crew.

Despite all warnings to Svat and Budala, the boys continue their dialogues with each other. Two, three days go by without mishap.

"What do you talk about?" Josip asks Svat one night in the darkened barracks.

"We talk about the kind of women we will marry. I want blond, Budala wants brunette."

"I will lend you a shoe", whispers Josip.

The boy bursts out laughing, and Josip is forced to clamp his hand over the idiot's mouth.

The next morning, as the crew packs slabs of limestone uphill, a second truck drives along and three additional guards hop off the back. Usually there are not enough trucks to go around to all the quarries, and as expected it drives away. The new guards join with the ones already present, chat with each other, and then spread out around the perimeter.

At water break, Propo whispers, "This is not good. Zmija and Zohar are here."

Snake and Cockroach. Josip needs no explanation.

"They're the worst", Propo adds. "No more dialogues today."

"Back to work! Back to work!" shout the guards.

An hour passes, during which the snake and the cockroach behave no differently than other guards. Then it happens: Svat is going up with a big slab of stone in his arms, Budala is coming down, and they meet halfway. Even at a distance of twenty meters, Josip can see that the boys pause in passing, just a few seconds, but enough to draw attention to themselves. Though it is too far to see lip movement, the way they hold their heads is classic discussion mode. Only a blind man could fail to note that they have spoken to each other.

"Stop!" shouts a guard. A whistle blows shrilly; again and again it shrieks, until all movement ceases within the quarry. Men put down their stones and stand at attention. Zmija the snake stomps down the track, grabs Svat by the collar of his burlap shirt and shakes him. The boy hunches his head into his shoulders, his face stricken with fear. Barking and whistles. A cuff to Svat's face. Another guard strides down into the pit and grabs Budala.

What is said cannot be heard by all. Slowly, Svat crouches and picks up his stone, and shifts it onto his back. With a kick, the snake propels the boy upward toward the crest. To carry stone in this way demands that the bearer bend at the waist so that the slab will not slide off his back. The snake unholsters his pistol and follows behind with gun in hand.

Svat arrives at the top and shifts the stone onto the carry platform of the truck. Another kick sends him stumbling down the track to the quarry floor. Arriving there, he stands with head bowed. Now the guard who is standing by Budala—it is Zohar the cockroach—tells Budala to load two stones onto Svat's back. Svat bends, Budala obeys. Svat turns toward the track and begins his ascent. He is moving at his normal speed, but his face is red with strain.

Again and again the procedure is repeated. Three stones, four stones. Now all the guards have gathered at the head of the trail and are placing bets with each other. Down Svat goes to the bottom of the quarry, his eyes staring at nothing but his feet, as his trembling legs take him back for another load. He bends. Budala, his chin on his chest from anguish and shame, places five slabs on Svat's back. The boy cries out, moves his legs, trying to turn. One step, another, and another. Now he reaches the base of the track.

The quarry is silent as guards and prisoners alike observe his progress.

The incline begins. Svat is groaning, gasping, his limbs trembling as he forces them to overcome weight and gravity. He is still only at the bottom, and the slope ahead has become for him a sheer cliff. He takes a few more paces, until the muscles simply cannot move. A leg gives out, and he sinks down on one knee, though he does not let the stones slide off.

"Up!" commands the snake.

Svat gathers every last gram of energy and slowly rises. Then, in an instant, everything collapses. His legs give way beneath him, he tumbles sideways, and falls a meter onto the quarry floor, a few of the slabs sliding down after him. None hit him. He lies on his belly, panting, as the snake casually strides down the trail and comes to a halt beside the prone boy. With a snap of his fingers, he calls the cockroach and Budala over, and commands the latter to pull Svat to his feet.

Svat is up now, with Budala holding him by the arm, but he cannot stand upright.

"Again!" shouts the snake. "If you make it to the top with six, you will live. Give up now, and you die." He smirks. "Load him", he barks at Budala.

Budala puts one slab onto Svat's back. Then another.

"Faster!"

The third and fourth are added, and now every ear can hear the whimpers that are forced from Svat's throat.

"Another!"

The fifth is added, and Svat's knees begin to shake and buckle. He resists, and straightens them.

"Now the sixth!"

Budala bends to pick up a slab. Suddenly he straightens and cries out, "Sir, sir, please let me carry it for him!"

The snake punches Budala in the nose; the boy staggers backward into the dust.

"Get up! Put the sixth on him!"

Budala gets himself to his feet and obeys.

For a few seconds, Svat quivers and sways, then collapses under the entire weight. He lies beneath the rubble without moving.

The cockroach squats near Svat's head. The boy's eyes are closed but twitching; his lips are trembling, his breath is whistling in and out.

"He's alive", says the cockroach.

"Then he can work", laughs the snake. "Seven!"

The cockroach pushes Budala forward. "He said seven. Put another on."

Sobbing openly now, Budala lifts a slab from a nearby pile and moves toward Svat. He is about to add it to the load pressing down on his friend, but he stops himself and with a wild animal yell hurls the slab at the snake. He throws himself onto him, pummeling with his fists. The cockroach grabs him, drags him away, rams the barrel of his pistol under Budala's chin, and pulls the trigger. The explosion echoes throughout the quarry. Budala's head snaps back, and he crumples at the cockroach's feet. The snake nods approval and dusts himself off.

With a jerk of his hand he tells the cockroach to finish the job. "Not with a bullet", he adds. "It has been a while since we made wine."

The other guards have unslung their rifles and are pointing them down into the quarry, lest the prisoners interfere.

As the snake stands by with a smirk playing on his face, the cockroach lowers a slab onto the stones on Svat's body. Faint groans come from the boy. Another slab is added. Inarticulate pleading.

Josip and Tata are standing nearest, convulsing interiorly, but keeping their masks in place.

"Courage", Josip breathes through his parted lips.

Slab after slab is added. Bones crack, a scream, and then silence.

"You two," snaps the snake, "get these bodies up to the truck!"

Josip and Tata pull the stones off Svat. When his head is exposed, they see that his eyes are open, unblinking. His skull is crushed, blood and brain-matter seeping out; his arms are broken, his ribcage is caved in.

Numb with horror, they pull the broken body toward the trail, leaving a smear of blood in the dust. Tata takes the boy's legs, Josip the arms, and they carry him up the trail to the truck, then roll him onto the platform behind the cab.

"Back to work! Back to work!" shout the guards, blowing whistles. All prisoners stir, shake themselves, turn away from the pile of rubble and gore, and resume their tasks.

"Get the other one!" a guard tells Josip and Tata. They go back down into the pit and retrieve Budala's body. Josip chokes and vomits when they pick him up, for much of the boy's face has been blasted away.

When both bodies are on the truck, the snake commands Josip and Tata to get on. A guard with a cocked rifle joins them.

The truck drives away. Rocking on the uneven road under the hot sun, Tata and Josip crouch beside the bodies, staring at each other in disbelief, two living prisoners beside the two dead. We are all dead, thinks Josip. The guard lights a cigarette and leans against the cab with a sour, bored expression. The engine has no muffler and is roaring loudly. No whispers are possible, though Tata's lips are moving. At one point, when the truck rounds a bend and begins its descent from the hills, the guard stands and faces the front, leaning over the roof of the cab. No one's going anywhere, his posture says, there are no escapes.

With thumb and forefinger, Tata traces a sign of the cross on Svat's forehead, then on Budala's. Josip holds Svat's limp hand. It is not yet cool, not yet stiffening. They pass the prison compound and descend further, going round a bend that arrives at a little bay.

The guard tells them to strip off the boots and throw the bodies into the sea.

Josip and Tata drag Budala's body from the platform and carry it to the water's edge. They throw it in. The body sinks a little and then rises, rolls onto its side, and sinks again, leaving a veil of blood in the water.

Josip takes Svat's body by the legs, the bare feet bobbing against his chest; Tata has the arms, the boy's head lolling and leaking fluids all the way. They throw him in. He slowly sinks, his mouth open wide as he goes down.

Krunoslav, Krunoslav! cries Josip silently. *I will not forget you!*

Then they are commanded onto the truck and driven back to work.

20

Hatred is an energy that gives and takes. It drains the soul, even as it seems to invigorate.

The night after they have thrown the bodies into the sea, Tata crawls across the barracks in the dark and whispers into Josip's ears:

"Now is the test that we all must pass through."

"What test?" Josip replies bitterly.

"When Cain slew Abel—if there had been a third brother, would he not have been put to this test?"

"Leave me alone, Tata. Long ago I figured out that you are a priest, but I cannot bear any religious talk."

"If the third brother allows himself to become Cain in turn, then evil wins."

"Go away."

"Do not give in to it, Josip."

Josip rolls onto his side, his back to Tata.

Now he is planning his escape in earnest. The east side of the island would be best because it is closest to the mainland. To go into the water there would cut the journey down by a kilometer or two, at least a third of the distance. However, the hills and cliffs are also highest there. To dive into the sea from such heights would mean self-destruction. Even so, there may be gradations of the terrain close to the shore—inlets or even small coves, as there are on the south side of the island.

He will escape, find his wife and child, and they will flee to freedom. This is his primary objective. Yet he has new motivation also, for he fully intends to track down Snake and

Cockroach at some point in his life and kill them. It will be justice, not the vengeance of Cain—so he tells himself. He broods on this dark and delicious dream, savors it, imagines it endlessly. Plans it and replans it according to the variations that might evolve with the passage of time and circumstance. The day will come, maybe after the Communists have fallen, when he will find one of the killers, will spot him at a café in Split, or Zagreb, or Dubrovnik, anywhere, and he will stalk him to his home. Later, in the middle of the night, he will knock on his door, and, when it opens, he will point a pistol at the killer's head. "I am from Goli Otok", he will say. "This is for what you did to Krunoslav Bošnjaković." Bang. Blow the top of his head off. Then the other killer: he will knock on the door, and, when it opens, he will point the pistol and say, "I am from Goli Otok. This is for Budala." Bang. And they will both be as dead as Uncle Jure.

He wracks his memory, searching for Budala's true name. What was it? Did the boy ever tell? Of the original conspirators, only he and Tata, Sova, Propo, and Prof remain. They no longer engage in dialogues—none of them—but with Prof there are still some whispered exchanges. Prof has been changed by the boys' deaths. He seems the most stricken, withdrawn; and something is harder in his demeanor.

"Do you desire to avenge their deaths?" Josip whispers in the dark.

"Yes."

"How would you do it?"

"We need not discuss this. If we survive, you will one day, perhaps twenty or thirty years from now, read in the newspaper about the unsolved murder of a former officer of the prison administration."

He will say no more on the matter.

"Did you ever learn Budala's name?"

"No. Go to sleep."

Every day for weeks, the snake and the cockroach hover above the quarry. Six hours a day—half a workday. Josip never glances in their direction, though he knows at all times where they are. If one of them crosses his line of sight, he memorizes and re-memorizes their facial features without appearing to. They pay him no attention. There are other brutal moments during this period, but no more deaths, at least not in this quarry, not in this crew of prisoners. Then they are transferred to a pit lower in the hills, and for a time the snake and the cockroach are seen no more.

"Your hatred is understandable," whispers Tata in the dark, "but it must be overcome."

"Why must it be overcome?" Josip replies in a voice as cold as death.

"What have you suffered in your life, I wonder?" Tata asks. "It seems to me that there is anger in you so deep that it is fathomless."

"Are you not angry?"

"Yes, very angry."

"Well, then, you have answered your own question."

"I do not think so. Your anger is different. Krunoslav's death has opened a deep hole of anger in you. I ask myself: What have you suffered? And did you run from that suffering, whatever it was? And now, because you can run no longer, does every evil blow you have received return to you?"

"You are no help! If what you say is true, the fact remains—there is no place to run on this island."

"Neither from the killers nor from oneself."

"So, I will release my hate. It will have its day, and then the *killers* will suffer."

"You would kill your oppressors if given the chance?"

"With pleasure", says Josip.

"Your vengeance will destroy you."

"Oh? Tell me, Tata, how does a man remain wise in hell?"

The priest does not respond to this. Instead he says: "A man suffers injustice. He resents it, and his resentment grows and grows and becomes anger. Anger, if it is fed, then becomes hatred. Hatred, if fed, opens the soul to evil spirits. And when they possess a man, he becomes capable of any atrocity. Afterward, he will not know how or why he became like that."

"I will know why. Go away!"

It is late autumn now, or perhaps early winter. Their trousers are longer versions of the canvas shorts, and their shirts have longer arms. Otherwise, it's much the same. In order to keep from shivering away one's energy, one must work harder. Cold winds sometimes blow down out of the Dinarics. The first snow has fallen on the peaks, though at sea level there are still days when the sun shines warmly on their backs and they sweat. Coughing and hacking are more common. A body can be sweating one moment, but in the next the sun drops behind the distant shadow of the island of Cres and the chill descends swiftly. Then a prisoner's sweat becomes his enemy. Three men in the barracks have died of pneumonia this month. Since summer, Josip has suffered three colds but has thrown them off.

Today they are in a natural ravine, not very deep, and the path up to the truck is a wide gentle slope.

As Josip carries a slab up, Tata passes him coming down.

"Budala's—" whispers the old man.

On the next pass: "name is—"

The next: "Dalibor—"

And finally: "Kovač."

Josip meets Tata's eyes when they pass again. *Dalibor Kovač.* He is grateful for the information but makes no reply.

Dalibor, I will not forget you!

At lunch break, they sprawl in the dust, the prisoners huddling close to each other for warmth. The guards permit it today.

"I heard his confession", whispers Tata, "the night before he died."

For this Josip has no reply. What difference did it make?

"He was a good boy," says the priest, "a good, good boy, though not wise."

On the homeward trek, shivering in their thin clothing, Tata says, "Krunoslav came to me the week before. A clean heart, a strong heart, wiser than Dalibor but—"

"But not wise enough."

The guard barks, a whistle blows, they are locked into the compound for the night.

In the dark, Tata approaches. "Josip."

"Go away."

"Josip, your heart is not at rest."

"That is true. I will not rest until the killers are slain."

"Do not become Cain."

"I am already Cain."

"Not true. Let us pray together. Death can come at any time."

"Go away."

"If only the *jugo* would blow", whispers Sova. They are in a small ravine, working with fine, pure-white limestone. The blocks are smaller, thinner, not so heavy. Some friend of the regime will enjoy excellent stone floors. Or perhaps these are being shipped to America—Propo overheard one guard telling another that the best stone is sold to the West. Money is flowing into Yugoslavia. The guards are fewer today, only four for the thirty or so prisoners in this crew. The path is steep and narrow, but it affords a little room for dialogue.

The *jugo* is the unpredictable *sirocco* that blows up from the south bringing African warmth to the North Adriatic. It is damp too and often causes rain—long overdue now. If it comes, they will walk to and from work with their heads tilted up, mouths open, drinking fresh water poured from the sky. Moreover, they will feel warm as they do it. For the moment, their bodies are cold, and their tongues are like parchment.

The *jugo* does not come—week after week it does not come. Instead, each day brings a new variation of torment, for the first winds of the *bura* are blowing. They come in the mornings, usually after a big cloud appears over the mountains to the northeast, wailing down the slopes and ripping up the channel into a frenzy of whitecaps, then racing over the islands and out to sea. Though such gusts are unpredictable, so far they have lasted no more than a few hours at a time, chilling, but leaving the atmosphere cleansed and sunny.

A *bura* can be a passing squall, but one of the prisoners warns that it can rise to the level of a tempest, and then to hurricane force, raging down from the northern Dinarics and roaring seaward for days at a time, bitterly cold, destroying men and ships. He says that it is often worst near Senj in the Kvarner region. Senj is only a few kilometers northeast of Goli Otok.

The increasing winds do not provide an excuse for letting up on work, though guards now sit in the cab of the truck with the engine running, two at a time. Two others stand on the crest in their heavy jackets and thick trousers and gloves, stamping their feet and hunching inside their collars, while keeping an unsteady eye on the prisoners.

Propo—clever engineer that he is—has shown the other conspirators how to slice pieces of canvas from the underside of their pallets. Using a sharp piece of scavenged stone, he makes pads that are worn next to the skin, doubling the wind-block. If the mutilation of pallets is discovered, it will mean punishment, but freezing to death is punishment, too, argues Propo. Several of the crew are hacking and coughing as they work. This past week, two others developed pneumonia and were taken away to the infirmary. The administration does not waste penicillin on donkeys, so it is probable that the missing will not recover.

"What month is it?" Josip whispers to Prof in the dark.

"December."

"The day?"

"I'm not sure. I gave up counting. Tata will know."

Josip crawls across the floor to the old man's pallet.

"What day is it?" he whispers.

"The seventh of December", whispers Tata, rising on his elbows. "Josip, we must pray—"

Josip hastily crawls away.

By morning a fierce *bura* is blowing, so cold that all prisoners simultaneously begin groaning aloud as they get up. Whistles are shrilling but as yet no guard has entered their barracks.

The conspirators stand at the narrow windows, watching what is happening outside. A malevolent hand is ripping clouds across the sky and tearing up small bushes near the rim of the compound. The wind whistling through the glassless windows is lighter, for the compound is low in the shelter of the hills, near the west end of the island.

"Up there it's a devil's dance", says Propo, jerking his thumb in the direction of the quarries. "It's a bad one. My guess is there will be no work today because the guards will want to stay inside."

This provokes hopeful looks all around. Rare is the day without hard labor. Even so, if they are to remain in barracks, they will need to huddle together for body warmth.

Later than the usual hour, a guard enters the room and grunts at them to line up and begin the usual trek into the hills. No one dares groan, though dismay is on every face: not even the masks will hide it.

The guards are in a nasty mood, for they do not want to work either. The prisoners file through the open gate and climb up out of the compound, then quail as the full force of the wind hits them. The guards, like a pack of snarling dogs, shout at them, warning that if they want some shelter they had better get moving. No one is beaten, but there are plenty of insults and backhand blows to the train of donkeys that winds its way too slowly toward the hills.

They work in the small ravine again, the source of fine slabs for American floors. It is hard not to resent them—the foreigners, that is—the wealthy, warm, well-fed foreigners with fine homes and more freedom than they know what to do with. It is hard not to spit on this luxury stone, curse it, and send an invisible message across the Atlantic embedded in it. But few are the men who would waste their spit today.

Up and down, up and down, endure this day, endure it—to hell with dialogues!

There is less wind in the ravine because it runs north and south on the flanks of a bulge in Glavina, at right angles to the path of the *bura*. The wind's roar is still deafening, with leaves and branches flying overhead. Once, a gull catapults past with feathers bending the wrong way. The water-break at mid-morning is longer than usual because the four guards have crammed themselves into the cab of the truck and are reluctant to emerge. To their amazement, the prisoners find themselves alone, though doubtless someone is keeping an eye on them from above. They are free to talk, as long as their mouths are out of sight and their body language expresses only fatigue. The water is like ice. Josip can feel every tooth in his upper jaw— half are gone, and as many are absent from the lower jaw. Sometimes he forgets this, but not today.

"Now is our time for escape", he says to Prof, who is lying inches from his mouth.

It is interesting to hear the sound of his own voice, loud and deep. Yes, he still has a man's voice! Yet he hates the garbled pronunciation that his tongue makes because of the missing teeth.

"How?" says Prof doubtfully. "There is no path out except past the truck."

"Not now, later."

"You're mistaken. They know what we're thinking. They will have extra guards and spotlights on the compound tonight. You can be sure of that. I've seen more than one fool die on days exactly like this."

Whistles blow. A single guard points his rifle into the ravine. "Get to work!" The other guards remain in the truck.

So it goes. At lunchtime the soup is cold; the wind has sucked all heat from the iron drum during its ride from the compound.

In the afternoon, another truck drives up, and the morning shift drives away. Now only two guards are watching them, yet both have machine guns. One gets back into the cab and stays there, while the other struts around the perimeter, scowling. Bundled in winter clothes, cap low on his forehead, this guard is not at first recognizable. From time to time, he pulls a bottle from his jacket pocket and drinks from it.

"Zmija", says Propo.

The snake is not happy. Though he makes no trouble, he bestows a look of hatred on every prisoner arriving at the top with a stone in hand. Up and down, up and down continues for a while. He keeps sipping and sipping until the bottle is empty. Then he starts on another one pulled from somewhere inside his uniform.

With each stone deposited on the carry platform, Josip notices that the snake's eyes are red, wandering, unfocused. The snake mutters to himself and smashes the empty bottle on a stone, kicks away the pieces, then pops the cork on a full one.

At one point, he shouts down into the ravine, "Don't try

403

anything!" Then he points the machine gun up toward the *bura* and gives it a few bursts. Instinctively, the prisoners duck, then slowly rise and resume their tasks.

The other guard leaps from the cab of the truck to see what is the matter. The snake growls at him and takes his place inside. The new guard is younger and not threatening. He paces back and forth with only cursory attention to the prisoners. His face seems absorbed in private thoughts. Two hours later, he rouses Zmija from his dormant inebriated state, and they change posts. Zmija is staggering now, still sipping from a bottle. How many of those little bottles does he have?

Then it happens: He steps too close to the edge, and, with a cry that is blown away on the wind, he tumbles to the bottom of the ravine. All prisoners are paralyzed, staring at the body lying at their feet. The snake has knocked his head on a stone and is semiconscious, groaning with closed eyes. His leg is broken, the jagged femur jutting from a torn pant leg.

Pausing only for an instant, Josip picks up a large stone and hastens over. His lips are parted in a savage grin as he lifts the stone high and is about to drop it onto the snake's head.

Suddenly, he is grabbed from behind and yanked backward. The stone topples sideways, narrowly missing the snake, and Josip trips and falls. Tata and Prof land on him, holding him down.

"Let me go, let me go!" he roars.

They will not let him go. He is stronger than any other man in the crew and is close to throwing them off, when Propo and Sova also pile on and keep him down.

With the palm of his hand, Prof hits Josip hard on the cheek. "Enough!" he bellows into his ear.

While the others restrain Josip, Prof stands and galvanizes the prisoners. As yet, the other guard has not noticed the commotion. If he does, they might all be gunned down. Prof gives hurried commands; then he and three other prisoners carry

Zmija up the trail and deposit the body on a heap of rocks behind the truck. He is breathing but unconscious. Prof jams the broken leg between two rocks, then takes a bottle from the snake's pocket and sprinkles alcohol over the jacket, in the hair, in the mouth. Commanding everyone to go back down into the ravine, he tells them to gather stones and get busy. Prof then waits a minute until the up-and-down procedure has resumed. He walks slowly to the cab and raps on the side window. He raps again, and again.

The door swings open, and a surprised guard pushes his way out, unslinging his machine gun.

"Sir," says Prof, bowing at the waist, "there has been an accident. The other guard has fallen down and does not get up. Come quickly."

Prof leads the way at gunpoint. Behind the truck the guard comes upon Zmija, and startles.

"Drunk!" he shouts, and breaks into curses. "Broke your leg, you swine! Well, you deserve it!"

Turning to Prof he says, "Get back to work!" Prof retreats down into the ravine. The guard blows his whistle again and again, and shoots burst after burst of gunfire into the air. A few minutes later another truck roars to a halt and several guards jump out, pointing their weapons down into the ravine.

"No, no, it's not the donkeys, it's him!"

They load the snake onto the back of one of the trucks, and it drives away. Well guarded for the remainder of the day, the crew completes its work and trudges back to the prison compound under a darkening sky, their bodies bending before the wind.

Night. The barrack is dark, the wind is howling outside. No one sleeps, everyone huddles close to others, begging some body warmth. Many are whispering about the demise of the snake. They are hoping he will die, but of course a broken leg

405

cannot kill a guard; broken legs only kill prisoners. Daring a look out, Propo and Prof examine the compound and report to the others.

"It's quiet. More spotlights on all fences; the gate is locked. No guards walking about, only those in the watchtowers."

"Are there more watchers than usual?"

"Of course."

"If Zmija blames us, we're dead."

"He might do that. Or maybe he lost consciousness before he knew he was falling. The other guard will give witness. And being drunk on duty—"

"Also, their little brains would never be able to imagine what nearly happened. If it crosses their mind to suspect it, they'll dismiss it no matter what Zmija says. They would assume that if he fell among us we would finish him off and make a break for it."

"That's true. Who wouldn't!" Sova nods.

"Brbljavac almost did. Good thing you stopped him, Tata", says Propo.

"He hasn't got over Kruno and Dalibor", says the old man. "Give him time."

"Why didn't the other guard notice?"

"I had to wake him up", says Prof.

"A close call—"

"We survived by a thread."

Josip is curled into a ball on his pallet, staring at the darkness, in the blackest mood.

Prof shakes his shoulder. "Josip."

"Leave me alone."

"Do you forgive me?"

"For what?"

"For striking you. I am sorry. You could have killed us all for a moment of revenge."

Josip sits up with his back against the wall and puts his head between his knees.

"You should sleep", says Prof.

No reply.

One by one, the others fall asleep. Josip remains awake.

Slowly he lifts his head. Moving carefully, so as not to disturb the others, he gets to his feet and turns over his pallet. Several pieces are missing from the underside, and these are inside his burlap shirt. Now he unfolds the entire pallet and with his bare fingers widens a tear in the center. He pokes his head through and lets the cloth fall down over his body. It is like a small tent, old and threadbare, a stained green army canvas that has lost its stiffness.

He is still undecided. Should he risk a run for freedom? Is this the night? The cold and the wind will keep some guards inside, but not all of them, and besides there are extra spotlights now. Is it the best time or the worst? He does not know.

Josip is on the verge of lying down and going to sleep when, in an instant, total darkness falls on the world. From beyond the barracks, shouts erupt, a whistle blows, though the *bura* carries the sounds away westward.

Dropping to his knees, he shakes Prof's shoulder.

"What is it?" he mumbles.

"A power failure. The wind has torn something; there are no lights outside."

"Is this true?"

"Look around you!"

"Yes, the generators are down. But for how long?"

"I am going. Come with me."

"Don't be a fool."

"I am going."

Prof grapples Josip's hand and shakes it. "Then God be with you!"

"Good-bye, Vladimir Lucić. I hope we meet again."

407

The barrack door is locked. If he had a tool, he might be able to break it open. Trying not to step on bodies in the dark, Josip makes his way to the windows. Only a child could squeeze through, but he knows of a place along the wall where a brick is loose, one of the verticals that divide the windows. He has tried to loosen it before to no good effect. He finds it, wiggles it, noticing as well that beams of flashlights are waving out there in the dark—along the fences, it must be. All else is blackness. Suddenly, someone is beside him, grabs his arm, pushes a sharp piece of stone onto his hand.

"You are going?" It is Propo's voice

"Yes."

"Well, then, let's get this brick loose."

Josip scrapes at the mortar while Propo wiggles the brick. It hardly moves, and their fingers begin to bleed from small cuts. They keep on trying, the wind screaming so loudly that there is no danger anyone will hear. Indeed, they can no longer hear each other. How much time passes? As the brick is loosening in its socket, there are fewer flashlights in the compound.

Finally, the brick is free. Now they use it as a hammer to bang the others loose. One by one they remove bricks until there is a gap wide enough for a man to pass through.

"Go!" shouts Propo into Josip's ear.

"You come, too!"

"No, I stay."

"Good-bye, Ante."

"Good-bye, Brbl", he shouts back. "If you make it, babble about us somewhere out there in the world, will you?"

"I will not forget you."

Then he dissolves, becoming a deeper shadow within a world of shadows. The tent is over his head in an instant, cutting down the chill. He crawls blindly to the barrack's firepit, where the wheat is reboiled. Spitting into his palms, he makes a paste of ashes and smears it over his face and hands. That done, he crawls along the building, flattening on the ground whenever a light flashes near the wall. There are many walls, and the guards are few. None of them want to be out in the storm. Besides, all barracks are locked, and the gate of the compound is also locked. The fence is twice as high as a man and is capped by barbed wire; it cannot be climbed with ease, even by a healthy man on a fair-weather day, and certainly not by donkeys who are locked inside their exhaustion.

Between buildings he crawls as if through a city of mausoleums, for no light or sound comes from any of the barracks. The ferocious wind snaps the tent wildly, sometimes slapping him in the face. He keeps his eyes shut as he turns toward the eastern end of the compound. Leaving the buildings behind, he scrabbles up the slopes and within minutes is bumping his forehead into the chain links of the fence. He removes the tent from his body and folds it into a compact square. Then, using all the force at his command, he hurls it high, hoping that it will pass over the barbed wire. But it falls back under the force of the wind and lands a few feet behind him. The *bura* is ripping the clouds away, and a slice of moon appears, a fiendish grin of a moon. The light is enough to show him where the canvas has landed. The *bura* is unpacking it, tossing it, and it is about to be taken away like a sail when he throws himself onto it and fights hard to bring it under control. Finally, he has repacked it into a tighter cube. Then he removes his boots and ties them together with the cord laces.

He must not make the same mistake twice. There is more light now, under the moon and the stars—very little, but enough to draw the watchers' eyes if any are turned this way.

He waits—the minutes creep by torturously. Suddenly, there is a drop in the wind's velocity, the world pauses for a second or two, inhaling between gusts. Instantly, he hurls the cube high, followed by his boots, and both land a few feet beyond the fence.

Now he leaps into action. The links are too small for his feet, but his big toes go through. Hand over hand, he swiftly climbs as the *bura* resumes its fury. Nearing the top, he struggles to hold on, for the pressure pushes against him with renewed force, seeking to tear his fingers and toes from the threads upon which he climbs.

Gripping the top crossbar, he pulls himself upward a few more inches. There are three rows of barbed wire above the bar, and if he tries to go through, they will rip him to shreds. Even if he were able to stand with his toes in the topmost links, it would be impossible to hoist a leg over without numerous cuts to the inside of his thighs. Paralyzed by indecision, he remains for some moments wobbling in space, debating with himself. Should he endure the tearing it would exact as the price for freedom? What would happen if he should make it to the sea, and then swim for hours leaving a trail of blood in the water? Surely the sharks would find him!

Desperation makes the decision for him. Gripping the topmost wire in two spots where there are no barbs, he pulls himself higher, with his toes pushing his body upward. This is the worst risk of all. If the wire breaks, he will fall to the rocks below, inside or outside will not matter.

The wire holds. Now his toes are on the upper links, his body is bent double, and his belly arches inward to avoid the barbs in the space between his hands. The wind drops for a second or two. Then, without thinking, he does it. Gripping the wire as tightly as he can, he flips himself over the fence and hangs suspended above the outer perimeter. The backs of his forearms are torn in two or three places by the lower wires and his spine is rammed into the links by the force of the wind. He commands his left hand to let go of the wire, and then twists his body around, grabbing the wire again. This time he has hit a barb, and it cuts into the mount near the thumb but does not impale it.

Now he descends, fingers and toes seizing the links as though they were life itself. The wind is helping because it holds him against the fence, no longer seeking to blow him off like a fly from a spider's web.

His feet flatten on cold stone, and he drops to the ground, curls into a ball, and flashes his eyes around to make sure no lights are pointing at him. None are visible nearby, though sparks can be seen beyond the barracks' roofs at the other end of the compound.

Boots quickly onto his feet, tent over his head, he crawls up through the uneven rocks toward the rim of the compound's stone basin. The last few meters are the worst, as the wind's scream is now deafening, and a horizontal rain of dust and flying gravel, twigs and weeds has begun. He has reached the rim, and with renewed effort he pulls himself over it and into a crevasse between the rocks. There he rests for a time.

Whenever there is a respite, a few seconds, he moves onward. How long does this silent crawling out of hell really take? Is it a matter of minutes or hours? He does not pause to think about it, nor to measure anything other than the fundamental elements of survival—the integrity of his body's resources, the direction in which he must go, and the velocity of the wind, which now seems close to thirty or forty meters per second, hurricane force.

He comes to one of the gravel tracks that lead up into the hills. He forces his body to standing position, sustaining it with effort against the *bura's* animosity. One step, two steps, three, he staggers toward the east, but even a strong man would not be able to resist its power for long. It is better to crawl. But would the gravel and sharp little stones shred his knees and make him more vulnerable to sharks? And how much energy would this crawling consume with a kilometer or two of rough terrain to cross? Well, he must begin.

He removes some of the extra canvas padding from beneath

his shirt and packs it inside his trousers, wadding it about the knees. He moves ahead, feeling the toll on the unused muscles he now needs for a constant crawling motion. He ignores their complaints, lashing them onward. He keeps his head down and his eyes to the dirt in front of his face, giving the wind as little sail as possible. The moon crosses a quarter of the sky. Will there be enough time? Will he reach the east shore before dawn, and will his absence be discovered early or late? It may be that the guards will leave all prisoners in barracks today because work will be impossible. If so, his escape might be undiscovered until the following day. But there is no predicting anything. If the *bura* dies down, the work routine will resume, and guard boats will be circling the island again, as it is said they do whenever there are no storms. They would spot him easily.

Now, though the wind does not cease its roaring, its force seems less. And yes, glancing all around, he sees that the track has entered a narrow valley. It runs due east, at an angle away from the trajectory of the wind. The hills are also swelling higher on the left. Now it is possible to stand and proceed with better speed. His body must still bend, however, but there is relief as his muscles uncramp, and he can stretch his limbs. A crouching run is possible in short bursts. It is of utmost importance to keep his eyes on the track, lest he step off of it and stumble, sprain an ankle or break a leg, and end like the horses that are regularly shot on this island.

An hour passes, then another. Are they hours, or are they minutes stretched interminably by distortions in the mind? How far has the moon traveled along its course? Oh it is far, far! Too swiftly, it is bringing the morning closer and closer— though in the east the sky is still black and riddled with stars, no hint yet of approaching dawn above the mountains.

The mountains? Yes, there they are! He can see the shadow of the Dinarics ahead, rising like a giant's fortress. He has come farther than he thought. Now the trail turns to the right and begins a descent. Where is it going? He does not know this path. Then it turns left again, winding eastward and higher, then north-eastward and lower, up and down, this way and that—yet ever toward the east. Whenever it passes through narrow defiles, or out into folds in the hills that are at odds with the direction of the wind, he runs. He is running as he has run only once before in his life. It is the same lurching-stagger of his return to Rajska Polja after the wolves came to Pačići, and the memory of it is in his flesh, his lungs, his heart. Is he once more running from terror into horror? He does not know. He knows only that he must keep going.

The trail ends. Glavina is on his left. The foothills below his feet roll over and begin their steep descent to the eastern shore of the island. The passage between it and the mainland is visible because the water is whipped into a frenzy of whitecaps, and the lights in the heavens illumine them sufficiently to present them as a blur of lesser shadow among the shadows of the world.

Now the dangers are changing. He must pick his way slowly and blindly down the slope, which is sometimes smooth lime-stone yet more often a maze of crevasses and precipitous drops. The drops may be no more than a meter or so but are enough to break a leg or smash a skull. His fingers are his eyes' pilots; the soles of his boots transmit other information. Combined, they guide him along, meter by meter. He is still too far south. At the shore, the route might be blocked by steeper drops and deep cuts in the stone, inlets and coves—if there are any—that would increase the number of steps he must take, slowing his progress toward the easternmost tip. Now he cuts to the left, descending diagonally in a line that will bring him abreast of a spark of light on the mainland.

Is it a village or a solitary house? He does not know the northern coast of the Adriatic, though he has a vague sense that a few villages and lonely farms are strung haphazardly along hundreds of kilometers of shoreline. He recalls that the distance from Rijeka in the north and his home in Split is about four hundred kilometers. The city of Zadar is about halfway between the two. Hundreds of islands and inlets are somewhere in all of this. He has no recollection from his life before arrest about the precise location of Goli Otok. The other prisoners have said that it is closer to Rijeka than to Zadar. He knows from his reading of maps where the great islands of Krk and Rab are, and during his imprisonment he has learned about the little nearby island of Prvić. But where is he, really?

No matter, he will focus on his destination. Yes, first to the distant shore, then to Split, to Ariadne, to the baby!

This thought infuses him with renewed strength, and he overcomes his terror of the near-blind descent, taking more and more risks. Despite a few tumbles, none are serious, and they give him only minor bruises.

Lower and lower he goes. There is no grass anywhere, no hint of shrubbery. The wind contains less debris, too, though it is now damper. The tent continues to shelter his torso, keeping vital energies within. Yet his head feels severely chilled, and his inner ears are aching. The wind is now at its maximum velocity with nothing to mediate it. Again and again, he is pressed down to the stone and can only slide. It is impossible to stand or kneel or even progress at a crouch. He slithers downward on his back, and the wind helps him, for it acts as a brake on the pull of gravity. From time to time, his feet hit a bump or a sharp protuberance, slowing him still further. The spark is now more visible—just there—across the water. Beneath his feet, a line of pale turbulence appears, indicating that the shore is near.

Then a great gift—his right boot dips over the edge of a ravine. He slows to a stop and considers. It is not possible to see how deep or sheer it is, but undoubtedly it descends directly to the waves that are now pounding against the rocks below.

Carefully, he lowers himself into the hole and gasps with

relief as his boots hit jumbled rocks. It is neither deep nor sheer. Little by little, he picks his way down, and within minutes he is huddling in the mouth of the ravine, with sea spray pelting his face. The scream of the wind and the roar of the surf swirl into a single unending shriek of pandemonium. For the moment, he rests.

What hour is it? The sky is entirely full of stars and still is not paling in the east. This means he will have some time. With luck he will reach the distant shore before sunrise.

Now the major hurdle: the wind is bitterly cold, and the water will be only a little less so. He cannot swim with the tent. If a storm-tossed abandoned boat were to float past, he would take it and use the canvas as a sail. But no miraculous craft appears. The bits of wood-wrack battering the rocks are out of reach, and doubtless these twigs and branches would not offer sufficient float. He needs swift, economical speed—against the wind, at that!

He can waste no more time. Fighting his physical reluctance, he removes the tent from his body and wraps a large stone in it. He throws it out into the water and it sinks. Now he is shivering. He removes the canvas pads from beneath his shirt and throws them into the water, where he hopes the wind will blow them elsewhere in the dark. Now the boots, a stone in each, and they too are gone. His trousers are so thin that they tear easily just above the knees. The arms of the shirt go as well. He will need the bit of canvas that remains on his flesh to slow the release of energy into the water. But he must retain only the minimum—anything more than this would increase the drag.

The windchill could kill him if he does not move quickly. He crouches again, his teeth chattering, his whole body shaking, and then comes a second or two while the *bura* pauses to catch its breath. He springs and leaps out into the water.

It hits like a hammer blow, but he does not succumb. Underwater he goes, using the breast stroke that is like second nature to him. His ears register the moaning of the waves and wind above, but it all seems quiet beneath. Lungs bursting, he kicks upward and thrusts his head into the roaring tempest, wind and spray pelting him and blowing him back toward the rocks.

Now he breaks into a swimmer's crawl. This desperate, hard-paced flinging of his limbs above the wind and waves succeeds in moving him away from the island by no more than a few meters.

Again and again he tries, using all the force he can muster, refusing to let the cold numb his will and his flesh. But it is no use. His head is aching with the windchill, and he must bob under to escape it.

He rises again, gasps for air, and begins a slower loping crawl, the classic method of doing laps that now returns to his muscle-memory. It has been more than a year since he was arrested, the muscles are weaker than they once were, and he has eaten little today; moreover, there is not a gram of fat on his body. Even so, there are reserves of strength that he had not suspected. After some minutes, he glances over his shoulder and realizes that he has made a little progress, fifty meters or so. He quickens his pace, spearing himself arm over arm through the whitecaps. Now the crests are shattering into sea foam, and sporadic gusts that would capsize boats blast the foam into mist. The spray is hard in his face by the time he is a few hundred meters from the island, and the effort to resist both wind and wave is sapping his strength. The top of his skull feels like ice, and he dives for a respite.

It is cold beneath the surface, but the windchill ends. Holding his breath, he kicks hard and swims underwater, hoping against hope that there are no strong currents. Perhaps he progresses a few meters, perhaps not. But he knows that if he continues to swim on top, every expenditure of energy will end as complete waste. He rises, gulps for air, takes a slap of salt water in his face, chokes, spews, and sinks again. A few more meters forward. He opens his eyes for an instant and sees nothing. It is dark above but darker below. Up he goes for air. The waves smash into him again and again, and he must go down.

Down—forward—up. Down—forward—up. It is impossible in this water-labyrinth to know if he is making headway or slipping farther and farther behind. Rising, he turns in the water and pops his head out for a quick view of the island. He can see Glavina as a shadow against the black west. Yes, he has been moving away from it, slowly, slowly. The hill seems a little more distant, though he is alarmed when he realizes that he is gradually being blown to the south.

Down—forward—up!

This oblique route will lengthen his journey to the shore, yet it might also increase his chances, for the wind is veering, blowing on his left cheek whenever he rises. Hour after hour he goes. Why does he not die? Why is his heart not giving out? The manic obsession with flight from all that lies behind is energizing him, but the limitations of the flesh cannot be expanded by will alone. He forces himself to slow down, to reduce the time above and the time below, and to make shorter strokes.

He is a boy again, going down to the Miljacka each morning, walking along the shore to a stretch of mud, and wading in. First, he learns to float in the shallows, then to dog-paddle, and finally to master the crawl with motions that are economical, graceful, and relentless. By autumn of that year, he is able to spear his developing limbs into the swirling waters of mid-river, going against the current a hundred meters at a time. He does not give up until ice forms on the banks of the Miljacka and the more challenging Bosna. This pushing of the outer limits of endurance is a game he plays with death. Who is the stronger? What secret reserves does he contain? His body wills to survive, his mind and heart sometimes will to die, but with every plunge into the mountain streams, the balances of life and death, energy and cold, will and despair, are shifted.

Down—forward—up!

Rising, he sees a spark of orange light ahead. It is still distant, but now the island seems farther behind. By its shape he can tell that he has not gone very far south, and is, in fact, still proceeding toward the coast.

Is he leaving a trail of his blood from the barbed wire cuts? Perhaps the water is so cold that the wounds have closed, the vessels contracted so tightly that no messages are trailing out for predators to read and follow.

O Jadransko more! he cries into the wind at his next rising for air. *Do not betray me!*

Down—forward—up!

He is slowing, slowing, his arms are aching, a leg is cramping, and his feet feel as if spikes were being driven through them. He rolls onto his back to float spread-eagled. Though there is some loss as the wind pushes him westward, there is a crucial gain as blood pumps through every extremity, his heart pounding as it never has before.

Down—forward—up!

On and on, until he is nothing but a will sending micro-impulses of command to the resisting parts of his body. He stops more frequently now and is blown backward each time. He must cling to the hope that his underwater progress is still a little greater than his surface losses.

Down—forward—up!

On the next gulp of air, he finds that the wind has declined significantly, and he remains on the surface, trying to resume a crawl. One arm over, another arm over, slowly, slowly. Head to the side, draw in air, head to the front, blow it out. Kick one leg, kick the other.

A bit farther, not much more, keep going!—see, the sky is pale above the mountains.

One arm over, head to the side, sucking in air, the other arm over, head to the front, blow it out, kick—*I am not an animal, I am not a number, I am not a machine—I will not stop—I am not an animal, I am not a number, I am not a machine—I will not stop!*

Now all strength is going, and his feet and hands are without feeling, though his limbs can still move a little; his face is ice, his lungs are fire. He is a *lastavica*, diving, rolling in the impossible trajectory, looping around his own body, wings cutting the liquid air, but he goes lower and lower and can no longer rise.

As he sinks, he cries her name:

O Ariadne! I am sorry, I am sorry, I am so sorry I did not come to you!

With the final lashing of his arms and thighs, he rises—and then the worst occurs. In the pale predawn light, he sees that the sharks have found him. Flanking him, two on his right and one on his left, they are swimming parallel and closing the gap. Their fins are slicing the whitecaps, angling toward him. He cries out, even as he knows that all human cries are useless against the powers of death when it comes. Now it is here at last, in one of its most terrifying forms. They will tear chunks from his living flesh.

Oh, my child! Oh, my child, Oh, my little child, I shall never see your face!

He sinks—and the sharks hit him.

There is no pain, though they buffet him hard.

O my God, O my God, I am sorry, I am sorry—O my God, let me drown before they eat me!

He sees for a moment the blue light of dawn beneath the waves, and the three sharks circling and buffeting and smiling at him.

Then his feet hit something solid, and his knees scrape on round white stones. He thrusts his head above the waves, coughing water from his lungs, crawling forward, staggering out of the sea, and placing his first foot on the fields of heaven.

THE WALKER OF THE WORLD

21

The singing wakes him.

He forces his eyes to open, then closes them immediately, for they are encrusted with salt, and stinging. All his flesh is burning from the seawater. Still, he feels warmer, and he opens his eyes again.

It may be, after all, that he has come only to the borderlands of paradise, for a little girl is approaching along the shore, singing to herself, dabbling a stick in the water. An orange cat strolls a few paces behind her, its tail pointing straight up. It does not like to get its paws wet, but it is willing to endure it when a dead minnow is spotted in the surf that washes onto the beach of white stones.

The girl is about five or six years old. She is wearing rubber boots and a heavy sweater. Her dress is bluer than the sky. She is blue upon blue. He knows this color, its meaning is returning after all these years. She is the essence of blue—that shade halfway between water and sky on bright days.

"Josipa!" he croaks.

The cat hears him and turns its head to stare suspiciously at the creature lying in hummocks of grass between a tumble of rocks at the base of the hill. He rises unsteadily on one elbow but can do no more than this. In this shelter, there is no wind, and the newly risen sun is cresting the mountains. His scraps of clothing are dry. The *bura* has declined to fitful gusts, no longer fierce but still capricious, winnowing westward over a rippling light chop farther out, leaving a band of near-calm by the shore. Where it strikes the sea, there is no spume on the whitecaps, no sea foam. In the distance lies the naked island, shining brilliantly in the morning light.

"Josipa!" he croaks again. The cat meows and saunters over to investigate. The girl does not hear because she is standing with the toes of her boots in the lip of surf, laughing and singing to something splashing offshore.

> *Dupin, dupin, dupin,*
> play with me, one, two, three,
> *dupin, dupin, dupin . . .*

"Josipa!" he cries.

Startled, she turns and stares at the hill, searching for the source of the voice. She is not Josipa. Now she sees the creature in the rocks and gives a little cry of alarm, turns on her heels, and trots away along the beach.

In the water, three fins cut the waves as they drive out into deeper water and plunge beneath.

He closes his eyes and falls back onto the grass, unable to move.

Later, a man's voice:

"No, no, the *dupin* cannot turn themselves into people. You imagined it—they and the man are your pretends, no? See, there's not a soul to be seen. Isn't this where you say you found him?"

"I can't remember, Tata."

"Besides, the *dobri dupin* swim only far out. Never have I seen one here, nor anyplace else along this shore."

"But I saw them—one-two-three."

"O Jelena, Jelena, what a girl you are! Was the man you saw one of the three?"

"No, he was another."

"You were imagining it. Let's go home."

"Look, Tata! There they are!"

"What! Yes, you're right and coming closer! And three of them, just as you said. Oh, what a tale we will have to tell Mamica!"

Josip opens his eyes, then opens the cave of his mouth and moans, *Zdravo!*

They do not hear him.

"*Zdra*—" he cries, "—*vo!*"

The man and girl turn in his direction, and startle. The girl seizes her father's hand and hides behind his leg. The man strides toward Josip and kneels beside him.

It is night, in a small room with space enough only for the cot he is lying on and a wooden chair beside it. At the foot of the cot is a black window, with a tallow candle burning on the sill. The walls are stone and the roof is timber beams and clay tiles.

He is under a blanket, and his head lies on a pillow of wadded cloth. His ears are aching as if skewers are turning within them. His face, hands, and all his skin are burning; his eyes too.

The man who knelt beside him on the shore now comes into the room from a side door. He is carrying a basin and towel. Behind him comes a round country woman with a steaming pot and a ladle. Both man and woman are in their forties. Their clothing is faded, their hands rough from a lifetime of physical labor. The man's face is humorous and wrinkled about the eyes in a way that indicates he has seen much in this life, has been surprised by a good deal of it, and likes to ponder what he has seen. Though his conclusions will not be complex, they will be sensible. All of this is visible to the man on the cot.

"He is awake", says the woman. Her face is a sweeter one, though not as humorous as the man's. Her eyes have seen much and suffered much. There is kindness in those eyes, but also a trace of fear. She worries about many things, and this too is visible to the man on the cot.

"Look how thin, so terribly thin", she says.

"A man can be thin yet strong", replies her husband.

"If he is a fisherman who was cast into the sea by the *bura*, why is he this kind of thin? I know what thin is."

The man laughs. "You know *what thin is*? What are you trying to say, Marija?"

"There is good thin and bad thin. This is starvation we are looking at."

The man sits down, puts the basin of water on the floor, wets the cloth in it, and wipes Josip's face. Then he helps him to sit up.

The woman spoons soup into his mouth. He swallows—again, and again, until the pot is empty.

"I will make more", she says, a hand fluttering above her heart, sighing as she goes out of the room.

"My wife", says the man. "Marija. I am Drago."

Josip looks at him. Drago looks back.

"Well, then, do you have a name?"

"Jo—" he murmurs, "—sip."

"Ah—Josip. Then lie down, Josip, and rest. Sleep if you wish."

And so he does.

Morning. How long has he slept? He is thirsty, and his ears are still aching. He struggles to rise in the bed. The window is small, a single pane of glass. Blinding light is coming through it, along with the rhythmic sound of surf not far away. Above a fringe of bushes, a band of blue can be seen, and beyond that—with a stab of fear—is the island. It is white and beautiful but naked and dreadful, and many evils are occurring on it, even as he lies here in safety.

Is it safety? These people who have taken him into their home—are they loyal to the regime or quietly enduring it?

The woman enters, clicks her tongue when she sees that he is awake and upright, clucks over him like a mother hen, then spreads a cloth beneath his chin and begins to spoon-feed him another pot of soup. It is thicker than yesterday's, and full of chunks of fish and clam meat. Because it is not very hot, he reaches for the pot and asks permission with his eyes to take it into his hands. She nods. He lifts the entire vessel to his lips and gulps it down as fast as his throat will allow.

"Ooh-ooh", she sighs, making the sign of the cross on her chest.

"You need water, poor soul. Now let the soup get into your bones for a while. Too much all at once and you will explode."

He cannot yet speak to her, because his throat is raw from the salt it took in during his swim from the island. His eyes continue to crust with salt as well. Or is it sickness that makes the crust? His ears are draining, putrid; his lungs are rasping, trying to cough up phlegm. He coughs and coughs and coughs. Between fits of his coughing, the woman brings him little bits of soaked bread and pops them into his open mouth. Like Sova and Propo and Tata did when he first arrived on the island.

His eyes cannot focus; he sees her face melt, and she becomes a bird. She is a pelican, stabbing her own heart to bring forth blood to feed her chicks.

Night. Josip wakes. His throat is swollen, permitting only a little breath to pass through. He is gasping, panicking from lack of air. The man holds him upright, thumps his back with the palm of his hand until more poison is hacked out into a basin.

Drago—yes, Drago is his name.

"It is a foolish thing to fight the *bura*", Drago mutters.

Josip remains afloat, though the cot is rising and falling.

"Better for your lungs you don't lie down for a while."

He props Josip up with his back against the wall.

For a time, they regard each other in silence.

"Josip", says Drago at last. "Josip who came from the sea, it seems you have good friends."

Since the sick man does not reply, Drago goes on:

"Do you mind if I talk? No? Well, permit me. I am a simple fellow with no thoughts to speak of between my two ears. But it seems to me that a man who falls into the sea must have very good friends if he lives to tell of it—yes, friends up above and friends down below. My own Tata drowned when I was a boy, in a storm just like the one that brought you here. The Jadran is not always friendly, as we know, but there are friends swimming in her. Three of them brought you to us, three made sure we found you. Now that's a hand reaching down from the clouds and dabbling a finger in the water, I say! So, I ask myself, who is this man from the sea who has been washed up on my shore?

"I have done much thinking about this. Yes, I think and think as I scrape the dirt in my little garden, and when I go up with my brother to his meadow above the great road—that's where we watch his sheep—he has a boat in Rijeka but owns the land we have here, and I look after it for him—and whenever I throw a net into the sea I think some more.

"So, I am thinking, as I mentioned already, about many things. Especially, I think as I watch the boats cruise along the shore and the men with guns asking questions about those who fall into the sea and are washed up on shore. And I say to myself, well, that's no concern of mine. The man who visits my family is not the one they are looking for, since it is the *dobri dupin* who brought him here, and if the *dupin* like him, who am I to argue?!

"So, you see, Josip, it is very clear to me—and to Marija and Jelena also—that you are a fisherman who fell out of his boat in the storm. Yes, that is what you are and nothing else. The men called to us, since their boat is too big to beach, and I told them I have seen no criminals washed up on the shore. Jelena—being very little—said that she had seen a man lying on the shore. And when they asked her where she had seen him, she told them it was not really a man but a dolphin that she and her cat had found, and the dolphins had all swum away. Then she sang them her dolphin song, so they left and have not returned. I feel sure that their boat is not the one you seek. I think you are a fisherman who has lost his own vessel, and you want to find her again, no? Perhaps it has sunk. Maybe it blew out to sea and is waiting for you somewhere. Or it might be riding at anchor in a nice cove, safe from the storm. I wonder where it is. I wonder where you need to go to find her.

"So, we will look after you until you are well, and then we will help you find her. But listen, I'm talking too much. It's your fault because you don't say a word, only your name, and I do not blame you for it, after all you've been through.

"But that is little concern to me. You can say nothing at all, if you wish. Besides, it's nice to have a listening ear. How often do I get a chance to talk, eh? Not often. My brother—the one with the sheep—now there's a talker. I am a silent man myself, very quiet, just like my Tata was. Though I forget much about him, I remember that! And Marija always has lots to say, that woman, a good scolder she is, but kind in the heart, and Jelena, my princess, is our jewel in the crown. My sons are all grown and working in Rijeka at the shipyard. One is married, two are engaged; such fine lads, but none of them wants the life of the sea. I wonder why? It's the best way of life, I say, though sometimes she kills, takes a little interest on what she lends. No, I said it wrong, for it's not really lending—she always gives, and if she takes back from time to time, who are we to begrudge her! It's we who are all wrong—thinking about it upside down—which, as I'm sure you know, is the way we are, we people, not at all like the birds and the dolphins and the squid. Do you like squid? Tonight we have it for supper. So tasty, cut into little pieces in a secret sauce my wife makes—Oh, I am sorry, do you not like sauce? Well, I will tell her, and you won't have to eat it with the sauce. She can fry it just as easily—Listen now, I am sorry, Josip—you needn't cry. Look, don't worry about anything—"

Now he is awake most of each day. How long has he been here? There have been three stormy days, overcast, and four or five sunny ones. All have had *buras*, though none as strong as the night of his swim. His lungs are clearing. Marija claims it is because she is pouring garlic into him and also the juice of crushed citrus seeds. It kills the little devils in the lungs, she assures him.

Our guest they call him, *Mr. Josip*. They do not probe for his full name. How much do they guess? He does not want to find out. Silence is best. Yes, he will remain silent. Now his throat can make low sounds, like speech, though he uses it only when the room is empty, when the man is down by the shore doing something with his net, or when the woman is scolding out back, shrieking at hens that have broken into a seed bin. There is a donkey as well. He has become fond of donkeys. He is one. No, he is not! *I am a lastavica. I am a dupin!* He knows this is fanciful musing, understands full well the fragility of his situation. But why do they help him?

One afternoon, Drago declares that Josip is well enough to try getting up onto his feet. Let's go, he insists, and will not take "no" for an answer. He gives Josip some of his clothes—undershirt and underpants, thin and full of holes but clean too, the first such garments Josip has worn in over a year. Then a wool shirt and wool trousers with cuffs that hang at mid-calf, and thick socks knit from the wool of his brother's flock. Then the host leads the wobbling guest out of the room and into a low-ceilinged kitchen, where it looks as if most of the family life happens. It is a two-room house. There are beds beside the stove, the man and woman have given him their room for the duration of his stay in their home.

430

Leaving the kitchen, they go outside into a dooryard, a narrow terrace flagged with uneven pieces of limestone and fenced by a low wall of broken red bricks.

"Sit here in the sun", Drago commands pointing to a wooden bench. "Soak it up, you're as pale as a cod's belly."

It is wonderfully warm here, shielded from the breeze, his back to the sun-baked stones of the house's front wall. Beyond the retaining wall, the land slopes down ten meters or so to the water's edge. Jelena is there with the cat. She is tossing pebbles into the waves, and the cat is tormenting crabs that are trying to escape it.

Goli Otok is to the west and north. Choking, Josip looks away from it. Drago, who has been deftly lighting a hand-rolled cigarette, keeping his eyes on the guest, drags in smoke and blows it out.

"A fine day", he muses. "A fine, fine day. And look at the white island, so bright, a man can hardly stand to look at it."

Josip nods and meets the other's eyes.

"A bad place, that! Once it was a good place. My grandfather sometimes took his sheep over there in his boat on a calm day. That was before the war. There were plenty of bushes and grass there at one time, though only on the other side—this side has always been naked. The wind strips everything down.

"Then in '48 or '49 they built something out there—some say a stone quarry. But why all those watchtowers, and why do the guard-boats circle the island all the time, eh? I tell you, Josip, it's a strange place. Ghostly it looks and maybe ghostly it is, though pretty enough when the sun shines on it. But at night, Marija says she can hear the cries of men coming from that place. Me, I hear nothing, but Marija, she hears things no other ears can hear. So, she prays for the ghosts who live over there. Jelena does too. All the time they pray. Me, I'm not much of a praying man.

"But I ask myself, why do they make a wall around that

431

island—not a wall you can see with the eyes, but a wall of fear. Did you know that people who live along the shore have sometimes been shot at from that island, if they go too close. Now, it is my opinion that ghosts do not own guns, and even if they did, they would not shoot them at us people. Whoever is shooting at ordinary fisher folk are up to no good. It seems to me—though I am not a smart man—it seems to me that a wall is something that keeps things inside and keeps other things outside. I do not like walls. A wall on a house is just fine, who could live without such a wall? And a bit of wall to keep the garden and the dooryard from sliding down into the water, that's a good wall too. But other than that, I don't like walls. There's something wrong about them."

Suddenly, Drago laughs aloud and slaps his knees. "Wait! What a fool I am! I live on a wall!"

Josip glances at him curiously.

"The Dinarics are a wall, are they not? Yes, the biggest wall in Yugoslavia. It keeps some things inside and other things outside. But I must say again that I am not fond of walls. Are you fond of walls, Josip?"

"No", Josip croaks, and looks away across the sea.

"I must tell you a little about myself", chuckles Drago. "Otherwise, how can we honestly say that you are our guest? If we don't speak from the heart, that means I am just a hotel keeper, and this would be an insult to you, Josip, for a guest is Christ himself coming into the home—that is what my grandfather taught me, and my father too, before he drowned—I remember that much. Then the hard times came, and a lot of things were forgotten, like a wall somebody built in everyone's head. A big wall, keeping some things inside and other things outside—and many things that should be inside our heads are kept out.

"Did I tell you I am a criminal. No? Well, let me tell you, it's not a pretty story, but I think you will find it interesting. I was never caught—as you can see from the evidence right before your eyes. Here I am, hale and hearty, and puffing my own tobacco, which I grow myself, with a door open to guests at all times. But I am losing track of my story, what was I saying?"

"You said", Josip murmurs in a low rasp, after clearing his throat, "that you are a criminal."

"Oh, yes, well it's true. This is what happened, and I'll tell it just like it was. When I was a young man, I walked all the way to Rijeka; that was before the war, before the Italians came. I was not fond of Italians because they are always trying to push the border from Trieste into our land, and besides they drink too much. Well, we drink too much too, but the way they drink is worse than ours, and they have hot tempers; well, ours are hot too, but theirs are worse. Has Croatia ever invaded anybody's land? No, never! Has Italy? Yes, always! So, I am not fond of them because of this, and also because they are a bit arrogant, though I guess we can be that way too, but always for better reasons than theirs—Anyway, where was I?"

"You walked to Rijeka."

"Oh, yes, so I was a young man and full of oats, and had not yet met my Marija, my sons and my princess were only sparkles in the corner of my eyes, but these eyes were sparkling a lot in those days I can tell you, me being about eighteen at the time and so good-looking that all the mothers from St. Juraj to Starigrad were trying to make a match for their daughters. But don't judge what I'm saying by the way I look now. Sad to say, we grow old. We grow older and older and older, and storm-tossed are we for most of our years, up and down on the waves, and sometimes under them. Well, there I was, not ready to make a family, but hungry to see the wide world. Though I was full of oats, they were not wild ones; I was also in the church every Sunday, and I kept a bench warm beside the confessional, and rubbed the wood raw with my backside, I can tell you, and wore out a few pant-knees afterward, I can tell you as well. I was not a bad boy, Josip, just really stupid. I am still stupid, as you can see, but I try to make up for my crime by doing what I can to help people, especially people who fall into the sea.

"So, there I am in Rijeka, just gaping about at the big city, with a few coins in my pocket. I stopped into a tavern and treated myself to a nice big fat lunch and some red wine—yes, too many sips of that devilish Italian wine did I have that day. So, after filling my belly, I staggered out into the city square, the biggest city I ever saw in my life—well, to be true, it was the only city I had ever seen—and I came upon a crowd of people shouting and waving red flags. There was a man on a box shouting back at them, making them all hot under the collar. He was one of those Communists from before the war, and he was the Italian kind too, a nasty bunch, not like our *friendly* Communists here in *Yoo—go—slavia*."

Josip eyes the man warily.

"Istria, as you know, is full of Communists now. They're really strong in that region, and I think maybe it's because the Italians were strong there first. Lots of agitation among the workers. Anyway, as a man of the sheep and the sea, I had little use for those factory boys and their shouting. When my family shouts it's for a good reason, not to work people up into hitting each other on the head. But as I told you, I was three sails to a strong wind that day, and getting hotter as I listened to those idiots. Fistfights broke out, some Ustashe types broke into the crowd, and then the Communists fought back. Oh, it got really bad. Now, I never liked Ustashe; they're as mean as sharks, though they had some good ideas about Croatia. But you don't make good countries by bashing heads, I always say, that's not the Croatian way, not since we made that promise to the Pope a thousand years ago, maybe longer than that. Anyway, as I was saying, I got pulled into the thick of it, and there I was swinging my fists too, like everybody else. Then this Communist thug with a red kerchief around his neck starts in on me with a stick!

A stick, bang-bang on my poor head. Never in my life have I been hit like that, leastways not on any spot besides my hind end, and that was because I deserved it, and my Tata knew it. Though I forget a lot of things, I remember that about him. Then a Ustasha starts hitting the Communist, and here the two are just whacking each other with sticks and iron bars. To tell you the truth, Josip, they were both crazy. I don't know what made me do what I did next. I had a bottle of wine in my pocket, with the cork still in it, none of it safely tucked away in my belly, and I tell you it was a heavy one. Quick as lightning, I had it out and banged the Communist on the head, and then the Ustasha, and they both went down—out cold. Just at that moment, the police swooped in and whistles started blowing and guns firing off in the air, and all hell broke loose. I ran for it, I can tell you. And to this day I do not know if they lived or died, but there was a lot of blood. Did I kill the one or the other or both? I just don't know. It bothers me still . . ."

Josip has listened to all of this with an open mouth.

"Of course I took it to confession, but I do wonder from time to time if I ended someone's life . . ." Drago looks down at the open palms of his hands and sighs. "To kill a Communist, this is not a nice thought. This is not a thought I would like to be known by others." He looks up suddenly and peers into Josip's eyes. Drago's face is an uncomplicated one, an open one.

"So, you see . . ." he whispers, then turns his gaze toward Goli Otok.

Josip nods, "Yes, I see."

22

The boat is *Morski Lav*, the *Sea Lion*. Despite her name, she is a little vessel about ten meters long, open topped, with a token pilot's cabin up front and an inboard diesel engine rumbling and blowing black smoke out the stern. It is the kind of vessel used by countless small-scale fishermen along the coast. Though old and battered, the hull has been brightened by a recent coat of white paint trimmed with royal blue.

Drago does not own a boat; this is his older brother's—a wealthy man, it seems, with a boat and a flock. The craft's draft is too deep to beach her, and she must sit offshore a stone's throw. Drago rows his skiff out to meet her, with Josip seated on floor boards that are soon swooshing water and smelling strongly of rotted fish. Banging the skiff alongside the larger craft, both men scramble on board, welcomed by a gray-haired version of Drago. The brothers embrace, and introductions are made. *Josip, this is my brother. Brother, this is Josip.*

"It's better you don't know our family name", adds Drago.

The captain of *Morski Lav* asks no questions, though Josip presumes that the man must either know, or has guessed, the truth of the situation. Even so, Drago runs through the prearranged script, telling his brother that this is the sailor who fell into the sea, and now he must be returned to his home port, which is Split.

"A long way from Split you were blown by the *bura*", says the brother, with an arch smile. "And against the wind, too! But that's the *bura* for you, full of surprises it is. Well, let's get going."

The skiff is hauled onto the back deck, then upended and secured to the gunwales with its line. The sky is clear and sunny, with a light wind swooping down from the mountains. The anchor is pulled up. In the cabin, the captain throttles the engine and then makes it roar.

Marija and Jelena stand on the beach and wave their hands as the *Sea Lion* gets under way, the boat rocking slightly when the waves hit her broadside, then accelerates and diminishes into the horizon.

For three days, they slowly proceed southward, encountering no difficulties along the way. Early on, they leave the inland "kanal" at the southern tip of the island of Rab and turn west into the channel between it and the northern tip of Pag. From there they enter rougher and deeper waters, then veer south again, keeping Pag on their port side. They stop only once to refill the fuel tanks, at a quay in Zadar. Here, Josip hides beneath the cabin floorboards. Here too, he learns that Drago's brother is fully aware of his situation.

A policeman, strolling along the quay and reading the names on the sterns, stops to chat with Drago and his brother. What jolly, simple-minded men they suddenly become, how without guile or grave interest to others they are! They offer the police-man a cigarette of home-grown tobacco, which he casually accepts. Then they offer him a sip of *slivovica*, but he declines, being on duty. He asks why they are so far from Rijeka in such a small boat.

The captain replies with humorous indignation that the *Sea Lion* is no ordinary dinghy but a mighty seafarer that has weath-ered more storms than the policeman has years! Then the captain explains that in Split, so he has heard, there are stronger nets to be purchased, and at good prices. He holds up an old net full of rot and gaping holes. Then the captain—true to Drago's description—launches a lengthy monologue about the strengths and weaknesses of various kinds of nets, and seems unstoppable. The policeman tips his cap in mid-sentence and saunters away.

Her tanks now filled, the *Sea Lion* growls and moves on. She passes two great islands on the starboard side before Drago brings Josip up from his hiding hole. The brothers pour water into his dry mouth and give him bread soaked in olive oil, adding strips of smoked fish.

Hour after hour, seated with his back to the gunwales, Josip ponders their faces. He is immensely grateful to them, but he fears for them, too, wondering if their generosity will bring them to ruin. Such men are the heart of Croatia. Even so, when they take rosaries from their pockets and pray aloud together, he cannot bring himself to join them. Though Josip admits to himself that an unexplainable dimension has intervened in his life, the mystery that man calls divine may be no more than . . . a mathematical tropism, a cosmic force. In any event, he cannot pray to it.

Now bitterness is mingled with gratitude—a strange feeling, pulling him inward. He buries his head between his knees as the brothers pray, folds his arms on his knees, closing his eyes.

Ariadne, Ariadne, soon I will find you. Soon it may become possible to think again about God. Until then . . .

At night, he sleeps wrapped in a blanket on the pilothouse floor. It seems that the captain sleeps little or not at all, though he naps a few times, letting Drago take the wheel—in the manner of elder brothers bestowing tentative trust. This occurs only when they have left the last island behind and have gone farther west into open sea, in order to sweep around the mountains of the headland above *Splitski kanal*. Rocking, rocking in the arms of the boat, Josip slides into half-consciousness.

O Jadransko—

Sighing, sore at heart, grateful and bitter, fearful and happy, knowing Ariadne is closer and closer, and their child, their beloved, this little soul—soon he will see the baby's hidden face, and soon he will fall into good dreams again, in his lover's arms.

The cosmos is a sea, his tired mind murmurs to itself, *we are diatoms, we are living glass—do not break us—do not break us—*

"We are here", says Drago, shaking Josip's shoulder. "Wake up."

Morski Lav is rocking gently beside a quay inside the harbor. The morning is warm, the light splendid. Across the bay, Diocletian's palace rises above swaying palm trees. Cars and buses rumble along the waterfront. Above his left shoulder, Josip sees the little mountain of the Marjan park, and to the right above the steeple of the cathedral are the treetops of the Manus district. She will be there with her mother in the family home. Then he recalls vaguely that Vera has fled and Simon is in prison. Maybe Ariadne was released from prison and has returned to their apartment. Yes, he will make his way slowly and unobtrusively through the maze of the palace compound, and climb the steps to the balconata. He will open the door without knocking, and there she will be standing, fresh from a bath, a towel wrapped about her, a sweet baby crawling across the floor toward him. He will step forward to embrace them both at once, he will swell with his love as wide and as deep as the sea, and they will swim in each other's love—all three—in the waters of bliss. They will close the door and lie down in peace, and they will speak to each other with their eyes and their hands forever.

"No time to lose, Josip", says Drago gruffly. "My brother and I must leave. There are plenty of watchers in the city. Now, come into the cabin and change your clothes. There's a gift for you from Marija."

It is a pair of brown wool trousers, an old pair of Drago's, which Marija has lengthened. Also a sheepskin belt without a buckle, a cotton shirt boasting a few holes and patches but clean as the seabreeze. A sack with bread and smoked meat in it and some dried fish wrapped in oil cloth. There are, besides, an extra pair of wool socks and a few coins.

"Now give me back my old trousers, there's a good fellow", grins Drago. When Josip is dressed in his new outfit and knotting the belt at his waist, Drago pulls the leather boots from his own feet and tells Josip to put them on.

"I cannot", he murmurs.

"Yes, you can."

"It is too great a gift."

"A barefoot man with a shaved head wouldn't survive ten minutes in this place without somebody asking questions. Do as I say, or I'll blow my whistle."

"You have no whistle, Drago."

"I'll find one. Now hurry. I don't want to loiter around here with people reading the names on our butt."

Josip puts on the boots and ties the laces, his hands shaking, his throat choking.

"Repay me when you can", says Drago. "When we are old men you can repay me—when we are old men who can give to each other our right names."

The little fisherman removes his cap, places it on Josip's head. "Very nice", he says, nodding approval. "Now you're just an ordinary nobody, a man of the sea. And you smell like one, too."

Drago shakes Josip's hand, then says gruffly:

"Enough, get out of here now! Go with God!"

So, Josip steps from the boat onto the wooden wharf and climbs the steps to the street above. The *Morski Lav*'s motor is rumbling, and she is already easing away, pointing her bow to the north. It is only after the boat has exited the inner harbor that he recognizes the spot on which he stands. It is the very place where he was reunited with the Lastavica of the Sea more than three years ago.

He slings the burlap sack over his shoulder and, staring at the pavement beneath his feet, walks toward the palace.

Passing through the Gate of Gold, he enters the maze. The cap low over his brow, he observes every face in the narrow streets and alleys, wondering if they suspect. Few notice him, and those who do, quickly look away or alter their course so as not

440

to brush against him. He supposes that their cursory glances register no more than a working man of rough—even squalid—appearance. Without interruption, he turns off Kreši-mirova into an alley that takes him toward the northern wall. From there he hits a cross street that he recognizes as one of his old running routes. There are more shops in the ground floors than he remembers, and there are foreigners gawking at the architecture with cameras dangling on neck straps. Even the local people seem more prosperous than they did before his imprisonment. East, then north again. Now he is entering the familiar little square of Carrarina Poljana, his heart's ever-increasing beat beginning to palpitate, his breath coming in short bursts. Then the last few paces into another alley and he is standing beneath the balconata, gazing up at it, blinded by tears.

He steadies himself and climbs the stone steps to his apart-ment. Breathing heavily from exertion, he pauses in front of the door to catch his breath. He reaches for the handle and turns it. It is locked. So, he must knock.

After a light rap, footsteps echo from within. Yes, her steps, her shoes on the hardwood floor. The door opens, and a face appears. The woman is about the same age as his wife, but she is not Ariadne.

"Is Ariadne here?" he mumbles in a low voice, hoping the neighbors cannot hear.

"Who?" asks the woman looking him up and down with a certain caution, perhaps with distaste. Josip becomes aware of the heavy fish smell of his body.

"The Lasta family lives here", he says nervously.

"There are no Lastas here. I do not know the name."

"But they used to live in this apartment."

"We moved in a year ago, my husband and I. The place was empty when we came. We didn't know the people who had it before us."

"Do you know where they have gone?"

She shakes her head.

"Do you know the Horvatinec family?"

She shrugs, "I don't know that name either. Now, if you'll pardon me, I am busy."

She shuts the door.

Standing before the closed door with bowed head, he reflects for a minute, then turns and retraces his steps down to the street. There is another possibility. Yes, and this is the more likely one. He crosses the imperial complex and exits through the east gate into the open market place. Though a few fish and bread and flower vendors have their stalls open for business, the market is not busy today. It cannot be a weekend. What day is it, then? For that matter, what month is it? February, March? Can it really be a year and a half since he lived here? It feels as if a lifetime has passed since he left, and now he returns to find that the whole world has changed and not even noticed his absence.

He circles around to the north wall of the palace and stares up through the tree branches. The window of their bedroom is open; unfamiliar green curtains with a floral print are pulled outward by the breeze blowing through the apartment. There is no seashell on the sill. Turning away, he crosses the park; then he continues onto a sidewalk of Zagrebačka and goes along it as far as a street that will take him up into the Manus district. Nothing seems to have changed. The houses are the same, the trees also.

Now he is standing in front of Simon and Vera's house. During his first interrogation, he was told that Simon was in prison and Vera had fled the country. Perhaps they have returned. It may be that Simon's Party connections have been able to reduce his sentence. The interrogators told him that Ariadne was in prison. They may have been lying. She was not directly involved in the Dolphins, and surely the state would recognize this, would try to maintain a modicum of law, even for enemies of the people. The law is unjust, but Ariadne did not break it. Her husband and father and mother, yes, they are criminals, but surely—

Gathering his courage, he climbs the front steps and knocks on the door.

It is opened by a young man in a business suit. His face registers surprise, caution, and distaste.

"Yes, can I help you?"

"I am looking for the Horvatinec family. Are they here?"

"No, there aren't any Horvatinecs here."

"But this is their home."

"Maybe a long time ago it was", the man shrugs. "I don't know who lived here before. This is the office of *Jadran*."

"What is *Jadran*?"

"We're a magazine. The Ministry of the Interior puts it out." He smiles ironically looking Josip up and down. "Maybe you know it."

Josip shakes his head.

"A good magazine. Culture. You should read it."

He closes the door.

Josip walks through the downtown core to the base of the Marjan. His energy is low, and he is very hungry. Remembering the food in his bag, he chews some strips of smoked meat with the side of his mouth that still has teeth. Then some bread. At a street fountain, he puts his lips to the spigot and drinks water. Then he climbs. The park is as he remembers it, and he spends the afternoon winding through the trees on trails that he recognizes as his old running path. Little by little, he sees where his feet are taking him. As the sun begins its descent toward the sea, he arrives at the heights, the rock on which he used to stand with arms spread wide, panting and exultant in the prime of his youth.

He sits on the warm rock for a time, looking out at the turquoise Adriatic, eating more bread, and waiting for his heartbeat and breathing to return to normal. It takes much longer than it did when he was young—a year or so ago—when he was young. Now he is old and very tired. He lies down on the grass beside the rock, in fetal position, and falls asleep.

In the morning, he wakes shivering, for his clothing is damp with dew; during the night the rock bled away all its heat. The sun has not yet crested the Dinarics, and the city lies in shadow. Out on the sea, the gray water is speared with glistening silver.

He sits up and eats dried fish, the last of the bread, and a strip of smoked meat. He has some hard thinking to do. He must find out where she is. She and the baby may be fine, living elsewhere. But how can he pick up their trail without revealing his own presence in the city?

By mid-morning he has made his way to the building which houses the university's faculty of medicine. He waits on the sidewalk, does not go in to inquire at the front desk. If he were to do that, his clothing, everything about him, would arouse suspicion. Perhaps a face he recognizes will happen along. Just after noontime, a man wearing a trench coat and carrying a black briefcase leaves the front entrance and comes down the walkway toward the street. The face is familiar, though Josip cannot place it exactly. He has just decided not to approach the man when he remembers where he last saw him. It was at his wedding. He is the doctor-friend of Simon's.

"Excuse me, sir", Josip mumbles, bowing his head, looking up from under the rim of his cap. The man slows his pace.

"Yes?" he says, though he continues to move forward, as if to say he is very busy and can spare only a few seconds.

"Sir," mumbles, Josip, "can you please tell me where I may find Dr. Horvatinec the surgeon?"

"Dr. Horvatinec is no longer at the university. Now, if you will excuse me—"

"He is at the hospital, then?"

The man glances at his wristwatch. "No, not at the hospital. If you have problems with your back, you should consult your personal physician. He can refer you to a surgeon."

"He is in prison?"

Now the doctor stops in his tracks and inspects Josip's face more closely. He frowns, but does not move.

"Who are you?"

"Josip Lasta, Simon's son-in-law. You were at our wedding."

The doctor glances nervously all about and swallows visibly. "What do you want?" he whispers.

"I am looking for my wife. Do you know where she is?"

"No."

"Where is Simon?"

"I have not heard of him since his arrest. If he is still alive, he is in prison. But what prison I cannot say."

"You do not know?"

"I know nothing. Now, please, I must go."

"Can you not tell me anything?"

"I've told you what I know. And why are you walking around like this? I thought—"

"I was in prison. Now I am free. I need to find my family."

The man shakes his head, nervously glancing in every direction, his eyes flicking left and right. Then he thrusts a hand into his pocket and pulls a coin from it, offering it to Josip.

"Take it", he whispers.

"I do not want it."

"Please, take it in case anyone sees us together. You are a beggar. If anyone asks, I gave a coin to a beggar, that's all."

Josip opens his palm and accepts the coin.

"Can you not suggest anything? Anything at all."

"There was a brother. Simon's brother is in the Party. He

might know something. Goran is his name. Track down Goran Horvatinec at the Ministry of the Interior and he might be able to—in any event, I must go. We have not met, we have not spoken."

The doctor turns and walks away with hastening steps.

The city is a thousand villages. So many streets, so many offices. To whom should he speak, whom should he avoid? At first, he wanders back down into the district around the palace and ambles here and there without apparent purpose. Perhaps an office building will appear before his eyes with a big sign on it, *Ministry of the Interior.* This is not likely. To find Uncle Goran will demand some deductive thinking and much caution. Already Josip has noticed a few policemen eye him as he walks by on the street. Though they do not stop him for questioning and identification papers, it is only a matter of time before one does.

He hunches his shoulders, lets his lower jaw hang a little, revealing his hideous smile. He will save the drool for very bad encounters. In the park by the palace, he takes the last of the fish from his sack, and, making sure that no one is watching, he crushes it in the palms of his hand, smearing its oils all over his hands, neck, and face. Then he puts the shreds into his mouth and chews without swallowing until it is a mash, and packs the mash behind his gums. After that, he continues on his way, shuffling, hunching, looking more and more like a poor soul who should be mercifully housed in a state institution.

An elderly woman is walking toward him, tapping a cane before her. Partly blind, a white moon in one of her eyes. When she is near enough, he says, "Excuse me, Madame. Can you tell me where is the Ministry of the Interior?"

She stops and peers up with a smile. "In Belgrade, it must be."

"They have an office in this city, I hear."

"Oh? Well, I don't know for certain, but I think there is a big government office down on the avenue near the archbishop's palace. Do you know where that is?"

"Yes, by the harbor."

"That's the one, though it's a pity the archbishop is not permitted to live there. It was taken from him, you know."

She stops herself, her good eye clouding with worry. "Not that I wish to criticize the government, I'm sure you realize."

"I understand", Josip says. "Thank you, Madame."

He finds it soon enough. But it would be reckless in the extreme to stand outside on the street for hours, waiting for a certain official to emerge. To go inside and ask for him would be madness. So, he walks. Up the street and down, keeping his eyes on the entrance all the while. Around the block, searching for back entrances. Once, twice, three times. It is early afternoon now. Maybe Goran will come out for lunch. Officials like late lunches. Maybe he will remain inside if there is a source of food in there. No, officials like to dine out, prefer to be served the finest in the best of surroundings.

Uncle Goran does not come out. Instead, a policeman stops Josip and demands to see his papers.

Josip breathes heavily through his mouth and drool runs down his chin.

"Papers—no papers—my uncle", he mumbles and laughs, spewing a little fish mash by accident onto the breast of the policeman's uniform. The man steps back a pace or two with a look of disgust.

"Who are you, and why are you lazing around here, you good-for-nothing?"

"I'm Jozo, no, I'm Bozo, he tol' me wait for him here, my uncle for bring me home."

"Well, Bozo, who is your uncle?"

"Uncle Goran", Josip dribbles and laughs.

"Goran Horvatinec?"

447

"Uncle—bring me home. See my mummy."

"Idiot, you came too early for your uncle. They don't go home until six o'clock. Now, go away and bother someone else. Come back when the big hand on the clock tower is at twelve and the little hand is on the six."

"Twelve? Six?"

"That's right, twelve and six. Don't you know your numbers?"

"No number. Hungry."

"Oh, damn, then have a bite on me."

He offers a coin.

"Here, take this—no, no, don't refuse. Take it! Don't argue with me, take it! And get lost. I have work to do."

"Thanks—nice man." Josip coughs and shuffles away toward the market.

He has received two splendid gifts. Goran will appear at six— when the big hand is at the twelve and the little hand at the six—and he can eat in the meantime.

With the coin, he purchases a bun and an orange and eats them after swallowing the near-liquid paste in his mouth. He consumes the peels and seeds of the orange as well.

Just before six, Josip returns to the block where the Ministry is housed, approaching its main entrance circumspectly. Fortunately, his particular friend, the policeman, has gone off shift, and the night patrol is on duty. Josip positions himself halfway down the block, hunches over, and holds out his hand. Whenever a pedestrian passes, he mutters, "cigareta, cigareta?" and has pocketed half a dozen by the time ministry employees begin leaving the building. He scans their faces from the corner of his eye. The policeman at the front steps glances at the beggar once or twice, then loses interest; he is busy tipping his hat to officials whom he knows.

Then Goran appears, silver-haired, scowling, buttoning a

fine greatcoat across his huge belly. He nods impersonally to the policeman, then turns and comes down the sidewalk in Josip's direction.

"Cigareta, cigareta?" Josip mutters as he passes. Goran pays no notice. Josip does not turn his head to watch where the man is going. Instead, he observes from the corner of his eye that he is walking at a leisurely pace in the direction of the promenade in front of the palace, a few blocks west. Popping an unlit cigarette into his mouth, letting it dangle, Josip crosses to the other side of the street, rounds a corner, and goes north, away from Goran. A minute later, he crosses back and heads west, entering the east gate of the palace, and then begins to move through the maze as quickly as possible. Within minutes, he has doubled back and is on the promenade, scanning the crowds of people strolling in the evening sunlight. Though the weather is cool, many are seated at outdoor cafés, sipping coffee and chatting with friends. Suddenly, he spots Goran just ahead, moving through the crowd at a slow pace, his shoulders set in the posture of an important man who need step aside for no one. He is looking for something, maybe trying to decide which café to enter.

As if coming to a precipitous decision, Goran suddenly turns right and enters the tunnel under the palace walls. Josip follows, keeping close to the pillars in case the man turns around. But it seems that he has no concern about being followed, and, at the end of the tunnel, he climbs the steps and enters the peristyle in front of Diocletian's mausoleum—the cathedral. He passes on, leaving it behind without a glance, and turns left onto cobbled Krešimirova. Josip is now so close on his heels that he can hear the sound of Goran's breath, wheezing from the exertion of climbing steps and a walk that is a long one for an overweight man. Without warning, he turns again and enters an alley, then proceeds along it several paces to a little hole-in-the-wall restaurant, and goes in. Josip waits a few minutes, then follows, passing the restaurant with his head averted. At the end of the alley, he comes to an old wooden staircase that is missing several steps. He sits down on the bottom step and waits.

During the two hours he remains there, not a soul goes up or down the staircase. People enter and leave the restaurant from time to time, but none give a glance toward the end of the alley, which is now in deep shadow. Looking up, Josip sees that the narrow shaft of sky overhead is deep blue, slipping into black, tinged with some red cloud. Soon it is all black, with only a few lights dimly glowing behind curtained windows along the alley.

At one point he shifts his feet, and his boot hits something that rings metallically. He picks it up—a short length of iron pipe.

The noise of the city continues unabated, though it changes to domestic sounds—muted conversation behind walls, cooking and laughter and scolding and bursts of dissociated music. He waits.

Rummaging in the bag, he finds the last crumbs of bread, puts these into his mouth, and swallows. Nothing can be wasted. Nothing. Does the energy expended by all the walking exceed the energy replaced by the meager food he has consumed today? He does not know. It only matters that the gap between him and his family is closing.

Finally, the restaurant door opens, and two men come out. By the light of the open doorway Josip can see that one is Goran, the other a thinner man. They shake hands, the door is closed, and the thin man goes away down the alley. Goran lights a cigarette, takes a few puffs, then stomps it out. He comes up the alley in Josip's direction, stops not ten paces away, and throws back his coat to unbutton his fly. He is urinating against the wall of a house when Josip presses the end of the pipe between the man's shoulder blades.

"Don't move," he says in a low growl, "or I shoot!"

"Don't shoot! I beg you, don't shoot! In my right pocket, lots of money, take it!"

"Don't make a sound. Don't call for help or your life is over."

"I won't. Please just take what I have and go."

Josip does not move. The man's hands are in the air.

"Take it and go", Goran pleads in a high voice.

"I don't want your money."

"Then w-w-what?"

"Answers."

"Answers?" he trembles. "What answers? Who are you?"

"Kneel on the ground. Put your hands on the wall."

Goran obeys; Josip keeps the pipe pressed hard into his spine.

"Where is your brother Simon?"

"What? My brother Simon—?"

"Where is he?"

"He went to prison. He is dead."

"And his wife?"

"No one knows. Who *are* you? A friend of his? Look—I had nothing to do with all that business."

"Where is Ariadne?"

"Who?"

Josip jabs the pipe harder into the spine, and Goran squeals.

"Where is she?"

Goran does not answer.

"Tell me or you are dead."

"All-all-right, give me a moment. I will tell you."

Without warning, Goran heaves himself sideways and with a backward swing knocks Josip's arm away. With surprising agility for so heavy a man, he lunges and throws a punch in Josip's direction, though in the dark it fails to connect. Josip staggers, rights himself, and grabs the man's collar, trying to jab the pipe into his chest. But Goran knocks it aside again while he is struggling with something in the pocket of his jacket.

"Back, back!" Goran shouts. "I have a gun. Drop your weapon."

Josip brings the pipe down hard on the space between himself and Goran, hoping it will deflect the aim. There is a howl, and the gun goes rattling away on the cobblestones.

Sprawled against the wall, Goran whimpers. With his left hand, Josip grabs his shirt collar and twists. He presses the pipe into the center of his chest.

"Where is she?"

"I will tell you, but don't shoot. I beg you, don't shoot. If you kill me you will learn nothing."

"Where is she?"

"I had nothing to do with it. I don't know anything."

"It was you who betrayed us!"

"No, no, not me!"

"Yes, it was you."

"You're wrong. I protected him as long as I could."

"Then you knew they were watching us. You knew, and you did not warn us."

"I heard only at the last minute. Time enough for Vera to get out. Simon didn't—"

"Where is my wife?"

Goran falls silent. His chest is heaving, his throat gasping for air.

Twice before in his life, Josip has come this close to taking a man's life. The first in Sarajevo, when he held Petar's axe in his hand above the sneering face of Uncle Jure. Then the rage that had burned in him had not been enough for action. Later, on Goli Otok, he had been ready, the hatred grown older and deeper, black fire in a cold wind, though another hand had doused that fire and pulled him back from murder. Would it have been murder? No—he was pulled back from justice!

The grotesque man of power, now cringing before him, embodies all that has destroyed his life, his people, his homeland. And in that face so full of ironies and contempt, in that voice so accustomed to speaking murderous lies in the calm tones of a bureaucrat, all evil is present. He can demolish it with one stroke, without much noise. A swift blow to the cranium, then blow after blow after blow until all the evil is pulverized and pushed out of the world forever!

He raises his hand to strike, and the black fire flows, his lips part over the cavern of his mouth.

"Where is she?" he whispers one more time.

"She's alive. If you kill me, you will never find her."

"Tell me!" Josip growls, ramming the pipe so violently into the temple of the man's head that he howls.

"She's dead!" he screams.

"Tell me the truth—everything—or you die now!"

"I didn't kill her. Nobody killed her. She was in prison, then they let her go. A week later, two weeks, the baby came—came too early. It died. And the mother—Ariadne—she died too. So much blood—they told me she lost too much blood."

The world ceases to move, all light fades. He is alone in an empty universe, standing with an iron pipe clenched in his hand, raised above the skull of a killer, a coward, a betrayer, a liar. But he can do nothing now. He drops the pipe to the cobblestones and walks away, leaving behind forever the alley, the sobbing man, and the world that was.

23

So, what is left?

Nothing. Nothing remains. A damaged organism still inhaling and exhaling, its mineral reserves consumed by its own self with nothing to replenish it. An organism that has no will left, neither to kill another nor to take its own life.

Life itself is taking his life—it's only a matter of time. Let it do what it will. It doesn't matter.

Until it completes the job, what is he to do? He will walk. He will move the organism forward so that the burning up of its cells accelerates, speeding his exit from this world.

Where? It doesn't matter. Just walk.

So, he walks, and his feet take him away in the night, upward from the palace of the emperor by the sea, over a hill and around a bay, and by morning he is still walking, with the sea on his left, boats far out, airplanes rising and falling over an island with red roofs.

Now the sun is high and beating him with an iron pipe, making his eyes blur and his legs shake. It doesn't matter. Just walk. One step after another, use it all up, that's what he knows how to do. Use it up until it is gone.

Now it is night, and the road rises steeply. He forgets some of what he is leaving behind. No, he remembers but cannot think about it. What purpose would that serve on this road that is just one of those he has trod before. It is the road of flight from the wolves of Pačići, the road to Mostar, the road to Sarajevo. It is all his roads and no roads, for every road is loss. He is a boy, he is an old man, it is the past, it is the future, but it is never the present.

He pauses at a stream falling from the mountains toward the sea, lies down beside it and drinks from it, sure that bodies trussed in wire will float past. But they do not, and he walks on again.

Night and day, followed by night and day. He sleeps sometimes, usually in jumbled rocks near the road. The road is important—he must not leave it—because it is the path that is leading out of this world, as surely as a bullet or a slab of stone dropped on his skull—though slower.

There comes a time when his body is being lifted onto something that moves. Is Alija putting him onto the donkey's back? Or is he Krunoslav rolled onto a truck driving down to a bay where he will be tossed into the water to sink after the boots are stripped from his feet?

It does not matter.

Someone traces the sign of the cross on his forehead. It must be Tata's fingers, though a priest should not touch him because there is no need to do this to Cain. No need, no need, it does not matter.

"Who are you?" a voice asks.

Be silent. You are dead.

"Who are you?"

I am a man with no name.

"Come on now, wake up and drink a little water."

I am the broken diatom.

"Where have you come from?"

The fields of heaven. But the fields of heaven are no more.

"Where are you going?"

To the land of oblivion.

"Look, he's listening, his eyes are open."

He is seated between two men, one on each side of him, an engine roaring, gears clanking, shifting up and down.

"He smells bad."

I am the organism dissolving in the cesspool.

"We should drop him at a hospital."

"What hospital? It's hours to the nearest one, maybe Rijeka itself."

"He looks too weak to be dangerous."

"Yes, but we have to get to Trieste by tomorrow."

"Let's take him with us. He'll die if we leave him here."

"What's one body more or less."

"Don't say that. Here, mister, drink."

His mouth opens, and water pours in because his tongue is dry.

"Whew, this guy's been through something. You have a big fight, fellow?"

Yes, a big fight.

He does not want to drink, but his body will not let him sink; it always betrays him when he tries to hide from the rain of blood that is falling on the world.

Joshko, you cannot swim! You and your friends only pretend to swim!

"Poor guy. Too many like him in this country."

You won the city medal, Josip! Not the Olympics, but almost as good. Soon you will be a national hero.

"Watch what you say, eh? This is a good country now."

"Oh, yeah, a very good country. Too bad about all the missing people."

"Shut up."

A scholarship, Josip! Now you see the result of all those years of study!

"If we're stopped, what do we tell them? This guy has no papers."

"We'll say he's a tramp we found on the road. Yugoslavia looks after its own, doesn't it?"

The inferential of the meta-universe is no more than tropism.

"Anyway, I don't mind if he comes along. You're so boring, this guy seems exciting."

"Pass me the bottle."

Stone slab.

Kruno sinking in the most beautiful blue waters in the world.

I'm Svat. Here, take this bread.

Ustashe killed him. No, Chetniks killed him! No, it was Partisans! No, it was the friends and strangers in my mountains, on my street, in my home, in my school, in my place of labor, and in my place of rest.

And all my striving, all my striving, all my striving is blown away on the wind.

It does not matter.

But it does.

And all my love—all the love I poured out. It is gone. It is gone.

"Hey, slow down! You nearly went into the ditch!"

"Relax, Pero!"

"We're not in Slavonia, Draz! These ditches are a thousand meters deep."

"Okay, okay. How's our passenger?"

"Sleeping, I think."

I cannot tell you what I love in you, Ariadne, because if I were to try I would not cease speaking.

"How much longer?"

"A couple of hours. Look, there's Krk on the left. A big island. After that, we go through Rijeka and then the border a few hours after that. Istria's not as up-and-down as this."

"Well, we'd better find someplace to leave him, because there's no way he can cross the border. The permit says just you and me."

"Right, keep your eyes open for a hospital."

"Maybe a police station."

"Nah, he's sick. They'd just throw him in a holding tank till they figure out who he is. That'd finish him off for sure."

"He's got trouble, whoever he is."

"Is it *policija* or *politika*?"

457

"Maybe just crazy."

"Who is he?"

I feel certain, my Josip, that together we will make a story with only joy in it.

"Where has he come from?"

He grieves the loss of one he wed, and a child within its mother-bed.

"Cut me some of that salami, Pero."

Your life was given to you, Josip. And beautiful is this life to me. So much, so much has been given to you and is given to me through you.

"My mama says, never eat salami without red peppers."

"Why?"

"The peppers kill the bugs. You know, in the gut. The ones you can't see. They're the worst."

I love you, she says. And I will not leave you.

You will be taken away, he replies. I know you will be taken away.

"My mama never made salami. Always it was Hvar prosciutto for us! As thin as a feather and meaty and smoky, and some red wine to go with it. The prosciutto my mother used to make took about eighteen months to dry, and it's the slow drying that gives it the best flavor, no matter how poor the pig it came from. But that's another story. Did you ever taste Italian prosciutto, Daz? Ooh, it's bad stuff."

"Maybe they think ours is bad stuff."

"You're right. That's the way people are."

I cannot be taken from you, because I am now, and forever, living in the sanctuary of your heart.

"The sky is lighter over the mountains. What time is it?"

"Don't know. Not long now. You'll be packing breakfast into your gut within the hour."

"You too! Watch out for the bugs!"

"And the ditches. Hold on, Pero, we're going to dive!"

"Slow down, slow down, slow down! It's really steep!"

Laughter.

It is dark, it is all darkness, as into the land of exile and ancient bondage they walk,—

"There's the city lights! Whew, it's a big place!"

—bearing the light in their arms.

At a petrol station at the edge of the city, he gets out and stands in the street, leaning against the truck, his limbs trembling, his eyes blurring. The two drivers ask if he wants them to find a hospital. He shakes his head and walks unsteadily away.

He will walk. He will move the organism forward, burn up the cells. Where? It doesn't matter. Just walk. So, he walks, and his feet take him through the streets, and no one stops him, no one sees him. Then the houses decrease in number, and he is walking along a dusty road with the sun striking his head again with the iron bar. He pulls the cap from his pocket and puts it on top of the bristles, wipes away the sweat from his brow, feels the scars that are there—he does not remember them, they were not there before, a long time ago in the world that is no more.

Now the road arches slowly upward into high hills speckled with villas, little farmhouses, and orchards. For half a day, he puts one foot after another, and then, as the sun slides toward the sea on his left, he feels himself bending sideways, and he falls to the side of the road.

Up in the branches of a nearby tree, a child is picking oranges. A little black dog sits at the base of the trunk, inspecting the man who has fallen but not approaching him. The child—a boy of seven or eight, barefoot, in dusty brown shorts and a stained undershirt—climbs down and stands beside the dog for a few moments. Then he walks over.

His pockets are bulging. He kneels beside the man's head, and the dog sniffs the man's boots. The boy slowly peels a winter orange, spotted with brown bruises. The man is resting, with his eyes closed and his mouth wide open. The boy sees that teeth are missing. He feels a wave of pity. Last night his mother read to him the story of St. Francis of Assisi, about whom he is not permitted to speak at school. Now a leper has fallen into his hands. He leans over and kisses the man's forehead. The poor leper does not stir.

The boy holds a sliver of orange over the open mouth and squeezes it. Juice drips down and fills the mouth, slice after slice. The leper swallows and groans. The boy empties his pockets, though for a moment he does not really want to do this. He has worked hard to pick this fruit, left on the tree for the birds by a neighbor. He peels the oranges, one by one, and squeezes the pieces, one by one, into the open mouth. The man swallows, though he does not open his eyes. Because the leper does not get up, does not thank him for this kindness, does not become Jesus Christ in front of his eyes, the boy goes back to the tree and picks a few more. His father has told him that oranges are children of the sun. He wants to take the sun home in his pockets, and now his pockets are full again.

He goes back to the leper by the side of the road. Though the little black dog has been watching its master curiously, it has not stirred from the man's side. The boy puts a single orange into the leper's open palm, then gets up and dusts off his trousers. He whistles to the dog, and they go away through the trees toward their home.

There are stars in the sky. He is shivering. There is something round in his hand—soft and firm. He sits up. What is this? He sniffs it. Then his mouth, without waiting for his permission, tears into it and chews and swallows, rips and chews and swallows again and again, until it is all gone. Then he licks his hands, hating his body for not letting him die.

The road is ever rising, up and down sometimes, but always climbing higher. The night grows colder, a chilling wind begins to blow. It does not matter. It will speed him toward the end. But it hurts, this cold. One may die without pain. It's the dying itself that is needed. Under the stars, he sees a shape looming in a field beside the road. All about are barrens, no longer any trees. He leaves the road and makes his way little by little through rocks and briars toward the shadow.

It is a shelter of some kind. He feels it with his hands, moving along its curving walls in search of a doorway. The building is made of unmortared stones piled upon each other. His hands push into empty space, and he goes inside. The smells of sheep droppings and straw are strong. He lies down on the floor and, without knowing it, sleeps.

Dawn floods the interior with light. Beyond the open doorway are dry rolling hills, already simmering in the sun. Here and there upon them stand round huts roofed with stone shingles. He rises and goes outside, finds the road again, and moves on. He walks because that is all that is left, this walking. Yet he is thirsty.

The road enters a dip in the hills. Soon he comes to a stone wall and sees a little house beyond it. Smoke is rising from its chimney. Chickens are clucking, and a pig is snorting, though none of them are visible. The gate in the wall hangs open, squealing back and forth, but what makes it move is unseen.

A white billy goat bursts from the gate onto the road, dragging an old woman after it. She has it by a rope around the neck.

"No, no!" she yells.

The goat leaps up on its hind legs and plunges, butting the air with its massive curving horns, this way and that, trying to get loose. It is very strong, and the woman is weak. She wails and scolds. The goat lands on four feet and turns around, paws the ground, and charges toward her. She swerves to avoid it, but the rope yanks her from her feet, and she sprawls in the dust.

Spotting the man on the road, she cries, "Help me!"

461

The goat goes up on its hind legs again and prepares to charge. Its front hoofs strike the dust as its horns flash and narrowly miss the woman. She scrambles to her feet and stumbles in the direction of her gate.

"Help me, help me!" she cries.

The man standing not ten meters away continues to stare. Then he shakes himself, bends down, and picks up a rock. He hurls it at the beast. It strikes the animal's rib cage. He bends for another. The goat jerks the rope from the woman's hand and charges the man. The man remains without moving, without fear on his face. Now death comes, he hopes. But though he welcomes it, he also hates it. He hates its willfulness, which so thoughtlessly and unswervingly seeks to destroy him.

He hurls the stone, and it clacks off the goat's horns. The goat tosses its head and kicks and spins in circles. The man picks up another rock and hurls it at the goat's head. Now it strikes the skull, and the goat drops onto its front knees, shaking its head as if to rid it of a fly. Then it is up again on all four feet, still shaking its head, unhurt but subdued.

The man grabs the end of the rope and ties it to the iron gate. Then he walks on.

"Wait, wait!" the woman calls after him. She scurries along behind and tugs at his sleeve. He pauses and looks down at her.

"Thank you, sir, thank you. Old Pohota might have put an end to me had you not come along. A bad one he is, never satisfied. He has three nannies of his own out back in the shed but got wind of the others at the farm down the road. I've had enough of his roving, and my neighbors have had enough, too!"

The man nods and walks on. It is not good to expose the death that is inside him, to let an old woman see that he is Cain and that he is fleeing from paradise, out into the desolation where he belongs.

"Will you stop for a sip?" she asks, trotting along beside him.

Once more he pauses and considers. His tongue is cracked leather. He does not need to die in pain.

When they return to her yard, she sits him down on a wooden beam between two stones and bustles into her house—more a shelter than a house—and comes out again with a jug and a cup. The jug is very fine, white with blue flowers, the flowers that grow on the slopes of Rajska Polja. The cup is an odd one, white stone hollowed by much chipping. Clicking her tongue, chattering in words he does not listen to, she fills the cup and goes back into the shelter, returning with a basket of bread and a handful of raisins.

"Drink", she says. "Eat."

The cup is heavy, heavier it seems than a rock that can fell a billy goat. He drinks from it and holds it in both hands between his knees. He stares at the dust of her dooryard. An orange rooster with a green crown passes before his eyes, strutting and inspecting him.

"Now, tell me, what is your name and where are you going?" says the woman. "We're far from any place, and it's farther to any that lie ahead."

He looks up into ancient blue eyes; he sees her green kerchief, bordered with red hearts, so much like Mamica's.

"Jo—" he whispers.

"Jo—*sip!*" she finishes for him, smiling with satisfaction. "Or is it Jo—*zo?* Some say Jo—*shko,* which is what I called my own boy. They are gone, my husband and my boys. They did not come through the war. But a home of my own have I, and my goat-ladies and this bad billy, and a pullet or two. An egg and some milk is all I ask of life."

They are gone, they are gone.

"More milk?" she asks, filling the cup without waiting for a reply.

In the end, she just hands him the jug, and he drinks from its

463

lip, tilting his head back, swallowing and swallowing until it is empty. She refills it, and he drinks again.

"Those are big hands," she mutters pensively, "and a big man you are, too, poor fellow. It's hard to find work these days, though things are better than they were. Where did you say you were going?"

He drops his eyes and does not answer.

Now she rocks back and forth beside him on the beam, humming a song, muttering a few thoughts to herself, sighing.

"Eat some bread too, Joshko. There's plenty and to spare, because I trade milk for wheat."

So, he dips the bread into the jug, and tears wet pieces from it, and puts them one by one into his mouth. And all the while he is staring at the tops of the hills, not wanting to look into her eyes. Eyes that have lost everyone, too.

When it is time to go, he stands and nods his thanks. She forces him to accept more chunks of bread, which she tears from a large loaf; in fact, she stuffs them into his pockets. Without another word, he goes out through the gate and, without looking back, disappears around a bend in the valley.

It is nightfall; the west is bleeding. His legs can no longer move; he sits down in the dry scrub to silence their protests. All around him birds and insects make noise. Why are they doing this? What makes them sing? Is it the presence of the sea? No, the sea is nowhere to be seen in any direction. The tips of the hills are glowing bronze and purple. On a distant hilltop, a tiny spire rises above the horizon, more or less in the direction where his feet have been taking him.

He eats a chunk of bread, though it is dry in his throat. After a while, he stands and continues along the winding road. All the colors have drained from the world by the time he nears the spire. There are no lights inside. The chill is settling upon the land, and he must lie down. Leaving the road, he follows a gravel path that is now only a pale mark beneath the stars, wandering through a rocky field to the heights. Arriving at the top, he finds that the spire is part of a building—or several buildings surrounded by waist-high stone walls. Behind this stands a little grove of olive trees, swaying in the wind. He knows their scent, but there will be no olives at this time of year.

The moon rises, round and red, as if it were presiding over a burning village. He sits down and watches it. He eats another piece of bread, swallowing it with difficulty, for his mouth is drier than before. As the moon climbs it turns from flame to gold, casting its glow across the hilltop. Beyond the wall, to the right of the grove, is a field of crosses.

Now he stands, and looks all about with night-eyes, searching for a way into the building—a church, he supposes. No, he cannot enter, because there will be a mutilated body lying on its steps. He will sleep in another building, then. And, yes, to the right of the church there is one of those round huts with a stone roof. Near it he spots a well. A rope dangles down into its depths. He pulls the rope and feels an unseen weight on it. Hand over hand he pulls, and when the weight emerges it is no more than a tin bucket with water sloshing inside. He sniffs the water, because sometimes bodies are thrown into wells. It is clean. He takes the bucket in both hands and drinks and drinks until his belly bulges. Then he drinks more. With his fingertips, he feels the walls on the moonless side of the hut until they find a doorway. It is blocked by boards hammered at angles across the opening. He pulls one off and crawls in through the hole.

The floor is stone. It smells of ancient dust and leather, of beeswax candles and incense. Is it a little church or just a storage place? He is too exhausted now to worry about it, and no body blocked his entrance.

Morning. When his eyes open, he finds himself knotted in a fetal position, shivering. The cracks of light from the entrance indicate that dawn is near. Not yet able to rise, he looks about the interior. It is not a church. It is a circular room containing wooden shelves along one wall and a prayer-kneeler facing the shelves. On the shelves are shadowy forms, like sticks. Little wooden boxes are sitting on the boards, up-ended so that what is inside can be seen. In the dim light he cannot tell what they are. Perhaps there is food.

He crawls across the floor to the kneeler and rests beside it. He is still shivering and wants to go back to sleep. He closes his eyes. Oh, it is cold in here, cold, cold, and it may be that he has come at last to the place where he will die. He longs for this because he can no longer walk, and even standing is beyond his power. There is nothing in his pockets to eat because the old woman's bread is long gone. He does not have the strength to go outside to drink from the well, though he is thirsty again.

Now, I go down, he says in his mind. *Now, I will go down into nothingness and will feel no more.*

As he waits for death with closed eyes, a light appears in his head. It is not in his thoughts, for it is nothing he can imagine, nothing he has ever experienced before. He sees it with eyes that are not the eyes of his head—a red spot approaching, expanding as it comes closer. The spot becomes a little sun glowing and heating his skull. This makes no sense, because the only source of light in the chamber is the entrance behind him.

The little sun pulsates and penetrates his mind, gently, gently, not invading, merely enfolding him and warming him. Now it is heat and light, and tears begin streaming from his eyes, tears without feeling. He cannot remember when he last cried—was it before the island or on it, when he was an animal in chains? No, this kind of tears came before—it was on a Christmas day long ago in a world that no longer exists, when a woman made bread for him with secret spice, or when he lay beside her in the dark with his hand on her belly, feeling the quickening of their child.

Is it you? Am I coming to you now?

The light slowly fades.

He opens his eyes, and to his dismay finds that he is still on earth. The tears cease. He sits up. He sees that the little boxes contain bones and scraps of clothing. Some of the boxes contain hands and feet—living hands, living feet—they have not decomposed. The fingers of a hand in a tin box are positioned in a priest's blessing. The wrist is severed, like Petar's. Though here there is only the hand, while back there in the fields of heaven there is only a body without a hand. On the wrist are fine golden hairs. Peering more closely, he sees other forms on the shelves. Before him is the shape of a person stretched out along the shelf, sleeping. It is a woman—he knows this because she is wearing nun's robes, black and white, and her hands are crossed over her belly, and a crucifix is about her neck. The skin of her face is dark brown, drawn tightly over the bones, but the little hairs of her eyelashes are visible.

The red sun pulsates once more from her face, and for an instant he is warmed again. Then—understanding—he jerks backward, a cry of fear leaping from his throat. He scrambles away from her on hands and knees, out through the hole in the door, and then he is up and fleeing as quickly as his legs will carry him. Now he is hobbling down the gravel path, now he is running. He runs until he reaches the road, and there his feet take him to the right because that is where he must go. And when the ruined buildings are far behind, he slows to a walk, and stumbles onward, deeper into the white hills, with a knife turning in the center of his chest.

It is night, and he is still walking. How is it possible, all this walking? He has eaten little since he left the goat-lady, a bite or two of bread; he has drunk nothing since the well beneath the spire. Yet on he goes. Now the road pitches downward under the stars, and because silence is upon the world the stars no longer sing. The moon rises, glinting on the sea. Yes, the sea has returned, on his left side, and far ahead, lights are twinkling in the bottom of a valley.

He trips and lands on his knees. Close to the road a hill is glowing beneath the moon. He crawls through the grass and comes to its base. He will rest here awhile. But dew is settling on him, and he has begun to shiver again. The shadow of a crevasse beckons. Into this he crawls, then deeper and deeper, until the stone closes over his head. A cave. He will sleep.

Tired as he is, he cannot sleep, for the memory of the pulsating red light remains, and it seems that the memory warms him a little. But there are other memories. He sees the exploded skull of his uncle, and his fist curls around the hilt of a hatchet, wanting to kill, seething with the lust to kill the Jure-face of death. Then the Zmija-face of death, which he wants to kill by dropping a stone on it, smashing all its bones, pressing poisonous wine from its brains. Then the Goran-face of death, and he is smashing and smashing its head with an iron pipe, splattering its snake-thoughts out of existence. And though the little sun fights with the three faces of death, it is no good. For as he slides down into wrath, he knows that *he* has become Jure and Zmija and Goran.

Gagging, choking on the poison within himself, he gropes about in the dark. His hand touches a rock, and he seizes it and strikes his breast with it. Again and again he strikes the bones in the exact center of his chest, killing and killing and killing his heart, the evil within this heart, until from blood and pain and exhaustion he cannot go on. He drops the stone and falls into unconsciousness.

Still he is not permitted release from this world.

Morning. Get up! Go on! Keep moving! Burn up all the cells, and today you will go down into the ruined houses of heaven. Let your skull rest among the burning books, shimmering down to ashes, and snow, and dust, and dry-cold wind. Two skulls become three skulls—mother and father and child—the children of Cain breeding Cain breeding Cain breeding Cain breeding Cain—

Get up! Go! So, he crawls away from this new torment and resumes his journey, trying to leave it behind.

The dusty road on which he has traveled for days comes to an end at a larger road of finer gravel. This runs along the sea coast and descends at a sharp angle. He turns right and goes down with it.

In time, he sees a fence blocking the road just ahead. On both sides of the fence are soldiers and flags. On this side is a flag with a red star sucking blood, on the far side is another flag, green-white-red, no star. Though there is blood on it, its fields are up and down. No flattened fields, no compressed sea, no sinking and crushing and sucking. So, he shuffles through the dust, approaching the fence and the buildings on both sides of it, and the soldiers and flags on both sides of it. He becomes invisible as he moves, for he is now transparent mobile glass that is no longer sessile, no longer spectacular for its qualities of light, no longer living on light, for it is the dying light, and no human eyes can see it.

A truck sits at the fence gate, vibrating and chugging black smoke from its tail pipe, an old truck with a cave of green canvas over its carry-platform. As he approaches its back end, the soldiers do not see him—of course they cannot, for he is too small to be seen and they are talking to the drivers. He lifts the canvas flap and climbs up into the dark interior. He lies down among piles of hard objects. Then the engine roars. The donkey moves, carrying him forward, then it stops, and voices are heard, then it moves again, and men's laughter and curses and songs resume, as they always do.

The donkey carries him, hour after hour, and he sleeps as it sways and rocks him along the road to Sarajevo. Now the truck is screeching to a halt. The heat is great, and he is sweating away the last of the water in his body. The truck does not move. Outside, men are pulling back the canvas from its roof of iron pipes. He sees now that he is lying under the pipes in a space among piles of limestone squares. Imprinted on every piece are sweat and tears and blood, for these are the ghost-stones from the island of death. He blinks and clears his eyes. There is no mark upon them except the sign of Cain. And when he slides down from the back of the truck and walks away unseen, he learns that he is not in Sarajevo but in a strange new land, and on the horizon stands a golden city, rising out of the sea.

24

He has walked all morning beside a paved road, along which automobiles run in both directions. He passes a house with a dark blue flag flying above it. On the flag is a falcon capped by a gold crown. To his left is a wide bay, on which boats with white sails are flying before the wind. On his right are rows of cypress trees and fields of black soil being turned up with tractors and plows. The golden city seems no nearer.

Then he comes to a roadside fruit stand. Under its awning, a fat man in an apron studies the walker suspiciously, then shrugs and tosses him a plum. When he sees the way in which the plum is eaten, he gathers a few more into his apron and approaches. He puts one into the hand of the man standing before him, and, after considering, pushes the rest into the wretched fellow's pockets. Then an orange and an apple. Still undecided, he goes back to his stand and returns with a little baguette of bread. Into the pocket as well. He shakes his head as if to say, *poor soul.*

"*Acqua?*" he asks.

Because the walker continues to stand there with his cracked lips parted, neither speaking nor leaving, the fruit vendor brings a metal pitcher and a glass. He fills the glass. The walker ignores it, takes the pitcher in both hands, and gulps its contents down. Then he staggers away alongside the highway, narrowly missing the end of his life, for many vehicles whizz past his elbow, honking their horns, though he does not hear them.

Evening. Twilight settles on a village decorated with yellow streetlights. A concertina is playing somewhere within the houses. Voices are rising and falling. At the edge of the village is a heap of rubble, hills of broken concrete, bricks, and clay tiles. Half-buried in it is a huge green machine with a cannon poking out of its nose. The walker climbs the hill and stops beside the machine. On its side is a white star. The metal around it is riddled with bullet holes. Its top is broken open, and there is a cave within, deep and cool and dark. He climbs inside.

The gray light of dawn spills in through the little holes and from the jagged opening above his head. When his eyes clear, he notices broken pieces of metal all around, a steering wheel, and a slit of sky above the wheel. The cannon juts upward from somewhere below it.

Slowly, slowly he examines the walls of the cave. Written upon them are the musings of many ghosts. *Sally B I love thee. FDR take us far. Back to Old Virginny.* He does not understand these words. He closes his eyes and gathers his strength, because he must travel far today, farther than he has ever walked before. He will walk into oblivion; he will walk so far that all remaining cells will be burned away, if he can overcome his body, if he does not allow it to force him to eat.

But as he gathers strength, he loses it again so swiftly. He falls asleep. He awakes when voices surround the cave—children shouting and screaming. Then clinking and clanking as bullets hit the outer walls. He understands now that he is inside a machine of war and that the war has continued without his knowing it. Now, because all soldiers are dead, children must take their places. Peering out through the slit above the steering wheel, he sees a band of them running about the piles of rubble, stopping from time to time to throw stones at each other. A few hold iron pipes and make noises as if they are firing machine guns.

He sinks down inside the metal cave and hides. He will leave when they go away. But all day long they play around him. Sometimes a child will stand on the roof of the machine, shouting taunts and firing his gun. Then a hail of stones will fly, and that one will run away, only to be replaced by another. He sees their shadows cross the hole in the roof, and once a little face, contorted with hatred, screaming words that he does not understand. The voices decline, return, fade again, and at last there is peace. Cocks crowing, women's voices, the smell of cooking food, and it is dusk.

Today he has not died. Tomorrow, then.

He can relax his vigilance in the dark, though he must shift his body with care, for there are points of metal wherever he turns. He should not spear himself; he need not die in pain. Death itself is the important thing. He lets his head fall back and looks up at the sky. It is overcast, no stars, no moon.

With a skip of his heartbeat, he realizes that something alive is moving within the machine. He freezes his body and holds his breath. It moves again, a soft sound, a rope coiling on canvas, then hissing—breathing or whispering. Another person has quietly dropped down into the hole with him. He chokes with fear, for the soldier-children might strike his head again and again with their iron pipes. It would not be right to die in this manner.

"They're gone", whispers the voice.

He does not move, does not speak. When his lungs are about to burst, he gasps for air.

"I won't betray you", says the other.

Throughout the long night hours, they converse together, the walker and this unseen companion, so quiet-spoken and considerate. In time, it seems to the walker that he no longer hears the voice with his ears, for the other's thoughts are in his mind.

"You see what they're like, don't you, those innocents."

His own thoughts are pictures, not words, but the other's are words dialoguing with the pictures.

Children who desire to kill. Children whose play is murder and contempt.

"Do you see what they have done to your world—the world that was? Do you see what they will do again and again with their freedom? And you, do you think you are walking to freedom, like the man pulling his cart into the north with a little toy boat on top, and a violin, and a wife and a child?"

Ariadne and the faceless infant. In the end, there was no pathway to freedom for them.

"These innocents who make war their game, are hungry, of course. They are brutal because they are empty. Their bellies and their souls, for they have no souls. How loathsome they are."

But this does not seem right, for the soldier-children are indeed brutal, but it is wrong to think that there is nothing inside them.

"Like the ghosts of the island of death", says the voice, in a calm and pleasing tone. "Though I see you have escaped."

"Is-is-is it you, Vladimir?" the walker stammers, in a hoarse whisper.

"No, I am not he. I am one who brings you bread. Are you hungry, do you want bread?"

"I am hungry, but I must not eat."

"Surely you must eat. All living things eat. They devour and are devoured, are they not?"

"I will escape from the devouring."

"But the devouring is inside you", whispers the voice reasonably.

"I did not wish it to be so."

"Yet it is so, and nothing can be done about it."

"Who are you, then? Tell me, for I do not know where I am, nor where I can go."

"Would telling show you the way?"

"It would help me speed to my end."

"I will speed you to your destiny."

"How?"

"You need not take the path you think is yours, for not every road leads to an end. I will show you a different way. See——"

The voice opens a path in the walker's mind and shows him a route that leads into another city, far along the path. And out of the air, bread and gold materialize and will fall into his hands if he wishes. And in that distant city his strength will return as well, and his beauty, and his voice, and his knowledge. Then men will heed him again and respect him.

"It takes but a little", explains the voice. "You choose to put your foot on one path and not another. Then your other foot. Onward you walk, faster and faster, and you rise into the places where no adversaries can confound you, and no hunger weakens you, and no authority rules over you."

"What place is that?"

"Freedom", whispers the voice reverently. "Freedom without submission. Come with me, and I will show you. We will enter together."

"What is your name?"

"You know my name."

"It seems to me I do not remember it. Though it may be I once knew you in the fields of heaven."

"No, that was another, and you saw how it all ended, the death of everything and the loss. All that loss, all that hunger, and the weakness upon weakness that came afterward, and the fear too. You remember the fear, and now you feel it again. I will take it from you. I will take all pain from you, if you follow me into my light, for I am master of light and of darkness."

"I forget so many things", says the walker. "I did not know you well, though I saw you crushed on the floor of the church in Rajska Polja and ate you with the blood and mud upon your flesh. You were with Fra Anto's body too, and you were there in all that horror and pain. But I was afraid. I was afraid that this is how we all end, but now you have returned to me, and I see it is not so."

"It is of another you speak, the one who died long ago, for he had no power. Now I will show you new things. I will take you by the hand and lead you out of this pit that men have made, and I shall take you higher. I will restore your mind, and with your thoughts and numbers you will amaze the cities of man. You can possess the fire from the heavens, and teach many about it. And if you wish, you can bring it down on those who have destroyed your life."

The walker pauses and wonders, for an unease has entered him. Though this voice speaks of life and light and fire, his words are unlike the other one, the man he once knew, the man in the brown robes who gave him sweet fire upon his tongue. In that weakness and poverty there had been peace. Why is there now no peace?

"Little do I ask in exchange", whispers the voice. "So little, so little—"

"There is nothing I can give you," says the walker, "for there is nothing left of me. I have come to my end, and beyond it there is nothingness."

"Yes, you have come to your end, yet I will show you another end, and if you accept it the end I give becomes beginning. For in me you will not enter nothingness, you will become as me, knowing good and evil."

"I hunger and thirst," says the walker, "but I know that mine is the path of weakness. Be it only hours or days left to me, this is my path and no other—I know it in my soul."

"But you do not have a soul", whispers the voice.

The walker falls silent. The dawn has crept in through the holes in the walls, and above his head is a scar of pale light. Now he sees the form of the other in the shadows, a man seated close

476

by, their bodies centimeters apart. The face comes forward out of the shadows. It is Zmija the snake.

"You have found me!" cries the walker. "How did you find me?"

"I followed your trail, the trail Cain always leaves in the desolation beyond Eden, for his evil drains out of him but is ever replenished. Yes, you are already like me, for you are me and I am you."

"No!" cries the walker.

Glancing about with desperate terror, he spies a spear of metal and thrusts his wrists upon it. He presses down, sawing the flesh furiously on the jagged edge, gasping and trying not to hear the whispering of the other.

"You escape from me into my arms," laughs the snake, "for there are no escapes."

Now his blood is spurting, and he falls backward against the hard metal floor.

Now another form slips down into the hole and strikes the shadow of the snake. The two forms clash, sword upon sword, until Zmija flies out through the hole and disappears into the sky.

The warrior kneels and takes the walker's wrist in his hand.

"Rise up," he says, "for you have work to do."

Then the warrior too is gone, and children's voices fill the air. A boy's face floats in space above him, peering into the pit, reaching down.

Then a cry—*Yankee-Yankee-Yankee!*—and the face disappears.

25

He is walking along a hallway, feeling groggy. The floors are green linoleum, and the walls are white. Where is he? How did he come here? Is this his own body?

Glancing down, he notices that his mind is riding on a body dressed in pale blue pajamas, with cloth slippers on his feet. The top of the garment has short sleeves. The arms are as thin as sticks, and the wrists are bandaged.

Beside him stands a little man, as small as a child, but rather old. He is chattering in a language Josip does not know. How strange is this fellow who holds his arm and guides him along, with his dark brown face and bright red hair and little white teeth that grin and click incessantly. Along one wall, sun-filled windows offer a view of old buildings tipped by spires and capped with domes. Flocks of pigeons wheel among the pinnacles and then drop between them. Stopping to look down into the street below, he sees that it is made of water. All the streets are water, and boats are being poled along them.

He can escape, he can swim away from this prison. He must look for a way out.

The little man takes him into a room where people in white clothing are standing beside a table. They make Josip lie down on it and bind his ankles and wrists. He wants to fight, but his body is too weak, and he is so sleepy that he cannot think. They put electric wires on his head. There is a bang, and his body jumps. It is the end, and he knows now that everything is over.

He wakes up in a room with white walls. A red-haired man enters through a door, helps him to stand, and takes him into a hallway. Down the hallway they go. He cannot remember how he came to this place. He has never seen it before. Now he waits at the end of a line of people. Others are waiting in pajamas just like his, old women, young men muttering to themselves, people crying with fear. One by one, they are taken into a room off the hall where there are voices and thumps and cries. He is very afraid. The bodies are taken from that room, wheeled away on rolling trolleys. Now is the end. It is time to die.

The little man takes him into a room where people in white clothing are standing beside a table. They make Josip lie down on it and bind his ankles and wrists. He wants to fight them, but his body is too weak, and he is so sleepy that he cannot think. They put electric wires on his head. There is a bang, and his body jumps; his mind goes black. It is the end. His life is complete.

He wakes up in a white room. He is lying on a cot, covered with a clean sheet. A red-haired man enters, helps him to stand, and then takes him into a hallway. Down the hallway they go. He cannot remember how he came to this place. He has never seen it before. What is his name? He could remember his own name, if he were to try, but he is too sleepy. Now he stands at the end of a line. Other people are waiting in pajamas just like his, old men and women moaning or staring into space, young men muttering to themselves, a girl crying with fear. One by one, they are taken into a room off the hall. He is very afraid for them, and for himself, but he cannot run away. One by one, the bodies are taken from that room on rolling trolleys. Now is the end. It is time to die.

The little man takes him into a room where people in white clothing are standing beside a table. They make him lie down on it and bind his ankles and wrists. He would fight them if he could, but his body is too weak, and he is so sleepy that he cannot. They put electric wires on his head. There is a bang and his body jumps. His mind goes black. It is the end.

He wakes up in a room with white walls. The red-haired man enters through a door, helps him stand, and then takes him into the hallway. Grinning, he holds up nine fingers. Down the hallway they go. He cannot remember how he came to be here. He has never seen it before. Now he stands docilely at the end of the line, hanging his head, sure that he must remember something, though it is not important.

"What is this place?" he asks, and only after speaking does he realize that these are his first words.

"*Italiano?*" cries the little fox excitedly. "*Credo di no! Austriaco? Croato?*"

"What is my name?"

"*Croato, sì, Hrvatsko, sì?*" says the fox.

Josip nods and drops his eyes, for he cannot bear the other's look of enthusiasm. Besides, he is about to be executed. A woman in a fine suit and a white jacket walks by, her high-heeled shoes clicking on the linoleum. She carries a clipboard under her arm. The fox stops her and speaks rapidly in his language. The woman replies in kind, though she examines Josip's face with curiosity. She hurries away. He is executed.

He wakes up in a room with white walls. A red-haired man enters through a door, helps him to stand, and then takes him into a hallway. Down the hallway they go. He cannot remember how he came to this place. He has never seen it before. They move past a line of people waiting to be executed and enter a room farther along, a large open space with tiled walls and floor, a row of sinks and toilets. The little man takes a toothbrush and tube of paste from his pocket and hands them to Josip. Then, as if to enlighten the ignorant, he imitates brushing motions. Josip turns and glances into a mirror above a sink.

Now he sees what he has become. How frightening is the creature staring back at him, this skeleton, this battered old man. He is hunching forward, his neck sunken in the collar bones and his shoulders sagging. His lips are parted to reveal a mouth like a graveyard, and there are hollows beneath wide cheekbones, over which parchment skin is stretched to the tearing point. Beneath the brows are purple shadows, and there are bags under blue eyes, which are distant and without expression. Most of the hair is gone, and what remains is wispy and gray. White scars score the sunburned forehead and cheeks.

After cleansing what remains of his teeth, he must shower with the fox standing guard nearby. Under the hot spray he closes his eyes and soaks. The fox reaches into the stall and fumbles a bar of soap into his hands. This soap smells of lemon, so fragrant and malleable that he wishes to eat it but does not. Afterward, he dries himself slowly with a towel, observing his body in the mirror. Yes, it's a skeleton with a large purple bruise in the center of the chest, all the ribs are popping out, and on one shoulder he bears a healed gash, roughly stitched a long time ago. The knees and elbows swell between vestiges of muscle in the legs and arms.

The fox observes it all, clicking and frowning and crooning sympathy. Then he helps Josip into a clean set of pajamas. After that, he is guided back to a small room at the other end of the corridor, gently taken into it, and then left alone. The door clicks shut behind him and is locked. There is a bed, a clean sheet, and a light bulb in a basket beyond reach in the ceiling. The window has a vent on top, through which fresh air is trickling in, but nothing human can climb back out. There are no bars on the window. He looks out through the glass and sees pigeons circling and boats slowly passing through the street below. In one, a man and a woman are reclining side by side, arm in arm, as the boatman leisurely poles them along.

Later the fox returns and takes him to a dining hall where people in blue pajamas are seated at tables, staring into bowls. Some are dipping spoons into them, eating bread and pasta, talking to their soup. Like them, he eats.

He is sitting alone in a room with two chairs and a desk. Through the window he sees a church dome, and a bell is booming from it. Pigeons fly around it. He watches them for a while and does not break his gaze when the door opens behind him and someone enters. A woman seats herself opposite with the desk between them. She is peering at her clipboard through ugly reading-glasses—an owl. She is about forty years old, maybe a little more. Her hair is dyed jet black, her cheeks are rouged, and she has a thoughtful face, not pretty.

"*Zdravo!*" she says with a smile, though her eyes are worried about something. "*Pozdrav!*"

He sits straighter and pays attention, but does not answer.

"You are Croatian?" she asks in his native language.

He looks away.

"What is your name?"

He resumes watching the pigeons.

"I am Dr. Mazzuolo. Can you tell me your name?"

He does not answer, neither does he look at her, though he notes that she wears too much lipstick.

"I am Croatian", she goes on in a friendly conversational tone. "I'm married to an Italian man, and I live here in Venezia. I was born in Croatia, but right after the war my parents and I got out. We fled across the sea in a little boat. I was younger then, engaged to be married, not to my present husband but to a boy who died. It seemed to me that the world ended when we left our home. Do you feel that your world has ended?"

He wishes she would stop speaking. He understands why she is doing it, why she wants to engage him in conversation. It is her job.

"I am your psychologist", she explains. "I hope you do not mind that I am a woman. It is not so easy for a man to talk to a woman doctor, I understand this. But you are older than I am, so you could think of me as your niece—" She smiles. "—a niece who is also a doctor. I am not a physician; that would be

482

a psychiatrist. But I studied at Bologna and did my graduate work in America. So, you see, I hope you will trust me in time, and then if you wish, when you feel you are ready, you can speak with me."

He glances swiftly at her and then away.

She looks down at her clipboard and writes something on the paper.

"So, you do not feel you are ready to tell me your name. But can I at least reassure you that you needn't hide information anymore. You are safe here in Italy, where there are no secret police or political prisons. You have been in prison, I know."

He ceases watching the pigeons, drops his chin to his chest, and clasps his hands between his knees. If he had the energy he would put his face between his knees and shut everything out.

"The doctors have described the wounds upon your body. I have seen wounds like this before. Sometimes people from our homeland are able to get out across the border. They walk a long way or they come by boats. And among them are a few who escaped from prison. I think you are one of them. Are you one of them?"

Now his head is between his knees. He is a breathing diatom, diving for the darkness of the deep waters. The woman is silent for a time. Then she scrapes back her chair and walks over and stands beside him. She puts a hand lightly to the back of his head and keeps it there, gently stroking the bristles and the scars.

"I am Slavica", she whispers. "Don't be afraid."

How long has he been here? There is a lot of rain. Is it spring or autumn? They have moved him to a part of the hospital where it is not necessary to lock the doors of patients' rooms. The ward is locked, however, so escape is still impossible. He has not yet spoken to the woman. Slavica does all the talking. She has told him there will be no more electroshock treatments. He has had nine—it was like being executed nine times over. She does not like the shock treatments; she thinks they are barbaric, but she is not a physician and has no say in hospital policy. However, she did get them to stop his treatment because it seems the shocks made no difference. They certainly were not helping. Does he feel better now? Is his memory returning?

He likes to listen to her. She talks about her husband, who is a dentist, and her two children, a boy and a girl, and what they are doing. The older child, a boy, is obsessed with soccer. The little girl plays the flute—she's gifted, says the mother, advanced beyond her years that child! Slavica is very proud of her. And of the boy too, he is so much like his father. They live in a good house on the mainland in the town of Mira. It means a bit of a drive to work each day, but they don't like the dampness and the frequent floods in the city. The tourists can be bothersome too. In summer, the family likes to drive up to the Dolomites and hike in the mountains. In winter, not every year but as often as they can afford, they go to Innsbruck for skiing. Does he know where that is? It's in Austria. Very lovely, though she prefers the Sud Tirol. Italy is unstable right now, she tells him, the Euro-Communists are always trying to get the better of the Christian Democrats.

He understands why she throws these fine filaments to him: she is hoping he will catch a thread and let her pull him in. Sometimes she is so naïve in her approach that he feels an urge to help her along, to suggest a few topics that would be better bait. Of course, he does not.

Most days he just eats and naps and eats. And eats and eats and eats. And walks the hallways. He knows the other patients now, not by name, but by their faces and their conditions. He feels pangs of pity for the truly insane, those who remain in agony. Usually such people are under heavy sedation. It is impossible to engage them in any way. He has tried once or twice to find within himself that mysterious current he first felt

484

in the cellar hospital of Sarajevo, when he looked into the souls of other sufferers and spoke to them with his eyes. Wordless messages from the swallows, consolation from a myth. But it seems that this too has been taken away.

Sometimes she makes him smile—not much, never in the beginning, a little as the months go by. Sometimes her eyes get wet. Her little boy has suffered a broken leg. A big boy kicked him hard during a game. An accident, but it does things to a mother's heart.

Three or four times a week, an hour per session.

He is picking up a few Italian words from the fox. No, not the fox. He is known to everyone in the hospital as "Chicklet". Slavica says that it's because the man makes clicking noises, as if he is always chewing gum with his little square teeth, and *Chicklet* is the name of an American gum. This is interesting. You learn something new every day.

"What year were you born?" she asks abruptly one day, changing the subject from alpine flowers to more personal questions.

Without thinking, he murmurs, "Nineteen thirty-three."

She leans across the desk and takes his hands in hers. He pulls away, disturbed not so much by her touch as by the fact that he has spoken without intending to.

"Your first words", she breathes, wiping an unprofessional tear from her eye.

He looks away.

"What is your name?" she whispers, pressuring for more.

He does not acknowledge the question. She tricked him, caught him with her thread. Who is she, really, and why is she so concerned about him? What does she hope to learn, and why does she want to learn it?

"Yes, enough for one day", she says with a sympathetic smile. "Though the year isn't right because that would make you only in your late twenties." Then the smile dies on her face, and she sits down again, looking closely at him. The months of plentiful food have been filling him out, and his hair is growing again. Perhaps he sits taller these days. The bruises are healed too. After a few moments, she jots something down on her clipboard, stands up, and in a muted tone bids him farewell until tomorrow.

He finds the neurotics most difficult. Psychotics elicit sympathy. Neurotics repel sympathy because they demand attention and in a language he cannot understand. They get very angry or very hurt if you do not play their games. The games are all inside their minds, and the rules are difficult to figure out. He would not play them even if he knew what they were. Slavica informs him that he is neither psychotic nor neurotic. He has suffered severe trauma and is recovering. The hospital windows, she tells him in a factual tone, are made of a kind of glass that cannot be shattered. In the old days, patients sometimes ran down a hallway, threw themselves against the glass, and fell to the sidewalk below, or drowned in the "street".

"But I know you would not do such a thing", she adds, glancing surreptitiously at the jagged white lines across his wrists.

Another month goes by. It is hot these days, but breezes sometimes blow in off the Adriatic. The days are growing shorter, autumn is approaching. He watches the pigeons a lot and walks the hallways. His strength is returning little by little. He can shower without Chicklet standing guard. He spends more time in the recreation room playing checkers with the deranged, or making paper flowers under the art instructor's eye. He spends a week putting together a thousand-piece picture puzzle of the world. The world is very large. The color for Yugoslavia is red. Italy is green. All oceans are blue.

Today they lend him a little safety razor (one from which the blade cannot be removed) and some shaving soap. He is scrap-

ing his face clean of bristles for the first time in—how long?—
straining to remember, he realizes that the last time he shaved
was —how long ago? how long ago?—it was just after Christmas—when—

Then he stares into the mirror and sees himself stripped to
the waist, needing a haircut, whistling as he shaves with the
Spanish straight-razor Antun gave him as a wedding gift, and
behind him Ariadne is stepping out of the bath, smiling to
herself, holding her large belly because the baby is now kicking
and swimming around in the inland sea. He collapses onto the
floor of the ward washroom, sobbing aloud. Drawn by the
noise, Chicklet and another orderly come rushing in. They help
him to his feet, take him back to his room, and call his psychologist. When she enters his cell, she finds him lying on his
bed with arms crossed over his face, weeping silently now.

She sits down on the bedside chair. He is aware of her
presence. No one comes in to give him a needle. No one
restrains him or locks the door. Only Slavica is here. She asks no
questions, offers no maternal pit-pats or chat. She merely sits
and waits with him.

He drifts into a light sleep and awakes to find her still present.
Now she will ask questions, he feels certain: Why is he crying?
What has he remembered? What is his name? Instead, she looks
back without tension or intent. She says nothing with her lips,
though she is telling him, I am with you, I am here.

At last, he sits up and whispers, "My name is Josip."

"Would you like to have a day out?" she asks, a month or two
later.

"Yes", he says.

"I will arrange it."

They have talked their way around a few things, but not
much so far, nothing that would open an inner abscess. Just a
few facts. She knows now that he is without family, has been a

political prisoner, and was once a professor at a university in Croatia. She says with a playful smile that she can determine his academic field (a pure conjecture, she admits, not a clinical diagnosis), because his temperament and character are those of a writer, and if this is true, she is certain he is a poet.

"Why do you think that?" he asks with a scowl that intrigues her.

"Your eyes. The way you watch things."

He angrily gets to his feet and paces about the room.

"I am not a poet!"

"What, then?"

"A mathematician."

"That is surprising", she says, raising her eyebrows. "I could not have guessed."

He wants her to go now, just let him be, enough is enough for one day. But she does not move a muscle. She just sits there and watches him stare out the window with his shoulders quaking, observing how his body grows still with the passage of minutes. He is looking at something out there above the city's skyline.

"What is it, Josip?"

In a subdued voice he murmurs, "*The wing's curve . . .*"

"What did you say?"

"*The wing's curve, the wind's curve, the earth's curve.*"

"That is interesting. What does it symbolize?"

"I don't know. They were my wife's words."

"You are married?"

"Her name was Ariadne."

The outing takes place a few weeks later. Slavica has come to an agreement with her husband that one of her patients will visit all day Saturday, have supper with the family, and then they will drive back to Venezia and drop him at the asylum as if it were a hotel.

After breakfasting at the hospital, Slavica and Josip drive across the causeway from the city to the mainland. Josip has doubts about the wisdom of the excursion. He is a little afraid of himself. She reassures him that this is to be expected after all he has been through. Add to this the months he has been locked inside that stuffy old hospital—nearly a year—and it's not surprising that he feels like a stranger in a strange land.

"I *am* a stranger in a strange land", he replies glumly.

"Emilio will make you feel at home."

"What does he think about a mental patient coming for a family visit?"

"He's looking forward to meeting you. He likes Croatians."

"Aren't you afraid I will hurt your children?"

She turns her eyes from the road for a second or two, peers at him over the rim of her owlish spectacles, and laughs. A much more effective response than anything she might have said.

"This is good, Josip", she says after a silence. "It's very good that you are honest. When a person is real, he speaks truth. I know you are a man of truth."

"Thank you. But I do not know what truth is."

"You know what it is. It's there."

"How honest am I permitted to be?"

"As honest as you like. Say what you wish."

"You wear too much lipstick."

She bursts out laughing. "It's true. Emilio tells me the same. He asks me, do you wear all that paint for me or for someone else? I wear it for *you*, my dear husband, I tell him, and I wear it for someone else. And do you know who that someone else is?"

"I would rather not know", murmurs Josip uncomfortably.

She laughs again. "The someone else is the lady I see each morning in my mirror."

Josip knows it is better to be tactful, but she has invited candidness.

"Do you not like how you look—how you look naturally?" he asks.

"I am not beautiful. I am not even pretty. Women want to be beautiful, even if it's just a fantasy."

"I thought you told me last week that fantasy leads to unreality."

"Yes, that's so. I prescribe the medicine, but I don't take it myself."

This makes Josip smile.

"Any more questions?"

"Are you still my niece?"

"No, I am your auntie."

Their home is a two-story brick villa—a very small one—near the Brenta, a river that runs through Padova to Venezia. The other houses on the street are real villas, their marble pillars and cornices reminding Josip of classical Rome. The Mazzuolos' home has no pillars, though from the outside it appears to be spacious enough. An enormous television aerial caps the roof, and the grass in the front yard is mowed like a fine carpet. Flowering shrubs hug the building, and old cypresses and poplars of various shapes and sizes border the property, whispering in the morning breeze. The sun is shining through the branches from the direction of Croatia.

They find her husband behind the house. He is a short, pudgy man with a balding head, practicing golf shots on the back lawn. A few steps away, two children are reading books as they lie on a blanket beside a little fountain and a pool of natural stones, over which a statue of St. Anthony of Padova is preaching to fish. The girl drops her book and comes running to her mother, chattering excitedly about a bird's nest in a tree—the peeping of baby chicks has begun this morning, but Papà will not let her climb up to touch them. She is five or six and possesses very pretty Slavic features.

"Chiara, Chiara, say hello to our guest." The girl smiles and

490

curtsies, and then runs off to the tree where she discovered the nest.

Slavica's husband has a wide friendly face, and his black eyes sparkle as he shakes Josip's hand.

"*Benvenuto*", he says with a smile. The clasp is warm and strong. He has fine teeth, well displayed. He switches to awkward Croatian. "Slavica has told me a lot about you. We're so glad you could visit us, Mr. . . . . Mr. . . . ."

"Lasta", says Josip, with a bow of his head. "Please call me Josip."

"Josip—and I am Emilio."

The boy glances up from his book.

"Mamma," he calls, "was Garibaldi a bad man or a good man?"

"A bad man", she calls back.

"A good man", grins the boy's father. "Paolo, come and meet our guest. No—our guest will come and meet you."

So, they all go over to the blanket and tower above the boy, who is about eight years old, with an unruly thatch of black hair and intelligent eyes. His leg is in a cast, and he can only roll over onto his side and stick up his arm for a handshake, then back to the book.

Josip glances into the pool. St. Anthony is preaching to real fish, gold and yellow and black, swimming around the stems of floating flowers.

They have a leisurely lunch on the patio, hours-long, Italian style, full of pleasant disconnected chat, mostly the important things the children want to talk about. No questions are asked of the visitor. Emilio is an excellent host, offering wine again and again, though Josip declines. He is happy with water. Afterward they take a long walk beside the Brenta, the father pushing his son in a homemade contraption of bicycle wheels and plywood—which they call "the limousine".

Throughout the day, Josip is content merely to be there. He says little. They demand nothing of him, not a hint of prying. Slavica speaks of her childhood in a village near the shrine of the Mother of God of Bistrica, the Queen of Croatia. She tells of the numerous little churches scattered throughout the mountains in that region north of Zagreb and about the pilgrimages she went on as a child, before the troubles. Emilio asks where Josip is from. Bosnia i Herzegovina, he replies and says no more.

"I've never seen it", muses Emilio. "Lots of mountains back there, I hear, beyond the Dinarics."

They have a supper in the evening, outside on the patio again. After the meal, Emilio lights a fat candle in a jar in front of the statue of St. Anthony and another in front of a standing crucifix on the table. The dishes, wine bottles, and baskets of uneaten food are not yet cleared away. The sky is burning red, then dusk settles quietly upon the land, and the heat of the day is replaced by a cool breeze from the ocean. The family prays the Rosary together in Italian. Josip sits silently throughout, feeling some pain, staring at the flagstones, or gazing up at the sky as he listens to the murmured prayers and the peeping of chicks in the nest. How strange, he thinks. Do Italian birds hatch their young in autumn? Maybe they are late-comers. He cannot recall birds doing such a thing in his homeland. Perhaps they do, and he never noticed. Or is it spring now? What month is it? Slavica told him, but he has forgotten.

There is too much to remember, too much that would crack him open, though he knows full well what it is: everything that he left behind beyond the wall of the Dinarics, the wall of the sea, and the wall within his own heart. He wonders if shock treatments wipe out essential things. If they do, you cannot know what is missing. Perhaps that is their purpose. As the prayers continue, he tries to remember a little mathematics, but the mental strain is too much. He focuses on the saint and the fish and the children's faces.

After the Rosary, they go inside the house to watch television. The living room has a thick carpet and imitation baroque furniture. Hanging on all four walls are religious paintings of the sentimental kind. Sitting on a shelf are a few pieces of Croatian pottery, a painted egg and a heart-shaped biscuit dipped in red glaze, inscribed with the word *Zagreb*. The sofa has a lace throw on it and red and white braided cushions.

"Have you been following the mess, Josip?" asks Emilio switching on the television set. "No? Well it's really bad, a big showdown. Kennedy has told the Russians to back off. If their ships bring any more missiles to Cuba, there will be war."

Slavica claps her hands and tells the children it is time for bed. There follows an elaborate ritual of kisses and hugs. Seated in a corner armchair, Josip watches it all, the pain in his heart increasing, not by the threat of war, but by the happiness of these secure children. Perhaps, too, by the braided cushions just like Mamica used to make. The boy crosses the room on crutches and bends toward Joseph, shaking his hand again. The little girl kisses his cheek, hugs him, and flies away toward a staircase, leaving the faint perfume of innocence in the air.

"Another war", sighs Slavica, after the children are safely tucked in. "And this one will be the last."

When the news program is over, she drives Josip back to the hospital and accompanies him into the building, lingering a few minutes by the entrance to his ward.

"Did I pass my test?" he asks.

"It was not a test", she replies with a hurt tone. "Truly, I wanted you to meet my family. We are both far from our homeland, we both have lost so much."

"Your husband will become jealous—yes, in time he will imagine things."

She smiles and shakes her head. "My husband and I love each other very deeply. And as I told you, he likes Croatians.

It is plain to see he likes you. We hope you will accept more invitations to visit us."

"If you wish", he mumbles, dropping his eyes.

"You are honest, Josip. You are also proud. But I think maybe it is not such a bad pride. I believe it is because your trust has been broken—badly broken. It can be rebuilt. Can you let us help you?"

"Why do you want to help me?" he asks in a neutral tone.

She does not reply immediately. Finally, she takes a deep breath.

"My father took his own life. That was after we came to Italy. He had lost everything: our family, our home, our life. I had lost the young man I loved, but my loss was not like Tata's because most of my life was still ahead of me. He could not learn this language or the ways of the people here—so alien to us. So deep were his sorrows that he sank and sank and did not rise. And when my mother died—I think from weakness due to all our hardships—he just went after her."

"I am sorry for your family's misfortune", says Josip.

"He was a writer, a professional journalist. Over the years he was arrested in turn by the Ustashe, then by the Italians, then by the Tito regime—and they all tortured him, then released him. Each time he was taken away, I was terrified, and I learned to pray as never before. And each time he was returned to us, I learned to be thankful.

"But our prayers weren't enough for him in the end. I don't know why. He was a strong man in many ways, a fighter, and very courageous. Perhaps his confidence was in himself and not in God.

"When the Communists arrested him that last time, my brother was arrested along with him. He was so much like our father, and he was beginning to say things in print too. He wanted to be a man of truth, and of course Tata encouraged him in it, despite the risks. In prison, they forced my father to

494

watch as they put my brother into a huge drum of water. It was not to drown him. No, they wanted something worse. They wanted to take his soul—my father's soul and my brother's soul. They put Pavao inside and closed the lid.

"The drum was on its side, so a person could only float on his back within it, with a couple centimeters of breathing space on top. For five weeks he remained inside that drum. There was air inside, he could rest, he could drink the water he floated in. There was a tiny pipe for ventilation, but the drum was entirely packed in layer upon layer of cotton. No sound could enter or escape. It was neither hot nor cold. My father later said he thought they were taking away his son's senses, one by one, so that in the total darkness inside that drum he had only his own mind, a little air, and no feeling. The mind alone, cut off from all outside communication, turns in upon itself. Some men survive this but are changed for life; most men disintegrate.

"My father tried to shout to Pavao and was beaten for it, but it was useless, because not a sound penetrated that evil cell. In the end, they took off the lid and pulled my brother out. He was alive but completely insane. Then they just shot him there in front of my father. Then they kicked Tata out onto the street, and he walked home in the dark from Zagreb to our village. Not long after, we decided there was nothing left for us in our land. We walked from the mountains, and later arrived at the coast, and from there we found a fisherman who smuggled us across to Italy."

Slavica pauses, sighs.

"My father was not only a journalist, he was something of a poet too—though his poems were a private matter. I thought you were a poet, because your eyes are so much like his. He was always observing birds, like you, not as others would watch them. He told me once, when I was a little girl, that they sometimes spoke to him. After he died, I was certain that he had suffered from clinical melancholia, and that the sickness had killed him. Now . . ."

"You no longer think so?"

"It may sound strange to you, Josip, but I no longer think in those terms. In fact, I no longer trust the assumptions of psychology."

"Yet you are an excellent psychologist. You have helped me."

"I am a poor psychologist. I did little for you. It is you who chose to live. Only you can choose to live or die, and no one else can make this choice for you. Indeed, you chose rightly." She smiles suddenly. "It has been a long day. Tomorrow I will see you again, and then I will have good news to tell you—if the Soviets and Americans have not incinerated the planet during the night."

Josip is now a patient at a private clinic on the mainland, about thirty kilometers inland from Venezia. The clinic is a large manor house surrounded by tilled fields, orchards, and greenhouses. He has a room of his own in an unlocked ward from which he can freely go in and out of the building and throughout the grounds. He no longer wears pajamas during daylight hours, just ordinary casual clothes—slacks and shirt and shoes. Visitors are never quite sure whether he is a patient or a staff member. He is undoubtedly a patient, and Slavica still sees him for an hour of consultation once a week when she is not at the hospital in the city. His new doctor has taken him off all medication and is pleased by the way Josip can speak calmly about the traumas of his childhood and his more recent experiences as a prisoner. Certain crucial details remain archived in Josip's mind, known to him alone. It is not necessary to tell everything. He no longer yearns to die—this afflicts him rarely, and then only when he is unusually exhausted or troubled by nightmares. The nightmares are declining in number and intensity. Depression and its accompanying ennui can return at odd moments, but they last no longer than a few days at a time. His depression is dispelled more quickly whenever he overcomes feelings of despair with an exercise of will—above all, the will to physical labor.

He spends most days weeding in the garden, pruning trees or burning underbrush in preparation for spring. Then summer returns, along with its crushing heat. Birds build their nests, hatch their young, and the young fly away. The planet is not incinerated. As summer turns to harvest season, he spends more and more time picking fruit in the orchard.

He is good with other patients, those who are able to respond. He is learning Italian, too, and can engage those who are more aware with his attempts to draw them out—out of the sealed drums of self. The doctor hints that part-time employment is a possibility, at least for a reduction of his fees.

"What fees?" Josip asks, with some surprise. The question of who is paying for his care, and who has been paying for it during the past year or more, had never crossed his mind. A bad sign, he thinks.

He asks Slavica about it the next time they meet. She tells him that when he was first brought to the hospital, it was as a ward of the state, but the authorities now no longer accept responsibility for him, because the worst is over and he is not an Italian citizen. She admits with some embarrassment that she and Emilio have been covering the clinic costs. Josip is appalled that they have taken this burden upon themselves. It is too generous! How can it ever be repaid? There is no need for repayment, she replies, as if it is no great matter.

But if he is to be released soon, he asks, what should he do? He is getting stronger day by day, so perhaps he will be able to find employment.

"I will work at anything", he declares.

"The authorities may not let you", she says with a look of anxiety.

"What would happen then?"

"They may deport you to Yugoslavia."

His hands begin to tremble.

"It might not come to that, Josip. I am working on it. I have a friend. Soon she is moving to Roma from America, and then I am sure she will spend a weekend with us. It could open some doors. I would like you to visit us when she's here. Will you do it?"

He nods, still staring into a black pit.

Dr. Amaliani, the physician in charge, says there is no problem obtaining a weekend pass because, frankly, this man is not mentally ill, it's a complete cure, he really shouldn't be here. It would be a loss if he goes back to Yugoslavia, a loss to the clinic as well, because he is proving to be a real help with some cases. The way he can get the speechless to speak, or the immobilized to move, or the despairing to give a little smile now and then. It is all quite marvelous, though of course there are no funds to hire him as an untrained assistant.

"A volunteer, then?" Slavica asks Amaliani.

"It might be arranged. Of course, there could be no payment of wages by ordinary means."

Amaliani and Slavica exchange smiles. It will be done the Italian way, they explain to Josip, no paper trail, a little cash stipend for his needs, a room in the clinic's service quarters, and all his meals for free. A splendid arrangement, is it not?

"But what about the danger of deportation?" he asks.

"It can be delayed as long as you remain invisible", replies Amaliani.

"And if I am noticed by officials?"

"Then we will be forced to admit that we do not yet have conclusive data about your origins or the nature of your pathology."

"He means, Josip," says Slavica with an arch look, "that we will cover for you and cover our own hides as well!"

"Indelicately expressed, Dr. Mazzuolo", frowns Amaliani, though his eyes are glinting with pleasure.

"If I were ever discovered," says Josip, "I don't know what I would do. I would kill myself before letting them send me back."

"Ah, excellent", says Amaliani staring at the ceiling, rocking back and forth on his leather chair. "In that case, if the authorities were to decide for deportation, we would argue that you are suffering from suicidal tendencies, indicating that your cure is not yet complete, and thus you would have to remain here as a patient."

"Wonderful!" declares Slavica, rising and shaking Amaliani's hand.

So, apparently he is no longer mentally ill. This is very nice, but it is rather shaky soil to stand on. What exactly is mental health? At what point did he cross the frontier from insanity? And are there not a lot of pieces missing from the puzzle of his inner world? There is so much he cannot bear to think about. People he cannot bear to remember—the good ones especially, those whom he loved. The lost.

Today he is picking oranges in the orchard with the sun on his bare back and a warm breakfast in his belly. At the base of the tree stands a psychotic youth, a boy from Verona he is helping to come off drugs. The lad is for the moment without hallucinations, and seems happy enough holding a basket at the base of the tree, into which Josip drops oranges and cheerful comments. Birds are performing aerial acrobatics in the branches. An excellent morning.

Suddenly, the smell of orange peel dilates his nostrils and sends an electric shock through his brain. He bursts into sobs and must cling to the tree lest he fall out of it. His father is with him as they stand side-by-side on a cliff above the sea; they have climbed up from the shore, and Josip is carrying little white stones; the beach is clicking inside his pockets, and he is chewing a winter orange with its juice dribbling down his chin. *Sweet*, he cries with joy, leaping into the air. *Sour*, says his father with a smile.

So, is he crazy or isn't he? No, says Slavica, he is definitely not crazy. He has suffered some serious blows to his heart and memory, and these sorrows rise to the surface from time to time. She would be worried if they didn't, she tells him.

Another day. It is early afternoon. He has recited passages from *The Odyssey* to the young drug addict, and though the boy does not comprehend them, he has been calmed by the cadence of the lines and the mysteries embedded in noble phrases. It has been a good challenge to translate passages from memory into the Italian language. Not quite as poetic, but still rather good. Josip likes to read dictionaries at night in his little room. If he can stay in this land long enough, it might be possible to become a citizen.

The boy informs Josip that since leaving Milan, where he was a prostitute because of the drugs, he has become Telemachus again, but no one else knows his secret. Josip promises not to reveal his identity, and says that Telemachus has a long journey ahead—it is always a long journey to find a missing father. The boy smiles gratefully and goes back into the clinic for a siesta.

Josip remains in the orchard, lying beneath an orange tree while all Italy takes its daily nap. His legs are crossed at the ankles, and his arms are lazing in the surrender position with hands open beside his head as he drifts into half-sleep. A few drops of orange syrup trickle into his mouth. He can taste it. He sits up, looking all around. No one is there. No oranges in the branches above are leaking their juice. He shakes his head and lies down as before.

Once again the juice drips onto his tongue. He hears some creature sniffing about his feet—a little dog, he supposes. His eyes fly open, and he sits up. There is no one there, no person, no dog, no leaking fruit. He swallows the juice. Or is it an illusion that slips so sweetly down his throat? He shakes his head again. It was imagination. How powerful the imagination is. He lies down and falls asleep.

Chicklet sends a message via Slavica. He is to be married on such and such a day. Will Josip honor him by being in attendance? *Sì, certo!* Of course he will.

The wedding takes place in the basilica of San Marco in Venezia, and Josip accompanies the Mazzuolo family to the celebration. For the occasion, he has borrowed a suit and tie from a staff member at the clinic. He is feeling elated because to be a wedding guest is a sign of restoration to the world of normal things—the glorious, extraordinary, ordinary things. As he and the Mazzuolos cross the piazza toward the wide stone steps of the church, they must walk carefully along a causeway of boards, suspended above the overflow of an untimely flood. As he approaches the front steps, an uneasiness grows within him, which quickens into fear, then terror. The big bells are booming, and a party of eager people are waiting at the doors for the bride's arrival.

Chicklet is dressed in a white three-piece suit and white tie, white leather shoes, a yellow flower in his button hole, a bouquet of orchids in his hand, all capped by his flaming red hair slicked down with pomade. The bride appears at the far side of the piazza and tiptoes carefully along the causeway, holding her voluminous white dress high above her ankles. She arrives safely, greeted by cheers, a child-size woman with bright yellow hair, no taller than the groom himself. Like her betrothed, she is about sixty years old. Taking each other's hands with adoring smiles, the bride and groom enter the basilica. No one notices that Josip lingers behind; and when everyone else has gone inside, he crosses the piazza and leans against the wall farthest from San Marco. Trying to calm his breathing, he works hard to keep sobs inside his throat. He cannot enter the church. After all this time, he still cannot enter. His mind tells him how ridiculous and irrational this is, but every other aspect of his being rejects the reasonable arguments. Fear wins.

In time, the bells ring again, and the crowd pours out behind Chicklet and his wife. The husband strides forth to the edge of the top steps, goes down on one knee, throws his arms wide, and in mellifluent poetics recites an homage to his wife, whom he addresses as "My dear Canary!" After much applause, the entire crowd crosses the piazza and parades behind the couple along the flood boards to another street, over a stone bridge, and into a square where they enter a hall for the wedding banquet. This, Josip is able to attend.

The music and dancing and kisses will be remembered vaguely in times to come. He will recall the happiness among the people that day, especially the euphoria of recaptured youth in the faces of bride and groom. Most of all, he will recall a moment when Slavica turns to him and remarks offhand that it is a joy to be a wedding guest. She uses the Croatian word, *svat*. His heart sinks, and he is silent during the remainder of the evening, though he masks his feelings for the sake of others.

I will not forget you, Svat, I will not forget you, he whispers in his thoughts as he is driven home late that night. And as he lies down in the dark to sleep, he recalls another wedding.

26

It is a hot afternoon in Slavica and Emilio's backyard, heavy with humidity, and there is not a breeze stirring the air.

Josip has joined the family for the day because in the evening the influential friend from Rome will arrive. At the patio table, sweating jugs of lime juice and water are emptied, refilled, and emptied again by the thirsty revelers. About four in the afternoon, Slavica brings sweet-melon from the kitchen and slices it into little boats. Emilio's mother is here today, too—the first time Josip has met her—a tiny olive-skinned woman in a long black dress, her white hair bunched in a net. Her eyes twinkle like her son's, but she is a person of fewer words. She brings two little tubs to the table.

"*Gelato, gelato, gelato!*" scream the children, pressing in close as the treat is scooped into the boats. They run off with these prizes to eat them under the shadows of the trees, where the air is cooler.

Only Emilio chooses the vanilla, a small scoop. Everyone else chooses the thick creamy chocolate, onto which Slavica grates hard chocolate and hazelnuts. Josip eats his slowly because he has not tasted ice cream in years, and never any like this. He holds it on his tongue as it melts. It goes down like a streak of ecstasy.

"The chocolate is the best," says Slavica, plopping a double scoop onto her own boat, "but poor Emilio hates it."

"I don't hate it," her husband replies, "I just don't want it."

"But, really, Emilio, how can a sensible person prefer vanilla? Only you touch the stuff, and we always have to throw so much away."

"His teeth are very fine ones", says the old mother. "It is best to protect them. And I wonder if it would be wise to do the same for the children?"

"The children's teeth are in no danger, Mamma", laughs Slavica. "As you see, they are not falling out of their mouths."

"Soon enough they will rot!"

"Well, it's worth it. Will you have some too?"

"Of course!" grins the old lady baring her gums. "Chocolate, if you will, and please be so good as to give me two scoops. I'll eat Milio's share."

"Mamma, what about your teeth!" cries her son.

"I have no teeth!"

Supper is pasta with a mushroom sauce, bread and olive oil and red wine. Josip drinks gallons of the lime-water and sweats profusely. It feels very good. He does not engage himself in the conversations or let himself become engaged, for he is simply enjoying the antics of the children, who have become more rambunctious as the evening approaches. The air is a little cooler, and they are full of sugar. They are up and down the trees, peering into nests from which the chicks have long flown. Later, the boy and his father kick a soccer ball around, while Josip and the women sit on deck chairs and observe it all in a spirit of companionship.

A car horn beeps just after sunset.

"She's here!" smiles Slavica, who, with a clap of her hands, jumps up and runs around a corner of the house in the direction of the driveway. Soon she returns with a woman of about forty years. She is wearing a light cotton dress and carrying her sandals in her right hand. She moves like a younger woman, and it is plain to see, even in the twilight, that she is still very beautiful.

The children run to her, and she goes down on her knees to embrace them. Emilio, throwing his chest out and smiling urbanely, gives a double-kiss to her cheeks. Finally, Mamma is introduced. The old woman simply nods, with caution in her face and perhaps disapproval. Josip is standing by the table, waiting. Slavica brings the woman over for introductions.

"Cass," says Slavica in English, "this is our friend Josip Lasta from Croatia. Josip, this is my dear friend Cass Conway."

"Well, hello there," says the woman extending a hand graciously, "it's so very nice to meet you, Joe-*seep*."

Instantly the impression is formed. She is wealthy, educated, appreciates mildly interesting experiences as long as they are sufficiently odd and can later be used as anecdotes at parties, and she is somehow connected to the embassy of the most powerful nation on earth. There are no scars on her face or hands, or on her over-exposed chest, arms, and legs. A large diamond glitters on a finger. She has been admired or adored all her life and never ignored. Moreover, she has called him *Josip*, not Mister Lasta.

He shakes her hand courteously, then releases it. There is a holding-on in her fingers; she wants the touch to linger, even if only for a micro-second. Perhaps it is merely the style of American women.

"How do you do", says Josip stiffly, with a bow of his head. Last week he purchased a Croatian–English dictionary, and he has been practicing. He has memorized numerous common words, plus a few useful idioms: It is raining cats and dogs today. The corn is as high as an elephant's eye. Can you direct me to the subway, please? Where may I purchase a hot dog?

Very strange, this English.

Fortunately, everyone can speak Italian, and that is the language in which they converse throughout much of the evening. They all sit down, and after Emilio has poured wine, and the children are led away to bed by the grandmother, the two women put their heads together and dive into English, launching a contrapuntal discussion unintelligible to the two men. Emilio listens with a whimsical expression, while both he and

Josip note the several names that surface in the conversation, as well as Slavica's extravagant body language, her facial animation, her happiness to be reunited with an old friend. The women have become mutual catalysts, the men invisible.

Emilio catches Josip's eye. "They knew each other in Boston", he explains in adequate Croatian. "That's where Slavica spent some time putting the feather in her doctorate. This woman—I will not say her name, for then she will understand that we are talking about her—this woman studied psychology as well, and that is how they became connected. But she married someone in the diplomatic service and never became a doctor. Now her husband works in Rome. They arrived a few months ago, and the wives have been visiting back and forth, renewing old ties. The children, as you may have noticed, adore her."

"I see", murmurs Josip, gazing up at the stars filling the sky.

"You don't like her much, I can see", smiles Emilio.

Josip meets his gaze, but says nothing.

"She is quite beautiful, is she not?" Emilio continues as he refills Josip's water glass with lime juice.

Slavica breaks off, and casts a scowl in her husband's direction. "Emilio, what are you and Josip talking about?"

"We were saying that there are few pleasures in this world as fine as drinking good wine under the stars in the company of two great beauties."

She throws a bun at her husband, who ducks, while the American woman looks back and forth between them with a puzzled smile.

"Well, stop that nonsense, and speak in Italian for the sake of our guest."

"Of course, dear."

The women put their heads together again and resume their outpourings. Emilio smiles broadly.

"So," he says in Croatian, "so, you do not like her. And this I can understand because to tell you the truth I myself am not fond of her, though I am able to hide it for the sake of my Slavica, of whom I am very fond."

"Why are you not fond of your guest?" murmurs Josip.

"Perhaps it is for a different reason than yours."

"My reason?"

Emilio pauses to consider before answering. This is the longest and most intimate exchange they have had since they met.

"You are angry about the unfairness of existence, I think."

Josip, too, ponders before replying. "That may be true. Yet I also realize it would be unfair of me to judge. I do not know this woman."

"There is always more to people than we think."

"This I *do* know."

"Then—we will drink and smile and pretend we are thrilled by her company, no?"

Josip chuckles.

"Emilio, what did you say to Josip?" Slavica demands, breaking off in mid-sentence. "What did you say that made him laugh?"

"Weren't you listening, dear?"

"I was listening in English with both my ears, and not paying attention to you torturing Croatian grammar. Besides, I told you to speak Italian."

"Did you? Oh, I'm sorry."

Everyone laughs, and even the American lady joins in.

"Ah, the Tower of Babel", she says in Italian, her eyes flickering toward Josip to check on his response. He looks away.

"Come on," says Emilio, slapping Josip on the knee, "lets take a walk."

The women hardly notice them leaving, and soon the men are strolling by themselves alongside the Brenta.

"I suppose you have told her about me", murmurs Josip.

"Yes, of course", says Emilio in a thoughtful mood.

"Then I think it would be best if I return to the clinic now. I thank you for your kindness, but the evening will be a waste. This woman will not help me. Such people—" He stops himself. "I cannot say with certainty, but it seems to me that such people move through life without seeing what it is like for others. They are ignorant of what really goes on beneath their station in the world. And she is very high in this world."

Emilio clicks his tongue. "Sì! That is often the case. But not always. It is a roll of the dice, this meeting."

"She has agreed to meet me, I think, only because she likes her old friend from university times. In truth, she will do nothing, and she will have excellent excuses for it."

"Do you really think it will turn out that way?"

"Yes. I am a mental patient who does not speak her language. I am repulsive to look at with all my scars, and she comes from a world of lovely objects and ordered experiences, and she has never known deprivation. Hers is a world of beauty and achievement. If I were to work in her world, I would become a constant reminder of the dangers of human existence."

"You sound bitter, Josip."

"Do I? Perhaps I am bitter. In fact, I feel sad."

"She might enjoy having such a reminder. Maybe you will help her find some depth."

"That would be worse. Then I would function as the pathetic unfortunate kept like a hideous ornament in her beautiful world."

"Ooh-ooh, Josip, how hard you are on yourself. And how hard you are on life. Are people really as shallow as all that?"

"Yes, Emilio, they are. And for all kinds of excellent reasons."

Emilio chuckles and halts in order to light a cheroot. He blows smoke upward into the sky, the same way Simon Horvatinec did in his garden in Split. How many years ago? Three or four—yet it seems a lifetime has passed since then.

"This is forbidden", he explains. "Slavica will have a fit if she smells tobacco on me. She is always and everywhere worried that the people she loves will suddenly die."

"There are excellent reasons for this."

Emilio says nothing, merely puts a hand on Josip's shoulder, drops it, and then they walk on.

They return to the house only to find that the American lady has gone. When Josip hears the news, he exhales with relief.

"Ah, well", sighs Emilio.

"She didn't have much time to spare", says Slavica. "Tonight her husband is visiting the Consul in Venezia, and it cost her a lot to break away from a social event. She begged our pardons but had to hurry back and change clothes for it. She said she would much prefer to be with us and hopes to return before winter."

They sit down at the table. Grandmother joins them and sips from a glass of wine. She is so short that her feet barely touch the patio stones. She rocks back and forth, as so many old women do, like the goat-lady of Istria and the midwife of Rajska Polja.

"That poor woman has suffered", she exclaims out of the blue. The others stare at her.

"I don't think so, Mamma", says Emilio, then goes on to explain the woman's position and wealth.

"Yes, yes, yes, Milio, but I can see better than you. She's still nice-looking for her age and must have broken many boys' hearts in her time. But she is not happy."

"Cass?" exclaims Slavica. "Cass not happy? Oh, Mamma", she laughs.

"It's true. All that smiling and fine manners, but not happy. Not happy at all."

Slavica changes the subject:

"Josip, she was very impressed by you."

"In what way?" he murmurs with a frown.

"She thinks you're very nice."

"*Nice?*" says Emilio. "Heaven help us, I think I will have a cheroot."

He lights up, igniting a chain reaction of scolding, which he ignores.

The boy from Verona has been released, only to be replaced by two more boys, both recovering drug addicts and both ex-prostitutes. Josip does not understand this kind of horror, but he sees in their eyes what the drugs and degradation have done to them. One runs away and returns to the street-life of some Italian city. The other remains at the clinic and with the passage of weeks begins to respond positively to recitations from *The Odyssey*.

"Yes, life is like that", he says to Josip one afternoon, as they pick plums together. "I've met men like the Cyclops."

"I once met a Minotaur", muses Josip.

"No!" says the boy astonished. "Tell me about it."

"It was a struggle." Josip shrugs.

"He tried to kill you?"

"Yes."

"And did you escape?"

Josip laughs. "Yes, I did."

"I'll bet you wondered if you would escape, back then, when you were fighting him."

"Yes, I wondered."

He still wonders. Has he escaped? And what was lost while he was wrestling with the monster? His bride died with their child as he was being blown out to sea.

"Do you think a person can change—after he has done great wrong?" asks the boy in a strained voice, keeping his eyes on the branches.

"Yes, I am sure of it. But he must fight for it. He must fight harder than if he were wrestling with a Minotaur."

"Or with a Cyclops."

"One does not wrestle with a Cyclops. That is why Odysseus has much to teach us."

"What can he teach us?"

"He is not like Achilles, because Achilles is all rage and physical strength and he lacks wisdom."

"Are you a priest?" the boy asks suspiciously.

"No", Josip laughs again. "I am a gardener."

"So, how does one defeat monsters?"

"A man may defeat a monster and yet be defeated by his own heart."

"I do not understand."

"Odysseus must learn that he cannot win in the way that Achilles won at Troy. He must win by another method, for the monsters are too great for him. He uses his mind. He uses cunning and skill. Though he is strong in body, he knows it is not enough. To succeed in his *nostos* he must—"

"What's a *nostos*?"

"The homeward journey."

"Oh", frowns the boy, thinking. "So, how does he do it?"

"He defeats the monster within himself."

Another day.

"They do a lot of eating in that story."

"Yes, it's true."

"The monsters and the humans—they all eat like gluttons. They eat each other too!"

"Unfortunately, this is so."

"So, what do they all want? Why is everybody eating each other?"

"They are hungry. Achilles hungers for glory, and—"

"Wait, wait, who is this guy Achilles? He's not in this story."

"Yes, he is. You cannot truly understand *The Odyssey* without *The Iliad*."

"What's an Iliad?"

"It's this."

He hands the boy a paperbound copy of *The Iliad* in Italian. Then an Italian version of *The Odyssey*. He had purchased them with his monthly stipend.

"Hey, thanks."

"Will you read them?"

"Maybe." And the boy stuffs them into his back pockets.

They return to their fruit picking.

"Hey, boy", says Josip after a while.

"What?"

He tosses the lad a ripe plum, catching him off guard. The boy fumbles it, recovers, and pops it into his mouth. Smiling, chewing, he regards the scarred gardener with new curiosity. Then he removes something from his pocket and throws it at Josip.

The gardener catches it. It's an orange.

Another day. They are raking leaves together. A cool wind is blowing in from the northern Adriatic, promising rain.

"So, this king, he comes home in the end", says the boy.

"Yes, he comes home."

"He had a lot of trouble getting there."

"He did. But it was worth it."

"Was it?"

"Yes, and that's part of the *nostos*. The not-knowing is important."

"Why?"

"So, when you return, you find that you have returned with your whole self."

"You lost me again."

"You'll understand one day."

"You think? What if I don't come home?"

"Do you have a home?"

"Nope."

"Then you must make your home in your own heart."

These are noble sentiments. He plants them wherever he may, and perhaps life will permit them to sprout in the damaged lives of these children. Yes, they look like men, but they are just children. And maybe the seed he plants will grow into a big tree and bear its proper fruit in time. He hopes for this. What else can he do? As for himself, his bride-queen is lost, and he has no son to search for him. The immovable wedding-bed was moved—in fact, it sank in a sea of blood. Even so, others may escape, and he can help them a little. And his marriage will remain unshakable within his heart.

Slavica rushes into the clinic that evening, waving an envelope and dancing around his room.

"A letter! A letter from Cass!" she sings.

He is not interested and lets it show on his face.

"But Josip, it's about you! She has spoken to the officials at the embassy, and they have agreed to give you a job there in Rome—yes, right at the embassy. They need another grounds-keeper."

"I do not want the job."

"Don't be ridiculous", she exclaims, her face falling.

"I am happy here."

"Yes, but for how long? There's no wage. You have no future in this. And there's always a chance the government will ship you back to—"

"No, I have work to do here."

"What? Pruning bushes?"

No. Planting seeds, he thinks to himself. *It's not much, but it's what I know how to do.*

"You can prune bushes and cut grass in Rome, and besides, if you make good friends there, they may even give you refugee status; then you won't be sent back."

This is hard to ignore. He must think. His mind is swimming. He must think when he has calmed himself.

Josip is sitting in Emilio's dentist chair in his office in Mira. His mouth is full of wet plaster, which is hardening quickly. How does Emilio know for sure that once the plaster has hardened it can be removed? What if he made a mistake? Will it be necessary to chip it out with mallet and chisel?

It slides out easily.

"Soon you will have your smile back!" declares the dentist, with an operatic flourish.

"Why do you do it, Emilio? You are very kind, but I do not understand why you are so good to me and the others."

"The others? What are you talking about?"

"I know that you and Slavica pay the clinic fees for those boys—the drug addicts."

He shrugs and in a gruff voice commands: "Rinse!"

"Who told you that nonsense?" he asks, as Josip washes out his mouth.

"Amaliani."

"Well, we can spare it. We're rich enough."

"Look at your car. It's falling apart. Why do you drive an old Fiat like that, if you're so rich?"

"I like Fiats. They're the best on the road!"

"Why not a new one, then?"

"Automobiles are unreliable and dangerous slaves. They frequently revolt and kill their masters. I hate them. The cheaper the better, I say."

"Do you hate them as you hate chocolate?"

Emilio smiles pensively, puttering about with instruments on a tray. "Yes, like that."

A dinner party. Josip is doing a lot of grinning this evening. His dentures are so realistic that everyone oohs and ahs over them.

Paolo demands frequent showings, while Chiara goes so far as to pull up his lip without asking permission. Hands are slapped, jokes fly about the dining room, and the food is brought in, course after course after course. The planet has still not been incinerated. Spring is coming, buds are showing on the olive tree in the backyard, and nests are being built somewhere out there too! There is plenty of wine tonight, including a bottle from Yugoslavia, though Josip will not accept a glass—not even of this. Fruit juice is enough for him.

Tomorrow he leaves for Rome. He is staying the night with the Mazzuolos, who will drive him to the train station in the morning. Tonight they will celebrate. They have come to think of him as part of their family. How long has he been visiting their home? Two years, three years maybe. No one quite remembers.

Dr. Amaliani drops in for an hour and brings news about one of the drug addicts: the boy has found a job and is staying clean, and he seems happy living with the religious brothers in Padova who work with the young. Amaliani gives Josip an envelope with a wad of *lire* inside, enough for train fare and a few meals along the way, with some left over for a new shirt. He has also brought a parting gift of shiny black shoes: giant-sized for giant feet, he says, not easy to find in this country! But he must leave early, with regrets, because his wife is waiting for him. They made a date with each other months ago—they are off to Venezia to see the new Fellini film. He shakes hands with Josip and says his last good-bye, with thanks for all he has done.

The doctor departs, and the feast continues. It does not so much end as it tapers interminably. Finally, *gelato* is brought in from the kitchen in fancy dishes, plenty of chocolate for everyone but Emilio, who seems well pleased with his little scoop of vanilla.

As everyone dips into the desserts, Josip scrapes back his chair and stands up. All eyes turn to him.

"I have some things to give you", he says. "They are not much, and maybe they are too simple, compared to all you have done for me."

"Oh, Josip, that is not necessary!" scolds Slavica.

"For you, Slavica", he says, turning to her, "I have only words to give. I wish it were more, but this is what I have. They are in memory of your father. They are also in memory of all fathers, and the father of your children too."

Silence falls on the table. Josip removes a piece of paper from his pocket, holds it before him and slowly recites:

In a father's toil-worn face can be read the epic tale:
Within his eyes is a boy I once knew
though we never met.
See how he carries you and carries me
And the offspring of his soul
as if we weigh no more than birds perching on his fingertips
yet are dearer to him than the stars.

It is there in his eyes, not easily read,
Each true man is like this, holding within himself
A world that once was, a world that may be made anew.
He knows himself as incomplete, sees his failures
As do all men before the ending of their tale.
Though with each ending a beginning is writ,
Each death is birth for which he knows full well the cost,
Yet this price could not be paid alone, without you.

Finished, he sits down. Slavica is leaning forward, her eyes beaming moistly as she glances at Josip and her husband. She claps her hands vigorously, and the children and old mother join in. Emilio leans back in his chair, his eyes fixed on Josip, a whimsical smile playing about his lips.

"Oh, sì, sì, Josip," says Slavica, with a lump in her throat, "the poem is so much like Emilio! Yes, that is our Papà! Thank you, thank you, and now let us kiss you, if you will permit us?"

The children rush over and kiss Josip, and Slavica gives a kiss to his cheek as well, and the grandmother grins with her naked gums and rocks back and forth in her chair. And still Emilio continues to gaze at Josip with a pondering expression.

"I have something for you too, Emilio", he says diffidently and stands again. Because the table is wide and the men are seated across from each other, Emilio must stand also. Josip stretches and into the other's hands places a package wrapped in foil.

"Thank you", murmurs Emilio shaking it curiously. "It's heavy. What is it? A gold bar?"

"Yes, a gold bar."

Emilio unwraps it and holds up a large bar of Swiss chocolate.

"Oh, that kind is so expensive!" gasps Slavica. "You shouldn't have, Josip, but what a fine gift!"

Emilio nods at Josip and sits down, looking with some puzzlement at the bar in his hands.

"But Mamma, this isn't right!" cries Paolo. "Josip got the presents mixed up. The poem is for Papà, and the chocolate is for you!"

"Tsk! Paolo, Paolo, Paolo, you rude boy! If Josip wants to give me a poem, that's his business. And if he wants to give your Papà some chocolate, that's all right, too!"

"But Papà hates chocolate!"

"He doesn't hate chocolate; he just doesn't eat it."

"He *must* hate it because I have never seen him eat it. Never!"

All heads turn in Josip's direction. He clears his throat.

"Emilio?"

"Sì."

"You have no brothers and sisters."

"Yes, that's so. How did you guess?"

"I know."

"You know? Maybe you made a wild guess. For a family in my country it is not usual, eh, to be an only child. Come on, who told you? Slavica?"

"Not Slavica. You were the only one to look after your mother when you came back from the war, weren't you?"

"The war?" Emilio frowns, waving a hand dismissively, "I was a boy then. A long time ago."

"When you returned from across the sea—"

"That's right," says his mother, "away he goes across the Adriatico, and then a few months later he comes sailing back again without a scratch."

"And that is when you made a promise", Josip continues.

Emilio looks up and gazes at Josip with great seriousness.

"Yes, that's when."

"A promise you have kept."

"Yes, always."

"You do not hate chocolate."

"I love chocolate."

"Now you must eat some, for your promise is fulfilled."

Emilio's urbanity and whimsical manner have completely vanished. He puts a finger across the bridge of his nose, head down, staring at the table top.

He opens the wrapper, breaks a piece from the bar, and puts it slowly onto his tongue. He closes his mouth and his eyes, as tears run down his cheeks.

"Now I will tell you a story", whispers Josip.

27

In the end, he does not take the train to Rome. He decides to walk. Slavica, Emilio, and the children drive him to Padova, and there they let him out of the car on the highway to Bologna.

In the folios of memory there are many tears, but this scene of tears is like no other. It is a convergence of rivers, draining the wide green valley of the Udine and flowing into the sea. He shoulders his knapsack, which they have stuffed with food and mementos. As he walks away from them down the road, he looks back again and again, seeing their souls fused into one form that diminishes in size and disappears into the past—waving and waving until it becomes entirely memory.

Now he is again the walker of the world, and he understands the necessity of this walking. No longer is it a fleeing-from, it is a going-to. It is the counterpoint of flight; it is the search for completion, the arc between departure and arrival. It is *nostos*. The home of his past is behind, the home of his future is ahead in the unknown territory he must cross. He knows that he will live in the fabled city for a time, yet as he walks through the flat farmland and orchard country of northern Italy he dreams of another home. It is ahead and undefined, yet it is already taking shape within him. It has no form or detail and may be far away or near—he does not know. This sense cannot be dismissed, for it tells him that a momentous turning point is walking toward him, even as he walks toward it.

What is remembered, what is forgotten? Why are some things stored away forever, while others resurface again and again?

Who sifts through the material, who sorts and files it? A Renaissance palace is swiftly forgotten, while blue wings slicing arcs in the wind will be remembered always, in tandem with swallows swooping in coordinated flocks. Also imprinted is a barefoot child at a gate with a lamb standing docile beside him, the lamb's neck looped by a cord of red wool held tightly in the child's hand. There is a stone thrown at the walker by an unseen hand beyond a fence, but a cup of water is offered by a girl who appears from behind another fence farther along the road. Such events are both strange and familiar. Simple exchanges link them together, the media of humanity: food, gestures, and sometimes words: *Grazie* or *Godspeed* or *Safe journey, Sir.* There is a jug of cow's milk purchased from an old man at his farmhouse door and a bowl of pasta purchased in a village café, served by a grudging matron whose disapproval and suspicion are an essential part of her maternal style. When he smiles at her, the scowl transforms into a smile returned, and an extra serving, free of charge.

There are beautiful churches everywhere in this region—Romanesque and Renaissance and Baroque—the latter in a city he passes through with hurried pace. Was it back there in Bologna? He cannot remember where it was.

He understands that his many small adventures along the way will also fade in time: the changing landscape, roadside water wells named for saints, atonal bells in impoverished stone chapels. Though he cannot enter them, he is grateful that someone built these structures long ago, and that invisible people still pull the ropes of their campaniles at eventide and dawn. So many people are encountered on his journey, and there is no explaining why this one is remembered and that one forgotten. It is all part of a whole, the kindness of strangers, the harshness of strangers, the mixture of good and evil in strangers. At the same time, an uncanny sense of familiarity is growing, as if he knows this land and this people very well. The impression increases as the road goes ever upward, and his feet find themselves passing deeper into the Appennino. At nightfall, especially, he is sometimes startled to see spires glowing red in the sunset, surrounded by hilltop towns that, in the dwindling light, are like castles in dreams. He dreams when he sleeps—good dreams, for in them dolphins leap in the sea spray, and children standing on white-pebbled shores speak poems to them as they speed away, smiling as they disappear.

The hills are dry, and in this too he senses his past, for it is not unlike Istria. The hills are now rising higher and higher, and they appear in the dawn as sawtooth ridges and peaks. The days are still warm, though at these altitudes a chill can settle in swiftly when darkness falls and the stars come out to sing. Each night he sleeps rolled up in his blanket beside the road, hoping that snakes will not find him. Sometimes he sits down on a rock beside the road for no reason at all and sometimes, while he is sitting there, he cries. He is not sure about the reason for these tears. Perhaps he is merely fatigued. Or it may be that he cannot always distinguish between his losses and blessings, and the release of tears reduces the pressure. He does not know. Generally, he feels happy and, at times, elated. The mountains are intimations of transcendence, which he is now free to pursue, and the walking writes messages in every cell of his body, telling him that he is not locked inside a cement box, nor in a water drum, but is moving forward. The walking and the sun, the air and the food, and the sensation of progress all conspire to strengthen him with every passing day. He does not drive himself overmuch but does persevere beyond the little complaints of his reawakening muscles. Both they and his stamina are growing.

Once, he kneels beside a natural pool at the bottom of a narrow valley. He drinks from it as a man, not as an animal, for he carries a tin cup in his backpack. When the ringlets of disturbance flatten out into a mirror, he sees his reflection and notices that he is not as old as he was in Venezia. His hair is light-colored and thick again and is growing blonder under the beating sun. His face is lean and tanned, and his hands are wide and strong, no longer the claws of a skeleton. And his smile, admittedly artificial, is sincere and not unpleasing. Though the eyes are not those of a young man exactly, neither are they the eyes of an old man. How old is he, then? What year is this? Oh, yes, it's 1964. He was born in 1933. This makes him—how old?—well, no matter. Adding and subtracting are for mathematicians. It is enough to live.

Now the Appennino range spreads its arms and expands its chest, and the route descends through foothills into the valley of the Arno. In the distance appears Firenze, its domes rising rose-red above a golden mist. Bells ring continuously, it seems, as he walks through its streets, pausing only a few times to absorb the meanings in faces—especially the very young and the very old. Then, by nightfall he is beyond the city and going deeper into the Valdarno. The energy needed to resist the city's distractions has tired him, and he rolls up in his blanket an hour after leaving it behind. He sleeps by a field of tomato plants. Their odor inebriates and pushes him into dreams. In the morning, he rises and shakes the dew from his blanket, shoulders his knapsack, and walks on.

Day after day he walks, the weather growing fiercely hot at times, succeeded by overcast and rain. It is pleasant to drink from the sky. The rain cools his body and soothes his soul, at one point gently pushing him from the road onto a path that leads him into the hills. There he loses himself in a thicket of wild trees and thornbushes, a place where people seldom seem to go. In a shadowed glade, he comes upon a man-made pool that looks ancient, its stone blocks overgrown with moss and cracked by the roots of bushes. Though floating lilies are taking over, the water is spring-fed and clean. He removes his clothing and stands beneath an outpouring of the heavens, as if it were the first day of creation. He washes his clothing, scrubbing it with hand soap, holding it up for the rain to rinse, and then sloshing it in the pool. He wades in as a child would wade, laughing and splashing about. When the sun comes out again, he drapes his clothes on the surrounding bushes and sits shivering and exposed to the light until they are dry. Then it is time to move on.

He is in Umbria now, with lovely hills rising to the left and the right. He passes roads that cross his path, leading off into the hills. At various junctions, there are signs with names he recognizes—Spoleto, Assisi, Rieti, Gubbio—places in stories that Fra Anto once told to the children of Rajska Polja. He would like to see Assisi, far up in the hills, but it would be impossible to enter the shrine of the saint. Perhaps he could go to Rieti, where St. Francis received the stigmata. No, that might hurt too much, to see it yet be unable to kneel and pray. Perhaps he could go to Gubbio, where the saint tamed a man-eating wolf. He stops and ponders these choices, trying to decide. In the end, he continues along the road toward Rome.

Before he knows it, he is crossing another river—the Tevere, the Tiber—and then walking beside it going south, always south. He carries a map but does not consult it, preferring to let the world surprise him. The river will bring him to the city, because it is the mother of Rome. The valley curves this way and that, and now great pine trees increase in number, their bare trunks soaring all the way up to wide-spreading black canopies. At their feet are a litter of seed-cones. He rests in the shadow of one such tree and is narrowly missed by a missile from a lofty branch, thumping to the ground only centimeters away. Picking it up he twirls it in his fingers, noting the spiral symmetry. He sniffs its sap, which is like incense, then puts the cone into his knapsack and continues on his way.

Memory will bring forth from its storage house things both old and new. Of that day's context, he will remember dust and stone, blindingly-white marble, and noise such as he has never before experienced. Streets are crammed with automobiles that speed and screech and honk and brake and lurch from stable positions at traffic lights into a blur of motion—all with the manic pace and the demonic roars of dangerous, unreliable slaves. The drivers' faces are the worst aspect. They are as intense as any he has seen in his life, even the guards on the island, certain interrogators, or various prisoners who would bolt from their chains in a hopeless run toward the sea.

He inquires of a pedestrian where he might find the American embassy and is told that he must continue into the heart of the city and cross over such and such a bridge—the Ponte Margherita—and then keep going till he reaches a park, the Villa Borghese. You can't miss it; it's very big. The embassy is below it, on Via Veneto.

So, he continues along the banks of the Tiber, preparing to cross over to his left, when he sees the dome of St. Peter's rising above the rooftops on the right. Of their own will, his feet take him in that direction. They bring him to a street that leads into a vast open piazza in front of the basilica. He takes a few steps forward and comes to a halt, gazing about with wonder and a certain unease. He has seen pictures of this place since earliest childhood. This is the center of the world.

Because he cannot enter the church, he turns to go, feeling the deepest sadness that he must leave. He recalls that his parents once desired to make a pilgrimage to this place. Now their son is here without their faith, and they are dead.

He pauses and goes back into the piazza. He will wait a few minutes in memory of his mother and father. He will look up at the sky, and perhaps his thoughts will shape a little prayer, like a clay bird formed in the hands, warmed there too, and he will breathe into its mouth. Perhaps the dead clay will quicken and shake its feathers and spring up from his fingers into the wind and rise toward heaven. *Do not break us—do not break us*, it will cry, as its wings beat against the force of gravity, its small eyes seeing for the first time the secret shape of the world.

He smiles, walking about the piazza, shaping the wet clay in his mind.

I do not know if what I have lost can be found again. I would ask you for help, if I believed, but I send you this bird instead, for it carries my request. It may be that you are there and will receive my messenger.

He throws his arms into the air, and the bird rises and disappears. He laughs to himself and turns away, intending to leave the piazza now.

There are many people here today, walking about, taking photographs, kneeling, talking, courting, praying, pointing, going into the basilica and coming out of it. Here and there along the pillared colonnade, a few priests sit on portable chairs. Some wear religious habits, some, black suits—all with purple stoles about their necks. Moving toward each are lines of pilgrims waiting to confess.

As he is leaving the piazza, he notices a priest in brown robes, alone in the shadows of the colonnade, where the sun cannot burn him, near the last pillar. He is seated on a box, his head bowed, fingering a rosary. He is a Franciscan of some kind, because his robes are like Fra Anto's. His head is tonsured in the old manner, a ring of white fuzz around the crown of his skull. His long beard is white, threaded with gray strands. His feet are shod in rough sandals. Only the movement of his fingers indicates that his lined face is not asleep.

Josip approaches, lingering another moment in memory of Fra Anto.

The friar whispers something. Thinking that the priest has called to him, Josip approaches.

"Please, I did not hear."

"I said, welcome", whispers the friar with closed eyes.

"Thank you."

"Come closer."

"I must be on my way—good day to you!"

"Come closer, and do not be afraid."

"I am not afraid, good Father."

"You are afraid, good son, but your message is heard."

"What did you say?"

"Your messenger has delivered its word."

Josip smiles indulgently. Poor old priest.

"Will you not hear *my* messenger?" the friar whispers.

For a moment Josip hesitates, and then, without knowing he is going to do it, he falls to his knees before the man.

"Wh-why do you speak to me this way?" he stammers.

"Do not be afraid", murmurs the friar, "Oh, do not be afraid of love."

"I-I am not afraid of love."

"The words you send to me are heard. Always they are heard. Now I speak to you, my son, from my heart. Bring your sorrows to me and give them to me, for no longer will you call yourself forsaken."

"I-I do not understand. Who are you and what are you saying to me?"

"Welcome", whispers the priest once more.

"I must go!"

"The door opens before you. Walk through it now, and everything else will follow."

"I cannot," he chokes, "I cannot."

"You can if you choose. You are free to choose. You are afraid of the pain."

"Yes", he whispers.

"And the blood in which you drowned?"

"Yes."

"I am with you, do not fear. Now you may confess and be cleansed, if you choose."

For some moments, Josip wrestles silently. His hands are by his side, his head bowed, and he sways on his knees. Still the priest has not opened his eyes, though his fingers continue to move on the beads.

"It has been—it has been—many years since my last confession—", Josip begins. He breaks down sobbing as the priest makes the sign of the cross over him.

"How many years?"

"I think I was twelve years old then, before—"

"Before the men of darkness came, and the blood."

Startled, Josip stares at the old man's face. Instinctively, he moves backward on his knees.

"Do not be afraid. See the door is opening."

"I can't see it."

"Just begin. You know how it must be, for you are one who walks. First a step, then another."

So begins his confession, his first since the world ended. How long does such a confession take when a lifetime of sin is remembered. The storerooms open one after another, the cellars too—though not all at once. The sun soars across the sky, and the shadows of the pillars move with it. Pigeons land nearby, strut about, then fly off. Sometimes people line up behind Josip, but his confession does not cease—it stretches into a suspension of time. They leave and find lines that move.

How is it so, all this sin he has committed? Why is there so much when he thought he was good? His youthful errors had been minor, his moments of great darkness had been both few in number and swift in passing. So, he had thought. Now, as he and the priest fall silent together, he knows there is more.

"Once, long ago," Josip whispers, "I desired to kill a man. And if I had not been a boy at the time, if I had been stronger, I would have killed him."

"With the hatchet."

"Yes", breathes Josip, astonished again.

527

"Yet you did not commit this act, and so it is the heart alone that sinned, and the guilt is lessened because no man died."

"But he did die. Later he took his own life, or it may be that another killed him. And I felt I had a part in it too, for I greatly desired his death and hated him."

Telling him what the eyes of wisdom see in events that occurred twenty years ago and in the conscience of a child caught up in them, the priest speaks to Josip's heart. Then he reaches into Josip's damaged thoughts with truth and grace so that the penitent begins to understand the measures of guilt and innocence concerning his own life. And so a burden is lifted from him.

"There are two more", says the priest.

"Two more?"

Then Josip sees the faces of Zmija and Goran. Yes, there are two more.

"The stone", the friar prompts. "And iron in the fist."

Josip is becoming accustomed to this priest knowing things that no man could know without witnessing them. Who is he? He glances at the friar's hands. They are ordinary hands, wizened and dry. There is no stigmata, no unnatural transparency. The blood pulses normally within a vein. He is neither an angel nor a saint revisiting the earth. An ordinary man, an ordinary priest. But why is he speaking this way, and how does he know these things?

"The stone", the friar prompts again.

Josip confesses his attempt to murder Zmija. On that day, he had become like Cain again, and only the hand of another priest had stopped him from becoming Cain in his act.

Once more the friar speaks to Josip with anointed words, words that will remain forever. Another burden is lifted.

"And the third", says the friar. "The iron in your hand that would have struck. Though it was not murder, it was the threat of murder, and the full rage of it was in your heart. You must bring this to the Lord, too."

And so he does, exposing what happened when he stood over Goran in a dark alley and was seized by a passion to smash his skull and destroy the evil within him, but blinded to the evil that would have leaped like a snake from that dying body into his own.

Now he sees it in the light of day and confesses it. There is more to tell, and it all comes out: his despair, the time he tried to take his own life—to murder himself. When he is finished, he is emptier than he has ever felt before, but there is peace in this emptiness and a sense of profound rest.

"For your penance, pray a Rosary for the soul of each one whom you desired to kill. Three souls, three Rosaries. Will you do this?"

"Yes", Josip whispers.

"Good", says the friar. "Yet more do I ask of you. Not as your penance; rather, this is for the strengthening of your soul. It is what Christ asks of each of us. For the remainder of your life, do good to those who harm you. Bless your enemies, and do not hate them. Pray for them, and do not hold them to account."

"I will try."

"In Christ's grace, you can do this. Though the sins committed against you are most grievous and would test the greatest of souls, you have been given a cross and a blessing that few can receive. Will you ask each day for the grace to forgive?"

"I will ask—for without God's help it is not possible. Each day of my life I will ask for the impossible."

"He is Master of the Impossible."

The priest hears Josip's act of contrition and absolves him, making the sign of the cross over him.

"You are free. The Lord is with you."

"Thank you, Father", whispers Josip, rising on trembling legs.

"Now, my son, go to the house of the Lord, to God, the joy of your youth."

Falling silent again, Josip turns and faces the wide-open doors of St. Peter's across the piazza.

"I-I do not know if I have the strength to enter."

"You do not need strength. You need the heart of a child. See, one comes to you now. He will show you the way."

Though the old man still has not opened his eyes, he points, and there at the end of his fingers, standing a few paces away, is a twelve-year-old boy in white shirt and white shorts, with sandals on his feet. When Josip meets his eyes, the boy smiles and extends his hand.

Puzzled, Josip takes the hand in his own and lets the child lead him across the square. Neither the man nor the boy speaks. No questions are asked. It is as if they have always known each other. They are father and son, yet, as they approach the staircase, he sees the body of a mutilated man lying there exposed on the top, and his heart beats hard with horror, and he no longer knows who is the father and who is the son.

Step by step, the child leads him upward toward the entrance, pulling gently, looking back with an encouraging smile. Now they are standing on the stone porch of the basilica; now they are moving forward, and the little hand is glowing like a small sun in his own.

Fra Anto's body is blocking the entrance, as it does on the steps of every church. But now a white robe floats down from the sky and covers him. Only his damaged face is visible, as well as his hands with their holes, and his feet with their holes. Josip can step over him, and he knows that he *must* step over him. He moves forward, but in that step he dies. Pitching headlong into those wounds, he falls and falls and falls—into terror and despair. Then, the little hand pulls him up. Now he is standing again and going forward past the body, and at last he enters the house of God, the joy of his youth.

28

The boy remains silently beside him throughout that first Mass. When Josip opens his mouth to receive Communion, peace flows through his body, like a current of warm oil. He closes his eyes as he kneels on the floor of the basilica, near the main altar, above the place where it is said the Fisherman is buried.

Later, when he opens his eyes and gets up off his knees, he looks about and sees that the boy has gone.

For three days, he resides in a pilgrims' hostel a few streets from St. Peter's Square. Silence is one of the house rules. Silence, plenteous simple food, and prayer. Several men sleep on cots alongside him in the attic dormitory. Many of them fall asleep each night whispering prayers, with rosaries in their hands. Wordlessly, an old man gives Josip his rosary, a cord of knotted string. Its cross is made of tin with five holes in it.

"From Rieti", the old man whispers, and goes away.

People come and go in the hostel, and none of them does Josip meet again in this life.

When he is able, when he is ready, he leaves that place and crosses the Tiber and makes his way through the streets to the Villa Borghese. Strolling on its pathways, he is like a man in a dream, carrying peace within and carried by peace as well. He is in no hurry to meet his future now. When time no longer exists, the present contains a new fullness, in which both past and future dissolve.

There comes an hour, however, when he knows it is time to leave the park and to resume his search for Via Vittorio Veneto.

Within minutes, he arrives at the grounds of the embassy. After showing his letter to a guard at the gate, he is permitted to enter and is led to the office of the day laborers. There an Italian foreman reads the letter and nods.

"Well, you're three weeks late", he grumbles. "But you have friends higher up, and they say to let you in and show you the ropes when you arrive. So, come this way, and I'll teach you your duties."

It is not much. In fact, it is not like work at all, simply a continuation of what he has been doing for the past two or three years. He sweeps the walkways in the back garden, gathers the leaves and dog droppings, scrubs the front steps with a brush and bucket of water, washes the exterior windows, and paints the iron railings. It is much the same for ten hours a day, five days a week, except that he will be paid in cash every Friday afternoon.

The foreman finds him a room in an old house near the city's rail terminal. The *padrona di casa* is a widow who takes in boarders, and she will give him low rent if he helps clean the building on Saturdays and fixes broken things now and then. His room is a dark cubby at the back of the house, with a private entrance off the alley. There is a cot, a wooden chair, and a cold-water tap that drains into a hole in the floor. Beside it is a washstand with a metal pitcher and bowl. Above that hangs a faded print of the Sacred Heart of Jesus. Josip is quite pleased with the place, though it is noisy night and day with the sound of trains and cars and yowling cats. The alley is crawling with cats, slinking in and out of crannies and between garbage cans, chasing birds and rats. There are a lot of cats in this city, and it seems that most of them have no owners. The foreman tells Josip that Romans respect the wild cats and never harm them because during the war the city was very hungry—many people were starving, yes, right here in Rome, and they ate cats to stay alive. Now the poor creatures have a special status, because people remember this.

One whole day Josip prunes the ancient olive in the embassy garden, a tree older than any he has ever seen. This excites the foreman's anxiety, because the tree was planted by a member of the Italian royal house a long time ago, when the embassy was a palace.

On his next day off—his first Sunday in Rome—he attends Mass at St. Peter's again. The boy does not appear, and Josip is able to enter through the front doors with only a little trepidation. Though the body of Fra Anto remains where it was, it is now possible to pass him with a prayer and a respectful bow of his head. Later in the afternoon, he writes a letter to Slavica and Emilio, telling them that he has arrived safely and is settling into his new life quite well. He mentions that he has been to the sacraments and is at peace. He prays now; yes, he has begun to pray a lot, and he is sorry that it has taken him so long to return to the practice. Among his prayers, he promises, are petitions for the patients at the clinic and the hospital in Venezia. He does not forget each member of their family and thanks them again for all they have done for him. He begs their continued prayers that he will find his path. Perhaps, if they keep praying for him, he will be able to stay permanently in their country.

Little by little, he becomes familiar with the city. If he rises early enough, he can walk across the Ponte Garibaldi and attend Mass at the chapel of Santa Cecilia in Trastevere, where the body of the saint is entombed, incorrupt since the third century. Some mornings, he recalls the incorrupt body of a nun that he saw when he walked through the hills of Istria and slept unheeding beside her in the little chapel with the well. He remembers the mysterious sun that warmed him and gave him strength to continue. Who was that saint, preserved by heaven for an unknown purpose? And whose hand was it that had been raised in a priestly blessing? Now he will never know, because it is impossible to return to his homeland.

So far Josip has not encountered Mrs. Conway. Does she live in this great palace? He would like to thank her for her help in obtaining the job. The foreman tells him that he doesn't know the names of all the Americans who work here. There are a lot of them, and maybe a few are supposed to remain secret. But he does know who Mr. Conway is—he comes to the embassy a few times a week, though he works in another building in a different part of the city—part of the United States Mission to Italy—mostly it concerns itself with money problems between the two countries. Or maybe other things—he doesn't know for sure. All that is too far above his head.

Josip meets her at the end of his third week of employment. It is a Friday morning, with plenty of sunshine and a strong evergreen smell baking in the hedge beside the "elephant steps", as they are called. He is sweeping this long staircase of wide steps that ascend from the garden to an upper prom-enade. The Italian princesses once led their pet elephant up and down on it. He is about halfway down when she appears at the bottom and glances up, her eyes assessing the scattering of leaves and brush. She climbs the stairs toward him, taking care not to soil her gold shoes in the debris. Her hair and her dress are gold as well. Her skin is also gold. There is gold at her earlobes and on her wrists. Speechless for a moment, he steps aside, clearing his throat, and is about to catch her attention. But she brushes past him, casting a brief smile and an apprais-ing look, then moves on.

"Mrs. Conway", he says in unsteady English.

She stops and turns around. "Yes?" she asks with upraised brows.

"Mrs. Conway, I wish to thank you for—"

Her puzzled look is replaced by sudden recognition. She extends a hand, which he does not see at first, but then notices and shakes once, manfully, and drops.

"*Joe-seep?*"

"Yes, Madame, it is I."

This makes her titter and cover her mouth. "Well, I wouldn't have recognized you. Not at all. You look as if you've dropped fifteen years since I last saw you. It's been, what, almost a year? But here you are at last!"

"You are part in it Mrs. Conway cannot be replaced, for new hope it gives to me this position."

Chuckling once more, perhaps because of his stilted English, she puts a hand on his arm, becomes willowy, and steps a little too close. "Oh, not at all. I did nothing really, just a word here or there."

"I thank you for it." He bows his head in deference.

"Well, I must be off. Please give my very best to dear Slavica. I don't know when I'll get up to Venice again, but if I ever do—" She turns to go, then pauses. "Oh, I forgot. Are you an Italian citizen now?"

"No, I am waiting because I do not see what I do. It may be they send me back."

"To Yugoslavia? Oh, I surely hope not!"

"I hope it not, too."

"Don't worry", she smiles reassuringly, patting his arm. "I'll put in a word here and there. Now, I have to go because the women are planning a garden party."

Off she goes up the elephant stairs, skipping and humming to herself—a strong and beautiful woman with a nice laugh. Well, it's nice enough if she is not laughing at him. Good-bye, American lady. I do not think so badly of you now, but why are you the way you are? Why do I feel like a simple-minded child when you speak to me? Am I still so repulsive, have I become the hideous ornament at your garden party, am I in need of your condescending pity?

Yes, Josip nods to himself. Yes, I do very much need your pity, because your pity may inspire you to help me, and your help may keep me from being torn to pieces by wolves and sharks, or being pressed into wine under the most beautiful limestone in the world.

The Roman Forum is a fascinating place: a metropolis for the imagination to reconstruct. After Mass on Sundays, Josip usually spends a few hours wandering about the ruins, trying to see it as it once was. He also likes to go to the Gregorian University now and then, because it revives a lost sense of his university years. There are evenings when he sits alone in his room trying to reconstruct the cosmology, the fragments he had composed in Split, which his interrogators seized and doubtless destroyed. He cannot remember much of it, a few pieces only.

As Christmas approaches, he thinks of Ariadne more and more, recalling every detail of their only Christmas together, before the world ended. Their child would be how old now? Five or six? Does this little soul see him, look down from paradise and think about its father? Was Ariadne able to baptize the baby before its death?

He attends the great Mass on the evening of the twenty-fourth and feels his sorrows anew. The sins committed against his family have left a gap in the world and a void in his heart. Is it a void—or is it a stable waiting to be filled? How hard it is to keep from falling under the tyranny of dark emotions. The desire to kill has left him, hopefully forever, but the feelings of confused rage and helplessness that sometimes rise up to overwhelm him have not yet disappeared. As the Pope lifts the Body of Christ above the altar of the world, Josip bows, worshipping and pleading, asking Christ's forgiveness for all the anger still inside him.

After Mass, he remains kneeling at the very back. When the crowds have thinned he goes forward to reverence the kiss-smoothed feet of the statue of St. Peter. Then it is possible to go out into the world again with peace in his heart, bearing no man ill will—repentant and poor and repulsive, yet grateful. In this manner, he passes the body of Fra Anto with respect and a prayer for his soul, without fear, returns to his room with the holy fire in his breast, and resumes his life of ordinary things.

Do I forgive? he asks himself as he sweeps the embassy driveway, between the arrivals and departures of limousines. Do I forgive everything? And how may I fulfill my promise? How can I do good to those who harm me? No one has harmed me here, and though the people I know are few in number, they are good and generous. The evil ones are all behind me in the past.

Now it is May. Flowers fill the market stalls everywhere, and the city has begun to bake in the heat of the growing sun. Josip has become a trusted employee. This remains something of a mystery. Who protects him; who upholds his status? Is he a unique category suspended between the worlds of the privileged and the absolutely dispossessed? How does he continue to float? Perhaps it is Mrs. Conway who has brought this about. If so, she is better than he thought, for it seems she has asked for nothing in return. He has seen her in passing a few times, waving from a distance with a lingering look before she enters the embassy. Has she put in a word here and there? Or has he merely been overlooked? Will the Italian government pry into his whereabouts, ask who is this man working at the American embassy without records or identification papers, and how does he pay his taxes? And why does he breathe Roman air as if it were his own? Are they like this, he wonders. Maybe not. Perhaps it is just his fears speaking to him. There are more Africans in the city now, people with scars on their faces and less visible scars within their eyes, so it may be that this country is kind to those who flee their nations without papers.

Occasionally, he must work at night inside the building, after the doors of offices are locked. An American guard will pace about the hallways while Josip and a few other servants vacuum and dust or wash the insides of windows. All wastebaskets are emptied by other staff—Americans only; then the papers are fed into shredding machines in the basement and incinerated in a furnace. Yes, the world is full of secrets.

On some evenings, the embassy is not deserted. There are parties in the salons of the upper floor and larger events in the ballroom below, with stringed instruments playing among ancient, very valuable Roman sculptures. The cleaning staff cannot go down there whenever a ball is in progress, nor can they vacuum because of the noise. But there is plenty to do nevertheless, such as stripping the wax from the hallways of the office floors and then washing, drying, and rewaxing. Usually by dawn the revelers are gone, leaving only the workers and the guards. Then he is permitted to drive the big polishing machine that turns the hallway into glass, making a fine smell like candles. He loves this part, he supposes, because he commands for a very brief time a powerful machine. Well, it is fun! When the work shift ends, he goes out through the gates, salutes the guard, and walks across the river, arriving at the tomb of Santa Cecilia in time for morning Mass. The city is quietest then. Afterward, he will see swallows swooping over the river as they hunt insects at sunrise.

He is sweeping the elephant staircase again today. What a clean-up job it must have been when the elephants went up and down it daily. Now it is used only by officials and special guests. What makes a guest "special"? It is hard to say. Perhaps it is anyone who has business dealings with the Americans, and possibly they have personal relationships as well. Yes, of course, they would—they are human after all!

He has just finished this musing when two figures appear from around the hedge, about ten elephant-steps above him. They halt at the top, and, as he shields his eyes from the direct rays of the sun, he notes that they are women. Indeed, one of them is Mrs. Conway. They have their heads together and are tittering and whispering. He does not like the sound of it. Very adolescent. They link arms and step down the staircase like new-world princesses. As they approach, he notes that their faces are coyly, conspiratorially smiling—again like silly girls talking about boys. They are eyeing him with interest.

He straightens and assumes his formal posture, useful for maintaining distance.

Mrs. Conway comes to a stop, gives him a smile, and says, "This is Joe-*seep*, our foundling." More titters.

"Joe-*seep*, this is my friend, Mrs. Sybil-Pfiefer."

"How do you do, Madame", he says with a nod of the head.

"Divine", says the woman, catching Mrs. Conway's eye.

She offers her hand in the exquisitely extended gesture of a genteel woman bestowing largesse. He shakes it and drops it as quickly as possible.

"Mrs. Sybil-Pfiefer is with the British embassy", Mrs. Conway explains. "Rather, her husband is. In any event, I wanted her to meet you because she has just returned from a holiday in Yugoslavia."

What to say? *Oh, I am glad you escaped! No one killed you?*

"Dubrovnik was splendid", effuses Mrs. Sybil-Pfiefer. "So warm and friendly, and the colors—all turquoisy and reddish, especially the big creamy castle. And, if you can believe it, oranges simply dropping into our laps wherever we turned. The Yugoslav government gave us guides who were *so* good to us. Wonderful hotels and meals that I can't describe—heavenly!"

"And the tallest men in the world", adds Mrs. Conway with a little smile, provoking another titter from her friend.

"I am happy you see it, my country", murmurs Josip. "It is beautiful, with many difficulty there now."

The British woman flutters her hand. "Well, you're so right

on that point. It wasn't *all* a bed of roses. In Dubrovnik, we visited an utterly fascinating aquarium with tanks full of fish and other marine creatures. But I must say I was appalled at the treatment one poor creature receives. It was a giant sea turtle paddling about in a tank like a hole in the floor. I mean, really, it had been there for decades and decades, and it looked terribly unhappy with its lot."

"It was well fed, I suppose", says Mrs. Conway.

"Oh, I expect so, otherwise it would have died. But really, how cruel to imprison a creature of the wilds like that in such a small tank! We lodged a formal complaint with the Yugoslav government. Hugh has connections, you know, because he's liasing our cultural exchange program with the President's office in Belgrade."

"Good for you, Sarah", says Mrs. Conway.

Josip resumes sweeping.

"Well, *lovely* to have met you", sparkles Mrs. Sybil-Pfiefer. The women continue on their way, with backward glances and heads together, comparing notes.

Good-bye, turtle-lady, good-bye gold America-lady, please do not speak to me again about your moral outrage. Please take a holiday on a white island in the northern Adriatic.

Josip rebukes himself and finishes sweeping the steps in record time.

Summer. He likes to walk about the city in his free hours, observing life's surprises. He sometimes stops and chats with people, gives coins to beggars, talking with them about their lives. He buys food for them and plants a few seeds in their minds too. It's not much, but it's what he knows how to do. He goes to a nearby library whenever he can and has begun to read in his field again, perusing texts of higher mathematics, though neither his Italian nor his English is really sufficient for it. Some of the symbolic language is recognizable but not enough to reconnect the severed portions of his memory. A little physics in German offers stimulation, and a Polish article on quantum mechanics—the Slavic roots of Polish and Croatian help the translation—but it proves to be more a source of mental strain than a step forward.

The Yugoslavian government has an embassy in the city, but he avoids it and its propaganda bookshop as if they were the gates of hell. Still, he sometimes longs to dash inside and ask if they have any technical publications in Croatian. This would be imprudent because the watchers among them would ask questions, would want to know who he is and why he is in Rome. They might even go so far as to follow him to his room or his workplace. Perhaps not, but it's better not to risk it. He cannot speak lies even to protect himself, and evasions would only incite their curiosity. Thus, he continues to study English and Italian dictionaries each night and to hope for a breakthrough. Is anything being done about his status? He must ask for a meeting with Mr. or Mrs. Conway. They will know if progress is being made. Paperwork takes a lot of time in this country. They are using their influence with the Italian government, he is sure, but the Italian way is ponderous, Byzantine.

Once again, he happens to meet Mrs. Conway alone. He is gathering hedge prunings when she appears out of nowhere and sweeps past, sliding her hand across his shoulder as lightly as a feather, then down his spine. She pauses with a lingering glance, a certain tilt of her chin, and a voice from deep in her throat says, "I'm doing what I can."

Though disturbed by the intimacy of her touch, alarmed even, he is more desperate to know if there is news.

"Mrs. Conway, excuse please, can you say if it is possible I get documents?"

"I haven't forgotten", she whispers. "I think about it a lot." Then another pause. "I think about *you* a lot."

Refusing to read any inference, he nods appreciatively.

"I thank you, Mrs. Conway", he says with extra formality.

She smiles and skips away. Yes, a forty-year-old woman skipping. He does not like it. It is very immature behavior in an older woman. He knows she must be about forty because there are little wrinkles about the eyes, though a person could easily think she was ten years younger. Thirty or forty, she is nevertheless a great beauty. Disturbed, attracted, his heart beating hard, he is so appalled by himself that he abruptly gathers the prunings and heads toward the outdoor incinerator with an angry stride, chastising himself all the way. Enough of that! When the shift is over, he leaves work with some relief, attends an evening Mass at Santa Maria Maggiore, goes to confession, and walks home in peace. Before crawling under a sheet on his cot, he prays for the soul of Ariadne, missing her terribly. He lets the pain of it move him, weeps, and drifts into sleep.

Another day. He is washing the floor of a little portico in the embassy. Wine-spills have spotted the white limestone, and it's his task to remove the stains. He is on his knees scrubbing with soap and water, but it's proving to be ineffective. The stones remind him of Goli Otok, and in an instant he is back there, staring into the face of death. At that moment he hears the tippy-tappy of a woman in high heels approaching the portico from the corridor. She enters behind him, but he does not look up. Suddenly a hand strokes his shoulder. Pulled violently from the island of death, he jerks away and struggles to his feet.

"Oh, sorry, honey, I didn't mean to startle you", she says in a velvet tone, pursing her lips with sympathy, standing too close. He steps back.

"Mrs. Conway," he murmurs without thinking, "you must respect your dignity." His tone is polite, in a quiet voice that no one else can overhear.

"My dignity?" she laughs, sliding the hand, as light as a feather, down his arm.

"Please!" he erupts, and steps back again.

Her face tightens, the smile disappears, and her eyes melt from sweetness into cool sarcasm. "Sorry if I offended you. Just trying to be friends."

He bows his head, frowning. "Of course", he mumbles. "I misunderstood."

"Yes, I guess you did." With a cold look she turns on her heels and strides away.

Back to the limestone. Down on his knees. Human relationships! he thinks. So complicated! Scrubbing, scrubbing. The wine stains are coming out, but not the stains in the soul. Where did these stones come from really? Carrara is expensive; Goli is cheap. Yes, it is possible that these very stones came from the island. If so, men died in chains while cutting them and carrying them, shedding their blood on them. His lips tighten to a line, his eyes snap with rage and contempt. He spits on the flagstone. Shocked at himself, he swears that never, never, never would he spit on the blood of the victims, never would he defile their sacrifice! No, it is the regime he spits on, and the contemptible blindness of spoiled foreigners he spits on, for they cannot see what occurs beneath the plateau of their pleasures and complacency! And if they knew, they would try to forget because their fine floors are more important to them than human lives. Yes, even these generous Americans are like that. He spits on their divided hearts. With one hand they offer freedom to the world, and with the other hand they give half a continent away to evil men.

Now he sees the stain of Svat's crushed brain on these stones. He bends and kisses the stain. Then, shaking with inner grief, he spits on death.

He does not realize that footsteps have returned to the portico. The American lady is back, and beside her is another woman, an official of the embassy. They have stopped in passing and are staring down at him with disgust.

"Why did you spit on the floor?" asks Mrs. Conway, somewhat irritated.

"A spot", Josip murmurs. "I am cleaning it."

"Oh, I see. Well, that's very diligent of you. But we don't need to spit on the embassy floor, do we? There must be plenty of cleaning fluid in the janitor's closet."

"Yes, thank you, Mrs. Conway. I will find it."

And off they go, clicking-clicking, leaving him alone, quaking with anger and sinking in dismay over his unruly heart.

Sunday. After early Mass and a bite to eat, he strolls from his room in the Ludovici district to the Palatino and enters the Colosseum. It is staggering in proportion to the little amphitheater of Solin, where he once played soccer with hungry urchins, so long ago. Are they still alive, those boys, grown into men as old as he is? Are they somewhere in Croatia or have they fled to freer lands?

He spends the rest of the day wandering about the ruin, touching the surfaces of stone blocks, mortar, and brick. He climbs from floor to floor and descends to the pit, hiding in alcoves so that he can pray undisturbed by the stream of tourists. Again and again, he stares transfixed at the oval arena: here and at the Circus Maximus countless people shed their blood as entertainment for the Roman people. He leans his head against a wall and is jolted when he hears a roar of blood lust erupt from the spectators. He hears the howling of wild beasts and, above all, the screams of children as they suffer unspeakable torture.

Night shift. He is in the basement with the foreman, sweeping and picking up paper litter. It's not the secret kind, just a lot of newspapers and magazines from all over the world.

"I do not understand these people", mumbles the foreman. "Half of my family now lives in America, but still I do not understand these people."

"Is that why you do not live there?"

"No, it's because I have a good job here. Besides, my wife will not let me go."

"She sounds like a good wife."

"She is, but still . . . I would like to see Coney Island. And Disneyland."

Josip shakes his head. "I do not know what those are."

"Play places for people who do not eat cats."

Josip laughs.

The foreman sighs and mumbles, "No, no, no, never will I understand these people."

The telephone rings, the one that connects to the service phones on the upper floors. The foreman answers it and barks, *Sì, sì, sì!*

"It's the cook", he groans, hanging up. "She's in a panic. They've run out of ice, poor souls!"

"Who?"

"Upstairs. They've got a big party on, and they need more ice. There's five ambassadors, and a troop of lackeys plus all their women, and you can be sure they will not be happy if there is no ice for the whiskey. But the iceman he went home, and the cake people refuse to go upstairs because their aprons are a mess, and the guards won't come down to get it. So, that leaves you and me to do the running."

"I'm a mess, too", says Josip, looking down at his sweaty T-shirt, soot-stained slacks, and cracked running shoes.

"Yes, but you are a good-looking mess. I am a slob, and please don't deny it", he says, slapping his empirical belly. "So, *who* does this leave?"

"Neither of us."

"No, it leaves only *you*!"

"No! I would be a dog with fleas running through their party."

"Don't be silly. You just go up in the elevator with a big bucket of ice, tiptoe into the room, and hand it to the wine waiter at his table. Then, quick as a flea on a dog's hind end, out you come, run along the hall, and hustle down the service staircase. Easy, no?"

"All right, I'll go. Say a prayer that no one sees me."

"Don't worry, don't worry. But go up by the gold elevator because they need the ice right now."

In the kitchen, the cook puts a big bucket of ice-cubes into his arms and thanks him profusely, promising him some cake and *gelato* when he comes back.

The elevator guard lets him into the cage, presses a button, and hops out before the bronze gates close. Up in the elevator Josip goes. On the fourth floor, it stops and lets him out. A maid far away at the end of the hallway waves to him frantically and points to the open double-door where she is standing. Josip hastens along the carpeted hall, bobs his head at the maid, and ducks into the room. Nearly a hundred people in evening dress are gathered there, a splendid roar of conversation, with the aromas of caviar and wine, cigar and perfume swirling all about. How can they hear each other? Josip puts the bucket down on the wine table, gets a nod and a *grazie* from the waiter, wheels, and beats a hasty retreat. The maid thanks him and goes back into the room. Done! Next, the *gelato*!

He is puttering along the hall, looking for the servants' staircase, when he hears a voice calling behind him:

"*Joe—see—eep!*"

Oh, no! He turns around, and sure enough, here comes Mrs. Conway, glittering and emanating her nimbus of gold light.

"*Joe—see—eep*, wait, wait, wait, don't run *ah-way-ay*!" she sings as if talking to a toddler or a poodle. "I have something wonderful to *tell-tell-tell* you."

Her gait is unsteady. She is weaving a little and dragging her heels, smiling in the way that sets him on guard. He would run if she did not have news for him. Instead he comes to attention respectfully, clasps his hands across his abdomen, and awaits her arrival.

"Yes, Mrs. Conway?"

"Oh, shweetie, how nishe to sheee you", she coos, trailing a gossamer gold scarf that loops around her neck and drags along the floor behind her. A wine glass is in her hand, and she is tipping it this way and that, unmindful of the drops sprinkling the pale carpet.

"Ooh, don't be so stand-offish, Joe-sheep. You know I won't hurt you." She pushes herself too close. "Are you jush a lil' bit scared of ol' Cass?"

"Mrs. Conway, I must go to my work below."

"Not show fasht, dear man, not show fasht. I wanna give you a progresh report. But first you gotta gimme a little kiss."

She drapes one length of the scarf about his neck and coils it around him. He takes a step back and tries to extricate himself.

"Please, you will respect your dignity", he murmurs, nervously trying to untangle the thing.

"Dignity schmignity! Again with the shmignity!"

"And mine", he adds.

"And your what? Oh, hell, Joe, you and me are grown-ups. I'm doin' a lot for you, and you can shpare me a kish!"

His eyes become slits, and his mouth tightens, every muscle of his body tenses for flight, but he knows that if he insults this woman she could punish him badly—in fact destroy him. He controls himself and says in English.

"You say, Madame, that news you have of my situation?"

"Did I shay that? No I don' think I shayed that."

"Then—?"

She throws the scarf around his neck again and pulls him

in—rather she reels herself toward him and wraps her arms around his chest. He is so taken by surprise that he is paralyzed.

"Never in my life, Joe-sheep, never in my entire life have I met a man as magnificent as you!"

Stunned, he merely gapes, and it takes a second or two before he can resume peeling her arms from his chest and then from his waist.

"You're a god," she exhales with ardor, "you're Triton comin' up out o' the sea, an' I'm gonna be your sea wife!"

He yells a wordless rejection in her face—a brutal sound—containing all his loathing for those who destroyed his wife and child. Though this woman had no part in it, their deaths are meaningless to her, and she wants only what she wants, regardless of whom she tries to take it from. She did not stop to wonder if he has a true wife waiting for him, their marriage bed unshakable beyond the boundaries of death.

"Foolish woman!" he roars, pushing her away. With a look of contempt, he stomps toward the staircase.

"What the hell!" barks a man's voice. "What's goin' on here, Cass?"

"Oh, Brad, Oh, Brad, thank God you're here!" she wails. "That man *insulted* me!" she shrieks. "He *assaulted* me!"

Josip hears this just as he reaches the staircase door. Before he can push it open, a hand grabs the collar of his T-shirt and yanks him back into the hall. He is slammed up against the wall, and in his face is a man hurling malice through his eyes, blinking rapidly, his teeth clenched. His tuxedo is askew, and his right arm pulls back to swing the fist toward Josip's face. He ducks, the fist hits the wall. The man's arm crumples, his face contorting in agony, and he shouts, "Guard, guard!"

Josip pulls the gold scarf from his neck and drops it onto the floor, pushes open the door to the staircase, and goes down. He does not run. In fact he feels no fear, only disgust. Step by step.

No one follows, no whistles blow, no crowd of guards swoops in with truncheons flailing.

He arrives in the kitchen, declines the cook's offer of *gelato*, then descends still farther into the basement level, and goes in search of the foreman. He finds the man sitting beside the furnace, reading a magazine.

"So," he says looking up, "mission accomplished?"

"I delivered the ice", says Josip buttoning his shirt as he heads toward the door.

"Where are you going? You have another two hours before shift's over."

"I resign today. This moment. Now. I am going."

"What? Are you crazy? What happened up there?"

"They will tell you. They will tell you a lie. I am finished with these people. I do not understand them. Even if I did understand them, I would not wish to see them anymore."

"Someone hurt your feelings?"

"Someone is going to call the police. Then I will die. You know my address. That is where I will wait. They can arrest me there."

"You're going to die? Did you spill the ice bucket down someone's dress?"

"I will die. You have been good to me, so I tell you the truth before God that I have done nothing wrong. These people are selfish, and I do not wish to work for them anymore."

He shakes the foreman's hand and leaves, forcing himself to walk without haste along Via Veneto.

He unlocks the door to his little room and enters, switches on the top light, closes the door, then sits down. He senses that each of these acts are final ones. He will miss them. The room is more pleasant than it was when he first moved in. There is now a small bedside lamp with dried flowers sealed on its parchment shade and a shelf of books containing his dictionaries, a Bible, and missals in Italian and Latin. A striped

Ethiopian rug lies on the green linoleum. At this moment, he desires what is impossible. He longs for a photograph of Ariadne. In the torturous minutes while he waits for the police to come, he would, if he could, simply sit here on the cot and look into her eyes.

He lies down and closes his eyes, gazes into her eyes as he remembers them, and hears her words as he remembers them. Then, before he knows it, he is asleep. And then it is morning.

He jumps up when a knuckle raps once on the door. Well, here they are! He opens the door to find only the foreman standing there, cap in hand.

"May I come in, Giuseppe?"

"Come in."

"I see you have not died."

"No, I haven't. Why didn't the police come?"

The foreman shrugs. "I don't know."

"Did they search for me?"

"Yes. But only a guard and an angry man with his hand wrapped in a towel. You must have fought him hard."

"We fought, but it was the wall that hit his hand."

"They should arrest the wall."

"Why did you come here?"

"To bring you your wages. Not for the whole week, as you see, because you resigned and brought it upon yourself. What a hothead you are!"

"Did they tell you a lie about me?"

"They told me nothing about you."

"Really?"

"Really. Look, Giuseppe, I think you should come back to work."

"No. I'm finished. I'm leaving this country."

"Where will you go?"

"I don't know."

"Where shall I tell the police to find you?"

"I—well—I just don't know for certain."

"Send me a postcard, and I can let them know."

"I will."

The foreman chuckles, and then slaps his belly.

"Time for a *cicchetto di vino*, eh?"

"All right, but I have none in the house."

"I carry my own supply wherever I go. Any glasses here or do you drink only from the spigot?"

"I have a glass. We'll have to share it."

"Even better."

So, the foreman, great-hearted fellow that he is, tries to throw wine onto the hothead's fire and with a single glass succeeds to some extent. Into himself he tosses glass after glass. But in the end, after they have talked for a few hours, nothing has changed. Josip says again that he is leaving the city—this city, which killed people for entertainment. He is leaving tomorrow or maybe the day after, if the police still have not come for him. It doesn't matter.

"Oh, don't say that", chides the foreman. "Come on, relax. No one's going to make hell of your life."

Josip fixes him with a doubtful look and says nothing. He shakes his head. He is leaving, he doesn't know where he will go. He will walk. Just walk.

Because the foreman is becoming too tipsy, Josip walks the man back to his own apartment building and delivers him to his wife, a long-suffering woman, who gives her husband a minimal swat and scold and puts him to bed. She thanks Josip for bringing him home. After that he walks to St. Peter's, where a priest hears his confession in the basilica. Then he attends Mass at a side altar. After receiving Communion, he feels some inner peace. Maybe he will be sent back to Yugoslavia, maybe not. Maybe he will die, maybe not. He is a little frightened now, but in a strange way not very frightened. He has no real options, and thus he must hope in God's help.

Well, he tells himself as he steps over Fra Anto's body, *I still have my dignity.*

Back at his lodgings, he learns from the landlady that the police still have not come. He lies down, prays a Rosary, and slides into sleep. In the morning, he gets up before dawn and walks to Trastevere for the early Mass at the tomb of Santa Cecilia. It is there that his peace is fully restored. Here, too, a light is given. After Communion, he remembers the counsel that the old Franciscan friar gave him—counsel that is no more than what the Gospels ask of all men. He now realizes that he has forgotten about this. Since he came to live in Rome, nothing harmful has happened. In fact, it seems that only good has come to him, save for the incident at the embassy two nights ago.

He is leaving this city. Soon. Maybe today. But it now seems that a reminder has been put before his eyes. The woman, no doubt, will be seeking vengeance. Her screams to her husband in the hallway certainly indicated a willingness to tell lies and to destroy his reputation. This is harm, plain and simple. She has ended his employment, and she may well be an instrument in ending his life. So, how can he repay this woman's evil with good? He will pray for her and think about other possibilities.

Throughout that day Josip walks the streets of the city, gazes into countless windows and enters many shops. In the late afternoon he leaves one, carrying a package in his hands. From there he plods to the American embassy and speaks to the guard at the gate. He asks for Mr. or Mrs. Conway. They don't work here, replies the guard. Mr. Conway has an office on the other side of town, and as for where they live, he couldn't say. Apparently, Josip has not yet been exiled from the embassy compound, and he is able to pass through the gates and go to the foreman's office. When Josip raps at his door, the foreman breaks into a grin and lumbers to his feet.

"Giuseppe, a surprise! You did not die!"

"I did not die. Can you tell me where I can find Mrs. Conway? Do you know where they live?"

"You're not going to kill her, are you?"

"No, I'm not going to kill her. There's something I must say to her."

"Well, you're out of luck because she's in the hospital. They took her to Gemelli because she swallowed too many pills a couple of nights ago. They say she was having trouble sleeping and took the pills on top of wine. Not a good idea, that. Anyway, she's pulling through, they say. But I wouldn't advise a visit."

He arrives in a wing of Gemelli Hospital after a certain amount of surreptitious behavior. It is still visiting hours, so there is not much of a problem finding her room. It's a private one, filled with flowers. No visitors are present. She is alone, sleeping. The hospital bed is raised at an angle. She is breathing lightly, in a blue nightgown, and covered to her waist by a sheet. Her face is haggard, without makeup. Her arms are resting on top of the sheet, and an intravenous needle is taped to one of her wrists. Fluid drips into it from a bottle.

Josip sits on a chair near the foot of the bed. He clears his throat.

"Is that you, Brad?" she murmurs without opening her eyes.

"Mrs. Conway?" he says.

"You're supposed to be at the reception, honey. You shouldn't have come back."

"I came to bring you a gift, Mrs. Conway. May I stay a moment?"

Her eyes blink open, and she sees him. She inhales sharply, her eyes full of fear.

"I do not want to trouble you", he goes on. "And I will leave if you tell me to go."

"I know what you'll say", she moans. "Go ahead and flatten me if you want to. I deserve it."

"No person deserves it", he whispers.

She begins to cry and covers her face with her hand.

"I will go if you wish."

"Stay, please stay. I'm sorry for what I said. And for what I did."

He sees what it costs this proud and lonely woman to say this. She cannot meet his eyes, and her face is turned away. There is no dignity left but what remains after purgation by shame.

"Once, when I was in despair, not many years ago," he says to her in a quiet voice, "I tried to take my life. I was in great fear. All love had been taken from me. My wife and child had been destroyed, my life also. It seemed to me that only evil remained in the world, and that I too had become evil."

She turns her face to look at him.

"You? Evil? You're good. That's the difference between you and me."

"You are wrong, Mrs. Conway. In each person there is good and evil, and we cannot choose the good unless we see that there is also evil. If we resist it, the good grows."

"So, you've come to help me see my evil?"

Josip shakes his head.

"I come to ask your forgiveness."

"Don't—" she cries. "I couldn't bear it."

"You do not understand what I wish to say. I have resigned from my employment at the embassy; perhaps I have already been dismissed. And even if it were not so, I would leave. I do not come to you to seek anything. I do not want this job, and I do not need you to help me from being sent back to Yugoslavia. I will not go there under any circumstances. I do not even come to you to prevent any trouble from police or authorities or from your husband. I do not look for anything from you. I come simply as one person to another. Can you understand this?"

"I think so", she whispers. "A little."

"When I shouted at you, I was afraid. I was afraid that I was falling back into the island of death."

"What do you mean?" she asks. "What is an island of death?"

"May I explain to you about it?"

She nods, no longer averting her eyes.

He tells her about his wife and child, about their deaths, his arrest, and his imprisonment. He speaks of his despair and rage, his fears and his terrors.

"So, you came to Rome," she says with eyes brimming and lips quivering, "and from all that hell you walked straight into a woman like me. A woman who—"

She begins to cry again.

"When I was praying for you this morning at the tomb of a great saint, she showed me that I was not understanding properly. She helped me to see that I must come and speak with you. I know it is hard for us to speak together. But I think it is good."

"Maybe it is", she whispers.

"I want to tell you that when I leave this room tonight, all that has happened at the embassy is forgotten and will not be spoken of in my life. We remember things, I know. I remember the wrong I have done in my life, and I am sad for it, but it has no more power over me. And this, I think, should be the way for you too. I ask it of you."

"You ask it of me?" she says, puzzled. "You ask me to forget that I hurt you, and could have really hurt you badly, maybe ended your life?"

"I ask you to understand and to forgive. Understand yourself and understand me."

"I will try."

"You can choose. May I give you a gift I bring for you?"

"A gift?" she says and breaks into fresh sobs. "You bring me a gift?"

"Yes. Here it is." He smiles. "Please open it. A little thing, but it is for you."

She takes it in her hands and holds it.

"It's heavy", she says.

"It is light," he replies, "like a *lastavica* sitting on your finger-tips, or a *dobri dupin* leaping above the waves."

She carefully pulls away the wrapping paper, and finds a glass sphere. In its center is a tiny blue dolphin.

He steps forward and bows his head, then stands to attention.

"Mrs. Conway, may I give you a little kiss?"

She stares at him in disbelief. She does not say no, so he bends and plants a brief kiss on her forehead.

He straightens and says, "Good-night, Mrs. Conway."

"Good-night, Mr. Lasta", she whispers.

Her eyes follow him as he leaves. Then, when he is gone, she sits for a long, long time, gazing at the dolphin within the sphere.

NOTES FOR A
RECONSTRUCTED
COSMOLOGY

(FRAGMENTS INFERENTIAL OF A META-UNIVERSE)

29

So! What is he going to do with this big catfish? It's as black as soot, weighs fifteen kilos, and it keeps sloshing around in his bathtub all night, keeping him awake. He caught it as food for himself, and now he is feeding *it*! Something is wrong in this arrangement. It doesn't want to die; it wants very badly to be taken back to the Hudson River and released. Can catfish hypnotize people the way snakes can? Probably not, but he must admit he has grown quite fond of the thing, against his will.

It's too big a fish for the freezer compartment in his fridge, even if he could bring himself to kill it. Maybe he could give it to the Franciscan Fathers over at the parish. Not a bad idea, but do Franciscans kill fish? It might be as hard on them as it is on him. It would be difficult to preach to the fish and the birds and then knock them on the head.

Maybe he should offer it to Mrs. Franklin. She works so hard cleaning the penthouses and looks tired all the time. She has some heavy crosses (and her skulker-scowler son is going to be one of the heavier ones, if he isn't already). Yes, he will give the fish to this fine lady, who has a family to feed. They are friends, in an oblique way, though she is reticent to share details about her life. Since he moved into the building seven years ago, they have struck up a habit of short conversations whenever they pass in the hallway. Not unlike the dialogues on Goli Otok. He and the woman share no confraternity of the unjustly imprisoned, but there is a rapport of sorts, for they both serve at the very bottom of the world: he cleans the building—keeps the hallways shining, the garbage carried out, and the boiler in the basement running—and she cleans the more expensive apartments on the upper floors. They are the feeders at the bottom of the river, like the catfish. Yes—it will go to her.

Wait! The fish is black. Will she infer a veiled reference to her color in this? Maybe not. She's a sensible person, in no way neurotic. But it must be hard for someone to have come from slavery—even if it was a hundred years ago. Well, he knows what slavery is, too.

Later in the morning, they happen to meet in the corridor on the sixth floor, where he has been fixing a leaky tap. She has a bottle of cleaning fluid and rags in one hand.

"Good morning, Mrs. Franklin."

"Mornin', Mistah Lastah. You look chirpy today."

"As do you, Madame."

Madame always makes her laugh, and she laughs with her whole body, her eyes dancing, too. She is very overweight.

Her full name is Coriander Franklin, and she knows that his name is Josip, but they stay with the Mr. and Mrs., mostly for the fun of it, but also because they both enjoy the dignity it bestows.

"I am wondering if I may give you something, Mrs. Franklin, a little gift for your family", he begins tentatively.

"What kinda gif'?"

"Fish."

"My daughter's got more than enough goldfish, so I better not."

"It is a fish for eating."

"Well, we like t' eat fish, so I ain't got no objections."

"It is a large fish—very large."

"How big?"

"Fifteen kilograms, perhaps sixteen."

"Say again?"

"About thirty or forty pounds."

"What! Where you get a fish like that!"

"I caught it in the Hudson a week ago."

"That's a lotta fish to pack into a freezer."

"It is alive still, and I think quite fresh which will improve the taste when it is cooked and eaten."

"Makes sense. But where you keep that fish—*alive*?"

"In my bathtub."

She looks at him for a moment, then bursts into giggles. "You da biscuit, Mistah Lastah, you sho' da biscuit."

Biscuit? An odd expression, but then most English idioms are inexplicable. In what way is he like a biscuit?

"I do not have the heart to dispatch it, that is my problem. How do you feel about killing fish?"

"I feel jus' *fine* about it. No problems there. Say, that is real good of you, sir."

She pronounces certain words like "fine" and "sir" as *fahn* and *suh*. Her use of language has sunshine in it—warmer than the Manhattan environment. He likes it a lot, this mysterious poetry in her speech, redolent of generations of southern cotton fields and a more elusive Africa. He feels sorry about the slavery but enjoys the soul-speech that evolved from it.

So, they go down to his basement apartment to have a look at the fish. She shakes her head when she sees it.

"My, that is *some* fish. How did you get that monster back here all the way from the river?" Pronounced: *Mah, thass sum feesh. Ha y' get thet mounstah hee-ah allaway from d' rivah?*

Well, his Slavic dialect must sound equally quaint to her ears:

"I have an excellent method. Not all my catches survive the trip home, I must admit, but catfish are capable of enduring much oxygen-deprivation." Pronounced: *I haf ecksillint met ode. Not ole my cat chess survife treep home, I mussed mitt, but catfeesh are capabile uf entoorink mutch oxychen-deprivat-yun.*

There are always pauses while the two brains translate.

He shows her the carrying case—a flexible plastic water-bag with a zipper on top, red handle, and a spigot at one end. The plastic is see-through.

"That's a mighty clever invention, Mistah Lastah, mighty clever. You have troubles getting it on the bus?"

"The bus driver looks at it, this is true, but he does not ask questions."

She belly-laughs. "And the people on the bus, they look, too?"

"They all look. None of them ask questions. I find this aspect of our life in the free world very strange, Mrs. Franklin. Here, people look at the most surprising things but are afraid to ask about them."

"I know, I know", she grins, still shaking her head. "That's city life for you. It wasn't that way in the South where I was born."

"In my homeland we had reason to fear. But what are *these* people afraid of? I ask myself all the time."

"Well, I can't say for sure." *Willa cain't say fo' shoah.* "I'll never understand these people myself. But I thinks they's afraid of themselves, mostly."

"Perhaps you are right. Will you take the fish?" *Veel yoo tek se feesh?*

"I'd be happy to take it off your hands. I can knock the dang thing on the head right here and cut it up, take it home in a shopping bag. That okay by you?"

He sighs. He does not like slaughter, especially not in his own home. He knocks fishheads sometimes, but always smaller ones. Slaughter follows by necessity. Still, he prefers to do it by a river bank. In summer, this is a risk because heat can spoil the fish.

"That is okay by me."

"Well, thank you very much, Mistah Lastah. I'll talk to Caleb tonight and get him to come by after school tomorrow. Him and me can carry the thing home."

"That is an excellent plan. Thank you for taking it."

"I'll leave you a few chunks for your dinner."

"That is thoughtful of you."

"And just as a bonus, I ain't gonna call you a heretic no more."

He laughs. "Thank you again and again."

This is a joke they like to spin along over the months and years. She belongs to a Pentecostal church up in Harlem and always wears a large cross on a chain about her neck, full of jewels and flashing lights, but no corpus. Their religious dialogue began about two years ago, when she noticed one day that his crucifix had fallen out of his shirt as he bent over the squeeze-bucket, pressing dirty water from the floor-mop. Until then they had enjoyed a relationship of courtesies, friendly but impersonal.

"Oh, my", she exclaimed, "You love the Lord Jesus?"

"I do", he answered solemnly.

"I love him too", she smiled. "He's my main man!"

So began their theological debates. She invited him to attend a Sunday service at her church, The Ethiopian Gospel Holiness Tabernacle (of the Ark of the Covenant) in Harlem, not far from her place. He declined, though he was touched by her invitation. In return, he suggested that she might enjoy attending Mass with him someday at Saints Cyril and Methodius parish, down by the Lincoln Tunnel. Its pastors were Franciscans, and a lot of Croatian exiles were attending it now. She declined, though she seemed touched by the invitation.

"That's real nice of you, Mister Lastah, but I gotta be honest. I just don't truck with no heretics. And I'm sorry to say, you's *heretics*."

Astounded, he said, "But Madame, I think, perhaps, it is you who are the heretic!"

She slapped his arm with a cleaning cloth, a gesture that sealed their friendship.

"Well, honey," she concluded, "I don't know what's gonna happen to either of us on the Great Day of the Lord. Maybe you gonna fry and I'm gonna go on up to glory, or maybe the other way around. But I knows one thing for sure."

"What is it, Mrs. Franklin?"

"We both loves the main man, and that's good enough for me."

So, back to the fish.

They are standing there in the bathroom, looking down into the tub, where the sinister creature swishes its tail and broods about existence. Its nose is an inch from the drainpipe; its tail scrapes the other end.

"He is very black", Josip muses.

"Still good eatin'."

"Black is beautiful."

She laughs. "Where you hear that?"

"Quite often in the newspapers, and on the radio."

"Well, it's true, but it sure soun' funny comin' from the mouth of a white man."

"Am I a white man?" he asks with some puzzlement. "Ah, yes, of course, my skin has very little pigment." He smiles and shakes his head. "The psychology of perception is always a problem in human affairs, is it not?"

"Say again?"

"We see the outside and think we know what is inside."

"Uh-huh, that's a very bad habit in human bein's."

"Very bad."

"So, you think you ain't white. That's got me mighty curious. Where you from, anyway?"

He tells her. She has heard of Yugoslavia but not Bosnia-Herzegovina or Croatia.

"So, you's from eastern Europe, then."

He corrects her, but she waves it away.

"All that's too much for me, Mister Lastah, but tell y' what, I'm gonna get you some sauerkraut to go with the fish."

"Please do not waste your money, Mrs. Franklin. I am not fond of sauerkraut—*kiseli kupis*, we call it."

She nods, thanks him for the fish, and says good-bye, because she has to get back to work. She will return tomorrow with the boy and two shopping bags.

The next day, Mrs. Franklin arrives with her son in tow. He is about eleven years old, scowling like a New York City policeman, and clearly unhappy about being put to work. Josip drains the bathtub, and she hits the creature on the head. A horrible amount of thrashing ensues, but in the end a large number of fish chunks get wrapped up in newspaper.

The boy doesn't say a word. From start to finish, he eyes the janitor with disapproval—even contempt. Josip does not know what to make of it. What goes on inside that young mind? Is he getting involved in drugs? Is he stealing? Is he breaking his mother's heart again (the father had left them some years back). The boy is not sad. He is angry—as Emilio Mazzuolo once put it, angry at the unfairness of existence. And it looks like this lad is going to make somebody pay for it, starting with his mother.

About two months later, a November evening. Puddles freeze at night, though no snow has fallen yet. The days are occasionally autumnal, full of fine light and spinning yellow leaves; but one can feel the approach of winter. Josip is talking with Gus-the-doorman in the entrance lobby and watching children playing stoop-ball on the steps of the apartment building across the way. Gus is restless, keeps patting every pocket in his uniform because he has run out of cigarettes, but he cannot leave work to buy a pack. Josip offers to go get him the cigarettes; there's a convenience store over on 9th. It's a rough neighborhood—not called Hell's Kitchen for nothing—but he has strolled through it many a night without a qualm.

It is a short walk from his own street, 52nd, to 9th Avenue, then a fair hike south to the store. Arriving there, he buys the brand Gus prefers, then goes back out into the street. He decides to lengthen the journey home by walking west to the river, then north on 11th Avenue, and back east on 52nd. He has been growing a bit of a belly lately, something that has never happened to him before. He can't explain it. Maybe puttering about a twelve-story apartment house is not what human beings were designed for. He has been neglecting his walking—just too much to do around the building. He stretches his legs and strides along at a good clip. *Nostos*, he thinks, and then wonders where the thought came from. He does the circuit and is just heading along a murkier section of 52nd, a few blocks from home, when three teenage boys bound out of an alleyway and block his passage. One pulls a knife and presses its point into the chest of Josip's coat.

He is not frightened, merely surprised. He has heard a lot about such incidents but has never worried about them happening to him.

"Gimme your cash", snarls the knife-boy.

Josip frowns. "You don't want to do that."

"I *do* wanna do it. Just gimme or I cut you bad."

Without warning, a shriek explodes in their midst. A whirring shadow suddenly descends upon them, a *bura* blowing and striking in every direction. Josip's assailants howl and run off, disappearing into the alley. And there in front of him, huffing and puffing, is Mrs. Franklin's son. Caleb the contemptuous. Caleb the bad boy who will break his mother's heart.

"Th-thank you", Josip says, blinking rapidly. "You appeared at the providential moment."

The boy is carrying an iron bar in his right hand. He smacks it on the palm of his other hand. He says nothing, just scowls, as if this white man has put him to a lot of trouble.

"What are you doing here at this time of night?" Josip asks. "Shouldn't you be at home?"

"My Momma, she's working tonight, cleanin' up for a party."

"You don't need to be out in the streets. You could wait in the lobby."

"I cain't wait there. Gus he tol' me stay outside. He don't like me."

"Well, from now on you can surely wait in the lobby. I'll talk to him, Caleb."

"How you know my name?"

"Your mother told me."

His scowl deepens. He is one tough boy and wants everyone to know it. He is capable of demolishing a gang of older adolescents. Nevertheless, he is too young to be running around in the dark on these streets. How old is he? As old as Josip was in Sarajevo when he carried an iron bar to fend off boys who leap from alleyways to steal other people's fish.

Josip reaches down and puts a hand on the crown of the boy's head. It is probably permissible to treat him as such. The gesture is absolutely paternal, even patriarchal. It is a hand that reaches out of the past, out of a world of fathers and their children.

He ruffles the springy black hair a little, only to find that it cannot be ruffled. It is like steel wool, rough to the touch, not a trace of Slavic silk in it.

Caleb barks, "Don' touch mah hair, cracker!" knocking the hand from his head.

"I apologize", Josip says, taking a step backward.

The boy puts his fists on his waist, braces his legs, and cocks his chin high in defiance.

"I save yo life, man, but I don't give you no rights ovah me."

"Yes, yes, I understand", says Josip, embarrassed. "I was not thinking. I did not respect your independence and autonomy."

"I don't givasheet bout no tonomy, just you watch yo hands, cracker."

Cracker again. Hair cracker and hands cracker. What do these expressions mean? Are they similar to biscuit, but when applied to anatomical parts they take on other significance, inferences that are still indecipherable to him? He has not yet discerned any similarities between himself and a biscuit, and now the word cracker has been added to the mystery. These expressions simply make no sense whatsoever. Even so, his constant perusal of the English dictionary has taught him that a cracker and a plain, salted biscuit are the same thing—the choice between which word to use depends on whether one is living in a British Commonwealth nation or in a nation that has revolted against the British. To decrypt the history embedded in language can be confusing at times, but it does offer a rewarding sense of mental stimulation.

Josip, as it happens, has a wax-paper bundle of soda-biscuits in his coat pocket. He never fails to carry this supply whenever he goes out into the city, just in case. Hunger is still a demon that haunts, yet it can be easily dispelled if you prepare ahead for any eventuality.

He digs out the package and opens it. Offering the contents to the boy, he says, "Would you like a cracker?"

Caleb stares at the crazy janitor, and then is struck by the humor of this whiteman's naïveté.

"Sho", he says, and drops his arrogance. Grinning, he scoops up all the biscuits and crams them one after another into his mouth. All the while he observes the man observing him and notes the sadness that has entered those watery blue eyes.

"Do you like figs?" asks Josip.

"Ah hates feegs."

"The children must eat", Josip whispers. "They are our fu-ture, they are our hope."

Mghmgh—mghmgh, mumbles the boy, with a full mouth.

"I beg your pardon, Caleb, what did you say?"

"I say I ain't no child!"

"Yes, this appears to be so. There is a maturity in you I had not anticipated."

Caleb is again chewing and swallowing, his eyes still somewhat suspicious, trying to figure out what kind of strange bird this man really is. Josip bows, turns, and walks on toward his apartment building. Oddly, his young combatant follows, then steps up along beside him, keeping pace. Reaching the front entrance, they come to a halt, and Josip says, "Good-night, then. Thank you again."

"Night", says the boy, wiping crumbs from his mouth. "You ain't no cracker, mistah."

Josip recognizes a supreme compliment and goes in.

Fragment:

I was twelve then, that time in Sarajevo. Or maybe I was thirteen. Yes, a bit older, because I had already learned to swim in the Miljacka. I remember the day my feet sank in blood and gore on a rust-colored field above the city, though it was only soil. During those years my poor mind was still confused, still healing from the catastrophe of Rajska Polja. Has it ever been entirely well since then?

I remember, too, the time I rode a white horse in thickest fog. We galloped together in the clouds. And when he took me back to the place that was my rank in the hierarchy of existence, he told me that I would ride him again someday. He has never returned. I know that I rode him, but were the words he spoke to me merely something produced in my imagination or in a dream?

From time to time, he is rehaunted by confusions, very brief moments of disorientation when he wakes in the morning and wonders where he is. He sits up, rubs his face, and thinks about getting the coffee pot percolating. But who is he, really? And what is this place? How did he get here? Then he remembers.

Usually months pass without Josip's recalling the final meeting with the American lady in the Rome hospital, the sphere with the dolphin in it, and the little kiss. He never saw her again after that visit, never heard a word from her. But a few days later, as he was sitting alone in his room listening to the trains screeching into Rome's rail terminal, pummeling his brains for a solution to his hopeless situation, and praying a lot too, there came a knock at the door.

And there stood Mr. Conway. Both he and Josip regarded each other with uncertain expressions, until Josip invited him in. The visitor sat down on the single wooden chair and nervously picked at the plaster cast on his right hand.

They looked at each other for some minutes before both, simultaneously, began to say something. Every time one of them tried to speak, the words died on his lips. In the end, they both knew that everything was understood between them.

"How is your hand?" Josip asked, trying to offer at least a token conversation.

"It will be all right", said Mr. Conway, bowing his head in embarrassment.

They nodded and nodded at each other, then smiled a little. Finally, Mr. Conway stood, put on his hat, and extended his left hand for a shake. And so they shook hands, and not long after that, a good deal of paperwork began. Then, for the first time in his life, Josip flew like a *lastavica*, and he found himself in a basement apartment on 52nd Street, tending a boiler and sweeping the hallways, narrowly escaping muggings, and catching fish in a river much deeper and mightier than the Miljacka, though not as beautiful.

Fragment:

The past comes with us—even when it seems to have vanished or to have merely faded. After Sunday Mass, a man came up to me on the steps of Cyril and Methodius and asked in Croatian if I had recently moved to the city and how I had come to live here. I felt no disturbance of my inner peace, and thus concluded that he is a legitimate exile, like myself. So, I gave him a vague account. It was pleasant to speak my native language but a little disturbing to find out how rusty it is becoming. Most of my conversations are in a variety of English dialects. Mrs. Franklin's, for example, and those of Gus, the Armenian manager of my building, and my confessor at the parish. I once spoke with an Australian. This was a disturbing exercise. It really should not be called English. And yet all these variations derive from the same source—my Webster's dictionary is technically reliable, but in conversational practice not always reliable.

I am digressing.

In any event, this man who was born in Zagreb and fled with his mother into Austria and then made it to America after narrowly escaping the Bleiburg massacre is now a wealthy businessman, not much older than myself. He plans to start a monthly newsletter for the Croatian expatriates in the city. It will be in our own language. He is collecting personal accounts of injustice from individuals and would like to publish them. He explains that most people decline the offer because they have family back in Yugoslavia and are worried about reprisals. Everyone is haunted by a feeling that we are being watched. True, so am I! It is ridiculous, of course, but I cannot shake this vague sensation we all carry.

When I, too, declined to write him a little account, his discouragement about our caution (or paranoia) was evident. So, I made a concession. I offered to contribute a poem. He did not look enthusiastic. Poems! his facial expression said. What use are poems! He is a businessman and very American in appearance and style of speech. After all, he was only a lad when he arrived in New York. But in the end he gave it some consideration, and we agreed that I would resurrect some of my old attempts at poetry from the *Dobri Dupin* journal. I think I can remember scraps, maybe the one about the family that pulls a cart toward the Drava River with a toy sailboat and a violin on top. Even as I struggled to remember it, I felt the old pain return. After all this time, it still hurts.

I warned him that it would be obscure and certainly not professional. He pursed his lips and told me that it would be better than nothing. Such good pragmatists these Americans are, new and old.

I also insisted on a pseudonym. I will write under the name Josip Marulić. He told me that I am being paranoid, this is a free country, there is no secret police here. Nevertheless, I did not budge. Paranoid I may be, but one can never be too careful.

It is a fine Saturday in spring. Josip is standing on a grassy patch in Central Park, several blocks northeast of his apartment building. It is his day off. His paycheck is not due for another week, and he lacks the necessary funds for the bus ride that would take him to his favorite fishing spot on the Hudson. There has been another warning on the radio about mercury poisoning from some fish. He does not worry about this, just ponders it a little.

Despite the terrors of mercury poisoning, the hole in the ozone layer, and melting ice caps, the world is still beautiful— moreover, there is an island of green within this city. He goes often to the Metropolitan Museum, on the east side of the park. Its Mesopotamian collection is fascinating, as well as a few select pieces of Scythian and Illyrian art, which for him are touch-stones. Nearby is the New York Public Library, a cathedral for the mind, where he spends much of his free time. And he sometimes visits the zoo, though he feels a natural empathy for the animals imprisoned there.

The park is primarily for salving his hunger for natural things, if an artificial park can be natural. He has his favorite trees. If he lies down at the base of one, the grass against his back is cool and the smell of organic things restorative, however fugitive they may be. If he squints his eyes, the ranges of high-rise towers become distant mountains, and he is in an alpine valley surrounded by the sounds of children laughing and calling and crying—as they do everywhere.

The birds are not unfriendly. They know him, he is sure of it. Well, to tell the truth, he has cultivated the relationship by feeding them. Ah, food—it never fails to connect creatures. He has developed a special affection for pigeons, which are generally disliked because of their great numbers and their droppings. What on earth do they live on? Popcorn? Sandwich crusts? A portion of his income is allotted for them. They are one of the city's great resources, though few residents realize it. The birds humanize the place. There is an illogic here, but nevertheless he feels it is true. He has written a silly short poem about it. He has not yet spotted any European pigeons, which are thinner, subtler, and more graceful in appearance than these brash new-world pigeons. He keeps his eyes open, hoping that one will appear, perhaps blown west on the *bura* of providence.

Today he is standing in a hollow of grass just south of the clockwork gate into the zoo. The clock's bells are ringing, and crowds of children are gazing at its revolving bronze characters. A few adults are among them, just as enrapt, but retaining their unnecessary aplomb. When the clockwork mechanism has completed its performance and the hour has struck with gong and bell, they disperse. Josip, too, turns away.

Where are his friends the pigeons today? Oh, here they come! How did they spot him? Thirty or forty swoop in low and land, clustering about his feet, strutting, jostling for position, bumping shoulders, and pecking at each other, vying for first place in his attention.

"Oooo, where are your manners!" he scolds. "Be patient, there is enough for everyone!" He speaks in English because that is appropriate for them, considering the land of their birth.

He scatters seeds and bread from the two bags he has brought with him, which is followed by frenzied feeding and a chorus of thanks, which they offer him in semihysterical coos. He longs to pick one up and hold it. He has succeeded in doing so a few times in the past and is ever-entranced by their startled eyes, their shimmering and chortling, and the feel of smooth wing-feathers beneath his fingertips. They do not like being held but will endure it for a minute or so before he tosses them up into the air.

He now bends into the mob, slowly, slowly, and they sidestep away from him, protesting with their alarmed little voices: You're too close, despite your benevolence! A young white one is rather more naïve than the others, and he scoops it up. Its eyes dart franticly, its head snapping this way and that, looking for paths of escape. It trembles in his hands and he can feel its heart's vibrations. It is warm. This is one of the few moments in Josip's life when he is able to touch, and be touched by, another living creature. He smiles, loves the little prisoner, and then lets it go.

A laugh! Has he laughed, or has someone nearby laughed? Glancing about, he sees a man sitting on a bench not ten feet away, observing him. The man is smiling. It is a fond, knowing smile, yet detached, because all human beings in this city are detached until they distill themselves into colonies and villages within the metropolis.

The man nods, and Josip nods in return. He is about fifty years of age, East Indian, dressed in a fine tweed suit with matching vest and flawless brogues. (Always pay attention to the shoes, Josip recalls. The shoes tell you everything.) Moreover, this man has been exquisitely barbered and wears a cream-colored cravat (does he know that *kravates* originated in Croatia?). A brown hand curls lightly around the staff of the black cane laid across his knees. The knob of the cane is an ivory elephant's head. By the man's side sit a leather valise and a wicker picnic basket.

"Good morning", he says in a pleasant and cultured tone.

"Good morning", Josip replies.

"You are fond of the pigeons", says the man. Though it is unclear if a statement or a question has been uttered, Josip nods again.

"I too am fond of pigeons", the stranger continues, leaning forward with an earnest smile. "In my home country they were the constant companions of my childhood. Many of the birds in this great park are variations of the rock pigeon. However, you have not, I presume, heard of the Nicobar pigeon, which is black with a shawl of string-like feathers and iridescent green sub-feathers and projects a most sinister appearance, nor have you heard of the Pompadour pigeon, which is lemon-green with red wings?"

Josip shakes his head, uncertain whether to approach or to depart.

"My favorite is the laughing pigeon—yes, this is its veritable and verifiable name—which is self-explanatory. While in appearance it is lovely, as are all pigeons, no, I should say *most* pigeons, it is among the humblest of the species, for it is only tawny-colored and does not attract the eye as do the others. As with many things in this world of ours, it is in disguise, which is to say, *in cognito*."

"May I sit down?" Josip asks.

"Yes, please accompany me. You have passed a great test."

"A test? I have said nothing."

"You have asked to sit down. This is something. Moreover, it is a trans-cultural event of epic proportions."

"You are gifted with language, sir."

"Yes, and more prodigious is this accomplishment because it is my third language, in a total of seven."

"You do not by any chance speak a Slavic language, do you?"

"I regret that I do not. I may be forgiven a presumption if I guess that you, sir, are of Slavic origins?"

"Yes. I am from Croatia."

"Ah, a Balkan exile."

"We do not consider ourselves to be part of the Balkans. We are an ancient nation."

"If you will permit me a quibble," the man goes on with an apologetic smile, in a tone of cordial exchange between equals, "may I suggest that all Balkan peoples consider themselves to be ancient nations."

"Perhaps that is so, but in our case it is true."

"That is quite how I feel about my native land. You are doubtless wondering if I am from Pakistan or Bangladesh, or Sri Lanka or Madagascar, or even if I am a Persian with an excess of dark pigmentation chromosomes."

"I think you are from India."

"This is correct."

"Are you an ornithologist?"

"I regret to say that by education I am an economist, though I have not yet obtained employment in this capacity and do not wish to pursue it as an occupation either, despite my doctorates, of which I am inordinately proud."

Josip smiles, recognizing a joke.

"Then you are a professor."

"No, I am a clerk at the Bank of India on Park Avenue. And may I be so forward as to inquire of your profession?"

"I am not unlike you, sir, in that I was a doctor of mathematics in my homeland, before emigrating to America."

"And are you suitably employed in that profession?"

"I regret I am not."

"The language barrier?"

"Yes, and the difficulty in obtaining my education records from the government of Yugoslavia."

"You are, then, not in their good favor?"

"This is so."

"I see."

Josip wonders if the other will end the conversation abruptly. But the man leans closer.

"Am I correct in guessing that you are a person who searches for truth?"

Josip gives this some thought before replying. "Yes, I suppose I am."

"I am the same. However, you will doubtless agree that intellectual brilliance is not everything. Indeed, a global intellectual in search of truth may be handicapped in his pursuits due to displacement—disorientation, if you will permit me a pun."

Josip does not detect any pun in the comment but replies with a grave nod, "Yes, I think it is a great problem."

"Do you mean the pun or the displacement?"

"The displacement."

"You have passed the second test. You are not only a nice man, you are an honest one."

It is hard to know how to respond. What sort of fellow is this, really? He is rather strange. Brilliant but strange. And what does he want from the encounter?

"Consider," says the man from India, "consider the causality and the odds necessary for this configuration of yourself and myself in a city such as this, which is a vast and perplexing amalgamation of human enterprise. Here we are, two minds, both exiles, one Christian (I presume so because the indelible mark is upon your forehead), one not a Christian, myself, in other words. Thus the dialogue will be multidimensional: origins, race, reason, soul, religion, identity—universality and particularity in human nature, filtered through human perception."

Josip chuckles and says nothing.

"You laugh?" says the other with curiosity. "Why do you laugh?"

"We do not know each other."

"Do you think that if we were to spend the next thirty years

577

sharing golf games and barbecues we would know each other better than we do now?"

"You are a philosopher, not an economist", says Josip with a smile.

"A pleasant epithet, though inaccurate. But we can discuss it another time. Where, may I ask, do you live?"

"On West 52nd Street."

"Really!" says the man with a look of surprise. "So do I? What number?"

Josip tells him.

Astonishment replaces surprise. The man stands and leans forward with both hands on the knob of his cane. "This is extraordinary! Absolutely incredible. That is my building as well. I moved in a week ago today."

A week ago today was Josip's day off. Perhaps a new tenant moved in while he was fishing on the Hudson.

The man sits down again and gazes at Josip with wonder. He continues to shake his head as if trying to compute the statistical odds or an impossibly convoluted theorem.

"Do you live with your family?" he asks.

This generates so much pain in the cellars of Josip's soul that he merely shakes his head mutely.

"Ah, the Balkans. Exile or loss?"

What a question! Exile *is* loss.

"Unfortunately, I lost my family after the Communists came to power in Yugoslavia. They have all perished."

"I am so sorry", says the man, with a look of profound sympathy. He glances at Josip's wrists. Usually Josip takes care to wear only long-sleeved shirts, which hide the jagged scars—the loud proclamations of his suicide attempt. Today, however, he has been feeding pigeons with his sleeves rolled up. He now rolls them down and buttons the cuffs.

"These are terrible times", the man from India continues. "It is estimated with some degree of accuracy that in this century one hundred and seventy million people have been murdered by their governments."

"Is it so?" says Josip, casting about in his mind for other topics, anything to pull the conversation out of its downward spiral.

The stranger sighs. "Yes, tragically it is so. And here we are coolly discussing the murders, which seem to us from this vantage point to be *true* yet unreal. Is this perhaps another kind of murder that has been committed?"

"What do you mean?"

"I mean that every such crime murders more than the immediate victims, it murders the consciousness of survivors."

Josip does not answer. How to explain to the man that a bomb was detonated on his childhood and that he is still dealing with his altered consciousness.

A silence ensues. Is the conversation over? How will this tenant treat him when he discovers that he has been discussing profound and personal topics with the building's janitor?

"I want to reassure you, sir," says the man, "that continued dialogues would not be a case of my plundering your mind or your life for reflective material. I seek understanding, not information. I seek a coherent system for knowing the world."

"I do not think I have much to offer", says Josip.

"A doctor of mathematics has nothing to offer?"

"I should correct your impression. I am—"

The man sighs. "Yes, yes, but you see, though I know many Oriental exiles, I do not really know any Occidental, or accidental, exiles from regions east of the Mediterranean."

With a sudden bright smile, he says: "Would you care to join me for a cup of tea?"

"I would be pleased to", says Josip.

"I have come prepared."

From the wicker hamper he extracts two china cups and two napkins, a stainless steel thermos bottle, and a jar of milk, all of which he carefully sets on the bench, between himself and Josip. He pours milk into each cup, and then the tea is poured into the milk. He offers one to Josip first.

Josip takes it, then hesitates.

"Ah," says the man, "we have only just met. Who is this stranger who offers me a beverage, you ask yourself. Perhaps the thought crosses your mind that I am an extremely intelligent thief. You suspect that I have read in ornithology and economics all morning as an elaborate preparation for the act I am about to commit. After all, it is not against the weight of statistical probability that a trusting scientist would appear in the park today, considering the decline of the humanities in the Western world and the promotion everywhere of science, and that such a person, given over as he is to the myth of pure *gnosis*, would also be somewhat naïve. Theoretically, let us say, I have drugged the tea with a sedative. I will pretend to sip from my cup, and you will swallow all of yours. Then, when you have drifted off to sleep, I will remove your wallet from your pocket. I will extract any money I find within it, as well as your credit cards. This will give me approximately one hour in which to make a great many purchases until you awake. With a certain margin of error, I may have perhaps a second hour of rampant purchasing, during which time you will gradually realize that you have been deceived and robbed. We will never see each other again, for to your chagrin you will discover that I do not really live in your apartment building. I warn you, I am extremely clever."

Josip drinks down the entire cupful of tea in three swallows.

"This is excellent", says Josip. "I much prefer its taste to tea into which the milk is added afterward."

"It is a British custom. Some say it is Irish. There is much debate over this." He pauses. "You will not fall asleep."

The man beams with satisfaction. "We have progressed very far with each other. Still I do not know your name." He extends a hand, "I am W. V. R. Kanapathipillai."

Josip shakes it. "How do you do, Mr. Kanapath . . . I'm sorry, it's hard to pronounce."

"Then, if you wish, please call me Winston V. It is Churchillian, for victory."

"Thank you, Winston V. I am Josip Lasta."

"Josip Lasta. Considerably more easy for me than it is for you. Ah, the human tongue, so conditionable, yet so intractable once it is conditioned. The children of Noah scattered across the face of the earth."

"You know Sacred Scripture."

"Yes, of course", says Winston V. "Though I was born and raised in a Hindu family, I attended an elite Anglican college in Bangalore when I was a boy. I played cricket passionately and remain to this day very fond of Shakespeare, especially *King Lear*, though I dislike rugby and Shelley. I am not so good at horseback riding. I liked polo when I was younger, but, alas, my physical stature is not suitable to that sport."

"What floor do you live on?"

"The seventh", says Winston, with a smile.

"Would you care to join me for a dinner in my home?"

"I would be delighted."

So they walk side by side back to the apartment building, saying little, both quietly musing on the improbabilities of life. Arriving at the front steps, Josip thinks to himself that it is now Winston V's turn to take a test.

"What floor do you live on?" Winston asks as they enter the lobby.

" 'Lo, Joe", says Gus-the-doorman before Josip can answer.

" 'Lo, Gus."

In the elevator, Winston smiles to himself. "What a country! Even in New York City they behave as if this is small-town America."

"It's just human, I think, and most pleasant."

"It is undoubtedly better than massacres. But don't presume

they won't massacre us if the political-economic situation worsens."

Josip glances at Winston out of the corner of his eyes.

"We are going up to which floor?" the latter asks, his index finger poised over the number buttons.

"We are going down to the basement," says Josip mildly, "for that is where I live. I am the janitor."

"Splendid", says Winston with real enthusiasm, pressing B. "Most splendid."

So they enter Josip's little cell and have a supper of rice and fish, finished off with more tea. And throughout it all, Winston gazes with discreet interest at the shelves of books.

"May I ask you an intrusive question?"

"Yes, you may."

"When I offered you the tea in the park, you took the cup, but then you hesitated. Why did you?"

"It was not because I felt any suspicion", Josip replies after some thought. "I was recalling that it has been several years since anyone offered me something to drink. I was remembering the last time it happened."

"Then you are really alone in this world?"

"I have no family, as I said."

"I too am without family. All connections to my past have been—how do I express it concisely?—terminated by my lack of interest in high-level economic and social advancement. For an eldest son, this is a disgrace. Not for any practical reason is it a disgrace, because it is purely symbolic. My family is quite wealthy. They have no need for my economic and social advancement, other than a perceived need based in unreality and ancient fears that long ago became groundless. The 1919 Amritsar massacre syndrome. Fear of the colonial power, alternating with aggressive overreaction to that power. A bristling pride, a bristling ambition."

"They have cut the ties?"

"They have."

Josip ponders this for no more than a few moments.

"Would you honor me with your friendship, Winston V?"

Winston V's face registers astonishment, which he quickly hides.

"It is you who honor me", he murmurs, in a subdued voice.

Later in the evening, Winston invites Josip to visit his apartment. Sure enough, a business card taped to the hall side of the door proclaims: *Dr. W. V. Ramamurthy Kanapathipillai, D.Sc., Ph.D. Econ.* He unlocks and they go in. Winston deposits his cane among a bouquet of umbrellas in a brass stand by the front door.

"Please, enter the temple of the elephant god", he says, throwing his keys onto a little table. Winston has a one-bedroom flat, with a window facing west toward the river. Not much of a view because there are a lot of buildings blocking it. A telescope at the window points heavenward.

"Useless", says Winston. "Its role in my life is purely symbolic."

The walls are lined with books. The furniture is antique British, and the rug is a garden of Tudor roses. There is nothing Indian.

As Winston makes a pot of tea for his guest in the kitchenette, Josip browses through the bookshelves. Economics and literature, astronomy and history, even some physics. He quickly pulls out one of the latter and flips its pages, translating concepts in his mind and matching the English words with the vocabularies of Croatian and German physics—the scraps still lingering in his memory.

Observing Josip's intense interest in something he has found in the book, Winston says, "You may borrow it."

"That is very kind of you."

Josip continues to devour the contents as they sit together without much social expectation, facing each other across a coffee table piled high with *The New York Times* and *The Times of India*. They are enjoying the rather unusual experience of it all—the sensation of a time-tested and comfortable friendship that is only hours old.

Winston nods at the book in Josip's hands. "Are you aware that many scientists assert that the only realities in the sub-atomic world are the De Broglie waves? For them, matter is an illusion."

"I must say, Winston, that it sounds very close to Hinduism."

"I agree with you, Josip", he chuckles. "What the rational scientist and the irrational cultist forget is that perception is limited. Of course, they both declare that they understand the limitations. The scientist tries to measure what can be measured, and the cultist promotes the cultic symbols as a mode through which the supra-physical may be apprehended. Yet both types of men are present *within* their modalities, thus altering the very modalities they assert as the means for attaining objective knowledge or objective experience."

"Yes, it is a problem in scientific method."

"A universal problem of perception, I think. Consider only one aspect of reality: the visible light spectrum. It tells us much, but we did not realize how little we knew until instruments were developed for registering forces beyond the sensory."

"So, you're saying there may be other dimensions."

"I'm saying I do not reject the possibility that they are there, that's all. I make no judgment about what they may be or what they may mean."

"Then you will admit the existence of meaning in the world."

"That is a big topic. Should we attempt it so soon in our friendship? Perhaps I will offend you by my critical doubts."

"On the contrary, I am heartened by your willingness to admit the possibility of the metaphysical." Josip pauses. "Have you ever heard of diatoms?"

And so it goes for three more hours. By ten o'clock, Josip is yawning. Tomorrow is Sunday, and he wants to attend the early Mass at the parish, which means setting the alarm clock. They shake hands, arrange a next meeting, and part.

Today is his feast day, March 19. He was born on the feast of St. Josip in 1933. This makes him, if his computations are correct, forty-two years old. This morning he receives a birthday card from Slavica and Emilio. It is, as usual, full of heartwarming news. Paolo will begin studies at the University of Bologna in September and hopes to major in medicine. He is presently tormented by a parallel desire to become a professional soccer player. They are a little worried about Chiara. She is so beautiful that all the Italian boys from Venezia to Padova are in love with her, but fortunately she has no interest in the suitors, who must be batted away incessantly. She thinks of nothing but her flute and piano. She is longing to begin her studies at a music college in Firenze. Emilio eats too much chocolate. His mother died this year, and they miss her greatly.

Slavica and Emilio have sold their home and moved to Padova, where they now live in a modest apartment. They have opened a private refuge for young prostitutes. Two houses: one for girls, one for boys. She is working together with the priests to heal minds and souls. It is a great challenge because the damage done to these young people is severe, mostly psychological. They feel worthless, often hopeless, and certain that they have ruined their lives. So much love is needed, so much healing—everywhere it seems.

Slavica asks if Josip recalls the American woman, Mrs. Conway, who was so helpful in obtaining his refugee status and eventual citizenship in the United States of America. She and her husband are in Vietnam but soon will be transferred to a European city where her husband is to become ambassador. This news is confidential for the time being. The situation in

Saigon is very bad, and the remaining Americans will probably soon withdraw from the country.

In the afternoon, Josip and Winston share another cup of tea in the park. Winston is trying to teach Josip British manners, which his Slavic mind cannot, will not, accept. He, in turn, is trying to teach Winston to be more relaxed, by mastering the art of the temporary capture of pigeons. He is a slow learner and has not yet succeeded. Today he is not interested in any of this and seems uncharacteristically angry. He is outraged by a statement in *The New York Times* posted by a group of scientists who demand the reduction of the planet's population, either by cooperation or by force. Josip points out to him that the Church's censure of Galileo was rather mild in comparison to this. The new high priests of scientism are much more intolerant than the old hierarchy ever was. Winston stares at Josip, then laughs. They play chess together sometimes. Today Winston merely replies, "You win, Josip. Checkmate."

Later, he comes down to the basement for a birthday supper. Josip had caught a fat trout on Saturday with the new fiberglass rod and stainless-steel reel that he purchased at Abercrombie and Fitch—an extravagance, but one he paid for by cutting back on luxuries for six months. He had no coffee or jam during all that time and did not indulge in a single book purchase. He is not sure how he survived it. But what a rod and reel this is!

Winston has brought coffee and Darjeeling tea from his apartment. As they sip their beverages and nibble at European pastries purchased for the occasion from a shop on the Avenue of the Americas, Winston says: "These scientists in their Harvard and Princeton laboratories are alchemists. They misunderstand practically everything."

Josip considers this a very good sign. Winston may be abandoning his habit of confusing data for wisdom. By the same token, Josip reminds himself not to confuse wisdom for data. Even so, he senses that the elephant god is dying.

There is a lot of craziness here in America. Well, lots where he came from too, but this is a new kind. He reads things in the papers, even Catholic papers, that astound him. Has the human race gone mad? Have Catholics gone especially mad!? Josip feels much love for this Pope who carries the burdens of the world on his shoulders. The newspapers are criticizing him these days, and his own theologians are too; they are the worst. They say he does not understand sex, that people are not baby factories, that theologians know better what is right and wrong in bed. For Josip, such thoughts are so evil that it is difficult not to slip into his old temptation to hatred. How blind they are! How proud and arrogant, to tell people it is fine to poison themselves with chemicals and mutilate their bodies at the very sources of life, just so they can escape children! As if children could ever—*ever*—be a burden! Death in disguise has entered the hearts of these theologians, and death will come from their teachings!

Whenever he spots their articles in the magazine rack at the back of the church, or attends a Mass in a parish where such ideas are expressed in homilies, he stares in disbelief. Then he wrestles silently with disgust and horror. Worried by such feelings in these holiest of places or in these holiest of moments, he turns his attention to the crucifix that still hangs above some of the altars. And when the Body of Christ is raised above the altar of the world, he bows and asks Christ's forgiveness—begs that all the anger still inside him will be washed away.

Fragment:

> My confessor, Friar Todd, is a husky fellow from Ohio. This morning I confessed my ongoing struggle to love my enemies, even those who are beyond reach—separated as we are by innumerable years and by a wide ocean. He told me that all the sufferings in my past are a gift. He is young. He plays a guitar. But he does love St. Francis, and he has the basics in right order.

"I know how glib it must sound to your ears", he said through the confessional screen. (Has he guessed my identity? Perhaps he has figured out my accent.) "And it's hard for me to say this to you because I've never really suffered. But our Lord has suffered, and I think he would say the same thing to you."

A gift that I lost Ariadne and the baby, my family, my people? A gift that I lost my learning and my vision of the cosmos? I know the truth of this, theologically. Still, how hard it is to accept in one's heart and soul.

Would I like to have the gift rescinded? Of course! Yet, in the strangest level of my self I know that it is a gift nonetheless. How else do we know God's rescue unless we have been drowning? Can healing be demonstrated without injury, or love be proven without trial? Still, there is an ache within me that cries out: what of those who were not protected, who are left unhealed, who do not know love?

The reply is articulated by—and can *only* be articulated by—God dying with us on our cross.

With us? Did I just write this very simple phrase? Have I not "died" enough? Yet it makes me wonder—if there is more to come, how could I, now so privileged in this new world, die with him?

Fragment:
[in English]

quirks: idiosyncrasies.

quarks: elementary particles in pairs, such as + and − charges.

quantum jump: an abrupt transition from one discrete energy state to another.

quantum mechanics: a theory of matter based on the concept of the possession of wave properties by elementary particles that affords a mathematical interpretation of the structure and interactions of matter (incorporating both quantum theory and the uncertainty principle).

quantum theory: a theory in physics based on the concept of subdivision of radiant energy into finite quanta and applied to processes involving transference or transformation of energy in the atomic or molecular scale.

[In Croatian]

I experience a moment of inflated pleasure as I copy these definitions from an English-language book. Then deflation follows, as I realize that I simply do not know what to do with this material. I begin to cry. I did not feel the tears coming because they were suddenly there, shaking my chest and swelling my throat without sound. I know what caused it: *Loss*. I have my mind still, but what I had thought to be my identity as a young man is gone, probably forever. I can tinker with little components of the "unified field theory", but I now realize that I can never again reconstruct it. Today, if I had a rock in my hand, I would beat my chest with it, like Jerome.

No, no, no, I would not! It is an evil thing to punish oneself for what was done to you against your will. Of course, it is feeling—dismay engendering terror or rage, initially. Then the rage tends to go outward, onto perceived enemies by transference, or inward, against oneself. In order to escape this island, one must swim away from it, draw a fresh breath of air, and see that the world has not ended. One does not need to recreate the cosmos or to fix it, but I can choose to love, despite everything. This is currency. Only God frees me to choose this because, without him, I would slide into the condition of the killers, the beast-men of Goli Otok. I am no better than they are. All men, without Christ, are capable of becoming Cain—though everyone would deny it.

That winter he reads his way laboriously through the *Summa Theologica* and is startled not a few times by what St. Thomas Aquinas has to say about angels. The angels guide the course of the material heavens and strive to help man with his freedom. They sometimes appear on earth, in disguise. This prompts an old memory—the boy who came to him in the piazza of St. Peter's in Rome. At the time, he had sensed that the encounter was mysterious—not strange, really, because mystery is a different thing from strangeness. Yet even now, over a decade later, he cannot say whether that boy was a wholly material being. Was he perhaps a supernatural being, and was the sensation of a physical hand tugging on his own a grace in the imagination? Was it like Raphael and Tobiah and the great fish? And if he was an angel, why did he not appear as a mighty warrior with a sword in hand, eagle's wings, and a valiant face, fierce and holy? If he was an angel, why was he sent as a child? Why was his age the same as Josip's was when his world ended?

30

Today he is playing chess with Caleb, a habit they began a year after the boy rescued him from an attempted robbery. Sometimes they walk together to Central Park, where it is not uncommon to see forlorn old men sitting on benches, with chessboards beside them, hoping to engage a stranger in a game. If strangers let themselves be hooked in this manner, the impersonality of the city shrinks to the dimensions of a village square. Or perhaps it is expansion. Whenever Josip and Caleb play chess in the park, passersby gather around, cosmic stragglers and wanderers, armchair military strategists, failed mathematicians, and kings—all in the vestments of the dispossessed. A few pigeons too.

Caleb is very intelligent. Undisciplined and unformed, yet capable of lightning decisions propelled by inductive rather than deductive reasoning. It is quite a challenge to bring him into check and an extremely rare event to checkmate him. He is as good for Josip's general mental health as Josip is for his. How old is the boy now? Sixteen, perhaps. He has shaved his head and become a beanpole—almost as tall as Josip—with the universal potential for rage in his posture, mediated somewhat by lingering African warmth. Yes, there is heart there, and while it is always guarded by the threat of violent eruptions, the taming process is under way. Formation will come later, if it is to happen, but freedom must be respected at every moment. One may invite but never force or coerce. In his back pocket, Caleb carries an ugly knife that can be unsprung and plunged into the flesh of an attacker within a second. So far, there has been no occasion to put it to the test. Every day Josip prays that one will never arise. The taming process is helped along by food. Food is soul-currency. Especially smoked-meat sandwiches, which Josip prepares in advance whenever they are to go on a chess excursion in the park—one sandwich for himself, three for Caleb. The boy also likes chocolate and cigarettes. These are better than heroin. Josip is willing to supply chocolate but no drugs.

"Let it melt slowly on your tongue."

"No way. This a whole bar y' give me. Fast-fast-fast, that's what ah like best!"

"It is the worst method, Caleb. You dishonor the people who made this bar for you."

"I don' know 'em."

"Yes, you know them. Your mother works in a chocolate-bar factory."

"You crazy, man? She don' work in no factory!"

"I meant it figuratively."

"Whatinahell's *figuratively* mean?"

"Symbolically. She cleans rooms in the apartment house. What if some sixteen-year-old boy living in that house were to toss his candy wrapper onto the floor she had just swept?"

"What you talkin' 'bout?"

"Take a little square and let it melt on your tongue. See if I'm right."

Caleb tries it, swallows, and shrugs; says he still prefers fast-fast-fast. Regardless, after three years of dialogues and shared experience, he is decelerating a little and taking a closer look at life.

Josip tries, as well, to expand the lad's universe by calling their trips to the park "hunting expeditions". They will search for surprises. Caleb thinks this is idiotic, childish, not very street-savvy. It is cosmic-savvy, Josip replies. We will collect clues to something bigger than what we see with our eyes.

"What you see is what you get", counters the boy.

"No, what you *cannot* see is what you get", says Josip and will explain no further. More and more he inserts such hints into their dialogues. For example, one day as they pass a woman in rags rummaging in a trash barrel, he turns to Caleb:

"You, of course, recognize that lady."

"Hell no, I don' recanize 'er. Who she anyway?"

"She is a queen who has fallen upon hard times. She should be living in her palace."

It is easy to hook the boy with the absurd—especially absurdities that contain encrypted truths.

Or simple actions that write messages in memory. They are walking from the monkey house at the zoo, when they spot a teenage girl sitting up against one of its walls, with her head between her knees. She is wearing dirty jeans and a sweatshirt. The front of her sweatshirt is pulled over her knees, the back hiked up over the top of her head. Her forehead, eyes, and a bit of greasy hair are exposed. Her eyes are clenched shut, and her skin is gray. Though it is a summer day, she is shivering, trying to stay warm in a patch of sunshine.

Josip and Caleb stop a few paces away.

"Tracks", mumbles Caleb with disgust, pointing to her exposed forearms, tattooed with lines of needle marks.

Josip kneels beside the girl, removes something from his pocket, and gently shakes her shoulder.

"Don' giv her no cash, Joe!" Caleb mutters contemptuously.

When the girl looks up with bloodshot eyes, she startles. Josip offers her a bread roll, a chocolate bar, and an orange. She takes them, staring at him uncomprehendingly. He closes his eyes and silently prays for her. And when she knocks him away with an elbow, he blesses her and walks on.

Caleb shakes his head all the way down 52nd street.

"You a bleedin'-heart liberal, man", he says as they approach the apartment house.

"Please, Caleb, explain this term to me."

593

"I meant it figuratively", he laughs.

Josip frowns. "What are you, then, Caleb?"

"I'm a conservative", declares the boy with a proud jerk of his chin. "Me'n'Momma, we vote Republican."

"Aren't you too young to vote?"

Caleb ignores this. "My Momma, she *always* vote Republican. She say th'othah people in Harlem, they's Democrats, and she got no truck with Democrats. She says they's bleedin'-heart liberals. She got a lotta people mad at her in my 'partment over it."

"Does she think I am a bleeding-heart liberal?"

"Nah, she say you a *heretic*, man. But why you give your stuff to that girl anyway?"

"Because I know her."

Caleb looks surprised. "Don' gimme that shee-it. You don' know her."

"But I do. That is myself I saw sitting there."

Caleb stops in his tracks. "What you talkin' 'bout?"

"When I was her age I was just like her. I sat against a wall in that posture, freezing and starving, with nowhere to go."

As they walk on, Caleb digests this.

"You ain't no Jesus Christ", he snorts.

"I realize this, Caleb. I cannot save her, but I am permitted to give her a little bread."

Currency.

"Let's go round the block again", mumbles Caleb, still shaking his head.

"All right. What should we see?"

"Nothin'."

But the boy sets a course directly to a corner store, commands Josip to wait outside, and goes in. A few minutes later he comes out with a paper bag in his hands. He opens it and extracts a package of soda biscuits. Without a word, he hands it to Josip, and then walks away.

"Where are you going, Caleb?" Josip calls after him.

"To the monkey house."

The Croatian newsletter has been launched, with its first issue doing a bustling business at the back of the church. The publisher/editor/newsboy tells Josip that copies have been mailed to Croatian parishes throughout America, and also to some Croatian nationalist organizations on the West Coast and in New England. It's a test run, he says, maybe there won't be a second issue, but there's no harm in trying.

Josip's poem is on pages 12 to 14 of the mimeographed periodical. Unable to recall his old poems from the Dolphin journal, he had written a new one. A hundred-line, thinly-disguised love poem. For a few short weeks, he fell into an illusory daydream of romance with a Croatian–American woman about as old as he is, late forties, graceful, courteous, and very devout. Friar Todd told him that she was a widow, a high-school teacher in the Bronx. Because of his various inhibitions, both natural and inflicted, he never spoke with her in any personal way. On the front steps of the church, he tipped his cap a few times, and they exchanged weather comments in Croatian, but no intimate information was divulged. However, there was something of the old current of attraction in their eyes.

Yes, he sensed a hint of gentle flame in hers. He was certain about his own feelings because he could have poured out his lonely soul in a single flare if she had given him a signal to proceed. But she did not, though he spent several restless nights wrestling over the finest inferences of her facial expressions. Even though he misinterpreted and hoped for his own interpretation to be correct, he finally understood that he was desperately trying to inflate an illusion into a reality. If anything were to have developed, he would simply have gone down on his knees like Chicklet to his Canary and proposed marriage. But in the final days of his infatuation, Josip realized that he was merely seeking a cure for his loneliness and was not really in love with her. Then she moved away to another part of the city.

Two blessings came as a result of this "romance". First, it expanded his heart again, and he remembered Josipa a little and Ariadne a lot, and felt the old flow of heart-soul passion. It hurt—hurt more than he thought it could—but there was an unexpected sense of vitality that returned with the pain. It was difficult to get through this period. The horror of Josipa's death surfaced, and he had to keep pushing the memory of that final day in Rajska Polja back into the locked cellar. His memories of Ariadne were grief rather than horror, and these he permitted to linger. The second blessing was that the poem seemed to write itself. The object of this creation, the Croatian–American woman, remained unnamed. He addressed it to Croatia, titled it *In the Homeland of the Soul*, and later understood that he was speaking to Love itself.

Fragment:

This passage from my one-hundred-line poem (to Croatia, to the lady, to love) keeps returning to my mind. Why this and not another?

Language, speech, the grammar of the heart,
expanding the vocabulary of the soul,
signal from the heart's lost lexicon:
Where do we come from?
What are we seeking?
Why do we run ever and ever onward
toward union and completion?
Yet speech impedes us, slows us, weights us,
for uncertainty lies between the speaking and the hearing,
in turgid eddies, cold slipstreams, vortex and whirling pool.

And fear, dark as the rotting beds of old oceans
sucks at the limbs.

Well, my great romance didn't turn out the way I had hoped. Perhaps she was struggling with her own memories and could not take on any new ones. The initial look of interest in her eyes, the latent affection, and the unexpressed depths of understanding were probably no more than a form of bread offered to a stranger. Currency of the soul. In any event, she has moved on.

The publisher/editor/newsboy informs Josip a month later that readers are enthusiastic about the inaugural issue. There will be a second. Some feel that Josip's poem is "interesting", though oddly inconsistent with the other material—Croatian nationalist politics, critiques of the Tito regime, and examinations of the struggles of the exiles. But since it has aroused some interest and a couple of letters of praise, he is willing to consider more poems as long as they are shorter (*much* shorter) and less obscure. Would Josip agree to that? Josip agrees, and so begins a working relationship that is to endure for more than twenty years and will lead to many surprises.

Winston has developed the habit of going away every weekend. He becomes evasive whenever Josip inquires about the reason. He is looking at some horses, he says—*polo* horses—as if this failed polo player cannot shake an obsession. After three months of evasion, he admits that he also visits a woman who lives in a place called Yale, in Connecticut (a strange name for a state—a connection that severs!). She is a teacher, and she likes horses. They both like horses, he adds.

"Oh, that is a congenial shared interest", Josip replies. Winston shakes with suppressed mirth, leaning on his cane.

"Would you like to come with me one weekend?" he asks.

"I am honored, Winston, truly, but I am not interested in polo. If the game were played with elephants, however, I would not hesitate."

"I regret, the only elephant present at the games is a small one made of ivory. But to be honest, Josip, I would like to introduce Miriam to my friends. Correction, to my single and singular friend."

"In that case, I will eagerly come."

Josip hopes that Winston's heart will not be broken. It seems to him that there are far more broken hearts in this world than there are fulfilled ones. Thus the statistical odds are not favorable.

It turns out that Yale is a prestigious university, with many faculties and fine old brick buildings, walkways, and a lavish number of trees. "This is quintessential New England", Josip's tour guide proudly informs him, poking his ivory cane here and there as they walk about the campus—as if to say that *this*, and not Oxford or Cambridge, is the center of the world. Indeed, for Winston it has become the epicenter, because there is a heart beating for him here. She is a professor of Asian Studies, and they are "betrothed." Josip worries that the beloved will turn out to be an American girl entranced by Winston's mystique, a purely cultural infatuation. That would be a recipe for a broken heart.

Before meeting her, they go to an early afternoon polo match at a park near the university. It is an elegant though brutal game—an interesting juxtaposition. At one point, a horse throws its rider, gallops in a circle around the grounds, then comes to a halt by the fence guarding spectators from the play. In fact, it stops right in front of Josip, whinnies, and stands there without moving, gazing at him with its dark eyes. It is a white horse. It is speaking, but what it says he cannot hear. He is instantly a boy again, and with an ache of longing in his throat, he thrusts his arms impulsively through the rails to touch its neck. It steps back a pace or two, smiles in a way that only a horse can smile, tosses its mane, wheels, and breaks into a gallop. It takes some minutes for its rider to capture it, and then the game resumes.

They have a late lunch in a restaurant in New Haven, and there Winston's beloved joins them. She enters the dining hall in a purple sari and Oriental sandals, carrying her briefcase. She is a lovely woman, quite a few years younger than Winston. She is East Indian. A Fifth-Avenue platinum wristwatch glows at her wrist as she shakes Josip's hand and lets Winston kiss her cheek. A small silver crucifix dangles at her neck. It is explained over oysters and wine that she is a Goa Catholic. Josip does not know the term. He guilelessly asks her when she converted to the Faith. She replies with a gentle laugh, "Actually, our family converted more than nineteen hundred years ago, when St. Thomas the apostle evangelized India." The Goa branch of her family were late-bloomers, converted by Portuguese missionaries.

This information affords Josip (supposedly ancient Catholic that he is) a little reflection. Her ancestors were disciples of Christ five or six centuries before his own barbarian forefathers were converted by the Romanized Illyrians they had invaded and overcome. Overcoming the overcomers. Life is strange. You learn something new every day.

But what about Winston? What does the agnostic Park Avenue banker make of all this Catholicism that has surrounded him and perhaps even threatens to metamorphose him? Does he feel himself to be the victim of a conspiracy? Does he wonder if a metaphysical chess player moved a Catholic friend to the square beside him, and then a Catholic maiden to the flanking square—and is he now boxed in? Checkmate?

They plan to be married next summer. In May, Winston will resign from his job and move to Connecticut to be closer to her. He has obtained a position as an associate professor of religious studies, explaining to Josip that his business card does not list all of his degrees. He is, as well, taking instructions in the Faith from the Dominican Fathers at the university, and his betrothed is teaching him to pray the Rosary.

Dumbfounded by these developments, Josip remains fairly silent on the bus ride home to Manhattan.

"You do not seem pleased, Josip."

"I am very pleased", he replies in a subdued voice.

"Do you not like polo? Was it a boring afternoon?"

"It was not a boring afternoon."

"Then you think Miriam is unsuitable for a person of my heritage . . . or personal qualities?"

"She is very suitable."

"What is the problem, then?"

"It is not a problem, Winston. I am merely trying to compute the statistical probability of two miracles occurring on a single and singular day."

Winston chuckles.

Arriving in the city in the late afternoon, they find a fish market not far from home, and there Josip buys a salmon to make a supper celebration. The lady who sells it to him is extremely rude. She is a Serb, he thinks. Though it's uncertain whether she has spotted him as a Croat, the fact remains that she is polite enough to other customers and treats him as if he is utterly despicable. Winston is outraged by the woman's bad manners; Josip is merely intrigued. It has been a day of surprises. Two pluses, one minus.

Now, this Serb-lady: There is something in her eyes that suggests a history of suffering, of crushing personal defeats. Yet she has survived, and she is here in the free world. Did Ustashe kill her family members? Or did she merely detect a whiff of Yugoslavia in Josip's accent and bristled with animosity to protect herself from the mayhem of the land she left behind? It's hard to know.

Nevertheless, after some prayer and not a little musing, he decides that God has offered him an opportunity to put into practice the counsel of the Franciscan friar of St. Peter's piazza. Though he continues to make excursions up the Hudson whenever he can afford the time and bus fare, he changes his routine significantly, doing more and more fishing at the market. Her scowls, her contempt, her eyes that grow icy at the sight of him, all are somewhat daunting—intimidating really. Whenever he asks for a specific kind of fish, enunciating clearly, she inevitably barks "What?" It makes other customers turn their heads in curiosity, because she can hear everyone else quite well. No pleases or thank yous for him but always good manners for others. Why does she treat a customer this way? Has she smelled a Croat and wrinkled her nose in disgust? Does race hatred come with the birthright, or is it a private grievance? Her employers do not seem to mind her behavior—perhaps they are oblivious to it or perhaps they are Serbs. Nevertheless, they really know fish, these people, and do their jobs very well. The place smells like the bottom of Drago's boat, but the quality and choice of fish are excellent. Wealthy people from the big avenues around Central Park are much in evidence, as well as less prosperous fish lovers. The woman treats rich and poor alike with moderate courtesy, though it is never effusive, and never cheery. For Josip, and Josip alone, she exercises something akin to diabolic loathing. It is so astounding that he takes it on as a challenge. He estimates that it will take three or four years to tame her, but he is resolved that even if he cannot tame her, he is willing to spend a lifetime enduring her as reparation.

The word springs unbidden into his mind: *reparation*? Reparation for what? he asks himself. I have not hurt this woman. We have never met before. My parents and ancestors surely did hers no harm. General reparation, then. He can accept the insult as a mild form of humiliation offered for her soul and offered as payment for sins committed against her people by

601

Croats. The disproportion in this, however, seems incredibly unfair, because most of the victims of Yugoslavia's confusion were not, are not, and probably will not be Serbs. Even so, she has an eternal soul, and he feels pity for her. Whenever she throws a dart, he takes it in the chest and says a silent prayer for her.

When she slaps the package of fish onto the countertop, he always smiles, always says *thank you*. Whenever he augments this by saying *thank you, Madame*, her scowl worsens. She throws his change onto the counter, but carefully hands other people theirs. What on earth is troubling this woman?

Caleb's academic ability is entirely latent, potentially outstanding. However, his actual achievement is pathetic. He hates to study, hates sitting in a classroom all day, wants to be out pounding the streets with his feet, drinking up life with his eyes in fast-fast-fast quantities. On those evenings when Coriander is working nightshift upstairs, the boy comes down to the basement, and Josip becomes his tyrant. A nice tyrant, rewarding the subject with chocolate and mysteries.

He purchases a low-power microscope, along with a tray of sample slides, and presents it to Caleb on his birthday, the date extracted from his mother.

"Why you give me dis?" Caleb barks, when he suspiciously unwraps the box and sees what is inside.

"To help with your biology studies."

"I hate biology."

"I know you do. Now you will go hunting deep into the interior."

"What interior?"

"Yours. Here, let me show you. Look into the lens."

"Shee-it, that some monster down there."

"Don't fall into its mouth."

A grudging smile from the street rat.

Street Rat is the logo Caleb has painted on his sweatshirt. He still asserts his mask, Mean-and-proud-of-it, and he still carries a switchblade in his back pocket. He now wears a gold ring in his earlobe. But he has accepted to be the slaughterer whenever Josip hosts a large fish in the bathtub. And sometimes, of his own volition, the boy will help carry heavy trash to the dumpster behind the building.

"I sho' don' wanna meet that creep in a back alley", he mutters, peering into the lens. "He one big'n'ugly."

Josip knows that the street jargon is part of the mask. He has got Caleb reading *Macbeth*. Homer will come later. Perhaps Virgil as well. He will see how it goes.

"I regret to inform you, Caleb, that this monster is already inside of you."

"No shee-it. Don't gimme dat!'"

"Unfortunately. it is true. There are approximately three million of his kind running around in your intestines."

Caleb looks disgusted, says nothing.

"Now, this one is worse", says Josip putting another slide under the lens.

"No joke, that one *bad* customer. How many of *him*?"

"About the same number."

Caleb shakes his head. "We should stir em up, get a fight goin'. Then they kill each other off."

"Did you know that Louis Pasteur came up with the same suggestion?"

"Whoinahell is Louie Pasture?"

And so it goes.

Winston and Miriam are married by a Dominican friar in a chapel at Yale. Josip is the best man—though he feels quite unworthy of this honor. After the nuptial Mass, there is a small celebration in a faculty lounge. Josip later recalls little of this event, other than the curry—curry so hot that it killed every single monster in his intestines. Also, the word *svat* passed through his mind more than once.

When Winston is baptized at Easter, Josip is the godfather. He feels an almost unprecedented joy as the water pours over the brown dome of the skull, a head so full of intelligence and skeptical considerations, yet submitting to the ancient rite with the heart of a child. He also feels a weight of apprehension because the responsibility is great. He must help Winston to arrive safely in paradise.

At Christmas, he purchases a little golden carp to bake for his solitary dinner (Winston is at Yale this year with his wife). As the Serb-lady wraps the fish in newspaper, Josip takes from his pocket a package of European cream-biscuits wrapped in red foil. Orthodox Serbs celebrate Christmas in January, not on the 25th of December, but perhaps she will accept the gift anyway. He pays for the carp, she slaps it onto the glass, and tosses his change beside it as usual.

"Thank you, Madame. I wish you a merry Christmas", he says in English and places the gift where her hands can reach it. She examines it from the corner of her eyes, steps away with her down-turned slit of mouth, and says nothing (not even "What!").

"Thank you for your dependable service throughout the years", he adds, tipping his cap and walking out the shop door into the street. He admits that he is not quite man enough to wait for her reaction, if there is any. He will leave it to her to deal with. Snow is falling heavily on the sidewalks, and the recent history of human comings and goings is written there. He beats a fresh trail toward Sts. Cyril and Methodius, where he will sit in the pews for a few hours, waiting for Midnight Mass. He always loves this time, so silent, so abandoned, waiting, waiting, waiting in peace. And the more alone he is, it seems, the greater is the peace.

Fragment:

(A progress report on the disunified field theory of human relationships)

Caleb:

Year one, he read *Macbeth*, hated it. Looked down a microscope, was intrigued, kept looking. Various discussions about street life, weird people, his career as a tough guy. Regrettably, he failed his year at high school and was enraged that he must repeat it. His mother informed me that he failed a number of grades at the lower levels. He carries a weight of discouragement, the false conviction that he is "stupid".

Year two, he read *The Iliad* (I began with that because he prefers brute fighting to strategy). This opened the door for more poetry to seep in. I gave him Kipling (more fighting). He added a couple of Kipling novels to this, very much on his own. Applied for a library card and apparently uses it. He graduated to the next level of high school—the second, I think. He was relieved, though he feigned indifference.

Year three, practically a throw-away year, but it was better during the final months. First, the boy fell into wholesale madness, a love interest. She demolished him and departed for Chicago to become an exotic dancer. He could not concentrate, and thus he failed another year at high school. Though he did not seem angered by this, he displayed something more worrisome, a dark despondency that gripped him month after month. He dropped out of school, got a job loading trucks at night, and was soon fired for failing to appear on time for work. Then he just disappeared.

Year four: He was gone for more than six months, and not a word did Coriander receive from him during all that time. She was sick with perpetual anxiety; all banter ceased between us; her eyes were often red from secret tears. She prayed constantly that he would suffer no harm. I did too. You may become a surrogate father by appointment or by default, but this does not guarantee authority. You may plant seeds and tend vines, but you are never the master of another's soul. It is the problem of freedom, again. Freedom and love. Yes, it seems that certain claims upon the heart cannot be erased: I was surprised by how much I missed him.

Then, suddenly, he was home. Chastened, bearing a new scar on his upper lip, he would give no explanations. And in September he returned to school. That autumn, I took him to Connecticut one weekend, and we stayed with Winston and Miriam. They treated Caleb like a visiting African royal. I felt quite "white" over the weekend, a real cracker-biscuit. The cumulative effect on the street rat was an evocation of his genuine self, perhaps even his royal self buried somewhere down deep in his "interior", overlayered by strata of democratic ethos, exile, and slavery. Dig deep enough and we are all kings, despite our rags.

Around Yale there is less sky glow at night than over New York City. Caleb was fascinated by Andromeda, which we saw through Winston's telescope. C frowned when W told him how far away it is. At first he wouldn't believe it, but of course he does believe it. Abstractions and sensory input are connecting.

Caleb earns money as a part-time pack boy at a local "super-market" and at Christmas gave me a present that he bought at a used-book shop. It was a quaint old volume printed in England, *The Compleat Angler*, illustrated with engravings of fish. The gift touched me, both the giving and the thought that went into it. When he dropped it off at my room on Christmas Eve afternoon, along with a cake his mother had made, his street jargon was worse than it has been in years. He now wears rings up and down the rims of both ears and a small one in his nostril. The mask. Yet choices and acts are the real man beneath the mask. He knows this, and he knows that I know, but for good reasons we did not start ripping off masks just because it was Christmas and he had displayed vulnerability.

Caleb grumbled about his literature teacher. She told him that he wouldn't pass his year unless he wrote a poem. He was very angry about it and wanted me to write it for him. I adamantly refused.

Year five, Miriam and Winston expecting a baby. Winston is happier than I have ever seen him—ecstatic, actually. However, he has become more didactic than ever (always a tendency in him), a fervent Catholic, extremely involved with devotions (perhaps predisposed by the rich symbolic life of his country of origin). I am the same but not quite to his degree. Winston has metamorphosed into an apologist of epic proportions. On a recent visit I teased him about it. He laughed at my teasing and laughed at himself—a good sign. He loves the Eucharist and our Lady especially and frequents the confessional weekly. He urged me to do the same. I already do, I assured him. Oh, good, he replied, with a whiff of disappointment. It may be he wanted to evangelize his sidereal evangelizer. Overcome the overcomer. However, it was all quite pleasureable for both of us. I have never seen him so effusively elated. The soon-to-be-born baby is his greater joy.

Winston and Miriam's baby was born, a tiny brown sweetheart whom they baptized Christiana. I am her godfather.

Caleb passed his year but wouldn't show me the poem he wrote. "It's crap!" he said.

The Serb-lady:
Year one of my campaign. I gathered all the slights and hurts and atavistic fears she had engendered in my little heart and offered them at Christmas Eve Mass for her soul. For two weeks I wondered what effect my Christmas package had

had on her. When I entered the shop the day after Epiphany, I learned that it had had no immediate effect. I bought some fish, endured another "What!", gathered up the tossed coins, repeated my customary manners, then departed. No visible changes.

Year two, more of the same, but somewhere in the middle of the year she dropped the "What!", though all the other symptoms of loathing continued.

Year three, she nodded at me one day when I said *thank you* and put the change into my hand. She still wouldn't meet my eyes, however, and kept her scowl firmly in place. Each Christmas I give a box of cream-biscuits and recite my thanks for her excellent services. Each year she pretends she hasn't heard. I never discover what happens to the biscuits. Does she trash them for fear of poison or moral contamination? Or does she open them secretly wherever she lives and wonder about the mad Croat who will not collapse before her arsenal? Alternatively, does she pass the box around to her fellow employees and make jokes about the idiot who brings them? If so, that is not my concern. It is not my business what other people think about me. The Serb-lady is around seventy years old and physically unwholesome, so of course no one would attribute my attentions to romance. If they laugh at me behind my back, it is only because I appear to be very stupid. Well, I will say it again: no matter! And stop being so sensitive, Josip!

Year four: No difference from year three.

Year five begins. Have I ever been able to predict anything? No. The surprises of the Lord have not come to an end.

That year he learns that the owners and employees of the fish market are indeed Serbs, an extended family of refugees. Freshly taped to the wall behind the cash register is a big tourist poster of Belgrade with English words beneath it: *Sunny Yugoslavia*, followed by the name and address of a travel agency. There are no Orthodox icons or religious symbols anywhere in the shop, so Josip concludes that these are not religious Serbs. However, as immigrants, even as citizens of America, they are perhaps anti-Communists or simply apolitical.

Croats are fairly certain about who Serbs are—you can tell by their faces, their expressions. Serbs, doubtless, can spot a Croat a New York City block away. Josip has been proven wrong before. Now he is certain.

The Serb-lady never speaks to him, nor does he speak with her other than relentlessly to maintain his courtesies and his annual Christmas gift. Still, she continues to put his change into his hand and no longer barks at him. She hears his requests for certain kinds of fish without asking him to repeat himself. Her eyes remain cold and her mouth is ever the dangerous inverted slit, but he has come to feel a strange affection for her. Who is she? What has she suffered? Where has she come from?

One summer day, he is in the shop buying a slab of white cod. Caleb is with him, and he wants to show the boy the best cuts of cod and how to cook it properly, which is to simmer it in water to remove the heavy dose of salt, then to marinate it in lemon juice, and finally to cook it in butter and olive oil with generous peppering. A Portuguese man on the third floor introduced him to sliced potatoes cooked in oil and pimiento sauce (minced, slightly fermented, sweet red peppers). Combined, they make an excellent meal. Josip likes to put pimiento on his cod also. Few North Americans know about this rare treat. It's time for Caleb to leave behind the disgusting habit of eating fast-food hamburgers.

The Serb-lady is not at the cash register today. She is standing (scowling as always) at a wooden chopping table behind the counter, dressed in a blood-spattered apron. She raises a stainless-steel cleaver above a fish and brings it down on the body like an executioner. Chop! Josip shudders. Caleb chuckles.

Josip places his order, smiles at the woman, and bows his head to her in deference, prepared as always to receive no good return for his efforts. Instead, she places the cleaver on the block and covers her face with her hands. Her poor old body trembles, then her shoulders heave with suppressed sobs. Fish gore is dribbling down her fingers. She begins to cry audibly. The man at the cash register glances at her, shrugs at Josip, then is distracted by another customer.

At first astounded, then impelled by a wave of compassion, Josip leans over the counter.

"Oh-oh-oh, Madame", he murmurs sympathetically. "Are you all right?"

Looking up, she stares at him with red eyes and snarls in Serbo-Croatian, "Get away from me, you UDBA bastard!" Following these words issues a string of foul invective that leaves Josip stunned to silence and Caleb grinning.

"B-but I am not UDBA", Josip stammers.

She steps up to the counter and leans over it, her face close to his, seething with hatred.

"You almost fooled me with those biscuits, but I saw through it. I know you came from *them*!"

"Wh-who is *them*", Josip whispers, shaking his head.

"I know who you are. I know! You killed my son!"

"I have killed no one, Madame!"

Then she begins her tirade: "He was a good comrade, he built bridges and dams for you, and then just because Tito betrayed the Cominform, you throw the loyal men into prison. My boy was all for Stalin, and then when Tito went to bed with the British, you destroyed him."

"Where was he in prison?"

"You know where! You know!" She picks up the cleaver, and an animal rage flares in her eyes.

"Was it Goli Otok?"

"See—you know!" she screams, preparing to throw the cleaver. The other employee leaps for her and grabs her arm, wrestling the cleaver from her. Now she is raging uncontrollably. Shocked and embarrassed, customers are scurrying out the door.

"I-I-I was a prisoner on the white island too", Josip says in a raised voice, trying to bring this torrent to an end.

When she finally absorbs this, she stops struggling, but her furor is unabated.

"You're a liar! You followed us here. You're always watching! I don't care if you kill me. If you come close, I will kill you first."

"No, no, no, Madame, I am not with the watchers."

Neither his English words nor his Croatian words make any difference to her. He unbuttons his shirt and pulls it open. The crucifix is exposed. The scars most of all.

"The UDBA put me in Goli Otok", he says. "The UDBA made these marks on my body. You see this. And this. And this—"

His shoulder is now bared, revealing the jagged scar and stitch-marks standing up like ridges. Trembling, breathing heavily, she falls silent, staring at the old wounds. The other employee lets her go and gapes. Caleb, too, is staring.

"An engineer from Belgrade sewed up this wound", whispers Josip. "He bathed all my wounds and kept me alive, gave me his bread. His name was Ante."

She covers her face with her hands and breaks into fresh sobs.

"Oh, my Ante", she wails. "My Ante, my Ante!"

So the three other human beings stand there helplessly, listening to the old woman cry. No customers enter the shop. Outside, the city's pavement is hot, and traffic noises are roaring. Inside, there is only stillness and the agony of memory.

When it seems that the woman is becoming a little calmer, Josip continues.

"I do not know if the Ante I knew on Goli Otok was your son, but he would be the right age, and he built bridges and dams for Tito, and he was a Communist. That is all I know. Perhaps it was another."

Wiping her eyes with the bloody apron, her lips trembling in the struggle to shape words, she asks in the voice of a child, "Is he still alive?"

"I do not know. I escaped in 1960, or it may have been 1961. He helped me to escape."

"Where is Goli Otok?" she asks.

"It's a small island not far from Rijeka."

Taking a deep breath, she comes to a decision, strides to the poster of Belgrade, and rips it from the wall. Her teeth are bared and gritted as she tears it into small pieces, crumples them, and throws them onto the floor. Then she stomps on them.

Josip buttons up his shirt. Caleb grunts, "C'mon, let's get outta here; this is a mega screw-up!"

"Be silent", says Josip, with a firmness he has never before used on the boy.

The woman returns to the counter, staring at the floor. Finally, she raises her eyes and says, "Did he tell you about his family?"

Josip shakes his head. "I'm sorry, nothing."

"What did he look like?"

Josip describes the Ante he knew.

"That must be him", she whimpers. "Was he brave?"

"Yes, very brave. He was one of the few who did not lose his honor—on an island where there was little honor."

"He did not betray the Party?"

"I know only that he did not betray his fellow prisoners."

She nods solemnly, then murmurs, "On this day in 1957, they took him away." She can say no more.

Heading back to the apartment with a package of cod under his arm, Caleb is quiet for most of the way.

"What all dat shriekin' about?" he ventures at last.

"The woman lost her son. I think I knew him."

"She sho' was pissed at you."

"She mistook me for someone else. We corrected our misunderstanding."

"So, you knew her son in the ol' country."

"Yes, we were prisoners together."

"Prisoners? Dat where y' get dem scars?"

Josip nods.

"Sheee-it."

"Caleb?"

"Yeah?"

"You are an intelligent young man. I like you very much. But I am exhausted by your act."

"What act?"

"I ask a favor of you. I entreat you to speak like the man you really are."

"What you talkin' 'bout?"

"You are not a rat. From now on, you will speak to me like a man."

31

Fragment:

Individual destiny is not produced machine-like from the "mills of the gods". Nor are we characters in a morality play. We are works of art, each work distinct, each a phenomenon, the art laboring hand in hand with the Artist to create the story. We are inside a poem. No, we are the poem. Oh, my mixed metaphors! Help me, imagination, to revolve the lens of microscope and telescope so that what I see is in clear focus.

The lens revolves:

On the seventh floor a family of six lives in a three-bedroom apartment, Sally and Steve McIsaac. Josip has frequently replaced electric fuses in the panel above their refrigerator, but somehow the McIsaacs continue to overload the circuits. Their life is a little out of the ordinary. Though husband and wife seem to love each other and their children, they are perpetually exhausted, and the reason is that they have an eight-year-old son who suffers from a severe mental disability. He is a grinning lad who lunges in and out of the building with a parent always gripping his hand firmly. He cannot speak, can only make grunting noises, and is hyperactive.

Today, the mother of the family phones down to the basement to explain that once again a fuse has blown, and there is no electric power in the living room. She cannot run out to buy more fuses because Steve is at work and the baby is sleeping, Jason (the handicapped boy) is in his crib, and all the other children are at school.

When Josip arrives at the apartment, he learns from the exasperated mother that the boy has stuck a bobby pin into a wall socket, burned his fingers, and fried the socket. He is now whimpering in one of the bedrooms. She apologizes for putting Josip to this trouble once again, is terribly sorry for her son's misdemeanors and explains his condition, as she has done several times before. Josip tells her not to worry and replaces the fuse.

"Jason doesn't sleep much", she sighs. "How he keeps going, I just don't know, because he never stops moving, burns up energy all day long, and most of the night too. That's why he has to be kept in the crib at night. He bounces in his crib night and day, making noises. The other kids have learned to sleep with it, but Steve and I are always on the alert. If he breaks out, he can get into the kitchen, turn on a heating element, and burn himself. He has done it a few times, but he never learns from his mistakes. You just never know when he'll do something crazy and hurt himself."

Jason is also epileptic and suffers grand mal seizures when he gets sick and develops a fever. The high temperatures are a real danger. Now Jason stops wailing. Though it is late January, a Christmas tree is still sitting in the corner of the living room. Josip plugs in the lights, and the tree blooms with its cascade of colors, the glass angels dangling from every branch, magnifying the lights, casting sparkles about the room. He notices a Bible open on a table beside the tree.

As the woman continues her apologies, Josip tries to reassure her, but the explanations are something she needs to say. She has said it so many times to him that he knows it all. There are dark bags under her eyes, and she is close to tears.

"We couldn't bear to put him in an institution, we just couldn't. We love him so much, Josip. I know he looks kind of hard to love, and our life's pretty stressful at times, but you can't imagine what he's brought to our family."

Josip can imagine. This family is full of generous, patient children with bright faces and a depth in their eyes that is far beyond their years. There appears to be no self-centered behavior, just an uncanny amount of happiness whenever they are not involved in a Jason crisis.

"I understand very well", he says. "It is a great cost—and a great gift."

Blinking rapidly, she pauses.

"You're the first person in eight years who's said that."

"It is so obvious; he is a pure soul."

She begins to weep and sits down on the ripped couch.

"You can't imagine the things people say to us", she chokes. "All those well-meaning sympathetic friends and neighbors, doctors and teachers and counselors, and even the check-out lady at the grocery store. Family members are the worst. Their bottom line is he really shouldn't exist, better for him to die, better for him never to have been born, and better for us too, that's what they really mean."

"Their thoughts are evil."

"Yes, evil", she whispers. "I just don't know what to say to people like that, because if you try to explain it to them, they go all vague and mushy, and then you can't see the killer beneath the kindness."

"Do they ever help you?"

"Of course not. They're very helpful with their advice but never with practical—"

Then a scream from the bedroom.

She jumps up and races down the hallway. Wondering if he can help, Josip follows her into a bedroom crowded with bunk beds and dressers and a unique kind of crib. It is made of wooden slats and a lid that latches. In fact, it is a comfortable cage. Inside are cloth animals and a jumble of plastic toys suitable for a two year old. Inside, as well, is the boy, an eight year old in diapers. Eyes in a panic, he is lifting his arms to his mother, who is scrambling to unlatch the lid, while his mouth chews on something, and blood dribbles down his chin.

"Oh, Jason!" she cries, pulling him out. "Oh, no, not again!" She pushes the boy into Josip's arms. "Hold him tight, please."

Jason begins to thrash, and it takes every bit of Josip's strength to keep him from catapulting onto the floor. While he holds the boy's head, the mother pokes her fingers into the yelling mouth and pulls bits of glass from it.

Later, as she sits on a rocking chair with Jason in her arms, dabbing his tongue and lips with an ice-cube wrapped in a washcloth, the lad calms down. Somewhat subdued, he is soon grinning and making his grunting noises.

"He thinks Christmas-tree bulbs are fruit. The red ones are his strawberries, and he likes real strawberries a lot", she laughs, wiping her eyes.

"Would it be good to take him to the doctor to check his mouth?" asks Josip.

"We've worn a path in his carpet with stuff like this", she says, shaking her head. "He'll just looks inside the mouth and tell us to keep an eye on him, and always—I mean always— suggests that he needs to be put in an institution."

"I think he needs to run", murmurs Josip.

"I try to get him out to the park at least once a week, but he's a total-care child, and I can't really do it with the baby. On weekends, when Steve's home all day, we go out as a family. Every Saturday we go to the zoo or have a picnic by the pond, but we can't go out at night. There are some rough characters roaming around, and strangers say things too."

"Mrs. McIsaac, would you let me help you?"

She furrows her brow and cocks an ear as if she has not rightly heard.

"I could go with you each day during my lunch hour, if you

think this would help. I can give more time during my day off, if you wish."

Gazing at Josip with something like wonder, she whispers, "I'll talk to Steve."

So begins two and a half years of almost daily excursions to Central Park. As a result, both Josip and the boy are looking healthier. The pigeons in the park will distract Jason for a few minutes, making him laugh and laugh and laugh like a very small child. They pull him into the flock, where he clearly longs to be, and he would rise with them into the air if he could, because he always raises his arms and sobs as they fly away. Josip understands. He was like this once, a long time ago.

Though Josip sometimes feels regret that his Saturday is not as free for fishing trips up the Hudson, he realizes that in the unfolding of the providential universe, he is now purchasing almost all of his fish from the Serb-lady. As a result of this, Ante's mother continues to thaw. They speak together sometimes. It is nothing extravagant, just basic human courtesies. The following Christmas, he gives his usual gift, and she gives him an extra little packet of smoked fish, now bestowed with a grudging smile and a flick of the eyes—an unspoken qualification that he shouldn't count on this every year.

Sometimes on a Sunday, Josip will accompany the McIsaacs to Mass at St. Patrick's cathedral, and they have in turn come with him once to the Croatian Mass at Sts. Cyril and Methodius. Jason is hospitalized a couple of times with high fever and convulsions, and Josip stays overnight in the ward with the boy, praying the Rosary, while Steve and Sally go home to sleep. Coriander babysits during crises.

Josip grows accustomed to the feeling of a hot sweaty hand in his, connected to a powerful little body that is ever in search of escape. Let go of that hand, and the boy bolts for the pond (drowning), the street (crushing by automobile), or into crowds (kidnapping). Sometimes, with a grunt, Jason holds up both arms to Josip and makes a high whistling sound that means, "Pick me up; hold me!"

So, a lot of hugging is added to the cost (gift) or gift (cost). In the end, it becomes all a gift, and there is no sense of cost. He loves the little monkey. In Jason's lack of rational language, there is an absence of lenses that separate him from those who love him. His soul recognizes and responds to love. He evokes love. Even dour, unemotive Gus-the-doorman has adopted the boy—in transit, because Jason always passes through the lobby without stopping, either lurching or staggering at the end of an adult hand. Without Gus, Jason long ago would have smashed through the glass at the front entrance. Regulars in the park recognize the boy now. The balloon man gives gifts, and the ice-cream lady as well. The pigeons maintain their caution. All in all, Jason has become a personage in the neighborhood. To some people he is a delight, to some a reminder of the fragility of human consciousness, and to others a scandal—dangerous because he wantonly destroys barriers. And for a few, Jason is a priceless gift—for precisely the same reason. If he accomplishes no other good deed in his life, he will on Judgment Day have to his credit the most important event that takes place in New York City that year:

Josip, hand in hand with him, walks into the fish market to place his usual order. Suddenly, Jason wriggles free from his grasp, gives a piercing cry of ecstatic joy, and then lurches behind the counter, throwing himself into the arms of the Serb-lady. Jumping up and down and crushing her ribs, he won't let go. Astonished, preparing to fight, she looks down at this strange child who, without warning, has demolished her fortress walls and burst into her gloom. Then the tremendous event occurs: her face melts and she puts her arms around Jason and holds him tenderly.

There are times when Jason throws his arms around Josip's chest and tries to crack his ribs, squealing with glee. Then

Josip's throat swells, and he must push memory away, because he feels in this closeness the absence of the child who is truly his, the one who died so many years ago.

Oh, my child, my child, my child, I did not come to you! I will never see your hidden face!

And Ariadne.

Ariadne, Ariadne, Ariadne—

On Palm Sunday, he is walking with Steve and Sally around the pond in Central Park South. The two older children have brought along the wooden sailboats their father made for them. Taking off their shoes and socks, they roll up their cuffs, jump in, and paddle around with exuberant faces, pushing the little vessels before them. There are other children pushing toy boats about the shallows, and others who possess remote-control devices that propel expensive sloops and yachts farther out. Josip does not quite approve of this electronic play. Something bothers him about it; something is detached that should not be detached. It is control amplified to the level of metaphorical loss. A child should get wet in the ocean, he should ride the deck of a ship or *become* the ship, if possible, but he should not drive it as if he were a dissociated god.

In any event, some children still play with toy boats in the old way. The McIsaacs stop to enjoy the scene while Josip walks on with Jason, intending to circle the pond. Jason is particularly gleeful today, not struggling to escape but dancing along on his tiptoes, making all his noises. Whenever he spots a flying pigeon, he raises his arms but does not cry, just laughs. They have just completed half the circumference when time seems to stop and an enormous stillness fills the world. Into this moment comes an awareness without words: this is the last time he will ever see Jason alive. He pushes away the sensation, certain that it is no more than subconscious worry. Time speeds up again, noise floods in, and he and the boy complete the circle.

620

About two o'clock in the morning, the phone rings beside his bed. It's Sally's panicked voice: "Josip, I'm so sorry to wake you. Can you come up and watch the kids? Jason's gone into grand mal, and he's not breathing right. We've got to get him to a hospital."

"I'll be there in a minute!"

Arriving at their floor, he races out of the elevator just as they are rushing into it with the boy limp in their arms.

"Pray", says Steve.

Josip and Caleb spend two days building the pine coffin, sanding it, varnishing it, and fixing brass handles to the sides. Coriander makes a thin mattress to go inside and sews a gold cloth to cover it. Then they take the coffin up in the elevator to the seventh floor. When the morgue delivers the body, Steve and Josip dress it in a suit and lay it in the coffin in the McIsaac's living room. Jason is stretched out as if asleep. Josip has never before seen him resting, because the boy has been in a state of perpetual motion since the day they first met. Now he reposes with a dignity he never enjoyed in life, hands crossed, a rosary in his fingers, his blond hair combed neatly, and his face absolutely pure. There is a small smile on his lips. It is easy to see how magnificent he would have looked if he had not been given his crosses. As Josip prays before the body, he comes to understand that Jason *was* a magnificent human being.

Mrs. Franklin brings meals to the McIsaacs' apartment, as do a few other people from their floor. Two days later there is the funeral. It is not an expensive one, because the family has so little money. Few people attend the Mass, and few cars follow behind the McIsaacs' station wagon to the cemetery. After the priest says the final prayers, Josip and Caleb shovel the dirt onto the coffin. When that is done, everyone stands around, gazing down at the barren hump as if it were inexplicable, as if it were an island imprisoning the evidence of death. Josip kneels and with a finger traces a cross in the soil. A light rain begins to fall. A pigeon swoops low over the grave, then soars high.

Josip does not say a word of condolence throughout these days. He speaks with his actions, and his tears, whenever he is unable to contain them. Most of all he speaks through a poem he writes in the middle of the night, the day following the boy's death. He looks everywhere downtown for a greeting card with a picture of a pigeon on it but cannot find one. Finally, in an artsy shop, he finds one with a bird picture—a photo of swallows lined up on a television aerial at sunset. It looks like *lastavice* on a cross.

He writes the following lines on the card and gives it to Steve and Sally:

> ### SOUL BIRD
> As you rise on the wings of grace,
> Jason,
> you grow larger and larger in our hearts,
> even as you disappear from our sight.
>
> Smaller and smaller you seem to the eyes
> as you reach the horizon
> where the great Wounded Hands reach down
> to receive you.
>
> You carry us now, On-flyer,
> as we carried you for too brief a time.
> Go with joy, for we are with you
> and you are with us.

Revolve the lens:

Temporarily housed in a two-bedroom apartment on the fifth floor are an elderly Russian man, his son, and the son's wife. The latter two are in their late thirties and speak some

English. The wife is depressed and bitterly ironic, the son is brooding and irritable, the old man is serene. Josip can never quite remember the names of the young couple, but the father is Sasha.

Josip meets them the day after they move in, when the son phones to complain about the condition of the apartment. He is angry about the lack of a fresh paint job, so Josip inspects it only to find that it is quite clean, though it smells strongly of cigarette smoke. The young ones are chain-smoking noxious Russian cigarettes. There are a few sticks of furniture, a mattress on the living room floor, a baby grand piano, and an easel with a half-completed canvas of a naked woman—semiabstract, surreal and hideous, without a tentacle of allure.

Josip explains that the apartment could not be painted in time for their arrival because the previous tenants had moved out the morning of the day they moved in, and that the Immigration Service did not give the manager enough time to prepare properly.

This explanation does not satisfy the young couple. They give Josip a bad time, shouting and gesturing, using plenty of irrational argument and recrimination. He does not take offence, promises to see the manager, and says that hopefully wall-painters will be hired—would they mind living with the smell of fresh paint? They insist that they be given a special apartment on the penthouse floor while their own apartment is being cleaned. He explains that none is available. They threaten to protest to the government about how badly they are being treated. All the while their manner continues to be arrogant and demanding.

"I was once a refugee", he tells them. They light cigarettes, and a look of boredom crosses their sullen faces.

The old man has listened to all of this without a word, and Josip supposes that he has understood none of it. He now says something in Russian, and the son interprets.

"My father would like to play for you. He is a pianist."

The two young people go off to the kitchen to prepare food and drink for themselves, while the old man sits down at the piano. He smiles at Josip.

He begins to play. The piano is out of tune, but there is a masterly hand at the keyboard. The piece seems to be improvised, but it goes on and on. It is moody and semiromantic, with bleak existential lapses. As its themes unfold, Josip sits down on the floor with his back to the wall and listens. He closes his eyes and lets the music take him where it will. In his imagination, he sees snow fields and frozen lakes, wind blowing through taiga forests, and trees white with crystals. The score infuses a sense of struggle, fate, death, and regeneration.

The son and daughter-in-law bring their food and drink back to the living room and stand by the window, nibbling caviar on crackers and sipping from glasses of vodka. None is offered to Josip or the old man, who continues to play without interruption.

"There is no end", laughs the woman sarcastically, after about twenty minutes more. The son barks at his father, the old man smiles self-deprecatingly and brings the performance to a close. Then he asks a question.

"He wants to know what you thought of it", says the son.

"I felt winter in it", says Josip. "I saw winter—and the longing for spring."

The son translates. The old man gazes at Josip and nods.

"Yes, its title is 'Winter'."

Then the following exchange:

"I can see that you hear my music in your heart", says the pianist.

Josip notes that the Russian word for *heart* is almost exactly the same as the Croatian—the Slavic roots.

"I think so, sir. Music speaks to the heart. It enters the soul through the heart." (The word *soul* is also nearly identical.)

624

"Yes, it is so."

"Music is a spiritual language that leaps across the oceans, through language barriers and cultural fortresses—from soul to soul."

"Yes, yes, this is true." (They make deep eye contact.)

Josip asks him a few questions, where are they from, how did they come to America, et cetera.

The son and daughter decline to translate. "You don't need to know this", says the son, suspiciously. "Who are you, anyway?"

"The janitor", replies Josip. He adds a few little facts about his own life. They shrug and change the subject and still do not translate it to the father. Then they put on leather coats and boots, and leave.

The apartment is repainted that week, and afterward everyone seems improved in disposition. Two months later, the son stops Josip in the lobby and asks him to come up to the apartment to change a light bulb. Unless they are infirm, tenants change their own light bulbs, but Josip hasn't seen the old pianist since their first meeting.

There he is again, improvising at the keyboard. Josip changes the light bulb. This time the son offers a glass of vodka. Josip thanks him but declines, he is on duty. But he is forced to sit down for five minutes to drink a cup of tea and eat some caviar on crackers. There are more possessions in the room now, costly new furniture, books in shelves and paintings on the walls, all semiabstract, surreal, hideous. The mattress remains on the floor, and now Josip notices with a skipped heartbeat that there is an unclothed woman lying on it, drowsing in half-sleep. She is not the son's wife. Josip hastily averts his eyes.

"My model", says the son, with a disgruntled toss of his head. "I pay her by the hour, so I can't talk to you long."

He swallows the last of his shot glass and picks up his brush. But this does not signal an end to the conversation. Thus, with averted eyes, Josip listens to the following story:

They are political refugees. The son was a professor at the Moscow Art Institute until five years ago, when he participated in a free exhibit in a city park—avant garde, antitotalitarian paintings. The State did not like it, and the KGB destroyed the exhibit. Several paintings were seized or ruined, some friends were arrested, and two committed suicide, though it might not have been suicide. He lost his job, and they began to starve. His father, who worked as a musician with the State Opera, took them into his little flat, and then they began a years-long effort to emigrate. The KGB dragged them in for questioning too many times for counting. There was no imprisonment, but much threatening. He is a nihilist, he declares, an antimoralist, because Marxism-Leninism is a *moralistic* system, and moralism must be resisted whenever and wherever it manifests itself. He hates all organized religion, and Communism, he believes, is a religion. Josip counters that it is a faith-system, a mythology, not a religion. This sets off another harangue.

During a lull in the monologue, as the son dabs purple splotches onto the canvas, Josip ventures disingenuously:

"How happy you must be now that you live in a free land."

The painter drops his brush into a pot of turpentine, rubs his fatigued eyes, and fixes Josip with a look of pity.

"I hate this country", he snarls.

"You hate it?" Josip asks, with some surprise.

"Yes, I *hate* it. In my country we were dying, my friends and I. We were starving and beaten and in prison, but we were alive. There they kill the body. Here they kill the soul."

Soul? What does this avant-garde amoralist-nihilist mean by the word? He never has a chance to find out. Ten days later the Russians move out, and never again does he meet them.

Revolve the lens:

A weekend in autumn. He visits Winston and Miriam to celebrate Christiana's third birthday. The family has moved from the university grounds to a little house (Cape Cod design, Miriam explains) at the edge of a woods. The road near their front door is well-traveled but is not busy during most of the day—only at off-to-work hours or home-from-work hours is there much traffic.

"Uncle Yosup!" the little girl cries, skipping down the stairs to the living room and throwing herself into his arms. "Did you bring me a present?"

"I brought you a present, Christiana, but you must wait until the party tonight to open it."

"Do you think I'm pretty?"

"You are the most beautiful young lady in all of Connecticut."

"I know. Daddy told me. Mommy says you'll take me for a walk because Daddy's sick in bed."

Poor Winston waves to Josip from the couch, where he is lying under a blanket, watching a Jane Austen video, and suffering from the flu. He offers copious eloquent laments for ruining Christiana's party and pleads with Josip to save this disastrous situation by taking her and Miriam for a walk in the woods. So, while Winston naps, Miriam reverses their Volvo out of the garage, and they drive over to the university chapel for Mass. Afterward they go north into wooded hill country, park on a side road, and step into glory. The trees have changed color now and are a riot of red and gold, and many shades of orange. They breathe the feral scent of dying leaves, plowed fields and haymows, the damp humus of the forest floor, and deer droppings and quail spoor scattered on the narrow path they follow through the trees. They are hiking toward a little river that Miriam knows, about half a mile from the road, a place where the water is absolutely clear, flowing down from a high hill. You can climb the hill, she says, and from the top you can see the world stretching away into infinity in every direction.

The girl trots ahead but stays in sight. As they stroll along behind her, Miriam describes what she has been reading lately—St. Augustine's teachings about word and sign. As Josip listens, he grows more and more excited because it is what he has been learning about language and poetics throughout his life—learning the hard way through blessings and blows, as well as through intuition and observation. Augustine's great mind articulated it all fifteen or sixteen hundred years ago!

Josip launches one of his forays into loquaciousness.

"Miriam, Miriam," he exclaims, "do you understand what this means!?"

"I think I do, Josip."

"It means that the world is radiant with signs. Heaven is pouring out continual messages, but we can hardly read them, you see, because we are blind and deaf and do not know who we really are. The signs in the earth, inanimate and organic, living and dead, are not divine in themselves, but they are creations of the divine, and this sense is being lost because we—"

He pauses to catch his breath.

"Lost, Josip? Perhaps mankind has never really found it?"

"Some have found it. Some—the great saints like Sveti Franjo—Saint Francis of Assisi."

"And John of the Cross", she adds with a smile, enjoying her guest's intense expressiveness, which in her experience of him is a rare outburst.

"Yes, and the great poets too!" Josip goes on. "And when a saint is also a poet, we have an amplification of the power of language."

"And if a poet is also a saint?"

"The same, but a true saint is first and foremost *alter Christus*, a kind of Christ living among us. He is never first and foremost a poet who happens to be a saint."

"Aren't you making a false distinction, Josip? If man is not a collection of components, his poetry will always be the language of his love for Christ, don't you think?"

"Yes, of course," Josip nods, "I said it badly. But, Miriam, is it not wonderful! Is it not splendid! We live and move and have our being within a vast masterpiece. Nature itself is speaking or, rather, God is speaking through nature—"

"Yes, everything speaks because it is given by the Creator of all things."

"His hand is upon it all, the damaged and the undamaged. We must learn to see the original intention even in the damaged."

As they continue to follow the path deeper into the woods, the mother keeps an eye on her daughter, but Josip is staring simultaneously inward and upward, and also connecting to the colors blazing all around him. "We are so blind, so blind!" he groans, flailing his arms for emphasis, his face flushing, his voice intense with the excitement of this new discovery. "It's as if heaven is raining miracles upon us, but we cannot see because we do not look. It's as if fabulous birds fall unceasingly from the skies!"

"Peacocks and ostriches?" she laughs.

"No, no, I mean fabulous because they *exist*—fabulous birds are—"

At the very moment when he flings out his right arm and says *fabulous birds*, a flash of blue catches his eye at the end of his hand. Halting abruptly, he gazes along his arm, off the springboard of his hand, and sees the stroke of blue lying in a pile of red leaves. He drops his arms and goes to it, kneeling down to find out what it is. It's a bird. A very little bird that is unfamiliar to him. Miriam kneels beside him as he picks it up in his hand and lets it rest there, as if it were sleeping. It is warm, it has died only a moment before.

"An Indigo Bunting", whispers Miriam. "I've never seen one before, never this close, I mean."

Christiana has come running back and is playing in the leaves nearby, singing to herself.

The bird's apparently insignificant form is so elegant, so perfectly shaped for the wind, its form and function so integrated, that the genius of whoever sculpted it is beyond question. Moreover, its feathers are a rare kind of iridescent blue, falling from the light turquoise of the head to the dark indigo tail in a perfect gradation through that part of the spectrum, without any discernible transition zones of shade or tone.

"*Who* designed this little masterpiece?" says Miriam shaking her head in wonder.

Josip lays its body on the ground and covers it with leaves.

"And so death entered the world", Miriam whispers. They walk on, and for a while can say nothing.

As she promised, the river is pristine. Josip, Miriam, and Christiana bend over a miniature waterfall and drink from it. When they are refreshed, the little girl looks upstream and startles. She tugs on her mother's arm, pointing. Before them stands an antlered deer, drinking from the same side of the river. It lifts its head and bolts away into the trees.

They cross on stepping-stones and then climb through red maples to the hill beyond. From the top, the view opens up in all directions, and it takes a stretch of the imagination to believe that human habitations, villages, towns, and cities are really there among the rolling hills. They rest awhile, then go back down, and make their way home.

That night, after the party and prayers and bedtime for Christiana, the three adults sit around the living room and engage in a long discussion about symbology. Winston, ever the master of didactics, even when he is sick, gives the history of the symbols of Christ drawn from nature: the fish and white hart, the kingfisher and pelican. Near midnight, he returns to the subject of the stag—particularly in relation to Charlemagne, St. Hubert, St. Felix, and others—arguing that this is the paramount symbol—a dying stag with blood pouring from its wounded breast, the fountain filling a chalice.

Miriam insists that the sick man must come upstairs to bed now, and Josip yawns and lies down on the pull-out couch in the room off the entrance hall. He drifts into sleep composing a little poem about the indigo bird and another about a white hart, the words blurring together until he is snoring.

Bang-bang-bang! He sits bolt upright, his heart hammering hard. The bedside clock reads six A.M. Dawn is near. He throws on his bathrobe and goes out into the front hall to see what is causing the noise, just as Miriam comes trotting barefoot down the staircase in her nightgown. She opens the door, and there on the steps is a weeping woman.

The woman stammers the explanation: she was driving to work, has just hit a deer; too heavy for her to drag off the road, and she's late for work. Would they do it . . . ?

Miriam agrees and, without putting on a coat or shoes, follows the woman at a trot back to the road. Josip feels self-conscious in a bathrobe and returns to the guest room, where he dresses himself as quickly as he can. Arriving at the roadside a few minutes later, he beholds a wondrous sight:

Miriam is sitting on the yellow centerline, cradling the head of an antlered stag in her arms. Its brown eyes are blinking, its massive chest heaving sporadically. There is no blood, but there must be internal injuries. Cars are backing up, their horns honking, brakes screeching, and engines roaring, as drivers swerve to go around the woman sitting in their path. A few even shake their fists.

"Miriam, we must pull the animal from the road. It could cause an accident."

She holds up a hand and silences him.

"Give us a minute. He is dying."

She rocks the hart's head against her chest, its antlers splayed like tree branches across her shoulder, and strokes its forehead and nose, singing softly. It closes its eyes, and then its chest falls into stillness.

"Now", she whispers. Together they drag the body to the side of the road. The traffic roars, honks, and flows on.

Later, Miriam phones some people at a farm down the road, and a man and his son come by and take the body away in their pickup truck.

When Winston stirs from his sleep around noon, they tell him the story. He finds it improbable. Surely his wife and friend are joking, or perhaps they are being metaphorical, building upon the discussion they had last night. They shake their heads no; it happened.

"What are the statistical odds?" Winston frowns, with eyebrows raised high. "Who will believe that we fell asleep speaking of a dying stag and woke up with a dying stag in our arms?"

"Do such things often happen here?" asks Josip.

"Oh, yes", says Winston dryly. "Deer die in our arms every day."

Revolve the lens:

Caleb is about to graduate from his high school. Although Harlem can be a dangerous neighborhood, Josip walks all the way from his apartment to the school without anyone bothering him. More and more of the people on the streets are black as he proceeds north through Manhattan. Almost everyone is black as he reaches Harlem, and when he climbs the front staircase into the high school he realizes he is the only white person to be seen in any direction. He is being watched by many eyes.

Doubtless people are noticing that he wears an ill-fitting suit, which he bought at the St. Vincent de Paul Society thrift store. They also see the bouquet of roses he carries in his hands—a gift for Mrs. Franklin. He finds a place in the back row of the school's auditorium, which is already packed with people. He does stick out dramatically—his color (or lack thereof) and also the scars all over the top of his head, his baldness too. His tallness is not what draws their eyes, he is sure, because several very tall men have likewise chosen to sit in the back rows, in order not to block other people's view of the stage. He wishes his appearance were better than it is, but that's life. You grow old. The flaws gain on the pleasanter parts then overtake them, and then become the new regime, ruling everything. Well, not everything, he smiles to himself, for there is the interior country, where you are always young.

Coriander comes trotting up the aisle, spots him in the crowd, and bustles over. She looks tremendously fine this evening, with her hair spun high in a beehive, her pearl earrings and necklace, and her shiny blue silk dress with matching high-heeled shoes. Her poor waist is put to the test by the shoes because they make it hard for her to walk upright—she is a bold parenthesis when seen from the side, but the glow in her eyes won't let anyone notice the gait for more than a second.

She scolds Josip for hiding himself away in the back, cocking her head and wagging her finger at him, making the people beside him laugh and slap their knees. Then she takes him by the hand, drags him from his chair, and pulls him down the center aisle to one of the rows nearer the front, where the family has been saving a place for him.

"Y' set down heah, Yo-sep. I don' wone no moah nonsense from the lahks o' yoo. You's fambly, an' I ain't gon' take no ahgamint 'bad it!"

It takes a moment for him to interpret her black dialect:

You sit down here, Josip. I don't want no more nonsense from the likes of you. You is family, and I ain't gonna take no argument about it!

"Tenk yoo sooo mutch, Corrhi-anterr. Yoo honorre mee—an honorre I to not tesserf."

It takes her a moment to translate his Slavic dialect:

Thank you so much, Coriander. You honor me—an honor I do not deserve.

She grins and gives him a little kiss on his forehead, then pushes him into his seat.

Caleb is visible in the rows of graduates immediately before the stage, dozens of young people in caps and gowns. He is a head taller and a fair bit older than the others. He is twenty-two years old now, a late bloomer. But the confident tilt of his head and the squared shoulders proclaim a personal victory over his years of failure. Sitting in the Franklin family row are several elderly women who nod and smile a welcome to Josip; they too are wearing their best dresses and jewelry. Also attached are a couple of old gentlemen with canes and a young man in military uniform, as well as Coriander's other children, three teen-age girls. Everyone is dressed like a Broadway star, and Josip feels very shabby by comparison.

The purple stage-curtains part, revealing a brass band in red uniforms and gold braid. When they strike up "The Star-spangled Banner", all in the crowd stand, put hands over their hearts, and sing with gusto.

To make a long story—longer—Caleb graduates with honors. He has the highest marks in his class, and he has won a scholarship to NYU. The crowd erupts in cheers when the news is announced. Josip is sure that Caleb has blushed. In any event the boy's eyes are blinking rapidly, and he is shaking a lot of hands up there in public, looking nervous and dignified all at once. How will he handle all that success?

Afterward there is a big party at the Franklins' apartment a few blocks away, just off Frederick Douglas Boulevard. This is the first time Josip has been invited to their home. It is a three-bedroom apartment with a balcony and a view over treetops and rooftops to the northernmost end of Central Park, which is about eight blocks south. If you squint your eyes, it looks like a decent section of the city. Inside, the rooms are packed with friends and family and people from their church—everyone drinking coffee and tea or fruit juice and eating cakes and cookies and candy from dishes spread out on every available tabletop. Plenty of Gospel scenes are arrayed on the walls: an

Anglo Jesus with bright blue eyes, a Semitic Jesus in Geth-semane, and a Black Jesus holding little children on his lap. Bibles and hymn books, red lampshades dangling with glass crystals, an imitation Persian rug, and a bright yellow sofa with matching chairs surrounding the large television set, which Coriander insists will remain off—"O.F.F.!" she shouts at one of the younger girls, who switches it on because she is sure that her brother winning the scholarship will be announced on the national news. Off it goes, and the hum of conversation grows louder. Though the decor is not to Josip's taste, the people surely are. And if the visuals and audios are disorienting, over-whelming him at first, he soon senses a strong peace in the place, a wholesome spirit, that makes him feel completely at home within minutes.

Finding an empty chair in a corner of the living room, Josip sits down quietly. He feels shy and does not want to force these good people into a position of having to make conversation with a person who is really not from their culture. This is an evening for warm-hearted celebration, not for social strain. He himself feels no strain, but it is quite possible that some of the people here tonight might be uneasy around him. When Caleb sweeps into the living room with his arm linked in his mother's, Josip grins and applauds like everyone else, though he does not want to push himself forward. The graduate is surrounded by his people, thumping him on the back and shouting advice and congratulations into his ears. Then there comes a moment when, in the midst of all this tumult, his eyes grow completely still for a few seconds and swivel unerringly in Josip's direction. The eyes flicker a message: *I see you. Yes, here we are.* A small smile flashes before he resumes his interaction with the others.

Josip sits down, just soaking it in.

An elderly woman is seated next to him on a couch, and beside her are three other elderly women. The one closest to him seems to be asleep. She looks rather frail, tiny and very black, with white hair freshly arranged by a beauty parlor. Pink dress, pink shoes, pink pearls, a big red cross on a gold chain. Her hands are long, with fingers as thin as slender shoots and very wrinkled, roped with purple veins. Her nails are unpainted. These are hands that have toiled and suffered. How many lives have passed through these hands? Is she Coriander's mother or grandmother? Was she once a slave?

He is still staring at these phenomenal hands when one of them reaches for him. The right hand gently covers his and enfolds it. It is cool, trembling a little yet holding him with a certain firmness. He does not withdraw his own.

"Oh, yes", says the old woman in a quavering voice. Josip looks up to see that she is gazing at him with huge watery eyes. "Oh, yes, oh, yes, I know that my Lord is good, for I see what he has done here." *Heah*.

"How do you do, Madame", says Josip. "I am Josip Lasta, a friend of Caleb's and Mrs. Franklin."

"Hello, Josip; I am Cori's gramma. Mah name's Naomi Johnson. It's so nice to see you."

So, they sit there and hold hands. Perhaps people notice, perhaps not. In any event, it feels very good, and Josip is content for it to go on.

"You know," says the old woman, "I look in your eyes, and I see right into your *soul*." She nods and nods. "And I see what the Lord has *done* in you."

Josip is somewhat uneasy about North American soul-readers. On the whole, they tend to be imaginative, and a few are manipulative.

"It is a small, poor soul, Madame."

"Oh, Josip, *all* our souls are small poor ones, don'tcha know."

"Yes," he nods, "I think it is true."

"It true, boy. It true. But he is *so* good. He is sure lovin' us *all* the time. An' we hardly knows it."

636

"Where are you from, Madame?" he asks, thinking it best to make friendly conversation. "It seems to me that your accent is not from New York."

She chuckles. "I'll tell you later where I's from. That's not why we been brought together—no, not at all why. Now I has a message for you, Josip." She leans closer, serious again, nodding and nodding. "I's lookin' into your heart, and I sees a whole lot of things there that move *my* heart."

There is not much one can reply to such a statement, so he says nothing, just keeps holding her hand and looking back into her eyes.

"No, I waren't no slave, but my momma was when she was a li'l' gal, before Abraham Lincoln. Now I am ninety-three years old, and I been livin' in freedom *all* mah life. I voted for the first time when I was *already* a ol' woman, back in 1964, and that was some experience, but it don't make for *freedom*, I try to tell these younger folk—no, that ain't what freedom is *all* about."

"What makes for freedom?" he asks.

"You *already* knows what makes for freedom, Josip. I see right into your heart, and there it is within you, it was just a-waitin' for me to look at it, and I didn' need t' say a *word* to put it there."

Now he feels perplexed. What is she saying?

"I sees that *you* have come up from slavery. I sees you beaten on the *threshin'* floor. You was broken under the wheel of the devil, but he could not break you *entirely* for the hand o' the *restrainer* was a-holdin' him back. And that is how you come to be *here*."

"You see many things rightly, Madame", Josip says. "How is it that you see these things?"

"Oh, I don' see with my poor ol' *eyes* and my poor ol' *head* which is full enough o' stuff an' nonsense, like most people's. I see with the *spirit*, and what he show me now is something else. It is something big, Josip. It don't look big in your *own* eyes,

637

because you's *inside* yo'self, and that's the way with us human bein's, seein' the *outside* for the inside."

"Yes, that is a very bad habit of human beings", Josip murmurs with a nod.

Naomi chuckles, her little voice and little body shaking. "I tells Coriander that too, and she got no objections to it. But it one *fine* thing to hear it from a boy like you."

Boy? The term is quaint and culturally interesting; he is familiar with its inherent social-historical problems. But he is not offended.

"You is a *runnin'* boy, I know." She looks down at the floor for a moment, whispering, "I know, I know, I know—" She squeezes his hand; a tear spills down her cheek. "Sometimes you was a *walkin'* man, and sometimes you was a runnin' boy, and I'm called to tell you, Josip, that all your walkin' ain't over. You gonna *walk* many a mile before you go on up to *glory*. You gonna get *older* and *older* and when you is as old as you can stand it, you is gonna become a *child*!"

Now he is not only perplexed, but somewhat disturbed. It seems that sound and time are decreasing steadily until they are alone in a room where the voices of angels become plausible.

"You is gonna take the hand of a little *child*, and he is gonna run with you. And no longer will you call yourself abandoned, Josip, no longer is you gonna put your head under your wing like a dying swallow—you's gonna *fly*."

She pats his hand, then withdraws her own. She falls asleep with Josip staring at her.

Later, the man in military uniform crosses the room with two bowls in his hands and stands in front of Josip.

"'Lo, there", he says. "Can't shake your hand as you see. Brought you a bowl of prawns in Cori's special sauce. She's my sister, Caleb's my nephew, I'm Carl Johnson."

"How do you do", says Josip, rising to his feet and taking one of the bowls. They clumsily shake hands.

"Balcony's deserted for the moment", says Carl. "Why don't we go on out there and get as much fresh air as is allowed in New York City?"

So, they step through a doorway in the living room wall out onto a narrow balcony and are hit by the roar of traffic.

Carl spoons down the prawns, and Josip follows suit. When they're done, Carl lights up a cigarette.

"Nice of you to talk to Grandma Naomi like that", he says. "Thanks for taking the time."

"It is I who am grateful. She is a great soul."

"Great soul? Well, yes, you could say that and wouldn't go far wrong. We all love her, but sometimes I wonder if she's getting senile."

"She sees better than most people, I think."

Carl regards Josip thoughtfully, then turns away, looking out over the city.

"That boy of Cori's is something else", muses the uncle. "I been trying to get him to join the army. I'm a sergeant now, and it's a good life, lots of benefits and discipline. And that's one boy who *needs* discipline, I can tell you."

Josip says nothing, hesitating to render assessments of a family member.

"I worried myself thin over him when he was growing up, and Cori, she wore out her knees praying. I don't know what would've become of him if—"

He doesn't finish the thought.

"He is an outstanding person", says Josip at last. "He does not quite realize it yet."

"Oh, he's smart," agrees Carl, "he's real smart. And he's going to go up in the world, but it ain't over till the fat lady sings."

Another idiom! Who, exactly, is the fat lady?

"Have you experienced any combat?" Josip asks.

"I was in Vietnam."

"Was it bad?"

"Very bad. I lost some buddies. Saw terrible things. That's the way war is—always."

"Yes, always."

"I pray to God to keep my hands clean. Every day I ask the Lord for this. But a country has to pray too, doesn't it."

"Yes, it does."

"That war, I don't think about it the way I used to. And I believe there's another one coming."

"Where do you think it will be?"

"Could be Europe, could be any number of places. Communism is rotting from the inside—collapsing *internally*. Ten years ago, who'd have guessed. Now it's close—real close."

"The end of Communism? It does not seem possible."

"Not if you read the papers, but I think we'll see it. Five years, ten, maybe twenty at the most, and there's going to be a whole new world over there. You're from Europe aren't you?"

"Yes. Croatia, a republic in Yugoslavia."

"Yugoslavia—now there's another potential hot spot. I think it's going to be a right big mess there when the Communists fall."

"Will they fall? It seems a dream to me that such a thing could happen in my native land. Only God could accomplish such a miracle."

"It'll take more than one miracle."

"What do you mean?"

Carl lights another cigarette and blows the smoke out over glittering Manhattan. "I mean there's a lot of people who won't be happy about it."

"My people long for freedom."

"Of course they do. Everyone does. But Belgrade has a pretty big army, I hear, and your people over in Zagreb don't have an army or much of a police force or anything really, do they?"

"They have their faith."

"That may be so," nods the American sergeant, "but they're also standing on the border of three worlds. Right in the path of everything that's going to happen."

"What do you think will happen?"

"It's not about freedom, Mr. Lasta. It's about power and wealth. And in our times power and wealth are all about oil."

Josip says nothing.

"I know, I know, it sounds like conspiracy theory and all that. Cartoon politics, bad guys and good guys trading hats. But it all comes down to some basic factors in the end. During the past ten years, I been tinkering away getting a political-science degree, took some history courses too. You ever hear of a writer named Aristotle?"

"Yes", Josip nods.

"It's not as simple as I used to think it was, and it's not going to get any simpler. If I had to make a bet, I'd wager that a lot of things are going to be battled out on your home ground. After that, Iraq, then Iran. Maybe Nigeria, maybe Mexico—who knows." He stomps out his cigarette and shrugs. "Give or take ten or twenty years, I think we're going to see Islam on the rise in our lifetimes, keeping us busy with more riots and killin' and oil politics. Then when we're real distracted and real worn out, China will swoop in and take the whole crap game. Oil, again. Oil and population and space to live the good life. Soviet Communism's finished, just a few last gasps to go and then it's over. Something new is coming, and it's going to be *real* bad."

"Can anything be worse than Communism?"

"Maybe we'll find out. Maybe not. Round and round it goes and where it stops nobody knows. Life's cheap, you see. Shouldn't be that way, specially shouldn't be that way in a country like ours. Inside and outside should be the same, don't you think?"

"I'm not sure what you mean."

"Domestic policy and foreign policy—there shouldn't be two sets of morals, a different code for each. If we try to live that way the center gets hollower and hollower till everything collapses. After that, it doesn't matter what happens outside because there's nothing left to protect."

"Is it really as bad as you think?"

"Probably not. There's a whole lot of good people in this country—the best. People like my sister and grandmother. And I'm willing to die to protect this country—I probably *will* die doing just that. But I'm not going to lie to myself about the way it's going inside our borders. We're rotting too—rotting fast. And life's getting cheaper every day."

Fragment:

Well, the Afro-American prince-in-exile has changed costumes and dialect and has become truly impressive. He no longer wears rings on his body. His vocabulary is about three times larger than mine (in English, I should say). He is quieter these days, when he is not emoting about literature. He is humbler too. Perhaps he was always humble and the blatancy of his arrogant mask was an admission of his powerlessness. We will soon see what he does with power. Yes, he will have power, and I pray that it will not be the worldly kind. He despises NYC politics, loathes federal politics, and hates militarism in any form. (I gave him Aristotle's *Politics* as a mild corrective, but he has not yet read it.) A newly forged idealist and humanitarian, Caleb does not really see the beast-man in human nature, despite the streets he has lived on all his life. He is reading American poets, focusing on black writers especially, though he likes some white poets from the previous century, for example a man named Whitman. I found some of the poems intriguing, notably one about lilacs in a yard on the day a president died. But there is a disturbing sense of the pantheistic spirit in the book. Perhaps I am misunderstanding him—the language barrier. Caleb is presently obsessed with Thoreau and recently took me on a weekend excursion to a place called Walden Pond. It is a little body of water, quite charming, but I could not get excited about it, even as I observed the religious fervor in the prince's face as we walked around it through the woods.

"It's very small", I commented.

"It's enormous", Caleb replied, bringing me to a stop as I strained to recall a lost memory.

He gave me Thoreau's *Journals* for Christmas, and it is wonderful, wonderful, wonderful (full of wonder). As Zoran once declared at a meeting of the Dolphins, philosophy is born of wonder. So is poetry. Where is Zoran? Where is everyone I once knew?

Caleb's infatuation with the poetics he once hated ("crap") gives me hope for his restoration to the transcendent universe. He long ago rejected his mother's faith, tells me that it is no more than "residual subservient assimilation" into white Anglo-Saxon religion. I reminded him that Jesus was a Semite with skin probably about as dark as his. "So?" he snapped back irritably. "What you cannot see is what you get!" We both laughed. He is fast and very, very clever.

"My Momma is the best," he summarized, "but she seeks her pleasure and consolation in borrowed tribal rituals every bit as primitive as the trance-frenzy of the animists of my native land."

"American trance-frenzy?"

"I meant Africa."

"Oh. Which country in Africa are you from?"

"I'm not sure. Somewhere between Pygmies and Watusis. If you were black, Josip, you'd be a Watusi."

"Your great-grandmother does not strike me as a trance-frenzy person."

643

"She's a Pygmy", he laughed.

I could not restrain a look of censure, and I'm afraid I said very gruffly: "Naomi is a giant. You should spend more time with her."

He shrugged and changed the subject. On the bus ride back to Manhattan, he informed me that he is the editor of a new poetry journal at the university. Somewhat timidly (he was still a little shocked that I had been angry with him), he asked if I would be willing to read what he has written lately. This was absolutely the first time he ever made such a request of me—in his entire life! An excellent development. I agreed, of course. He has been reading my poems, too. I translated a few for him, awkwardly, into English—a frustrating exercise. Ideas cross the ocean intact, the poetry drowns somewhere in mid-Atlantic. If only I had been created a musician!

Facet:

THE HART OF MANHATTAN
I am walking by night from the mountains of my home
lordly beneath this crown, though no man knows its weight,
white-antlered as if I am a mountain crested with two oaks,
the foothills green and gold by the sea of blood
part to let me pass, and when I ask if I am ever to return
they bow in silence
—no eyes see my approach.

Pausing upon a bridge made by human hand,
spanning land and sea and river and sky, I ponder
what they have made,
then knowing my task I leap forward onto the island
—none see my arrival.

I have brought the mountains into the city;
it is my gift to you; and the sky which is my breath,
and the sea as well, for all oceans are in my eyes,
and all this I bring to you,
for all has come from me
—none see me pass between the towers.

I lift my head and sound the bugle call
to rouse the city from its sleep, but the city awakens into
    deeper sleep
and dreams itself awake when I am among them.
Why is it so, this reversal of intent?
Why, though I do them no harm,
do they fear me?
—none know who I am.

Who shot me, who made me fly on panicked feet?
Leaping, leaping, tossing my head before I fall to the
    pavement
and my crown rolls along the streets
as you gather round to see a marvel brought down.
Who has done this? Who?
Speak! The arrow quivering in my chest with the last pulse-
    beats
does not condemn you, nor do I condemn you, my slayer,
but you should know me, for I was born for this.

If my blood is needed to show you to yourself,
to refresh you or awake you now, I will give it.
Here it is, take it.
But understand as you drink that even the mighty
strain their eyes for a final glimpse of stars,
longing to rest like children in their mother's embrace.

This dialogue between Josip and Caleb, after the latter soliloquizes about T. S. Eliot and Pablo Neruda, takes place over Josip's bathtub while cutting up a grass carp, which the old man caught at Peekskill on the Hudson three days ago—2.5 kilos.

"So, how did you like *Giraffe Wars*?"

"I regret that I did not like it, Caleb."

"Oh, thank you very much."

"However, I did notice your technical competence, and your growing sense of creative intuition."

"Oh, then it's my hypothesis you reject."

"Poetry must never be a vehicle for ideology."

"That's ridiculous. Poetry is *always* a vehicle for somebody's ideology! Look at Ezra Pound."

"I cannot read him. His Fascism disturbs me, just as Picasso's paintings disturb because they derive, consciously or subconsciously, from his Communism."

"I like Picasso—a lot!" the boy says in a challenging tone.

"You should go to the Metropolitan and spend time with Chagall."

"Who is Chagall?"

"I will take you to meet him on Saturday. He is in his painting what a poet should be in poetry. These heroes you are fond of, Picasso and Pound, they disturb not in the way a painting or poem should disturb. Instead they create a malfeasance in the subconscious—and in the soul."

"And you're saying that's what I did?"

"I am offering you a little caution. Your concept is clever. The giraffes have lost patience with the rhinocerasauruses, yes?"

"Rhinoceri."

"And so they have a war. The metaphor of tribal hatreds is immediately obvious."

"Right. And territorialism and class-conflict."

"Your Marxist-Leninist presumptions are my real concern."

"What! I'm not a Communist!"

"No, you don't want to be, but you are presently a material-ist, and it is my hope that you will recognize the dangers inherent in its mythological impressionism."

"I'm for freedom."

"So am I. But what do you mean by freedom, Caleb? Can there be freedom without responsibility?"

"The giraffes are *very* responsible."

"Yes, but only to themselves. And that is perhaps what I am getting at. The poet who sees himself as a hero or a prophet, or a priest of the socio-political forces to which he is loyal, which he believes are the historical necessities of his times, too easily becomes a puppet. He has no external measure with which to assess reality. Whether he submits to the forces or rejects them, he becomes a parody of himself, and then without knowing it submits his gifts to the demons of his era. He loses his place in the continuity of time. He becomes dependent on social affir-mation and the drug of exalted feelings common to all revolu-tionaries. He destroys, even as he thinks he creates."

"Whew! I shoulda got into basketball."

Josip laughs. Caleb's humor is sometimes irresistible.

"So, you think I'm a bad apple, Joe?"

"No, you are merely young. And your desire for exultation is really a damaged longing for the transcendent."

Now Caleb is frowning hard, thinking hard. Silently he wraps the fish pieces in waxed paper and leaves the room. The fridge door opens and closes. Josip is washing the bathtub when Caleb kneels beside him and sprinkles cleaning powder on the stains.

"I don't get what you're saying. Could you write it down for me?"

"Of course, if I can remember it. I have already forgotten what I said."

"Something about fake prophets, I think you said."

"Did I say that? But that is not it exactly. I think the real challenge for the poet is to distinguish between his tendencies to genuine creative intuition and the impulses of the self-centered ego."

"How does he do that?"

"By seeking to understand himself without falling into the trap of self-obsession. By suffering. And most of all, by loving."

"Love?" Caleb rolls his eyes.

"Yes, Caleb, love. Love costs. It always costs. Sometimes it costs everything."

Josip's article on Goli Otok sparks a reaction from Yugoslavia. He has been pressing for years to have it published (his promise to Ante to "babble" about what is happening), but the publisher/editor/newsboy has resisted until now, feeling that Josip exaggerates the severity of Tito's camps. In the end, he decides that Josip should be trusted and publishes the article, despite the lack of confirming evidence from other sources. A week after the issue is mailed, someone tries to break into the publisher's apartment, but he scares him off without catching a clear sight of him. Now Josip is grateful that he has maintained his pen name. No one tries to break into the basement cell of Josip Marulić—simply because it cannot be found.

The next night, a freak fire breaks out in the newsletter office, burns up the files, the subscriber list, the back issues, and the galleys for the issue being prepared for the printer. Fortunately, someone walking past the parish hall smells smoke and calls the fire department. The building is saved, but it seems the magazine has gone up in smoke.

It is a terrible blow, but, strangely, the publisher appears to be quite pleased when he tells Josip about it on the steps of Cyril and Methodius.

"It's a good sign", he smiles. "Yup, a very good sign."

He explains that he is scheduled to give an interview about the incident to *The New York Times*. Also, as a precaution, he had made a duplicate copy of the subscriber list and kept it in the safe at his commercial office downtown. Twenty-eight hundred names is nothing to scoff at.

Revolve the lens:

Josip is yawning, sitting on his cot in his underwear, sipping his first cup of coffee. He glances out the window, which opens onto the light-well. A blue-yellow hue—so there is sunshine out there. It will be a long day—"garbage day" for his building. As usual, the dumpster in the back alley will be heaped high, and the lid won't close.

After breakfast, he goes out to clean up any litter that might have fallen off the dumpster. There's not much—a broken tricycle, a few plastic bags leaning against the metal bin. He tosses them onto the top. Then he spots a black plastic garbage bag wedged between the back of the dumpster and the alley wall. He pulls it out. It's heavy, ripped.

A miniature human hand appears within the rip; then he can see an arm and a shoulder. An abandoned doll, he supposes. The doll is . . . blue. He carefully places the bag on the ground and chokes. Kneeling, he widens the tear. Inside is an infant with part of the umbilical cord attached. It is dead.

Josip remains immobile, staring. At last, he closes the bag and picks it up in his arms. He turns and goes down the alley and out onto the street. Without conscious decision, he makes his way along 52nd to Tenth Avenue and heads south, seeing nothing, feeling only the weight of the child in his arms. A sword is slowly revolving in his heart. He would yell, he would cry, if he could, but now there is only numbed horror. The city is utterly silent, as if nothing moves in all the frantic traffic. He crosses streets against the light and cannot hear the car horns blasting. Finally, he arrives at the church and goes up the front steps.

A few people are scattered among the pews, praying their

rosaries; others are making the Stations of the Cross. He proceeds down the aisle and into the sanctuary. There he kneels in front of the tabernacle. Head bowed, lacking any words to say to God, he remains there. Silence and stillness and emptiness. There is no sense of minutes or hours. He is simply a consciousness before the court of heaven, waiting for something—he does not know what. Waiting, waiting, waiting. And it seems to him that he is presenting not only this child to its creator, but himself also. He must explain, but he has no explanations. He must speak, but he cannot speak.

When at last he can cry without sound or visible tears, he unwraps the body and lays it on the top step beneath the tabernacle. He prostrates himself face-down, and waits.

That is where one of the friars finds him. "Josip?" says a voice.

He slowly lifts himself to his knees and sees Friar Todd staring at him and the baby.

"What—what's going on?" stammers the friar.

Later, he brings water and baptizes the child conditionally.

"We should give a name", says Josip.

"You choose."

"Abel." Then, after considering: "Abel Kristijan Bogdan."

The friar wraps the infant in a white alb and brings it and Josip into the rectory; and he phones the police. The police come—Josip cannot thereafter remember what happens next, but in the end it is decided that, according to the law, no murder has occurred. The baby was about eight months old within the womb. Abortion, in this country, is not a crime.

Three days later, the city morgue releases the body to Josip and Friar Todd. The friar has borrowed the parish car to collect it. He drives; Josip sits on the passenger side, and the body, wrapped in a red cloth, lies between them on the bench seat. They cross the George Washington Bridge into the Bronx and head up-country toward Massachusetts. There's a cabin in the Berkshire hills that friends of the Franciscans let the friars use for hermitage days. Neither Josip nor the priest say a word throughout the entire journey. Josip keeps his hand on the little body. Sometimes words come to his mind that he would like to speak to the child, would have said if they had been able to know each other, and perhaps these words can now be heard in eternity.

He remembers Tereza and Josip's baby, murdered by Partisans in Rajska Polja, shot through the chest even as it took its first breaths. He also remembers the swell of Ariadne's belly, containing his own child who died at birth. There are no visual memories of this baby, because he did not see her. Yet *this* personal loss is the sharper, a relentless turning of the blade. And now the aborted child beneath his hand, unnamed and unknown, unloved even by its parents, embodies for him all such losses.

It is early afternoon by the time they turn off the road onto a gravel driveway that winds higher through mixed woods. At the top, they come to a cabin overlooking a small pasture and thicker forest. Friar Todd parks the car and gets out. He removes a shovel from the trunk, while Josip gathers the baby in his arms and stands by. In a clearing behind the cabin, the friar digs the grave. Josip kneels and gently places the body into the hole. Then Friar Todd puts a purple stole over his brown robes, opens a book, and prays aloud in the name of the whole Church, past, present, and to come. He blesses the tiny body and the grave. Then they fill it in, the priest with the shovel and Josip with his bare hands. A crucifix is plunged into the soil.

That done, they stand in silence for a while, looking down at the hump.

They get back into the car and return to the city.

Facet:

CHAGALL'S ABRAHAM AND THE THREE ANGELS

It is not what you expect:
The three angels are seen from behind
and you are the invisible servant who approaches the table.
Six great pigeon wings are folded politely
as the old patriarch stands before the guests with the
nervous reverence of a man
who must serve dinner to God.
Behind him, Sarah brings a bowl of stewed lamb, scowling
over the inconvenience
and the waste—it is she who must reckon the sum of
investment, gain and loss—
accustomed as she is to barrenness.
The old man is not sterile—no, the fault is hers—so she
keeps an eye on the larder
and on the issue of seed among the underlings.
Her wrinkled eyes observe the angel reach for a bottle of
       wine
and she laughs at his presumption while on a black hill
beyond the camp
a little sapling grows.

              —Caleb Franklin, New York, 1989

32

And so the years flow into the reservoir of memory, where even the events of recent years are sometimes blended and divided by unseen currents, until Josip can no longer recall exactly those which came earlier and those which came later. Rationally, he knows that time is like a river, in its more sensory aspect—that is, it is linear. Intuitively, he senses it as a fathomless sea, continuously replenished by the streams of experience. Time's purpose is to be found in the meaning it brings to the surface.

He is—how old? What year is now ending? Oh, yes; 1989.

On the first day of January, he glues a colored print of Zagreb's St. Stephen's cathedral over the Statue of Liberty on his new 1990 calendar. He tore the print from a brochure of "Sunny Yugoslavia" that he had bought in a used-book stall on the sidewalk of Central Park east. Tito is moldering in his grave, and so are the hundreds of thousands of his victims. Now the rivers of blood have become the "Riviera of the Adriatic". How quickly people forget—enforced erasure and willful absentia.

Fifty-six years old. He feels ten years older, but no matter. He has a good job and stability, prayer, his study of literature (he is learning Greek in order to read Homer in the original), and his poetry. He has lost count of the poems he has written—"facets", he calls them. Nothing comprehensive, no unified field theory in literary form. They are bits of a puzzle or pieces of a broken mirror or even faces of a cut diamond. Stop that, now! No more metaphors!

Fragments are prose, facets are poetry—though he will admit that sometimes his prose is more like poetry, and his poetry more like prose. No matter. He is what he is, and it is not his business what other people think about him.

He does not consider the possibility that his poems are publishable. Only in small ethnic journals, perhaps. Over the years, several dozen have appeared in the old parish newsletter. It has swollen into a national journal now and is published every month, boasting full-time employees in the downtown Manhattan office and a subscriber list that recently passed thirty thousand. Last week a Croatian-language journal in Vienna negotiated for four of his poems (rather, Josip Marulić's poems) to be republished over there. There is no fee involved, because everyone knows that the small of the earth should be grateful for a public forum. The editor chose the white horse, the white hart, the dolphin, and the swallow. Nothing political—nothing *overtly* political.

This is very pleasant, but he knows his limitations. He has never formally studied poetry. He often reminds himself that he is a janitor, a man who takes out the world's garbage and scrubs its murky mental droppings off the walls. Graffiti is the fugitive poetics of those who feel they have no voice, and their fugitive politics too. He understands and would like to be lenient about it, but the rules of the building prohibit the spread of this strange new art. Its aesthetics are appalling, and his interest in it is probably disordered in some way—perhaps it is only because he remembers the graffiti scratched on the cell walls, latrines, and stones of Goli Otok. One stands out in memory, a little stick man etched into a piece of limestone left by the side of a path—a public forum of sorts. Beneath the tiny *ikon anthropou* was a name and a cry:

Andro I was here.

Did Andro write it, or was a nameless one calling to Andro?

What is art? Moreover, *what* is poetry? And why should he be permitted to write it, let alone have it published? He is a man

654

who doesn't know a pentameter from a tetrameter, even though he can give an intelligent discourse on the tetragrammaton and knows what a marvel the chambered nautilus is. He can describe the Hebrew name for God and the offspring of the sea in the same breath, not so much conflating as relating both as words of a secret language. And he would say this to anyone who would care to listen. He would make his listeners fall in love with that language, its countless measures discovered and undiscovered, if he could, but no one would be interested. He has at last admitted to himself that this is the case. They like a bit of verse as emotional prompts on greeting cards or as page-filler in periodicals, but they do not dive deep. Perhaps they do not know the deep is there. The pace of modern life, television, subways, fast food—these all work against the sublime illuminating moment when the distance between utterance and reception is closed in an embrace.

"What can you say to them, Josip?" he declares into the little mirror over the bathroom sink, as he shaves the gray bristles from his chin. "Should you stand on the street corner and shout, 'Slow down, everybody!'?"

There are already a lot of shouters out there. Nobody listens to them, and why should they? He is not interested either—except on occasion, when he stops in the street and cocks an ear for the hidden springs of poetry that do sometimes leak out of the mouths of the deranged.

Into this category, he places the following characters: politicians, media personalities, drug dealers, dishonest merchants, and certain kinds of academics. He has never in his entire life met a politician or media personality—but these, he believes, are the criminally insane, for the effects of their crimes are more far-reaching than those of the street-level cheat. He knows madmen aplenty—the guilelessly insane. He knows only a few good academics—Winston and Miriam, and of course Caleb, who will always remain the boy whacking his palm with a metal bar, ever ready to strike down marauders. But there is one whom he regards with particular distaste.

She is a resident of his apartment building. On her bad days she does not see him at all when they pass in the hall. He is invisible. That's all right; as far as he is concerned this makes it a good day for him. On her good days (his bad days) he ceases to be invisible and her eyes glint, her mouth tightens, and a little dividend of verbiage emerges when she has caught his attention. "Good morning, Mr. Lasta, the halls are looking cleaner lately, but I'd appreciate it if you would scrub the graffiti off the wall on the third floor, thank you."

The tone is condescending. Her "thank you" is a command wrapped in the cotton-batting of an ersatz smile and delivered while she is in motion toward the entrance foyer. However, she does say "Mister", and in this he finds hope for her redemption.

It is not that he strongly dislikes her, nor does he envy her reputation and salary. In fact, he pities her. He tries not to judge, truly he does try. In his moderately unkind moments he considers her to be a pampered baby driven by pathetic desperation to feed her false persona; in his worst moods he considers her to be a shark. She bites chunks out of human beings, therefore she is a shark. On good days he tries not to entertain negative thoughts about her and simply prays for her soul.

In her late thirties, she is handsome and overflowing with determined vitality. She has a chair at some university in the city, is a book reviewer for one of the big papers, and has authored two books of literary criticism. Last but not least, she is a devourer of men, "devourer" in the sense of putting them firmly in their place, keeping them emasculated. The Serbs would have been proud of her, though of course she is an Anglo-Saxon.

In the privacy of his room, he sometimes reads what she writes in the papers. He laughs and contradicts, shakes his head, then wraps fish heads in the page and takes it out to the dumpster. Her articles examine only to demolish what does not fit into her narrow agenda—which of course she promotes as the broadest possible worldview. She does not seek out literature that reveals the miraculousness of life, and he is sure that she would make mincemeat of his poems. Fortunately, she would not be able to understand them even if something of his did make it into print in an American periodical. She reads English perfectly but is completely illiterate in soul-speech. Doubtless, she reads no ethnic journals.

Men and women of creative genius are dissected by this lab technician only according to her strict social criteria: she is a liberal democrat with not-so-subtly disguised socialist leanings and (he suspects) a slight, though not terribly serious, infatuation with Marxist terrorists. This part of her geo-psyche never reveals itself in print, but he knows that it almost inevitably comes with the package, the new-liberal being a romantic at heart, a peculiarly repugnant kind of romantic, he adds with a shudder. It would be a mistake to presume that she is a Communist. She is not a Communist. She is simply full of contradictions, all of which are resolved in her own mind by the historical necessity of her upward mobility.

Caleb reads her articles religiously. Whenever he storms into Josip's room, waving one of those newspaper clippings, excited by her talent and wit, Josip prepares himself for an exercise in cautious debate. He does not want to alienate Caleb, nor does he want to appear as a hidebound reactionary.

Josip will sometimes admit to himself that he is prejudiced against her. After reading her more provocative articles, he puts his head in his hands and scrutinizes his conscience. Why does he dislike her so much? Why does *he* examine *her* writing only to demolish? Is there nothing good here? Well, there is plenty of good in her words, but it is mixed with so much blind nonsense—and that is the problem. She has come to represent for him the triumph of materialism. She is a very talented, charming, and sanitized Partisan. In her reviews, she sneers with exquisite irony at what she calls "moralism" and is at her most eloquent when attacking books that might undermine the licentious socio-cultural revolution and impede the march of progress. She exalts only those authors who help propel the revolution ever onward into the glorious future.

Is he bitter about her? Yes, he supposes that he is; he cannot lie to himself about it. But why is he so bitter? Is it because she represents something he can neither fight nor run from? Yes, that must be it, because she does indeed represent the new order. What the Communists and Fascists failed to achieve through violence, materialists have accomplished without firing a shot.

He is not afraid of her. If she were to complain to the owner of the building, it would not be a great problem, even if he were to lose his job. Nor is he afraid of her on the more instinctual level—the psychic stratum that imprisons a growing number of men who collaborate with aggressive women so as not to be hurt by them—because they are unequipped to be put perpetually on the defensive.

For more than a week now, he has not seen her comings and goings. Perhaps she is away vacationing in Cuba or Yugoslavia. Communism with a human face. He sighs, and goes down to the foyer to chat with the doorman. He knows that Gus is in a state of anxiety over his wife's health—she has been diagnosed with cancer. When Gus is left too long without conversation, he begins to stare into the street and to overlook the people who need the door opened for them. There have been complaints. A few residents want him to be dismissed.

Sure enough, Gus is staring out into the street. But it is not the massing of his personal woes that has caught his attention at the moment. On the front step, a cat has captured a pigeon and is mauling its wings and head with its paws while trying to get its jaws around the throat.

Josip races out and picks up the cat by the scruff of its neck, and shakes it.

"Let go!" he says in his native tongue. The cat is feeling particularly bloodthirsty this day, or perhaps it has employed a complicated strategy of stalking its prey, and for either or both of these reasons it will not let go. Blood speckles the pigeon's wing, and for once Josip is too impelled by the imperatives of justice and mercy to let himself be distracted by the beautiful juxtaposition of magenta upon a field of shimmering violet-gray.

With his free left hand, he lightly bats the cat on the back of the head. At this most inauspicious moment, the academic rushes through the doorway and stomps to a halt before him. Her chest inflates with outrage and her fists thrust down at her sides. Her feet arch upward, the silk-covered heels lifting from their suede clogs.

"Don't you dare strike this animal!" she seethes.

"Do you mean the pigeon, Madam, which, as you see, is suffering an assault?"

"I mean the cat. Let it go, this minute!"

"If I let it go, both the victim and the aggressor will fall to the concrete", says Josip in a reasonable tone. "Thus, both creatures may be hurt."

"You are hurting the *cat.*"

"I am separating the aggressor from the victim. This is a policy of the United Nations Organization, is it not?"

This brings her tirade to an abrupt halt, and she examines Josip with keen, if hostile, interest.

He now places thumb and forefinger at the base of the cat's neck and squeezes.

"You are causing it pain!" the woman cries, with a note of wildness.

"The cat is causing the bird pain", Josip replies in a meditative tone. The cat opens its jaws and with its hind legs rakes

Josip's forearm, shredding his sweater. Then it leaps for the pavement and bolts away. The pigeon trembles in the crook of its rescuer's arms and buries its head.

The woman is breathing hard. Joseph recognizes a psychic weather front in her face that carries with it the threat of certain rain, possibly a hurricane. He calmly prepares himself inwardly. When you have been beaten with truncheons, a woman like this is not a serious threat.

"I don't know what people are like in the country you came from," she says in cold, evenly spaced words, "but in this country we do not abuse defenseless animals."

"The abuse of birds is permitted?" he asks, without blinking an eye.

"They are wild, the cat is someone's pet", she says, as if explaining the obvious to a difficult child. "If you knew cats you would understand that it is a very valuable Siamese. The bird is a pest. They breed like vermin. Their droppings spoil the monuments and buildings throughout the city."

"Ah, so you are saying they ruin the aesthetics."

His use of the word *aesthetics* gives her pause; in fact, it silences her as she examines him more closely. Her gaze is unblinking, ferocious actually, as if she would cleanse the world of all superabundance, all superfluous fertility and virility. She opens her mouth to say something.

"The Siamese cat", Josip blocks in a quiet voice, with a whimsical smile, "rather spoils the aesthetics of the neighborhood, don't you think? It is a most unpleasant breed of cat. It has a sinister voice and a sinister appearance, though of course it is not sinister in the ontological sense. Have you not winced at its hideous screech in the alley at night, so unlike the orange tabby or the tortoiseshell, of which I am quite fond."

"So, it's a question of breed, is it?" she mutters coldly, drawing back and lowering her heels. She crosses her arms and stares at Josip with unconcealed contempt.

"Yes, a question of breed, though I admit it does have a right to exist."

She snorts.

"The pigeon, also, has a right to exist", Josip goes on. "And as a fellow creature, I have the right to defend its right to exist. This is my prerogative."

He feels a little ashamed of throwing in that word so soon after *ontological* and *aesthetic*, but she is a formidable force, and, after all, it is her native language.

Three or four seconds pass while she sizes up this new species of male, one she is destined inevitably to demolish, but whose demise might demand more complex methods. Her eyes alone are capable of splitting the shell of an Adriatic clam.

"You're an Eastern European", she says in an analytical little voice.

"No," he corrects, "I am not an Eastern European. I am from Croatia which is allied in culture, intellect, and spirit with Vienna and Rome. We are distinctly Western, though we are not without affinity for *Mittel Europa*."

She snorts again, then continues her probe.

"So, how many lives did *you* defend during the War?" she asks.

He flinches inside but does not let it show.

"I was a child during the war."

"And the death camps? What about those Nazi death camps? *Croatian* Nazi death camps."

He replies gently. "Many of our people died in those camps, Madam, and most Croatian people hated and feared the Fascist Ustashe. Even more did they fear the Chetniks and the Partisans, who committed most of the crimes."

He is feeling defensive but cannot let her see this. Her mind is shaped by media and revisionist history that has been pumped full of Serbian propaganda.

From the corner of his eye, Josip notices Caleb leaning

661

against the banister at the bottom of the front steps, books under his arm, taking in the whole scene through wire-rimmed spectacles. He is wearing green corduroys now and a tweed blazer with Oxford shoes. He is an Afro-American intellectual listening with studied interest to the conflicts of Caucasians.

"Chetniks and Partisans committed most of the crimes", Josip repeats.

She tosses her head and looks down her nose. "So *you* say. But the Partisans created the most humane socialist state in Europe. Would you have preferred Hitler or Stalin?"

Her swords strike so deep, eliciting so many memories, so much horror, that his suppressed feelings of disgust over the superficiality of the North-American mind now threaten to crack open. Not since Goli Otok has the impulse to shout like this arisen in him. He does not give vent to it, nor does he let a flicker of it show. He looks down and with his forefinger strokes the pigeon's head and coos soothingly. He smiles reflectively. It is a mirthless smile, but it's the best he can do at the moment.

"No, I would not have preferred Hitler, nor would I have preferred Stalin", he says at last, in a quiet voice. "I was a prisoner in a concentration camp established and managed by the most humane socialist state in Europe. Many of my friends died in it, innocent people, teachers and students, thinkers and writers like you. They were shot or beaten or starved to death."

He is curious to know how she has taken this. How hard an ideologue is she, really? At the same time, he administers a little mental rebuke to himself. He has never approved of the way some survivors use their victimhood to manipulate others. Tempting as it is, he does not mention the fact that hundreds of thousands of his countrymen died in slaughter pits at the hand of the most humane socialist state in Europe. He does say the following:

"Many people were killed by Tito."

"Propaganda", she retorts.

"History", he says. "Search the index of your library for Bleiburg and Maribor."

"Bleiburg? Maribor?" she snorts again.

"Seek," he says, "and you will find."

She rolls her eyes. As they stand there facing each other across an abyss, so many thoughts cross his mind. He does not tell her that his parents were murdered in his home village by the people who helped establish the most humane socialist state in Europe. He does not mention that his mother and father were beautiful souls who hated both Fascism and Communism. Would she understand the term—*beautiful souls*? How could he mention Josipa? What would his sudden upwelling of grief have said if it had been permitted to erupt? I am remembering my childhood friend who was always kind to everyone, and very bright too—you value brightness, do you not, Madam—she would no doubt have gone on to study at university because she loved to read the books my father gave to her. She learned rapidly and with understanding of everything. I found her body tossed in a heap of bodies when I was a child. Do you know what this has done to me? No. Never. Never. Never.

He cannot say it, he can only permit the memory to flash before his eyes for a second before shoving it back into the cell.

"I lost many friends", he manages to say, his voice beginning to tremble for the first time, continuing to stroke the bird.

"Haven't we all", the woman counters. "And for various political reasons."

Political reasons. For various political reasons, all Josipa's songs, her little gifts, and luminous glances are buried now in the fields of heaven.

"*Rajska Polja*", he whispers.

"What!" says the woman.

He shakes himself and draws a breath.

"There is much I could tell you about those times", he says

aloud. "But perhaps you are busy. Perhaps you have an article to write."

She snorts again. He prays it is her last, because if there is another it might be impossible not to say unforgivable things to her unspeakably arrogant face.

"Why do you approve of the extermination camps here in America?" he asks instead.

"What do you mean? There are no extermination camps in *this* country!" she retorts.

"They are everywhere in this land", he replies, peering straight and deep into her eyes. "The women's clinics."

She flinches for a moment, then counters by flushing with rage. Leaning forward until her nose is an inch from his, she says, through slightly parted teeth, "Every child a *wanted* child."

"And every literary critic a wanted literary critic?" he replies evenly.

She has had enough; she turns on her heels and storms away.

Smiling to himself, Caleb climbs the steps and says in a erudite accent, "Having a little tension are we?"

"A little", Josip answers.

"Can you spare a cup of coffee?"

"Of course. Did you find the book?"

"I found it in the Old English section at the library. And what a poem it is! Opened a lot of doors for me."

"Excellent. Would you read it to me?"

"I'd be delighted", Caleb says, then adds "Sho'-nuff" for effect.

Down in the basement apartment he sprawls on an armchair. Caleb is now taller than Josip, which makes the lad over six feet, five inches tall—a mega-Watusi. No chair can really contain him. He sips coffee while Josip rummages around trying to turn a cardboard box into a temporary hospital room for the pigeon.

"How come you're such a laid-back guy, Joe?"

"What on earth is a laid-back guy?"

"Mellow. Like *mell-low*. Like smooth and calm. Like nothing flusters you."

"Many things fluster me. I am a seething cauldron of displeasure and dissatisfaction."

Caleb rolls over with laughing.

"You're too much, Joe."

"You're sure the biscuit, Caleb."

The graduate student in literature holds his belly and guffaws. My goodness, was it really that funny?

"Caleb, please, get control of yourself. You are under too much tension writing this thesis. You are becoming hysterical."

"Yup, I sho is."

"You should take a holiday. Leave the books aside for a time. If we do not run away occasionally, we will never be at home."

"Hey, that's deep!"

"If we do not waste time properly, nothing will be accomplished."

"Okay, okay, I got the point."

The outcome of the dialogue with an American academic is that Josip is called to the manager's office the next day and told to explain himself. Josip describes the incident accurately, without prejudice, resisting the urge to supply commentary about the woman's character and mentality. Gus-the-doorman is called in to verify. Gus places all blame on the woman, who was "in a state" that day, he says, "and looking for trouble". The manager is an Armenian, a longtime card partner of the Greek who owns the building, and they both understand a few things.

"She is always looking for trouble", the manager mutters, and tells Josip and Gus to *faggedaboudit* and get back to work.

Faggedaboudit is an English word that means: don't waste another thought on the matter.

During the following months, whenever Josip passes the

woman in the hallway, she looks away. He is now *always* invisible. He delays scrubbing the graffiti from the walls of the floor where she lives. He regrets this lapse, this self-inflicted blemish on his honor, yet he cannot help himself and hopes to improve his disposition as time goes by. When her lease expires later that year, she moves to another apartment building, who knows where. It's a big city, ten million people. She continues to publish her eloquent articles, books, and speeches and to teach a new generation of young Americans. But what can one do about such matters? Stand on a street corner and shout?

More important, the pigeon lives in Josip's room, gathering strength, healing from its bruises and bites, and enjoying the constant food supply. When at last he puts it on the windowsill overlooking the alley and tells it to go, the bird hesitates. It shuffles back and forth on the sill, looks at Josip questioningly as if to say, you don't really mean it. Go, go, he mutters, like a doting old uncle who must have his privacy, and pokes it gently to underline the point.

So it launches itself, flutters about in the light well, then returns to the windowsill, staring at Josip, coo-cooing. Let me in, let me in, it pleads. He sighs and scoops the little fool into his arms. Up they go in the elevator to the roof, across the flat walkway to the edge—ooh, be careful, watch the wind, not too close to the precipice! He strokes its head and then throws it into the air. How wonderful are the dynamics of its flight path, the way it opens its wings wide before the plunge—for it is at first a plunge—downward a few feet, and then, with the merest tilt of its wings, upward between the canyons toward the sky, where it belongs.

EYE OF THE PILGRIM

33

Speak, O my memory! Disclose the fragments and facets of the on-flying years. Do not hesitate, do not take a step back. Come, you can do it: blow the dust off the archives, open the grave, lift the lid of the dumpster, sever the rib cage, and reveal the heart's palpitations and its woes!

If he had been given a choice, would he have chosen to be a man of sorrows and acquainted with grief? Never. It was given. It is gift and cost—and in time the cost may become entirely gift. It is hard to know if that will be the end of all this striving, impossible to guess when the next blessing or blow will fall.

Naomi has died, ancient and revered, though it must be that she was once a child holding a pink hibiscus in her hands. At the funeral in the Ethiopian Gospel Holiness Tabernacle (of the Ark of the Covenant), a little girl approaches Josip as he sits alone in a corner while many black people dance like David before the Lord. She puts a flower into one of his hands and takes the other, as if she is a princess and he a field slave. She then leads him out into the aisle (the aisles are wide, the pews narrow) and teaches the stiff old white man, sad and without rhythm, to dance with abandon. First she shows him how to stick his arms up into the air and to clap and wave his hands. Though he cannot say the words that she and everyone else sings or shouts—*glory* and *hallelujah* and *praised be*—he throws his own mute cries into the air and watches them become little clay birds into which the breath of life is blown, rising, rising through the ceiling of the church toward a distant mountain, as feathers fall from the sky, blue and white and black.

O Naomi, I did not know you very well, but I feel you close! See me dancing, message bearer, see me dancing, I am a fool. Is this what you wanted me to learn?

As the dancing souls sing out their spontaneous harmonics, rising, soaring, taking with them all those gathered into the ark—yes, even him—he is profoundly grateful. Now he can cry as he dances, cry for her passing, feel the loss and longing that prefigure the communion for which they were created. And he can weep with Caleb, who is dancing too, flinging his arms in the air, sobbing like a child for all his losses, and in gratitude for what was given, no longer concerned about trance-frenzy, for there is no hint of trance—it is all holy passion.

Naomi, I have not walked yet, I have not run, but I have taken the hand of this little child who leads me, who brings me into this great dance. Is she the one you promised would come?

He cannot turn the experience into a poem. It would be wrong to try to capture it, translate it. It must remain a mysterious parting of the veil. Is it right, is it wrong? Are they deluded? Have they drawn him into their delusion with their arts of worship, as well as by his love for them? They are not Catholic; they are, indeed, heretics.

"Can they pray the Nicene Creed and mean every word of it?" Friar Todd asks him during their post-confession discussion on the matter.

"I think so—yes, I'm sure of it", Josip replies. "They really love Christ."

"There are a few things missing in their relationship with him. We can't pretend there's a union when we really aren't united", says the friar.

"I know, I know", sighs Josip, rubbing his forehead in consternation. "But I do care so much for them, and I think a few of them care for me."

"Well, that's probably the key to the situation. We and your friends believe in the same Lord, and maybe at this stage of history the big thing is to love each other and pray for each other. We can't share sacraments, but we can share our hearts."

In the parish hall of Sts. Cyril and Methodius, a new thing is happening, a prayer meeting, with a kind of singing very much like the singing at the Ethiopian Gospel Holiness Tabernacle. Though there is not the same abandon as there is among the black believers, there is passion such as he has never heard before among his own. Here too they raise their arms and pray and cry and sing, these exiled Croatians, their long-oppressed ardor surfacing at last! Sometimes they dance as they pray, and the friars dance among them, the followers of Sveti Franjo, who loved to dance toward heaven.

It is also the dance of Jason, leaping high and tugging toward eternity, his arms reaching for pigeons, his inarticulate cries calling to the transcendent among the towers. It is Abel Kristijan Bogdan's dance too, for Josip sometimes gets to his feet and walks about the room with his throat open, singing soundlessly with the baby in his arms. He lifts the invisible child high in his hands as lament and offering, as protest and as love. And sometimes he simply raises his arms empty-handed among his countrymen, not in imitation or assimilation, but as a child, because for an hour or two each week he is the child. And though most of his days are spent as an aging man of woes, he now understands that the soul of the child has not been lost, that there is no separation between this prayer-fire and the Holy Eucharist-fire, or the consolations that come from the Rosary of the Mother-Gospa. It is all one. It is all the sea of love.

Thus, he learns that there is good surrender and bad surrender: in reawakened memory he is a child in the snow-yard of Pačići, raising his arms in terror as a man points a rifle at his head. Then, in the blink of an eye, he is a man raising his arms in peace, in a warm and comfortable room in a wealthy city in a free land, far from the catastrophe.

Does good surrender wipe out bad surrender?

See, O Lord, I have no weapon in my hands.

A publisher in Vienna has put together a book of Croatian poems, written by contemporary poets in exile. Six of Josip Marulić's are included in the anthology. Letters pour in from Europe and America inquiring about the author. Who is he, what is his story? The New York publisher always replies without supplying the information they desire, explaining that the poet wishes to maintain a private life.

Winston and Miriam have a newborn son, whom they name Thomas Xavier.

The McIsaacs buy a small farm in the Mohawk valley of New York and move away, insisting that Josip must visit them someday.

Gus-the-doorman retires to look after his wife during her dying months.

Carl Johnson has been promoted and is living on an army base in Georgia with his wife, who is a schoolteacher. They have three young children. Carl writes articles for U.S. military journals and sends copies to Josip. He likes to quote a French writer named de Tocqueville. Josip replies, quoting from Aristotle, Plato, and St. Thomas More.

Coriander has surgery on her hip. She can no longer work. She has a little pension, but it is not enough to live on. Caleb supplements the family income with his wages as an associate professor of literature at Columbia University.

Caleb marries a woman whom he met at the university. She is working on her master's degree in sociology. She is from Eritrea. A guerilla war is under way there, a vicious and dirty one—worsened by drought and famine and years of Marxism. It will soon escalate, she believes, into full-scale war between Ethiopia and newly independent Eritrea. The church in Harlem has changed its name to the Abyssinian Gospel Holiness Tabernacle. The woman is the only true Abyssinian who visits the church. She is, in fact, a Catholic, educated by nuns in Asmara. Shy and graceful, she is devoted to Coptic art, Dante, and Caleb. Her name is Miriam. One of her brothers is an Olympic runner. Seven family members were executed by the Communists. Caleb is entirely, reverently, and poetically in love with her. They are married in St. Patrick's cathedral. Though Caleb does not convert to Catholicism, he takes premarriage instructions and agrees to the nuptial Mass.

Because the bride does not have any family members in America, the people from Caleb's family and congregation sit on both sides of the aisle. A few of her university friends are also present, talking aloud, indifferent to the presence of God. Miriam is working on them, slowly but surely. She wears the traditional wedding dress of her people. There is a lot of classy clothing among Caleb's people and much humming and swaying during the Mass, though out of respect for cultural differences they do not give full vent to their religious passions. However, they are reverent. Much of the liturgical music is provided by a folk ensemble from the university, young Catholic friends of Miriam. The recessional hymn is sung by the choir from Caleb's church. It is a trans-cultural event of epic proportions, as Winston would say. Pouring out the front doors and down the steps, the wedding party encounters an unexpected demonstration: a group of angry people dressed (or rather, undressed) in scanty clothing are throwing rotten eggs, small pieces of rubber, and coat hangers at the door of the cathedral. Life is strange. You learn something new every day.

Within a six-month period, all of Josip's remaining teeth fall out. The dentist tells him that this is unusual in such a young man. Young? He is, what, fifty-six or fifty-seven years old now. "You don't have a single cavity or filling", the dentist comments. "No gum disease either, so early malnutrition is probably the cause." He pauses and glances uneasily at the patient. "You must have had a rough childhood."

Full dentures are made. He likes his new smile and uses it overmuch until he more or less forgets about it. Faggedaboudit.

The Serb-lady retires from the fish market. At some point after Jason destroyed her fortress walls, she told Josip that her name is Ljubićica—Violet. He now dares to ask the Serb owners her family name. With Yugoslavians this is a risk.

Why do you want to know? is implicit in their eyes.

In any event, they tell him: Czobor.

Now he knows his fellow prisoner's full name, Ante Czobor.

Three of Caleb's poems are published by a big New York publishing house in an anthology of young African-American poets. The book is widely and positively reviewed. A small press in New Hampshire invites Caleb to submit his work for publication. He does not hesitate. The book is being edited now for release under the title *Distant Shores: Selected Poems of Caleb Franklin.*

One evening in May of 1990, Josip arrives at the parish hall of Cyril and Methodius to find the people of the prayer group standing about in animated clusters, talking intensely. They are enthusiastic but worried by news. The *Sabor* in Zagreb has passed a decision on the sovereignty of Croatia, following a referendum. An independent Republic of Croatia has been declared!

Now Josip begins to study the newspapers in earnest. Day by day, the situation worsens. Belgrade is refusing to acknowledge the new country. It is brandishing its sabers and encouraging Serb minorities in Croatia to rise up and overthrow the legitimately elected government. People are being killed.

Serbia invades Croatia, Slovenia, and Bosnia. Full-scale war has broken out. The small republics have little defense other than their police forces, for the Serbs control former Yugoslavia's army, navy, air force, weapons, money, and all instruments of intimidation.

The first scattered reports appear in the papers—civilians are being killed by the Yugoslav army wherever it goes. Cities are bombed. Vukovar is being pulverized. Its citizens are resisting the massive onslaught of Serb troops and heavy equipment with only small handguns. Mysterious death squads are roving about, mainly in Bosnia, killing Muslims and Croats. People are fleeing the country in great numbers. They are cut off and herded into zones, raped, tortured, exterminated—bands of merciless killers wear the uniform of the state, but the death's-head insignia is branded in their souls.

It cannot be happening. This is not real! This is what genocidal shock troops do; this is like a world war concentrated into a micro-zone.

Josip prays fervently for proliferating intentions—the preservation of innocent lives, the conversion of guilty lives, for the survival of a nation, for democracy. Month after month his anguish grows. He feels helpless and ashamed. Though he knows that this shame over his safety is groundless, he cannot understand why he has been pulled from the fire only to watch from the sidelines the immolation of his people. The odds against Croatia are staggering. The people are practically weaponless,

675

possessing hardly a rifle with which to defend themselves. Though they are rallying, arms embargoes have been placed by the world on the new republics, as if denying them weapons of defense will ensure peace. Don't they understand? The peace that follows will be a trussed pigeon handed over to a hungry cat!

The editor of the Croatian journal tells Josip that weapons are being smuggled into Croatia and a resistance army is being built from the base of the small republican police force. Money is needed, and he is trying to channel funds to Zagreb. Josip contributes everything he can, lives on bread and water for weeks, sells some of his most precious books, even his fishing rod and reel, anything that people will buy. "It's not much", he tells himself. "I have not truly sacrificed."

In December of 1991 the Vatican recognizes the independence of Croatia and Slovenia, as do Iceland, Ukraine, Latvia, and Lithuania. In January, Germany, Italy, and Sweden follow suit. Strangely, the most conservative nations of the West, notably Great Britain and the United States of America, are reluctant to grant official recognition. The latter's successive secretaries of state are strongly critical of Germany for recognizing the new nations, arguing that such recognition merely escalates the war. Carl Johnson sends Josip a clipping from a Washington newspaper, an opinion piece that notes the strong economic ties that American banking and industry have with Belgrade. *Oil*, Carl concludes. For the most part, the media focus on horrific imagery and minimalizes, when they do not avoid altogether, the actual architecture of the situation.

Josip's anguish grows and grows, fed by his outrage over the distortions in the American press. It is a combination of platitudes, humanitarianism, rhetoric about democracy (as the real thing is being sabotaged), and clever propaganda bottle-fed to the media by Serbia and its friends. Occasionally, other reporting trickles through and gains some momentum. Journalists on the ground send reports about the actual situation, revealing the motivations of the several nations involved. The situation cannot be distorted completely. Even so, mixed messages continue to pump into the consciousness of the free peoples of the West. For most, it is just another conflict in "the Balkans", the zone of madness, the old cockpit of European hegemonies. Whenever Josip tries to explain it to others, they merely regurgitate the info-bites that television news has given them—a nation of the impressionable controlled by impressionists.

It is hard to sleep properly these days, little more than a few hours snatched from the constant anxiety, fleeing from awake-pain into dream-pain. Restless dreams become nightmares. He is a boy running from a village in flames; he is a youth drowning in blood; he is a man crushed beneath slabs of stone. He is alive and dead, screaming silently.

At every Mass, month after month, he pleads with Christ, "Why am I here? Why did you save me? Why are so many people dying? Why does evil go on devouring the good? Why do men of malice have so much power? Why do men of freedom help them?"

Each day Josip remains kneeling before the tabernacle long after most people have left the parish church, but the silence of heaven just grows and grows. Occasionally, he feels again what he felt that day when he laid the body of Abel Kristijan Bogdan before the tabernacle. It is the silence of Calvary, the muting of creation as the mouthpieces of the killers babble on about freedom and democracy even as they stab and stab with their lances, even as a fountain of blood and water pours from the wound.

On Good Friday, Josip makes a prayer during the liturgy of the Passion of Christ. Approaching the cross to reverence it, he is slowly moving forward in a line of fellow parishioners when a light appears within his soul. He perceives it as a form, not as actual thoughts. It shows him that he has been pulled from the fire for a purpose, though what the purpose is he cannot know. Then, in his mind's eye, he is kneeling on the stones of St. Peter's piazza, confessing to the friar who read his soul, and he sees as well the counsel he was given: You shall love your enemies; forgive those who harm you.

This he has tried to do, with much success and some failure, throughout the nearly thirty years since that turning point.

"Teach me to die like you", he asks, as he kisses the bronze feet of the corpus.

On Holy Saturday morning, Winston phones. This year Josip is to spend Easter with the Kanapathipillai family, and he intends to take the bus to New Haven later in the day.

"Josip, I guess you saw yesterday's *Times*? Look, if you want to go to the event, we'll understand."

"What event are you speaking about?"

"Don't you know? Sunday evening, there's a benefit concert at Carnegie Hall to raise funds for Croatia. American and Croatian musicians will be performing."

"Would you mind if I go?" says Josip. "I could come to you on Easter Monday."

"Miriam and I are driving down for the concert too. Why don't we meet you there and bring you back to our place afterward?"

"Good", says Josip, "Very good. This is wonderful news."

At last something is being done. He can help. He can do a little to protect his homeland and perhaps to save lives.

He meets Winston and Miriam in the lobby as arranged, and they find seats together about halfway to the front. The hall is full, with standing room only. The orchestra is tuning up in the pit below the stage. The curtain parts, and an introductory speech by an American-born Croat begins the evening. Then come brief speeches by Croats in exile, including the editor of the monthly in which Josip's poems are published. The applause is loud, impelled by the release of passions long-suppressed by helplessness.

As singers, musicians, and choirs perform, Josip feels his heart tear open again, exposing the reservoir of sorrow. Though he weeps silently throughout, his grief is mingled with an inexplicable joy and the whole is subsumed in supernatural peace. He is also surprised by a sense of consolation—the kind he has felt only after receiving Holy Communion.

Finally, as the evening draws to a close, a second curtain divides, and a grand piano is exposed. A man enters from stage right and seats himself at the keyboard. One by one, other musicians enter and stand nearby—three violins, a bass viol, cello, flute, oboe, and a long-necked bandura.

Silence falls as a stagehand brings a microphone to front and center of the stage. A dignitary, speaking in Croatian, introduces a Mr. Robert Finntree, the organizer of the concert. The latter is a distinguished, silver-haired man in a tuxedo. He apologizes for his lack of Croatian blood, for he is pure Irish, he says, drawing scattered applause from the audience. He goes on to say that he is married to a Croat and that his children are half-Croats, therefore he claims some rights. Appreciative laughter, stronger applause.

He continues with moving words about the war and about the peoples of former Yugoslavia who are falling victim to naked aggression, are invading no lands, and are merely defending what is their own. The Croatian people are doing this practically without material means and without a spirit of vengeance, he says, and are an example of courage for the whole world.

Finally, he introduces the concluding performance, "In the Homeland of the Soul".

As Mr. Finntree leaves the stage, Josip's scalp begins to tingle. He sits straighter, and chills wash through his body.

Can it be? Can it be the same piece composed by Iria more than thirty years ago?

The pianist begins, slowly, slowly, striking a minor note as if it were the deep booming of a heartbeat. More minor notes arise, the pulse of blood quickens, and the melody begins, quietly at first as if a soul is awakening. The violinists lift their instruments and draw their bows across their strings. The central theme emerges, growing complex with alliances, then the wind instruments enter unobtrusively and gradually increase in volume. Themes blend and part and reunite, and all the while it remains meditative and melancholic as the Slavic passion is released. The composition is Iria's.

It has been refined with the passage of years, but still present are the faintest residues of the Orient and the cool northern exultation of Europe, followed by the heat of the Renaissance and the suction of the Turkish tide rising from the south, and then the final movement, when the tide is repelled at last by valor and faith and love for what must not be lost, for what has been purchased by immeasurable sacrifice. The cries of mankind are heard by the mysterious presence within the music, a vast consciousness who is suffering with his people.

The spirit of the composition has been preserved almost wholly intact. In the pauses between movements, the silence in the hall is like a suspension of breath in which the murmur of a thousand pounding hearts can be heard. They have left behind all thought as they rise into a realm that is never seen with the eyes and is rarely felt in the homeland of the soul.

When it is over, not a sound can be heard. No one speaks. No one applauds. There is only stillness, attention to the indefinable presence.

The musicians lower their instruments, bow their heads, and then the subdued weeping of a woman comes from somewhere in the audience, a child calls out, and a baby begins to cry.

Now the audience rises and breaks into thunderous applause,

countless voices are cheering, it goes on and on as if it will never stop.

Josip too is standing, crying openly, as are so many others in the seats around him. Blinded by tears, he cannot see the performers and does not hear the voices at the microphone calling for silence and the final words of thanks. Throughout all of this, the audience remains standing, breaking into applause again and again, while Josip is flown across the years and is once more within the parlor of the Horvatinec home in Split, seeing Iria's face as she plays her composition, seeing Ariadne playing the same piece. Finally, he looks up and wipes his eyes. The past, the present, and the future are concentrated in this moment, this eye of the needle.

Mr. Finntree is surrounded by people on the stage; he has just finished his final words, and a little girl comes forward and presents a bouquet of red roses to him. A little boy comes forward at the same time and presents a bouquet of white roses to the woman beside him.

Josip steps out into the aisle. He moves through the crowd toward the stage, longing to ask so many questions. Perhaps this man will know how the composition came to America, how it survived. Did Vera and Iria take it out of the country when they fled? Surely it must have happened that way. Was it 1958 or 1959? Yes, it must have been 1959, because he had been married a year, the baby was due within a few months, and Christmas had just passed. Thirty-three years ago.

He is closer to the stage now, and hundreds of people are milling about the floor in front of it, clapping and shouting things to Mr. Finntree. More people are filling the stage from both wings to hug and kiss the musicians. Though he is talking to those who crowd him, Mr. Finntree keeps his arm around the woman's shoulder, a white-haired lady of noble bearing. Her refined face is reposed and glowing. Yes, it is the man's wife, because the woman's right arm is around the man's waist, her left arm dropped by her side. She holds a violin in her hand, and on the wedding finger is a diamond ring.

The woman is Ariadne.

Josip halts. No, it is not Ariadne. This is merely how his bride would have looked after thirty years. It is another woman, but for the moment the similarity is difficult to absorb. He can move no closer since the uncanny resemblance evokes too many memories at once. He steps away from the crowd and sits down on an empty seat, a few rows from the front.

Shaking his head, Josip glances at the program, searching the titles of the musical pieces and the names of musicians who performed them.

"In the Homeland of the Soul"—yes, it is attributed to Iria. He must find a way to speak with Mr. Finntree, ask him by what paths the composition found its way here after all these years. The musicians are listed. And there among the violinists is a name he knows:

Ariadne Finntree.

He cannot remember how he is returned to his basement room—he vaguely recalls Winston and Miriam asking if he feels ill, a postponement of the Easter visit to their home, a drive in their car. Unlocking his door in the basement, he goes into the darkened room alone, shuts the door and locks it. He sits down on the bed without turning on the lights. His mind is without thoughts of any kind. He sits for measureless time, staring into the night. Finally, he rolls over onto the bed and curls into fetal position.

As has so often happened during his life, he does not remember how the following days are spent. For three days he is alive, yet held in the grip of darkness. There are knocks on the door, followed by silence; a phone rings several times, followed by silence. The knife is turning and turning silently in the heart, within the larger silence of God. He will later recall that it is like lying in a tomb, and that it is Wednesday morning when he awakes and sees light in the window.

Later that day, the lock rattles, and the hallway door opens wide. Coriander and Caleb are standing there next to the manager of the building. The Franklins come in and turn on the overhead light. Coriander puts her hand to Josip's forehead, checking for fever, while Caleb takes his pulse and asks questions. The old man does not respond, though he looks back with consciousness in his eyes.

"Maybe just a bad flu", says Caleb to his mother. "You go on home, Momma, I'll stay with him."

When Coriander and the manager leave, Caleb sits down on the end of the bed.

"Feel pretty sick, man?"

The formation of words is too far beyond him.

Caleb brings a wet cloth from the bathroom, washes Josip's face and hands, then removes his shoes and socks, washes his feet as well, and pulls the blanket over him. He sits down on a wooden chair beside the bed with his elbows on his knees, looking and looking at the old face that is now completely a mask.

"Say something", he mutters at last. "C'mon, Joe, tell me something."

No reply. Eyelids shut, head turns toward the wall.

"Got any pain?"

No reply.

Another day and night like this. Caleb tries to get him to sit up in bed and drink some soup. Josip keeps his lips firmly closed except for a single glass of water, because only dying is needed, and he need not die in pain.

After one more day of this, Caleb loses patience.

"Look, Josip," he says in his serious professor tone, "you either tell me what's wrong or I call an ambulance."

Josip rolls over and faces the wall.

"Go away, Caleb", he whispers.

"I'm not going away. What's wrong?"

"Please, go away."

"Sheee-it!"

No reply.

"I've never seen you like this. What happened to you? Tell me!"

No reply.

Caleb reaches for the phone and begins dialing for an emergency ambulance.

"No", whispers Josip before the call is connected.

"Waddayamean, *no*?"

"A hospital will not help."

"Did you have a heart attack? Any pain in your chest?"

"No. Please go away."

"A stroke? Can you move your limbs?"

"My body is fine. I need to die."

Now it is Caleb's turn to make no reply. He places the receiver back on its hook and glances at the jagged scars on Josip's wrists.

"What do you mean you need to die?" he says in a quiet voice.

"I want to be alone. Leave me."

"You feeling suicidal?"

"No."

"Then what are you talking about? Maybe you're just depressed."

"I have to be alone."

"I'm not going until you tell me what's wrong."

No reply.

Josip turns away again, his back to Caleb. Caleb grabs Josip's shirt and yanks the old man fiercely until the body rolls over, facing the room.

"Talk to me!" he growls.

Josip shakes his head.

"I said talk to me!" Raising his voice, he repeats, "Talk to me!"

"I have lived too long. I am a mistake. I must die now."

Caleb lets go of the shirt, drops his hands.

"You can't do that", he stammers.

"I can."

"You can't!"

"Go, now."

Caleb breathes heavily, shaking his head, covering his eyes with the palm of his right hand.

"Don't kill me", he whispers in a child's voice. "Please don't kill me."

Suddenly, Caleb jerks forward with a look of rage and terror.

"Don't go away!" he shouts.

He grabs the shirt in his fists and shakes the old man violently.

"Don't leave me!" he roars into his face. "Don't leave me! Don't leave me!"

Draw the veil. Remember this, but do not speak of it. It is private and holy. Only say that Josip sits up and places a hand on the trembling shoulders of the sobbing man.

"Caleb. I am very thirsty", he croaks. "Can you bring me a glass of water?"

34

And so the months go on, and life returns to its pace. He carries a numb place in the exact center of his heart. When he works, when he prays, when he eats the fast-food that Caleb sometimes brings him, and even the next Christmas when he opens the gift from Winston and Miriam (a new rod and reel), he feels none of the usual emotions. People are dying, the chronicles of human malice mount high, hundreds of thousands of people are driven from their homes, perhaps hundreds of thousands killed. Stories of atrocity leak into the West, Omarska and Trnopolje and Manjača, concentration camps that are in fact extermination camps. Muslims and Catholic Croats are being killed in vast numbers. There are orphans in abundance, homeless people everywhere, homeless, homeless, homeless. And then the rapes followed by abortions, degradation of the image of God, more and more and more until the mind goes numb.

And now Josip begins to notice the emergence of the very thing Winston predicted so many years ago in Central Park when they first met—the abstraction of catastrophe. The killers murder not only their immediate victims; they spread death into the souls of survivors. The free men of the West abstract those hundreds of thousands of violent deaths in terms of geopolitical strategy. What to do with the Balkans? How to make peace? The men of power who preside over foreign affairs do not see people, they see only mass structures and shifts in the configuration of the world. Amritsar syndrome, Auschwitz syndrome, Hiroshima syndrome, Gulag syndrome, Cambodia and Ethiopia and Jonestown syndromes—yes, all the proliferating syndromes. What is a syndrome if not another name for a phenomenon that occurs when evil strikes good and hell is unleashed through the human heart—and the good who survive recoil and seek forgetfulness.

Father Tomislav said it on Goli Otok, and now his words reach out across the years and echo in Josip's ears. In the darkness of the prison cell, he approaches:

"Josip, your heart is not at rest."

"It will not rest until the killers are slain."

"Do not become Cain."

"I am already Cain."

"Not true. Let us pray together. Death can come at any time."

"Go away."

And later:

"You would kill your oppressors if given the chance?"

"With pleasure", says Josip, seething.

"Your vengeance would destroy you."

"Oh? Tell me, how does a man remain wise in hell?"

The priest does not reply directly. Instead, he says:

"A man suffers injustice. He resents it, and his resentment grows and grows and becomes anger. Anger, if fed, becomes hatred. Hatred opens the soul to evil spirits. And when they possess a man, he becomes capable of any atrocity. Afterward, he will not know how or why he became like that."

"I will know why. Go away!"

Now, after all these years, Josip prays and fasts and offers his second loss of Ariadne for the saving of the victims—perhaps some will escape. He clings to the Cross and lets himself be nailed in his own way and understands that this union saves him from the dangers of vengeance and apathy. Of his loss he cannot speak. None of his friends realize what has happened. He makes no approach to the Finntree family and does not seek to learn anything about them.

Gradually it dawns on him that there is a moral problem involved in his situation. He and Ariadne are man and wife. She and someone else are man and wife. Which of the marriages is valid? Neither? Both? One or the other?

During the Serb bombardment of Dubrovnik, the world is outraged by the destruction of heritage buildings in the city, not so outraged by the countless murders that continue in Serb-occupied zones. Though U.N. troops strive to keep the peace, there are incidents in which they help the Serbs load prisoners onto army trucks that drive away to slaughter pits.

Posturing and strategizing, impression-making and money-making, while the spilling of blood continues. Somewhere during all of this, Josip realizes that his own small woe must be resolved. Thus, he brings it at last to Friar Todd. The priest is stunned and silent. He can think of nothing in his theological training or in his pastoral practice to resolve it. He will check with the moral theologians and get back to Josip.

In the interim, Josip plans to resolve it in his own way.

I will walk, he declares to the Presence in the tabernacle. *I will no longer run from* paklensko polje, *the fields of hell. I will enter them. I will walk into the midst of this war and bring my armless body in its path. Then my life will end, and I will fly up to you.*

I offer it to you, he repeats, but there is no reply.

Josip obtains a passport and with his meager savings purchases a flight to Sarajevo through Budapest. In Budapest, he learns that the Sarajevo airport has been closed and that no flights are landing there other than military aircraft. He waits a week in a hotel near the Budapest airport, but the situation does not improve. It dawns on him that he might try walking into Croatia across the Hungarian border. He travels by bus as far as Pécs, where he learns that no one is permitted to cross the frontier because there is fierce guerrilla fighting under way in the Slavonija region. Regardless, he tries to make his way south on foot.

For two days he walks, and during this time he ponders and prays and listens.

"Am I offering myself, truly?" he asks. "What is the intention of my heart? Am I trying to take myself out of existence because I want to escape suffering and reject God's will in my life? Am I subtracting myself from her life, finally and absolutely? Is it for her sake or for mine? Or is it grace in my soul that draws me into this field of war? Is it holy sacrifice or is it suicide? Speak to me, O my Lord, speak to me, I beg you!"

He hears no reply and continues to walk. While crawling under a fence that divides Hungary from Croatia, he is caught by a border patrol and forcibly returned to Budapest. Exhausted, with only enough money to rebook his flight home, he returns to New York.

Friar Todd takes him into the rectory office, brings two cups of coffee, and closes the door.

"Whew!" he begins, shaking his head. "You sure threw me a curve ball!"

While idioms continue to perplex him, Josip understands that the friar's research into the status of his marital situation has not been easy.

"I want to do what the Church teaches", murmurs Josip. "I will do whatever is right, but you must tell me what is right."

"I've been trying to make headway with this, Josip. But you have no idea how clogged the marriage tribunal is these days. Trying to get an appointment with one of the moral theologians is like asking for a private audience with the pope. The crowds pushing at the chancery door are bigger than at a Yankees game."

Josip waits while the friar vents a little, rubs his flushing face, and blinks rapidly.

"All those people eager to dissolve their marriages, and here you are trying to figure out what's the right thing to do!"

He goes on to describe his perusal of Canon Law and theology texts, and a few phone calls to moral theologians here and there in the country.

"It's a mess, Josip—the state of moral theology in America is one big mess. But the bottom line is, the good, the bad, and the ugly all agree that there's no moral culpability here. Especially if both spouses believed the other had died. I'm presuming your wife thought you were dead, too."

Josip bows his head, the pain of this is so great. "I'm not sure. She knew I went to prison, and in those days most people did not survive prison. It has been thirty years since we parted, and she had no word from me in all that time. So, it is likely she believes I am dead."

Friar Todd grows quiet, observing Josip struggle.

"Did you wonder if she had written you off?"

"Written me off—what does this mean?"

"Did you wonder if she washed her hands of you, living or dead?"

"I do wonder about that. So much has happened, I cannot think clearly. It is complex."

"Very."

"I think it best that she does not know about me. But if the Church tells me to, I will contact her."

"So, you haven't contacted her yet. Is she still a Catholic? Is she married sacramentally to her second husband?"

"I don't know; I don't know", Josip whispers.

"Do you know her married name?"

"Ariadne Finntree."

The friar grows absolutely still.

"Is she married to Robert Finntree?"

"Yes, that is his name."

"Oh, Lord", breathes the friar. "Then she's married in the Church. Bob Finntree is a big benefactor of the archdiocese. He's a Knight of Malta, and the family is . . ."

"Is what?"

"Is very devout."

They remain in silence for some minutes. Finally, Friar Todd stands and puts a hand to Josip's shoulder. "I'll keep trying", he says. "I have an appointment scheduled for seven months from now. Sorry it's not sooner. Can you hold on?"

"Thank you for your good efforts, Friar Todd."

"Maybe you should contact your wife to let her know you're alive."

"What would be the purpose? To heal an old grief that may in fact be long healed in her heart? To rejoice in a miraculous resurrection? We cannot restore what we once had. It was long ago. My return would probably create more pain, a great confusion for her new family, especially between herself and her husband. I will do it if the Church says I must. Until then, I cannot."

Shaking his head with a mixture of sympathy and perplexity, the friar bids Josip good-day.

It takes a few months to earn the price for another flight. Winston will not lend him any money for the venture, nor will Caleb. They both tell Josip that he is being reckless, that people are dying over there. I know, he replies, that is why I must go. Still they refuse to help. Nor will any bank give him a loan.

Finally, after he has saved enough money by missing meals and selling a few possessions, he is able to board a commercial flight from New York to Frankfurt, and then from Frankfurt to Split. He makes it as far as Split, landing in thick fog. He can see nothing from the aircraft's windows. He is held by Croatian officials in a security zone in the airport because of his lack of funds and no adequate explanation for his presence in the country. He is given a cot to sleep on in a locked hall with other unexplainable people. He is treated courteously and fed well. He tells what he can to guards and an investigator, but it is not enough to admit him into the country. One perceptive official asks him if he is trying to get into Bosnia. Incapable of lying, Josip nods in the affirmative. "It's where I was born", he says. The official tells him that it would be impossible for him to pass through the border, let alone through military lines. They lock him up again with a comfortable bed, regular meals, courtesy, and apologies, but neither they nor the unopenable window in the room permit him to escape. Rain falls every day that week, and a low overcast hides the mountains. He is in Croatia, yet he cannot see it. Finally, he is escorted onto a flight back to America.

Arriving at his building on 52nd Street, he finds several notes and letters in envelopes pinned to his door, a couple from Winston and several from Caleb. Winston and his Miriam want Josip to come live with them, if he ever returns from Bosnia. Caleb and his Miriam have moved into an apartment on the ninth floor; please call them immediately if he ever returns from Bosnia. Josip goes up in the elevator and knocks on their door, which is decorated with an ancient Coptic cross. The door opens, Caleb flings wide his arms and gives the old man a few back thumps. He goes all inarticulate, then tries street jargon, and then lapses into silence with a smile. Miriam plops baby Jefferson onto Josip's lap and heads off to the kitchen to make supper for them all. Caleb says he has translated a few of Josip's poems into English with the help of a dictionary. Pretty cumbersome stuff has resulted. You could hardly call it poetry. Can they work together on it? All right, Josip nods.

Life goes on, as it must. The manager has been persuaded not to fire Josip. Many tenants missed him while he was away. His unplanned "holidays" messed things up around the building, garbage and graffiti accumulated, et cetera, but, well, a good janitor is hard to find, says the Armenian. Faggedaboudit!

Friar Todd sits him down in the rectory office. There is strain in the friar's good face.

"Well, Josip, I have a bit more for you to think about. I've talked with a moral theologian from the archdiocese and a couple of other people and their advice tallies. Here's the situation in the Church's eyes, at least the Church in New York. As I told you before, there is no moral wrong in this second marriage. Everyone involved is in good conscience. In the 1960s, they were married by a bishop, a friend of the Finntree family. They have five children, all practicing Catholics. You had what's called in theology a 'natural marriage'. It was a civil union under a Communist government, and the Church respects such unions as genuine marriages. But a sacramental marriage takes precedence, especially in cases where there's a factor they call 'disparity of cult'. Ordinarily, the Church would demand that an engaged couple formally dissolve any civil union they had with someone else before being married in the Church. That's not always possible, for all kinds of reasons, and so in certain exceptional cases, Canon Law allows that it's not necessary to dissolve the civil contract whenever the dissolution would be extremely difficult to obtain. For example, if one of the spouses disappears—usually that means one of them takes off and isn't heard from again. He or she may be alive but can't be found. Or, say a civil ceremony was performed in a tyrannical state from which records would be difficult or impossible to obtain. Are you following all this?"

"Some of it", Josip murmurs.

"Simply put, it's a kind of *de facto* dispensation."

"What should I do?"

Friar Todd takes a deep breath, exhales.

"Basically, it's your call, Josip. The Finntree's marriage is valid, but that doesn't stop you from contacting them."

"Must I contact them?"

"Only if you want to. It seems to come down to a pastoral discernment question. I guess the question you need to ask yourself is, what would bring about the highest good for everyone involved."

"Do you have a suggestion for me?"

"You're free to make your own decision about contact. I can only offer what every other theologian I talked to said about it. They all thought you should probably leave the Finntrees in peace, let them get on with their lives, and you can get on with yours."

Josip nods and puts his face in his hands.

"I'm sorry, Josip. I wish it were easier."

What would *easier* be? And what is this he feels? Is it relief, anguish, loss, resurrection, death, execution, rebirth, a beginning, the end? It is all one. He sighs and lifts his head at last.

"I'm driving up to the Berkshires this weekend", says the friar. "Want to come along?"

"Yes. I would like to visit Abel's grave."

Thus, more is asked of him—the abyss of longing, as well as the inner resistance necessary to repel the magnetism of a phone directory that might divulge the address of the Finntree family. He reads newspapers sparingly, only articles about the war. He attends no more Croatian-American benefits, fund-raisers, or social events. He donates what he can but becomes more invisible than ever. For the time being, he continues to send in new poems to the magazine—shorter, darker, more melancholic ones. He is growing nervous that the publisher might slip and mention the poet's name in an unguarded moment—thus broadcasting it far and wide through the human "grapevine", as Americans call it. Josip extracts a renewed solemn promise from the man that under no circumstances is his real identity to be divulged.

"Paranoia!" grumbles the publisher.

"That's right, it's paranoia", Josip nods. "Please indulge my mental afflictions."

It must remain this way because it is always possible that Ariadne will pick up a copy of the magazine and notice his name. Marulić will mean nothing to her. In a glance, he had understood her new life, her good marriage, her good husband, her five children. He could not bear to become a tragedy returned, a long-healed memory erupting into pain. He will not permit what remains of his life to haunt her or destroy her happiness.

"If I die now, at this very moment," he declares to the stars, "it has all been worth it. For I have seen that she exists. She is on the earth with me."

He will bear this absence, this silence, this permanent separation. He will take it entirely upon himself, and no one needs to know. Yes, he will offer it to the crucified Christ. He will offer it for Ariadne and her family, and he will unite it to the Lord's sufferings so that lives will be saved over there in the war.

35

In 1995, the war in former Yugoslavia ends. In the autumn of 1996, Josip flies to Zagreb and is admitted into the country as a tourist. This is his first sight of the northern regions of the land. He walks on foot from the city to the mountain shrine of the Majka Božja Bistrička—a day's journey around Mount Zagreb and through wooded hill country, gentle valleys, and fields—about thirty kilometers. His pilgrimage is slow but unflagging. Sometimes he passes others who are heading toward the shrine, usually the elderly and infirm or women with small children. Sometimes vigorous walkers pass him, older or younger than he, striding eagerly toward the shrine, while he approaches step by step, as if each passing meter has a significance of its own. He sleeps at a pilgrims' inn on the way and arrives the next morning.

Now he has come to the place where his father often spoke of taking him when he was a boy. There they would have prayed for Josip's vocation—"whatever it might be", Tata had said. Now the old man sees what he and Tata would have seen together if a journey had been granted to them. Though his vocation in life never materialized because all possible forms of it were atomized by the malice of God's enemies, he can still offer what remains, offer it for others, the known and the unknown.

Wandering about the grounds, he comes to a large crucifix and stands before it with bowed head. His body begins to shudder with interior sobbing. It is not normal weeping. It is something else, as if his soul cries. Then, with closed eyes, he sees a human form approaching. He knows—though he cannot explain how he knows—that it is a father, a father given to him. It is not Tata, but someone else—a soul he does not recognize. Is this the materialization of longing in the imagination, the father who should have been here with him long ago? Or is it a guardian for his soul sent from beyond the perceptions of man? Who is he? Josip does not know, does not need to know. Now the presence takes Josip's old man's hand and transforms it into a child's. Thus he is led from holy place to holy place around the holy valley, his mysterious father showing him everything. As they walk together, Josip begins to understand his own loneliness in full measure, feels it anew, sees its foundations, and becomes certain that only the ground of poverty opens the soul to such consolations. He gives thanks for this after Communion in the basilica, and when he stands for the final recessional hymn, he senses that the invisible father has departed from his imagination—or perhaps he has merely stepped away a pace.

Returning to Zagreb on foot, Josip finds a cheap hotel room, falls into peaceful dreams, and awakes with words ringing in his ears, *The surprises of the Lord have not come to an end.*

In the cathedral of St. Stjepan, he attends Mass, prays before the tomb of the martyr Alojzije Stepinac, and remembers the calendar in the kitchen at Pačići the day the Partisans came.

From Zagreb he travels by bus through the coastal mountains. It is a shock to see houses, indeed whole villages, that were bombed into ruins and have not yet been rebuilt. At the town of Senj on the Adriatic, he hires a local fisherman to take him out among the islands. The boat is not unlike the *Sea Lion*, which long ago took him south from this region and dropped him at Split. This boat does not have a name, only a number, but its captain is no cipher. He is old enough to have weathered some storms, young enough to have been born after Josip fled to Italy. As his craft chugs across the Velebitski kanal toward the island of Prvić, he keeps up a stream of commentary above the thrum of the inboard engine.

"I remember when they abandoned it", he says, pointing into the distance, where a white knob is rising above the heat haze. "That was in 1989. We used to sneak over there for years to pick up bits of metal they left behind. There was stone for a while too, limestone squares. Very nice they were, but they disappeared pretty fast. They call it the naked island, and that's its name too. They called it that long before it was a prison."

"So, you know it was a prison?" Josip says.

"Everyone knew, but no one said a word about it because none of us wanted to go live over there, you can be sure. Then a few years ago, after the Communists were kicked the hell out, people began to talk. The homeland war changed a lot of things, and I'm glad of it. Though I'm sad, too, because I lost some friends. They were in the army, and we had nothing to fight with, no navy or air force, not many guns on the ground either. It was a miracle we won that war. One hundred percent miracle, just like the old days."

Josip continues to scan the horizon as the heights of Glavina slowly rise before him.

"Why do you want to see it?" asks the captain with a quick look.

"I was a prisoner there."

"Ah, that's too bad. Good to see you made it through. Will you tell me about it?"

Josip drops his eyes.

"It was a hard place", he murmurs.

"Many of our people died there, it's said."

"Yes, many."

Thirty thousand, perhaps as many as fifty thousand.

"We'll have to land on the other side because there are bays over there and a landing dock. It's too steep here."

Yes, too steep. Now they are passing close to the precipitous slope down which he slid in the dark, a skeleton man in flight from hell, not knowing the hell that lay ahead. Is that the ravine he descended to reach the shore? Yes, it must be.

His heart is playing tricks on him now—racing, then stopping, and racing again.

The captain cuts back on the throttle, turns the wheel, and eases the boat around to the north side of the island; then they slowly proceed to its western end. There they make another swing and cruise along the south side. Trees and thickets of bushes are now growing here. A cove appears on the left.

"That's Vela Draga, where they dropped off the prisoners. Or maybe it's the place where they picked up stone. I don't know."

He spins the wheel, and the bow turns toward the wharf.

"I've changed my mind", says Josip. "Don't land, just go around the island."

"As you wish."

Once, twice, three times around, and during much of this time Josip remains with his eyes closed, facing the island, whispering prayers as the cries of countless souls reach for him across the water.

Finally, the captain, who has been patiently quiet for a time, asks if Josip wants to return to Senj.

"Not yet. Can you take me a little farther?" Josip replies, nodding toward the mainland a bit to the south. As the boat cruises in that direction, Josip stares down into the waves, seeing a pale human shape desperately swimming underwater.

Down—forward—up!

Within twenty minutes, the boat is idling, slipping toward a beach below a small stone house that stands alone among fruit trees at the base of a high hill. The boat's draft is shallow, and the captain kills the engine, letting the bow rustle onto the pebbled beach.

"Should I wait for you?"

"Please. I won't be long."

"Take your time. You've paid for the day."

Josip drops over the bow onto the beach, shifts the knapsack onto his shoulder, and climbs a winding path through the weeds toward the house. When he arrives at the courtyard, he sees that it has not greatly changed. On the rough flagstones there are still potted flowers, and the house is better shaded by fruit trees larger than he remembers. There is a driveway on the other side of the house, and an old car sits there. Beyond it is a gravel road that climbs toward the coastal highway, which is hundreds of meters above.

Seated on a plastic lawn chair, with her back toward him, a woman is speaking to a child sitting on her lap. The woman's voice is reciting in a sing-song. Josip clears his throat and says, "Zdravo."

Zdra—he croaks—*vo!* as the dolphins speed away into the deeper waters, smiling as they dive.

The woman yelps and jumps from her seat, turning around with the child in her arms. She is in her early forties, handsome and strong. A book drops from her lap—she has been reading to the child, a three-year-old girl. She is startled by this man who has come up out of the sea, but she does not seem afraid. The little girl examines the stranger curiously, stands beside the woman, and takes her hand.

"Can I help you?" asks the woman.

Josip nods.

"I—I am looking for Drago and Marija. Do they still live here?"

The woman's face saddens. "I regret that they have both passed away. My father some years back, my mother this winter. You hadn't heard?"

"I knew them a long time ago. I am sorry about the loss of your parents, Jelena."

Startled again, she asks, "How do you know my name?"

700

"I knew you too", he smiles. "You were as young as this child at the time."

"Really? A long time ago it was, then. What is your name?"

Josip steps forward and offers his hand, which she shakes in a hesitant way, her kindly face somewhat puzzled.

"I am Josip Lasta. Your parents knew me only as Josip. And I never learned your family name."

"Oh", she says. "I'm sorry, but I don't remember you."

An orange cat comes out onto the patio from around a corner of the house. Its tail is pointing straight up in the air. The child runs to it and picks it up, cuddles and strokes it, sings into its ear.

"Do you remember the poem?"

"The poem?" she laughs.

> "*Dupin, dupin, dupin,*
> play with me, one, two, three,
> *dupin, dupin, dupin . . .*"

"I don't know any poem like that."

"It is your own. Those words came from your lips. And I think those little words helped save me."

She shakes her head, then pauses, and looks away toward the sea, as if straining to remember something. She frowns, then looks back at Josip.

"Were you the man who came from the sea?"

"I was. I am."

"Yes, I remember now", she nods. "Mamica and Tata talked about you for years. Not your name—only *the man who fell into the sea*, that's what they called you."

"When they took me from the sea, they brought me into your home and cared for me because I was very ill. Later, your father and his brother took me in the *Sea Lion* to Split."

"The *Sea Lion*! My goodness, then it's true. You know, that boat is still in the water. My older brother has it in Rijeka. He uses it to fish sometimes, though he's not really a man of the sea."

She offers to bring him food and drink. He thanks her but declines. He cannot stay long.

"I had hoped to give something to your father and mother", he says, opening his knapsack. "When they rescued me that time, they gave me gifts—from the little they possessed—clothing for a man who had no clothing. They were very brave and generous. They saved my life. They and the dolphins."

"Dolphins", she smiles. "I have always loved them, but we seldom see them this close to shore. Years go by without seeing one."

"It was they who guided me to your shore. And it was, I think, your poem that honored them and thanked them, for at the time I was unable to speak and was close to death."

She regards him thoughtfully but says nothing.

He offers her several packages, which she accepts with a look of curiosity. Opening them she finds a pair of men's trousers and a fine shirt, a leather belt with a metal buckle, and a new fisherman's cap. From the knapsack he also takes out a box marked with the symbol of a New York shoe company and gives her that as well. She takes it hesitantly and opens the lid.

"Oh, what fine boots!"

"Please accept them."

"If you wish. I appreciate it. Though my Tata is gone, these will fit my husband." She is still examining them with a look of wonder when he says, "Now I must go. Thank you, Jelena, for everything. I pray you will remember your poem. And perhaps you will teach poems to your child."

"My grandchild, this little one is", she corrects. "When you came up out of the sea, just now, I was reading poems to her."

She smiles into his eyes. He bows to her and goes back down to the shore. On board the boat, he sits near the bow and looks up at the little house on the hill as the craft draws away. The woman and the child are standing there, waving.

At Senj he catches the bus to Zadar. He has been to that city before, but he has never seen it, for he was hiding under the deck of the *Sea Lion* as it was being fueled. How odd to have been in a place and to have no visual memory of it. It's like being a blind person. Soon he will see it, but during the two-hour journey he can sit back and try to absorb the meaning of his return to Goli Otok. It will take time. He is too close to that epicenter for real understanding, but the assimilation has begun. He holds the image of the white island in his mind, for it is a place he has never seen as a whole. Its interior he knows all too well, and it now provokes sorrows and ponderings.

He sees again the faces of his fellow prisoners, those who tended his demolished flesh after his arrival, sewed up his wounds, washed him, fed him, and helped him to stand and walk again. Those who advised him and whispered with him and engaged in the forbidden dialogues that awakened the atrophying mind, and in the end held back his hand from the act of Cain. Those few whom he had known among the countless nameless ones, were they too among the hosts of the lost? Or did they survive? Were Sova the owl and Fr. Tomislav and Ante Czobor ever released, or did they die in their chains? And what about Vladimir Lucić? While he was in Zagreb, Josip checked the telephone directory, recalling that the professor once taught in that city, but no such man was listed. Neither did the university's information office know of him. Did he perish among that vast cloud of witnesses? Everywhere Josip goes, he checks directories, finding nothing.

Now he turns his thoughts from the old pain. He knows it will return because it always has. And it may be that this pain is an essential part of his mission—one of the reasons he was permitted by providence to escape and to live, so that he might

703

remember them always and pray for their souls. This he now does, as he has so often done since his restoration to faith.

The face of Jelena smiles at him again, simultaneously as the child and as the middle-aged woman. How swiftly life passes, full of partings and reunions, some accidental and some intended. She had not remembered the words of her dolphin poem, while he has remembered it ever since, each word distinct within its whole. What is this mysterious overflow of the soul's secret languages, so close to the surface in the heart of a child but buried deep under the weight of experience or crowded aside by practical matters as the years unfold? The voice of mankind speaking its thoughts and singing its songs and breathing its poems. Little dreams that evaporate almost upon leaving the lips. Where do they come from, and where are they going? And who are we, if such mysteries pour from our mouths?

Later, he recalls Zadar as a mixture of beauty and devastation— a lot of bomb damage, rubble, and burnt-out buildings, but St. Donat's cathedral on the island is intact, and the surrounding streets show signs of recovery. A little boy eats a ripe fig with a smile of gratitude to his father, a mother sings a hymn in the old Roman forum, pouring music into the sky while her adolescent children prance about reading historical plaques and trying to imagine a lost empire. There is a very old woman pushing a baby carriage with a crying infant in it, and two young lovers stroll aimlessly as they dissolve into each other.

Above all he will remember the cathedral. A long line of people trails into the church and Josip follows it. He does not know what the line is for. Perhaps it is for Mass, and if so he would like to attend. People nearby are talking about a relic, and thus he learns that today is the feast of St. Simeon and that the prophet's relic is inside. This is the one day of the year when the public may see it. It had been brought to the city during the Middle Ages by a Venetian ship returning from the Holy Land.

Blown hard by a *bura*, the vessel had sought shelter in this harbor. When the storm passed and the Venetians were ready to leave, the people of Zadar insisted that the relic remain in their keeping. The Venetians departed after much debate, and there ensued centuries of dispute over it. But here it remains.

As the line inches forward he supposes he will kiss a gold container containing a finger bone or a lock of hair. As he enters the cathedral along with hundreds of other people, a hush falls on them all, and now, slowly, slowly, he approaches a great silver casket on a dais above the high altar. Its front panel is dropped, and a form can be seen inside behind glass. He climbs narrow marble steps toward it. Now he is here, and suddenly he is frozen in a state of attention, because the case contains the body of a man who lived two thousand years ago, lying as if asleep. Though the skin is dark brown and dry, he is neither a waxed effigy nor a mummified corpse. Very short and thin he is, just an old man. The head is centimeters away from Josip's face, and he can closely inspect the shape of the skull, the wisps of hair at the temples, the eyelashes, the pores of the skin—all visible and incorrupt.

Josip drops to his knees and plunges into the timeless stillness that has been given. It would be easy to question, to demand documents and proof, but he simply knows. He is only perplexed that the entire world does not line up to enter this church and see the lips that spoke the incandescent words.

This child is destined for the rising and the falling of many in Israel. He will be a sign of contradiction—

Who is this little man from whom such words poured forth? Where did he come from, and what formed him? What impelled his spirit to cry out at the sight of an ordinary man and an ordinary woman and an ordinary child entering the temple, bearing the light of the world in their arms?

—a sign that will be rejected, that the thoughts of many will be laid bare, and a sword shall pierce your own heart.

Now the sea rides at his right hand, and it seems to him that the ships of ancient heroes no longer sail upon it as they once did. There, so bright that he cannot stare at them for more than a second or two, are angels walking upon the sea of glass, even though the turquoise of the water is stronger than he thought it would be.

Split is near, and the bus is descending on the coastal highway; the Dinarics are white-crested above it, and the Adriatic is shimmering to the West. There are the hill of the Marjan rising between the bays and the ivory city capped by red roofs and bell towers. Here, at last, after thirty-five or more years, the intervening time is dissolving as the past becomes present.

The bus takes him to Stari Grad, the old downtown core near the imperial palace. He carries his luggage from the drop-off point on the waterfront promenade to Marmontova Street and to a hotel, a minute's walk from the shore. It is also a minute's walk from the church of St. Francis. After he has checked into his room, he goes back down to the street and makes his way directly to the church. So much returns as he approaches its entrance. The crucified body of Fra Anto, holy and beautiful, is on the steps as always, yet he is now standing, robed in white, with open arms and light pouring through the wounds. His smile welcomes Josip home. Though the original catastrophe took place on other steps, all churches are forever that place.

Here too, in this very spot, Josip had his last conversation with the Lastavica of the Sea, forty years ago.

Let us go in, said the man with no arms.

I cannot, said the youth, shaking with nameless terror.

Josip now enters the church, blesses himself with holy water, and kneels on the marble floor. There are no other visitors. He may speak without disturbing anyone. He wants to say thank you, aloud—many words of gratitude, aloud. Yet, as always whenever he is upon those bridges that span oceans, especially those bridges uniting time and eternity, all spoken words repose in the source of words, which is silence.

Christ is alive here. The flickering red candle signals it, yet the clearer affirmation is within Josip's soul. He bends and kisses the floor, once, twice—then five more times in honor of the wounds. He is kissing the wounds of Christ, he is kissing the wounds of Fra Anto; so, too, he is kissing this land and this people who have been forged in the furnace of affliction. Their tortures and humiliations have given birth to a new country. And within this country, though it is still young and unstable, there prevail wisdom and valor that have long been declining elsewhere in the world.

He wonders: Is there any virtue antecedent to the wills they define; is there any good without sacrifice; is there a true home without abandonment as its herald? Yes, there can be, he reminds himself, for we are not mechanisms. Much good begins in us before we learn to know its name. Our Father is patient with us, for he loves.

Josip eases from his musings into prayer and remains there until the pews begin to fill with people. The great prayer begins, Holy Mass. Then follows his first Communion in the new world. And peace.

Josip passes through the Gate of Gold into the imperial compound and walks at an unhurried pace toward the northeast corner. He must not rush things, especially the important reunions—most of all the ones that might reopen old sword-wounds that were once, long ago, pushed so deeply into the heart. He will walk slowly through the labyrinth, for all Minotaurs are dead, and he, the king, is returning to the palace. This way and that, through the streets he moves, until he comes to a halt and looks up at the balconata, to the doorway leading into the apartment where he and Ariadne lived and conceived their child. It has not changed. Children are boisterously running up and down the zig-zag steps. He remains for a time in silence, gazing at every detail, and looking within himself as well. There is peace in this reunion, peace and sadness and gratitude. A year of joys was given to him, a year of hopes, and though it was taken away, he now thanks God that it was given, for not everything was destroyed. He prays for Ariadne, casts his mind across the ocean to the city of New York, where she is living, unaware of his existence, and he is grateful for her new life as well. If he would truly live, he must live with an exposed heart, with both blessing and loss.

Turning away, he returns by the way he came and goes out onto the waterfront promenade, and the peace comes with him. He intends to return to their first home many times in the days to come, but for now he is hungry and needs to rest his old legs for a while. He will eat a little and afterward bask in the ethos of his homeland. The palm trees are sighing in a stiff breeze from offshore. In the harbor, a large white pleasure-ship is nosing toward the docks, full of tourists from Italy and elsewhere, he supposes.

He finds a table at an outdoor café and sits down to watch the people strolling in all directions. It is good to be here after all this time. He can turn in any direction and find a memory associated with it:

There to the right is the wharf where the two brothers dropped him after his escape. There too, he was reunited with the Lastavica of the Sea. Above is the green mountain of the Marjan where he used to run. He will go there tomorrow and remember his youth, remember especially the times he lay down on the rock during his courtship of Ariadne, and how she slept with her head on his chest while he stroked her hair, with his eyes fixed on the pale fracture line of sea and sky, the metaphors of infinity.

Look to the left, and there is the tunnel under the palace

walls where he followed Goran Horvatinec. Beyond is the cathedral, where he prayed beside his father. He will go there to pray after he has enjoyed his two or three cups of coffee and a dose of bright October sunshine, as well as a stronger dose of turquoise hungrily absorbed through the eyes. Coffee and a basket of bread are brought to his table. What a pleasure it is to pay the young fellow with Croatian currency untainted by servitude or tyranny. To sip the coffee slowly, to tinkle the tiny silver spoon in its depths, to breathe salt air, to squint at the young lovers and feel again the joy he once felt while walking here with his betrothed, their hands molten gold, their eyes full of stars and their hearts brimming with the eternal—which is love.

So, this is the way it happens, he muses, this is what it is to be old. You return to the past only to find that it returns to you. Nothing is lost, even when everything has been lost. Or is it the other way around? For the moment he is unsure, but he brushes aside the question. Is it really always necessary to ruminate on imponderables, on symmetries and structural chiasms and fanciful syllogisms? No. He is merely happy to be here. Though he is alone and should have been sitting here with an aged woman who was the great love of his life, he need not banish the sadness of her absence, for sadness is part of love in this world, and it is even part of the joy he feels this day. She is alive and has had a long and happy marriage, a life he did not share with her. Perhaps she sits alone sometimes and remembers him. Or it may be that he has faded into her past and blended into the tragedies she left behind when she departed for the new world. Her loss is unlike his loss, for she is married with a family that loves her.

Is he alone? Yes, he is alone, and yet, not alone. Beyond all sorrows, he has the fire of Holy Communion with Christ, as well as friends and fishing and the central grace of his life—his mission to forgive. Returning good for evil wherever he stumbles across it, within the streets of the great city where he lives and also within himself. In all of this, he has been blessed with a life of interior riches, with the added gift of poetry. Though this creative power is falling into disuse in the present age, it abides. It will not be lost, and perhaps he has added his little fragment of bread to the feast.

He will leave in a moment, after just one more cuplet of coffee. Europeans know how to make it right! This is the best in the world, better than the specialty brands he experimented with in the delicatessens on Fifth Avenue. Europeans understand that flavor is not about sensory stimulation, it is about evocation. It is art and memory. It is reunion with exalted moments, and such moments are never solitary ones. In short, life without coffee is not really life. The waiter brings it to him and tells him it's on the house! A smile from the lad and a bow of his head. What elicited this gift? Perhaps it is house policy: three paid, get one free! Maybe it is simple human kindness. Yes, kindness prevails in the world, gratuitous and unsolicited. This bodes well for the future of mankind.

He senses again Fra Anto's presence with him. The friar seems to be lingering for an unusual length of time today. Maybe it is the proximity of the church, added to the promptings of memory and grace. Yes, hallucination has been transformed into a vehicle of grace. O life! O very mysterious life! What can we say about you—only that you will never cease to astonish us.

There are a lot of old fellows sitting at tables along the promenade, most of them in groups of three or more, chatting, smoking, and drinking coffee or herbal *loza*. Scattered among them are tourists drinking from large glasses of red wine. He can tell which ones are tourists. They do not wear certain kinds of discretionary masks, hiding their thoughts. Their thoughts, shallow or deep, happy or sad, are visible to Josip. Their shoes are a giveaway too. Always check the shoes.

Take the man sitting under the awning at the next table. His shoes are Balkan design and down at the heel and scuffed. He is a portly fellow about five years older than Josip, overweight, with high-blood-pressure symptoms in his face. But he has a neat silver moustache, and silver hair, recently cut. His right leg is stretched out straight, and a cane is leaning against the table. A war veteran, no doubt. Which war? There's a heavy overcoat to guard his chest against the autumn chill. What memories does he hold dear, what treasured lore, what losses? He is drinking *travarica* from a small glass and sits alone.

A returned expatriate cannot help imagining the personal histories of strangers. Just like legs, poetic imagination needs daily exercise. So, what harm is there in asking himself who these old fellows are, what their lives were like in Yugoslavia while he was safely tucked away across the Atlantic? He has made a guess as to what their stories must have been, but he also knows that it is his own mental construct. Look at that face. Not a bad face, though a history of troubles is written in it. Was the man formerly a Communist or a freedom fighter? A betrayer or a victim? Now that everyone is being let out of prisons and offices of power, and is walking about in the sunshine, it is hard to know. Perhaps he is a retired factory worker with a pension, or a banker from Zagreb, or a Dalmatian fisherman. He can't be a banker with shoes like that, nor a fisherman with a belly like that. And (Josep thinks) what about his own rather rotund middle, which, despite all his janitorial sweating, grows larger with each passing year? Maybe the man's bad leg has prevented him from exercising. Maybe he has some heavy crosses to bear. Look at that face, so strained, so full of memories, whatever they are. There are traces of bad mistakes in the eyes—nothing you could put your finger on, but they're there. Plenty of faces like it pass by on the promenade or sit together at nearby tables. Such faces are everywhere in the world, and more of them in New York than in Split, he would wager.

Ah, well, he will never know the truth about their lives. In this environment, a stranger who asks personal questions would be perceived as a threat. Excuse me, sir, I have been exercising my creative intuition on your life and would like to have my suppositions confirmed. Do you mind answering these four hundred simple questions, please?

This is not America, Josip reminds himself. Enough ruminations for one day. It's time to go.

Though he is tired and needs his nap, he pauses a few minutes longer, gazing up at the palm branches and letting the breeze stroke his cheek. He closes his eyes for a moment, just to take a rest before leaving. And then he overhears a word or two from the next table.

"So, here you are at last", says a man's voice.

"The ship was delayed leaving Bari", replies another. "It just docked, and I came as fast as I could. It's good to see you after all this time."

"Thirty years and more, it must be. You have changed."

"You too have changed."

"Life has treated you well. Nice clothes."

"Thank you."

Josip opens his eyes to see two old men shaking hands and sitting down side by side. One is the fellow with the cane, and the other is a thin gentleman dressed casually in tan slacks, olive polo shirt, and a jacket imprinted with the insignia of crossed golf clubs. His shoes are very fine—green alligator with tassels—it cannot be doubted that he is a man of means.

"You're not as I thought you would be", says the portly one. "When you wrote to me, I wasn't sure if this was for the best— our meeting. Things are different now."

"I understand the situation. I read the newspapers."

"And how do you like it over there in Los Angeles? Are you very rich?"

The other laughs. "I'm not doing badly. I don't have to work anymore, if that's what you mean. I own three apartment buildings in Pasadena, but they're small ones."

"I'm glad for you. You can play a lot of golf, then. Am I correct, that's what they play over there?"

"They play everything over there."

The conversation continues in this line, and is so banal that Josip's mind begins to wander. He is just nodding off into another doze when he overhears the words "white island".

Curious, he opens his eyes a slit. Can it be? Did one of them just make a veiled reference to Goli Otok? Closing his eyes again, he listens with great attentiveness, though he appears to be asleep.

The conversation continues, opaque to anyone who might be listening. There is more about golf and pensions and general politics, and then another reference to how things are different now—so different from the way it was on the island.

What island? Josip asks himself. There are a thousand islands in the Adriatic.

"It's better to forget all that", says the portly one with the cane.

"I forgot it long ago—everything."

"Still, it's good to meet up with old comrades."

"It was a surprise when your letter came. How did you find me?"

"It wasn't so difficult to track you down. The old lines of information are crumbling, but a few remain."

"I always wondered what happened to you, after you left", says the thin one.

"They put me to work at a desk. Thirty years at a desk in Belgrade and Zagreb."

"And since the new people took power?"

"Records disappear, memories too. I'm content with retirement. But it's not as much fun as we used to have."

The thin one laughs without mirth and lowers his voice: "Well, we did our part to clean up the mess."

"Yes, it was a mess. The country was a shambles then."

"Did you ever have trouble—afterward?"

"Never. Donkeys, as you know, don't speak."

Josip's eyes remain closed. Nothing in his manner visibly changes, though he knows that the two men, seated only meters from him, must be aware of his presence. He is just an old man dozing in the sunlight, the same as a dozen others at the surrounding tables. He does not look at the two beside him, but he knows who they are. Zmija and Zohar, the snake and the cockroach.

"Let's go get a drink", says the cockroach. "I'm booked into the Hotel President. We can talk privately there."

"Good idea. This is too public."

They get up and amble away.

Exhaling loudly, Josip bends over and puts his face into his hands. He pants for breath, and then, when the beat of his heart slows enough, he gets to his feet and walks away in the other direction.

He enters his hotel room, locks the door, and sits down on the bed. He is no longer able to rest. A terrible heat flushes his body, rising from within. His head is pounding with blood, and he cannot think. At first he is merely numb, then the currents of rage and hatred—and fear—begin to flow through him. He tries to pray, wants to run as fast and as far as he can. He wants to head straight to the airport and return to New York on the next jet leaving Split.

Wave after wave hits him. He grits his teeth so hard that they are in danger of cracking, and his fists are clenched, bloodless. He tries to pray again, to cast out the dark angel that has entered the room and now strikes him again and again with its truncheon, within and without.

He would like to cry out but can only sit there trembling. He pulls his rosary from his pocket and merely grips it in his right hand. The words of the prayer are impossible to speak. He tries, but each word is a slab of stone that must be carried up a steep incline. Then it seems that all prayer dries up like a river blocked at its source. He is silent, and for a few moments he feels his life seeping away. How strange is this mixture of riotous feelings and deadness. It is as if his entire life has led him on circuitous and astonishing paths to this final moment, this end. Is this what he was spared for?

At last he is able to lie down on his back and throw his arms over his face. Wide awake, he cannot imagine what to do. What *is* there to do? Nothing. Be silent, you are dead. Now the only alternatives to despair are rage or terror. Terror is unsustainable because it demolishes the interior, but rage can galvanize energy, direct it outward, bring it to its conclusion. A consummation of justice, at last.

At last. In the end. In the end, in the end . . .

When he awakes, night has fallen. He drinks a little water and then lies down again in the dark. Throughout the following hours, he remains sleepless, staring at the black ceiling of a cement barracks, hearing the barks of guards and the groans of prisoners. He sees also the two boys who died at his feet. Svat's skull crushed beneath the stones, all witnesses helpless before his cries and pleading, and in the end his silence, the brain matter and blood oozing into the dust of the quarry. Then the face of Budala shattered by a bullet, a rag puppet thrown away, crumpled in the white dust. The good have died, and the evil have prospered, grown fat on the riches of this world. They sit at cafés under the unheeding sun, laugh about their pasts, and speak of the necessity of their acts. They would grind the face of God into the dust if they could—or a young Christ with his features blasted into fragments. If God died in Goli Otok, Josip will not let it be the final word. The end of the cosmos will not go unprotested. Against the weight of the entire world, he will be the lamb's cry for justice. He will make a gesture, futile though it may be. And as the sun crests over the Dinarics, he knows what it will be.

Later, when the city awakes, Josip leaves the hotel and wends his way through the streets of Stari Grad and beyond, toward the modern section of the city. Not far from the northern wall of the palace, he finds a little shop that specializes in antiques. Inside the dim interior, he asks the proprietor if he has any weapons for sale. Yes, quite a few, the man replies; step into this room, please. See, we have sabers and swords—old Croatian from the days of the kingdom, also Austrian cavalry, and even a Turkish scimitar. And these pistols in the case are from the Austro-Hungarian empire. Very fine this silver one with the ivory handle.

"Very fine", murmurs Josip. "Does it still fire?"

"Yes, I fired it myself last month at the armory show in Vienna. And of course we keep every item in the best condition. I cleaned and oiled this pistol with my own hands a few days ago. It comes with a certificate of reliability. I would suggest, sir, that if you are interested in the item, you might want to make a decision soon, because a museum has expressed some interest in it."

"I will take it."

"Do you wish to know the price?"

"It doesn't matter."

So, the purchase is made, and Josip leaves the shop with a package containing the pistol and bullets.

From there, he walks over the hump separating the old city from the new and goes down into the warren of industrial enterprises. There he locates a masonry shop, and is led by its proprietor to a yard full of bricks and stone. He purchases a single block of yellow-white limestone, about twelve inches square and three inches thick, and pays for it to be delivered to his hotel. Then he goes out onto the street and catches the next bus for downtown. Back in his hotel room, he sits in the gloom with the curtains closed, and waits for the stone to arrive. He drinks more water but can eat nothing.

Shortly after one in the afternoon, the stone is delivered to the lobby desk, and the porter rings up to say that a package has arrived for him. Josip puts the pistol case into his knapsack, shoulders it, and goes down to the lobby. There he receives the stone, which is wrapped in newspaper, and loads it into the knapsack. He leaves the hotel and heads straight to the church of St. Francis. He passes Fra Anto, who is gazing at him somberly, and enters the church. He stands at the back for some minutes before going down on his knees. He kneels for a length of time, then bows to the tabernacle and goes outside again onto the promenade. Walking north on Marmontova in search of Starčevićeva Street, he proceeds with determination until he arrives at the Hotel President and enters its lobby.

He cannot ask for the thin man and the lame man because he does not know their real names. Inquiring of a porter the way to the bar, he is directed into a cocktail lounge. The snake and the cockroach are in the room, hunching over drinks at a table in the corner farthest from the door. Josip takes a seat near the entrance and orders and pays for a cup of coffee, which is brought to him shortly. After he sips it, he removes the heavy package from his knapsack and places it on the table, keeping an eye on the two in the corner. They do not notice him, deep as they are in their conversation. He removes the pistol from its case and sticks it into the inside pocket of his jacket. There comes a moment when the room is deserted, save for himself and the snake and the cockroach. After unwrapping the stone, he picks it up and carries it to the table where they are sitting.

He stands before them. They flicker their eyes at him, thinking he is the waiter. Their faces register a little surprise to see an old man standing there with a limestone slab in his hands. When he drops it onto the table between them with a boom, they jerk back in astonishment.

Josip pulls the pistol from his jacket and points it at the killer's head—the snake.

"I am from Goli Otok", he says in a low voice. "This is for what you did to Krunoslav Bošnjaković."

He pulls the trigger. *Bang!*

Swiftly he points it at the head of the cockroach.

"This is for what you did to Dalibor Kovač."

He pulls the trigger. *Bang!*

The snake and the cockroach stare in amazement, mouths hanging open, their eyes blazing with fear but for the moment paralyzed.

"What?" stammers one. "Who?" says the other, for the *bang* is not the firing of a gun but a whisper.

Now the old man takes something else from his pocket. Before the snake he places a wooden crucifix. Before the cockroach he places another.

Taking a step back, he says to both men:

"Unless you repent of your crimes, the winepress of God shall extract from you full payment. Know that judgment is soon to be upon you in the court of heaven."

With that, he pockets the pistol and leaves the room. He walks away from the hotel without haste and goes back down the streets leading to the sea. Arriving at the shore, he stands on a wharf and throws the pistol far out into deep water, then the bullets. After that, he returns to the church of St. Francis, climbs the front steps with trembling legs, bows to Fra Anto, and enters the house of the Lord. He remains there for the day; and when he returns at nightfall to his hotel room, he falls onto the bed and sleeps.

36

The modern maps of Bosnia-Herzegovina have no trace of Rajska Polja, nor of Pačići, and as far as Josip can tell, no older maps ever revealed the presence of those two villages. Days spent in Sarajevo's city library and also in the national archives turn up nothing. Yet he knows his home was there. He came from somewhere, even if history has erased it. No one in the city knows of a village by that name. The Communists changed the names of many places, so it probably has another now. Of course the people still living there will know its traditional name. But he must search for it by sight, dredging in the murk of his past and trusting that landmarks will aid him.

The car-rental terms are decent enough, and his pockets are full of American dollars, which open every door. Because he has never bothered to learn to drive, he hires a man to take him to the fields of heaven. The car is a white compact. The driver, it turns out, is a young fellow named Alija, the same name as a man on a donkey more than half a century ago. His full name, he informs his passenger, is Alija ibn Yosuf al-Bosnawi, but this cannot be integrated into Josip's pilgrimage of memory. The man on the donkey had a family name, of course, but what it was, Josip had never learned.

The drive along the highway south from the city begins pleasantly enough. It is a warm autumn morning. The war is over, peace-keeping troops are everywhere, and the native people proceed about their business as they have for millennia. But the evidence of catastrophe is soon abundant—a bombed-out town, burnt, abandoned vehicles along the highway, and then a larger center with many shattered windows in apartment buildings, bullet holes sprayed across the walls, and dark-eyed children learning to play again in streets where murder reigned only a short while ago. The country is full of thousands of orphans. A quarter of a million people died here. Hundreds of thousands of others fled to Croatia and have not returned. Even so, minarets are being erected again above many a village, and, less frequently, the spires of small churches.

Alija hums to himself then breaks into a deep-throated melancholic song, a Muslim poem translated into Croatian:

> Over Sarajevo flies the falcon,
> Searching everywhere for shade to cool him.
> He finds a black pine in Sarajevo,
> by a well of sparkling water.
> Near its fountains are Hyacinthe the widow
> And Rose the young virgin.
> He glances down, the falcon, and thinks to himself:
> Shall I kiss the solemn Hyacinthe
> Or the fair now-blooming Rose?
> Then admonishes he, most wisely, to himself:
> Gold, long tested, is far better
> Than finest silver freshly poured . . .

And so forth. The falcon, clever bird that he is, kisses both women. Alija's eyes dart to see how his customer has taken this bit of local color, so Josip smiles and nods appropriately. The song is not the way the poem is supposed to be, the young man explains. He changed it and likes his own version better. In the original, the falcon kisses old Hyacinthe, and that makes Rose lose her temper. She curses the stupidity of men, for in Sarajevo youths love older women and old men love maidens. Alija's thoughts drift away on a trail of chuckles.

And all the while, Josip is pondering. As the mountains sweep past, his eyes linger on a lake that appears on the right, the artificial reservoir made by the dam at Jablanica.

"Jablansko Lake", says Alija, good tour guide that he is. "The Neretva used to flow here; I guess it still does underneath."

Yes, the Neretva. It was the river in which he saw the bodies of priests floating, the waters from which he drank.

Those waters gave him his second baptism—a death and a rebirth—the first of the many he was to experience. He had met Christ in it, a bound and trussed and murdered Christ floating by. Christ had called to him there, asking him to enter the water in a way that he had never done before, not even by the shores of the sea when, having hurled himself under the surf, he had been pulled up again, against his boyish will, by his father.

Then Christ had pulled him under. Had it been a pulling or an invitation? In a sense, it was both, the dialogue between freedom and ignorance, between providence and fate, between the call to good and the vulnerability to evil. And so, he had gone down, deeper still into the unseen currents, where he had begun to learn that knowledge itself cannot save. Christ, he had learned, always drew his followers into deep waters, even, at certain points, to the brink of literal drowning, for in this immersion was the beginning of wisdom. It pulled the soul from the merely horizontal perspective into the vertical, the cosmic one, which is so much higher than it is broad.

Is this so in every age, for every generation of men? Has it been so for him? Will it be so in the future? And will the return to his birthplace, which he has long dreaded and so yearned for, be another drowning? He is not sure; he knows only that he must return and that there can be no more delay. It is no longer necessary to avoid the *apokalypsis* of memory at all cost, for this practice of avoidance, which he has pursued for most of his life, can now be left behind. The only certainty is that it will contain pain. Yet this pain is life. If drowning contains the promise of rebirth, then pain contains the promise of joy. He hopes for this. Yes, the journey is not so much about knowledge as it is about hope. Here, at the latter end of his years, he may begin again.

His meditation is interrupted by the driver, who is now smoking a Turkish cigarette and has just broken into Josip's thoughts by offering him one. He politely declines. Alija asks if he recalls any particular road coming down out of the mountains, because there are a number in the region. Josip shakes his head, straining to recall the contours of the land as he once knew it. Surely they cannot have changed, surely they will not fail to offer evidence of his past. But they do not yet do so. They are beautiful but vague.

"There was a bridge", he murmurs. "I crossed a bridge."

"Then you must have come from the west side of the river", says Alija. "The highway is on the eastern shore from just south of the lake all the way to the Adriatic."

Shortly after, Josip glances out the driver's window and sees a great rock flash by on the side of the road, then another, followed by a third. They are natural phenomena, yet the evocation of the sacred in this trinitarian configuration cannot be dismissed. There is a sense of familiarity but no clear identification. The sense might be caused by anything from actual memory to a theological inference, or simply his visual interest in the stones. Even so, as the car rounds another curve he sees in his mind's eye an old woman leading a pig by a rope and raising her walking stick in warning, *Steal my pig, and I will break your head!* Is he mixing memories—was it before or after the bridge?

Ten minutes farther along the highway they come to a bridge, and on the other side is a road that descends from the foothills of a narrow gorge. Soaring beyond are very high mountains, stark and brutally sharp.

"Stop!" Josip says.

Alija pulls over to the shoulder and idles the car.

"Is that where you want to go?" he nods toward the mouth of the gorge.

"Yes, there."

The car reverses, turns off the highway, crosses the bridge, and begins to climb. Gearing down, the driver makes the engine roar. The surface under the wheels is rougher than the highway pavement, yet not difficult to navigate. It is well used, with no encroaching overgrowth. This stage of the journey is slow because the route continually twists and turns, rises and dips as it gradually ascends to higher altitudes. Now and then, they pass isolated farms, small stone houses and sheds standing among modest groves. Some of the trees are faded now, and some still have the remains of wild fruit. The older oak woods and the beeches along the way are crowned by distant stands of dark pine, and above these are the more barren heights of the range, with new snow cloaking the crests.

The day is growing warmer. Josip and the driver roll down the windows, welcoming the fresh alpine air into the car.

Because time has slowed, or simply is resting from its usual pace, it is difficult to know how long they drive through this sparsely populated countryside. They see no people on the way, though they pass a few goats crowding resentfully to the side of the road to let them by. At one point, an aggressive billy chases the car and clangs its horns on the back bumper. The driver laughs, and Josip smiles.

Coming to a fork in the gorge, the route divides into two rougher gravel tracks.

"Turn right", says Josip. The gravel is soon replaced by narrow tire ruts winding upward at a steeper angle. Now the track is hardly navigable—only a path wide enough for a car. It climbs interminably, and Alija is worried about the engine overheating. Just as they are about to give up, they come to a dead end in a yard surrounded by five or six houses. Alija brakes, turns off his engine, and glances at Josip for confirmation. The passenger nods.

Josip opens the door and gets out. It is Pačići. The houses are much the same as they were when he last saw them. The surrounding trees are higher, their trunks thick. Between two houses, he can see a glint of water, and upon it geese are paddling. In the courtyard, more geese are strutting, with goslings frantically following on their heels. Chickens peck about, a donkey chews on hay and examines the visitors. There are automobiles parked in front of some of the houses: two black sedans, a white farm truck with open back, and a red motorbike. Perched on the roofs of two of the houses are small satellite dishes pointing to the heavens.

A door opens in the nearest house, and a man steps out onto the porch. About fifty years old, he is clean shaven, wearing jeans and sandals and a sweatshirt with the word *Hajduk* written beneath a soccer ball decal. He approaches, wiping his hands on a dish towel, his expression curious to know their business.

"Are you lost?" he greets them.

The driver steps back and lets Josip answer.

"Is this Pačići?" he asks.

"Pačići, no", replies the man with a furrowed brow. "No ducklings here. Though, as you can see, we raise geese. But we don't really sell from the front door. On Saturdays we bring them to the market in Mostar. That's the best time to buy."

"I did not come to purchase anything", says Josip, with an apologetic dip of his head. "I used to live near here when I was a boy. I have come to see it again."

"Ah", says the man, with a smile of interest. "You lived here, in this place?"

"Not here, but deeper in the mountains. We used to pass through Pačići to get there."

"Well, I regret to say we're not Pačići. Maybe you took a wrong turn somewhere. I don't know of any place by that name."

Josip pauses and glances around the yard. The houses are the same, placed exactly where they were when he last saw them.

He knows that if he looks too closely he will see a man raising a gun above a boy collapsed on the snow of this yard.

"It seems the name is now lost", he murmurs. "But this is the place. A clan of people once lived here. Their name was Dučić."

"Dučić is a common name—there are several in the hills between here and Mostar, and north toward Sarajevo, I would wager. But no one by that name lives here. Let me go and ask my aunt, she may know."

He calls toward the open door of his home, and a woman comes out. She is about the same age as Josip. Introductions are made all around; the Muslim driver is treated cordially. The man's name is Branko, the woman is Teta Ana.

The man explains the situation to his aunt.

She puts a hand to her cheek, as if trying to recall something.

"Yes", she says. "There were Dučićs here before the war—I mean the war when the Italians came. None of the family survived those times. We got this house in the 1950s. The buildings had been empty for years, just falling into ruins. When the government started to move people around and make the collectives, we had to leave our place down by the river, where I was born. One of my cousins married a Dučić, but that branch of the family lived farther out from here. She's still alive, and so is her husband."

Josip's heart skips a beat. Is it possible?

Then, with a sudden ripping in his chest, he sees Petar with a split skull, his arm without a hand, lying in a pool of frozen blood.

"They raise sheep", the woman adds.

"Where is their home?" asks Josip.

Teta Ana points toward the east. "Over there about five kilometers. You can't drive it, you would have to walk."

Josip can walk there, but he knows it is not what he is looking for.

"You said you once lived near here", says Branko. "Where was it?"

Josip turns and faces the forest to the north. He does so without hesitation, by the interior orientation that requires no thought.

"There", he whispers.

Branko and Teta Ana are puzzled.

"There's nothing there", says the woman. "No one ever goes that way, only the sheep."

"There is a valley up there. It's where I lived as a boy."

"Yes, there's a valley", says Branko. "I've been to it a few times, but there are no houses."

"Rajska Polja", Josip murmurs, choking.

The man and woman shake their heads. They do not recognize the name.

"You must mean Roško Polje on the other side of the mountains, near Tomislavgrad."

Josip shakes his head. "This is the place", he whispers.

Branko and Teta Ana frown. There is nothing more to be said, really. They cannot think of anything else to suggest.

"Would it be possible for me to go to that valley?" Josip asks. "Is the road still open?"

"There's no road, only a path for the sheep. It's a long walk."

"Then it can be walked?"

"I don't think it would be too hard", replies Branko. "If you're willing to walk, you'd be there in a couple of hours. The shepherd takes the flock there each spring and brings them down in the autumn, so the path will be open."

"The owners would not mind?"

"There are no owners. It doesn't belong to anyone."

By now it is noon. The man and his aunt invite the guests to lunch in their home. Inside, the stone walls have been papered in bright floral patterns, the wooden floor varnished and shining. Everything is spotless. A generator hums, the source of electricity. Now there is a refrigerator, cooking range, and a color television set on which cartoon characters are playing. There are no religious decorations to be seen anywhere, nor are there political ones. Family photographs and sports insignia predominate. The single window in the kitchen is where it has always been. Though no pig tries to enter the house through it, Josip can almost hear the trotters clacking on the sill.

After lunch, he pays the driver, who prepares to make his departure, promising to return on the evening of the following day. Branko lends Josip a rucksack and fills it with bread, cheese, sausage, and a water flask. Teta Ana lends a roll of blankets and a woolen farmer's jacket. They refuse all attempts at payment.

"I would go with you," says Branko, "but I have to pick up my son later today. He's studying at the university in Mostar and wants to come home for the weekend." He grins and taps a cell phone hanging from his belt. "No escape!" he quips.

"Are you sure you want to go there alone?" asks the aunt, with a worried frown.

"Yes, alone", Josip replies, with a smile of reassurance.

They take him to the edge of the forest and onto a footpath leading to the northwest. As he sets off along this narrow, muddy track, they watch him for a minute, then return to their lives.

The trees on both sides are no longer the sun-filled woods they once were, during his boyhood. Now they are a forest of beech trees blocking the view of the surrounding mountains. It is difficult for Josip to believe that upon this path he once ran at top speed to save a life, which in the end was not saved. Two lives. Many lives. From time to time, his eyes become moist, yet it is the happiest memories that now return to him. He holds them and does not let them go too quickly. He realizes that the memories of his last day will soon rise up to receive him, though in what form he cannot guess. His heart beats quickly, yet he suffers no wave of the terror one would expect to feel when returning to a scene of catastrophe. He is surprised at himself. It is not quite what he had anticipated.

Perhaps a half century has numbed certain portions of his mind. Much of that day and night has blurred, though the crucial scenes have never left him. At present, they are in the background of his thoughts, perhaps because their pain has decreased with the passage of time. There have been other drownings, other blood, other deaths and rebirths. Yet he knows that this rebirth, long overdue from his first death, is not yet complete.

After two hours of steady walking he notices that the forest is giving way to a woods of younger beech, their paper leaves crackling in the breeze. Birds are still singing. High above in the open blue spaces, a falcon circles slowly, then plunges like an arrow. The woods become a scattering of saplings, as thin as rods. A hundred meters farther on and the trees end. Josip comes to a halt and gazes out over the valley of Rajska Polja.

It has changed. There are no buildings here. Random patches of meadow are knee-high in grass and wildflowers. Solitary trees now stand tall and rich with foliage where once there was open pasture and cultivated gardens. Black pines have crept down into the edges of the valley floor, narrowing it still farther. Toward its far end, near the ancient pass into the north, a land-bound cloud meanders across a patch of green—the flock of sheep that is still brought here each summer. There will be a shepherd with them.

For a measureless space of time, Josip does not move. He sees a silver thread winding through the valley and knows it is the brook that served the people of the village. The sun glints on its surface. The warm wind blows in his face, bringing with it the perfumes of all growing things. He inhales and moves again, slowly, through the wild grass toward the place where the village once stood.

He arrives at the bank of the brook just south of where the houses were. The lane that bisected the dwellings is no longer there. Yet the sheep track wanders along beside the water, staying true to the path long ago trodden by human feet. It passes between two rows of grass-covered humps, six or eight to a side, then beyond a larger one at the end of this formation and out again into the fields beyond.

Josip stops at the first hump.

Everything has flown from his mind. No memory of fire and blood roars in to take its place. He is simply in that state of suspension he has experienced a handful of times. He is conscious that this is extraordinary, that it is given to him only at the most pivotal moments: when time ceases, but motion continues in the world around him. He feels an unusual calm. There is pain in it, and sorrow, but there is also the throb of joy, for in this very place was his beginning and his end. The end that led to other beginnings. He would like to pray, but it is not necessary. He knows that the entire experience is a wordless prayer subsumed in the presence of God. He squints as he looks briefly toward the sky and the wheeling of eagles and doves.

The current ebbs and flows, sometimes gentle, sometimes threatening to break out in sobs. But whether this is caused by happiness or grief, he does not know, nor does he question. He takes a few steps forward, and the street opens up to receive him, materializes as both a row of grassy humps and as a habitation with a name. Its walls rise before his eyes, and the sound of laughter and music fills his ears. His eyes are streaming now. A few more steps and he is home.

It is the fourth house on the right. A little above it, on the rise of meadow, is the hump of Svez's shed, and beside it is the rock on which he so often sat pondering the shape of the world. For a few moments, he stands by a flat stone that must have been the doorstep, once raised, now half buried. He puts a foot forward and plants it gently onto the exposed stone. Then he removes it. He looks at the hump of green. A few hewn blocks are visible on its sides, covered with moss. The hump is a foot or two above the level ground. Inside it are the bodies of his mother and father. It is a tomb. Miroslav and Marija. Two skulls in the burning embers of the thoughts of men, shimmering down to ashes, and snow, and dust and wind and seed and the droppings of generations of sheep that have summered here for fifty years.

They are gone.

He bows his head, chin on his chest. He is a dead boy, seated in a bare room in the house of his parents' killer, fed by the woman who brought him back to life again, beside the many waters that flow through the habitations of man. He is a boy with no face, gazing into the mirror of the past, seeing himself again, knowing himself as his own grandfather, yet without issue, for there were other deaths to come.

Are they gone?

They are gone.

Now he cries. It is soundless, as fathomless as the sea.

He would kneel if he could, but his joints are aching from the long hike and threaten to collapse. His back is sore. Slowly he circles the house and goes into the yard behind. A few steps farther and he has reached the rock. Beside it is the rotting stump of the oak that was old when he was young. Mamica tied a rope between it and the house so that her washing would catch the wind. He sits down on the rock. It is hot from baking in the sun. The sky is bright as silver. He cries for a time and remembers.

On this very rock he found the flowers and the blue feather Josipa gave him in their first exchange of gifts. And the little crucifix that she made for him, is it still here? Are the white stones from the Adriatic still under the house where she lived? Is the little doll he made still there, does it rest with her? Yes, they are here. They are reduced to ashes, but they are not gone.

Because he is tired, because he is old and full of memories, he stretches out on the rock and sleeps for a while. He cries in his sleep and then awakes. Just as he is sitting up, he hears a whistle from the north end of the village and sees a human form striding in his direction at an unhurried pace. The figure spots Josip, pauses a moment, waves, then continues along the sheep track toward him.

As he approaches, Josip gets to his feet and waits. It is a tall youth. Then, with a shock of recognition, he sees that it is Petar!

With a cry, Josip stumbles forward to meet him, but as they close the gap, he trips and falls. The boy rushes forward and helps him up. They stand facing each other, both astonished, both blinking rapidly. Yes, it *is* Petar. It cannot be, but it is! The same face, the same eyes, the same black hair poking out in all directions.

His heart is palpitating now, and he is gasping for breath.

"Petar", he breathes, at last.

"Who?" asks the youth, laughing and puzzled.

"It's me, it's Josip!"

"I thought you said your name is Petar."

"No, no, *you* are Petar!"

"You are mistaken, sir. I'm Ivo Dučić. Who are you?"

Josip rubs his face, shakes his head, cannot answer.

"Are you lost, sir?"

"No", says Josip. "I have come home."

"Home?"

"I lived here when I was a boy."

Now the youth's bewildered expression is replaced by curiosity. "Ah", he says. "I always thought people lived here long ago. No one knows the name of this place, no one remembers."

"I remember", Josip whispers.

"Who are you?"

"I'm Josip Lasta."

"You're from the city?"

"I am from America, the city of New York."

"New York? I have not heard of it."

"It is where I now live. But when I was a child, Rajska Polja was my home. This place was Rajska Polja."

"The fields of heaven. It is surely that. I come each spring with my father's sheep and go back before the snow falls. I never like to leave it."

Ivo Dučić leads Josip to the rock beside the brook, and they sit down on it. From this rock, Josip has dipped a bucket into the water a thousand times. On this rock, he left the letter J in round white stones from the sea. Here Josipa in a blue dress found them and knew instantly who had left them there, for her.

Josip glances up the east slope to the mountain of Zamak. There, at the edge of the lower oaks, he sat beside her the day she cried for her parents.

Where are you going? she asked.

To the cross, he replied.

Now the old man from New York gazes higher, toward the place where the watchtower once stood. The white cross is no longer there.

"Have you ever climbed up to the fort?" he asks.

Ivo smiles. "Many times, though it's just ruins."

"Yes, it was ruins in my day too. And is the cross still there? I do not see it."

"It's still there, but it's fallen and broken into pieces. I don't know who broke it. My father says the Partisans did it or maybe the Communists who made Yugoslavia did it later."

"Are you a Catholic?" Josip asks

Ivo shrugs. "I guess we're nothing."

"It was not always so. I knew your family. My friend Petar was a Dučić. He lived here, too."

The boy does not know what to say. Names are so easily blown away by the winds of time.

"He looked like you."

Ivo grins. "Some of my cousins look like me. The hair—"

"Did any of your family live here high in the mountains?"

Ivo shakes his head. "I don't think so. Well, maybe. But that was a long time ago. My father was born down there—" He points in the direction of Pačići. "On a farm past where those houses are, the people who raise geese. My grandmother told me before she died that Dučićs lived there before the war. I mean the war when Italians and Germans were here, not the war when the Serbs invaded. Now we are Bosnia-Herzegovina. I don't like the peace soldiers, because they aren't from our land. They shouldn't be here, but maybe they keep the Serbs from hurting people."

Ivo offers a few more thoughts about the recent war. As Josip listens, he is hearing voices from the past.

My father says someday we will have a real Croatia.

Petar shrugs. *My father doesn't think so. The British will rule us just like everybody else tries to.*

Maybe Ustashe and Chetniks won't let them, says Josip.

Maybe Partisans won't let them, replies Petar.

They all kill people, Josip muses. *Why do they kill people so much?*

I don't know, Petar replies shaking his head. *They are angry.*

Fra Anto says we must not do what they do.

He's right, but when they try to shoot you, what can you do? You shoot back.

Ivo is still talking, remembering things his grandmother told him. She gave birth to his father on a night when Partisans swept through the region, slaughtering people. She lost family members.

"From Pačići?" Josip asks.

"Pačići? I don't know where that is. She lost some aunts and uncles. She didn't like to talk about it. It always made her cry."

The sun is dropping into the western range. Josip tells Ivo that he will stay the night. The boy invites him to sleep at his camp at the end of the valley. When they arrive there, Josip sees a large canvas tent and a crude stone fireplace, a paddock of rails, boxes with food, an old rifle leaning against a stump, an axe, and a barn lantern. Ivo goes off for a while to gather the flock into the paddock for the night.

When he returns he makes tea over the fire, then fries sausages and potatoes, enough for himself and his guest. Josip contributes the food Branko gave him. As the stars come out, they eat their meal and drink their tea. The boy grows talkative. He tells about his youth, his interests, and his desire to travel. He would like to go through Europe and see the world, maybe even farther to America. There's a special girl in a town halfway between Mostar and Sarajevo. Every two weeks, his father hikes here and stays for a day or so, to bring food and to check on him. He has begun to read history. He finds it very interesting, realizes that a lot of the things he learned at school before the Communists were booted out are not true. An uncle in Split sent him some books last winter.

Ivo lifts a volume and waves it in the air.

"This one is so interesting. It's my favorite."

"What is it?"

"It's about a man who goes on a long journey, on a ship. He has a lot of trouble, but he gets home in the end."

Josip peers at the title. *The Odyssey.*

"Do you like poetry?" he asks.

"No. But I like this book."

It is early evening, and the mountain chill is settling in. Ivo tells him that he's welcome to sleep in the tent, but Josip wants to fall asleep watching the stars. He lies down on the grass, rolls himself in the blankets, and looks up. Ivo lights the lantern and reads for a time. The old man blinks, and it is dawn.

The boy is gone; he is somewhere in the valley with his sheep. Throughout the morning, Josip retraces his steps through the village, moving ponderously from house to house. He remains motionless for a long time before the largest hump, where the church of St. Francis once stood. There are no artifacts to be found. Whatever remains is buried: the broken glass portraying the poverello's life, the dented chalice and burnt prayer books, and the body of a martyr. Here he fell in love with a girl before the altar of God. Here he ran toward the sanctuary of the tabernacle moaning, *O-o-o-o, Jesus!* Here, too, he consumed the sacred hosts, muddied and bloodied by killers. The very place where the crucifixion of a child's heart cast his life into a pit, into the end of everything. Though it was not the end.

Josip kneels. He experiences again the sense of suspension, where the frontier of time dissolves into eternity. As on the day before, it is not prayer with words, but absorption into the presence.

Later, he goes to the house where the blind woman rocked him, from there to Petar's house, and from there to the most terrible place of all.

This heap of grass was the schoolhouse. Though he jerks his head away, he sees again the heap of naked bodies, the women and girls. His mother is not among them, for she is already burning in her home. He forces himself to look at the bloody mattress and finally at the body of Josipa. He sees everything as if it occurred seconds ago. Though he did not witness the killings with his own eyes, it now seems that he hears screams and sobbing and the pleading of the women and the laughter and curses of the strong men. The horror has remained within him all these years, known but unexamined, because to stare at it for more than an instant is to be pulled headlong into absolute darkness. The negation of everything is hell, and he must not go there. Now, it is possible to look. Now, the powers of negation can only wound, not destroy him. He examines everything that he saw in a single flash more than fifty years ago. It takes no more than a minute, yet it cracks him open. So wide is the fissure that it gapes before his soul as an abyss of despair, and it drags him forward onto his hands and knees. He chokes, chokes, chokes, and then vomits.

It is as if he is vomiting all that darkness out and must see its every detail as it leaves. Now he faces it—knows that his beloved *lastavica* was raped by the soldiers before they cut her throat when they had enough of her. Before his eyes he sees her, as if he were a boy again and it happened only a minute ago, the two pools of blood crying out to him, the little pool in the hollow cavity between her collar bone and her neck, and the larger pool at the exact center of her body, halfway between the head, which is the crown of all sublime thought, and the feet, which are the humble bearers of burdens.

Then a low, dull, retching scream from an old man's ravaged throat. So horrible and ugly is this sound that it would be unbearable for another human being to hear it. He can hardly bear the sound of it. Gradually it subsides, and he is empty. Then he weeps—hours of weeping—and with the tears there slowly grows an inner calm. In this calm, he is able to acknowledge the loss that is at the very core of his being. He has lost the most beautiful gift in the world. There were other gifts, before and after, yet this was the purest of all, the one that first drew him into the holy fire. It is gone, it will never return. And he has lost the children who might have come from their love and the many who would have come from those children, the generations upon generations who will never be.

Ivo finds him lying on the hump of grass in mid-afternoon. Worried that the old man has fallen again, he runs to him and shakes his shoulder, like the shadows of the dead who cannot be roused from their sleep. Josip sits up. The boy helps him to his feet.

"Are you all right?"

736

"I am all right."

"Come, I have made a lunch", he says, brushing grass and dirt from Josip's clothing. "Well, not quite a lunch because it's getting late. But you can think of it as an early supper."

Seated on stumps beside the campfire, they drink tea. The boy hungrily downs a pan of food, while Josip eats nothing.

"I have to go", he says. "A car is coming to pick me up this evening at the house of the people who raise geese."

"It's a long walk", says Ivo. "I'd like to go with you, but I can't leave the flock."

"That's all right. It has been so good to meet you. You are a fine boy."

Clearly, this is somewhat embarrassing for Ivo. He pretends he did not hear it and keeps eating.

"Do you have a pen and paper?" Josip asks.

"Hmmm, I think I have a pencil."

He jumps up and rummages around in the tent, returning with a stub of pencil.

"Sorry, no paper. What do you want it for?"

"I want to leave you something."

"Oh."

"May I write on a blank page of your book—your favorite book?"

"Sure. Let me get it for you."

Josip, with the book in his hand, turns the pages slowly. There are four blank end-pieces. He sits down on the stump and writes. From time to time, he looks up at Zamak or toward the end of the valley or the ruins of the village, then goes back to writing. When he is finished, he hands the book to the boy.

"What did you write there?" he asks.

"My address in New York. If you ever come to America, you can find me."

"Ah, this is good!" declares Ivo with pleasure.

"There is more", Josip goes on in a quiet voice. "I have

written some lines that you will not understand. As you grow older, you will understand them. Will you keep them?"

"If you wish", he nods.

"I ask you to keep them", Josip says. "They will be of little value to you at this time, but later you will see."

"I will keep them and read them again."

"Good. Now I must go", says Josip, rising.

He and Ivo shake hands.

"Good-bye, Mr. Lasta. It was nice to have company."

"Good-bye, Ivo. Thank you for your welcome."

With no more to be said, Josip turns and walks through the village toward the pass that will lead him to the south. He is leaving his home now, and he knows he will never return. Yet he is going toward home as well, there in a distant land.

Ivo watches the old man until he has disappeared into the trees. Then he sits down on the stump and opens the book. He reads:

LOSS
Of those times
which we the living and the unremembered dead
live again as if we have not ceased
in tides of memory to swim,
we know:
The past is present and will be all that is to come.
With final breaths we tell what we have learned
in words you do not know:

There was fire and there was snow,
there were hands held tenderly and striking fists,
there was each year's returning sun
and the first fruits on the laden trees,
the milk swinging in buckets, sweet waste
and nourishment, warm breasts, a father's toil-worn face;

there were birds that landed fearless on our wondering
    fingertips,
filling our minds with images of flight
and our mouths with laughter.

I see the eyes of children I once knew
who through those dark pools beheld the killing
of mothers and fathers, the ones who gave them their names,
for no child lacks a name, the great and the small.
And thus, sinking, they reached for what was gone,
for what was beyond all hope, clutching their names as
    survivors cling
fiercely to the unsustaining debris of shipwreck.

What would such a child say to me as he drowned,
if he were to speak at all?
What sole legacy hurled above the abyss, what sound
as his final contribution to mankind?
For what far sanctuary would he strain in his last gesture
as he went down?

Were I to reach for him as a bird without hands,
capable of rising above his soon-forgotten fate,
yet unable to assist,
my only strength would be to carry his words,
and sing them out across the void.
What would these words be? Surely it is these:
    "I do not ask why;
    I do not seek to be as you,
    though I am you.
    I seek the ocean that is above me
    and within me, for it is one sea;
    and I leave behind
    the island of the world."

THE FLIGHT
OF THE LASTAVICA

37

Caleb hands Josip a bundle of paper crawling with typewritten text. He is bursting with anticipation, affection for the old man brimming in his dark eyes. So much intelligence in them, a wily street survivor, this well-published literary man, yet curiously childlike too. Or perhaps this is a rare moment of complete guilelessness.

"What have you got for me, Caleb?" asks Josip, taking the papers gingerly. "Is this a new collection of your poems? Do you trust me to critique?"

"I trust you, Josip, but they aren't new poems. These are the galley sheets for my intro to *your* selected poems.

"Your intro? What do you mean, *your* intro?"

"The publisher asked me to write it. Of course, I knew what you'd have to say about that, so I made an executive decision. You ain't gonna escape fame, brother Joe, no matter how far y' runs or how hard y' tries t' hide."

"I am not running, I am not hiding, but, shh-shh, let me read it."

The document takes quite a while to go through, and by the end Josip is thoroughly appalled. It is fairly accurate, but he wonders how Caleb has obtained all this biographical data. Doubtless he has gleaned it from their years of conversations, and by his uncanny skill in observing the nature of white people. Has he really revealed so much personal information to the boy? Boy? No, the lad he met more than twenty years ago is now a doctor of literature, married to a sociologist, and father of a prodigious little child of the metropolis; moreover, he possesses the subtleties and complex manifestations of character and historical damage that are the particular patrimony of the despised and rejected. A former slave sees things from the ground up, from the inside out. Of course, Caleb has never known slavery, but he has experienced the residue of slavery's mark upon his society. He has from childhood onward (especially during the years when he wore his sinister camouflage) been avoided or regarded with suspicion by strangers. Throughout his life it has been of utmost importance for him to read properly the character of the race most dominant on this continent. Josip smiles ironically—he can relate.

He loves Caleb and his family, though his cosmological sympathies lean toward the wife, who remains always, despite her alien temperament and exotic Eritrean culture, a sacramental Christian. He sighs. How complex the universe is—a mine field of difficulties. Nevertheless, he must not be bamboozled (a curious English term) by this upwardly-mobile shiny copper penny just because of love. There is no love without truth, Josip reminds himself.

So, what is true here? Is this glowing mini-biography the truth? The details are flawless, but the meaning is as far off the target as an arrow shot in a windstorm.

Stop the metaphors, Josip! he admonishes himself.

"Well, do you like it?" Caleb asks leaning forward.

"I am honored, Caleb, that you have applied such an effort of concentration and energy, not to mention mnemonics, to an insignificant life."

"You don't like it", Caleb mumbles, his face falling morosely.

"It is not me."

"What do you mean, not you!"

"In the poetic sense."

"It's prose."

"Yes, it's prose. But I don't believe one can express the truth of a life with prose."

"I think we disagree on that."

"I know we disagree on that, of this I am very certain. Please, you will not publish this."

Caleb clears his throat, he has worked hard getting the biography just right. There's the old hurt look in his eyes, the look that fatherless men sometimes revert to without realizing it.

Josip reaches out and pats Caleb's shoulder.

"No man could have done a better job writing my life, Caleb. However, it must be honestly admitted between us that my life is in my poems, not in such words—fine as these words are. And they are very, very fine."

"Don't guff me, ol' man."

"Okay. I will speak frankly. I am embarrassed by them. I am afraid of the naked facts. It is better to be silent about facts."

"Why?"

How to explain to this energetic North American the consciousness of a boy drowning in a river of blood—drinking from it as bodies float by—a dead boy found on a road in the middle of the night. Or a skinned rabbit.

"It's just better, that's all."

"You're not being coherent today, Josip."

"True. But what can I do?" he shrugs.

"And another thing—it's ridiculous for you to keep using the pen name. Why not use your own? What are you scared of? The Communists aren't going to track you down and mess up your life. Those days are over!"

The battle continues for two or three hours. Josip interrupts from time to time to make Caleb a cup of coffee, and once to show him the seven-kilo catfish brooding in the bathtub. Caleb just stands there, looking down into the water with hands on hips, shaking his head.

Perhaps it is the absurdity that breaks up the categories of his thought—his assumptions about how literary biographies should be written.

"So, you refuse", he says at last with a groan of resignation.

"You can do as you wish."

"Don't give me that! You know I can't do it if you aren't going to be happy about it."

"You're a free man. This is a free country."

"Uh, yeah."

"Thus—?"

"*Thus*—what do you suggest?"

"If you are desperate to have an introduction, and if the publisher insists upon it, I can think of no better person to write it than yourself. However, I request that you delete all informational data from it."

Caleb shakes his head again. The old poet is proving to be a barbed catfish—and after all these years!

"Okay, Josip", he says glumly. "I'll rewrite the damn thing."

That autumn the book is released under the title *The Seraph of Sarajevo: Selected Poems of Josip Marulić*. When Caleb drops by one blustery November evening to deliver a packet of six complementary copies from the publisher, his facial expression is cheerily enthusiastic, his bass voice announces the happy birth as boisterously as a presiding uncle, yet his eyes are qualified. Though he is the midwife, doctor, and family member all in one, the baby is not quite as he had hoped it would be. Josip interprets this mild tempering of the original enthusiasm as a double compliment. Caleb, it seems, is not unattached, and that is nothing less than a sign of how much he cares. After a cup of coffee and a quick check into the bathroom to see if there are any fish in residence, Caleb opens the package and presents the first published copy of Josip's poetry in the English language to the poet himself.

It is one of those moments when silence is as it should be—good and full.

Josip flips pages, reads a poem or two, his own words translated into a foreign tongue. He notes the Calebite changes, not bad at all—very well done, in fact, and a few are actually improvements.

"Excellent," he says, "excellent."

He likes the weight of this hardbound edition, its purple cloth and its shiny jacket too, which displays a hieratic skyline of Sarajevo with a burst of flame above it—presumably a fire of angelic holiness.

Then, with some trepidation, he turns to the introduction and reads it from start to finish, while its author looks on with a neutral expression combined with body language that signifies intense anxiety.

Thus, Josip reads the revised summation of his life:

Introduction

At long last the poems of Josip Marulić appear in English translation. Though his individual poems have been acknowledged by the expatriate Croatian community in Europe and America for several years now, they have been published by small journals and circulated only among the Croatians in exile. As the editor of this, the first English-language edition of his work, I was honored with a responsibility due entirely to the operations of fate and friendship. Mr. Marulić is my neighbor and the janitor of the building in which I live.

He is an unassuming man, in his mid-sixties, of moderate frame but unusually tall, his height mediated a little by the stoop of age. His appearance, though clean and groomed, is not one of style or opulence. He performs his work in the building fastidiously, and no resident other than myself knows of his stature in the world of letters. There is nothing to distinguish him from the hundreds of thousands of other immigrants who live in the surrounding streets.

Upon the hall-side of the door to his one-room basement apartment there hangs a shield: the red and white checkered crest of his homeland, and above it a simple sign in English:

Custodian. One enters his residence as if through a looking glass, penetrating a world of memory and artifact, though the latter is scant and the former largely invisible, revealed slowly, over many years, in conversation. For Marulić, objects are words and words are objects, though they are primarily so in the sense of *objets d'art*. Even this must be qualified, for in Marulić's mind art is never static. He speaks of words (with words) as living beings, not dead letters, not even true dead letters. Language should be, he says, as fluid as love and as stable as marriage.

The interior of Marulić's room is spartan. There is a cot, a dresser, a hot plate for his beloved coffee, a small refrigerator, and a desk and chair. The single window looks out upon the brick wall of a neighboring tenement. There is no radio or television, no desktop computer, no satellite dish at the window. A black dial-telephone sits on the floor beside the bed, though it appears little used, considering the dust on it. Such a room is, I would guess, like many a janitor's room throughout this great city, with the differences that there is a manual typewriter on the desk and the walls are lined with books. The books are in several foreign languages. They appear to be, for the most part, literary and historical works. The room contains, with one exception, no other distinguishing features. The exception is simple and, like its owner, inexplicable: above the desk hangs a fine intaglio print of a bird. It is, I think, a swallow in flight.

Who is he, then? For me, the answer is to be found only in the collage of my memories of him. For example, as a boy I once stood beside him at a fish market and observed him transforming the mundane act of buying a piece of cod into a mysterious experience of communion between himself and an irritable old woman who held a cleaver in her hands above a bloodstained chopping block. He spoke to her with his eyes, with his tone, and with a slight bow of the upper body that reawoke her respect for her inherent dignity and her lost charms. In the end, she smiled. Later, as a youth, I observed him playing tortuous games of checkers for hours in the park with a mentally deficient octogenarian, with whom he shared no common language—no spoken language, that is. Fast forward a few years to a press conference launching my first book of poetry. Josip Marulić was present that evening as my guest. By then, I knew that he was the great poet and I no more than a "promising" young amateur. Yet he beamed throughout the event like a child at a surprise party. Indeed, for him, life is always an unending series of surprises, at one moment grievous, the next brimming with delight.

Toward the end of this party, however, the smiles died on his face when an aggressive academic of great renown, having been informed that my guest wrote poetry, launched into a condescending, facile disquisition on classicism, the demise of which the speaker roundly approved. With several deft strokes of his Herzegovinian saber, Marulić demolished the glib assumptions. However, it is to his credit that no one in the room could have taken his ripostes for insults, so gentle was the tone my friend used, so quiet was his voice. Yet with what compelling clarity, what intransigent authority did he press his points home—an authority that needed nothing more to underline its rights than the power of truth. The personage departed shortly after.

Though Marulić is an even-tempered and whimsical man, he can be roused to intemperate emotion by two things, as far as I know, though I admit that the existential spectrum of the New World is not quite the same as that of the Old World, especially his portion of that world. Even so, I have learned that he is capable of unruly passion. One need only speak of the pace of modern life to provoke a furrowing of brow, a tightening of mouth, or a cast of the eyes that is both ironic and angry. The second thing that provokes him is the false assumption, held by most people, that they have a right to *know* about the most intimate details of other people's lives. He calls this tendency "chthonic". It is a measure of the man that he is at ease with such terms but can be confused over the various meanings of the word *bar*.

The translations from the original Croatian language are by Marulić himself. My adjustments to the text were sparing, employed only when the author used a nuanced English term that clearly meant something other than his intention. It is, of course, a dangerous exercise to presume upon a poet's intention. However, certain word choices were obviously the casualties of a second language learned in part through literature and through the lesser, though by no means insignificant, element of street lexicon. In other words, slang. But this is no street poet. He is a poet in the classical sense.

Considering the extraordinary quality of his writing, and his long and not undramatic personal history, I felt it important to piece together what Marulić said would be, in his ironic phrase, "a volume of vast insignificance", that is, a provisional biography. From the stories he told me about his past, I compiled a brief "Life", which was to have been the preface to the poems. Before going to press, however, and having read the preface, he insisted on the deletion of any significant biographical data. He maintained that while such matters are important "for the soul" of a man, the understanding to be gained from them is for the man himself, and not for anyone who, from idle interest or "more perilous *curiositas*", as he called it, presumes to enter into the realm of another's private memory. Thus, all glimpses into the interior come through the poems themselves. Josip Marulić is, to the end, the custodian.

Caleb Franklin, Jr., Ph.D.

Professor of Literature, Columbia University

Looking up, Josip smiles, reaches over, and ruffles Caleb's unruffleable springy hair as he once did when the doctor was a street rat. Caleb grins, leans forward, and ruffles the absent hair on the dome of the old man's head, as he has never, until now, dared to do.

They both laugh, say no more, and call it a night.

The folios of exultation fill quickly. There are reviews in major papers but always on the back pages of the weekend book section. The review by Caleb is a big help and draws attention that *The Seraph* would not have otherwise received. Josip's old adversary, the literary critic who once lived in his apartment building, also writes a review. Devastating. It may be that she does not know the identity of the poet, does not connect his name to a scruffy fellow who defends pigeons from unpleasant cats. Even so, she has scented blood and uses all her weapons to kill her prey.

Josip reads her critique, winces a little, then wraps fish heads in it and takes it out to the dumpster. His book is a three-day wonder that is quickly forgotten, for there is an unending supply of writers in this land. Fifty thousand new titles a year are published in English, Caleb informs him, just to set the record straight, just to keep things in perspective.

In any event, the seraph is now out there in the world. It may be that someone reads it with interest. Perhaps lives are expanded or encouraged or instructed.

"What can I teach anyone?" Josip asks in a low moment—a rhetorical question. Unfortunately, this little groan is overheard by Caleb, and the young African-American laureate replies with a fiendishly eloquent and somewhat lugubrious rebuke. Josip is suitably chastened. Let God, then, deal with his pride. Humans are unreliable, in praise and condemnation alike.

Perhaps out there in the world wherever poems are still read, there is a child who would stare at him obliquely if they happened to meet, yet who is like Josip as he once was, walking along the shore of a Bosnian river in the predawn light, testing his damaged soul against the insurmountable. Does he plunge in and learn to swim against the current at the command of an inner voice, or in response to messages delivered by unlikely prophets, or impelled solely by the exigencies of youth? And does he, in winter, roam the heights, dreaming before the vast fields of heaven and hell, a child extremely sensitive to the metaphysical impressions provided by natural phenomena? Is there one such child in each station of the human dream? Filled with inarticulate longings, indifferent to the ordinary dreams of warriors and drawn beyond them to less visible conflicts, the existence of which he can only dimly apprehend? And is there a confraternity of these few, scattered like seed throughout all nations, ensuring the preservation of man's diversity?

Perhaps it is so. Perhaps not. He will hope for it nonetheless.

The following year, more of his selected poems are published in English, under the title *Beelzebub in Brooklyn*. He wanted it to be titled *Moloch in Manhattan*, but his publisher felt that this was too "political". Caleb writes a review. The sales are not so great. On the other hand, the Vienna publisher puts together a Croatian language collection of his later poems under the title *Loss*. This is republished shortly thereafter by a Croatian firm in Split, along with two other volumes of his poetry, *The Island* and *In the Homeland of the Soul*.

There is a distressing event that he is forced to attend. *The Seraph of Sarajevo* is nominated for the National Book Award in the poetry category. Josip is certain that dear political Caleb is behind this, though he denies it. The banquet, held in a big hotel ballroom in Manhattan, is an ordeal. He feels throughout that he has become what he has so often anticipated—the hideous ornament at a feast of beauty, the gargoyle in the garden. He does not win, thank heavens. Caleb is crestfallen.

It is all quite amazing and still quite unreal. He asks himself: Who, really, is this man Josip Lasta—or Josip Marulić—who writes those poems?

38

Josip swings his legs over the side of the bed and yawns.

Oh, look, I am still old. I have not grown younger during my dreams.

When you are this old, you need a few minutes to orient yourself, you rock a little, gather momentum like a boy on a swing preparing to fly, back and forth, higher and higher— Now! Let go of the chains, slide from the seat, and *weee!* you are airborne!

Ho-ho, he yawns again, rubbing his eyes. Get up, now, Josip, make the coffee. Check out the window. Oh, too bad, a gray day. Low pressure, sluggishness, and a little tug toward depression. Not a big problem, just something to push against.

His bathtub guest is sloshing vigorously, aware that the host is awake. It's a trout, 4.5 kilos. A trout with lampreys attached to the gills. Josip hates lampreys. They look like what they are. Caleb will drop by later in the morning to help cut up the fish. With his terrible cigarettes he will burn away the lampreys, drop them down the toilet—flush! Lampreys are like devils. They quietly attach themselves to the life forces and slowly suck away vitality. Poor fish.

The phone rings. He looks at it. He should get rid of it. It is covered with dust. Sighing he picks up the receiver, yawns *Good morning* into it, scratching his bare legs as he listens.

It is Winston on the line with news. I thought you'd like to know, he says, thought I should call you since you hardly ever read newspapers.

Josip nods, closes his eyes, says *Thank you*, places the receiver on the hook, bends over, and puts his face into his hands.

Winston has told him that New York's Croatian community is in mourning. Remember that concert in support of Croatian independence about ten years ago? The wonderful violinist? Her funeral will be at such-and-such an hour on such-and-such a day at the cathedral.

Hundreds of people attend the funeral Mass. The cathedral can seat thousands, so it does not seem full. The replica of Michelangelo's Pietà is three times larger than the original, on which Josip once meditated in St. Peter's. He prays before it while waiting for the Mass to begin, prays for Ariadne's soul, recalls Miriam and the dying stag which in his memory has been transformed into a white one. Then he finds a quiet place at the back, and a few minutes later the coffin is brought in as the bells in the tower ring and the choir sings a Mozart requiem.

A bishop and nine priests concelebrate. The choir sings traditional Latin and Croatian hymns. There are a lot of weeping people here. Josip sits alone in his pew, not weeping, solemn and still. He goes forward in a long line to receive Communion, and as he passes the coffin in the center aisle, he touches his hand to the top for a few seconds then steps forward and opens his mouth for the sweet fire.

As the coffin is taken out in procession, he stands. He is aware that it is followed by a crowd of family and friends but he does not look closely. The husband goes past, a dignified man in his late sixties, a stricken man, Mr. Finntree. Out on the steps and sidewalks of Madison Avenue, most of the mourners wait while hearse and limousines drive away with their passengers. It is a chilly day, everyone blowing frosty breath as if exhaling soul. Josip would like to go to the cemetery, wherever that may be, but does not know how he can do it. A woman standing beside him turns and says, "Did you know Mrs. Finntree?"

"Yes", Josip nods.

"So did I", the woman breaks down crying, covering her eyes with a handkerchief.

"I am sorry for your loss", whispers Josip.

"We played together for years in the symphony", says the woman. "I was cello, Ari was violin." She pauses and glances at Josip's poor overcoat.

"Did you know her well?"

Josip nods again.

"Are you going to Calvary?"

He stares at her dumbly.

"Calvary Cemetery in Woodside."

"I had hoped . . . But I do not have transportation."

"Oh", she says. "Well, why don't you come with us? My husband is just bringing the car around."

"I would be grateful."

At the graveside he stands at the back of the crowd. He can see nothing, knows no one. She was greatly loved by so many people—many, many. It is like other funerals he has attended, the body is mortal and must return to the soil, both the good and the bad lives, the good and the bad deaths. Red stars sucking blood above the cenotaphs of killers, or crucifixes planted in the garden of discarded infants. It is not possible to speak now. He is blinded, stares at his shoes, remembers, remembers.

I feel certain, my Josip, that ours will be a tale with only joy in it.

He waits until more people leave, only a dozen or so remain. Who are they? He does not know them, yet they grieve.

Finally, he is able to kneel beside the heap of soil, which is completely covered with flowers, flowers in winter under falling snow. With his right hand, he clears away a few blooms and places his palm on the cold soil. He closes his eyes and sees her face, he senses her love, as he has countless times since he lost her. Still, he cannot weep. The world is simply empty, like the silence after the end of a story.

He stands and brushes the slush from his knees.

"We can take you there", says the cello lady.

He nods without thinking, without really knowing what she means, knowing only that he needs to return to the city and to his room. They drive silently across the Williamsburg bridge into lower Manhattan. He pays no attention to where the car is taking him. Soon they turn off a main avenue onto a side street in Greenwich Village, full of stately town houses, three and four stories high. They park, and Josip gets out. Now he realizes that they have not dropped him at the cathedral, where he had assumed they were going. He had intended to walk from there back to 52nd Street. The woman and her husband tell him something, but he cannot quite hear them. He follows them because that is where his feet take him, perhaps to a reception of some kind. He can spend a moment or two there and then leave without being noticed.

They climb the steps of an old brownstone house, where dozens of people are standing and talking on the wide porch, while others are going inside or coming out. He follows the cello lady into the entrance foyer. On a table near the door are a violin and bow; beside it is a guest book; beside this is a framed photograph of Ariadne, about forty years old; beside her is a younger Mr. Finntree and five children. All very beautiful children, three girls and two boys. Two of the girls resemble Ariadne, the boys their father.

At the end of the crowded hallway, they enter a large living room filled with antique furniture and paintings, and people, and tables full of food and drink. The noise of conversation makes it hard for anyone to be heard, and the volume increases. From somewhere comes the sound of a Paganini violin concerto.

Mr. Finntree and his children are standing in a line receiving visitors. The children seem to be in their thirties and forties— yes, there are five of them alongside their father, all red-eyed, letting their tears flow, embracing newcomers or holding hands with all these people whom Josip does not know, these many who knew Ariadne so well. He remembers to remove his cap, holding it in his hands, uncertain about what to do. He does not want to meet her family. Quietly he moves out of the line, turns away, and retraces his steps down the hallway. But there is congestion of new arrivals at the door, people hugging each other, blocking his exit. He steps into a side room off the hall, intending to remain there for a few moments, alone, to remember her. When the entrance clears, he will leave without being noticed.

The room is a woman's small study. It has a scroll-top desk, a music stand, impressionist paintings, and shelves of books with Croatian and English titles. A crucifix hangs above a small marble fireplace, and on the mantel beneath the cross is a carving of some kind. He looks closer. It is a wooden swallow. Beside it is a smooth white stone, the size of a dove's egg.

He is staring at it, wordless, when a voice interrupts.

"Hello."

He turns to find a woman in her early forties gazing at him curiously.

"I—I was just leaving", he murmurs. "I am sorry to intrude in this room. The hall was crowded."

"That's all right", says the woman, still gazing at him, not unfriendly, not suspicious, but plainly interested. "Did you really want to go so soon? I saw you come in; then you left so quickly. Maybe you'd like to say a few words to Dad."

He shakes his head, glances at the floor. "Thank you, no."

"Did you know my mother?"

Josip nods.

She offers her hand. "I'm Maria Finntree", she says with a sorrowful smile. He shakes her hand, feeling helpless and confused. "Please feel free to stay awhile. I should go greet the other guests."

757

"Thank you."

She turns away then pauses, looking back at him.

"Where do you know my mother from?"

He cannot answer. He looks away. He hopes she will leave so he can go out the front door before he is completely blinded, down the steps unseen, away.

She steps toward him, searches his eyes. For a moment the two of them remain without moving or speaking. Then her eyes begin blinking rapidly, and she glances at the swallow.

O memory, how blithely we discard you, for you baffle us endlessly, and we cannot endure the confusion, the doubts engendered by our loss. Forgetting, forgetting the severance that connects, losing the possibility of reunion and completion. We are unable to keep vigil under the cross, and even less are we willing to be nailed to it.

Maria is still standing there, looking at him, her mouth opening a little. She does not let go of his hand. A handsome woman with dyed hair, reddish sable, tastefully cut with spears over her brow, so much like her grandmother's brow, a woman of Rajska Polja. A fine black dress, miniature white pearls at her neck. A wedding ring on her hand. She has her mother's eyes, but her face is Lasta.

Each time she tries to speak, she chokes. He, the same. They sit down on a sofa. Still, she will not let him go.

"Marija", he whispers and begins to cry. She puts her arms around him.

"My father", she breathes. "O my father, my father, my father."

Draw the veil over this. Let it rest. Weep if you must, laugh if you must—but remember that laughter should enfold all weeping.

Now he falls asleep each night, feeling grief and joy as one thing—a sun in the breast. There is much that he replays in his mind. The meeting with Ariadne's husband, the man she wed nearly forty years ago. A man who married a refugee and adopted an orphaned daughter as his own. A refined man, successful in the world, yet somehow a faithful believer too. Now devastated by his loss, he cannot really focus on what it means, this return of the original husband. His children are interested, even fascinated for a while, but it is Maria (Marija) who truly understands. She absorbs it, lives it, and begins rebuilding the severed connection. The husband is not really capable of participating in the process, though he makes a good effort during the single meal they share at the family home.

Marija is older than Ariadne was when she and Josip were last together in the palace by the sea. Sadly, Marija is separated from her husband and has returned to her family name—that is, Finntree. Her only child, Ryan Collins, is studying architecture at Princeton. She hopes to connect him to his natural grandfather when he is next home.

A month passes, then two months go by, and more blanks are filled in. There are meals at restaurants, a slightly embarrassing visit to Josip's basement room, the fish he neglected to remove from the bathtub.

One Sunday, while Josip is visiting Marija at her apartment, Ryan blows in unexpectedly. He is unusually tall for nineteen years old, wears trendy clothing, and drives a sports car of his own. His blond hair is in short spikes. He is distracted in his manner, mostly worried that the resurrected bio-grandfather could pose a threat to his mother's equilibrium or identity. None of this is spoken, but it is in his eyes. He does not really want to hear the stories of old people, either. He is courteous but somewhat detached. His mother is frustrated by him, takes him into another room and an argument ensues. The boy has made a date to see a Broadway musical with a girl—*Les*

Misérables. She lets him go and returns to the living room, where Josip had been telling her the missing portion of her own tale. She is upset about her son's indifference, hides it, and they resume reconstruction.

One evening in January, Marija takes Josip out to dinner at a popular restaurant near Park Avenue. She tells him many things about her mother, the wonderful memories. He tells Marija about her mother's youth, the two or three years when they knew each other. Marija asks about the Croatian side of the family. Does Josip know what happened to all those people? Nothing, he shakes his head. Nothing. He asks if she knows what happened to Vera Horvatinec, her grandmother?

"Oh, yes, we were very close. The three of us came from Vienna together. She lived with us after Mom and Dad were married. I think I was seven or eight years old when Bakica passed on."

Josip bows his head.

"Tata, why didn't you contact us when you found out we were alive?"

This is the hard question they have been circling around for months.

"If I had known that *you* were alive, Marija, I would have. Instantly I would have. I had been told that you both died during childbirth. Then, when I discovered that your mother was alive, I assumed that only she had survived. I never dreamed—"

"You stayed away. You didn't let her know."

"I couldn't, Marija. The one time I saw her, I understood that she had been happily married for many years. Our marriage was brief, little more than a year. It was a civil one, you know, and she was now married sacramentally to a good man."

"Yes," Marija nods, "Dad is a good man, the best. But still I think—" She pauses reaching for his hand. "I think it would have meant a lot to her, to know that you were alive."

"Do you think so?" Josip shakes his head, sighing. "Perhaps. Or it might have been like a ghost returning to haunt her."

"It never would have been that."

"Did she ever talk about me?"

"Of course. She told me all about you, many wonderful things. You were the great love of her life, Tata." Marija stops and takes a few moments to collect herself. "But she knew we had to go on. She was sure you were dead. When we were in Vienna, somehow the secret police found out where she was. They couldn't touch her because we had friends in the Austrian government, but they tried to hurt her. A message came out of nowhere, a heartless message, unsigned, but with an official Yugoslavian stamp on the letter."

"Do you know what was in it? Do you still have it?"

"No. Mama cried and cried over it, then she burned it. I was only four at the time, but I can still remember her weeping. I had never seen her like that, and I was very frightened by it. Years later, she explained that someone in the Communist government wanted her to know you were dead—that you had died in prison."

"Why? Why would anyone lie like that?"

Even as he asks the question, he knows the answer. When they cannot kill you, they spread death in any form they can.

"Even though I did not know my Tata, Mama kept your memory alive for me—and, I think, for herself as well. I missed you so badly for years, tried to imagine what you looked like. We had no photos, nothing. We escaped with only our lives."

"And with the swallow."

"Yes, the swallow and the stone, that's all. She didn't tell me what the carving and the white stone were about until I was married. She didn't want me to think that she loved her second husband any less. But I understand now that while she loved him very much, she had loved you as no other in her life. This never changed. I know that sometimes when Dad was away on business, she would hold the swallow in her hand and remember. Sometimes she would close the door of her study and play violin quietly to herself. I think she was trying to reach back across the years to you as well. Once I found her asleep in the armchair—the one beside the fireplace in her room. The violin was on her lap. The swallow was resting in one hand, and in her other hand was the stone."

A month later, they return to the same restaurant. They plan to make this a ritual. After supper, Marija tells Josip about the company she established five years ago, how well it is doing. She is a successful businesswoman. She also relates a little about the husband from whom she is separated. It is hard for her father to absorb all this, the intimate history of a woman who is closer to him than any other person on earth, yet who remains something of a stranger. They are linked by blood and stories, but by no shared experience. Even so, they both fully intend to remedy the situation.

By coincidence or divine humor, they are suddenly interrupted by Caleb, who happens to be in the restaurant and is passing by their table on his way out.

"Joe, my main man!" he exclaims with rather too much street accent. "Why you here in *this* upbeat dive?"

"Caleb, allow me to introduce to you my daughter."

"Your *daughter*?"

Caleb becomes all manners and royal black graciousness. It is sincere, the real Caleb. He sits down with a wondering expression to learn more about his friend's mysterious past. He listens enrapt, solemn, his mouth dropping open a little, turning his eyes back and forth between Josip and Marija as they take turns narrating their portions of the story.

"Wow", says Caleb at last. "That is some awesome! Finding each other after all this time. It must have been a surprise for you to hear that your Dad's been in this city all your life."

"A surprise for both of us", Marija smiles. "But God has the final word."

"In this life or the next", nods Caleb, Abyssinian Gospel Holiness man that he is.

"Where is Miriam this evening?" asks Josip. "I would so much like her to meet my daughter."

"She had to teach a class at the university tonight, and I had a supper meeting with my publisher. Let's get together soon, Josip. I'll talk to her about it and give you a call."

Caleb pauses, cracks a grin, and continues in street jargon. "See that man over there in the corner, he give me a cigar!" Pronounced *see-gar*. Caleb's accent is reverting by default, or perhaps he deliberately uses it with strangers whenever he is in a mischievous mood, just for the fun of demolishing stereotypes a moment later. "That man he try t' buy mah soul, but I tell *him*, no way, Mister, mah soul don't come cheap, it already been bought on a hilltop long ago. He want me to chill out the symbols, you know, make my stuff more *die*-gestible to the zeitgeist literary Nazis, but I *dee*-clined in spades. Full house, don't give me no sheet, I tol' him! He back down, promise me full scale *pub*-licity for mah new book next spring."

Caleb scrapes back his chair, stands, and stretches his spine. "Anyways, Jefferson, he's with my Momma tonight. She cain't get enough o' that boy, packs the candy into him, then eats him alive. She turnin' him into a butterball! I gotta go pick him up now. Nice to meet you, Marija, very nice. Take care this ol' man for me, willya?"

"I will", she laughs.

After he leaves, Marija leans forward and says, "Was that Caleb Franklin the poet?"

"Yes."

"You know him?"

"Yes, I've known him since he was a boy."

763

"He's very famous", she says. "I have some of his books. How do you know him?"

She is shaking her head whimsically, trying to understand how a man *that* famous came to be on such familiar terms with a man like her father.

"Well, it is a long story", he replies, frowning with embarrassment. "He was kind enough to write an introduction to my book."

"Your book?" she replies with raised eyebrows.

39

In June, Josip attends Jefferson Franklin's first Holy Communion. Caleb and his Miriam now attend Mass at Sts. Cyril and Methodius. They enjoy the multicultural environment and feel like American founding fathers compared to many of the other parishioners, who are more recent immigrants. Caleb still resists "swimmin' the Tiber", as he calls it, but he is studying the Catechism and is, paradoxically, more reverent than many a Catholic. Miriam sometimes attends her mother-in-law's prayer meetings in Harlem. There she dances and sings as she prays.

Josip has always been intrigued by the languages of worship and how people understand them, indeed how they reconcile them.

"It's interior and exterior, Josip", Miriam explains. "Well, there's both in each language, of course, but the formal rituals and especially the presence of the Eucharist help us to go very deep."

"Like a dolphin", Josip suggests.

"Hmmm, good image. Yes, like a dolphin. He dives deep, leaps high, and always remains a dolphin—just what the Lord wants him to be."

That month, Josip also attends Christiana Kanapathipillai's graduation from high school. She is valedictorian and delivers a graceful, erudite address, quotes from Solzhenitsyn's Harvard speech and John Paul II's *Centesimus Annus*, and concludes by exhorting her classmates to defend freedom and moral character. She makes her parents and godfather very proud and not a few people in the audience terribly uncomfortable.

November in New York is unusually gray and blustery—the month of all souls, the season of mourning. For the first time in decades, the manager of the building invites Josip to his apartment. They share a meal together and reminisce afterward. The manager tells long stories about the Armenian massacre, the martyrdom of countless Christians by the Muslims at the beginning of the twentieth century. Josip speaks about what the Turks did to his people. There are so many histories embedded in hearts, often where one would least expect to find them. Faggeddabouddit, says the manager as his eyes fill with tears—meaning, remember it, but do not condemn, for we are all sons of Adam. Remember, lest the past become present again.

A card from Slavica brings the news that Emilio has died after years of suffering from Alzheimer's disease. His last food was a bite of chocolate. He was always happy. Slavica now lives in a retirement home in Venezia but remains active in several organizations, notably the communities for troubled youth she helped establish throughout Italy. Her daughter Chiara is married, with three children, and plays in a symphony orchestra in Firenze. Paolo is a respected physician, married, and a grandfather—a very young grandfather, she adds. Yes, this makes her a great-grandmother! Her only regret is that her parents did not live long enough to see the darkness of their times begin to turn toward the light.

Throughout that year, there are reprintings of his poems by various publishers. In New York, Vienna, and Split, the revised editions appear under his real name.

Josip's Christmas is quieter than usual. The Franklins have gone to Jamaica for a month. Winston's mother died in India not long after being reconciled with her son, and the family has flown to Bangalore for the funeral and for further restoration.

Though it is now a year since Ariadne's death, the Finntrees have gone west to Aspen, Colorado, for a skiing holiday, trying to get their minds off their loss.

Thus, in this hiatus of solitude bestowed by an uncanny convergence of absences, Josip senses an ending and another beginning. He listens for it as he strolls through Central Park night after night, enjoying the Christmas-tree lights and the sparkling snow. He listens as he circles the pond in daylight, wishing he had some strawberries to pop into Jason's mouth, the tug at his hand and the cry in his ear nearly sensible. He listens as he scatters bags full of crumbled bread to his good friends the pigeons and offers sandwiches to royal beggars. He listens as he drops off an anonymous gift at the office of his old enemy, the literary critic—*Gift from the Sea*, by Anne Morrow Lindbergh—and he listens as he leaves his usual package of biscuits at the fish market. Now he listens as he visits Ariadne's grave, praying for her soul, missing her. He listens to his sorrow grow gentle and then come to rest, for love is stronger than death. He does not try to take his mind off his loss, has no desire to do so, for it is a return to their last Christmas together before the darkness fell.

On New Year's Eve, he attends the vigil Mass for the feast of the Mother of God, and after Communion receives a particular grace—the knowledge of what he must do.

In March of the year 2004—March 19, to be precise—on the feast of St. Joseph, he leaves the new world behind. Now it will become the old world. Caleb and Jefferson drive him to Kennedy Airport. Jefferson is somewhat bored, and is miffed that his father has forced him to miss school for a day. As they leave the towers of Manhattan behind, crossing the East River into Queens, he tells Josip that he has changed his name. He is now Jefferson Airplane Franklin the Third.

"Where you get that name, boy!" his father growls.

"From you, Dad."

"No way, you never hear that name from me, and what's with this *Third*, anyway? You ain't no third and you ain't no airplane."

Jefferson goes off into giggles. Father-baiting is fun, though you don't want to push it too far.

Caleb grows silent and fierce with the sense of impending separation, but he is trying to hide it. They make small talk, promise to write letters. Josip invites him to visit when he gets settled in Croatia, and of course bring Miriam and Jefferson. Caleb assures him they'll come, can't wait to come. He tells the old man that he should get on the Internet. E-mail is as fast as lightning, he says.

"Like lightning that fell from the heavens", Josip murmurs.

The rest of the banter is of the mundane kind. Jefferson in the back seat plugs himself into his digital music player and bounces through Long Island. Staring straight ahead at seventy miles per hour, Caleb reaches back and pulls the plugs from the boy's ears. A howl of protest, and an argument breaks out. Good-bye, America.

As they park at the airport, Josip notices that Caleb's eyes are getting wet. He's feeling moisture in his own eyes, too. Should he tousle the untousleable hair one more time, as a parting word? No—such tousling remains something of a risk, a culturally mixed message, stirring up the residual effects of centuries-old paternalism, does it not? A benevolent slave-master, but still, a slave-master. Or would Caleb understand and see the gesture as the airing of an old fear that they can now laugh about—the airing, as well, of an old breakthrough between them. Should he say all the unsaid things? No—that would be too much of a departure from their habit with each other. Implicit words are more powerful than the explicit, which can so easily evaporate, or get lodged in memory as something other than what they are.

Josip is unsure, feels the ache in his throat. What to do! Should he speak like a Lastavica of the Mountains addressing a Lastavica of the City, tapping into whatever remains of that old grace, as the armless man once spoke to him? Why not? He has always been unarmed.

Caleb and Jefferson take his luggage and carry it into the terminal, man on one side of him, boy on the other. Their arms rub close. Such physical people. Josip is wistful that other dear friends are unable to be here. He had the tearful good-bye weekend in Connecticut, another in Harlem. Most of all he feels the absence of his daughter and grandson. They are busy; they have full lives. He has not known them a long time. Well, they had a last supper at the restaurant two nights ago and then the final good-bye on the phone. Marija has a big meeting today with some Dutch people who want to invest in her company. They have flown in from Amsterdam just for this and will fly out again tonight. She feels terrible about it, but it's impossible to get away. Ryan is unable to drive in from Princeton because he has an exam today. If he skips it, he's a dead man, the year's blown! Thus, they have reached the end of some awkward yet soulful exchanges. The boy has grown curious about his ancestors and has begun to ponder on a wider field than his known world. Growth, expansion—perhaps even new depth. It's hard to say what will become of him. In any event, he plans to visit Croatia next year, bicycle from Trieste to Dubrovnik; and has asked if he can bunk in with his newfound grandfather when he gets to Split. He'll be coming for sure— unless he wins a scholarship to Oxford.

During the past month, Josip has laid a trail of bread crumbs through the forest: little gifts that say: this is who I am, here is how you can find me. You will find me when you know who I am. He gave the picture of the swallow to Ryan, gave Marija the first editions of his books (Marulić) and the revised editions (Lasta), inscribed to her with loving and heartfelt words. At her apartment in Greenwich Village, she has several copies of each title. She is always going into bookstores to ask if they sell the poems of Josip Lasta, never letting on that she is related to him.

Caleb interferes during the check-in, wants to do all the talking at the airline counter, as if Josip, who has traveled by air before and is familiar enough with the process, is a doddering old fellow who needs minding. The airline woman is black, too, and her face registers some irritation. Josip smiles. These psychological cultural-sociological dynamics are interesting to him.

Caleb is trying to assert his authority, straining to sound proprietary and knowledgeable, but the pose is not working. He interrupts the lady and supplies the answers before she asks the questions. She does not like his manner. Pretending she cannot hear Caleb, she asks Josip the usual questions in the proper order.

"Did a stranger ask you to carry anything in your luggage, sir?"

Josip shakes his head.

"Do you have any inflammable or explosive items, knives, scissors, or other weapons in your carry-on luggage?"

He hesitates. Inflammable items, yes—his mind for example. Explosives? Well, there have been moments . . .

She begins to restate the question, but Caleb interrupts:

"Sistah, this man ain't gonna hijack yo' jet. He's a very famous poet, runna-up fo' National Book Award, and he's about the best—"

She ignores him. Turning to Josip, she asks, "Is this gentleman your taxi driver, sir?"

"No." Josip shakes his head.

"An employee, then. Your chauffeur?"

"He is my son."

All discussion instantly ceases. The lady raises her eyebrows, tilts her glasses down the bridge of her nose, and peers ever so ironically at Caleb.

"That's right, sistah, this mah *Dad*." Pronounced *dayad*.

She turns to Josip, puts the tickets and passport down on the counter before him, and says, "There you are, Mr. Lasta. Please proceed to the security gate, and on the other side you go to the Czech Airlines counter at gate 44. You'll transfer in Prague to Croatian Airlines and pick up your luggage when you arrive in Split."

"Thank you, Madame", he says, offering his hand. She shakes it and smiles warmly. "Have a nice flight, Mr. Lasta."

Time to proceed farther into the labyrinth. Caleb and Jefferson are allowed to go as far as the security gate. Man on one side, boy on the other, lots of body contact. Caleb does something he has never done before, not in all the years they have known each other. He drapes his arm around the old man's shoulders, and holds him tightly all the way.

"You said *son*."

"I said *son*, Caleb."

"I know you meant it. I know."

There in the distance, a jaw gapes wide to receive those who intend to go up in the air. Josip must pass through its electronic dentures, the green and red lights, and the men in uniforms with their amazing batons. There is a lot of beeping, and long lines of people are waiting to be swallowed.

"I love you", says the black giant in a choking voice. "I love you, and I thank you for all you did for me."

"I love you too, Caleb. It is I who thank you."

Caleb lets the tears run down his face without trying to hide them.

"A man is himself and no other", Josip says. "He is an island in the sea of being. And each island is as no other. The islands are connected because they have come forth from the sea, and the sea flows between them. It separates them yet unites them, if they learn to swim."

"You already taught me this, Josip, a long time ago."

771

"As you taught it to me, Caleb, and as you are teaching it to Jefferson."

From behind comes the sound of running steps clattering on the floor tiles. A young man in a flying raincoat abruptly halts beside them, huffing and puffing. It is Ryan.

"Had to come", he wheezes. "Had to come."

"Ryan, what about your examination?"

"To hell with my examination!"

He takes the old man's hands in his own, his grandfather whom he is just getting to know and whom he may never see again.

Neither the old man nor the boy say another word. They just stand there looking at each other, the islands connecting across time and oceans and the blows of fate—a fate that has transformed itself into providence at the very end.

The boy kisses his grandfather on both cheeks, European fashion.

No matter what comes, my beloved, we will not be defeated.

Then a guard barks, and Josip must go through the tunnel to the other side. His belt and his religious medallions cause some delay, but when he is through into the secure zone, he turns and waves. There they are, over there in the unsecure world, Caleb, Jefferson, and Ryan side by side, waving back. Caleb puts his massive hand to his heart and keeps it there—a final word. Ryan has his hands thrust deep into his coat pockets, chin on his chest, though his eyes are looking up, gazing across the abyss at his grandfather.

For a moment, Josip is startled, for it is as if he is again in Sarajevo in a small apartment filled with darkness, staring at a photograph of his own grandfather. And now, in this way, he sees for the first time his grandfather in the flesh. Their faces are the same, all three: a youth of the West, a man of the mountains of Bosnia, and the one who is the bridge between them.

Images stream inward, albums of his mind filling with new things that once were old. First, the beginning of the slow descent into Split. There, in the west, are the little boats under sail as they have been since the voyage of Odysseus. The turquoise of the Adriatic is so intense that to gaze upon it is to fall headlong into worship. Passing below are the red-tiled roofs of the island town of Trogir; then, more turquoise. To the east, the Dinaric Alps are higher and whiter than ever before, the peaks still sleeping under heavy snow. A stewardess informs him that it has been a very cold winter; the city has suffered twice from frost!

It is spring at sea level, and as he steps outside the terminal into the air of Croatia, he breathes it in, opening wide his arms. The olive trees around the airport are sprouting new leaves, and the breeze is full of the spices of the earth. It is heaven, all this warmth and perfume and light, a light like no other on earth.

A bus takes him toward Stari Grad, the downtown core. There are many new buildings; the city is growing. Nine years have passed since he was last here. That time when he was tempted, when he almost took vengeance and killed the killers, but did not. There are the palm trees, and, oh, there is the Marjan! He bounces in his seat, cranes his neck as if he were nine years old, sitting beside his father when they had just spotted the sea as they descended from the mountains. Was it more than sixty years ago? I will add and subtract later, he smiles to himself. Mental pocket-calculators are for mathematicians. Oh, look at that emerald mountain, and look at the ivory palace, and the steeples shaking as their bells ring and boom in the pristine air. Look at the gulls and the shore birds, and look at all my people!

He carries his luggage from the drop-off point on the waterfront and makes his way to Marmontova Street and into the hotel where he stayed last time. It is a short walk from there to the shore and a minute's walk to the church of St. Francis. After he has checked into his room, he returns to the street and goes directly to the church. Fra Anto is there waiting for him, as always, but his face is now fully restored, and he stands robed in white, with his arms extended and light pouring through the open wounds. *You are home at last, Josip*, say his shining eyes. *Here you will stay.*

"You're here too", the old man replies.

Let's go in.

Now, for the first time in all the years he has known him, the friar does not remain outside. His priestly robes flow behind him, his bare toes with a bandage or two, his face of burnished bronze illumines the shadowy entrance. With some surprise, Josip notices that another person is walking with them—a barefoot twelve-year-old boy dressed in white shirt and trousers. The boy takes his hand.

So, with the friar's hand in one hand and the boy's hand in the other, Josip enters the church. There are other visitors, but their presence does not inhibit him from dropping to his knees and prostrating himself on the marble floor. Fra Anto and the boy do likewise, bending before the Presence in the tabernacle.

Holy, holy, holy is the Lord God almighty!

The old man kisses the dust because the earth was made holy and it is the Lord's. Then he kisses the wounds of Christ, and in this movement he understands at last that he is kissing his own wounds too. He is also kissing this land and this people, from whom he will never again depart. All crucified churches are resurrected churches, some within the boundaries of time and some only in eternity.

Much good begins in us before we learn to know its name, sighs the old man. *Our Father is patient with us, for he loves.*

Rising, he sees that the friar and the boy have gone.

40

It is high summer in Split, very hot. The *mistral* breezes blow in from the northwest from time to time, bringing some relief. Josip loves both hot and cool. It is all good.

His one-room apartment in a crumbling building five blocks from the waterfront is splendid. The water pipes clang, paint peels from the walls, yet the view from the window is superb. It faces away from the sea, unfortunately, so it is not exactly paradise but close to it. The building is on the slopes of the Marjan, surrounded by trees. From his window he can observe red roofs and courtyards filled with potted flowers. He sees mothers hanging laundry, children playing with balls, and contemplative cats. Beyond these are the swaying spears of poplars, the fans of palm trees, and the mighty spread of blacker pines. The Marjan's pathways offer a variety of opportunities for strolling and for observing the pleasant activities of birds, animals, and human lovers. He goes there daily, two or three hours at a time, good exercise. His lungs are not what they used to be, and his legs—well, the legs have from his earliest years threatened to betray him. But that's fine, that's what seventy-two-year-old legs are supposed to do.

His room—oh, this room is like a miracle. Not too expensive. His small janitor's pension and the semiannual royalties from his publishers are enough to cover the rent and to provide his food, to buy a few books and socks, and to leave a little extra for envelopes and stamps for letters to family and friends. He likes to go out to a restaurant once a month—one of the poorer places, not for tourists—and dine on freshly caught squid, rice boiled in its ink, brown trout and carp just fished from the estuary of the Neretva, plus inexhaustible platters of bread and bowls of salad. Dinner is always finished off with a basket of juicy figs. Most days he eats at home, subsisting on bread and olive oil, a bit of dried fish and his coffee. Life without coffee is not life—this is a lie, he knows, but one he can live with.

This room is smaller than his room in New York. It has an alcove with an electric stove and a metal sink for washing dishes. There is a bathroom with a small porcelain sink and toilet, but no tub, no place for fish to come visiting. He bathes once a week by wading into the sea in his swimming trunks, stepping off the very wharf where he was reunited with the Lastavica of the Sea when he was a student. On cooler days, when the aged must guard against chills, he gives himself a sponge bath in the privacy of his room. He worries about becoming eccentric—and "aromatic", as he calls it. A little incontinence, but no real prostate trouble, thank heavens!

The room has books in it, those he brought from America along with the new titles he has purchased here. He hires a man to build him shelves. Excellent shelves, they are, fresh pine boards carefully beveled and notched, built without hurry. For the entire week, as the carpenter works in Josip's room, scattering sawdust and smoking his pipe, Josip keeps him supplied with cups of coffee and snacks and stories. Because old men can be candid about their lives, he tells Josip that he was in Molat concentration camp. He is impressed that Josip survived Goli Otok.

"Few lived to tell of that hell", he shakes his head, chomping reflectively on his pipe stem. "Life is strange. But God has the final word."

Josip takes a slice of dry bread and breaks it in two. He gives one half to the carpenter and keeps the other for himself. The carpenter gazes at the piece for a moment and then meets Josip's gaze, steadily, understanding the gesture. They are both well-fed men, far from hungry at the moment. They eat the bread slowly, without speaking, then resume their tasks.

His books are few in number compared to what he once owned. There are twice as many shelves as he needs at present, but he hopes to fill them as time goes on. Can a dwelling place without books ever truly be a home? He has donated his collection to the new Catholic university in Zagreb, and last month he received a letter of thanks from the director. Caleb had packed them all and sent them to the university in a big container, by sea; the shipment arrived without mishap. Caleb must have stuffed a copy of *The Seraph* into the lot, because the rector, who is fluent in English, says that the translations are very good, not every word exactly what he would have chosen but still expressing the essence of "creative intuition". A person who uses such an expression is someone Josip would like to meet someday, a person with whom he might discuss obscure topics with mutual enthusiasm and occasional thrills of illumination. Nevertheless, he does not want to encourage any public persona of himself: the poet-in-exile-returned-home-at-last!

There have been probes: invitations to give lectures at faculties of literature in Split, Zagreb, and Sarajevo, three or four journalists knocking on his door. All of this he has declined. Let the poems speak for themselves! No need to inflate the persona with public relations that doubtless he would ruin anyway. It is preferable to remain what he is: a retired custodian, a person of no particular interest to others. It is essential to have nothing in order to keep the riches he has been given. Yes, he is rich—he is a man who can distill sight and insight onto bits of salvaged paper; he is a man who can enjoy taking the garbage down to the corner; he can chat with fishermen and carpenters and housewives, never as condescension but as the replenishment of his true self. Every day he can swim in the greatness of the ordinary. This is freedom, and he is very grateful for it. It is all good, just as it is.

A year passes. He attends daily Mass at St. Francis, Sunday Mass in the cathedral of St. Domnius. He never passes its wooden doors without a prayer for his father's soul. It is odd what one remembers, what one forgets. A single look of fear sixty years past is remembered, while a thousand hours of discussion are forgotten; the flicker of an azure wing cuts an incision that remains permanently open, while quantities of more dramatic events recede, taking up their residence deep inside the archives of the mind.

He does not return to Rajska Polja or to Sarajevo, though he knows that a journey to both places would engender a good deal of fruitful reflection and the most poignant feelings. He is not afraid to go. In a sense, it has already been accomplished. The sea is enough for him.

He does indulge in one short bus ride south along the coastal highway. By examining a map of Dalmatia he deciphers the route they must have taken when he was nine years old, the time his father first showed him the waters on which the *Argo* sailed. At the juncture of a road that comes down out of the mountains, the bus stops and lets Josip off by the side of the pavement. Old as he is, he feels weightless, a boy again. Picking his way down the slopes, however, he goes carefully through well-tended olive groves and occasional stands of orange trees. They are bending with ripe fruit now. The single windfall he eats is very sweet.

How he knows where to go is something of a mystery. All but the formations of land and water have changed. Perhaps it is subconscious orientation, aided by the configuration of a plateau immediately below and the island of Brač across the straits. There is no solitary tree growing at the very edge of the mainland, beneath which he might find a man and a boy eating sour oranges. He cannot in this way rediscover himself as himself—rather, the self that was, before the destruction of his childhood.

Arriving at the edge, he peers over and discovers that the compass of memory has not failed him. There below is the beach of white stones, a little to the right a cliff of hard sand, and before it, a flurry of activity in the air. The swallows are building their nests in the holes and feeding their young.

It takes a while to get down to the shore, for the last hundred feet of incline are rough with brush and rocks. He makes it without a tumble. When he stands at last on the beach of round white stones, blinding bright under the sun, he discovers that nothing has changed here. The sea heaves gently, more swell than wave, and the stones chatter where they meet the lip of water. He takes off his shoes and socks and wades in up to his knees. The water is cool, pleasantly so. The rounded shapes beneath the soles of his feet are familiar, stimulating. The sea is breathing, and he breathes with it.

So much space above the ocean! The sense of infinity that opens before him is a feeling that only limitless air above limitless water can give. His heart begins to beat wildly. It is that certain beat one feels only when falling in love. Though this is not first love, it is a return to the first illumination, when he had gasped with wonder over a love that would make such a world, that is present in it and speaks tender words through it.

If he were a little more foolish than he is, he would strip off his clothes down to his undershorts and plunge beneath, forgetting to breathe, trusting that some large hands would pull him up again and drag him to shore. Instead, pressing against the ocean's power with an old man's remnant of strength, he delights in its resistance. It would be worth drowning in it just to have a moment of such play, but it is not necessary. Long ago, he learned that it is possible to penetrate the infinite without force or folly—as spouses do in their acts of love, who, by submitting, learn to give and through their giving find submission.

Now it is time to visit his old friends the *lastavice. Ho-ho, there you are*, he calls to them, laughing, *there you are after all this time!*

Standing below the wall of their apartments, he watches the little heads pop out for an instant, take a look around, then go back in. Birds on the wing swoop down and enter this or that hole, others leave. It is still a very busy place. He imitates their calls, which draws their attention. The patterns of their flight, their arrivals and departures, change for a few moments then return to normal. He leaves the swallows, goes back to the shore, and sits down by the edge of the surf. His knees are under his chin, arms wrapped around his legs, as he gazes out at the horizon. For a time, he closes his eyes and listens to the surf. Perhaps as he rests, a swallow will make its high cheeping sound nearby, floating on a draft, and then it might land on his fingertips.

None of the swallows come near him. That's fine, he tells himself, they must do what they do. How often in a lifetime can a person expect such a visitation? Once only. Any more than that is opulence.

He stays a few more hours and then says good-bye to the beach and the swallows. After loading his pockets with stones the size and shape of doves' eggs, he begins the arduous climb back up the hill. Dusk is settling in as he reaches the highway. There is a lot of high-speed traffic, and the cars have their headlights on. He crosses to the other side and sticks out his thumb. He is beyond the age of threat to others. He is unarmed, he laughs to himself. Within five minutes a car stops, a vehicle crammed with a big family—a father and mother and their several children. To make room, the youngest ones must sit on laps. Josip is given a three-year-old to hold, a little girl sleeping. It's such a warm feeling. He has missed this since Jefferson and Christiana ceased being toddlers. They drive out of their way and take him right to the corner of the promenade and Trumbićeva. They all wave good-bye to him, young and old shouting, "Safe home! Peace!" and the new expression, "*Bog, Bog, Bog!!!*"

He walks up the street to his apartment building, his little hole in a cliff. Inside his home, he unloads the white stones from his pockets and lines them up along the windowsill, falls into bed, and sleeps.

It is autumn again, his seventy-third year of life in this world. It is hard to believe how swiftly his life has passed. So swiftly, so swiftly, and now it is surely nearing its end, though one never knows. There very well could be more surprises. Life itself is the great surprise, and all that is within it is an unpacking of subsidiary wonders. From time to time, he feels a few sharp stabs in the heart—physical only—though nothing to see a doctor about. The tip of the sword has poked at him since his earliest years, ever since he ran from the fields of heaven, that time. Nothing new in this department.

In November, his collected works are published for the first time in Croatia—his five slender books gathered together into a single volume, under a new title: *Homeland*. Meaning the eternal home toward which we all journey. The office of the publishing house is right here in Split. The founders and their staff are a bright and energetic bunch, fervent young Catholics, and very literate—world-class, really. Genuine heroes, they launched their company underground before the fall of Communism and now are flourishing. It does not take long before it seems to him that they are his family. He loves them. He would not dare to tell them this because he feels so unworthy of them.

The assistant minister of culture flies down from Zagreb for the book launching, which is celebrated in a magnificent reception hall at the archbishop's residence. It is quite an event; he did not expect all this! Other national officials are present as well, one or two of them poets in their own right. Also public figures from Dalmatian and municipal governments and numerous writers and musicians, playwrights and literary journalists, all fine men and women. He is again overwhelmed with love and unworthiness. They like to laugh. They are very witty people, and they lack the cynicism he grew so accustomed to in America. Their ironies, if they employ them at all, are purer, closer to gentle satire than to sarcasm.

Elaborate care has been taken to make the event a festival of culture: a soprano from the national opera sings arias, the cathedral choir sings Latin hymns, and another choir sings rousing folk pieces. Throughout the latter performance, Josip feels the awakening of latent dimensions in his soul, songs half-remembered from kitchen feasts in his childhood home, where family and villagers crowded together into the small rooms, cramped, yet wide open to what rises from within the heart and what is poured out from above. As it returns, some of it is joyful, some of it is sad, all of it is good.

He is embarrassed by the attention he is getting. He wishes he had some better clothes to wear, but what a waste of money that would be! Still, clothing is a language of respect, he reminds himself, a world of manners that is the basic level of human charity. He wishes he had thought about that before climbing into his only suit, the one he wears to Sunday Mass. Now it is painfully obvious to him that the jacket no longer closes across his belly. His single necktie is no lavish Croatian *kravate* but a droopy thing that he had purchased at a discount store in the Bronx in 1973. His shoes—well, he won't even think about those shoes! His white shirt is washed, however, and most of its wrinkles are hiding beneath the jacket.

After the banquet, after the speeches by visiting and welcoming dignitaries, after the press conference introducing the book, and after the interviews with numerous television cameras and journalists writing in notebooks (heaven knows what he says to them!), he is ready to go home and have a good nap. He did not make it to daily Mass this morning, Our Lady's Saturday, and whenever that happens he feels a little hunger, a certain loneliness. He really should go home now. And, oh, did he remember to water the sapling growing in a pot on his windowsill? It's a fig tree—rather, it will be a fig tree someday if his mind doesn't go first.

A famous man walks to the front of the room and takes the microphone. He praises Josip and lists his accomplishments. Not expecting this, Josip merely stares at his hands on his lap and sees the jagged white scars on his wrists. He closes his eyes.

Finally, he is asked to say a few words—publicly, to a rather large crowd of people. Oh, dear, oh, no, what shall he say? He shakes himself, breathes deeply, and gets to his feet.

Well, he thinks as he approaches the microphone, *it is enough to be who you are. That is the word you bring into the world.* He need not try to appear rational or erudite. He is neither. Logic is the province of beginners, reflection the sphere best suited for the end of years, though both should be employed by young and old. He will open his mouth and out of it will pop anything that rises from within. Elderly people are forgiven just about everything.

Oh! Oh, look at all those faces looking back at him. So very, very beautiful those faces. The young and the old alike—all beautiful, the lovely and the plain, all beautiful. See their souls, these *lastavice*, so beautiful. They are his own, his countrymen, and above all they are his family.

A hush settles on the crowd. Several experienced and knowledgeable people in the front rows send him smiles of encouragement. Go ahead, Mr. Lasta, their eyes tell him, say whatever you like, you are among friends.

Everything now rising from within, the ocean of wisdom and love that he desires with his whole heart to pour out for them, cannot be formed into a single rivulet of sound. An ocean cannot become a brook; it is the other way around, always. But it seems they are asking him to try. He knows there is no need to speak of poetry or politics, nor of history's woes and victories. That is not his task. Yet he longs to speak words that have taken a lifetime to coalesce, to become distinct and ripe, so that they may shimmer at last under the open sky and drop into outstretched hands, so that they may be eaten and transformed into youth and hope. What should these words be, then? What is most needed at this moment, at this place in time? He is not sure. He takes a breath and simply speaks.

"You are generous and good, and I thank you", he says, in a trembling voice. "These honors that you give to me are not for me alone. They are for those who, dying young, now sleep in the earth with their unspoken poems, waiting for the Last Day."

For a few weeks afterward, he must deal with the several avenues that now open up for him in the academies, the media, and elsewhere, the offers of friendship, dialogues, and correspondence. Though these would be stimulating and in their own way consoling, he knows they are not for him. He would too readily become attached to all that, scatter his energies, and lose the central gift, which is based in solitude. So, he declines all invitations.

The excitement of last month has been unsettling. He has written nothing since then. Well, not exactly nothing. A few lines about the fig, incorporating his mental images of fruit in the supermarket up on Frankopanska Street with the scriptural baskets of good figs and bad figs in the book of Jeremiah. It still remains undeveloped and unresolved, and in poor meter as well. He will work on it when things return to normal.

An official from the ministry of culture is in town, one of the poets he met at the book launching. He pays a surprise visit to the apartment (Josip has no telephone) and takes him out to lunch at the restaurant in the Hotel President, the very room where he confronted Zmija and Zohar. The place is crowded today, but the waiter finds them a good table in a quiet corner.

Over their meal, they discuss poetry and politics and the essayists and thinkers whose work they both know. Finally, the poet sits back and smiles. As he removes something from his briefcase, Josip irrationally wonders if the man will drop a limestone slab on the table.

In fact, it is a book.

"It seems there is more than one published Josip Lasta in this world", he says in a playful tone. "I should have given you this the last time we met, but I will admit I was reluctant at the time to part with it."

He slides the book across the table. It is a copy of *Equations Inferential of a Meta-universe*, by Dr. Josip Lasta. The dust jacket is missing, the cloth cover is stained, and the inside pages are yellow with age and smelling of mold. Josip fans the pages, letting equations flush out from between the leaves and fly away.

He says nothing, merely looks at it.

"I suppose a poet would have no interest in mathematics", says the poet from Zagreb. "But it *is* a coincidence—the names—so I thought you might like to have it."

Josip swallows hard and nods, unable to look the other in the face.

"Where did you find this?" he whispers.

"Oh, that's a long story, too long for a sunny day. Besides, I know little or nothing about the other Josip Lasta."

"I am interested, if you know anything about him, please."

"I was in prison when I was younger. The UDBA arrested me in the late sixties, along with other young writers in an underground circle we had formed. A show trial was scheduled, but before it took place the guards beat me too hard and broke my spine. Three vertebrae cracked, the disks were ruined. They didn't want to take me into People's Court in a wheelchair, which would have been bad publicity for them. So, I was sent to a prison hospital for surgery while we were awaiting trial. The surgeon fused the vertebrae, and I spent a few months recovering in his ward. He would come by every day to check on me. We would chat a little. Not easy to talk openly, of course, because we were both prisoners."

"The doctor was a prisoner?"

"Yes, a man named Šime. He told me his full name, but I'm sorry to say I forgot it. I was in pretty bad pain at the time, and a lot of things just didn't stick in my memory. But I never forgot that he was Šime. He was an extraordinary fellow, not just a scientist but a real thinker. A philosopher of sorts, I would guess. In any event, whenever we could snatch a few moments without the big ears listening, we would talk. He was a fervent Catholic, and it was he who brought me to the Faith. I should say, he began the process. I converted in another prison, after my trial. There were many priests and seminarians behind bars in those days."

"Were you on Goli Otok?"

"Goli Otok? No, thank heavens! I was in Sremska Mitrovica in Vojvodina for years. I was released after Tito's death." He pauses, then asks curiously. "So, you heard about the naked island even over there in America?"

Josip nods.

"That's news. I thought the regime covered their tracks."

"Šime gave you this book?"

"No, he told me about a friend of his, a doctor in Split to whom he had entrusted a few of his most precious belongings. When we parted, he said he would never be released, that he suffered from degenerative heart problems and he thought he probably had only a few months to live. He wanted me to have his belongings, few as they were. It seemed to me at the time that this was very strange because I was on my way to my trial and certainly to a cell for a long, long time. What made him choose me, I will never know."

"Did you tell him about your underground literature group?"

786

"Yes, I must have."

"That is why he chose you."

The poet ponders this. "Maybe."

"Did he tell you anything about himself?"

"Yes, though the years have erased a good deal of what we spoke about. I recall that he said he had been betrayed by his brother, a member of the Party. But, before his arrest, Šime sent his wife away to Austria. He had done so on a feeling the day before the UDBA came. He had tried to contact his daughter and her husband all that day, but they were away, he didn't know where. In desperation he put a note under their door, begging them to contact him the moment they got home. He never learned what happened to them, but constantly prayed that somehow they had escaped."

Josip looks down at the book, holding it tightly in his hands.

"About fifteen years later I found myself in Split and remembered Šime's last words. I tracked down the man he told me to find. All I knew was that he had been head of the medical faculty at a university. That was quite a search, I can tell you. By then, he had retired from practice and was living on the coast south of the city. When I found him, he was very glad to hear news about Šime and in the end agreed to give me his belongings. It wasn't much, just a few books, and this was among them. Apparently the author was Šime's son-in-law. I hope I haven't bored you. Everyone has stories, and many of them are more tragic than this one."

"May I tell you a story?" whispers Josip.

His only real excursion that autumn is a drive around the bay north of the city. He hires a driver to take him. At a spot where a path comes down through steep forested slopes beneath a rocky crag, the car stops and lets Josip out. The driver will return in six hours to pick him up by the side of the road. On winding footpaths he climbs to the base of the cliff, where there is a little stone chapel, stuccoed on the outside and painted creamy yellow. Its walls are covered with prayer requests that people have scratched or penned onto the plaster in numerous languages. The pleas are interesting, but he draws back from reading more than one or two. These are private conversations between souls and God.

He goes higher. His breathing is labored, and his heart is palpitating a bit too much perhaps, but he feels an exhilaration that is irresistible. Where the trail ends, rough stone steps climb a few more feet to a crack in the face of the cliff. A locked iron door covers it. Josip sits down on a stone, puts his forehead to the door, and then kisses it. It is said that this is the cave where St. Jerome lived before he went to the Holy Land and tamed a lion and translated the sacred Scriptures into the common tongue for all to read throughout the Roman world.

O God, have mercy on me, I am a Dalmatian, the saint had cried, beating his chest with a rock, ashamed of his short temper, for which he was as much renowned as he was for his lion.

"O Lord, have mercy upon me," Josip murmurs, "I am a—"

For once his descriptive powers fail him. What is he, then? A poet? As the Lastavica of the Sea told him long ago, a man is what he *is*, not what he *does*. Yet a poet is what he is, poetry is never what he does. Josip sighs—this kind of self-examination can be quite confusing. Is self-identification ever trustworthy? It is better not to dwell on it overmuch. But is he an ex-Herzegovinian, an ex-Isle of Goli Otokian, an ex–American, an exile from exile? No matter, God knows what he is. Have mercy on me, a sinner. Have mercy on me, a Lasta and a *lastavica*.

On the wooden table by the window in his room, he keeps three straw baskets. One is for figs. He is perhaps too fond of them, but he cannot help himself. In another he keeps pieces of broken bread—for birds mostly but also as a token of his calling. In a third, he keeps letters. Today there are several waiting to be posted:

Dear Winston,
Thank you for your most recent letter and the splendid photographs of Miriam and Christiana and Thomas. Give my kisses to each of them.

One photo of your good self struck me as indicative of significant changes in your life. It displayed "a trans-cultural event of epic proportions". Is that really you, grinning, with a hunting rifle in your hands, standing among a cohort of hunters? Truly, Winston, this worries me, since it appears that you are telling me something with the image. Here in Croatia the image of a gun functions in an entirely different way from in America's woodlands. Are you hunting deer? And what will you do if you find yourself aiming your rifle at a white stag with a crucifix in his antlers? Will you be surprised if he speaks to you?

I asked myself, is my dear friend becoming assimilated? What is it I see with my own eyes, a red cap, a fluorescent orange vest, a rifle with what looks like a telescope attached to it? Will he attempt to shoot Andromeda or Pegasus? What has become of his real telescope, the one through which he watches the stars and ponders infinity? Has he become a golfer? Does he host neighborhood barbecues? This is not an accusation. I merely inquire.

Of course, I am teasing you. I laugh and laugh and laugh because I see the joke you send me in this picture. You are in disguise. You are in cultural camouflage. You will offer poisoned tea (which is not really poisoned) to your fellows in the hunting party and thus shake their perceptions a little, an avocation you have often pursued with me and with others. You would not hurt the tiniest sparrow—not because you are a recidivist Hindu, but because you are so sensitive to death entering the world, as is your beloved bride, and thus you do not wish to reduce the number of living symbols in our existential spectrum.

Do not repeat the above to your hearty companions. My words would not fail to sound like something very different from what they are. I am not against guns. The people of my birthplace might have survived if they had had enough guns to defend themselves. If your children were hungry, you would shoot the great white stag without a moment's hesitation, and you would be entirely correct to do so. And so would I shoot it, if I were starving. I have rediscovered my taste for mutton and prosciutto, though rarely can I afford it.

What am I saying to you? Perhaps it is only this: man does not look deeply at the world. He lives by habit and pleasure and impulse. He does not read the poetry in things. And so I say, if he must kill a creature, that is his right, but he should see its beauty before taking its life and understand its presence as language. Moreover, he must understand that blindness to the miraculousness of existence makes it easier for him to pull a trigger and end a human life. Do I exaggerate? We both know the 170 million answers to this.

Salutations to you, singular friend,

Josip

My dear Christiana,

How delighted I was to receive your letter so full of good news about your studies. I understand how torn you feel at this time of your life, for youth is a stage when we leave childhood behind and are not yet fully adults. You have wings but have not yet flown!

What you tell me about your two desires does not in the least disturb me. In truth, they both make me more happy than you can imagine. You wish to raise horses, you say! And you wish to try your vocation as a religious sister. Is it beyond the realm of possibility that somewhere in the world there may be a convent that has a stable full of horses? This is farfetched, I admit.

I have placed the drawing you made of the white horse on the wall of my room. I look at it frequently. When I was young, I once rode a white horse. That was the only time I have ridden on a horse. Will you believe me when I say that he spoke to me and made me a promise? It is true. I will tell you about that another day.

For now, my goddaughter, I enclose this simple and rather amateurish poem, and I hope you like the little gift I send with it. This carving of a white horse was made by an elderly woman who sells such marvels in the market only a few blocks away from my home here in Split. She lives in a stone hut on an island, and she comes to the city by boat. Her name is Kristijana—the same as yours, in Croatian. That is a nice coincidence, isn't it? Life is strange. You learn something new every day.

My love and prayers for you, always.

—your Josip

WHITE HORSE

Beauteous is the filly and full of fire,
who dances on the fields of green and plunges
underneath the bower, heedless of the snare or hour.
Before the wind she flies, tossing head and heel,
prancing high and headlong free the pulsing choreography
equestrian jig and reel.

Her master sees the fire and loving well that light,
He knows how swift extinguishes the blaze of youthful life,
for leaping where the wind would take, as impulsed as a
        storm,
she flings her future here and there,
heedless that a filly will be
more beauteous when a mare.

The bit is cold and hard in mouth, she cries and clamps the
        steel;
it seems the end of all the dance, no more than this can feel,
the anger-embers in the heart ignite to fury race,
but He who knows her better still, commands a measured
        pace.
He sees ahead the leap that breaks and ends the ardent zeal,
He will not let her bound the fence that boundaries her reel.

Yearling on the fields of light, in seer and sacred green,
races cross the heaving land in bridle strap a queen.
Over ditch and hedgerow now, she leaps without a fault
the water-race and brindle bush and flamed foxy path,
the thorny brake and stony wall and heedless human wrath.
The steeplechase is long and far and tumbles riders down,
bit-broke now, the yearling-mare runs onward to her crown.

Dear Caleb,

Thank you so much for sending me your latest book. It is ever encouraging for me to see a man of your generation resisting the "zeitgeist literary Nazis", as you once called them. And it seems that you have discovered a parallel truth: zeitgeist literary Communists are an alternative danger, as are the proponents of any other collectivist ideas that present themselves to the mind as solutions to "the problem of man". I include in this category the new globalist's models of what is now called universal "governance". As all ideologues do, they offer us superficial either/or choices. Supposedly, one must choose between war and world government. They do not understand that globalism will not change the fundamental human condition. Globalism is ultra-nationalism expanded to a planetary scale, without the safety measures of cultural and religious diversity. Believe me, world-shapers (rather, world-reshapers) are long familiar to those of us who have lived through political experiments. Claiming my rights, I dare to remind you that beneath their constructs, and even beneath their supposed humanitarianism, you will always find a killer. Presumption and arrogance over mankind brings forth, in time, the fruit of death.

Oh, I am in a melancholic mood today. But do not be hurt by this, my son. Your new poems lifted my heart greatly. I wish you were here so that we could enjoy a rigorous and satisfying argument.

Love, Josip

Dear Slavica,

You asked about the situation here in our homeland. Though the war ended ten years ago, I find myself among a devastated, heroic people. I have met many vital, ingenious individuals striving to build a healthy society—primarily through the restoration and development of culture. However, there is at the same time among our people widespread discouragement. A quarter of a million are missing from my land of birth, Bosnia-Herzegovina, murdered by Serbs. As many have been displaced through what our enemy calls "ethnic cleansing". In occupied Croatia, twenty-five thousand noncombatants were killed. It is rare to meet a Croat and not talk with him about the war—everyone has lost someone.

Anyone who denies his negative feelings toward our historical enemy is not being honest with himself. Aversion, mistrust, and resentment are all there in the heart, and they do not disappear at will. Our emotions and our spiritual wounds cannot be erased simply from our memories—it is not humanly possible—though we can train ourselves not to act on these emotions. Over and over again, we hear the word "forgiveness". But how do you forgive someone who does not express remorse and who, moreover, claims to have been the victim in a war that he planned and instigated? In many hearts there is an unspoken cry: When will the justice of God come?

These and other countless frustrations have led to suicides—more than fifteen hundred veterans have taken their own lives. Here is the cross upon which so many now suffer. Despair or faith—you either go insane, or you turn to Christ for answers and consolation. Then you begin to pray harder, and you also try to pray for the enemy, because you know that God loves him and that it is His holy will that he be saved through your prayers. What does loving one's enemy mean? If our enemy does not respond to divine mercy and to our own crippled attempts at mercy, if he does not repent, what is to become of him?

The Serbian people have a saying: "He who avenges himself is sanctified." The Croatian people say: "He who does not seek vengeance is sanctified." In the middle of the fighting, in the nineties, our late Cardinal Kuharić spoke these simple but unforgettable words: "If someone has set fire to your house, do not set fire to his." Indeed, the Serbs destroyed hundreds of Catholic churches in the regions they occupied. For our part, we destroyed not a single Serbian Orthodox church on our lands or elsewhere. In our churches, we hear the repeated exhortation to forgive—to forgive everything. Now I understand that the Holy Spirit is calling us to be Christ among the nations. A sign of contradiction, as we have been for untold generations.

As we forgive we must not forget, lest history repeat itself. In a spiritual climate such as this one, which is so demanding psychologically and spiritually, and in a social climate that reeks of injustice and corruption, the nation withdraws into the so-called "Croatian silence", a phenomenon almost continually present in our history because oppression has been continual. It refers primarily to the passivity of leaders and their unwillingness (due to fear or resignation?) to verbalize the thoughts and best desires of the majority. Even so, Slavica, I heard a holy woman once say that when Croatia is silent she is steeped in prayer. I am now convinced that this is true. It is not the prayer of the entire people, but of a sufficient number of genuine and discerning faithful who are the spiritual backbone of the country. As always, it is the hidden sufferers who preserve us.

Isn't it a basic truth that we are brought to prayer only by passing through suffering? In this respect, the war was a blessing because it taught this generation how to pray, and it taught us the power of prayer. We learned that it was prayer that preserved us against impossible odds and only prayer that brought us independence. Dare I write these words—O God, how dare I write them?—yet I cannot be silent. The war was a catastrophe, but in Christ the worst catastrophe can be transformed into a blessing. The war renewed awareness of our centuries-old Christian identity and prepared us to be steadfast in these times which, with every passing day, are resembling more and more the end times. Our horrible war taught us "in the flesh" about the Great War that will last until the end of time.

Despite our heroes, the confusion and ideological invasion continues. Moral erosion pours in from the wealthy materialist nations, and we gasp and swim to keep our heads above the waves, even as many cooperate with it—human nature is the same everywhere. Have we cast off Moscow and Belgrade only to succumb to London, Paris, and Manhattan? We need not succumb, need not become the clone creatures of a globalist social revolution. We are blessed with something unique in our character, but I think we are too close to ourselves—inside of ourselves—to recognize it. While it is true that we must beware the danger of mythologizing our character (the mystification of self-love), there is another danger. That is to fall back into the spirit of resignation, which is thinly disguised despair, allowing our vital energies to be sapped or to lie dormant.

Why do so many of our people emigrate? Are we fleeing our memories, trying to sever the connection to our most devastating wounds? Are we searching for an earthly paradise, fleeing the challenges of the future, the responsibility that is asked of any human being in this world who hopes to build a family or a nation? Will we retain our colorful decorations and our music and our language in those distant lands of plenty and forget what is in the heart of the soul? And for those who remain here, what will they inherit? Will the young of this generation be able to know themselves?

Men speak of peace, but they do not know what they mean by it. Is it absence of conflict? Is it passivity and compromise? Is it the peace of the grave, or is it the peace of an active and wise love that doesn't count the cost?

Forgive me this disordered letter, I am presently a jumble of questions. I am a man who possesses only fragments, a beggar who wanders into a feast of materialism, offering to the guests a basket of broken bread.

Christ's holy peace be with you,

Josip

My beloved daughter,

I realize that this is the fifth letter I have written to you this month, which all too easily could place a burden of reciprocity upon you. Please do not apologize one more time for not replying letter for letter. (As I write this, I am sending you a smile across this wide ocean.) I know how busy your life is. We need never count the quantity of exchange as the measure of its quality.

I hope that in telling these stories of the life that your mother and I spent together, from the moment we first saw each other until the night of our parting, they will give to your mind (and your heart) a form for what is, in fact, already a part of you. Perhaps they will become nearly visual if I tell them well; perhaps they will become like a happy memory for you.

You must surely know that it is one of the greatest griefs of my life that I was not there for your birth, that I could not help you learn to walk and speak and love and laugh. To see you grow into a fine young lady and then into a wonderful woman. Yet it seems to me now that even such terrible absences can become a blessing if we do not lose heart, if we keep swimming in the many waters of God's grace, if we give him time, if we permit a little space for his mercy.

Now we can fill in small portions of the past for each other, though they are not in essence mere pieces of a puzzle; they are not a problem that must be solved. Are they not more like a work of art, which is always mysterious, always pointing to and revealing something beyond itself?

For most of my life, I have been a very quiet person—nearly wordless except on paper—and that too has not been great in volume. As I become older (and older and older), it seems to me that a messenger is in his words, if the messenger is truly himself. His life is his primary word, and his spoken words bear his life. He learns to be this when he has discovered that a man can give to others only what he truly is.

(Oh, now I am speaking too much, my words like a frozen mountain stream unleashed by the spring sun, tumbling down and spreading too thinly as it spills over its banks.)

Here is a prayer/counsel that I wrote for my own eyes—no other eyes have seen it but yours. I try to live by this instruction to myself:

> Seek nothing for yourself.
> Stand ready to serve
> in quietness,
> demanding nothing,
> expecting nothing,
> sacrificing and praying without anyone knowing.
> Silence
> Silence
> Silence

This silence before God and man is the *presence* of being. Such silence speaks! Then when one's spoken words flow, they come from the true heart of one's unique identity. An identity that only the Father in Heaven knows, for it is hidden even from our own eyes.

Here is an old, anonymous Latin poem I love so much:

> *Pauper sum ego.*
> *Nihil habeo.*
> *Cor meum dabo.*
> (I am a poor man.
> Nothing do I have.
> I will give you my heart.)

I give you my heart, my Marija,

Your Tata

He spends Christmas Eve with his publisher's family, in a newly built house in a hillside suburb, above a villa where Tito spent his vacations—one of several villas that socialism-with-a-human-face stole from their former owners. The publisher's bungalow is no villa. It is rather small but big on windows, light from all sides. Below, the tips of cypress trees sway in the wind, and beyond is the open vista of the Adriatic. After supper, Josip sits in an armchair looking at the scene and falls asleep while small children crawl all over him. Later, his publisher drives him back to his apartment—the family is off to Midnight Mass, Josip to his bed. They wish each other a blessed Christmas.

"*Bog*, Josip!"

"*Bog*, my friend!"

Alone in his room, Josip sits down at his desk and tries to write a poem about the day. He calls it "Christmas after a Season of Fury" but gets no farther than the title and a few phrases before he falls asleep. In the morning he cannot recapture the inspiration.

At the morning Christmas Mass, which is celebrated by the archbishop, Josip kneels near the tomb of St. Domnius, his forehead on his arms, arms on the chair-back in front of him. He is praying his thanksgiving after receiving Communion. He feels the peace, as he does most days. Yet he is also missing his family in New York, Marija and Ryan, Caleb and Jefferson, and his other family, gone these many years. In a word, he is lonely. Not unpeaceful, but still—lonely. He does not mind, for it is a familiar feeling. He unites it to the loneliness of Christ. There are no thoughts or images in his mind.

Then, without warning, an image comes. He sees it in his imagination, yet it is as if it has not come from his imagination and is almost three dimensional. He is within what he sees. He is sitting at the feet of Christ, who is seated on the grassy slope of a pasture above Rajska Polja. Josip is about eight years old. He knows that the Savior of the world is but a meter away, but he cannot look up at his face. He is ashamed of his dirty clothing and his sins, the blood he has swallowed in his life and the blood on his hands. He cannot lift his face, which is pressed into his knees, arms wrapped tightly around his own legs.

Josip, says a deep voice, as warm and vast as the sea.

He knows whose voice this is, but he still cannot look up.

Josip.

He is unworthy, he cannot!

Josip.

The third utterance of his name enables him to look up. He is not yet able to meet the eyes of the Savior of the world, yet he can glance hesitantly at the large hands opened before him and look right into the holes in the palms.

Put your hands into mine, says the voice.

He obeys, but shame and grief and loneliness mingle into one sense, a conviction that this is not the way he should have been. For here again after all this time is the blood he has struck from the faces of others.

Waves of love come to him from the hands of Christ, even as the boy realizes that his own hands are pressing the wounds.

Does it hurt you? Josip asks.

Yes, it hurts me, Christ gently replies. There is no reproach in the words, only an assurance that he desires to bear this for love's sake.

A bell in the tower rings, the Mass has ended, and the people around him are leaving. Josip blinks open his eyes and stands. He returns to his apartment in a state of wonder not unmixed with puzzlement.

During none of the daily Masses at St. Francis church is this extraordinary experience repeated. Yet at the following Sunday Mass in the cathedral, it happens again. Everything about it is the same as the first, except that after they hold hands, Christ asks him to stand up and walk with him. Josip stands, and they stroll slowly hand in hand through a forest meadow toward a distant snow-capped mountain. Josip still cannot look at Christ's face.

The tower bell is ringing; the Mass has ended. Josip rises and goes home.

He wonders if he is producing this experience in his overactive imagination, if it has come from his own creative powers. Perhaps it is a grace of his union with the Eucharistic Jesus combined with those human powers. He does not know. He cannot understand it, really. But the next Sunday it happens again. Now Josip is strolling once more with Christ. Christ is a grown man, Josip is still a small boy. For most of his life he has tried to walk with Christ, though never has it taken a form in his mind—certainly not a form like this. Today as they walk together, Christ asks him—he does not command—asks him to look up and see his face, and to do so while holding the large hand in his own, even though Josip's fingers are hurting the wound. He looks up and sees the face of God, the warm and strong face, gazing at him. Christ's expression is serious, gentle, and pleased that Josip has trusted in his love, trusted enough to believe that God is taking all his sins into his own hands and heart, and has forgiven him.

The bell rings; the Mass has ended.

Throughout these weeks, a convergence of odd things happen in the realm of the exterior—a veritable traffic jam of troubles. He trips down the stairs of the apartment building and breaks his right index finger, which must be set in a cast and continues to cause him some pain. He cannot sleep well because of it. Nor can he write. A chunk of plaster falls from the ceiling and smashes onto his bed, which he had vacated only a moment before. A man he passes on the street spits on him for no apparent reason. Then a rock band from America arrives and practices its raucous music for three days in the rented apartment on the floor above, and their drunken parties continue until dawn. They perform to a crowd on the promenade and depart, leaving a foul taste in the air.

Worst of all, an unsigned editorial appears in a daily newspaper, still run by former Communists, that purports to have unearthed the poet Josip Lasta's secret past. He was raised by an uncle who was a Chetnik. Lasta, too, was a Chetnik and is still in favor of Greater Serbia. To correct the lies would demand an exposition of the truth that, in some ways, is more horrifying. His uncle was not a Chetnik but, rather, a Communist Partisan who fought side by side with Chetniks and killed countless men, women, and children. His uncle may even have killed Josip's parents along with other beloveds in his home village. How to say all that! It would sound insane! Not to mention the fact that it probably would confuse things even more. He writes a reply to the paper, stating simply that the accusation is untrue. He was raised by a Communist aunt after the death of his parents, who were killed by a Partisan unit that had Chetniks and Communists in it. His parents were devout Catholics, not political. His reply is never published.

The following Sunday, he hastens to Mass with expectation, hoping that there will be another meeting. He knows that every Mass in the world is an encounter with Christ, but he is eager for this new revelation. And after Communion it happens again. Josip greets him with a smile this time, takes the offered hand and looks down with some worry that he is hurting it, then looks up again. Christ smiles, reassuring him, and they resume their walk. They stop in a field beneath a sun brighter than any Josip has ever seen before, yet it does not hurt his eyes. It is a light that the eyes cannot register, and it is coming from the Lord's face.

Christ smiles again. Josip takes his large hand in both of his own, and looks up into the face as once little Saša gazed adoringly into the face of Fra Anto. Josip makes a skip, hesitant at first, then jumps up and down. The Lord lifts his arm, and Josip's arm raises with it, his feet performing a dance, twirling in a circle and growing in confidence as he abandons himself to laughter and delight—it is good, it is all good, the joy that fills him now. And so, he dances before the Lord as they walk onward toward the mountain.

The bell rings; the Mass has ended.

That week an article appears in a scurrilous Zagreb paper accusing Josip Lasta, the *cause célèbre* of Croatian letters, of spying for Serbia during the Homeland War. Casual acquaintances refer to it in passing, assure Josip that they do not believe it, yet their faces reveal uncertainty—such is the power of accusations. His parish priest tells him about it too but does not show him the paper itself. Flustered, Josip denies everything. The priest assures him there is no need to defend himself, tells him to relax, this sort of thing is to be expected. He knows him well, knows his past and his soul.

As they drink coffee together in a bistro not far from the waterfront, Josip asks him in a general sort of way, a theoretical way, about spiritual blessings and consolations. A certain person whom he knows has begun to experience such blessings even at a late age in life.

"What are these blessings, precisely?" asks the priest.

"Images in the mind after Communion, very strong, almost three dimensional. With very consoling feelings. Time goes away for a while and he is *inside* what he sees. He has dialogues with the Lord."

"Audible?"

"Not with the ears. Heard in the interior but coming from an exterior source."

"Is your friend feeling concerned about it?"

"A little. He wonders if it's just his imagination getting carried away. He's a bit worried it might be self-deception, or worse, diabolic deception."

The priest has a doctorate in theology from a university in Rome, and he is also spiritual. He ponders and replies, "Well, such phenomena must be weighed carefully because spiritual pride is always a danger in human nature, pride of any kind, really."

"Why, then, does God permit it to happen?"

"You have to remember, Josip, that consolations are a great gift. Many people have them. Some in our parish do, and I think if we inquired we would find that it happens in every parish."

"There must be many holy people in St. Francis parish, then."

"There are many striving for holiness. Isn't that the best any of us achieve, this striving? Consolations are not a reward for piety. They are not in proportion to one's personal sanctity. They are given for a purpose."

"What purpose?"

"It varies from person to person. I think they are given in order to encourage someone, to help him persist in a mission for which he might not otherwise have the strength."

"Does everyone have them?"

"Not everyone receives consolations. Many saints didn't; many saints did. So, you see, it's related to the mystery that God is working in each particular soul. There are known principles involved in discernment, but it's not a science."

"We're not mechanisms", Josip murmurs, as if addressing himself.

"That's right, we're God's children, even God's lovers."

"I will remind my friend not to be worried about it."

"Remind your friend that if he's also experiencing an increase of trials, especially humiliations, this is a good sign. Even better if he bears them without complaint or anger."

The next Sunday the meeting with Christ is repeated. After the dance, they come to the brow of a hill and look out over a rolling plain. Then a light descends from the sky unlike any light ever seen by man, but with something solid within it. Josip cannot make out what it is. This image lasts no longer than a moment, and there is an incompleteness to it.

The bell rings; the Mass has ended.

The trees are unfurling new leaves now that the warm season is returning. To honor it Josip scavenges a windfall orange in a park. It is a winter orange, the kind that people and birds are not much interested in.

Sour? he wonders. He peels and eats it.

"Sweet", he says, swallowing the last bite with a grin.

The following Sunday, Josip kneels after Communion and puts his forehead onto his arms and closes his eyes. Dare he hope that these meetings will continue? Indeed, the Lord does come. *He is here, he is here, he is here!* Jesus greets him with the look of love, his hand reaching toward him.

Josip reaches too. Then, he stops and jerks his hand back. He sees that it is old again, gnarled with blue veins, covered with brown spots. He sees that his body is stooped with age, sore of heart and fatigued in mind. He is mostly bald, the fringes of hair at his temples are white, and his skull is covered in scars. His face sags, and his eyes are watery and exhausted. Yes, exactly as he is now.

Jesus takes his hand. He wants Josip to walk with him as usual.

"But I am no longer a child", he protests.

The smile of the Savior tells him that this is no impediment.

As is now their practice, they walk slowly hand in hand toward the brow of the hill, passing through the forest and the meadows. The Lord stops, turns to Josip, and says, *Come, let us run.* With these words, Christ becomes a child in a white robe, girded with a golden belt, his arms open wide. He is radiating light and joy and a love so great no human heart can contain it.

Come, he says again and takes Josip's hand. The Child's little hand is pierced through from side to side. Stricken with grief, the old man drops it and falls to his knees. He cannot touch such a wound! And he is too old to run; please do not ask this of him!

The Child runs ahead, gazing back, encouraging Josip to follow. The old man gets up and stumbles forward with aching limbs, sore lungs, and swords poking at his heart. There, in the distance, the Child is waiting for him on the brow of the hill.

Josip falls to the ground and can't go on. No, no, he's too old, too tired!

The Child returns to him and takes his hand, lifting him to his feet.

Come, he says once more.

So, Josip continues to stumble onward, hand in hand with the Child. As he goes, he becomes steadily lighter. Now his legs are moving, and he is running, and as he runs he grows younger and younger and younger until he is a child again. When he arrives at the hilltop, the other boy turns to look out at the valley beyond. He lifts an arm, pointing to where Josip must look.

A city has filled the valley. It is the celestial city, given from above. Beyond the valley it spreads in all directions, even onto the surface of the sea and inland over the hills and forests, rising higher and higher above all the mountains. The city is gold. The city is light. And it is full of happy people.

It will come down to earth, Josip, and here you will live with me.

41

There are no more such meetings after that. He longs to see the Child again. He tries to make it happen in his imagination, but he cannot, and that is evidence that the meetings have not originated in himself but were given. So, life resumes, as it must. He returns to ordinary time. His usual habits of prayer and sacraments continue as before, and in them he experiences less dramatic consolations and desolations.

As spring becomes summer and passes into autumn, the consolations decline and then cease altogether. In their place, a simple quietness grows. He no longer writes down the glimmers of illumination extracted from the glory that is continuously manifested in the world. What is a poem if not a substitute for its source? He reads Scripture for hours each day, as if hearing it for the first time. These words are not pieces of a large thought-machine, nor components in a coded manual, they are—well, what are they? Like nothing else on earth. They are surely alive, and they are also a summit upon which he stands and looks into time, awaiting the arrival of the celestial city.

He prays for the souls who have hurt him. He remembers them all, one by one, and there is no longer any pain in this. He prays also for the souls he has hurt—hurt mostly through indifference and neglect.

His habits have simplified, and he has begun to fast more often, bread and water only on Fridays, never any meat. A little fish. A little less coffee. There are other forms of penance, humiliations being the best, because he does not like those at all. Occasionally, he goes on parish pilgrimages to various shrines. Within the city there is one he can go to on foot, near Solin. He can walk there and back in a day with lots of time to pray. There are other local places, too, not the miraculous ones that are farther afield. He knows that they are all miraculous, both the near and the far.

A postcard comes from Ryan, a photo of the towers of the World Trade Center, missing these past few years. Subtraction—absence as sign.

> Dear Djedica Joseph,
> Mom gave me a dictionary. I won't see you this year. I won the scholarship to Oxford. Bicycle from UK to Split summer after next. Can I stay with you? Hardly know you. Let's fix that soon.
>   Love,
>
>   Ryan (unuk)

Can you stay with me, beloved stranger, my grandson? Yes, you can—yes, you may. Come soon, stay a lifetime if you wish.

A letter from Marija:

> My Tata,
> I keep and treasure all these letters we have been exchanging, the mysteries of the past solved one by one. Of course, I agree with you when you write that nothing is solved, that our lives are not picture puzzles that must be completed in order to be understood. I think your poems complete it in a better way— resolve rather than solve. One may solve a broken car by consulting a manual. One does not solve human lives. Need I tell you!
>   Since you left, I have been slowly going through Mama's papers. Last night I came upon a silver box that she kept in the bureau drawer in her bedroom—I know this drawer to be the place where she kept the most treasured things of her life. Her Bible and rosaries, a photograph album of her children's momentous events. Dad's letters to her and her mother's wedding ring. Of her years in Croatia, as you know, there remain only

the swallow and the white stone. In the box, I discovered something more from those days. And it is these that I send you. A ship load of mementos could not equal them.

I hope to visit you before too much more time elapses. My company demands all my focus because we are on the verge of tremendous growth. I will write about that another day.

I love you, my Tata.

Marija

Inside the envelope are two old letters. The paper is yellow and brittle, the folds torn by opening and reopening over half a century.

The first in his own handwriting:

. . . I have seen you with my own eyes, though this does not necessarily mean that you exist in any realm accessible to me. Are you real? Did you see me that evening as I saw you?

I do not wish to compromise the purpose of the cultural group, to use it merely as an excuse to enter the palace where you live. Yes, your father's house is now a palace. To do so would be dishonest of me, at the least a mixed motive. For you I must have only the purest motives, even though it may cost everything, indeed the consequence of never again seeing you in this world.

You are here (whether in this world or not).

I am here.

I will say no more.

The second is Ariadne's:

. . . Will it be that I shall read this to myself when I am a very old woman? And will I smile over that moment long ago, when I met a young man who was all that my heart ever desired, to whom I desired to give my whole being? And will I feel no more than a mild regret that he was here for a moment only, and then he passed on and disappeared out of my life? Or will it be that he becomes my life? If you read this at some point in the future, if you read it when you are young or when you are old, or read it unbeknownst to me, or never read it, Josip, you will not fade from the sanctuary of my soul, neither in this world nor in the next.

How much time does he have left? Is he seventy-three or seventy-four, or older? He cannot remember. Well, no matter. Years, years, what are years? Circlings of the sun, an arbitrary measurement. With God, a thousand years are as a day, and a day is as a thousand years, and if the days remaining to him be many or few, does he really need to know? To know is not his task. Everything gets simpler and simpler as he grows younger and younger. You learn something new every day. You discover that you never really knew what you thought you knew. You cease running from what is behind and race toward what is coming.

Mass, Rosary, prayers to St. Josip, intercession for his beloveds, intercession for his enemies, then more penance for those with the most hardened hearts, a category in which he places himself. He knows how much he has been given— throughout his life he has been given priceless, immeasurable treasures, even during his season of unbelief—yet how little the good he has done with it, how great his neglect of others. He does not understand everything about this, the guilt and the innocence. He leaves all that to the Child and offers what he can during his remaining time.

The essentials are so easily forgotten, he reminds himself. Too readily do we allow ourselves to become machines, our words converted into utilities and numbers. It must be resisted—always, it must be resisted. Resisted with love and mercy, with kindness and truth. For truth without mercy is not truth, and kindness without truth is not mercy. Only mankind needs to learn this. The other creatures live without betrayal. Only mankind fails in this, none excepted, the good and the evil. We seek to rise, yet we all stumble and fall to the earth, which is the station of our learning, our labor, and our love, until the time of our rising.

How can one speak about this to the new generation of souls springing up everywhere in Croatia? How to let them know how beautiful they are and awaken them to the certainty that they must not lose what has been purchased with so much suffering?

Does he need to tell them? How could he tell them? He is an exile returned home. Though he has his badge of honor from the sufferings of Goli Otok, he has lived most of his life in relative safety. While it is true that atrocities endured do not bestow moral authority, safety merits even less. Still, a man may speak of what he knows and does not know because authenticity begins in the heart, always in the heart.

What can he say that has not already been spoken by poets more gifted than himself, by thinkers in this land whose minds are far superior to his own, and by heroes and martyrs all about him, both the living and the dead?

Nevertheless, he jots down a few final thoughts, a little legacy, as men he once knew scratched messages on the walls of their cells, as Josipa inscribed the image of Christ onto a twig, and as the Lastavica of the Sea gave him the carved wooden bird that recalled him to his truer self at the moment when he was about to lose it.

Josip writes letters to those among the living who are dearest to him. Into each envelope, he adds a sheet of paper on which he has written a new poem, worked up into verse from his "final thoughts". He mails them the next day. He completes another such letter to his publisher, of whom he has grown quite fond. And another is for the carpenter who made his bookshelves. He writes another for Ivo Dučić, but it cannot be mailed to him, of course, because Rajska Polja is still not on any maps, nor is Pačići, and as far as he can tell, they have not been renamed. What the boy's exact address is, he cannot guess. However, into the publisher's envelope he adds an explanation and a map to the fields of heaven. There, a shepherd and his flock may still be found.

He is quite exhausted after completing all this, fighting a cough and sore throat as well, not to mention the chest stabs—nothing really to worry about. He will lie down now. He will take his rest. First a cup of coffee, then a glance out the window. The trees are thrashing wildly on the flanks of the Marjan, and rain is pelting down. It is somewhat thrilling, a good sea storm sweeping inland. The plants are drinking, cats are hiding under awnings, and children are dancing in the backyards, laughing and leaping in the rain. It is good—it is all good.

He sits at his desk and strains his mind, wondering if he has overlooked anyone who might appreciate reading his final thoughts. The young are probably not interested in such exhortations from the old. Yet they are the future. They must be fed. So, he addresses letters to the very newspapers that have assaulted his character and his life. Despite all that they have done, he will believe that they are still capable of listening. If they do not publish his new poem, that is regrettable, but he has done his part.

Seek the pure act that lives as a sign in memory.
Seek the indestructible, the true,
seek, if you wish, this art through which a soul
gone these countless years now speaks to you,
and you may know him as your own.

Seek all waters, be they waves of fear or wells of peace,
seek in unexpected places,
the creeks and rivers of release!
Seek the snow falling on sleeping fields or sighing hills,
seek the rain, yet seek the sun a moment before dawn,
when the forest to the east bursts into flames
and the lake is as blue as a pauper's crown.

Seek the tent of those abandoned in the desert!
Seek those who have known many paths, many woes,

yet have retained their dignity.
Seek the silent and listen to them speaking!
Seek the prisoner released.
Seek the wedding feast,
seek love, which is the royal wedding feast!
For with all its imperfections it is the work of art
before its final form is complete.

Seek the lost kingdom at the feet of mountains,
seek the interior palace!
Carry the great treasure of your burden
and serve it to the guests.
Run across the thinnest ice, laughing—or weeping if you
     must—
as you must, as I must, as each man must—
yet remember that laughter should enfold all weeping.

Seek the eye of childhood!
Seek the eye of purified old age!
Seek those who value good fools,
seek those who have mercy on bad fools.
Seek the wise but remember they are only dust,
seek the innocent, but remember the trials ahead of them.
Seek the strong and the weak, and love them equally,
know that their tests are only variations
on the unified theme.

Seek the eternal in the present,
seek the past and the future,
link them with the trajectory of your course,
for you are
you are
you are
you are the vessel.

He knows it is incomplete. As always, it is incomplete. But he has done what he can.

He lies down and naps. It is an old man's snooze, dreamless, and he rises from it a few hours later to find that the storm has passed. The rain has stopped, and the pitter-pattering of drops falling into the courtyard is soothing.

Children's voices can be heard through the open window—names, nouns and verbs, phrases, exultation, protest and good laughter—it all coalesces into random poetry. The fig tree on the sill yearns toward these voices, the leaves along its stem unfurl in expectation.

Somewhere in the nearby buildings a violin is playing. It is faltering—the hand of a beginner is on the bow. A peg is turned, a string tightened, then the music continues.

The ache in his chest is unceasing now as the old man gets up from his bed and goes to the window. He sits and watches the lights of the city winking on. It is ancient, this city, and new. It is shining and rising, rebuilding and moving ever onward into the future along the flow of time, seeking—though it does not know it is seeking—the celestial city.

As he continues to watch in the night, a swallow cuts its arc through the air, then flicks its wings and returns. Facing him, it hovers on a draft, tilting this way and that. It is no more than a meter away. He opens his hands to it.

It darts forward and lands on his fingertips. It quivers there, gazing at him, its feet dancing on his fingers, its tiny heart vibrating.

Who are you?

Now it cocks its head, and, across the abyss that exists between the ranks of creatures, they regard each other with attention.

Where have you come from?

It is not afraid. It would remain as long as he wishes. Yet it is time to go. A flicker of wings, and it soars upward, rising into the dark until it is seen no more.

Where are you going?

There is no need to ask.

It is already spoken.

Voyage

Selected Poems of Josip Lasta

(PUBLISHED POSTHUMOUSLY)

TOY SHIP IN A SHOP WINDOW

Odysseus in the city streets,
between his place of business and his home,
arrested by the shock of sails encased in glass,
is for a moment paralyzed, unable now to pass.
He stares into a mirror of himself, or memory of childish
    dreams,
hears again the heroes shout as they fight and love the sea.
He calls to them, but to himself he speaks:
I do not know what I have lost,
do not remember when.

A captain calls to him from on the heaving deck:
I will tell you the tale, he cries,
of what I have learned upon the sea.
For this is what she teaches,
of losing and finding,
of answering and quests:

A voyage is a movement embraced by departure and arrival,
an arc between speaking and hearing.
More it asks of us than we of it.
Look neither to your right nor to your left, my mariner;
see the bowsprit tilting northward to the axle of the world,
and beyond it the star-dipper full of quenching dreams,
and farther still the arching bow, the quiver full, the future
    waiting.
Will you dream with me the long-abandoned ways,
and be with me again the father-king and his valiant son
well met upon the sea?

Odysseus in the city streets then dares reply:
I hear your songs and groans, he cries,
but where are those who might have been?

What would I impart if they were by me now?
Seek now the glorious moment, I would say,
the act that lives as a sign in memory.
Seek the indestructible truth, I would declare,
seek, if you wish, this art or toy through which a soul,
gone these many years, now speaks to you.

Seek all waters, be they waves of fear or wells of peace,
seek in unexpected places,
the creeks and rivers of release!
Seek the snow falling on sleeping fields or mountain peaks,
seek the rain, seek the sun a moment before dawn,
when the forest to the east bursts into flames
and the lake is as blue as a pauper's crown.

Seek the tent of those abandoned in the desert!
Seek those who have known many paths, many woes,
yet have retained their dignity.
Seek the silent and listen to them speaking!
Seek the prisoner released.
Seek the wedding feast,
seek love, which is the royal wedding feast!
For with all its imperfections it is the work of art
before its final form is complete.

Seek the lost kingdom at the feet of mountains,
seek the interior palace!
Carry the great treasure of your burden
and serve it to the guests.
Run across the thinnest ice, laughing—or weeping if you
        must—
as you must, as I must, as each man must—
yet remember that laughter should enfold all weeping.

Seek the eye of childhood!
Seek the eye of purified old age!
Seek those who value good fools,
seek those who have mercy on bad fools.
Seek the wise but remember they are only dust,
seek the innocent, but remember the trials ahead of them.
Seek the strong and the weak, and love them equally,
know that their tests are only variations
on the unified theme.

Seek the eternal in the present,
seek the past and the future,
link them with the trajectory of your course,
for you are
you are
you are
you are the vessel.

WHAT IS MAN?

Consider the four gospels
consider the controversies and convergence,
consider the contradictions which are the authentification
of true events.

Consider the holy apostles in debate and misunderstanding.
Consider this: that even they needed time and steadfastness
and faith and prayer to find clarity and mercy and peace—
and from this the fruitfulness heaven desired.

All men are tested.
All servants of the King are tested mightily.

The steadfast man says, "Here I will stay. I shall not be
　　moved."
And in this his soul speaks: "Here is the place where I accept
　　to be killed."
Yes, on this battleground. In this desolation. In this place of
　　defeat,
will the victory be found.

And with all men be of single heart, listening to the eternal in
　　them;
be not dissuaded nor convinced by every tale formed on their
　　tongues,
for even in the mouths of the best, a tale takes another shape
　　than its true meaning,
and even in the mouths of the worst, a truth may be found.

Love all equally if you can,
but trust the few,
and even with these few, understand they are not perfection,

yet in their imperfections they carry their poverty toward
    eternity,
and in this way, with hammer and saw and wood and stone
and laughter and tears, they forge the shape
of the reliable word.

Look neither to the left nor to the right,
look not to opposing poles to find the true center;
do not measure equidistant from them,
for the earthbound poles shift
and the poles in men's minds are more unreliable than these.

Be not a slave to the apparent,
but seek the perspective of a higher vantage point.
Climb the mast with patience,
endure the abstinence of the immediate
for the sake of what is beyond the arc
(the spin of the arc, which men call horizon,
which men call the line of horizon,
which is not in fact a fixed line,
for it is a wave,
the hiatus between matter and infinity).

Seek the true center, which is above.
See the true center, which is above.

BENEATH THE WAVES

To you, the one who came on the waters of time,
like a swimmer, you passed in front of my eyes at the very
    moment
when hope was sinking as low as saturated wood.
You were there, a sudden presence, a form, a fire,
slow silent fire, the incandescent colors of your own past,
among the thickets and water-weeds of memory.

Unknown to me, you passed
in front of my eyes in the holy place,
in the troubled waters of the heart.
The ranks of your love and your burden were with you,
were written in your brow, your eyes, your tension.
They were beautiful in my eyes, for they were yours,
though I did not know you.

Later, as the waters drew us together, we spoke,
soul looked at soul, unknown at unknown,
and the knowing began its utterance of speech.
It was hesitant at first to move beyond its habitual state;
hunger was insufficient, could not reach across the void of
    uncertainty,
yearning to offer a little to you, or more,
if you would accept a word of consolation.

It was not the form alone,
the mass and weight and design.
Nor was it the first shaping of words; it was not these that
    drew us.
It was a knowledge that met in mid-current,
startled, simultaneous, unprecedented, unexpected,
each of us becoming a new thing,
for purposes we had yet to see.

To the shore I beckoned you, to the shallows,
but you proceeded on your course,
for you had come from a far place and were bound for
    another.
And I, resigned to permanence and exile,
could not then hope that you also had arrived
at the place which was your goal.
Was this no more than a shape that longing takes
in the theater of the heart?
Did it mean one thing for you, and another for me?

Into the water I dove,
into the deep waters,
and for the briefest moment we swam together,
as the current took us with laughter and tales;
memories which were unknowable
became familiar,
words like gold, split and shared as coinage,
small flags and pebbles, emblems offered back and forth,
given-received—given-received
expanding the vocabulary of the soul.

What is this form
composed of its parts yet greater than its sum?
Its shape, its color, its bright feathers,
its movement and its internal music,
no less its internal silence?
For there is silence and silence, and I must ask:
Are we silent together or has a parting begun?
The tide moves on but where is it taking us?
Will the current divide and pull you away?

Or will I, anticipating your departure,
turn away first?

Turn away from the unbearable potential:
the false or true certainty of loss?
Turning, turning, slowly—
infinitesimal flicker of eye, flicker of wing,
signaled from the heart's lost lexicon?
For an instant I gaze at the distant shore,
and in that fracture of attention I lose you.

Farther and farther from me, you part the waters slowly,
hesitant, wearying, head sinking beneath.
Now you rise again, resolved,
your arms slicing the rising waves
in strong, unhurried, measured strokes.
Then I see that you intend to spare yourself a drowning,
and with this I begin to sink.

Why did I turn away? Why?
Why did you turn away? Why?
Why did you proceed upon your course alone?
Now at the base of the unthinkable descent,
a hand grips mine and pulls me to the surface.
Gasping we break the ceiling of our world and take the clear
    air,
air charged with the indestructible, the faithful, the true.
It is you. You have returned.
I too am drowning, you say with your eyes.
We are rising, I say with mine,
and we will rise together.

Language, speech, the grammar of the heart:
Where does it come from?
What is it seeking?
Why does it run ever and ever onward
toward union and completion?

Yet speech impedes it,
slows it, weights it,
for uncertainty lies between the speaking and the hearing,
in turgid eddies, cold slipstreams, vortex and whirling pool.
Fear, dark as the rotting beds of old seas
sucks at the limbs.

Still, the question is in our eyes,
though neither of us understands the answer.
Neither can we speak,
for a word once spoken cannot be taken back.
How did we so swiftly lose our common tongue,
the silence which in an instant can become true speech,
or at a whim of thoughtlessness condemn
true speech to the suction of abyss?
Speak to me with your silence, Oh, speak,
for I still dream the drowner's dreams.

O form, finely wrought,
fire upon the water,
O word of love,
I see you weakened by the long exertion,
by sacrifice,
by energies demanded for the buoyancy of weight and mass.
Tell me in our own tongue what I am to you?
What may I be for you?
What shape and presence, what speech and silence
am I to you?
What form?
What true word
am I to you?

A VOYAGE TAKEN

The compass breaks, the mast is down
my soul heeds this: the world is round;
the rising heart,
the dream and pulse,
on a sea-wind carries us.

The birds are dipping under waves,
the fish bolt upward on their wings
and we, the captain and the crew,
suspended over the abyss,
hold the wheel and rig with faith
as this frail vessel dives beneath.

Good sire, we cry,
the waves are high!
Good youth, he answers from the sky,
beyond the fracture line of land and air
your port is near, your home is there.

THE ASCENT OF THE DOVE

The dove, soaring, sees the distant curve of the earth,
and trembles at its shape—vast, architectural,
the sea surrounding it deeper than fathoming.
Rising higher, he looks down to the small orderings of man,
into valleys, along rows of tilled earth, the threads of roads,
    the sprinkling of snow,
and lights coming on, one by one, in homes hidden among
    the folds of mountains.

Then up again he glances, as the last tint of green streaks the
    horizon,
and the rose fades into violet,
blue bleeds into the black of space.
The stars are there, choruses of singing stars.
He forgets all language, all origins of thought,
for thought itself is fluid light.

But this question still afflicts his flight:
Where am I going in the fathomless waters above the earth?
And why has this voyage begun at the very moment I wearied
and began to prepare for an end?
Why?
Night is coming on, the cold wind takes me
higher.

Higher on the tangent of the wing's curve, the wind's curve,
    the earth's curve,
the broad-flung arc of the orbit, then beyond into the realm
of infinite expansion.
There is no longer any thought of descent.
Still, the question: how will these small wings carry me?
How, when I am so alone?

In this dark, where distant songs recall
the firmament of solid places, of permanence and order,
I hear a presence beside me, sudden, unseen, there—
the wing-beats match mine.
I speak, who are you?
But there is only silence,
a language I have not yet learned.

Speak to me, Oh, speak, I cry.
Though the silence deepens, the presence does not depart
and we fly together our course through space and time.
It is undefined, this union, this abandonment
as one by one we leave behind the powers of cognition
which sovereign the self no more.

Higher now, propelled by the purified intention of ascent,
afloat above the currents of fear, not yet swimming in the
    liquid grace
of faithful and indestructible trust.
Now I remember, sighs the dove, I remember such moments,
it was, yes, I recall it was a different shape, but in essence
the same: those days when I was young,
when harvests of hay in the creaking wagons simmered in the
    sun,
and at end of day I plunged into spring-fed pools carved in
    the rocks,
scattering the million silver minnows of the fractured sun.

Even then I was not alone, though I felt alone,
for in those days the nights made scented vineyards chant with
    the love
encoded in all fertile growing things,
the plum and the wild currant and the roses bending with the
    weight of their fruit,

and you became a shape parting the night with your presence.
Though then, as now, you were unseen with the eye,
the eye ever-yearning for shapes to give form and place to the
     word,
for in this passion was the all-giving, the non-taking,
the concord and the emblem of our ascent.

Having seen, at once I feel the gyre veer, the tangent curve
     steep,
the wing-beat beside me audible as it pitches away,
beginning the parabola of descent.
Plunging, I see the distant curve of the earth,
and tremble at its shape—
for it is not the shape that was seen at the ascent;
its balances of orbit and of spin,
the equilibriums of planetary weight and stellar mass,
hold each close in a titan's dance.

Where now? I cry to the void once filled by you;
where, when the ascent has just begun, are you going?
Then the silence answers:
Back to the place which is the station of our labor and our
     love.
My own wings' tangent takes me too,
sure of knowledge that I did not know was mine,
yes, down to the heaving seas, the swaying forests,
the dark sleeping fields, the cold and barren lands,
where the indestructible, the faithful, the true
is needed.

No longer do I see you, no longer hear you,
but you are here.
If you were to speak at last, what would you say?
And if I were to speak at last, what would I say?

In the language which is beyond all speaking:

I am here,
I am here,
I am here.

There is no need, there is no need for this,
it is already spoken.

ARGO AWAITING

Let us go to the farthest shore beyond the white mountains
    under the moon,
to the hidden cove where beloved *Argo* lies at anchor, the surf
    lifting her bow, the wind yearning to billow her sails,
    waiting for us, waiting for the children of Odysseus our
    father to rise again and seek the horizon where sky and sea
    meet in dimensions
where only the brave will go with their presence.

Or if we cannot, let us dream of it and not call dreaming folly.
For if we fail to dream, all will fall
into disremembrance and neglect,
and the fires that shape the world, which are the heart of
    the world,
will grow cold
and the splendid art of existence
will become a solitary's prison cell.

As you stand in your prisoner's uniform, think of these:
the wind and dreams,
the fierce and beautiful eyes of captains,
the dance of the grieving giants,
the songs of the frolicking dwarfs,
the laughter of children as they run leaping
along the white beaches of infinite play,
listening to the chant of the sea.

And if it is not to be,
if it is never to be,
at least we thought of it
and loved it
and longed for it,
and in this manner we were changed.

If by face to face we never see,
nor touch, hear, smell, or taste
the love that is within the heart of the world,
let us remember this:
within our dreaming minds we met
and were set free.

A FACE REFLECTED IN A SHOP WINDOW

And so the glass behind which little sea dreams swell
has spoken to the heart in which true dreaming dwells.
I cast my eyes to pavement now and walk away,
leave the tokens of my quest for fairer day.

What I have seen will not be lost:
the well of longing has no brim;
Odysseus cannot be quelled in a city's maze,
nor drowners break their upward gaze,
nor will there cease the poetry of slaves.

Let not by my neglect or grief
the memory of unknown shores grow dim;
though voyage undertaken takes us
where we would not choose to go,
better far to seek and fail
than never to seek and win.

J. L., Split, Croatia, A.D. *2006*

The Island of the World

In Rajska Polja—
Josip Lasta, the central character, a boy of nine years as the
novel begins
Miroslav Lasta, his father, a village schoolteacher
Marija Lasta, his mother
Fra Anto (full name forgotten), a Franciscan friar, pastor of
the parish
Josipa (full name forgotten), a girl Josip's age, his first love
Petar Dučić, Josip's closest friend
Sister Katarina of the Holy Angels, Marija Lasta's sister, a
nun in Split
Emilio, an Italian soldier

In Sarajevo—
Aunt Eva (married name withheld), sister of Marija Lasta
and Sister Katarina
Uncle Jure (name withheld), Eva's husband, a Partisan
Alija (full name unknown), a man on a donkey
The Lastavica of the Sea (name unknown), an armless man

In Split—
Simon Horvatinec, a surgeon and professor of medicine,
founder of the resistance movement *Dobri Dupin.*
Vera Horvatinec, Simon's wife, a retired concert pianist
Ariadne Horvatinec, their daughter
Goran Horvatinec, Simon's brother, a Communist official
Antun Kusić, Josip's friend at the university
Ivan Radoš, a biologist

Various members of *Dobri Dupin:*

Tatjana (full name unknown), a poetess from Belgrade

Stjepan (full name unknown), a Croatian novelist

Vlado (full name unknown), a Macedonian sculptor and nihilist

Iria (full name unknown), a classical composer, half Portuguese, raised in Bosnia

Zoran (full name unknown), a Croatian philosophy student

Ana (full name unknown), Zoran's sister, a medical student from Zagreb

Ivan (full name unknown), a Croatian from Bosnia-Herzegovina, a musician

On Goli Otok—Prisoners:

Vladimir Lucić, known as Prof, a professor of history from Zagreb

Ante Czobor, known as Propo, "preacher", an engineer from Serbia

Krunoslav Bošnjaković, known as Svat, "wedding guest", a seventeen-year-old Bosnian youth

Dalibor Kovač, known as Budala, "blockhead", an eighteen- or nineteen-year-old Croatian youth

Tomislav (full name unknown), known as Tata, "papa", a Croatian priest

Sova, "owl" (real name unknown), a Slovene

Prison officials:

Zmaj, "the dragon", the camp commandant (real name unknown)

Sokol, "the hawk", the commandant's assistant (real name unknown)

Zmija, "the snake", a guard (real name unknown)

Zohar, "the cockroach", a guard and toady of Zmija (real name unknown)

In Dalmatia and Istria—

Drago, Marija, and their daughter, Jelena, a family on the
shore of the northern Adriatic (family name unknown)

"Brother", the older brother of Drago

Draz and Pero, two truck drivers

A little boy (name unknown), a disciple of St Francis

A lady with a goat (name unknown)

Sleeping saints (names unknown)

In Italy—

A fruit vendor

Slavica Mazzuolo, a psychologist, born in Croatia

Emilio Mazzuolo, a dentist, Slavica's husband

Paolo and Chiara, their children

Emilio's mother

"Chicklet" and "Canary", a married couple (real names
unknown)

A Franciscan friar (name unknown)

"Cass" Conway, wife of an American diplomat

Sarah Sybil-Pfiefer, wife of a British diplomat

"The foreman" (name withheld), director of Italian service
employees at the embassy

In New York—

Mrs. Coriander Franklin, a cleaning woman

Caleb Franklin, her son, a "street rat"

Miriam Franklin, Caleb's wife, a sociologist

Jefferson Franklin, Caleb and Miriam's young son

Naomi Johnson, Coriander's grandmother

Carl Johnson, Coriander's brother

Winston V. Ramamurthy Kanapathipillai, a natural
philosopher

Miriam Kanapathipillai, Winston's wife, a university
professor

Christiana, Winston and Miriam's daughter
Friar Todd, priest of Sts. Cyril and Methodius parish
Abel Kristijan Bogdan, a child
Jason McIsaac, a child
Steve and Sally McIsaac and their other children
Maria Finntree, a businesswoman, Josip's daughter
Ryan Collins, Maria's son, a student
A literary critic (name withheld)
Violet Czobor, a fish vendor

In Bosnia-Herzegovina and Croatia—
Two old men at an outdoor café (names unknown)
Ivo Dučić, a young shepherd
Alija ibn Yosuf al-Bosnawi, a tour guide
Branko and Teta Ana, people of Pačići
A poet, an official of the Croatian ministry of culture
Šime, a doctor/prisoner

Author's Afterword

Dear reader, all that is most improbable in this tale occurred. Only the "ordinary" is invented. Wherever you may be in this world, please know that I presumed to write about your memory, your blood, your loss, as if it were my own, only because I live with you in the lands that are east of the Garden we once knew. In eternity, we will know fully; in Him, we will see face to face. Then we shall understand even as we are understood, and love even as we are loved.

Michael O'Brien, Combermere, Canada
Feast of Saint Joseph the Worker, May 1, 2006